ELEMENTARY MATHEMATICAL METHODS

ELEMENTARY MATHEMATICAL METHODS THIRD EDITION

Diane Thiessen
University of Northern Iowa

Margaret Wild
Aberdeen, South Dakota

Donald D. Paige
Southern Illinois University

Diane L. Baum
University of Northern Iowa

Macmillan Publishing Company
New York

Macmillan Publishing Company
866 Third Avenue, New York, New York 10022

Collier Macmillan Canada, Inc.

Library of Congress Cataloging in Publication Data

Elementary mathematical methods / Diane Thiessen . . . [et al.].—3rd ed.
    p.   cm.
  Rev. ed. of: Elementary mathematical methods / Donald D. Paige,
Diane Thiessen, Margaret Wild.
  Includes bibliographies and index.
  ISBN 0-02-390320-1
  1. Mathematics—Study and teaching (Elementary)   I. Thiessen, Diane.
  II. Paige, Donald D.   Elementary mathematical methods.
QA135.5.E35 1989
372.7′2004—dc19   87-17371
                                         CIP

Printing: 1 2 3 4 5 6 7 8   Year: 9 0 1 2 3 4 5 6 7 8

PREFACE

TO THE INSTRUCTOR

The chapters in this text reflect the strands taught in the elementary school mathematics curriculum. It is not assumed that all chapters will necessarily be studied due to the varying number of hours allotted for methods courses. The ordering of the chapters is fairly arbitrary. One order of studying the teaching of elementary school mathematics is suggested by the table of contents. Other variations are equally suitable. For example, the chapters on problem solving, calculators and computers, and organizing for instruction are relatively independent and could be included at any time throughout the course. Many of the later chapters, such as measurement, geometry, probability and statistics, integers, or number theory could be taught earlier if desired. The chapter on ratio, proportion, and percent should be sequenced after common and decimal fractions and their operations are studied.

You may prefer to introduce problem solving by having the students study the first section and then include the other sections later in the semester. Calculator skills are needed throughout the text and the problem sets. Students could use the calculator skills quiz to determine whether or not they need to use Appendix A to improve their calculator skills. The chapter on elementary school textbooks could be studied at any time throughout the course. If students are unfa-

miliar with the structure of teacher's editions of elementary school mathematics textbooks, they should at least read through the chapter before studying the remainder of the textbook.

You may prefer teaching whole-number operations immediately following whole-number numeration. Similarly, you may prefer teaching common and decimal fractions and their operations separately. Common fractions and decimal fractions were included in the same chapter of this text to place emphasis on the fact that they are both fractions. Often students conclude that they are not related and treat them as totally disjoint subjects. Although addition and subtraction of common fractions are taught together in the elementary school curriculum and are usually followed later by addition and subtraction of decimal fractions, these topics are included in the same chapter in this text to emphasize the similarity of the concepts. Similar commonalities are noted in all the sections dealing with operations on common and decimal fractions.

Also, it is not assumed that all classes will study all the chapters in the same detail. Detail has been included in the development of some topics, as it is the opinion of the authors that many elementary school mathematics textbooks do not provide adequate teacher's notes on development.

Throughout each chapter are collections of problem sets that divide the chapter into sections. A number of these problems are similar to lessons that could be used with elementary school children. For example, some problems in the addition and subtraction chapter ask the reader to write problems that contain more than one condition. This is one type of activity that can be used to extend problem solving in the elementary classroom. Other problems are related to professional resources for teachers, such as professional journals, teacher's books, and children's books. These resources include topics such as activities for units and lessons, research findings, philosophical issues, how to construct games, and so on.

There is a selection of problems for the instructor and the students to choose from. It is suggested that the students *read* all of the problems. However, it is not reasonable to expect that they would write out complete answers for all of them. Instead, some of them could be used as discussion topics for the whole class or for small groups. After reading the problem, students could be asked to describe the purpose of doing such an activity with elementary children or to tell how this activity could be implemented into the elementary classroom.

TO THE STUDENT: AS YOU BEGIN THIS COURSE

The backgrounds and experiences of you and your peers are probably diverse. Some of you will have had experiences as elementary students or as college students participating in an elementary classroom or in other mathematics courses for preservice teachers with calculators, problem solving, estimation, or models such as base-ten blocks or fraction bars. Some of you will have taken a number of mathematics courses and be confident in your abilities in this area. Many of you have had the opportunity to observe and to experience the teaching and learning of mathematics with meaningful, effective methods. As you reflect on those experiences, you should be aware that those experiences were not "memorize this rule." Weren't the students and the teacher actively involved in a discussion or an activity? Weren't the questions of the nature that called for thinking and explanation? Weren't the students aware of what they knew and what they were trying to obtain? *And they knew when they understood the idea.*

This text is about developing mathematics with meaningful effective methods. Just as models are essential in teaching elementary mathematics, they are also essential in this course. Throughout the textbook, examples of how to use models to develop topics have been included; these examples include textbook pages that illustrate good development, pictures of how to use models step by step, and samples of appropriate teacher questions. You may find it helpful first to read the assignment quickly and glance at the diagrams to obtain an overview of the ideas. Then reread, carefully thinking through the text and each part of a diagram. It would be more helpful to study this text with a calculator and models available so that you can try the ideas as they are presented.

Questions sets are included throughout each chapter. Some of the questions are designed to help you evaluate whether or not you understood the section. Some questions involve other resources, such as *Arithmetic Teacher* or yearbooks from National Council of Teachers of Mathematics. The complete bibliographic entries are at the end of each chapter. The resources that were selected to be shared with you are some of the best available. In some of the questions more than one resource is mentioned; often they are not similar. You may wish to pursue more than one of them or read them at a later time. As you read these articles, you will find a number of teaching ideas that you can use as an elementary teacher. For future reference, you will probably find it most helpful to obtain a copy of the reading and write your comments and evaluation on the article itself.

The purpose of the resources is twofold. One purpose is to help you develop your own resource files. Files should be set up by topic, such as whole-number numeration, addition and subtraction of whole numbers, or measurement. For folder topics you may choose to use the chapter titles. By setting up the files by topic you will find that whether you are a first- or seventh-grade teacher you will have ready access to a particular topic. As a beginning teacher you will find it difficult to find the time to organize your notes, readings, and handouts from your methods courses. The second purpose of the resources is to acquaint you with *the resources* that are available so that you can continue to grow as an inservice teacher.

We hope that you will enjoy the semester as you pursue learning to teach mathematics effectively.

D.T.
M.W.
D.D.P.
D.L.B.

CONTENTS

5 TEACHING NUMERATION OF COMMON AND DECIMAL FRACTIONS

155

6 TEACHING ADDITION AND SUBTRACTION OF WHOLE NUMBERS

187

7 TEACHING MULTIPLICATION AND DIVISION OF WHOLE NUMBERS 253

8 TEACHING ADDITION AND SUBTRACTION OF COMMON AND DECIMAL FRACTIONS 337

9 TEACHING MULTIPLICATION AND DIVISION OF COMMON AND DECIMAL FRACTIONS

385

10 TEACHING MEASUREMENT

425

11 TEACHING GEOMETRY 469

12 TEACHING RATES, RATIOS, PROPORTIONS, AND PERCENTS 531

13 TEACHING STATISTICS AND PROBABILITY 573

1
TEACHING PROBLEM SOLVING

Ms. Lu presented a problem situation to her students. She observed that most of the groups were actively working on the problem but that one group was just sitting there. When she asked about their work, one student responded, "We don't know how to do it, so we can't work on it." How do you help students "who don't know what to do"?

In the elementary school, children begin studying many varied mathematical concepts, such as geometry, probability, estimation, measurement, and numeration. All these topics of mathematics are similar in that they can be approached through problem-solving techniques. Since children should study elementary school mathematics through problem-solving techniques, prospective elementary teachers must learn to teach using these techniques. This chapter and the remaining chapters are written with this point of view in mind.

Many people's concept of elementary school mathematics is that it is merely the study of arithmetical operations, namely addition, subtraction, multiplication, and division. Such a view is limited because arithmetic is just one branch of mathematics. Knowledge of other branches of mathematics—probability or geometry, for example—is essential for the informed citizen in today's world.

Every day, people encounter problems that must be solved. The problems an adult encounters range from "What shall I have for supper tonight?" to "Can I afford to buy this house?" to "How do I keep my business from going bankrupt?" Children, too, encounter problems that range from "What shall I wear today?" to "Should I do my homework before watching television?" to "How do I cope with my parents' divorce?" Some problems are familiar situations that can be easily worked out because they are similar to problems we have solved in the past. Other problems are unfamiliar because they are quite different from anything for which we have previously worked out a solution. The teacher's job would be easy if the schools could simply teach easy answers to all the problems a person would encounter in life, but this is not possible. Not only is there an impossible number of answers to learn, but there are also many problems no one has yet solved. Furthermore, as the world constantly changes, new problems arise every day. It thus becomes apparent that the school must try to teach some general techniques of problem solving that will be applicable over a broad range of diverse problems.

The importance of problem solving in the elementary mathematics curriculum can hardly be overemphasized. The National Council of Teachers of Mathematics (NCTM) in its recommendations for school mathematics of the 1980s lists as the number one priority that "problem solving be the focus of school mathematics in the 1980s." The second priority states that "basic skills in mathematics be defined to encompass more than computational facility."* Too often computational skill has been stressed almost to the exclusion of concept understanding and problem-solving ability. While some computational ability is certainly necessary for problem-solving success, the NCTM report points out that a disproportionate amount of class time is spent in teaching students the type of computation that can be done faster, easier, and with greater accuracy by a $5 calculator.

PROBLEM-SOLVING SITUATIONS

Exactly what is problem solving? Is any single problem a problem-solving situation for everyone? What sort of problem-solving situations are found in current elementary textbooks? To become effective teachers of problem solving, we need to determine what are problem-solving situations. When the

---

*National Council of Teachers of Mathematics, *An Agenda for Action: Recommendations for School Mathematics of the 1980s* (Reston, VA: The Council, 1980).

term "problems" is used, it is used to describe a variety of very different situations. For example, Ted remarked that he had just finished ten long-division "problems"; Ty was working on a "problem" to find the sum of the numbers between 100 and 200; the "problem" that Rosemary selected was to determine the cost of new carpeting for the family living room. To define problem solving, we need to classify the various types of problems that are encountered in the elementary mathematics curriculum. Six types of problems are identified by Charles and Lester in *Teaching Problem Solving: What, Why, and How.* Problems are classified as to whether they are drill exercises, simple or complex translation problems, process problems, applied problems, or puzzle problems.

TYPES OF PROBLEMS

Computational or Drill Exercises

Examples of this category include problems such as $23 - 17$, 34×56, $6 + 2$, 16% of 56, or $2\frac{1}{4} \div \frac{5}{8}$. In some situations both speed and accuracy are important; in other cases just accuracy is desired. Often the purpose of these exercises is to reinforce answers or practice procedures. National Assessment results (the National Assessment of Educational Progress is an evaluation given nationwide to a sample of 9-, 13-, and 17-year-olds over a range of selected topics) indicate that, in general, students do very well with this type of problem. The results also show that their ability to perform these procedures is much higher than their understanding of the procedures. For example, one situation from the National Assessment involved multiplication of fractions. When students were asked to estimate the answer to 3.04×5.3, only 21% of 13-year-olds were able to select the right answer. Since other responses,

such as 1.6, 160, and 1600, received similar percentages, it appears that many students were guessing. To help students understand computation, algorithms (an organized procedure for computing a numerical answer, for example, the addition algorithm, the decomposition subtraction algorithm, or the equal-additions subtraction algorithm) must be taught with meaning and with a greater emphasis on estimation.

Simple Translation Problems

Other common names for this category include one-step story problems or routine one-step verbal problems. "Routine verbal problems" refers to problems like most of those in student textbooks. Examples include: "Susan packed eighteen books into each of nine boxes. How many books were packed?" and "Keith had $\frac{3}{4}$ of the job completed. He assumed the entire project would take him six and a half hours. How many hours has he worked?" Overall, National Assessment results show that students perform quite well on routine one-step verbal problems.

Complex Translation Problems

These situations are often referred to as multistep story problems or multistep verbal problems. Examples include: "Chuck spent 20 dollars each day over a period of 6 and $\frac{1}{2}$ weeks. How much did he spend?" and "After Susan finished packing ten books into each of five boxes, she weighed one of the boxes to determine postal rates. She determined that it would cost her $2.45 per package. How much change will she get from a $20 bill?" National Assessment results show that students have many difficulties with multistep verbal problems. It is assumed that students do not have adequate experience or instruction in solving these problems.

Applied Problems

These problems are much more complex than the traditional one-step or multistep verbal problems involving applications. Examples include: "How much water is used in your school over a period of a year? Could some of this be conserved? How much money could be saved?" and "How expensive is it to rent an average two-bedroom apartment in your community? What expenses would need to be figured in a budget for housing?" These problems involve a number of mathematical skills. The students would have to decide what data to collect and how to collect it. Students will need to apply what they know about such topics as measurement, computation, geometry, estimation, and statistics. As students work through these situations, they should have a greater appreciation of the uses of mathematics.

Process Problems

In a process problem the student has no previously learned procedure or algorithm that can be applied for a quick solution. Examples could include finding the number of squares on a checkerboard or finding the sum of the numbers one through one hundred. In these situations students will have to find or devise a strategy to help solve the problem. National Assessment results show that students do very poorly on these types of problems. Mathematics has traditionally been taught in our schools as a topic to be memorized, a low-level mental process. Students have not been introduced to higher-level mental processes.

Puzzle Problems

The sixth category that Charles and Lester describe involves puzzles. Two puzzle problems are shown in Figure 1-1. The solutions to these problems often involve looking at

Without lifting your pencil; draw four straight line segments that pass through all nine dots.

Remove four toothpicks so that exactly three squares remain.

Remove five tooth picks so that exactly three squares remain.

FIGURE 1-1.
Puzzle problems.

the problem in an unusual way. These problems may not necessarily involve mathematics or any particular strategy. Solving one of these problems may not help in solving any other problems. Students who have solved the problem may find that as they analyze the situation, they cannot determine why or how they suddenly "saw" the solution.

DEFINING PROBLEM SOLVING

The definition below is based on the definition of a problem by Charles and Lester. A problem will be considered a problem-solving situation when:

1. The person has a *need or desire to solve the problem.*
2. The person has *no established or easily accessible procedure* for solving the problem.
3. The person *tries* to solve the problem.

Notice that a problem-solving situation is defined relative to the person. Any or none of the six types of problems described in the preceding section could be a problem-solving situation, depending on the person involved. For example, students in the seventh grade should be able to solve all of the problems listed under computation. But for younger students these could be problem-solving situations. First graders may have been introduced to the addition concept and the plus symbol, but they are just ready to discover new methods of solution, such as counting on from six to find the answer to 6 + 2. Second graders may know how to solve two-digit subtraction problems that involve no regrouping, but they may be puzzled by a problem such as 23 − 17. At first the children may think it is impossible as 7 cannot be taken from 3. These situations would be problems for these children as—assuming they are interested in them and willing to work on them—they do not have a readily developed procedure to solve the problems. The teacher could help the children solve the problem by using problem-solving strategies such as using models to represent the problem. Computational procedures can be taught through a problem-solving process that will help children understand the procedures. Also, children will gain in their problem-solving abilities if they are *actively involved in developing* the algorithm rather than being *told* what steps to follow.

Simple and complex translation problems may or may not be problem-solving situations, depending on the persons involved. We often predict what students know by considering their grade levels. We assume that the "average" student has studied particular topics by a certain grade level. Whether or not the students have mastered these concepts depends on their abilities and motivation. Both in-school and out-of-school experiences are very important. National Assessment results show that nonroutine one-step story problems are just as difficult for students as routine multistep verbal problems. Situations that are nonroutine, or textbook problems where students have not

been given help in developing strategies, have remained unsolved problems for students.

Depending on the sophistication of the problem and the experiences of the students, applied problems may or may not be problem-solving situations. If the students had worked through some of these situations earlier, the problem could be reduced simply to gathering and recording the data. For example, if the problem were to determine the cost of carpeting a house, some students may have been involved in helping their parents measure rooms, determine areas, and compare different types and prices of carpeting. These students would be aware of the various decisions needed and could quickly collect the data in an organized manner. Students without these experiences would gradually realize the number of decisions that would need to be made based on the use of the room, size and special shape of the room, and budget parameters. For these students, assuming that they were interested in and willing to help redecorate the room, this would be a problem.

Did you try, and were you able, to solve the puzzle problems? If you had not encountered these puzzles before, they probably were problems. If you had solved the first one before and remembered that you needed to go outside the borders of the array, this was not a problem for you. For people who do not attempt puzzles through lack of interest, it would also not be a problem. To solve puzzle problems, students need to be flexible in their thinking and be able to look at the problem from various perspectives. Since some people simply don't like puzzles, discretion should be used in any assignments on puzzles. Puzzle problems should be available for students who are interested in them. These problems will provide enrichment for these students and may stimulate further work in recreational mathematics. Also, as they work on these puzzles and other students see their interest and enthusiasm, the others may decide to become involved.

For many students, just computing algorithmic operations represents a problem situation. However, the drill on techniques for solving these problems can be replaced by the hand-held calculator. So the problems that will be emphasized in this chapter are process problems and translation or verbal problems. These topics are expanded in the next two sections. Part of the discussion focuses on traditional textbook problems. Some strategies for solving and suggestions for teaching translation and process problems are included in this section; other teaching strategies will be discussed later.

MORE ON TRANSLATION PROBLEMS

Most problems traditionally found in elementary mathematics textbooks might be called translation, algorithmic, or operational problems because once the students understand the problem, they can apply an algorithm or operation previously learned for solving that type of problem. If students recognize that the problem requires multiplication, they can apply the previously learned multiplication algorithm by plugging in the appropriate numbers. Too often what passes as problem solving in the elementary school is actually nothing more than doing exercises in computation. The "problems" merely present a few facts to be manipulated in one step. Since a whole group of subtraction story problems are usually presented immediately following practice in subtraction skills, students often do not even bother to read the problems. They merely pick out the two numbers and subtract the smaller from the larger. Results of the National Assessment (Carpenter and others, 1980) also indicate this difficulty with one-step translation problems.

Even when story problems using all four operations are grouped together, there are many tricks students can use in place of real problem solving. For example, they may formulate rules such as the following:

1. If there are more than two numbers, add them.
2. If there are two numbers similar in magnitude, subtract the smaller from the larger.
3. If one number is relatively large compared to the second number, divide. If the division answer has a remainder, cross out your work and multiply.

With such rules students can correctly solve many story problems without even reading the problems. They simply pick out the numbers and do an operation according to their rules.

Another trick students often use to solve story problems is reading key words. Again, students do not read the problem; they only read the key words and the numbers. Furthermore, it is very easy to find all the numbers quickly since usually they are all written in numerals and not in words. For example, the word "total" usually indicates addition, but this is not necessarily the case. "Elizabeth and Freddy have a total of 5 toy trucks. Jerome has 8. How many more does Jerome have?" Instead of analyzing the situation, students may pick out the word "total" and the numbers 5 and 8 and add, thus obtaining an incorrect answer.

Although students should be taught to analyze the context in which terms are used, they also need to learn *about* key words. For example, results from the Third National Assessment showed that 48% of 9-year-old students were able to solve 313 − 298 when it was written in algorithmic form, but only 17% were able to solve "subtract 298 from 313." In this case most students were not able to translate a simple expression that listed the numbers in a different order. A variety of wordings and situations needs to be presented to students to help expand their concepts of all operations.

Traditional one-step story problems that are all the same operation should not be discounted. Story problems that are at the end or throughout a chapter are used to exemplify situations in which an algorithm can be used. If the students do not read and think about these situations, they are losing an opportunity to learn how to solve problems in the real world. Their skills will be restricted to manipulating numbers. To maximize learning through textbook story problems, the teacher can engage the students in a class discussion about the situations. This can be expanded by having the students work in groups where they discuss selected problems and other situations where this operation is applied. These discussions to develop and extend operation concepts should not be restricted to lower elementary classes. They are also needed in middle school and junior high as the students study topics such as decimals, fractions, and percents.

Outside the classroom, problems do not come in nice neat packages containing key words as guides, including only the numbers necessary for solving the problem, and requiring only a single computation to reach a solution. Students who have had these varied experiences with story problems are better prepared to solve problems in the real world.

Student groups should also generate their own problems for other groups of students to solve. Being able to write or develop problems is a skill that is seldom addressed, but it does give students another experience that helps their own problem-solving ability.

MORE ON PROCESS PROBLEMS

In a process problem the student has no previously learned algorithm that can be applied for a quick solution. This does not necessarily mean that there is no such algorithm, only that the student does not yet know it. The same problem may be a process problem for some students and an algorithmic problem for others. Alternatively, the same problem may be a process problem for a student one year and an algorithmic problem for the same student the next year. In fact, the common practice is to use a story problem when introducing a new concept—for example, multiplication. At the outset a problem such as "Freddy and his mother are baking cupcakes. If each pan holds 6 cupcakes and they have 4 pans, how many cupcakes can they bake at one time?" is a process problem since the students have no previously learned algorithm for solving it. After the students have studied multiplication concepts, the same problem becomes an algorithmic problem.

Many current elementary mathematics textbooks do include some process problems. Sometimes they are given such labels as "brainteaser" or "for the experts," thus conveying the idea that they are suitable for only the brightest students. Also, they are usually placed at the end of the page and are to be done only after the regular assignment is completed.

It has been found that all levels of students benefit from problem solving. Interestingly, low achievers are more likely to be successful in problem-solving situations than in regular course work. Most of the curriculum is based on mastery of previous related topics. If they have been unsuccessful with the prerequisite skills, it is very difficult for students to acquire the new skills. One advantage for low achievers is that process problems are usually not dependent on prerequisite skills that they have not mastered. Organization and reasoning skills are often needed for success in problem solving. These skills are required by all students, and they need to be taught to all levels of students. This increases the chance of success for low achievers.

In solving process problems, students gain skills that are useful in solving many different types of problems. An example might be the following. "Allen, Freddy, and Sean all live on the same street. It is eight blocks from Allen's house to Freddy's house. It is three blocks from Freddy's house to Sean's house. How far is it from Allen's house to Sean's house?" At first glance this may appear to be a simple algorithmic problem. Most elementary students will give the answer as eleven blocks. A few may give an answer of five blocks. Almost none will give both answers at first unless they have already had some effective teaching in prob-

lem-solving strategies. A diagram or model can help greatly in solving this problem. When the situation is put in a drawing so that students can visualize it better, most will be able to understand that there are two possible answers (Figure 1-2).

Once the students have grasped the idea that two possible answers are equally valid for the given information, the problem can be varied and extended. "What happens if Sean's house may or may not be on the same street as the other two? What if all three houses may or may not be on the same street? What if Allen's house and Sean's house are on the same street, but Freddy's may or may not be on that street? What if Freddy's house must not be on the same street as either of the others?" The solution of a process problem is not complete until many possibilities have been explored.

SOME PROBLEMS TO SOLVE

As you work through parts of the chapter, you, the prospective elementary school teacher, will need to be involved in problem-solving activities. It is important that *you* become an effective problem solver. To gain an understanding of the process of problem solving, one needs to solve problems. Select one of the problems below that is a process

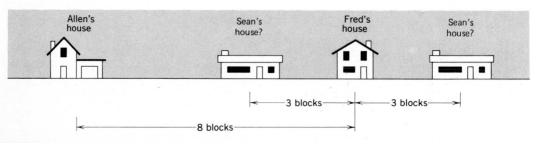

FIGURE 1-2.
Diagramming a process problem.

problem, that is, one that you are interested in solving and one that you do not know a procedure for solving.

McGillicuddy Pond
Today one blade of grass took root in McGillicuddy Pond. Every day the grass population doubles—that is, tomorrow there will be two blades of grass, the next day four blades, and so on. On the tenth day, how many blades of grass are in the pond? If the capacity of the pond is one million blades of grass, on what day will it be filled up? Guess first and then figure it out. On which day will almost half the pond still be open water?

Who Am I?
I am a counting number. All three of my digits are even and different. The sum of my digits is 12. The product of my digits is less than 40. The sum of my hundred's digit plus my one's digit is less than my ten's digit. Who am I?

Circle Table Mats
The table mat shown in Figure 1-3 is made of black and white circles joined so that black circles are along the edge and white circles in the interior. Twenty black and sixteen white circles are used in the example. There are two such mats made with *equal* numbers of white and black circles. What sizes are they?

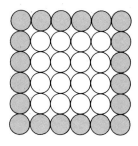

FIGURE 1-3.
Circle table mats.

FIGURE 1-4.
Calendar cube.

The Garden Fence
A gardener has 30 feet of fence to keep animals out of the garden. What is the largest area of garden that this fence will enclose? What about 36 feet of fence?

What's on the Cube?
Given the desk calendar in Figure 1-4, what are the remaining numbers on the dark and light cubes? Remember, all dates from 01 through 31 must be possible.

Take some time to work on at least one of these problems before continuing.

QUESTIONS AND ACTIVITIES

1. What are the six different types of problems defined by Charles and Lester? Define each of these in your own words.

2. Select a chapter on computation in a fourth- or fifth-grade mathematics textbook. List the publisher and copyright date.
   a. What is the purpose of the chapter? Classify the problems as computational, simple translation, or complex translation.
   b. Evaluate the quantity and quality of the verbal problems.
   c. How could you supplement the verbal problems so that some problems are included daily.

d. How could the simple translation problems be modified to become complex translation problems?

e. How could you involve your students in supplementing the translation problems in this chapter?

3. a. Choose any two chapters in an elementary mathematics textbook. Compare the verbal or translation problems.

b. Extend two simple translation problems from each chapter to complex translation problems.

4. a. The application problems as defined by Charles and Lester go beyond the usual definition of applications. These problems can involve other subjects, such as science, social studies, geography, health, and writing. Using their definition, consider an application project of your choice or choose from the following questions:

How could electricity costs at school (at home) be cut?

How could litter be removed from the school environment and this environment kept clean?

What is the best breakfast cereal?

What costs are involved in running a home (car)?

How do plants grow from seed under various conditions?

Brainstorm with another student to devise a list of activities to show how this project includes other subject areas as well as mathematics.

b. As you can see, these projects can lead in a number of directions and become very involved. To consider or explain an entire project at once could be overwhelming to both students and teacher. Describe how you would plan and introduce one small segment of this project and how this could lead into a second phase of the project.

5. Find two puzzle problems, one from a lower-grade textbook and another from an upper-grade textbook. Copy and solve each problem. What hints could you give students to help them understand the problems? To help them solve the problems?

6. *For your resource file:* There are numerous sources for process problems. Some of them are described in the articles by Barson, Slesnick, and Thompson. Read one of these articles and add it to your resource file. Work through one of the problems in the article.

7. Define problem solving in your own words. What factors need to be considered for a situation to be considered a problem-solving situation? Compare your definition to the one by Charles and Lester.

8. Do you use key words to solve problems? Why is it important to be aware of key words but not dependent on them? Why should students analyze the situation?

POLYA'S PROBLEM-SOLVING STEPS

You may have encountered difficulties in trying to solve the foregoing problems. Even finding an appropriate starting point may have been difficult. We face the same difficulties in many other problems that we confront. However, it is possible to develop a general process for problem solving. George Polya proposed four steps that are generally recognized as essential to all successful problem solving.

Polya's four steps are listed below. Within each step, different suggestions or strategies have been devised to help us successfully complete each step.

1. Understanding the problem

Read the problem and restate it in your own words.

Decide what is to be found.
Find the relevant data.

2. Devising a plan

Act it out or use models.
Draw a diagram or picture.
Guess and check.
Make an organized list.
Construct a table or a chart.
Write an equation or a number sentence.
Look for a pattern.
Relate to a similar problem.
Work backward.
Use logical reasoning.

3. Carrying out the plan

Use relevant information.
Check your work.

4. Looking back

Consider reasonableness of answer.
Check results in the original problem.
Determine whether there is another solution.

The remainder of this section is an expansion of this outline. To exemplify the various strategies for "devising a plan," problems have been included. To understand and appreciate each strategy and to gain more experience in problem solving, solve one problem included with each strategy. You may choose to work through these problems with another student. In cases where more than one problem is presented, choose the problems that are of interest and that are at an appropriate level of difficulty. Some of the problems have been adapted from *Problem Solving: A Basic Mathematics Goal.*

As you read this section you should notice that some of the concepts presented for each step overlap. Also, there is overlap among various strategies given in "devising a plan." Because problem solving is a continuous process, the steps are not rigidly defined. Although these steps are artificially imposed and overlap, they serve to outline the problem-solving process.

When students are introduced to problem-solving situations, the teacher should spend considerable time discussing the problem in terms of the first step so that all class members understand the problem. Whenever possible the situation should be related to real-life situations or school experiences that students either have had or will encounter.

A number of unsuccessful problem solvers try to start with step 3. When they realize that they cannot solve the problem, they often give up as they are unfamiliar with strategies. Another common occurrence is that when students skip the first step, they start working on the wrong problem, as they have misinterpreted the situation.

Read the Problem and Restate It in Your Own Words

Reading or hearing the problem is necessary but not sufficient. To determine whether students understand the situation, the teacher should ask them to retell the problem in their own words. Other class members should decide whether the retelling is a correct interpretation of the problem. Also, there may be unfamiliar terms or phrases that need to be explained.

Decide What Is to Be Found

Students should identify what is to be found. Sometimes this is referred to as the "unknown." Answers could include such results as geometric figures, measurements, or number or word statements. If a number is to be found, students should estimate the size of the answer and discuss what units the answer should be expressed in, such as dollars, square centimeters, or kilograms.

Find the Relevant Data

The students should identify relevant data. Sometimes these are referred to as the "knowns." If the necessary information is not given in the problem, students may need to collect some or all of this information. They should also be able to identify which information is unnecessary to the solution of the problem. As they identify the known information, they should discuss the relationship among the knowns and the unknown.

To help students with this step, the teacher might ask some of the following questions. "What is given? What do you know after reading the problem? Do you know a related problem? Have you ever solved a problem like this one? What are you looking for? What is the question to be answered? What is the relationship between the given(s) and the unknown(s)? Can you restate the problem in your own words? Does the problem contradict itself? Can you draw a picture or a diagram to illustrate the situation?" Many more questions specifically related to the problem being studied can be asked to guide students to an understanding of the problem.

DEVISING A PLAN

The second step is also very important; time and care are needed in devising a plan. Sometimes students solve problems by trial and error. If this is their only method, they will not make efficient use of the time they spend on solving problems, and they will usually not be successful. Students who have learned a variety of strategies are more successful than students who have a limited number of strategies. A number of strategies were listed for the second step. Depending on the problem and the person solving the problem, one or more of these strategies could be used for any particular problem. These strategies are discussed below. Sample problems have been included with the explanations to illustrate problems that could be worked with different strategies.

Act It Out or Use Models

With some problems students may choose to act out the situation or use models to represent the situations. In a number of cases, this strategy will also help them to understand the problem better. Read through the problems that follow. After you understand the factors in the problem that you select, make an estimate as to a reasonable answer. Then use this strategy to act out the problem with pennies, play money, or slips of paper to represent bills. After you have solved the problem, reflect. Was your estimate the same as your results from acting it out? Did the action help clarify the situation? Was the action an appropriate strategy for solving the situation?

Alisa buys a bike for $60, sells it for $70, buys it back for $80, and sells it for $90. How much does Alisa make or lose in the process?

If a penny is rolled around a second penny as shown in Figure 1-5, will Lincoln's head be facing up or down when rolled halfway around?

FIGURE 1-5.
Penny puzzle.

Draw a Diagram or Picture
In a number of situations, drawing a diagram or picture can take the place of using models. As problem solvers draw diagrams to devise a plan, they often notice new variables about the problem that they had not considered in the first step. Solve the following problem by using this strategy.

> A yard is to be fenced off with 96 feet of new fencing. The neighbor's existing fence will be one side of the rectangular enclosure. What are the dimensions of the largest area that the new and existing fencing will enclose?

Your diagram probably made you aware of the factors to be considered in the problem. Did it also help you solve the problem? You could check your solution by determining whether 96 feet of fencing was used, but how do you know if you found the best solution? Did you restrict your answers to whole numbers? If fractions, common or decimal, are considered, will the answer change? By using your calculator to check decimal fractions that are near your result, you will soon determine whether your results are correct.

You may have recorded your data in a list and reorganized the list as more data were collected. To help you visualize the pattern of the data, you could have used a graph to record your information. The data will form a curve, and the peak of the curve represents your answer. Constructing a graph is more sophisticated than drawing a picture. When data are collected, a graph is often used to indicate the pattern of the data. A graph of the data from the fence problem is shown in Figure 1-6. The Questions and Activities section stresses that the *Arithmetic Teacher* also contains many hints about problem solving. The October 1984 issue contains a good example of drawing pictures.

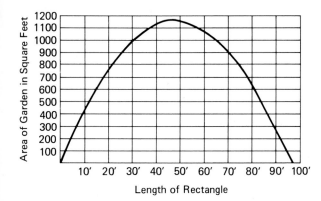

FIGURE 1-6.
Fence problem graph.

Guess and Check

Sometimes students use "guess and check" to solve a problem. This is similar to trial and error, but strategies should involve more *educated* guessing. Some students may randomly pick numbers and try different combinations. Although they may gain some insight into the problem, in most cases this is not appropriate after a couple of trials. Students need to be encouraged to stop and think about their guesses before they start to work.

In the section "Some Problems to Solve," you may have worked the problem, "Who Am I?" If not, reread and solve the problem. The strategy that you probably used was a form of guess and check. You probably listed the even digits, as you did not need to consider such numbers as 1 or 5. Then you probably determined which combinations of digits added to 12 and when multiplied gave a product less than 40. You may have focused on the zero as a factor if you were thinking about the multiplicative property of zero. As you discuss with your classmates how you solved this problem, you should observe that the process varied among individuals.

Some students did more thinking and may have found the answer on their first "guess." Some students would list all combinations of digits that add to 12, then work on the last condition of the problem. For a problem with a small number of combinations, the time needed for this may be unimportant, but most problems have a larger number of possibilities. Whole-class discussions should be structured so that students will be encouraged to become educated guessers. Considerable time should be spent discussing the options as a whole class *before* determining which combinations will meet these conditions. These dis-

cussions also help broaden their experiences as the students listen to how others approach the same problem. Use this strategy to solve the following problems.

> What two numbers have a difference of 5 and a product of 84?

> Find the dimensions of a rectangle that has a perimeter of 26 centimeters and an area of 30 square centimeters.

Make an Organized List

As you worked through a problem in the preceding section, you may have used lists to organize your thinking. You may have marked the entries that were not solutions. This strategy also helps you keep track of which combinations were tried so that you do not repeat your work and so that you try all combinations. This is another strategy that is as appropriate for adults as for young children. At first you may observe that some children's work is randomly scattered over their papers, so that it is difficult to determine what work has been done. Making an organized list can be taught by doing problems with the entire class. Data can be listed on the chalkboard. Different lists can be formed so that children can compare and discuss the advantages of organized versus random lists. The children should have individual practice in rewriting data from lists into organized lists. Solve the following problem using this strategy.

> Find an even three-digit number that is divisible by 5 and the sum of whose digits is seven. One pair of digits differ by four; another pair differ by one. The largest digit is in the tens place.

Construct a Table or a Chart

This strategy is similar to an organized list but differs in that labels are used to help organize the data into different categories. You may have been using this strategy in the problem involving area and perimeter if you wrote your data in separate columns. In addition to organizing the data in this manner, children need to be taught to label the information. Labels are helpful, as they make the students focus on exactly what data are to be collected. Labeled information is more easily read by the other students or when it is referred to at a later time. Use this strategy to solve the following problems.

> There are only two rectangles whose sides are whole numbers and whose perimeter and area are the same number. Determine the dimensions of the rectangles.

> You have seven coins in your pocket which are worth a total of one dollar. What are the coins?

Write an Equation or a Number Sentence

As you were solving the problems above, you were either writing or solving different number sentences. Some students may have solved the problems in "Guess and Check" by writing and solving the system of equations, $x - y = 5$ and $xy = 84$. Similarly, an equation, $2x + 2y = xy$, could have been written to express the problem in "Construct a Table or a Chart." The students would then need to use the strategy "guess and check" to solve this equation. Write number sentences to solve each of the following problems.

> Nicole is three years older than Jody. Together their ages add to twenty-one. How old is each girl?

> A rabbit hops completely around the edge of the garden fence, all 42 feet. The garden is twice as long as it is wide. What are the dimensions of the garden?

You may have recognized these problems from your first studies with algebra. They can be solved using equations, but they can also be solved using strategies such as "guess and check" or "construct a table." Children need to be introduced to these problems at earlier grade levels using strategies appropriate to their maturity.

Young children also use this strategy when they are beginning their studies of operations. They will write number expressions such as $13 - 7$ or $3 + 5 - 4$ to express the relationships among numbers in verbal problems. Then they will answer the problem by solving the equation.

Look for a Pattern

Another strategy that is used to solve problems, particularly in mathematics and science, is "finding a pattern." To find patterns, the student must organize the data in a sequence, list, or table. Very young children can be introduced to patterns through attribute blocks. (Attribute blocks are described in detail in Chapter 4.) Children can use these blocks to build trains (patterns) in which each block differs from the one before it by just *one* characteristic (Figure 1-7a and b). In the first train shown (Figure 1-7a), the differences, in order, are shape, shape, size, color, and thickness. Attribute trains in which the pattern is two differences can also be made (Figure 1-7c and d). In the last train (Figure 1-7d), the differences, in order, are shape–color, shape–color, size–thickness, shape–thickness, size–color.

Children also explore patterns in number sequences such as 10, 9, 8, 7, . . . or 3, 5, 7, 9, ... As the children mature mathematically, the patterns become more sophisticated. Solve the following problems using patterns.

1, 1, 2, 3, 5, 8, 13, ____, ____,

____, ____

0, 1, 4, 9, 16, ____, ____, ____,

____

Polygon	Number of Diagonals
Triangle	0
Quadrilateral	2
Pentagon	5
Hexagon	
Septagon	
Octagon	

To solve the second problem above you probably also used other strategies, such as "drawing a diagram" and "checking your guesses" by using the number sequence and the results from your diagrams. Finding a pattern is often used with simplifying problems.

Relate to a Similar Problem

Often problems are too difficult for students to work directly on the question that is asked. For example, the final problem in the section "Look for a Pattern" could have been to find the total number of diagonals in a 100-sided polygon. Since it would be too tedious to work the problem with diagrams, a simpler problem should be solved, such as the problem as given in the preceding section. The students need to find a pattern or a relationship between the number of sides and the number of diagonals in a polygon. Once this pattern is found, a generalization can be made. Use this strategy to solve the following problem.

How many diagonals are there in a 100-sided polygon? In an *n*-sided polygon?

Another aspect of this strategy is that when we are working new problems, sometimes we start thinking, "I've solved one like this before." By recognizing the similarities among different problems, students can find it easier to apply an appropriate strategy.

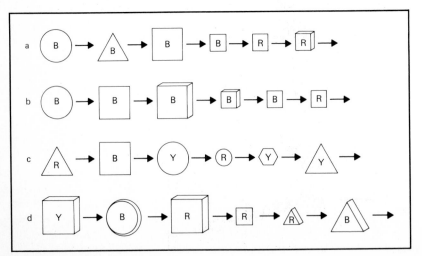

FIGURE 1-7.
Attribute trains.

When effective problem solvers encounter new problems, they *recognize* problems where strategies such as "finding a pattern" or "writing an equation" would be helpful. Sometimes not only can the new problem be solved by the same strategy, but it is actually one they have solved before that has merely been written in a new setting. Use your previous experiences to solve the following problem, which is similar to one that you have solved before.

> Loren walked into a party where he was introduced to ten people by the host. All of the people except the host were strangers to each other. How many introductions were made?

Work Backward

Sometimes when you encounter a problem, it helps to work backward. You may have found that in some problems you changed the order in which you had planned to work because this made the problem easier. Working backward is simply a variation of this method. In the following problem, use this strategy. Locate 100 and work backward.

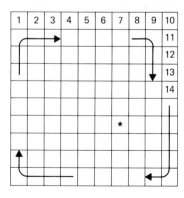

FIGURE 1-8.
Working backward.

	Red	Blue	Yellow
Not			

Place the attribute blocks in the appropriate spaces.

FIGURE 1-9.
Logical reasoning.

Figure 1-8 shows a grid with numbers in it. If you were to continue the number pattern until you got to the star, what number would you put in the star's square? Can you determine this number without filling in or counting all the numbers between?

Use Logical Reasoning

Problem solvers of various ages use this strategy. Young children can be involved in classification activities using logic blocks or other materials (Figure 1-9). The ordering activities described earlier also help develop logical thinking. Logic problems which are more sophisticated are given following. Solve one of these problems using this strategy.

> During three successive seasons, the Boston Celtics, St. Louis Hawks, Cincinnati Royals, and New York Knicks each reached the playoffs in professional basketball. A different team won each year. But the Hawks never beat the Celtics; the Knicks lost all of their games; and the Royals never lost to the Celtics. Can you complete the championship brackets (Figure 1-10) for each of the three years?

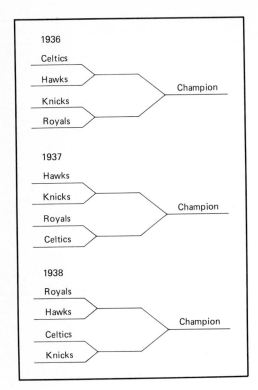

FIGURE 1-10.
Who won?

Using the 60-piece attribute set as described in "Prenumber Activities" in Chapter 4, define each of the three sets (Figure 1-11) so that all the pieces, except those *small* pieces shown, are in at least one of the sets. Place each of the 60 pieces in the appropriate section.

The focus of this section has been to acquaint you with various problem-solving strategies. At first, children need to learn how to use a particular strategy and apply it to many situations. After they have mastered the strategy, the students should be given problems for which they will have to decide which of several known strategies to use. The class should discuss strategies—both

appropriate and inappropriate—and why each strategy should or should not be used.

The teacher should give hints and ask questions to guide the students as needed. In asking questions about the particular problem, the teacher should be as specific as possible. Merely telling children to "Think" or to "Read the problem again" is usually not much help. However, the teacher should resist the temptation to *tell* students what to do, but rather should try to guide them in devising their own plan. Use of their own plans, however unusual or inefficient, will do more to aid students' learning than following any plan laid out by the teacher.

CARRYING OUT THE PLAN

This step simply involves carrying out the plan designed in the second step. More data may have to be collected and analyzed. Decisions will need to be made, but most of the major decisions have already been made in the first two steps.

Use Relevant Data

In some cases the students will be using the data that they identified in the first step with the strategies in the second step. Some of the simplest cases may involve the strategy "writing a number sentence or equation." In the example about Jody's and Nicole's ages,

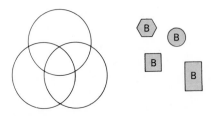

FIGURE 1-11.
Define the sets.

Erica selected the strategy of writing equations. In this step she referred to the relationships that were observed in the first step and wrote appropriate equations. Nicole (N) is three years older than Jody (J). $N - 3 = J$. Their ages add to 21. $N + J = 21$. Then Erica substituted $N - 3$ for the J in the second equation resulting in $N + N - 3 = 21$. She then solved the equation: $2N - 3 = 21$, so $2N = 24$ or $N = 12$.

Check Your Work

This is an important aspect of this step. When Erica was writing equations, she first wrote $N + 3 = J$ and $N + J = 21$. She checked her first equation by pretending Nicole was 5 and Jody was 2 since these ages fit the first condition that Nicole was three years older than Jody. When she substituted these ages into the equation, $N + 3 = J$, she obtained $8 = 2$. Consequently, she went back and rewrote her equation correctly as $N - 3 = J$.

In other problems where data are collected, errors can be very problematic. If students are trying to "find a pattern" and one piece of data is incorrect, the pattern will be very difficult to find. Students are more likely to find the error if they collect more pieces of data. As they analyze their entries, they should look for data that appear inconsistent. These data should be checked. Sometimes problem solvers will discover the right pattern but discard this result as it does not fit all of their data.

Students should be encouraged to use the calculator as a useful problem-solving tool. The calculator takes the stress out of computation so that students can focus on the problem-solving process. Calculators make it possible to use much larger numbers than students would otherwise be able to deal with successfully.

LOOKING BACK

The final step, looking back, is the one most often overlooked. When the solution is the main focus of the work and a right answer is more important than a correct process, the tendency is to stop working as soon as *any* solution is reached. Instead of allowing this, the teacher should use appropriate questions that guide the students so that they look back and check the answer. "Is your solution reasonable? Did you use all the pertinent data? Can you show that the result is true? Can you simplify any part of your work? Can you achieve the same solution by a different method? Can you use your solution to help you solve other problems?" The problem-solving process is complete only when this looking-back phase is finished.

Consider Reasonableness of Answer

During step 1 when students were getting to know the problem, they discussed what was a reasonable answer. If the answer was a number, what sizes and types of numbers would be reasonable. Some examples of answers that students have recorded for different situations include:

Age of Jeremy	-16
Age of grandfather	5
Number of cars needed for trip	5.8333333
Area of room	46.3 cubic meters
Volume of coffee cup	3 liters
Time needed to run a mile	2 hours 15 minutes

If these students had *thought* about their answers rather than merely recording them, they would have realized their errors.

Check Results in the Original Problem

In the section "Check Your Work," Erica realized her error when checking her procedures during step 3. She also made an error in her final solution. She solved the equations correctly but did not answer the problem. The question was to find *both* girl's ages. Erica needed to include both answers and *labels;* Jody is 9 years old and Nicole is 12 years old. Erica's strategies and work were correct but she did not answer the question. Other errors can result from miscalculations. These errors result primarily from carelessness rather than from faulty thinking. More critical are the thinking errors, which are due to not understanding the problem or to choosing an inappropriate strategy.

Determine Whether There Is Another Solution

In the section "Constructing a Table or a Chart," the second problem involved seven coins worth a total of one dollar. Is more than one solution possible? How many solutions are possible? In mathematics classes, both elementary and secondary, we often look for *the* answer. Traditional textbook story problems usually have one and only one answer, which leads students to believe that this is true for all problems. Due to this overemphasis on one answer, we often stop working after finding one solution. Students need opportunities to solve problems in which *more than one* answer or *no* answers are acceptable solutions.

QUESTIONS AND ACTIVITIES

1. Answer without consulting a resource.
   a. What are Polya's four problem-solving steps? What is the importance of each?
   b. Describe different aspects of the first and last steps.
   c. List at least ten strategies for the second step.

2. What are the advantages of knowing several strategies for devising a plan rather than only two or three strategies?

3. *For your resource file:* In 1984 a new column, "Problem Solving Tips for Teachers," was started by O'Daffer in the *Arithmetic Teacher.* Along with other tips for teaching problem solving, a series of columns highlighted various strategies. From the list below, choose two strategies that you would like to learn more about. Read and evaluate the article. Copy and add these ideas to your resource file.

   Guess and Check (September 1984).

   Draw a Picture (October 1984).

   Make a Table (November 1984).

   Make an Organized List (December 1984).

   Find a Pattern (January 1985).

   Use Logical Reasoning (February 1985).

   Solve a Simpler Problem (March 1985).

   Work Backward (April 1985).

   Write an Equation (May 1985).

4. The following problems are from the second-grade edition of *Harper & Row Mathematics,* 1985. These types of problems are found in the "Thinking-Skills Activity" for each lesson in this book. Solve six of these problems to gain an appreciation of the problem-solving emphasis in today's textbooks.

   There are more apples than oranges in a basket and more oranges than pears. If you add 2 to the number of oranges, you will get the number of apples. The number of apples is double the number of pears. If there are 3 pears, how many apples and oranges are in the basket?

A stop sign has 8 equal sides and angles. If you had a stop sign made of paper (without the post), how many ways could you fold it in half so that both halves were exactly on top of each other?

A bar graph has four bars: red, yellow, green, and blue. The longest bar is red and is double the length of the yellow bar. The shortest bar is blue and is one square shorter than the yellow bar. The green bar has four squares and is double the length of the blue bar. How long is each bar?

Be a detective and figure out who this number is. Here are the clues. It is an odd number between 382 and 414. It has no tens. If you add all the digits in the number, you get 7.

A chart has ten rows and each row has ten numbers in it. Numbers are put in the chart starting in the upper left with 414 and reading consecutively left to right to the last number in the lower right, which is 513. What number is in the seventh row and seventh column?

The builder built four rows of houses. Each row had 6 houses. He painted one third of the houses white and the rest in different colors. How many houses are not painted white?

Arrange the digits 1, 2, 3, 4, 5, and 7 to form two numbers that add up to 976. How many different ways can you do it?

A farmer has 5 animals. Some are rabbits and some are chickens. Altogether the animals have 14 legs. How many rabbits and how many chickens are there?

A red GRUBLE is worth 6 blue ZURKS. Mac had 7 red GRUBLES and 2 blue ZURKS. He bought a widget for 13 ZURKS. How many GRUBLES and ZURKS did Mac have left?

5. Choose two of the problems that you solved above. Write out teacher questions and hints that are explicit to each problem for:
   a. understanding the problem.
   b. devising a plan.
   c. looking back.
   Remember, these problems are for second graders.

6. Solve two of the following problems. You may want to work with another student. What strategies for devising a plan could be used for each of these problems?
   a. How many squares can you find on a checkerboard? (*Hint:* Include all one-by-one squares, all two-by-two squares, and so on.) *Extension:* Answer the same question for all rectangles with a ratio of 1:2 between their sides: those with a ratio of 1:3; those with a ratio of 2:3.
   b. Find the sum of the first hundred numbers. Develop a formula that can be used to find the sum of the first n numbers, where n is a positive integer.
   c. *The Tower of Hanoi:* Given the situation illustrated here, transfer the three disks from the peg at one end to the peg at the other end by following these rules: Only one disk may be moved at a time, and a larger disk may never be placed on top of a smaller disk. What is the smallest number of moves necessary to transfer the three disks? *Extension:* What is the smallest number of moves necessary if you start with 4 disks? With 5 disks? With n disks? Suppose that you have 4 rods instead of 3. How does this affect the problem? What about 5 rods? Or n rods?

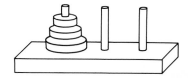

d. Locate a dripping faucet. Measure in milliliters the amount of water that is wasted in ten minutes. At this rate, how much water is lost in a day? Find out what the water rates are in your community and calculate how much the drip costs in one year. Find out the cost of a washer to fix the faucet. How long will it take for the washer to pay for itself by the water it saves?

e. A gardener has 30 feet of fence to keep animals out of the garden. What is the largest area of garden that this fence will enclose? What is the situation with 36 feet of fence?

7. a. Strategies for devising a plan need to be taught explicitly to children. A number of problems using a particular strategy should be solved so that the students can master that strategy. Below and to the right are lessons from a third- and a fourth-grade textbook on the strategies "guess and check" and "make a table." Read the lessons and write your reaction to the purpose of each lesson.

b. After students have had sufficient time with a strategy, another strategy should be introduced and studied. Later, problem sets can include problems that would involve more than one strategy. On p. 24 is a lesson from a fourth-grade textbook. The students are given the list of strategies that they have studied. What strategies could they use to solve each problem?

8. Read the children's book *Venn Diagrams* by Froman. Write a short paragraph evaluating the book. How could you use this book to help teach children the strategy "logical reasoning"?

9. The article "More Problems, Please" by Masse is about logical reasoning. Read the article and do any five of the problems involving classification and sets. Add these ideas to your resource file.

10. Read and work through the activities described in the children's book *Yes–No; Stop–Go: Some Patterns in Mathematic Logic* by Gersting and Kuczkowski.

(From A.V. Buffington A.R. Garr, J. Graening P.P. Halloran, M.L. Mahaffey, M. O'Neal **Merrill Mathematics: Grade 3, Student Edit** p. 207. Copyright © 1985, Merrill Publishing Company.)

Solve. Use guess and check.

1. Clara paid 24¢ for six erasers and pencils. How many of each did she buy? 2¢ 5¢

2. I am thinking of two numbers. Their sum is 7. Their difference is 1. What are the two numbers?

3.
A
2
4
3

B
7
5
6

C
9
8
10

Which block should you move so the sum of each stack equals 18? To which stack should you move it?

4. Put the numbers 1, 2, 3, 4, 5, 6, 7, and 8 into two groups of four. No number can be the sum of two other numbers in that group.
Hint:

1 2
7 8

3 4
5 6

These groups are not correct because 8 = 7 + 1.

PROBLEM SOLVING
Using the Strategies

Use one or more of the strategies listed to solve each problem below.

PROBLEM SOLVING STRATEGIES

CHOOSE THE OPERATIONS

DRAW A PICTURE

GUESS AND CHECK

MAKE A LIST

MAKE A TABLE

FIND A PATTERN

WORK BACKWARD

USE LOGICAL REASONING

1. Jolene took a math test. There were 20 problems on the test. Jolene got 10 more right answers than wrong answers. How many answers did Jolene get right? 15

2. The school play was about a king and a queen. Four boys, Nick, Preston, Robbie, and Donald, wanted to be king. Two girls, Hilary and Tess, wanted to be queen. How many different ways could the teacher choose a king and a queen? 8

3. The tallest girl on the team is the center. Peggy is taller than Linell. Ginny is shorter than Linell. Nancy is taller than Peggy. Edie is shorter than Peggy. Who is the center? Nancy

4. The basketball team and baseball team have a total of 24 players. There are 12 basketball players and 18 baseball players. How many players are on both the basketball team *and* the baseball team? 6

PROBLEM SOLVING

PROCESS PROBLEMS: TEACHING TECHNIQUES AND USING POLYA'S STEPS

If problem solving is so important, how does one go about teaching it? Aren't good problem solvers born and not made? The answer to the second question is yes and no. Some characteristics of good problem solvers are essentially beyond the influence of the teacher. However, even such an "innate" characteristic as intelligence can be fostered or crushed depending on the classroom atmosphere.

Research has identified certain characteristics of good problem solvers. These characteristics, and explicit teaching methods to enhance these skills in all students, are presented in this section. A more detailed discussion is found in "Untangling Clues from Research on Problem Solving" by Marilyn N. Suydam and "Mathematical Problem Solving: Not Just a Matter of Words" by Mark Driscoll. These articles were used as the primary reference for this section.

Good problem solvers can quickly comprehend the essential features of problems, particularly the purpose, and ignore irrelevant information. They also understand mathematical concepts and terms.

Good problem solvers are adept at applying Polya's first step, understanding the problem. Other students need more guidance in understanding the problem. Teacher hints and questions should be used to help them explore the problem and its purpose. The students should determine what information is necessary and what is irrelevant. Unfamiliar mathematical terms and concepts should be discussed. Teachers should try to choose problems for which students have the prerequisite skills. They should also review these concepts and terms as needed.

Good problem solvers make good estimations and check the reasonableness of their results.

As the students study the problem, the teacher should have them make estimates as to what types of answers are acceptable. If the answers are numerical, the students should have a sense of what is a reasonable answer. As they devise and work through their plans, such estimations should make them more aware of whether or not their plans are appropriate. If an inconsistency occurs, they may need to revise their estimates or plans. These estimates are also used in the last step to check the reasonableness of their results.

Good problem solvers analyze, evaluate, and select from alternative strategies to solve problems.

A variety of problem-solving strategies were discussed earlier. All of these need to be introduced to and used by the students. Some of these are explicit topics in the mathematics curriculum, such as "number sentences" and "charts and tables." Others, such as "using models," "drawing diagrams," and "looking for patterns," are more general strategies that are used throughout the year in developing mathematical concepts. By acquiring a variety of strategies students will have more options available when solving problems. If they only know a few strategies, the students may find that these are all inappropriate or inefficient for a particular problem.

When devising a plan for specific problems, various strategies and their appropriateness should be discussed. Part of *Look-*

ing Back should also be discussing other methods of solving the same problem. Students should discuss the different procedures that they used and also determine if there are other appropriate procedures. Through such discussions students should expand their repertoire of problem-solving strategies.

> Good problem solvers learn from their errors and are flexible in changing strategies when they realize that their current strategy is not appropriate.

As the different processes for solving a problem are analyzed and evaluated, students should decide if certain strategies are more appropriate than others. These discussions can take place during as well as after the problem-solving situation. Students should learn to become flexible in their work. They can learn to become receptive to alternative methods. They also need to learn from their mistakes and be willing to start over. Similarly, the students need to know that *mistakes are part of learning* and it is okay to be incorrect.

> Good problem solvers approach problem-solving situations with less anxiety and more confidence in their ability to solve problems than do other problem solvers.

As students' abilities improve, they gain confidence in their skills, and their attitudes toward problems will become more positive. Research has shown that one teaching strategy to improve students' problem-solving ability is to have them solve a lot and a variety of problems. Problems should be diverse rather than similar so that students will not be solving the same problems over and over. As with most skills, the more that we use them, the more comfortable and skillful we will become.

Good problem solvers can transfer their understanding of one solved problem to other similar problems. They are able to discern the general structures of problems. They are also good at noting likenesses and differences.

Through class discussions students can become aware of the general structures of problems. New problems should be compared with other problems that students have already solved; the similarities and differences should be explicitly noted. In the section on strategies, the problems on the number of handshakes and the number of diagonals were discovered to be similar. By comparing the settings, the questions, and the process, the students will see the general structure of the problem and realize that the setting was incidental to the problem.

Another teaching strategy to help students see the structure of problems is to extend the problems. To extend a problem, a component such as the setting, the numbers or variables, the conditions, or what is known and unknown can be changed. After a problem has been solved and discussed, extensions can be suggested by the teacher or by the students. The new problem can then be considered by the class. They should find that solving the new problem is *similar* to their process for the original problem.

An example of an extension is given in the situation described below. Throughout this example the teacher structures the situation to guide the student. More experienced problem solvers would need less guidance. *The goal of problem solving is that students will become independent problem solvers and will not need guidance.* To help them become good problem solvers, teachers need to give them effective strategies.

The following dialogue is an actual conversation between an adult and a third grader as the student developed a formula for the sum of the first *n* positive integers. It begins with a "brainteaser" problem such as might be found in an elementary mathematics book.

Problem: Steven's clock strikes the hours. At 1:00 it strikes once, at 2:00 it strikes twice, and so on. How many times does Steven's clock strike in one day?

Elizabeth: Oh boy! At 1:00 it strikes once, at 2:00 it strikes twice, that's 3 times. At 3:00 it strikes three times and that gives us 6. It's already struck 6 times.

Ms. Fox: How do you know? What are you doing?

Elizabeth: Adding. I added the 1 and the 2 and got 3. Then at 3:00 it strikes three times so I added that to the 3 I had and got 6. (Goes on figuring.) At 4:00 it strikes four times and that makes 10. At 5:00 it strikes five times . . . that makes 15. It's already struck 15 times in five hours. (Figure 1-12 shows what Elizabeth was writing as she talked.) At 6:00 it

strikes six times . . . I'm trying to think. I don't know what 15 + 6 is. Wait a minute . . . 16, 17, 18, 19, 20, 21 (using fingers). All right, it strikes 21 times in six hours. Now it's . . . Do we have to include the twice? ("Twice" refers to the two revolutions of the hour hand during one 24-hour day.) After we get our final answer can we add that with the other half so that we don't actually have to write down the whole thing—it strikes this many hours at this time and all 'cause there are 24 hours in a day? . . . 21 + 7 is 28 in seven hours. Boy, this is getting tricky. 29, 30, 31, 32, 33, 34, 35, 36 . . . (Works silently.) Okay, in nine hours it strikes 45 times. 46, 47, 48, 49, 50, 51, 52, 53, 54, 55 . . . In ten hours it has struck 55 times. Is that okay? Umm 55 . . . 56, 57, 58, 59, 60, 61, 62, 63, 64, 65, 66. Now I'm up to 66. I'm up to 66; I'm not through—in eleven hours 66 times. (Works silently.) It strikes 78 times in half a day so

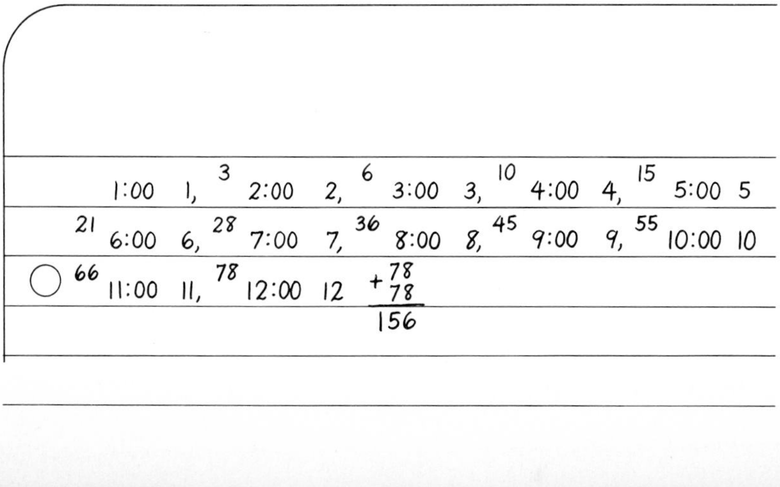

FIGURE 1-12.
Solution of the clock problem.

1:00 1,	^{3} 2:00 2,	^{6} 3:00 3,	^{10} 4:00 4,	^{15} 5:00 5
^{21} 6:00 6,	^{28} 7:00 7,	^{36} 8:00 8,	^{45} 9:00 9,	^{55} 10:00 10
^{66} 11:00 11,	^{78} 12:00 12	$\begin{array}{r} 78 \\ +\,78 \\ \hline 156 \end{array}$		

78 + 78 . . . Let me write this down . . . In one whole day it strikes 156 times. Correct or not?

Ms. Fox: How did you figure it out? (Note that the adult does not immediately *tell* Elizabeth whether she is right or wrong. Rather, appropriate questions are asked to help Elizabeth clarify and explain her thinking so that she can find her own mistakes, if any.)

Elizabeth: 1 + 2 = 3, 3 + 3 = 6,
6 + 4 = 10, 10 + 5 = 15,
15 + 6 = 21, 21 + 7 = 28,
28 + 8 = 36, 36 + 9 = 45,
45 + 10 = 55, 55 + 11 = 66,
66 + 12 = 78, 78 + 78 . . .

Ms. Fox: Why did you add 78 and 78?

Elizabeth: Because there are 24 hours in a day and 12 plus 12 is 24 so 78 + 78 = 156.

Ms. Fox: In figuring this problem out, you have just added the first twelve numbers. But suppose you wanted to know the total of the first 100 numbers.

Elizabeth: I don't know. I don't want to count that far tonight.

Ms. Fox: Why don't you want to do it?

Elizabeth: Because it'll take a long time.

Ms. Fox: Why will it take a long time?

Elizabeth: Because you have to keep going and going.

Ms. Fox: Do you suppose there might be any pattern?

Elizabeth: That would get you there faster?

Ms. Fox: Yes.

Elizabeth: Oh. 10, 20, 30, 40, 50, 60, 70 . . .

Ms. Fox: That won't get you to the total of the first 100 numbers.

Elizabeth: Oh.

Ms. Fox: You just found the total of the first 12 numbers. I want you to find the total of the first 100 numbers.

Elizabeth: Oh, no, not tonight. Please not tonight. Well, I already know the total for the first 24 numbers.

Ms. Fox: You do? Are you sure?

Elizabeth: Pretty sure . . . if my problem here is right.

Ms. Fox: Is the sum of the first 24 numbers going to be the same as twice the sum of the first 12 numbers? Let's figure it out with the calculator.

Elizabeth: (Adds the numbers 13 through 24 to 78 using the calculator.) 300.

Ms. Fox: Is that the same as 78 + 78?

Elizabeth: No.

Ms. Fox: Well, why do you suppose it's not?

Elizabeth: Because . . .

Ms. Fox: What was wrong with your thinking when you said they'd be the same?

Elizabeth: Because I forgot to add all the next hours going on. Now can we go on with our problem? We're at 25 . . . I want to find out the total of the first 100 numbers. (Starts to continue adding using the calculator.)

Ms. Fox: But I want to know if there isn't an easier way to do it. This is doing it the hard way. Even with a calculator, this is the hard way.

Elizabeth: No, you just keep punching the numbers and plus.

Ms. Fox: I know, but look how long it took

you just to get to 24. Suppose you wanted to go to 3000.

Elizabeth: I don't think the calculator would hold up that long.

Ms. Fox: We want to see if we can find a pattern. What might you do to help you look for a pattern?

Elizabeth: I don't know.

Ms. Fox: What helps you to see a pattern?

Elizabeth: Hey, I think I see a pattern.

Ms. Fox: What?

Elizabeth: As you count up to 100 . . . Let's say we have 10. You double that which is 20 and add 1 . . . 21. You double it and then you add.

Ms. Fox: Double what?

Elizabeth: Double the number.

Ms. Fox: What number? I want to know what number you're doubling. Are you going to double 78?

Elizabeth: No, 10.

Ms. Fox: Why are you doubling 10?

Elizabeth: Oh, I don't get this. I'm not sure why I'm doubling 10.

Ms. Fox: Could you make a table?

Elizabeth: (Makes a table using information already found.) Like this? (Figure 1-13).

Ms. Fox: Can we draw a picture of these

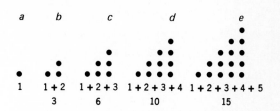

FIGURE 1-14.
Dot representation of the clock problem.

numbers? (Draws dots as in Figure 1-14.) What shape do you see?

Elizabeth: It's a triangle and half a square.

Ms. Fox: It's half a square. Does that give you any ideas about how many dots we might have? If we have a square and we know it's four dots on a side, how do we find how many dots it has altogether?

Elizabeth: It has four rows with four dots in each so it has $4 \times 4 = 16$ dots.

Ms. Fox: If this were a square, how many dots would it have? (Figure 1-14d)

Elizabeth: 16

Ms. Fox: But it isn't a square.

Elizabeth: It is a triangle.

Ms. Fox: So how many dots should it have?

Elizabeth: I think it should have 13.

Ms. Fox: How do you figure that?

Elizabeth: If a whole square is 16, a half a square should be 13. No . . . Half of 16 is 8.

Ms. Fox: But how many dots do we know are in that triangle? Are there 8?

Elizabeth: No, there are 10.

Ms. Fox: If it were half and we wanted to know about 100 without doing all

Time	Total Number of Strikes
1:00	1
2:00	3
3:00	6
4:00	10
5:00	15

FIGURE 1-13.
Partial table of the clock problem.

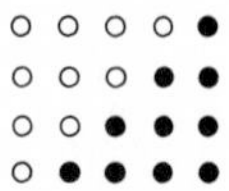

○ ○ ○ ○ ●
○ ○ ○ ● ●
○ ○ ● ● ●
○ ● ● ● ●

FIGURE 1-15.
Rectangles from triangles.

that adding or drawing all those dots . . . If it were half, we could say (100 × 100) ÷ 2.

Elizabeth: But it's not half.

Ms. Fox: When we tried half the square, it wasn't enough. What if we tried putting two of our triangles together? (Draws a picture; see Figure 1-15.)

Elizabeth: You would not get a square.

Ms. Fox: What did I get?

Elizabeth: You got a rectangle.

Ms. Fox: Do you notice anything about that rectangle?

Elizabeth: It's got one more line than a square.

Ms. Fox: Okay, one side has one more than the other side, right? So it has one side that's 4 and another side that's 4 + 1. If we want to find out how many dots are in that rectangle, what would we do?

Elizabeth: Multiply 4 × 5 = 20.

Ms. Fox: Now how did we make the rectangle? How did we decide to make a rectangle?

Elizabeth: You added one more stripe and you filled in all these other dots.

Ms. Fox: How is the rectangle related to the triangle we had before? (Figure 1-14d)

Elizabeth: It has the same black area that

this has and it has white dots and this one doesn't have white dots but it has the black dots.

Ms. Fox: Okay, but how many white dots does it have?

Elizabeth: It has . . . (Pauses to count.) 10.

Ms. Fox: How many black dots does it have?

Elizabeth: 10.

Ms. Fox: Hm, does that suggest anything?

Elizabeth: That's a square.

Ms. Fox: Oh, but it's not a square.

Elizabeth: No, it isn't. That's one thing about it. You made the dots different ways. Hey! As I thought; if we turn this over it looks exactly like we had before. This is up. Now I have it.

Ms. Fox: So if we want to know just about the triangle, how does it compare to the rectangle?

Elizabeth: It's half as much as that rectangle.

Ms. Fox: Oh, now what size is that rectangle?

Elizabeth: 20.

Ms. Fox: How did we get the 20?

Elizabeth: It's 4 × (4 + 1) or 4 × 5.

Ms. Fox: And that is how much too much? The black dots that we want to know about are how much of the total rectangle?

Elizabeth: One half.

Ms. Fox: 4 × 5 = 20. 20 ÷ 2 or one half of 20 . . .

Elizabeth: Is 10.

Ms. Fox: Well, well, and that's how many

black dots we had. Do you suppose that would work for other numbers?

Elizabeth: Maybe.

Ms. Fox: Let's try it for a couple of other numbers that we know about and see if it works. Let's try it for the triangle with 8 dots on the bottom row. What does the formula say to do?

Elizabeth: First we multiply how many dots . . .

Ms. Fox: What's that number?

Elizabeth: 8×5?

Ms. Fox: Why would we multiply 8×5?

Elizabeth: Well . . . no. 8 by 9.

Ms. Fox: Why would we multiply 8 by 9?

Elizabeth: Well, if we do it as we did with this . . . and have a rectangle that would be right because . . . 8×9 . . . all right . . . here we had 8 and . . . no, 4 and $4 + 1$ so here we'd have 8 and $8 + 1$.

Ms. Fox: And then what else do we have to do if we want to find just the triangle?

Elizabeth: Split the thing in half.

Ms. Fox: Okay, let's use the calculator to do that.

Elizabeth: $8 \times 9 = 72$ and $72 \div 2$ . . . equals 36.

Ms. Fox: Now let's look back up here where you were working the first problem (Figure 1-12) When you got to 8:00, is that what you had?

Elizabeth: Yes, 36.

Ms. Fox: Well, that one works. Now how do you suppose we'd find the sum of the first 100 numbers.

Elizabeth: $(100 \times 101) \div 2$ . . . equals 5050. (Using the calculator.)

Ms. Fox: Let's go back and check that the long way with the calculator. (They verify the 5050.) Now suppose we wanted to find the sum of the first n numbers.

Elizabeth: What do you mean n?

Ms. Fox: I mean we don't know for sure what number n is. So n could be 100 or n could be 372 or n could be 4968. It could be anything. Can we write a formula for finding the sum of the first n numbers? What would it look like?

Elizabeth: I'm not sure. What do you mean n? Like what?

Ms. Fox: Okay, suppose $n = 100$. What did you do?

Elizabeth: It was times 101.

Ms. Fox: It was what times 101.

Elizabeth: 100×101.

Ms. Fox: Now if $100 = n$, we could write the formula as n times what?

Elizabeth: All right, times 101 . . . no or times n, divided by n . . . no, 2.

Ms. Fox: But is it $n \times n$?

Elizabeth: No, not actually.

Ms. Fox: What is it?

Elizabeth: It's $n \times 101$.

Ms. Fox: Only if n is 100. Suppose n is 4. It's $n \times$ *what*?

Elizabeth: 5.

Ms. Fox: Can you write this part with n?

Elizabeth: Yes.

Ms. Fox: How?

Elizabeth: I don't know . . . As 5?

Ms. Fox: But it's only 5 when n is 4. When

a mathematician writes a rule, it should work no matter what n is—no matter whether n is 4 or 8 or 36 or 100.

Elizabeth: Well, then it's $n \times n$.

Ms. Fox: But that would be 100×100.

Elizabeth: No . . . $n \times n$ 1 . . . $n + 1$. So it's $n \times (n + 1) \div 2$.

Ms. Fox: Whatever number you used, whether it was 4 or 8 or 100, you added 1 to it. So another way to say that is $\frac{n \times (n + 1)}{2}$ Now that's a formula! Now we can substitute any number we want for n. If we say $n = 978$, we can put that into the formula and say $(978 \times 979) \div 2 = 478{,}731$ and that's the sum of the first 978 numbers.

This discussion shows that Elizabeth attacked and solved the textbook problem easily. When Ms. Fox began trying to extend the problem, Elizabeth experienced some difficulty. Some of this difficulty came from mathematical immaturity. Elizabeth was not really familiar with mathematical formulas and so had some trouble understanding what was being asked. She was unfamiliar with the idea of using a letter (n) to stand for any positive integer. She also made some unproductive attempts because she was in too much of a hurry to do something with numbers. But in spite of all this she was able, with guidance, to solve the problem. Because of the processes she used in solving this problem, she is better prepared to solve other problems she encounters.

Most third graders could solve the original clock problem by a series of addition computations. Few, if any, will find a pattern for solving the problem; they will simply do the required additions. When asked to find the sum of the first 100 numbers, students will recognize the need for a pattern. By using their computations for the original problem, some students, with appropriate guidance from the teacher, can find this pattern. A very few of those students who are able to find a pattern for the sum of the first 100 numbers will be able to generalize this pattern to the sum of the first n numbers. However, most third-grade students will need additional time and many more experiences to develop the mathematical maturity needed for this level of abstraction.

TRANSLATION PROBLEMS: TEACHING TECHNIQUES AND USING POLYA'S STEPS

Some teaching methods were described in earlier sections. The purpose of this section is to discuss additional guidelines for helping students solve translation problems. Examples of how problem-solving strategies could be used with a class have also been included.

Students need many and varied experiences with story problems. In an earlier section, National Assessment results were given which show that students do well on routine, one-step verbal problems but have a lot of difficulty with multistep and nonroutine one-step verbal problems. But even single operations can cause difficulty. National Assessment results also show that few students could estimate the answers to addition and multiplication problems involving common and decimal fractions. Some students cannot even *identify* the operation needed in verbal problems involving common fractions such as the following:

The mower ran out of gas after Lisa had mowed $\frac{5}{8}$ of the lawn. She had been mowing for the past $2\frac{1}{4}$ hours. How long will it take her to mow the entire lawn?

Although we may not use fractions as often as whole numbers, the difficulty the students were experiencing is due to a lack of understanding of number *and* operation concepts.

When students don't recognize the operation(s) needed, other problem-solving strategies such as "using a model" are required. In the case of the situation described above, students could use the strategy "solve a similar problem." By rereading the problem using whole numbers or other, easier-to-use common fractions such as "one-half," they will soon decide that this is a division situation. This is similar to a teaching strategy where problems are read without the numbers so that they *cannot* be solved numerically. Since students cannot find a numerical answer anyway, they must concentrate on the process of problem solving. They simply discuss what is to be done and identify the operation or operations needed. They should not be asked to solve the problem.

To help children focus on operations, read to them a situation with no questions. Give them directions such as "devise a mathematics question that could be asked about this situation." Sometimes give them explicit directions such as making up a question that involves subtraction or one that involves addition *and* multiplication. Another variation of this strategy is to show a picture and have them make up a story or question involving mathematics.

Textbook problems could readily be adapted to this activity. Read various situations to the students and have them write questions. These questions should be shared with the class who can then decide what operation or operations is/are involved. At first a number of students will write statements, not questions. They will also give the answer or tell how to do the problems in their

"questions." The class will need to discuss what questions are appropriate. With experience and feedback their techniques will improve. Writing questions for operations is more difficult than identifying or solving problems. It is a good technique for extending students' abilities to solve simple and complex, routine and nonroutine verbal problems.

Other problem situations involving applications can be adapted from the newspaper and other resources. Real-world application problems do not have to be made synthetic so that the numbers will fit a nice, neat mold. Instead, these problems can use the numbers that would be appropriate in reality. With the aid of a calculator, a problem such as the one about the grass in McGillicuddy Pond could be extended to questions about the growth of human population.

The same procedure of writing problems should be extended to nonroutine problems that contain too much or not enough information. Explicit separate lessons on problems with too much information and on problems with not enough information should be taught. These problems should be discussed as a class with the students identifying what information is not needed or is missing. In the latter case, they could describe what is missing, and when possible, identify what type of units, such as apples, minutes, chairs, or meters, are involved and estimate what size the units should be. For example, when given only one dimension of a room and asked to determine how much carpet is needed, students should be able to give a reasonable estimate of the other measure.

The order in which information is presented is also an important factor. Research indicates that children find problems easier to solve if the numbers are given in the order in which they are to be used. However, "real" problems do not always occur in this order. Interpreting problems in which the order of information varies is an acquired skill that needs to be explicitly taught.

One of the reasons that children have difficulties with all these types of problems is a lack of experiences. After the initial lesson is taught, children need continued practice in such skills. Throughout the remainder of the year, assignments and warm-ups should occasionally contain some of these nonroutine problems. Some textbooks have *a page* on problems with too much or not enough information, and throughout the rest of the textbook all problems contain only the appropriate numbers. In these cases teachers need to supplement their textbooks. Other resources can provide problems to be used as assignments or problems to be done in the first part of the mathematics period. Again, writing problems should follow identifying and solving such problems. As students learn to write these types of problems, their examples can become the source of more problems.

These are some of the general teaching strategies for studying story problems. Another aspect to helping children solve problems is using Polya's four steps to explore individual problems. In spite of their shortcomings, traditional textbook story problems can be used to teach real problem solving. Since these problems are mostly short and generally require only one previously learned operation, getting to know the problem is usually not difficult. An effective check of the first step would be to have the students retell the problem in their own words.

For steps 2 and 3, making a plan and carrying out the plan, students can explore more than one strategy. The greater the number of strategies they know well enough to use, the greater their chances of solving the problem successfully. Some strategies

that are helpful include estimation, drawing a diagram or using a model, using smaller numbers (working a similar problem), organized lists, finding patterns, working backward, and equations or number sentences. In the past there has been undue emphasis on choosing an operation or writing a number sentence. If children don't *recognize* a situation as a particular operation, too often they have no other strategies for solving the problem.

As students work on problem solving, the teacher may sometimes need to suggest particular strategies. Other times, the students will think of the strategies, but the teacher can help by verbally labeling each strategy as it is suggested. This technique helps the students to focus on the process involved so that they will use these same strategies appropriately in solving new problems later. It also emphasizes the strategy for those students who may not have thought of that approach. The following sample illustrates the kind of discussion that might occur in a fourth-grade classroom as the students work through Polya's steps 2 and 3 with a typical textbook problem. The objective of the lesson was to find as many different ways as possible to solve this problem.

Problem:	Kessler's grocery store has canned corn on special this week. In the last three days they have sold 390 cans of corn. If each case holds 24 cans, how many cases of corn has Kessler's sold in the last three days?
Ms. Biorn:	Now that we understand what information the problem gives us and what the question is, can you think of a strategy that might help us solve this problem? (Pause to give students some

time to think about possible strategies but not long enough for them to find an answer.) Who has a suggestion of what we could do?

Kerry: We could just divide 390 by 24 to see how many cases were sold.

Ms. Biorn: Yes, direct computation could give us an answer. Is there another way to solve this problem?

Jesse: I wrote a number sentence describing the situation. 24 × ? = 390.

Ms. Biorn: Number sentences help us to see the relationships between what we know and what we are trying to find.

Jerry: I'm not very good at division so I started making a table (Figure 1-16).

Sandy: A table like that takes too long. I figured if they sold 240 cans that would make 10 cases so it must be more than 10. But it would take 480 cans to fill 20 cases so it has to be less than 20. Then I would try numbers between 10 and 20 to see what works.

Ms. Biorn: Jerry is using a table. Sandy has started by simplifying the problem and will finish with guess and check.

Jackie: I just guessed. I thought 390 is a lot of cans so I guessed 25 cases. Then I would multiply 24 × 25 to see if that's right. (Continues, thinking out loud.) Let's see . . . 24 × 25 (Pauses to compute.) 24 × 25 is 600. Ugh! That's too much. Maybe I should try 23 cases.

Sandy: Don't try 23; I already found out that 20 is too many.

Ms. Biorn: Guessing is often a good way to start a problem. When a guess turns out to be too much or too little, we can change it and make a better guess. Did anyone try to solve the problem another way?

Dale: I like to be able to see things so I started making a diagram. It shows 24 cans in each case, and I could just keep going till I get to 390 cans (Figure 1-17).

Lynn: I have trouble with division too so I would use the base-ten blocks. I would get out three flats (hundreds) and nine longs (tens) (Figure 1-18). Then I would trade the flats for longs and some of the longs for units so I could arrange the blocks in groups of 24 and count the

Cans of corn	Cases
24	1
48	2
72	3
96	4
120	5

FIGURE 1-16.
Problem solving: using a table.

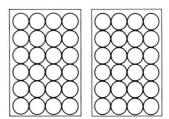

FIGURE 1-17.
Problem solving: using a diagram.

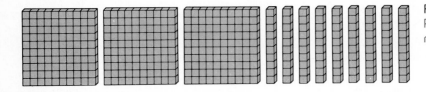

FIGURE 1-18.
Problem solving: using models.

groups. (Division using base-ten blocks is shown and discussed in detail in Chapter 7.)

Ms. Biorn: Dale used a diagram, and Lynn is experimenting with a model, base-ten blocks. Both of these methods help make it easier to visualize the numbers we are dealing with.

Kerry: I just had another idea. A couple of weeks ago we were learning about graphs. Could we use a graph to solve this problem? If we put the number of cases along the bottom and the number of cans up the side, then we could draw a line showing that for every one more case there are 24 more cans. Then we could come over from 390 until we hit the line and then go down from there to find how many cases.

Ms. Biorn: Good idea! That uses graphing, a new strategy we have just been learning (A group of students used this strategy; see Figure 1-19.)

As students found different ways to solve the problem, they were reinforcing and extending their operation concepts. The relationships among operations were also reinforced and extended as the students decided that a division situation could be solved as repeated subtraction, missing factor, or division. The teacher named each problem-solving strategy used by the class. This is an important teaching method, as it identifies and emphasizes the uses and types of a variety of strategies.

After this discussion, the students, working individually or in small groups, can use their strategies to *solve* the problem. Finally, they should look back and evaluate the work they have done. In this type of problem, they should all have the same answer. Anyone with a different answer needs first to check back through the work step by step to see where the mistake has occurred. Of course,

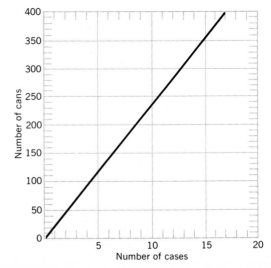

FIGURE 1-19.
Problem solving: using graphs.

it may be that the difficulty lies in having devised an inappropriate plan. When everyone has obtained an answer, a class discussion should follow so that students can compare the various methods used.

The teacher must be flexible enough at this point to accept any mathematically or logically sound method of solution regardless of how unusual it may be. For example, in the preceding problem, a student might suggest that in the real world, Kessler's might just check their computer inventory at the end of the third day to determine the number of cases sold. Or, knowing their inventory prior to the sale, they could count the number of cases left at the end of the third day and subtract that from the beginning inventory to determine the number of cases sold.

GUIDELINES FOR IMPLEMENTING PROBLEM SOLVING

It is recommended that problem solving be a daily activity. The amount of time for problem solving on any particular day would vary depending on the type of problems being studied, such as translation problems versus process problems. Charles and Lester recommend daily experiences that compose one third of the mathematics instruction time. They found that teachers, to provide time for problem-solving experiences, increased the pace of their instruction without affecting quality or quantity of instruction.

Selecting Problems

For the development of good problem solvers, good problems are essential. Some characteristics of good problems have already been discussed. In addition, good problems are those that the students perceive as useful, interesting, or entertaining. If students do not want to solve the problems, they will not put forth sufficient effort to learn problem-solving techniques.

Your textbook may have a problem-solving program incorporated into the units. The variety and number of problem-solving situations will vary considerably from one elementary textbook series to another and from one grade level to another. For most elementary teachers a particular textbook is the primary source for teaching problem solving through mathematics.

Good problems come from many sources. Depending on the quality and quantity of the program and the abilities of your students, the text may or may not need to be supplemented. Care must be taken in supplementing or designing a problem-solving program. The teacher will want to write supplementary problems based on the interests and abilities of particular groups of students. Books and articles on mathematical puzzles and games are another good source of problems. Finally, the students themselves usually enjoy writing their own problems and solving those posed by their fellow students. These can run the gamut from real-life problems—those based on the students' own experiences, articles from the newspaper, and the like—to pure fantasy problems.

At the beginning of the school year relatively easy problems should be selected. For low achievers the problems could be modified or more hints provided. Extensions and other more challenging opportunities should be provided for higher achievers. The problems should be chosen so that all students will be successful. Students, like other people, enjoy being successful. Developing positive attitudes should be a primary goal at the beginning of the year. As the students' confidence and abilities increase, more challenging problems can be introduced.

Grouping Students

Students should be involved in whole-class, small-group, and individual problem-solving situations. Whole-class instruction should be used to introduce and discuss new strategies. It should also be used to explore some problems as a large group as well as to summarize solved problems. Students also need to work individually in order to become independent problem solvers.

Small-group work combines some of the best elements of both individual and whole-class activities. Small groups provide an opportunity for students to be more actively involved in the process of problem solving. Due to the sharing of ideas, the students are more likely to be successful and to develop positive attitudes. It has been found that students who work in small groups solve more problems than if they had been working alone. It is also easier for the teacher to provide appropriate guidance for small groups than for students working individually. With this approach, the teacher has only 5 to 8 groups to interact with rather than 25 to 30 individuals. However, in contrast to whole-class instruction, teachers can tailor their hints and questions according to the small group's needs.

Time is a critical factor for small-group, individual, or whole-class work on problem solving. Students must be given sufficient time to work. With some process problems it is helpful to introduce and discuss the problem during the first time interval. Over the next few days the class may discuss their progress on it briefly. Later in the week the class can draw closure on the problem. Some process problems are particularly good for "problem-of-the-week" formats. The problem is introduced on Monday and discussed briefly each day. The solution and extensions are discussed on Friday.

Evaluation

Just as students are evaluated on other course work, they should be evaluated on their problem-solving skills. Topics in the curriculum should be evaluated by looking at the entire process rather than just at the answer. This is especially true of problem solving, where the emphasis is on the process, not the product. Group work or individual work should be collected. Students will need to show all work; subsections of their work should include all four steps. The teacher could write comments about the

Understanding the problem	0—Completely misinterprets the problem 1—Misinterprets part of the problem 2—Complete understanding of the problem
Solving the problem	0—No attempt or a totally inappropriate plan 1—Partly correct procedure based on part of the problem interpreted correctly 2—A plan that could lead to a correct solution with no arithmetic errors
Answering the problem	0—No answer or wrong answer based on an inappropriate plan 1—Copying error; computational error; partial answer for problem with multiple answers; answer labeled incorrectly 2—Correct solution

FIGURE 1-20.
Point system for assessing students' work. (From **Teaching Problem: What, Why, and How** by Randall Charles and Frank Lester. Copyright © 1982 by Dale Seymour Publications. Reprinted by permission of the publisher.)

process selected, how the process was carried out, and whether the information was correctly interpreted, as well as about the answer. Since the entire process is evaluated, the answer is deemphasized.

Charles and Lester suggest a point system for evaluating students' problem-solving skills (Figure 1-20). This method is useful as it helps the teacher and the students analyze their work. By such evaluations the students, as well as the teacher, are aware of what phases of their work need more attention.

QUESTIONS AND ACTIVITIES

1. a. Find a picture from a magazine or newspaper. What mathematics problems could be motivated from this picture? Include simple and complex translation problems.

   b. Clip an article from the newspaper and write several problems based on the information in it. Include two simple and two complex translation problems. Write two problems with too much information or not enough information. Include details for the solution of your problems.

2. *For your resource file:* Read one of the following articles and add it to your resource file. "Problem Stories: A New Twist on Problem Posing" by Bush and Fiala, "Ideas" by Ockenga and Duea, "Writing Techniques for Problem Solvers" by Fennell and Ammon, and "Another Look at Applications in Elementary School Mathematics" by Wirtz and Kahn. All of the articles describe strategies for involving students in writing story problems.

3. a. Write a situation that would interest students at a particular grade level and from which they could write questions

for various operations. State the grade level chosen.

   b. Write a situation for which students could generate questions that involve more than one step.

4. Why is it a good teaching technique to have students write translation or verbal problems?

5. a. Why do students need to have problems that include too much information? Too little information?

   b. Why should these problems be included throughout the year?

6. Read "Let's Do It: But It Can't Be Done" by Leutzinger and Nelson. To gain an appreciation of these types of problems, try solving some of them before reading their "solutions."

7. *For your resource file:* In "Ideas," Scheuer and Williams include activity sheets and descriptions of lessons for helping children analyze problems. Most of these problems are nonroutine. Read this article and add the ideas to your resource file. What were two new ideas that you learned from the article that you can use in your teaching?

8. Select a particular textbook chapter from a grade level of your choice. State the grade level. Find a page with a number of verbal problems. How could you adapt this lesson so that it was an oral activity where the students discuss devising a plan or choosing an operation? How could the lesson be adapted so that they revise the questions to involve more than one operation or different operations?

9. The approach to implementing problem solving varies among textbook series. To focus on three different approaches, work through the following problems. Cite grade level and textbook pages where you found evidence to answer each question.

   a. Consult the opening pages of a teacher's edition of *Harper & Row Mathematics.* Find the information on problem solving. Do they use Polya's steps or another problem-solving plan? Where is the daily problem solving found?

Analyze a chapter. Are there other lessons or parts of lessons that include additional problem solving? Are explicit strategies highlighted?

Is there an extra resource on problem solving for the teacher? How is it organized? What strategies for devising a plan are taught in this series? Does it give special helps such as teacher questions? Student activity sheets? Evaluation?

b. Consult the opening pages of the teacher's edition of *Addison-Wesley Mathematics.* Find the information on problem solving. Do they use Polya's steps or another problem-solving plan?

Consult the opening pages of three different chapters. What types of information about teaching problem solving are given?

Analyze a chapter. Are there lessons or parts of lessons that include problem solving? Are explicit strategies highlighted? How often is problem solving included? Under what different sections did you find problem solving highlighted?

Is there an extra resource on problem solving for the teacher? What strategies for devising a plan are taught in this series? Does it give special helps such as teacher questions? Student activity sheets? Evaluation?

c. Consult the opening pages of the teacher's edition of Scott, Foresman's *Invitation to Mathematics.* Find the information on problem solving. Do they use Polya's steps or another problem-solving plan? Where is problem solving found? What problem-solving strategies and skills are taught in this series?

Analyze a chapter. How is problem solving integrated in the chapter? Are explicit strategies highlighted?

Is there an extra resource on problem solving for the teacher? How is it organized? Does it give special helps such as teacher questions? Student activity sheets? Evaluation?

10. *For your resource file:* In "The Role of Problem Solving," Charles gives three guidelines on how to implement problem solving in the classroom. What are these guidelines? Add these ideas to your resource file on problem solving.

11. *For your resource file:* Two resources on problem solving are the February 1982 issue of the *Arithmetic Teacher* and the National Council of Teachers of Mathematics 1980 yearbook, *Problem Solving in School Mathematics.* These are extremely good references for ideas on teaching problem solving. Skim the articles of one of these resources to determine the main ideas in order to use them as future reference. Read at least one of the articles and add to your resource file.

12. *For your resource file:* For information on formation, chase, and elimination games, read the article "Games People Play" by Barson. He describes a number of strategy games.

13. As a chapter summary, read "You Can Teach Problem Solving" by LeBlanc. How did this article help you perceive yourself as a teacher of problem solving?

14. *For your resource file:* If you have observed young children, you know that they are actively engaged in problem solving. For suggestions for the mathematics curriculum, read Spencer and Lester, Bruni, or Wheatley and Wheatley.

15. In the article "Solving Verbal Problems: Results and Implications from National Assessment," Carpenter, Corbitt, Kepner, Lindquist, and Reys describe students' abilities in solving story problems and give suggestions for teaching such problems. Read the article, summarize the main points, and list the suggestions.

16. *For your resource file:* Periodically, the National Council of Teachers publishes an update of the research on problem solving. For further information, read the article by Suydam, "Update on Research on Problem Solving: Implications for Classroom Teaching." Add these ideas to your resource file.

17. In "Problem-Solving Opportunities," Easterday and Clothiaux describe four problem-solving situations that arose out of class situations. How does this article help you see how to incorporate problem solving from student questions?

TEACHER RESOURCES

Barson, Alan. "And the Last One Loses!" *Arithmetic Teacher 33* (September 1985): 35–37.

———. "Games People Play." *Arithmetic Teacher 29* (January 1982): 54–55.

Bruni, James V. "Problem Solving for the Primary Grades." *Arithmetic Teacher 29* (February 1982): 10–15.

Bush, William S., and Ann Fiala. "Problem Stories: A New Twist on Problem Posing." *Arithmetic Teacher 34* (December 1986): 6–9.

Carpenter, Thomas P., Mary Kay Corbitt, Henry S. Kepner, Jr., Mary Montgomery Lindquist, and Robert E. Reys. "Solving Verbal Problems: Results and Implications from National Assessment." *Arithmetic Teacher 28* (September 1980): 8–12.

Charles, Randall I. "The Role of Problem Solving." *Arithmetic Teacher 32* (February 1985): 48–50.

Charles, Randall, and Frank Lester. *Teaching Problem Solving: What, Why, and How.* Palo Alto, CA: Dale Seymour Publications, 1982.

Charles, Randall, Frank Lester, and Ian Putt. "How to Teach Problem Solving Step by Step." *Learning 15* (November/December 1986): 62–66.

Driscoll, Mark. "Mathematical Problem Solving: Not Just a Matter of Words." *Research Within Reach.* Reston, VA: National Council of Teachers of Mathematics, 1980.

Duea, Joan, George Immerzeel, Earl Ockenga, and John Tarr. "Problem Solving Using the Calculator." In *Problem Solving in School Mathematics,* 1980 Yearbook of the National Council of Teachers of Mathematics, pp. 117–126. Reston, VA: The Council, 1980.

Easterday, Kenneth E., and Clara A. Clothiaux. "Problem-Solving Opportunities." *Arithmetic Teacher 32* (January 1985): 18–20.

Fennell, Francis (Skip), and Richard Ammon. "Writing Techniques for Problem Solvers." *Arithmetic Teacher 33* (September 1985): 24–25.

Jacobson, Marilyn H., and Frank K. Lester. "Making Problem Solving Come Alive in the Intermediate Grades." In *Problem Solving in School Mathematics,* 1980 Yearbook of the National Council of Teachers of Mathematics, pp. 127–135. Reston, VA: The Council, 1980.

Krulik, Stephen, and Robert E. Reys (Eds.). *Problem Solving in School Mathematics,* 1980 Yearbook of the National Council of Teachers of Mathematics. Reston, VA: The Council, 1980.

LeBlanc, John F. "You Can Teach Problem Solving." *Arithmetic Teacher 25* (November 1977): 16–20.

Leutzinger, Larry P., and Glenn Nelson. "Let's Do It: But It Can't Be Done." *Arithmetic Teacher 27* (April 1980): 6–9.

Masse, Marie. "More Problems, Please." *Arithmetic Teacher 26* (December 1978): 11–14.

Nelson, L. Doyal, and Joan Kirkpatrick. "Problem Solving." In *Mathematics Learning in Early Childhood,* Thirty-seventh Yearbook of the National Council of Teachers of Mathematics, pp. 69–93. Reston, VA: The Council, 1975.

Nuffield Mathematics Project. *Logic.* New York: Wiley, 1972.

Ockenga, Earl, and Joan Duea. "Ideas." *Arithmetic Teacher* 25 (November 1977): 28–32.

O'Daffer, Phares. "Problem Solving Tips for Teachers." *Arithmetic Teacher* 32 (September 1984–May 1985).

Problem Solving . . . A Basic Mathematics Goal. Columbus, OH: Ohio Department of Education.

Scheuer, Donald W., Jr., and David E. Williams. "Ideas." *Arithmetic Teacher* 27 (April 1980): 27–32.

Slesnick, Twila. "Problem Solving: Some Thoughts and Activities." *Arithmetic Teacher* 31 (March 1984): 41–43.

Spencer, Patricia J., and Frank K. Lester. "Second Graders Can Be Problem Solvers!" *Arithmetic Teacher* 29 (September 1981): 15–17.

Suydam, Marilyn N. "Untangling Clues from Research on Problem Solving." In *Problem Solving in School Mathematics*, 1980 Yearbook of the National Council of Teachers of Mathematics, p. 34. Reston, VA: The Council, 1980.

———. "Update on Research on Problem Solving: Implications for Classroom Teaching." *Arithmetic Teacher* 29 (February 1982): 56–59.

Thompson, Alba G. "On Patterns, Conjectures, and Proof: Developing Students' Mathematical Thinking." *Arithmetic Teacher* 33 (September 1985): 20–23.

Wheatley, Charlotte L., and Grayson H. Wheatley. "Problem Solving in the Primary Grades." *Arithmetic Teacher* 31 (April 1984): 22–25.

Wirtz, Robert W., and Emily Kahn. "Another Look at Applications in Elementary School Mathematics." *Arithmetic Teacher* 30 (September 1982): 21–25.

CHILDREN'S LITERATURE

Burns, Marilyn. *The Book of Think (Or How to Solve a Problem Twice Your Size).* Illustrated by Martha Weston. Boston: Little, Brown, 1976.

———. *The I Hate Mathematics Book.* Illustrated by Martha Hairston. Boston: Little, Brown, 1975.

Charosh, Mannis. *Mathematical Games for One or Two.* Illustrated by Lois Ehlert. New York: Crowell, 1972.

Frédérique and Papy. *Graph Games.* Illustrated by Susan Holding. New York: Crowell, 1971.

Froman, Robert. *Venn Diagrams.* Illustrated by Jan Pyk. New York: Crowell, 1972.

Gersting, Judith L., and Joseph K. Kuczkowski. *Yes-No; Stop-Go: Some Patterns in Mathematic Logic.* Illustrated by Don Madden. New York: Crowell, 1977.

Thiagarajan, Sivasailam, and Harold D. Stolovitch. *Games with the Pocket Calculator.* Menlo Park, CA: Dymax, 1976.

2

USING CALCULATORS AND COMPUTERS IN ELEMENTARY SCHOOL MATHEMATICS

An irate parent calls you expressing the view that their third grader should not be using a calculator. What would you do in this situation?

CALCULATORS

Should sixth graders use calculators in their classrooms? For their homework? What about first and second graders? Should calculator use be restricted to certain topics? Do students and their parents use or need calculators for situations in their daily lives? Are school activities becoming less realistic if calculators are banned from the classroom but used in other life activities? When and where do children learn how to use calculators? These are some of the questions teachers are encountering as calculators become more readily available. What are your thoughts on the use of the calculator in the elementary schools? What is your opinion about each of the following statements? Decide whether each statement is true or false before reading the next section.

1. Children should not have access to calculators in school before the fourth grade.
2. Children should master their basic facts before being introduced to the calculator.
3. Calculators have been found to enhance students' problem-solving skills.
4. The majority of elementary children have access to calculators.
5. Overreliance on calculators has caused children's arithmetic scores to go down.
6. A classroom set of calculators is not appropriate, as they could be broken or stolen.
7. Calculators can only be used for developing skills not for developing concepts.
8. Calculators are only appropriate for above-average or gifted children.

As you read in the next section about the role of the calculator, check your answers. These true and false questions have been answered by research.

CALCULATOR USE IN THE ELEMENTARY SCHOOLS

As the price of calculators has decreased, they have become more readily available to the public and to schools. Individual family members can acquire their own calculators. It has been found that the majority of children own or have access to a calculator; in a number of districts 80 to 100% of the children had access to calculators (Suydam, 1982). As the price of calculators has decreased, more schools have purchased classroom sets. These schools have found that, due to increased technology, maintenance of calculators was not a problem. The costs in replacing batteries or the time involved in recharging batteries can be eliminated with solar-powered calculators. Schools have also found that calculator security is not a major problem (Taylor, 1980).

Some teachers and parents are concerned that students will become calculator dependent. No evidence has been found to support this statement. Students do not use calculators in inappropriate situations or when it would be just as convenient to use mental computation or paper and pencil.

A number of parents and teachers are concerned that the ready access to calculators by children would be detrimental to their development of arithmetic skills. In a summary of research on calculator use, Suydam (1983) stated that achievement scores were just as high or higher when calculators were used for instructional purposes as compared to instruction without the calculator. However, results from National Assessment show that students who used calculators took longer to take the assessment and consequently the *completion rates were lower* for both computation and problem-solving tests than for noncalculator groups.

In spite of doing fewer problems the calculator group scored substantially better on the problems involving only computation. Fifty percent of the nine-year-olds solved $28\overline{)3052}$, although most of them had not been introduced to the division algorithm. For problems that were strictly computational, students with calculators did much better on division problems but worse on decimal problems than did students without calculators.

Mixed results were found for word problems. Students did substantially better on a strictly computational problem than if the same computation were embedded in a story problem. The calculator group achieved higher scores on division problems with whole-number answers. The noncalculator group did better on division problems with remainders that required interpretation of the results. Similar results were found on the Third National Assessment, where students needed to be able to interpret calculator results with respect to the problem (Lindquist and others, 1983).

Although more work is needed to help children understand computational concepts and interpret calculator results, calculators have enhanced children's problem-solving scores. If children know how to solve the problem situation but cannot do the necessary algorithms, they can use the calculator to do the computations. Students were more willing to tackle problems with more difficult numbers when calculators were available (Suydam, 1982). The calculator is being used as a tool to aid children in solving the problem. It is also helpful because students can focus on the problem-solving process rather than the computations. But if they do not know how to solve the problem, the calculator will be of no use. Meyer in the article "When You Use a Calculator You Have to Think!" suggests a number of activities that support the premise that calculators enhance problem solving.

It has also been found that students with physical or mental handicaps benefited from instruction using the calculator. Their test scores were higher; they worked faster and attempted more problems. Students who were blind or partially sighted were taught how to use the calculator via cassettes. Mentally handicapped students learned to use the calculators with a minimum of instruction but had difficulty with clearing the display and using estimation (Suydam, 1982).

How do students accept calculators? Is it a motivational tool? Although teachers report that students are motivated by calculators, research has not shown this to be true (Suydam, 1982). Most studies reported no changes in attitudes. This is probably due to the fact that attitudes are changed over long periods of time and most research studies are conducted over short periods of time. It has been found that teachers and parents have become more accepting of calculators since preliminary research in 1976. They are more accepting of calculators in the upper grades than in the lower grades. Teachers' attitudes become more positive as they experience inservice work on calculators. As with most areas of study, as individuals become more knowledgeable about calculators, they are more confident and more positive about their abilities in that area. With an increase in their own expertise, teachers are more able and more likely to share this knowledge with their students.

Calculators have been used in some classrooms to check answers. This procedure can be detrimental to positive student attitudes. Students may have spent an hour working on the problems and then find that the entire assignment can be checked in

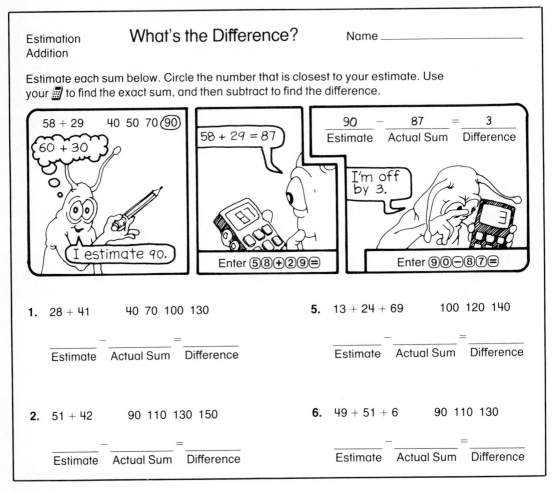

FIGURE 2-1.

Calculator and addition estimation. (From R.E. Reys, B.J. Bestgen, T.G. Coburn, H.L. Schoem, R.J. Shumway, C.L. Wheatley, G.H. Wheatley, A.L. White, **KEYSTROKES: Calculator Activities for Young Students: Addition and Subtraction,** Creative Publications, 1979, p. 43. © 1979 Creative Publications.)

less than five minutes. One strategy that uses calculators to check reasonableness of results is to give the students a set of problems that are already solved. The students can go through the work and estimate which answers appear to be unreasonable. They can then check using their calculators.

Calculators can also be used to teach estimation. Samples from *Keystrokes*, a resource book for calculator activities for the lower grades, are shown in Figures 2-1 and 2-2. Each page includes an introductory example showing how to estimate first and then check using a calculator. In both cases the students are being encouraged to compete with themselves to make a best estimate.

FIGURE 2-2.
Estimating in multiplication. (From R.E. Reys, B.J. Bestgen, T.G. Coburn, H.L.
Shoen, R.J. Shumway, C.L. Wheatley, G.H. Wheatley, A.L. White, **KEYSTROKES:**
Calculator Activities for Young Students: Multiplication and Division, Creative
Publications, 1979, p. 41. © 1979 Creative Publications.)

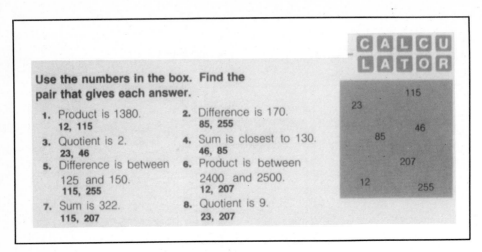

Use the numbers in the box. Find the pair that gives each answer.

1. Product is 1380.
   12, 115

2. Difference is 170.
   85, 255

3. Quotient is 2.
   23, 46

4. Sum is closest to 130.
   46, 85

5. Difference is between 125 and 150.
   115, 255

6. Product is between 2400 and 2500.
   12, 207

7. Sum is 322.
   115, 207

8. Quotient is 9.
   23, 207

FIGURE 2-3.

(From Joseph Payne et al. **Harper & Row Mathematics, Teacher's Edition, Grade 4**, p. 271. © 1985, Macmillan, Inc. Reprinted with permission of Scribner Educational Publishers, a division of Macmillan, Inc.)

These pages should be introduced by doing a similar activity with the whole class. An example from a fourth-grade textbook is shown in Figure 2-3. These exercises involve problem solving, estimation, and number sense.

Students need to use their estimation skills to check the reasonableness of the answers they obtain on the calculator. Would they be able to recognize unreasonable answers such as 44 + 23 = 21, 720 ÷ 9 = 90, 560 ÷ 70 = 80, or 234 × 26 = 1404? Experiences developing concepts of number, concepts of operations, and estimation strategies are essential. An unreasonable answer can be obtained by pushing the wrong number or operation key or by choosing the wrong operation or numbers. Even though students are able to manipulate larger numbers using the calculator, it should not be assumed that they are able to comprehend large numbers and the situation.

It is clear that calculators are here and they aren't going to go away. Children enjoy using them and calculators can be used effectively for instruction. *Calculators should be used in all elementary classrooms.* Exactly how and where they should be used in the curriculum is being explored. A number of resources are available that will help teachers learn to integrate them effectively into their classrooms for conceptual and skill development. At the end of the calculator section are samples of some of the available activities.

SPECIAL KEYS

For each calculator code below, predict the display. With a calculator, push the buttons in the order given in the code to check your answers. Results will vary slightly among different types of calculators.

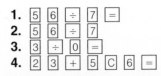

1. ⑤ ⑥ ÷ ⑦ ＝
2. ⑤ ⑥ ÷ ⑦
3. ③ ÷ ⓪ ＝
4. ② ③ ＋ ⑤ C ⑥ ＝

5. [2] [3] [+] [5] [CE] [6] [=]

6. [3] [4] [+] [−] [1] [2] [=]

7. [2] [×] [2] [=] [=] [=] [=] [For problems 7 through 9, some calculators need to have the operation sign pushed twice ([2] [×] [×] [2] [=] . . .) or the constant key must be used ([2] [×] [K] [2] [=] . . .).]

8. [2] [×] [6] [=] [8] [=]

9. [1] [2] [−] [3] [=] [1] [0] [=]

10. [5] [×] [6] [=] [M+] [4] [−] [6] [=] [M+]

11. [5] [×] [6] [=] [M+] [4] [−] [6] [=] [M+] [RM]

12. [3] [×] [1] [0] [=] [M+] [M−] [RM]

13. [8] [×] [6] [+] [2] [=]

14. [2] [+] [8] [×] [6] [=]

15. [8] [×] [2] [5] [%] (For some calculators, push the equal key also.)

The answers using one calculator are as follows:

1.	8	6. 22	11. 28
2.	7	7. 32	12. 0
3.	0 E	8. 16	13. 50
4.	6	9. 7	14. 50 *or* 60
5.	29	10. −2	15. 2

How well did you know your calculator? Did you know the functions of the basic keys? If review or instruction on the calculator is needed, work through Appendix I before reading the rest of the chapter.

It is important that children be introduced to the calculator and its special functions at an early age. As they mature mathematically, they should be introduced to other keys and their more sophisticated functions. One of the first things they need to realize is that they, not the calculator, are in charge. Bestgen in "Calculators—Taking the First Step" describes how she introduces the calculator to her students. The students discuss who is smarter and faster—the calculator or the children. A problem is posed to the children and to the calculator lying on a desk. For example, "How many tickets do Lance and Peggy have if Lance has 3 tickets and Peggy has 9 tickets?" The children answer promptly. The class discusses that the calculator is of no help unless someone keys in the appropriate code in order to answer the question. Through discussion the children realize that the calculator is a tool to help them and that they are the ones that make the decisions.

As children study the addition concept and are introduced to equations, they should explore the function of the equals key. They should compare the results of [3] [+] [5] to [3] [+] [5] [=]. It should be discussed that when they press the equals key they obtain another name for the expression 3 + 5. As the children are introduced to the operation keys, properties such as the commutative law will be reinforced as they discover that the order in which they enter data may or may not make a difference, depending on the operation being used.

One of the first keys the children learn about is the clear key. They need to learn to clear the display before entering new data. Children should also be introduced to and experiment with the clear entry key. They could compare codes such as [8] [+] [2] [=] with [8] [CE] [2] [+] [2] [=] and with [8] [+] [2] [CE] [6] [=]. They will find that the key acts like an eraser. In addition to changing numbers, children should be introduced to changing operations. Exploring calculator codes such as [8] [+] [−] [3] [=] or [7] [×] [−] [3] [=] should help them form a generalization.

The constant function can be used across a number of grade levels. First graders can use it for counting by ones. The children can be instructed to code in [1] [+] [1] [=] [=] [=] · · · to generate the sequence 1, 2, 3, and so on. As they push the equal key, they can orally count "one, two, three," and so on. A variation of this code can be used for counting by 2s, 3s, 5s, 25s, 100s, and so on. Counting on from numbers other than one can be coded; for example, to count on by 5s from 25, the code would be [2] [5] [+] [5] [=] [=] [=] ⋯. Counting backward can be generated by codes such as [5] [2] [−] [1] [=] [=] [=] ⋯ or [5] [2] [−] [2] [=] [=] ⋯. As noted earlier, for some calculators the operation sign must be pushed twice or a [K] (constant) key must be pushed to obtain the constant function.

The constant function changes if numbers are inserted between the equal signs. For example, what happens with the calculator code [1] [+] [5] [=] [8] [=] [1] [2] [=]? This is a helpful function when the same number is to be added to a series of other numbers. When students are practicing the counting on strategy for adding 2, they could count on to find the sum before pushing the equals keys to check their answer. The code for this activity could be [6] [+] [2] [=] [3] [=] [5] [=] [9] [=] [6] [=]. Similar activities can be planned for multiplication, division, and subtraction.

One of the special problems with the constant function is to determine what number remains constant. The constant may be either the first or the second number entered, depending on the particular calculator. For the code [2] [5] [+] [5] [=] [=] [=] ⋯ given earlier, one calculator generates the sequence 30, 35, 40, ... Another calculator, which requires pushing [+] twice, generates the sequence 30, 55, 80, ... Similarly, with some calculators the code [5] [2] [−] [2] [=] [=] [=] . . . will generate the sequence 50, 48, 46, ... Generating this same sequence with other calculators requires the code [2] [−] [−] [5] [2] [=] [=] [=] . . . . Although this type of constant function can be obtained with most general-purpose calculators, the necessary code varies somewhat. The teacher must be aware of these variations in order to help students who encounter difficulties.

At first when students are solving problems that involve more than one operation, they may use paper and pencil to record different displays as they work through the problem. As students learn more about calculators, they should learn how the memory of the calculator can store some of this information. The memory of a calculator is particularly important for problems involving several operations as information can be stored until it is needed. For example, to determine the cost of 3 cans of taco sauce at $1.45 each and 6 cans of cat food at 33 cents each, Cheryl used the code [3] [×] [1] [.] [4] [5] [=] [M+] [6] [×] [.] [3] [3] [M+] [RM].

Many inexpensive calculators have square root and percent keys. To find the square root of a number, the number is entered and then the square root key is pressed. The calculator will then display the square root of the given number in as many decimal places as the display allows. However, to introduce students to the *concept* of square root, a procedure in which they guess and check using multiplication should be used. For example, to find the square root of 91, a student may think, "9 × 9 is 81 and 10 × 10 is 100, so I'll guess 9.4." Since 9.4 × 9.4 is 88.36, the student may then try 9.5 × 9.5. This process would continue until the desired result was determined to the nearest tenth, hundredth, or other place value.

The procedure for using the percent key requires an understanding of the concept of percent and operations with percents. In most cases individuals are more likely to use mental computation or estimation to figure percents. If the calculator is used, individuals often change the percent to a decimal fraction rather than using the percent key. If students are to use the percent key effectively, they must first be taught percent concepts. An overview of using the percent key is found in Appendix 1. Also see Chapter 12.

Neither percent nor square root keys are necessary on calculators for use in the elementary classroom. Calculators that have large, easy-to-use keys with the symbols printed on them should be purchased. It is advantageous, but not essential, for all students to have the same type of calculator during whole-class activities. This prevents confusion since not all calculators are used in the same manner. It is not necessary to have one calculator for every student; a pair of students can work together with the same calculator.

Knowing how to use one's calculator effectively doesn't "just happen." It needs to be taught. Children should gradually be introduced to the different functions of their calculator over the course of their elementary years. To give you a better grasp of the kinds of calculator activities that have been designed for elementary students, a sample is included in the following problem set.

QUESTIONS AND ACTIVITIES

1. Write a calculator code to solve each of the following problems. Use the memory when appropriate. If you need a review on order of operations, consult the appropriate section of your textbook. Use your calculator to check your results. Discuss any special problems with other students and your instructor. Discuss how you would help your students with these concepts.
   a. 31 + 5 × 81
   b. (31 + 5) × 81
   c. 3 + 525 ÷ 15
   d. 42 ÷ 6 × 6
   e. 45 ÷ (15 − 5 × 3)
   f. Take 13 from 5.
   g. Divide 15 by 5.

   h. How many times does 16 divide 8?
   i. How many times does 21 "go into" 7?
   j. 3 to the tenth

2. Children often find that spelling words with their calculators is fun. This activity can be used as a motivator when teaching how to read or write calculator codes. Solve the following two problems on your calculator, and then read the display upside down.
   a. [9] [×] [3] [0] [=] [−] [5] [=] [×] [1] [0] [=] [+] [3] [=] [×] [2] [=]
   b. [(273 + 8) × 12 − 1] × 30 + 4
   Although these puzzles are somewhat gimmicky, most children enjoy them and the results are self-checking. This activity can easily be changed to a problem-solving activity by having the children write their own problems. To appreciate this problem-solving aspect, design two word codes of your own. Write the numerical expressions and word codes for each.

3. What is the smallest number you can write on your calculator? Predict and then check. What is the largest number? Add one to this number; what happened? Some calculators change to scientific notation rather than display an error message.

4. The problems below have been adapted from a *Calculator Information Bulletin* by Miller. Solve these problems using a calculator. What concepts are being reinforced?
   a. Given the following numbers:
      32 563   2670   1526   9043   2345
      3218

      (1) Add the numbers which have a 5 in the hundreds place.
      (2) Find the sum of the numbers that are less than ten thousand.
      (3) Subtract the numbers that are between twenty-five hundred and thirty-five hundred.
   b. Predict the answers to the following problems and then use your calculator to check your responses.

(1) [1][0][+][1][0][=][=][=][=][=][=]
[=][=][=][=][=][=][=]

(2) [3][0][+][1][0][=][=][=][=][=][=]
[=][=][=][=][=][=][=]

(3) [3][0][0][−][1][0][=][=][=][=][=]
[=][=][=][=][=][=][=]

(4) [6][+][+][=][=][=][=][=][=][=][=]
[=][=][=]

(5) [1][0][×][×][=][=][=][=][=][=]
[=][=][=][=]

(6) [2][0][÷][÷][2][=][=][=][=]
[=][=][=][=]

c. Enter a code in your calculator to generate the next numbers in each of the following sequences. Record the tenth term of each sequence.
   (1) 212, 210, 208, . . .
   (2) 75, 85, 95, . . .
   (3) 3.5, 4, 4.5, . . .
   (4) 2, 4, 8, . . .
   (5) 0.2, 0.4, 0.6, . . .
   (6) 0.1, 0.01, 0.001, . . .

d. Is the first expression equal to, less than, or greater than the second expression in each of the following problems? Estimate, write the appropriate sign in the circle, and then check your estimate with a calculator.
   (1) $304 - 37 \bigcirc 367 - 37$
   (2) $404 - 52 \bigcirc 352 + 62$
   (3) $327 + 45 \bigcirc 322 + 350$
   (4) $(34 \times 85) \div 75 \bigcirc 92$
   (5) $46 \times 88 \bigcirc 23 \times 176$
   (6) $81 \times 23 \bigcirc 162 \times 11$
   (7) $\frac{3}{8} \bigcirc .3$
   (8) $\frac{7}{9} \bigcirc .8$

e. Use the completed multiplication problem below to help answer the other problems given. Check your estimates with a calculator.

$$\begin{array}{r} 368 \\ \times\ 234 \\ \hline 1472 \\ 11040 \\ 73600 \\ \hline 86112 \end{array}$$

(1) $3.68 \times 23.4 = $ _____
(2) $40 \times 3.68 = $ _____
(3) $50 \times 36.8 = $ _____
(4) _____ $\div\ 2.34 = 3.68$
(5) _____ $\div\ 20 = 36.8$

5. With some calculators a game for two people using the constant key can be played. One person selects a number and an operation and enters them in the calculator as constants. For example, [6] [+] [=] or [3] [×] [=] may be coded. The player then hides this code by keying in another number and an equal sign. For example, after entering the code [6] [+] [=], the student could enter [5] [=]. The display would show 11, so the number 6 would be hidden. The calculator is handed to the other person, who keys in another number and equals, such as [4] [=], and observes the display obtained. This player gathers more data until the original number and operation are guessed. Play this game with another student. (*Note:* The codes must be adapted according to how the constant function operates on your calculator. On some calculators when the constant function is in use, the operation symbol shows on the display. In this case, how could you adapt the rules so that the second person would still have to guess the operation as well as the number?)

6. Triple Nines, a game for two or more people, is described by Thiagarajan and Stolovitch in *Games with the Pocket Calculator.* One person enters a secret number in the calculator and gives two clues to the other players. One clue must give the number of nines in the display; the second clue must be about one of the other digits, but not the place values of the digits. The other players suggest a number which is then added to the number on the display. Play continues until the display is 999 with a minimum number of turns. An example of a clue is: "There is one nine and there is a three." The other players may suggest adding 70. If the players suggest a number

that would result in a display of more than 999, they are given an opportunity to change their guess.

7. Enter the calculator code 4 5 × 1 5 % on your calculator. What is your result? What problem have you solved? Is this procedure commutative? Enter 1 5 % × 4 5. What can you conclude?

8. a. Imagine building a triangular-shaped tower with blocks. For a tower three rows high there would be three blocks in the bottom row, two in the next row, and one block in the top row. Use your calculator and problem-solving strategies to determine the number of blocks in a tower 10 blocks high. A tower 50 blocks high. A tower n blocks high.

   b. Change the shape of the tower so that in a tower 3 blocks high there are five blocks in the bottom row, three in the next row, and one in the top row. How many blocks are needed for a tower ten blocks high? A tower 100 blocks high?

9. The following problems are adapted from Morris's *How to Develop Problem Solving Using a Calculator.* Use estimation and your calculator to solve the problems.

   a. If a number is multiplied by itself and then 24 is added, the result is 700. What is the number?
   b. If a number is multiplied by itself and then 6 is subtracted, the result is 1290. What is the number?
   c. If a number is multiplied by itself and then the original number is added to that product for an answer of 1980, what is the number?
   d. Five is added to a number and that result is multiplied by a second number. Forty-nine is then added for a result of 1151. What is the number?
   e. Make up your own puzzle and give it to a friend to solve.

10. Work through the problems in Figures 2-1 through 2-3. Write an evaluation of the problems.

11. The problems below are from a third-grade textbook. What calculator functions are being taught or used? What mathematics concepts are being studied?

CALCULATOR

Use a calculator to find the missing numbers.

1. $0.75, $1.50, $2.25, ■, ■, ■, ■   . 7 5 + = =
2. $1.25, $2.50, $3.75, ■, ■, ■, ■   1 . 2 5 + = =

CALCULATOR

A calculator can *store* a number to be added.
To store 9 press 9 + = . "Add 9" is stored.
To add 6 + 9 press 6 = . 15 is the answer.
To add 3 + 9 press 3 = . 12 is the answer.
Find the answers.

  1. 9 + 7   2. 9 + 82   3. 9 + 125   4. 9 + 385   5. 9 + 764

How can you store 999? 9 9 9 + =

(From Joseph Payne et al., **Harper & Row Mathematics, Teacher's Edition, Grade 3**, pp. 75 and 15. © 1985, Macmillan, Inc. Reprinted with permission of Scribner Educational Publishers, a division of Macmillan Inc.)

CALCU
LATOR

Bonnie's Restaurant

Salad	35¢	Banana	15¢
Grilled Cheese....	65¢	Fruit Salad......	28¢
Hamburger.......	$1.25	Yogurt..........	42¢
Hot Dog..........	75¢	Milk..............	30¢
Juice Drinks.......	25¢	Lemonade.......	30¢

Find the cost of each order.

1. 3 salads
   2 juice drinks
   1 banana

For Exercise 1:
3 × 3 5 M+ 2 × 2 5
M+ 1 × 1 5 M+ MR

2. 2 hamburgers
   4 milks
   4 yogurts

3. 7 grilled cheese
   3 hot dogs
   4 fruit salads

4. 2 lemonades
   5 hamburgers
   9 salads

5. Choose an item from each section of the menu.
   Buy two of each. How much is your bill?

6. You be the waiter. Let other students give you their orders. Let them estimate how much the bill will be. Add to check their estimates. The student who gives the best estimate will be the waiter next.

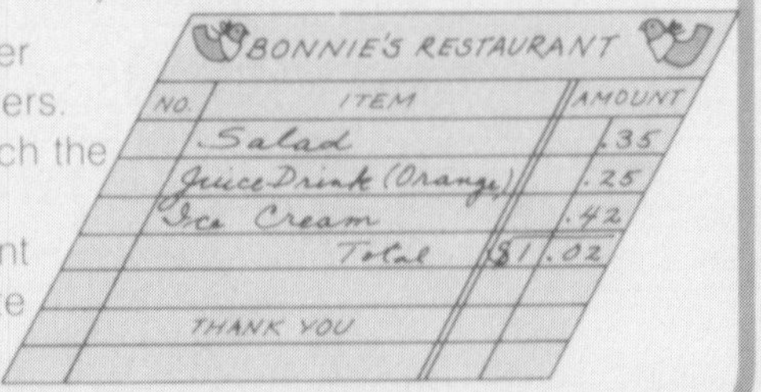

BONNIE'S RESTAURANT

NO.	ITEM	AMOUNT
	Salad	.35
	Juice Drink (Orange)	.25
	Ice Cream	.42
	Total	$1.02

THANK YOU

12. To gain a better perspective of how to use calculators effectively in the classroom, read "Calculators—Taking the First Step" by Bestgen or "When You Use a Calculator You Have to Think" by Meyer. Bestgen describes a series of lessons that she has used with students in grades one through six. Meyer describes her experiences with her fourth-grade class.

13. Williams includes further instruction on using a calculator in "The Language of Calculators." Hannick discusses three activities using the memory function in "Using the Memory Functions on Hand-Held Calculators." Read one of these articles and add it to your resource file.

14. Read "Problem Solving with Calculators" by Morris. Use a calculator to solve at least six of the activities described in the article. Record your results.

15. Read "Minicalculators in Schools" by the NCTM Instructional Affairs Committee. List the justifications and solve one of the problems under each justification. Record your results.

16. Should calculators be banned from the classroom? Read "Calculators in the Elementary Classroom: How Can We Go Wrong!" by Reys. Summarize the main points presented in the article.

17. Read "Calculators in Testing Situations: Results and Implications from National Assessment" by Carpenter, Corbitt, Kepner, Lindquist, and Reys. What were the results of the assessment? What were their recommendations?

18. Read and evaluate the children's book *Calculator Fun* by Adler.

19. The focus of the February 1987 *Arithmetic Teacher* is calculators. Read through the issue and look for articles that:
   a. justify why the calculator should be used in the elementary classroom.
   b. discuss using the calculator for problem solving.
   c. show other activities for the calculator.

COMPUTERS IN THE ELEMENTARY CLASSROOM

Think about the year you were in second or third grade. Did you have a computer in your classroom? Did you even know what a computer was? There were computers around then, but they were not the common item that they are today. From using and hearing about computers as an adult, you probably have formed some ideas about their use in the classroom. Answer the following true-false questions before you read the rest of this section.

1. Computers make good teachers.
2. Computer use improves student achievement.
3. A second grader can learn to write a program.
4. A second grader should learn to write a program. (Note the difference between statements 3 and 4.)
5. The increasing use of the computer will have no direct effect on the elementary mathematics curriculum.
6. Students who work with the computer will become isolates.
7. Using computers and knowing about computers are two different things.
8. The mathematics classroom is the only place for computers.

Unlike the questions on calculators, some of these questions cannot be answered with clear-cut answers that have been researched completely. Although there have been some studies done, more time and more studies are needed before there will be enough research to evaluate the effect of using computers in the classroom.

Many of the questions that were raised a few years ago about using the calculator in the classroom are now being asked about using computers. There are strong recommendations that students in the elementary school use the computer (NCTM, 1980; NCTM, 1984). Although the discussion here will be about using the computer for mathematics in the elementary school and the recommendations noted earlier came from mathematics groups, the computer has many other uses in the elementary classroom. Perhaps the most notable one is its use as a word processor. A student can use it to write, edit, and print stories, reports, newspapers, and other things. Also, there are computer-aided instruction (CAI) programs to be used with many elementary subjects. This should give you an idea of what the computer can do. It is not *just* a supercalculator that can also keep a record of what a child has done. It is a teaching tool. Although it is quite different from a movie projector, the computer has many uses that are similar to those of films and projectors. (*Note:* If you did not answer "false" to question 8, go back and reread this paragraph since the rest of this section will be about using the computer in the mathematics classroom.)

Children can use the computer in two ways in the mathematics classroom. They can run programs that have already been written (CAI programs) or they can learn to use the computer to write programs to explore certain mathematical ideas. The objectives of these two uses are completely different, and they will be discussed separately.

COMPUTER-AIDED INSTRUCTION

There are many commercial programs available today for use with mathematics lessons. Some of the ones available are to be used with a specific mathematics text and are produced and distributed by the specific textbook companies. Others are more general and are available from software companies or from educational agencies. Commercial programs are of four types: drill and practice, tutorial, games, and simulation.

Before you use any program there will be certain attributes you will want to evaluate just as you would for any other teaching aid. You might look for the following in a CAI (computer-aided instruction) program.

1. Is it appropriate material for the students who will be using it? For example, many programs are concerned with practicing addition, but some include just basic facts while others have three-digit addends. A basic-fact program might be appropriate for your students. However, if you wanted them to have practice with two-digit addends, the basic-fact program would not be appropriate.

2. Does the program give clear directives to the students? If students must type in an answer, does it *tell* them that they must type the answer? Or does the screen just show a flashing question mark and assume the students will know that they should type in the answer?

3. What provisions does the program make for a wrong response by the student, and what kind of a response do you want it to make? For example, if a student is asked to estimate the answer to 385 + 407 and responds with 2200, do you want the program to indicate that the response is wrong and give the students another chance, or do you want the program to indicate that the response is wrong and then tell the student the correct answer? Or do you want some other combination? In this example, you might want the com-

puter to respond one way if the answer is close, say 700, and another if it is way off, say 2200.

4. How is the student allowed to respond to a question? For example, if a student is doing the addition problem 421 + 343, written vertically, does the answer 764 have to be typed 7, then 6, then 4, or can the 4 be put in, then the 6, then the 7? (The latter, of course, is the way students would do this problem with pencil and paper, while the former is the common way for doing mental computation.)

5. Is there reinforcement built into the program? Do the students receive some sort of praise for getting a right answer and some sort of encouragement if they miss a problem? Also, is there some record at the end of the program on how well a student has done? For example, a program might tell Penny that she has tried 20 problems and answered 18 of them correctly. This would enable Penny, and her teacher as well, to keep a record of her progress.

6. Does the program use graphics? The use of pictures, and perhaps color or sound, can make a program more interesting even though it does exactly the same thing mathematically as one that does not have these features.

Studies show that when computers are used as a supplement to the regular curriculum there is increased student achievement. One might get the same results, however, if the teacher dressed as a clown every day for the math lesson. Anything that is different and interesting can motivate students, and the result is usually increased achievement. You must continue to watch the research and see if these results continue as the computer becomes more commonplace in the classroom. There need to be and there will be more studies done in the near future to evaluate the effectiveness of the computer in the elementary classroom.

Drill and Practice Programs

The commonest type of program available is the drill and practice type. As you use a program like this, the first thing you must ask is "What are the advantages of using the computer for this?" If the answer is, "There are none," then don't use it! This may seem to be a strong statement, but there is a reason for it. At this time computers are not as commonplace as the calculator, and you may have only one or two for the entire elementary school. Since there are so many good uses for the computer, you shouldn't be wasting the computer time on an activity that can be done as well or better some other way. When there are four or more computers in your classroom, the answer could change to "go ahead and use it," provided that there are no disadvantages.

Some CAI programs have record-keeping capabilities that allow the teacher to have a record of how a particular student did on a certain program. This function may vary from just reporting the number of correct responses to giving a listing of the problems missed by the student and the incorrect answers given. These records allow the teacher to plan additional learning experiences for the student. Some programs are also designed to determine when a student needs additional practice and to provide that practice.

Tutorial Programs

A tutorial program is one that develops a new skill or concept. It very carefully takes the student through a series of small steps to develop the skill or concept. Again, the teacher must ask, "Is this the best way (or at least as good a way as any other) to accomplish the task?" Your answer might be "yes," "no," or "maybe." Surprisingly enough, you may have all three answers for the same tutorial program. It might be "no" when you are going to develop a new skill for the class as a group. It might be "yes" when José and Sue return to class after being absent during the development of the lesson for the whole class. It might be "maybe" when you see that Rico, who hasn't been absent, still needs some further work on the development of the idea.

Some tutorial programs can do things that seem to be hard to do with some of the other teaching aids. For example, because of the graphics that can be used, certain concepts can be shown more easily. For example, children can be introduced to ideas about transformational geometry that have not before been part of the elementary curriculum.

The computer and the program can teach, but they can't *be* the teacher in the complete sense of the word. The computer can ascertain whether a student is giving the correct response and can keep a record of these responses. It can repeat questions if the program is written to allow the student to indicate a need to go back in the lesson and review a frame. Depending on the percent of correct responses on a given lesson, the computer can be programmed to tell the student to go back to the previous lesson, repeat this one, or proceed to the next one. However, the computer cannot be programmed to make the one major decision of whether to use the program at all.

Game and Simulation Programs

There are many computer games available for the elementary classroom. Some of these just involve coordination and do not belong in the mathematics curriculum. It is true that they do give the student practice in using the computer in a nonthreatening situation and therefore make the student more receptive to using the computer for other things. However, it isn't the computer that is part of the mathematics curriculum; it is what we do with the computer that involves it in the mathematics curriculum.

There are games that do involve mathematical concepts. "Guess My Number" is a game of chance, but it can bring up questions about random numbers, a topic that until this time has been relegated to a much later time in the mathematics curriculum. Also, the idea of coordinate geometry is quickly comprehended when playing some games that require the student to locate a position on the screen.

In addition to coordination games and games of chance, another category of games are those that involve logic. There are educators who state that these are definitely a part of the mathematics curriculum because they develop the logical thinking one needs to do mathematics. However, this should not imply that mathematics is the only place in the curriculum where a student does logical thinking.

Some programs are called games but are really drill and practice programs. Drill and practice programs are relatively easy to write, particularly those on computational skills. (See Appendix I for further discussion of writing drill and practice programs.) When these programs are disguised as games, they are often used more and enjoyed more by students. However, drill and practice programs are still qualitatively different from game programs.

"Lemonade" by MECC is an example of another type of program. It is a simulation program that can be used in the elementary school. A simulation program is one that simulates a real-life situation, and the user makes choices as to what to do under the given conditions. For example, if you make a choice to produce more lemonade and then it rains, you will lose money; but if you make the choice not to make the lemonade and the weather is hot, you will not make the profit you could have. Most programs of this nature for elementary school are in areas other than mathematics.

QUESTIONS AND ACTIVITIES

1. Go to your resource center and run at least three programs. Classify them as (1) drill and practice, (2) tutorial, (3) games, or (4) simulation.

2. Look at the most current issues of magazines such as *Arithmetic Teacher, Classroom Computer Learning,* or *Popular Computing* to see what recent research has been done relating to the question of the effectiveness of the computer in the classroom.

3. Discuss with your group "When is a game a game?"

4. Examine some textbook series to see what disks there are to accompany the texts. Are they drill and practice only? Are there disks with programs that help the teacher manage by keeping track of certain records? If a teacher management disk is available, read the manual and try it out.

5. Assume that you are a fourth-grade teacher. Using the six points given in the text, evaluate the programs you ran for Problem 1. (If fourth grade is not appropriate for the programs you ran, change the grade to one that is.)

STUDENT PROGRAMMING

An examination of elementary mathematics textbooks of today will show a wide variety of lessons and activities that have the students construct their own programs or do activities that prepare them to construct a program. To help children understand the idea of the sequence of commands, activities range from putting a series of pictures in order to writing a flowchart to describe how to do something a child does. Figure 2-4 shows a lesson on flowcharts from an elementary textbook.

The child must learn to use various commands so that the computer knows what to do. One of these is the PRINT command. Figure 2-5 shows lessons from a first-grade and a third-grade textbook on this command and how it works. The programs on these pages use BASIC, one of the languages used with elementary children.

Another common computer language is Logo. In elementary school the Turtle Geometry is the most widely used function of Logo. An example of this from an elementary school textbook is shown in Figure 2-6.

One of the advantages of Turtle Geometry is that the children can teach the turtle to make a certain shape. The turtle starts out with only four commands, and then it can be taught new words, such as "circle," "triangle," and so on. The geometric ideas are easier to develop in Logo than in BASIC because of the types of commands that the language uses—forward (FD), backward (BK), left (LT), and right (RT). Logo has the capability of doing other things besides graphics, but in the elementary school it is not widely used at this time for anything else.

When using any form of Logo the idea of a procedure is developed. Simply put, a procedure is a segment of a program that

NAME   Unit 6

Finding Out About Computers

What is a Flowchart?

A flowchart is a list of steps that shows how to do something. The steps must be in order.

Here is a list with 5 steps. It tells what to do when you go shopping.

Steps:

1. Make a list. Take enough money.

2. Walk to the store.

3. Find items on the list.

4. Buy the items.

5. Walk home.

Here is the flowchart for these steps.

Flowchart:

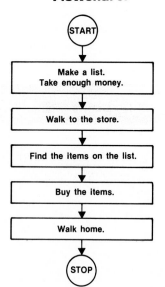

On Your Own

Make a list of steps for something else you do. Then draw the flowchart.

FIGURE 2-4.

Flow charts. (From Charles E. Allen et al., **Houghton Mifflin Mathematics: Teacher's Resource Book, Level 2**, p. 122. © 1985 by Houghton Mifflin Company. Used by permission.)

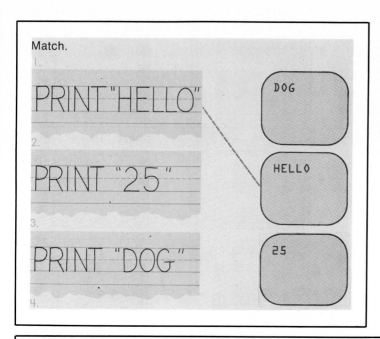

FIGURE 2-5.
(From Joseph Payne et al., **Harper & Row Mathematics, Student's Edition, Grade 1**, p. 347, and **Grade 3**, p. 368. © 1985, Macmillan Inc. Reprinted with permission of Scribner Educational Publishers, a division of Macmillan, Inc.)

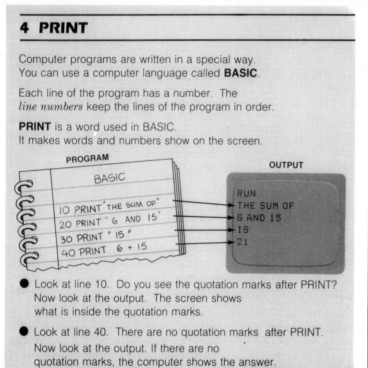

4 PRINT

Computer programs are written in a special way.
You can use a computer language called **BASIC**.

Each line of the program has a number. The
line numbers keep the lines of the program in order.

PRINT is a word used in BASIC.
It makes words and numbers show on the screen.

● Look at line 10. Do you see the quotation marks after PRINT?
Now look at the output. The screen shows
what is inside the quotation marks.

● Look at line 40. There are no quotation marks after PRINT.
Now look at the output. If there are no
quotation marks, the computer shows the answer.

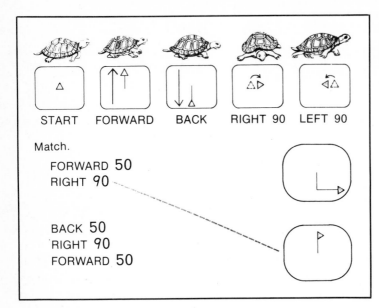

FIGURE 2-6.
Turtle geometry. (From Joseph Payne et al., **Harper & Row Mathematics, Student's Edition, Grade 1**, p. 351. © 1985 Macmillan, Inc. Reprinted with permission of Scribner Educational Publishers, a division of Macmillan, Inc.)

does a part of the thing you want done. For example, you can generate directions to draw a square and save them. Then give the directions to draw a large triangle and save them. Finally, you might write directions for a small triangle and save them. All of these are procedures, and in Logo they can be packaged in a file called SHAPES. Other languages also have procedures or constructs similar to procedures such as subroutines and remote blocks. Some upper grades are using Pascal, which is another language that has procedures.

Another concept that is developed is the idea of loops. In Logo the command "RE-PEAT" makes the program do what it has just done (Figure 2-7). In BASIC the "for-next" loop has the program repeat a block of commands. This allows the student to explore some of the same mathematical ideas, such as counting by 1s, 2s, or 5s, that you read about in the section on calculators.

Some examples of these types of pro-grams are shown in Figure 2-8. Shumway used these counting programs with first graders. After the children learned what each step of the program did, they learned to modify the programs. Children can suggest changes for line 20, predict the outcome, and run the program to see if their predictions are correct. Also, if they want a certain outcome, they need to decide what to put in at line 20.

Using BASIC and the graphics commands, a child can learn about coordinate geometry and certain geometrical ideas. Programs can show how each pair of numbers represents a position on the screen (Figure 2-9). An extension of writing a program to generate this segment would be "How can we make a segment parallel to this one?" or "How can we make a segment perpendicular to this one?" Finally, "What will we need to tell the computer to do to make a square?" Other geometric ideas can be introduced and explored in a similar manner.

```
10 FOR N = 1 TO 12
20 PRINT N
30 NEXT N

10 FOR N = 1 TO 12
20 PRINT N,N+N
30 NEXT N

10 FOR N = 0 TO 50 STEP 5
20 PRINT N
30 NEXT N
```

FIGURE 2-8.
Counting programs.

COMPUTER

LOGO: REPEAT Commands

In LOGO, the Turtle is a small triangle on the computer screen. This Turtle can follow commands that make it do special things. This is a REPEAT command.

```
REPEAT 2 [FD 50 RT 90 FD 20 RT 90]
```

A REPEAT command has two parts. The first part is a number that tells how many times to repeat a list of commands.

```
REPEAT 2
```

The second part is a list of commands that are inside two brackets [ ].

```
[FD 50 RT 90 FD 20 RT 90]
```

This REPEAT command tells the Turtle to complete the following commands twice: move forward 50 units, turn right 90 degrees, move forward 20 units, turn right 90 degrees.

When these commands are followed, the Turtle draws a rectangle. The length of the rectangle is 50 units. The width is 20 units. The perimeter of the rectangle is 140 units. The area is 1,000 square units.

Give the perimeter and area of the rectangle made by the REPEAT command.

1. `REPEAT 2 [FD 10 RT 90 FD 5 RT 90]`

2. `REPEAT 2 [FD 40 RT 90 FD 10 RT 90]`

3. `REPEAT 2 [FD 30 RT 90 FD 5 RT 90]`

FIGURE 2-7.
"REPEAT" command. (From L. Carey Bolster et al., **Invitation to Mathematics: Grade 5, Teacher's Edition**, p. 337. © 1985, Scott, Foresman and Company. Used by permission.)

As shown on earlier textbook pages, there is a wide variety of material being introduced in the elementary textbooks. Some textbook series now include programs for computer-aided instruction. Some include beginning instruction on programming. Some teach computer terminology. Some have lessons on the workings of the computer and the binary numeration system which is used by computers.

Camp and Marchionini, in "Programming and Learning: Implications for Mathematics Education" in the 1984 NCTM yearbook on computers in education, suggest a developmental sequence for programming. Stage 1 is to explore and discover the general concepts. Stage 2 is to use a subset of a standard language such as Turtle Graphics from Logo. Stage 3 is to study and use a high-level language such as BASIC, Logo, or Pascal.

At this time there are conflicting and changing views of what language, if any,

```
10 GR
20 COLOR = 7
30 FOR N = 1 TO 20
40 PLOT 5,N
50 NEXT N
```

FIGURE 2-9.
Coordinate geometry program.

should be taught in the elementary school. The discussion usually centers around whether to use BASIC or Logo. Again, because of the relative newness of the area and the lack of research in it, considerably more work must be done before many of the questions about what language, what age, how much, and so on can have reasonable answers. This is an interesting and exciting period in the development of this topic.

QUESTIONS AND ACTIVITIES

1. Each month in the *Arithmetic Teacher* there is a department called "Computer Corner."
   a. Find one activity from this section that would be suitable for the grade you intend to teach and try to run the program.
   b. The December 1986 and the February 1987 are two issues that have the same program written in both BASIC and Logo. If you have access to Logo, try running both versions.

2. Enter and run this program in your computer:

```
10    FOR K = 1 TO 10
20    PRINT K, K*K, K^K
30    NEXT K
```

Were the results what you expected? If not, try to find someone who can explain why you got the results you did.

3. Look at the scope-and-sequence charts for several elementary mathematics series and see what is introduced in the computer section.

4. If you can obtain the previous editions of the series used in Problem 3, do the same analysis for them and then compare your findings.

5. Write and run the rest of the program in Figure 2-9 so that you get a square. Then make a square inside of this one.

6. Obtain a Logo disk and do what you did in Problem 5 (i.e., have the computer draw a square and then another square inside the original).

7. Discuss Problems 5 and 6 with your classmates. What were the difficult spots for you in either of them? What are the differences? Which seemed easier to do? Why? Would the same be true for a child?

8. Work through the lesson in Appendix I.

9. a. Predict the output for the programs shown in Figure 2-8.
   b. Check your predictions using a computer.
   c. Write two different modifications for one of these programs.

10. Answer Problems 1 through 3 in Figure 2-9.

11. Read the children's book *It's BASIC: The ABC's of Computer Programming* by Lipson. What is your reaction to the book? How could you use this book with your students?

TEACHER RESOURCES

Alterman, Alan E. "Pulling in the Reins on Free Wheeling Logo." *Classroom Computer Learning* 6 (September 1985): 61–65.

An Agenda for Action: Recommendations for School Mathematics of the 1980s. Reston, VA: National Council of Teachers of Mathematics, 1980.

Bestgen, Barbara J. "Calculators—Taking the First Step." *Arithmetic Teacher* 29 (September 1981): 34–37.

Billings, Karen. "Developing Mathematical Concepts with Microcomputer Activities." *Arithmetic Teacher* 30 (February 1983): 18–19, 57–58.

Camp, John S., and Gary Marchionini. "Programming and Learning: Implications for Mathematics Education." In *Computers in Mathematics Education,* 1984 Yearbook of the National Council of Teachers of Mathematics, pp. 118–126. Reston, VA: The Council, 1984.

Carpenter, Thomas P., Mary Kay Corbitt, Henry S. Kepner, Jr., Mary Montgomery Lindquist, and Robert E. Reys. "Calculators in Testing Situations: Results and Implications from National Assessment." *Arithmetic Teacher 28* (January 1981): 34–37.

Clithero, Dale. "Learning with Logo 'Instantly.' " *Arithmetic Teacher 34* (January 1987): 12–15.

Doyle, William H. "A Discovery Approach to Teaching Programming." *Arithmetic Teacher 32* (December 1984): 16–18, 27–28.

Fillman, Paula K. "Guidelines for Introducing Microcomputers in the Schools." *Arithmetic Teacher 30* (February 1983): 16–17, 56.

Hannick, Francis T. "Using the Memory Functions on Hand-Held Calculators." *Arithmetic Teacher 33* (November 1985): 48–49.

Hatfield, Larry. "A Case and Technique for Computers: Using Computers in Middle School Mathematics." *Arithmetic Teacher 26* (February 1979): 53–55.

Hembree, Ray. "Research Gives Calculators a Green Light." *Arithmetic Teacher 34* (September 1986): 18–21.

Hodes, Carol. "Some Cautions for Courseware Selection." *Educational Horizons 63* (Spring 1985): 102–103.

Johnson, David, and Roger Johnson. "Cooperative Learning: One Key to Computer Assisted Learning." *The Computing Teacher 13* (October 1985): 11–15.

Kraus, William H. "The Computer as a Learning Center." In *Computers in Mathematics Education,* 1984 Yearbook of the National Council of Teachers of Mathematics, pp. 54–59. Reston, VA: The Council, 1984.

Lindquist, Mary Montgomery, Thomas P. Carpenter, Edward A. Silver, and Westina Matthews. "The Third National Assessment: Results and Implications for Elementary and Middle Schools." *Arithmetic Teacher 31* (December 1983): 14–19.

Meyer, Phillis. "When You Use a Calculator You Have to Think!" *Arithmetic Teacher 27* (January 1980): 19–21.

Miller, Don. "Motivational Activities for Low (and Higher) Achievers," Columbus, OH: Calculator Information Center, September 1982.

Morris, Janet. *How to Develop Problem Solving Using a Calculator*. Reston, VA: National Council of Teachers of Mathematics, 1981.

Morris, Janet Parker. "Problem Solving with Calculators." *Arithmetic Teacher 25* (April 1978): 24–26.

Moses, Joel. "The Home Computer in Your Future." *Graduate Woman 75* (July/August 1981): 42–47.

Mulkeen, Thomas, and Toby Tetenbaum. "Logo and the Teaching of Problem Solving: A Call for a Moratorium." *Educational Technology 24* (November 1984): 16–20.

National Assessment of Educational Progress. *The Second Assessment of Mathematics, 1977-78: Released Exercise Set*. Denver, CO: Education Commission of the States, 1979.

National Council of Teachers of Mathematics. "The Impact of Computing Technology on School Mathematics." Report of an NCTM Conference. Reston, VA: The Council, 1984.

NCTM Instructional Affairs Committee. "Minicalculators in Schools." *Arithmetic Teacher 23* (January 1976): 72–74.

Nelson, Harold. "Learning with Logo." *On Computing 3* (Summer 1981): 14–16.

Papert, Seymour. "Computers and Computer Cultures." *Creative Computing 7* (March 1981): 82–92.

Reys, Robert E. "Calculators in the Elementary Classroom: How Can We Go Wrong!" *Arithmetic Teacher* 28 (November 1980): 38–40.

Reys, Robert E., Barbara J. Bestgen, Terrence G. Coburn, Harold L. Schoen, Richard J. Shumway, Charlotte L. Wheatley, Grayson H. Wheatley, and Arthur L. White. *Keystrokes: Calculator Activities for Young Students: Addition and Subtraction.* Palo Alto, CA: Creative Publications, 1979.

——. *Keystrokes: Calculator Activities for Young Students: Multiplication and Division.* Palo Alto, CA: Creative Publications, 1979.

Shumway, Richard J. "Young Children, Programming, and Mathematical Thinking." In *Computers in Mathematics Education,* 1984 Yearbook of the National Council of Teachers of Mathematics, pp. 127–134. Reston, VA: The Council, 1984.

Slesnick, Twila. "Bunk! Computer Myths We Can Live Without." *Classroom Computer Learning* 5 (February 1985): 31–33.

Suydam, Marilyn N. "Achieving with Calculators." *Arithmetic Teacher 31* (November 1983): 20.

——. "The Use of Calculators in Pre-college Education." Columbus, OH: Calculator Information Center, August 1982.

Taylor, Ross. "Computer and Calculators in the Mathematics Classroom." *Selected Issues in Mathematics Education,* edited by Mary Montgomery Lindquist. Berkeley, CA: McCutchan Publishing Corporation, 1980.

Thiagarajan, Sivasailam, and Harold D. Stolovitch. *Games with the Pocket Calculator.* Menlo Park, CA: Dymax, 1976.

Thomas, Eleanor M., and Rex A. Thomas. "Exploring Geometry with Logo." *Arithmetic Teacher 32* (September 1984): 16–18.

Watt, Dan. "Computer Evaluation Cometh." *Popular Computing 9* (July 1984): 91–94.

Wiebe, James. "BASIC Programming for Gifted Elementary Students." *Arithmetic Teacher* 28 (March 1981): 42–44.

Williams, David E. "The Language of Calculators." *Arithmetic Teacher 28* (January 1981): 22–25.

Zukas, Walter, L. H. Buka, and Judith Martin. "Teaching Fourth and Fifth Graders About Computers." *Arithmetic Teacher 28* (October 1980): 24–27.

CHILDREN'S LITERATURE

Adler, David. *Calculator Fun.* Illustrated by Arline and Marvin Oberman. New York: Franklin Watts, 1981.

Ball, Marion J., and Sylvia Charp. *Be a Computer Literate.* Morris Plains, NJ: Creative Computing Press, 1977.

Berger, Melvin. *Those Amazing Computers.* New York: John Day, 1973.

Graham, Ian. *The Inside Story: Computer.* New York: Gloucester Press, 1983.

Harris, Dwight, and Patricia Harris. *Computer Programming 1, 2, 3!* New York: Grosset and Dunlap, 1983.

Jacobsen, Karen. *A New True Book: Computers.* Chicago: Children's Press, 1982.

Lewis, Bruce. *Meet the Computer.* Illustrated by Leonard Kessler. New York: Dodd, Mead, 1977.

Lipson, Shelley. *It's BASIC: The ABC's of Computer Programming.* Illustrated by Janice Stapleton. New York: Holt, Rinehart and Winston, 1982.

Simon, Seymour. *How to Talk to Your Computer.* Illustrated by Barbara and Ed Emberley. New York: Crowell, 1985.

Srivastava, Jane Jonas. *Computers.* Illustrated by James and Ruth McCrea. New York: Crowell, 1972.

Watson, Clyde. *Binary Numbers.* Illustrated by Wendy Watson. New York: Crowell, 1977.

Willerding, Margaret. *From Fingers to Computers.* Chicago: Franklin, 1970.

3
ORGANIZING
FOR INSTRUCTION

Ms. Kosarchyn replied to Mr. Goodnature, "National Reading Association? School Science and Mathematics? National Council of Teachers of Mathematics? National Council of Teachers of English? I can't join all of them!"

"Yes, that would be expensive. Joan, Marta, Don, and I each join one organization and then share the journals. Want to join our group?"

Professional journals? Conferences? National and state organizations? What do you know about these opportunities to continue to grow professionally after you have graduated?

For many prospective elementary teachers this is the last course relating to mathematics they will take before they begin their student teaching experience or obtain their first teaching position. A preservice teacher may be considering many questions, such as the following: What grade level will the students be? What will the students be like? What will they already know? Will they have a foundation on which to continue building problem-solving skills? What textbooks will be used? What topics will I be teaching? Will the textbook explanations be given so that the students will comprehend the concepts?

In the first section of this chapter, features of elementary mathematics textbooks are described. For most teachers the primary resource for teaching mathematics is the teacher's edition of the textbook. However, the order of topics and the topics themselves may vary among publishers. Also, the quality varies among different textbook series as well as within each series and within individual textbooks. Even though a teacher may be using a high-quality textbook, it is assumed that the textbook will need to be supplemented to meet the class's needs. The purpose of this section is to acquaint preservice teachers with one resource, the teacher's edition of a textbook.

It is assumed that the reader has studied theorists such as Piaget, Gagné, and Bloom in previous courses. Their ideas and theories will be related to the teaching of mathematics and the design of elementary school mathematics textbooks.

ELEMENTARY SCHOOL TEXTBOOKS

As you analyze current elementary textbooks, you will note that there are differences among current textbooks depending on the philosophy and teaching style of the authors. There are also major differences in textbooks over time. Textbooks are changed due to the current research on learning, trends in learning, and changes in society. A strong influence on current texts was a position paper published by the National Council of Supervisors of Mathematics in 1978 (Figure 3-1). During the 1970s there was a back-to-the-basics trend that was interpreted by many as drill, drill, and more drill. In response to this trend the NCSM defined what they considered the ten basic skills for elementary school mathematics. The effect of this position paper can be observed by analyzing the current content in elementary school textbook series. An overview of the content in textbook series can be found in the scope-and-sequence charts in the teacher's manuals of elementary mathematics textbooks.

SCOPE AND SEQUENCE

"Scope" refers to the range of mathematics topics taught in the elementary school grades such as place value and counting, addition of whole numbers, problem solving, measurement, estimation, decimals, and percent. "Sequence" refers to the order in which the topics are introduced. The topic place value and counting, from the scope-and-sequence charts of an elementary mathematics textbook series, has been reproduced in Figure 3-2. The various subtopics in place value and counting are listed in the order in which they are presented in grades kindergarten through eight. The bold type indicates that a topic is being introduced for the first time. The regular type means that the topic is to be mastered, reviewed, or extended. The numbers following a topic indicate the pages where that topic

TEN BASIC SKILL AREAS

Problem Solving

Learning to solve problems is the principal reason for studying mathematics. Problem solving is the process of applying previously acquired knowledge to new and unfamiliar situations. Solving word problems in texts is one form of problem solving, but students also should be faced with non-textbook problems. Problem-solving strategies involve posing questions, analyzing situations, translating results, illustrating results, drawing diagrams, and using trial and error. In solving problems, students need to be able to apply the rules of logic necessary to arrive at valid conclusions. They must be able to determine which facts are relevant. They should be unfearful of arriving at tentative conclusions and they must be willing to subject these conclusions to scrutiny.

Applying Mathematics to Everyday Situations

The use of mathematics is interrelated with all computation activities. Students should be encouraged to take everyday situations, translate them into mathematical expressions, solve the mathematics, and interpret the results in light of the initial situation.

Alertness of the Reasonableness of Results

Due to arithmetic errors or other mistakes, results of mathematical work are sometimes wrong. Students should learn to inspect all results and to check for reasonableness in terms of the original problem. With the increase in the use of calculating devices in society, this skill is essential.

Estimation and Approximation

Students should be able to carry out rapid approximate calculations by first rounding off numbers. They should acquire some simple techniques for estimating quantity, length, distance, weight, etc. It is also necessary to decide when a particular result is precise enough for the purpose at hand.

Appropriate Computational Skills

Students should gain facility with addition, subtraction, multiplication, and division with whole numbers and decimals. Today it must be recognized that long, complicated computations will usually be done with a calculator. Knowledge of single-digit number facts is essential and mental arithmetic is a valuable skill. Moreover, there are everyday situations which demand recognition of, and simple computation with, common fractions.

Because consumers continually deal with many situations that involve percentage, the ability to recognize and use percents should be developed and maintained.

Geometry

Students should learn the geometric concepts they will need to function effectively in the 3-dimensional world. They should have knowledge of concepts such as point, line, plane, parallel, and perpendicular. They should know basic properties of simple geometric figures, particularly those properties which relate to measurement and problem-solving skills. They also must be able to recognize similarities and differences among objects.

Measurement

As a minimum skill, students should be able to measure distance, weight, time, capacity, and temperature. Measurement of angles and calculations of simple areas and volumes are also essential. Students should be able to perform measurement in both metric and customary systems using the appropriate tools.

Reading, Interpreting, and Constructing Tables, Charts, and Graphs

Students should know how to read and draw conclusions from simple tables, maps, charts, and graphs. They should be able to condense numerical information into more manageable or meaningful terms by setting up simple tables, charts, and graphs.

Using Mathematics to Predict

Students should learn how elementary notions of probability are used to determine the likelihood of future events. They should learn to identify situations where immediate past experience does not affect the likelihood of future events. They should become familiar with how mathematics is used to help make predictions such as election forecasts.

Computer Literacy

It is important for all citizens to understand what computers can and cannot do. Students should be aware of the many uses of computers in society, such as their use in teaching/learning, financial transactions, and information storage and retrieval. The "mystique" surrounding computers is disturbing and can put persons with no understanding of computers at a disadvantage. The increasing use of computers by government, industry, and business demands an awareness of computer uses and limitations.

FIGURE 3-1.
NCSM position paper. (© 1978 National Council of Supervisors of Mathematics).

Kindergarten

Place value and counting

Same number, 45–48, 53, 77, 78, 81–83, 87
More, less, 49–52
Counting 0 through 5, 55–67
Counting through 10, 75–82, 85–87, 89–94
Counting practice, 68, 69, 73, 83, 84, 96
Order of numbers through 10, 70, 88, 97, 131
Ordinal numbers *first, second, third,* 71, 72
Counting money, 105–111
Writing numerals through 10, 113–117, 119–123, 125–128
Counting through 20, 147, 148, 151–158
Writing numerals through 20, 147–149, 151, 153, 157, 158
Order of numbers through 20, 150–159

1

Matching sets, 3, 4
Sets and the numbers 0–10, 5–16, 21–28
Counting and writing the numerals 0–10, 6, 8–15, 21–28
Number words, 5, 7, 11, 13, 15, 21, 23, 25, 27
Order of numbers 0–10, 26, 28, 51–52
Counting money, 3, 4, 17, 18, 47, 48, 129, 130, 163, 165, 183–188
Order of numbers on the number line, 51, 52, 147, 148, 161, 166
Comparing—less, greater, 53–56, 60, 148, 159, 160, 172
Ordinal numbers through *fifth,* 137–140
Sets of 10, 141, 149–152
Place value through 19, 142–146
Place value through 99, 153–156
Numbers in table form, 143–144, 153–156
Order of numbers through 99, 157, 161, 162
1 more, 1 less, 158
Skip-counting by 2, 5, and 10, 163–168
Projects on numbers and counting, 32, 170
Extra Practice, 301, 302, 304, 307–309

2

Counting and writing numerals to 10, 2
Ordinal numbers through **eighth,** 39, 40, 134
Place value through 19, 41, 42
Place value through 99, 43–46
Numbers in table form, 45, 251–253
Order of numbers through 99, 47, 48, 164
Comparisons, 24, 52, 56, 87, 88, 129, 130, 176, 270, 290, 296
Counting on the number line, 49, 50, 258
Counting backward, 50
1 more, 1 less, 51, 259
Skip-counting by 2, 5, and 10, 53, 54
Counting money, 33, 55, 56, 125–130, 149, 150, 170, 265–268, 289
Odd and even numbers, 248
Place value through 999, 251–256
Order of numbers through 999, 257, 258, 260
10 or 100 more, 10 or 100 less, 261, 262
Comparing using $<$, $>$, **and** $=$, 263, 264
A project on numbers, 270
Extra practice, 311, 312

3

Place value and counting

Ordinal numbers, 36, 37
Place value through 99, 38, 39, 42, 43
Numbers in table form, 38, 40, 54, 59–63
Number words, 38, 39–43, 54–56, 60–63
Comparing using $<$ and $>$, 44, 45, 58
Place value through 999, 40–43
Counting by 1's, 10's, and 100's, 42, 43, 46, 47, 55, 57, 61
Before and after (1 more, 1 less), 43
The number line, 44, 45, 50–52, 161
Rounding to the nearest ten or hundred, 50–53, 88, 118–121
Thousands, 54–57
Ten thousands, 60, 61
Hundred thousands, 62, 63
Counting by 1000's, 57
Commas in large numbers, 60–63
Even and odd numbers, 161, 163
Extra Practice, 353, 354

4

Digits, 24
Place value through 999, 24, 25
Numbers in table form, 24, 30, 32, 40
Number words, 24, 31–33, 40
The number line, 26, 28, 38
Rounding to the nearest ten or hundred, 26–29, 38, 39, 312
Thousands, 30, 31
Ten thousands, hundred thousands, 32, 33
Millions, 40
Commas in large numbers, 32, 33, 40
Comparing using $<$ and $>$, 36, 37
100 more, **10,000 more,** 36
Rounding to the nearest thousand, 38, 39
Even and odd numbers, 125
Place-value game, 37
Project on number patterns, 43
Extra Practice, 353, 354

5

Digits, 2
Place value—thousands, 2–5
Numbers in table form, 2, 4, 12, 14
Expanded numerals, 3, 5
Number words, 2–5, 12–15
Commas in large numbers, 4, 12, 15
Comparing using $<$ and $>$, 6, 7
Rounding to the nearest ten or hundred, 8, 9, 32
The number line, 8, 10, 65
Rounding to the nearest thousand or ten thousand, 10, 11
Millions, 12, 13
Billions, 14, 15
Roman numerals through thousands, 16, 17
Even and odd numbers, 65
Extra Practice, 349

FIGURE 3-2.
Scope-and-sequence chart for place value and counting. (From C.A. Dilley, D.W. Lowry, W.E. Rucker, **Heath Mathematics**, D.C. Heath & Company, 1983, Grades 1,4,7, p. T24. Reprinted with permission of D.C. Heath & Company.)

can be found for the particular grade-level textbook.

Some topics, such as place value, are repeated at several grade levels. In first grade place value of two-digit numbers is introduced, and it is studied further in second grade. Also, in the second grade the children are introduced to place value of

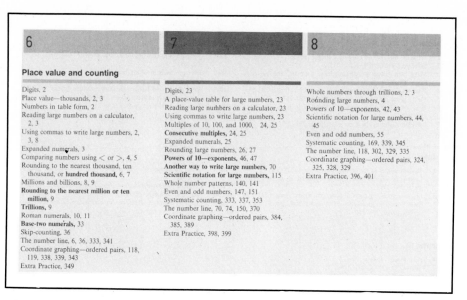

FIGURE 3-2.
Continued.

three-digit numbers. Place value continues to be studied, with larger numbers introduced at each grade level. In successive grades the topic is reintroduced with more complexity and more abstraction. This is called the spiral curriculum.

In the lower grades pictures dominate the student pages. In reading the lesson plans for either lower or upper grades, descriptions are found for using manipulative aids. The lower the grade level, the greater the emphasis on models for developing concepts. Developing concepts through models is supported by research and advocated by learning theorists.

One theorist who supports the use of models for teaching children is Jean Piaget. In his study of the intellectual growth of children he describes four sequential stages. Children proceed through these stages at different rates and different ages, depending on the influence of many factors. In addition to experiences, both intellectual and psychological, Piaget cites physiological maturation and social environment as factors that affect development at various stages. Also, an individual may be in more than one developmental stage at the same time. This person may be ready to think abstractly about number but still be in the concrete stage for geometric concepts.

Children in the early elementary grades are most likely to be in Piaget's preoperational stage. They need to manipulate objects and observe the results of their actions on the objects. For example, children at the beginning of this stage lack conservation of number. If they count out two sets of ten objects each and place the objects in one-to-one correspondence, they will probably decide that there are the same number of objects in each set. However, if the objects in one set are spread out, the children may conclude that this set contains more objects

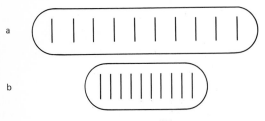

Preoperational child: "There are more
sticks in set A than in set B."

FIGURE 3-3.
Conservation of number.

than the other set (Figure 3-3). Experiences in counting, comparing, and rearranging objects and observing their actions on the objects will help children become conservers of number.

As preoperational children mature intellectually, psychologically, physiologically, and socially, they will proceed gradually into the concrete operational stage. Children in this stage still need to manipulate concrete objects, particularly when a new topic is being introduced. However, if the object is not available, they can sometimes imagine pictures of that object. For example, instead of manipulating blocks, they form pictures of blocks in their minds and mentally manipulate the pictures. Since these pictures are based on previous experiences, a number of activities using models must be provided to help the children build these images.

Piaget's fourth stage is formal operations. At this stage individuals are able to think abstractly. They are not dependent on real or imagined objects. They are able to consider possible ideas as well as real and representational ones. They are able to formulate hypotheses and draw logical conclusions from them. Many children do not reach this stage during their elementary school years.

Often, Piaget's theory is inappropriately

cited as stating that only young children need models for learning. However, research has found that models are also very important at upper grade levels for introducing and exploring concepts such as geometry and decimal or common fractions. Adults also benefit from models and diagrams in studying a new idea. The main difference in the use of these materials with the more mature student is that the model will not be used as long.

Research shows that increased student achievement is more likely to occur when models are used in lessons than in lessons in which models are not used. These results have been found across *all* grade levels, at *all* ability levels, at *all* achievement levels, and for a variety of mathematics topics (Suydam, 1984).

Research and theories of how children think are reflected in lessons at different grade levels. The intellectual maturity of children is an important factor in planning appropriate learning experiences for them. As the children grow in maturity and experiences, the lessons should reflect those changes. The differences in how topics are introduced across various grade levels can be noted by examining elementary school textbooks. Examples of place value lessons from the teacher's editions of elementary textbooks are shown in Figure 3-4. Note the sequential development of the content and the gradual change in the diagrams to conceptually more abstract models.

The simplest of the topics for first graders is shown in Figure 3-4a. The students are asked to circle each group of ten objects after they have counted each group of ten. Before using this textbook page, children should count and group actual objects such as blocks, sticks, and erasers. Sufficient experience in manipulating actual objects will prepare children for the more abstract activity of circling pictures of objects. In Figure 3-4b the objects have been grouped in bundles of ten for the students. The students record the appropriate numbers of tens and ones. As with the previous exercises and those that follow, the assignment would be preceded by a class activity in which the children used counting sticks.

In another example from a first-grade textbook, base-ten blocks are used to illustrate two-digit numbers (Figure 3-4c). Base-ten blocks are conceptually slightly more abstract than counting sticks. With counting sticks, children physically bundle 10 ones to

FIGURE 3-4a.
Groups of ten. (From Joseph Payne et al., **Harper & Row Mathematics, Grade 1**, student edition, p. 123. Copyright © 1985, Macmillan Inc. Reprinted with permission of Scribner Educational Publishers, a division of Macmillan, Inc.)

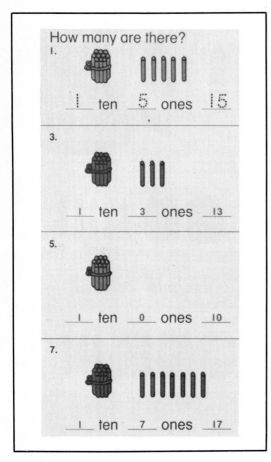

How many are there?

1.
__1__ ten __5__ ones __15__

3.
__1__ ten __3__ ones __13__

5.
__1__ ten __0__ ones __10__

7.
__1__ ten __7__ ones __17__

FIGURE 3-4b.
Grouping and recording tens and ones. (From Robert Eicholz, Phares O'Daffer, Charles Fleenor, Randall Charles, Sharon Young, Carne Barnett, **Addison-Wesley Mathematics Book 1**, p. 116. Copyright © 1985, Addison-Wesley Publishing Co., Inc.)

FIGURE 3-4c.
Writing standard numerals. (From A.V. Buffington, A.R. Garr, J. Graening, P.P. Halloran, M.L. Mahaffey, M. O'Neal, **Merrill Mathematics: Grade 1**, Merrill Publishing Company, 1985, pp. 156 and 160. Copyright © Merrill Publishing Company.)

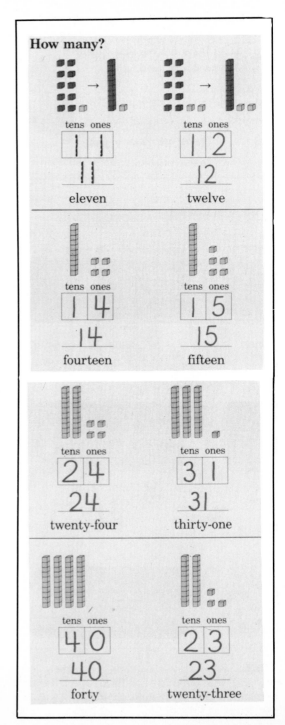

How many?

tens	ones
1	1

11
eleven

tens	ones
1	2

12
twelve

tens	ones
1	4

14
fourteen

tens	ones
1	5

15
fifteen

tens	ones
2	4

24
twenty-four

tens	ones
3	1

31
thirty-one

tens	ones
4	0

40
forty

tens	ones
2	3

23
twenty-three

form 1 ten whereas with base-ten blocks, they trade 10 units for 1 long. In this lesson the base-ten blocks and the place-value tables are linked to the numerals and the oral names.

The lesson in Figure 3-4d reviews place-value concepts introduced in the previous grade. The relationship between 10 ones and 1 ten and between 10 tens and 1 hundred is emphasized. Through discussion of such activities, children should realize that our number system is based on grouping by ten. In this lesson the children are also asked to read the numbers in two different ways.

In Figure 3-4e the numeration pattern is extended to thousands. Base-ten blocks and the place-value table are the primary models used to explore this concept. An example using the abacus is also shown. Each rod of the abacus stands for a different place value, such as ones, tens, hundreds, or thousands. The disks on the abacus are all the same size, so their place values are determined by the rod on which they are positioned. The disks on each rod are usually color coded to represent different values. This feature of the abacus, which relates different place values to position rather than to

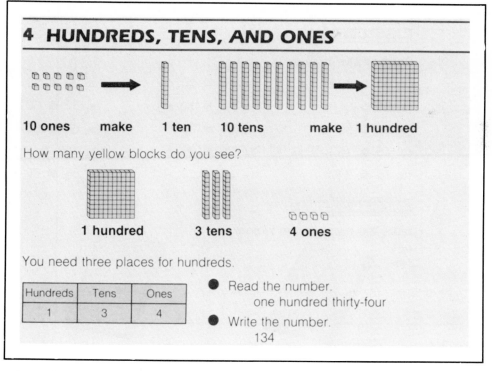

FIGURE 3-4d.
Extending place value to hundreds. (From Joseph Payne et al., **Harper & Row Mathematics, Grade 3**, student edition, p. 36. Copyright © 1985, Macmillan, Inc. Reprinted with permission of Scribner Educational Publishers, a division of Macmillan, Inc.)

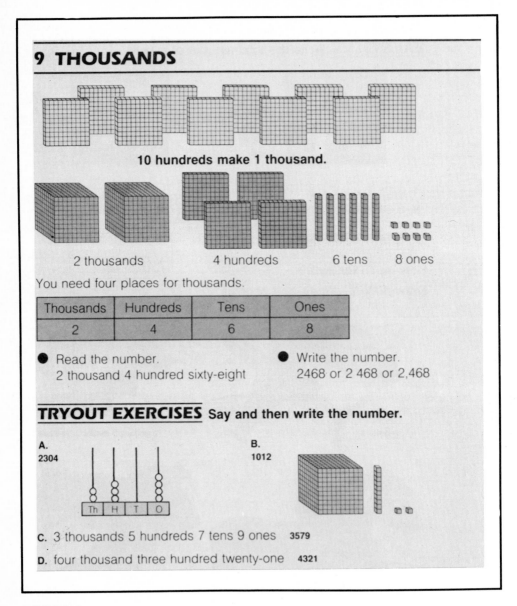

9 THOUSANDS

10 hundreds make 1 thousand.

2 thousands   4 hundreds   6 tens   8 ones

You need four places for thousands.

Thousands	Hundreds	Tens	Ones
2	4	6	8

● Read the number.
2 thousand 4 hundred sixty-eight

● Write the number.
2468 or 2 468 or 2,468

TRYOUT EXERCISES Say and then write the number.

A.
2304

Th | H | T | O

B.
1012

C. 3 thousands 5 hundreds 7 tens 9 ones   3579

D. four thousand three hundred twenty-one   4321

FIGURE 3-4e.
Four-digit numbers with base-ten blocks and abacus. (From Joseph Payne et al., **Harper & Row Mathematics, Grade 3**, student edition, p. 46. Copyright © 1985, Macmillan, Inc. Reprinted with permission of Scribner Educational Publishers, a division of Macmillan, Inc.)

different physical size, makes the abacus conceptually much more abstract than the base-ten blocks. The teacher's notes in this textbook chapter give ideas on how to relate the abacus to the place-value table.

Place-value lessons from fourth- and fifth-grade textbooks are shown in Figure 3-4f and g. Millions are reviewed and billions are introduced by using a place-value table and an abacus. In both cases the pattern of place value developed concretely with smaller numbers is extended more abstractly to larger and larger numbers.

Throughout the pages from elementary mathematics textbooks that were used to illustrate the scope and sequence of teaching whole numbers, various models were employed to illustrate number. At first it might appear that one model would be sufficient to illustrate number, but a variety of experiences are needed. This approach is supported by Zoltan Dienes, a theorist who has a background in both mathematics and psychology. He states that a concept must be presented in a variety of situations. This is called the perceptual variability principle.

Activities should be designed so that they *appear* to be different but each illustrates the same concept. For example, if children are continually asked to count poker chips, they may think that number is only a property of poker chips. From experiences

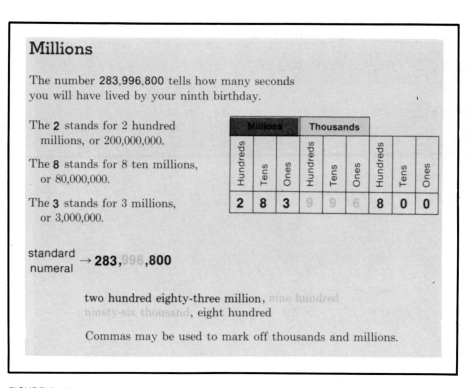

FIGURE 3-4f.

Reading numbers in millions. (From C.A. Dilley, D.W. Lowry, W.E. Rucker, **Heath Mathematics**, D.C. Heath & Company, 1983, Grade 4, p. 40. Reprinted with permission of D.C. Heath & Company.)

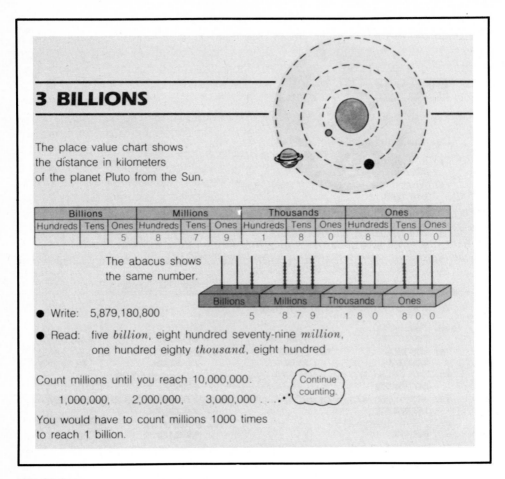

3 BILLIONS

The place value chart shows
the distance in kilometers
of the planet Pluto from the Sun.

Billions			Millions			Thousands			Ones		
Hundreds	Tens	Ones	Hundreds	Tens	Ones	Hundreds	Tens	Ones	Hundreds	Tens	Ones
		5	8	7	9	1	8	0	8	0	0

The abacus shows
the same number.

Billions	Millions	Thousands	Ones
5	8 7 9	1 8 0	8 0 0

● Write: 5,879,180,800

● Read: five *billion*, eight hundred seventy-nine *million*,
one hundred eighty *thousand*, eight hundred

Count millions until you reach 10,000,000.

1,000,000,   2,000,000,   3,000,000 . . . .

Continue counting.

You would have to count millions 1000 times
to reach 1 billion.

FIGURE 3-4g.
Extending place value to billions. (From Joseph Payne et al., **Harper & Row**
Mathematics, Grade 5, p. 6. Copyright © 1985, Macmillan, Inc. Reprinted with
permission of Scribner Educational Publishers, a division of Macmillan, Inc.)

that involve counting people, cubes, pencils, books, lima beans, and so on, children will abstract the concept of number as an idea that is not inherent in any particular set of objects. In the examples relating to place value, many aids or models, including counting sticks, interlocking cubes, base-ten blocks, abacuses, and place-value tables, were used to illustrate number.

If models are so important, why don't all elementary and junior high school teachers use them? Many teachers incorrectly believe that models are appropriate only for young children; as stated before, research has shown this to be false. Some teachers have simply lacked access to models. However, most textbooks now have models incorporated in their resources, including punchout models or black-line masters for making models.

Having access to models is important; knowing how to use them is essential. The quality of teacher's notes on how to use models to develop a lesson varies. In most cases these notes will need to be supplemented by the classroom teacher. Many teachers did not have a methods course in their preservice education that gave them an opportunity to learn about models for teaching mathematics. Too often inservice education has consisted of one or two hours of formal presentation rather than an organized, long-term, hands-on program that teaches the teacher how to use the models effectively. Teachers can continue their professional growth through sharing ideas informally with other teachers, participating at conferences, and reading professional journals such as the *Arithmetic Teacher*.

This overview of the scope and sequence of elementary textbooks discussed only whole-number concepts. As you analyze other topics in the elementary curriculum, you will observe similar development across various grade levels. Scope-and-sequence charts help you become aware of which topics are introduced or developed or reviewed in the elementary curriculum and at what grade level. The chart can also be used to note what topics were introduced or reviewed in the previous grades and how they will be continued in the students' next year of study. Additionally, you will need to start thinking of a yearly plan to encompass the scope of the curriculum.

PLANNING FOR THE YEAR

At the beginning of the year the teacher needs to organize the entire year's work in order to maximize learning. It has been found that teachers who plan for the entire year move at a faster pace, include more content, and produce higher student achievement than those teachers who merely start at the beginning of the book and proceed through it without planning for the year. Yearly planning does make a difference. Some of the factors that need to be considered are content, time, pacing, grouping, and activity.

Is it possible to include all of the chapters for a particular grade level within the parameters of a school year? If not, what topics should be omitted? Which topics should be emphasized? Who makes those decisions? In observations of different classrooms, it was noted that some teachers skipped topics such as fractions or geometry. Through interviews, it was found that the variables that affected teacher choice of content were their enjoyment of teaching the topic, their perception of whether it was a difficult topic for their students, and their perception of the effort required to teach the topic (Berliner, 1984). Note that these decisions were not based on student needs or on concerns for a balanced curriculum.

The most important variable accounting for student achievement is the opportunity to learn a particular topic (Berliner, 1984). If the teacher omits certain topics, student opportunities have been limited. If teachers find that they are omitting certain topics, they should be aware of why they make these curricular decisions. If their decisions are not educationally sound, they should discuss how to teach these topics with other professionals. Learning how to teach a topic effectively should also enhance their enjoyment of the topic.

To help teachers, a plan for the year is included in the teacher's edition of most elementary mathematics textbooks. The plan will recommend the number of days to be spent on each unit. Depending on the backgrounds and the abilities of the students, the teacher can choose among two or three different plans. The time allotment and the chapters suggested will vary accordingly. The teacher should then coordinate this plan with the school's schedule, indicating which month each of these topics will be studied.

Another consideration is the structure of the class. Should the class be grouped by ability? It has been found that when teachers grouped for instruction by ability, the pace of instruction was dramatically different between the high and low groups. The low groups were paced too slow, and consequently the gap between the groups increased further. Although most teachers believe that instruction should be differentiated according to student needs and abilities, it was observed that their instruction did not change between high- and low-ability groups (Berliner, 1984). If grouping is to be done in mathematics, the criteria should be related to the topic being studied and the grouping should be changed continually to meet the changing needs of the children.

Over the years teaching trends have included the gamut from individualized instruction to whole-class instruction. At the time, each structure was proclaimed to end all problems. Each structure has its strengths and weaknesses. Rather than rely on one type of structure, the teacher should use a variety. Whole-class instruction is effective when presenting new topics to the class because a large block of time is needed to present new concepts and skills. Also, students learn from each other's comments and questions. Mathematics should be presented in an active, process-oriented atmosphere through dialogue among the teacher and students.

Small groups and individualized instruction give teachers an opportunity to interact more closely with individual students. Small groups also provide an opportunity for students to interact with each other in exploring problems. By the very nature of the size of the group, more students will become involved in asking and answering questions and discussing and explaining situations. Also, individual students and each group will become more independent and more confident in their thinking and less reliant on the teacher. Burns in "Groups of Four: Solving the Management Problem" describes the benefits of small groups that are randomly chosen and regularly changed. She also describes guidelines for implementing small-group instruction. Small groups can be used during various activities such as problem solving, measurement, or games to build various concepts or skills.

Individual activities are equally important. Students need time to work on their own, concentrating on and being responsible for their own work. In addition to tailoring instruction to individual students and groups and to knowing appropriate teaching methods, effective teachers also need to be well organized for individual units and on a daily basis.

QUESTIONS AND ACTIVITIES

1. In the past decade some people advocated "back to the basics," which often was interpreted as "drill, drill, drill!" Throughout history, there have been many different approaches to teaching arithmetic. For a thorough discussion on three approaches—namely drill, incidental learning, and meaningful learning—read "Psychological Considerations in the Learning and Teaching of Arithmetic" by Brownell. Define each approach and list the advantages and disadvantages of each.

2. In a reaction to the slogan "Back to the Basics," the National Council of Supervisors of Mathematics formulated a position statement on what constitutes the basic skills in mathematics.

    a. List the ten basic skill areas as defined by the National Council of Supervisors of Mathematics. Define each in your own words.

    b. If you had made a list of ten basic skill areas in mathematics before reading this chapter, would your list look like the NCSM's? If not, how would it have differed?

    c. What is the rationale for the areas that they defined?

3. Why are estimation and mental computation included in the curriculum? Read "Mental Computation and Estimation: Past, Present, and Future" by Reys to gain a perspective.

4. Consult two textbook series. What evidence can you detect that the National Council of Supervisors of Mathematics has influenced the curriculum of these series? What specific recommendations do you find included? Omitted? Are they included in the lower grades and the upper grades? (*Note:* Some recommendations, such as "alertness to reasonableness of results," will not be listed as a topic; it is a philosophy that should be included throughout the year in the students' and teacher's thinking.)

5. Portions of scope-and-sequence charts that relate to place value and counting and to addition of whole numbers have been reproduced in Figures 3-2 and 3-5. Find the scope-and-sequence chart that relates to one of these topics in a different elementary textbook series. Compare the two charts and find their differences. Are the subtopics the same? Are the subtopics introduced at the same grade levels?

6. What topics in mathematics are taught in the elementary school? Consult two different elementary textbook series. For each series list the main topics found in the scope-and-sequence charts.

7. Children are not little adults and therefore cannot be treated as such. Explain how this relates to a child's learning experiences in an elementary school classroom.

8. Both Piaget's and Dienes' theories describe the importance of concrete materials. Discuss how their theories relate to the following statement: "Models do not develop mathematical concepts; children develop mathematical concepts."

9. Note the topics included in the kindergarten mathematics curriculum by reading a scope-and-sequence chart and looking through a kindergarten textbook. Read the article "Kindergarten Mathematics—A Survey" by Kurtz; it reports the results of a survey on children's competencies at the end of kindergarten. If you were a first-grade teacher and these results were typical of your new class, what implications would this have for your plan of instruction?

10. a. Should manipulatives be used in middle school? Read "Research Report: Manipulative Materials" by Suydam. What does this say to the classroom teacher?

    b. The February 1986 *Arithmetic Teacher* is a theme issue on manipulatives. Read, copy, and evaluate one of the articles.

11. Representations of whole numbers were used to illustrate the perceptual variability principle by Dienes. What would be some examples of common fractions to illustrate perceptual variability?

12. *For your resource file:* In this chapter and throughout this textbook, *activities* using models and oral language are described that precede the students' work in their textbooks. Diagrams of models and written work should follow the activities with models. Read and summarize "Is One Picture Worth One Thousand Words?" by Poage and Poage and "What Do Children See in Mathematics Textbook Pictures?" by Campbell for discussions on children's interpretation of diagrams. Add these ideas to your resource file.

13. Select an elementary school textbook of a grade level that you are particularly interested in teaching. List the series and grade level that you selected.
   a. Find the outline for the yearly plan. Does it suggest alternate plans depending on the students' abilities? How many days are alloted for instruction? Testing?
   b. Are all chapters included in the yearly schedule? Which chapters do you think you will enjoy teaching the most? For which do you feel the best prepared?
   c. Are there chapters that you think you will not enjoy teaching? If so, list them. What types of experiences can you plan to change your perceptions?
   d. For which chapters do you feel the least prepared? What types of experiences can you plan that will help you become a more effective teacher of these topics?

14. *For your resource file:* Read Larson in "Organizing for Mathematics Instruction" for a discussion on planning and management for the year with regard to time, ability groups, curriculum, and evaluation. Or for further information on research on grouping, read Suydam's "Research Report: Individualized or Cooperative Learning."

15. Read "Groups of Four: Solving the Management Problem" by Marilyn Burns. What guidelines are given to each group? How are the groups formed? What are the positive benefits that you perceive in organizing small groups? When and how often would you use this organization?

16. Learning centers can be used by individual students, or by pairs or small groups of students. Many elementary school mathematics textbooks include suggestions for setting up learning centers; some textbooks provide one for each chapter.
   a. Consult an elementary textbook series. Where are suggestions for learning centers described? Read through the descriptions of two or three of the centers. What was the purpose of each?
   b. Centers can be developed around the topic currently being studied or an enrichment topic. The center can be required or optional. Throughout this textbook, children's books are listed in a section at the end of most chapters. These books can be used for whole-class instruction or in learning centers. Read one of the books listed at the end of the problem solving, calculator and computers, or whole-number numeration chapters. List the book you read and briefly describe how it could be used in a center.

17. *For your resource file:* Gilbert-Macmillan and Leitz describe how to set up small groups for problem solving in "Cooperative Small Groups: A Method for Teaching Problem Solving." Copy the article and add it to your problem-solving file. Write a paragraph describing your reactions to the ideas described in the article.

18. Read from the *Arithmetic Teacher*, "Development of Elementary School Mathematics Teaching in the United States" by Paul C. Burns. Discuss briefly the history of one of the following topics.
   a. Purpose of teaching mathematics
   b. Process of pedagogy of teaching mathematics
   c. Content of mathematics curriculum
   d. Training of prospective elementary school teachers

19. What are other changes being suggested for the elementary curriculum? Read "The Elementary School Mathematics Curriculum: Issues for Today" by Lindquist. Do you agree with her recommendations? Why or why not?

UNIT PLANNING

In the previous sections, an overview of the content and sequence of elementary school mathematics textbooks and various aspects of yearly planning were discussed. In addition to a yearly plan, a plan is needed for individual topics. As teachers plan individual units, they will use other features of the teacher's edition, textbook resource packages, and other resources. In this section the components of an individual unit and its supplementary materials are examined with regard to planning the teaching of a particular topic. These parts could be categorized under the following headings:

1. Purpose.
2. Prerequisite skills.
3. Developing a new topic.
4. Practicing/mastery of the new topic.
5. Review of previously studied topics.
6. Story problems/applications.
7. Problem solving.
8. Enrichment.
9. Evaluating student progress.

Each of these sections will be defined and illustrated by discussing units on addition of two-digit whole numbers with regrouping from various second-grade textbooks. These units were selected because they *introduce* a topic rather than *reviewing* a previously developed one.

PURPOSE

In planning the presentation of a topic, teachers should first consider whether the topic is new or has been introduced earlier. If it is new, what are the prerequisite skills? Do the students have the prerequisite skills? If it is a review topic, when was the topic first introduced? How well did the students master the topic earlier? How well have they retained it? How is the topic extended in this unit?

Another main consideration is what type of topic is taught in this unit. Are concepts

such as whole numbers, integers, three-dimensional shapes, or measurement division taught in the unit? Or are the students learning to acquire an algorithm or skill such as estimating the quotient, applying strategies for learning the basic facts, or learning the procedures in adding three-digit numbers?

The purpose of each unit is discussed in the overview found at the beginning of each unit. There are usually three to seven objectives for any one unit. These objectives are related to individual lessons in the unit. It has been found that throughout the unit it is important to focus on the main purpose of the unit and on how it is related to the lesson for that particular day.

To help the students focus on the purpose of the unit, most textbooks begin each unit with a picture that can be used to motivate the topic. In the teacher's edition, suggestions for a class discussion and sample questions about the picture are included. Suggestions for learning centers and bulletin boards are also included in most textbooks.

Although the textbook explicitly identifies objectives of the unit, the teacher has the responsibility of adapting the unit to the background of the class and of individual students. The textbook offers many helpful procedures, but it is the *teacher's* responsibility to implement the suggestions and guide and direct the learning.

PREREQUISITE SKILLS

Before teaching a new concept, the teacher must analyze the task and decide what skills and knowledge the students need to possess in order to accomplish the new task. The skills and knowledge needed for a specific task are called prerequisite skills. If students do not have all the prerequisite skills necessary to accomplish a task, the teacher must design appropriate learning activities

Adding whole numbers

K

More than, 49, 50
Addition readiness
   horizontal form, 133–136
   vertical form, 137–140
   Addition game, 145

1

Sums through 6, 35–44
Using pictures to add, 35–38
Order property, 41, 42
Adding money, 49, 50, 81, 82, 251
Sums through 10, 61–64, 67–70
Sums through 12, 195, 196, 201, 202
Adding in horizontal form, 73, 74, 196, 202,
   276, 282, 290
Families of facts, 199, 205, 279, 280
Three addends, 207
Adding two-digit numbers—no regrouping,
   241–244
Adding in table form, 241, 242
Sums through 18, 275, 276, 281, 282, 289,
   290
Shortcuts for addition, 207, 290
Projects for addition, 58, 84, 214, 296
Addition games, 78, 208
Practice, 43, 44, 65, 66, 71, 72, 75–77
Mixed practice, 97, 98, 125, 126, 200, 206,
   249, 250, 287, 288
Extra Practice, 303–305, 310, 311, 313, 314

2

Basic facts—sums through 10, 3, 4, 6–14
Sum, 3
Order property of addition, 5, 85
Adding in horizontal form, 11–14, 73, 74
Families of facts, 26, 28, 97, 98, 107
Basic facts—sums through 18, 61–65
   67–70, 73, 74
Adding money, 33, 111, 147–150, 169, 293
Missing addends, 38, 66, 79–82
Three or more addends, 83, 84, 227, 228,
   278, 280, 293
Addition games, 86, 152
Completing an addition table, 92
Addition-subtraction boxes, 116, 178
Adding two-digit numbers
   without regrouping, 135, 136
   in table form, 135
   regrouping ones to tens, 137, 138,
     141–143, 163, 277, 278
   in horizontal form, 143, 163, 282
   regrouping tens to hundreds, 279
   more than one regrouping, 279, 280

Adding whole numbers

3

Basic facts review—sums through 10, 2–5
Addend, sum, 2, 8
Order property, adding 0 property, 4, 12
Basic facts—sums through 18, 6–11
Addition equations, 8–11, 13, 18, 19
Missing addends, 10, 11, 13, 20–22
More than two addends, 12, 13, 78, 79, 85
Addition and subtraction are related,
   18–20, 22
Families of facts, 18, 19
Adding 2-digit numbers
   without regrouping, 70, 71
   with regrouping, 72–75, 78, 79
Adding in horizontal form, 71, 73, 79, 83,
   87, 93, 119
Checking addition, 78
Adding 3-digit numbers, 80, 82–87, 116,
   117, 119
Estimating sums, 88, 119–121
Adding 4-digit numbers, 92, 93
Addition and multiplication, 158
Shortcuts, 7, 13, 23, 73, 79, 207
Mixed practice, 19, 103, 125, 169, 195,
   203, 289, 294, 295, 339, 342
Extra Practice, 352, 355, 356

4

Basic-facts review, 2, 3
Addend, sum, 2, 4, 6–8
Order propetry, adding 0 property, 4–7
Grouping property, 6, 7
Ordering addends, 7
Missing addends, 8, 9, 11, 12
More than two addends, 5–7, 58, 59
Using grouping symbols, 5, 12, 13, 78, 113,
   148, 149, 250, 304
Adding without regrouping, 48, 49
Adding in horizontal form, 49, 78, 148
Adding 2- and 3-digit numbers, 50–53
Adding money, 53, 59
Estimating sums, 54, 55
Adding larger numbers, 56, 57
Using addition to check subtraction, 76,
   77
Shortcuts, 4
Addition games, 13
Projects for addition, 19, 101
Mixed practice
   paths, 109, 141
   using a rule to make a table, 143, 304
   target-number game, 149
Extra Practice, 353–355

5

Properties of addition, 24, 25, 28
Addend, sum, 24
Missing addends, 25, 29
Basic-facts review, 26, 27
More than two addends, 28, 29, 36
Using grouping symbols, 28, 48, 49, 72,
   122
Adding 2-digit numbers, 30, 31, 36
Adding money, 31, 33, 35, 241
Estimating sums, 32
Adding 3-digit numbers, 32, 33, 36
Adding larger numbers, 34–36
Using addition to check subtraction, 40
Shortcuts, 25, 29, 36
Mixed practice
   target-number game, 49
   paths, 73
   using a rule to make a table, 73
Extra Practice, 349, 350

FIGURE 3-5.
Scope-and sequence chart for addition of whole numbers. (From C.A. Dilley,
D.W. Lowry, W.E. Rucker, **Heath Mathematics**, D.C. Heath & Company, 1983,
Grade 1,4,7, p. T24. Reprinted with permission of D.C. Heath & Company.)

Adding whole numbers

6	7	8
Addends, sum, 12	Whole number review, 2-5	Whole number review, 6, 7
Adding 0 property, commutative and associative properties, 12	Addend, sum, 30, 56	Properties of addition, 62
Using grouping symbols, 12, 15, 25, 39, 58, 59, 92	Adding with regrouping, 30, 31	Extra Practice, 396
Basic-facts review—speed drill, 13	Estimating sums, 30, 31	
Adding with regrouping, 16, 17	Three or more addends, 31	
Adding money, 17	Adding money, 31	
Three or more addends, 18, 19	Using a calculator to add, 33	
Using addition to check subtraction, 20, 21	Using grouping symbols, 36, 57	
Estimating sums, 24, 25	Properties of addition, 56	
Project for addition, 31	Mixed practice, 36	
Repeated addition and multiplication, 36	Extra Practice, 396, 399	
Mixed practice, 43, 58, 59		
Extra Practice, 350		

FIGURE 3-5.
Continued.

so that the students develop these desired skills.

This process of analyzing a task into specific, ordered components is part of the learning theory advocated by Robert Gagné. A behaviorist, Gagné explains the growth and development of thinking as being the result of learning; in contrast, Piaget claims that the growth and development of thinking is related to ordered biological factors that progress through a given sequence. Gagné's learning theories lead to a curriculum-centered approach to teaching. This curriculum is broken down into small, carefully sequenced learning steps. Children's skills will determine at what step they should enter the learning experience for any particular task in the curriculum. Piaget's learning theories lead to a child-centered approach to teaching. The children's stage of development will determine whether they are ready for a particular learning experience. Elements from both theories are useful for teaching mathematics.

In designing a learning experience for addition of two-digit whole numbers with regrouping, the teacher should analyze what the prerequisite skills are for the task. A scope-and-sequence chart on addition of whole numbers can give an overview of what addition skills are prerequisite for this second-grade topic. As shown in the scope-and-sequence chart, first-grade children study addition of two-digit whole numbers with *no* regrouping (Figure 3-5). In the overview of the unit, there is a discussion of prerequisite skills and how they are related to the topic to be studied. The prerequisites need to be reviewed prior to the introduction of the new skill. As shown in a sample lesson, the prerequisite skill is reviewed prior to the first lesson on addition with regrouping (Figure 3-6). In some textbooks the prerequisites are reviewed in the previous chapter in sections designed for daily maintenance or review.

Another prerequisite skill essential for the new task is regrouping ten or more ones

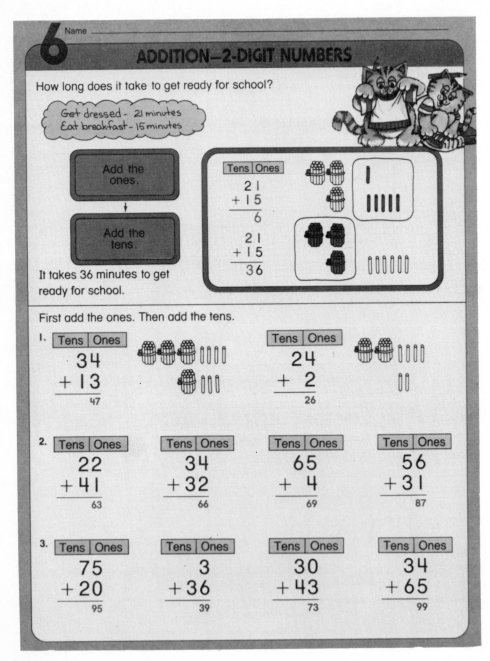

FIGURE 3-6.
Practice—addition with no regrouping. (From Robert Eicholz, Phares O'Daffer, Charles Fleenor, Randall Charles, Sharon Young, Carne Barnett, **Addison-Wesley Mathematics Book 2**, p. 153. Copyright © 1985, Addison-Wesley Publishing Co., Inc.)

FIGURE 3-7.
Regrouping 10 ones
to 1 ten.

2 tens 14 ones   3 tens 4 ones

a   b

to the appropriate number of tens and ones. Figure 3-7 shows how children can practice this prerequisite skill with counting sticks. First the children record the name for the counting sticks in tens and ones as they are shown (Figure 3-7a). Then they regroup 10 of the ones as 1 ten and record the tens and ones in this representation (Figure 3-7b). This lesson emphasizes place value. The concept that 10 ones are equivalent to 1 ten is an essential prerequisite skill for this lesson.

Chapter 6   Pretest   Name _____

Add. [Obj. 6-1, pages 135–136]

32	40	24	43	61	74
+ 21	+ 38	+ 42	+ 44	+ 28	+ 12
53	78	66	87	89	86

Add. [Obj. 6-2, pages 137–138, 141–143, 151–152]

43	16	56	41	37	48
+ 28	+ 35	+ 35	+ 29	+ 56	+ 47
71	51	91	70	93	95

Solve. [Obj. 6-3, pages 139–140, 144–150]

I saw 26 🚐
I saw 12 🚐   26
                    + 12
How many did I   38
see in all?

I saw 17 ✈
8 ✈ flew away.
How many ✈   9
were left?

I bought 🚗 46¢
I bought 🚙 39¢
How much money did 85¢
I spend?

I had 🪙🪙
I bought 🚙 9¢
How much money did 6¢
I have left?

Copymaster S23 or Duplicating Master S23

FIGURE 3-8a.
Pretest for addition with regrouping. (From C.A. Dilley, D.W. Lowry, W.E. Rucker, **Heath Mathematics**, D.C. Heath & Company, 1985, Grade 2, p. 135d. Reprinted with permission of D.C. Heath & Company.)

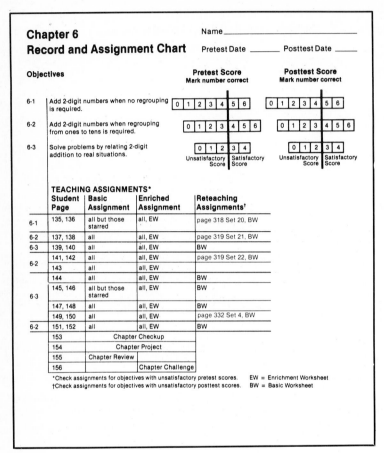

FIGURE 3-8b.
Record and assignment chart for two-digit addition. (From C.A. Dilley, D.W. Lowry, W.E. Rucker, **Heath Mathematics**, D.C. Heath & Company, 1985, Grade 2, p. 135d. Reprinted with permission of D.C. Heath & Company.)

After the prerequisite skills are identified, the teacher should determine whether students have mastered these skills. Teachers cannot assume that students have mastered the skills simply because they have been introduced to the concepts in previous grades. By means of diagnostic tests, conversations with students, and observations of students' work, teachers can determine which students have the necessary prerequisite skills. In this case teachers could carefully observe individual work on the lessons on prerequisite skills shown in Figures 3-6 and 3-7. Individual errors should be analyzed to determine whether they are conceptual or careless in nature. Learning experiences must be designed and sequenced for any prerequisite skills the learner has not yet mastered.

Some teacher's editions of textbooks contain pretests on the prerequisite skills and the chapter's content (Figure 3-8a). Each section of this test is written with regard to specific objectives (Figure 3-8b). For each section of the pretest, a cutoff between satisfactory and unsatisfactory scores is given. If the children are unable to add two-digit numbers with no regrouping (objective 6-1), reteaching assignments are given in the chart of teaching assignments.

LESSON PLAN

OBJECTIVE

To add a two-digit number and a one digit number
with renaming

WARM UP: Fact Speed

Use fact speed master 17 in the *Tests and Additional Resources* with Problem Set 10 on page T358.

TEACHING SUGGESTIONS

MATERIALS: Bundling sticks

USING MANIPULATIVES: Use the bundling sticks to
show 26 + 7 and write it on the chalkboard in vertical form. **When we add tens and ones, what do
we join first?** *(the ones)* Combine the ones in the
model. **How many ones are there in all?** *(13)* **Are
there enough ones to make 1 ten?** *(yes)* Regroup 10
ones to make 1 ten. **How many ones are left after
regrouping?** *(3)* **Combine the ten from regrouping
with the 2 tens in the problem to get the total number of tens. How many tens in all?** *(3)* **What number is shown by the bundling sticks now?** *(3 tens 3
ones or 33)* **Look at the problem on the chalkboard. What do we add first?** *(ones)* **What is 6 + 7?**
(13) **Are there enough ones to make 1 ten?** *(yes)*
How many ones are left? *(3)* Show where to write 3
ones in the answer. **What do we do with the 1 ten
we got from renaming?** *(add it to the tens)* We
write 1 in the tens column above the top number.
Now add the tens. **What is 1 + 2?** *(3)* **Where do we
write the 3?** *(below the tens place)* **What is 26 + 7?**
(33) **Is that the same answer we got with the sticks?**
(yes) Repeat with other problems adding a one-
digit number to a two-digit number with renaming.
Have a child show the problem with the bundling
sticks. Have another child write the problem on
the chalkboard and add. Be sure they write the
renamed ten above the top number in the tens column.

USING PAGES 223–224: Discuss the example at the
top of page 223. Make sure the children add the
ones first and write the renamed ten above the top
number in the tens column. On page 224 guide the
children through the example before they add.

FIGURE 3-9.
Suggested lesson plan for addition. (From Joseph
Payne et al., **Harper & Row Mathematics, Grade
2**, p. 223. Copyright © 1985, Macmillan, Inc.
Reprinted with permission of Scribner Educational
Publishers, a division of Macmillan, Inc.)

This can be helpful when the topic has
been introduced previously to the children,
as it can be used to measure what they have
retained. If the topic is totally new to the children, they cannot be expected to have mastered the topic. Some textbook series provide pretests that focus only on the
prerequisite skills for the chapter.

DEVELOPING A NEW TOPIC

The most important segment of learning is
developing new topics. A large portion of
class time should be utilized in activities that
develop the new ideas. Research summar-
ies state that when 50 to 75 percent of class
time is devoted to developmental activities,
as opposed to drill or practice exercises,
students are more likely to be able to retain
and apply the new concept. Throughout different textbook series, the teacher's editions
contain teacher's notes on how to present
the lesson to the children (Figure 3-9). These
notes often describe activities involving
models. Some textbook series describe activities with models at the beginning of each
chapter of the teacher's edition.

Using models to develop topics is advocated by theorists as well as researchers.
One theorist, Dienes, believes that children
should be involved in learning activities that
are meaningful and motivating. The dynamic
principle, formulated by Dienes, refers to the
active involvement of children in their learning. Carefully read the "Teaching Suggestions" in Figure 3-9. These suggestions describe activities exemplifying the last stages
of the dynamic principle.

In the first substage of the dynamic principle—the play stage—Dienes states that
children should be involved in unstructured
activities to become acquainted with the materials and their attributes. Like Piaget,
Dienes believes that children need concrete

models to help develop concepts. It is not sufficient simply to have models in the classroom; children must be actively involved with the models and they must *think about their actions* and the consequences of their actions. As suggested in the teacher's notes, the children should each have their own counting sticks to count, group, and regroup. As children work with the counting sticks and observe the results of their actions, they are gaining information that may help them solve related problems.

Dienes further states that after children have had an opportunity to experiment, their activity should become more structured, the next substage. As noted in the lesson plan, by asking appropriate questions on grouping by tens, the teacher can guide the students to discover various concepts. The structured activities should be designed so that they aid the children in developing the mathematical concept.

In this case the children first combined two groups of ones into a set and then regrouped 10 ones into 1 ten. By carefully observing individual students as they work with the counting sticks, the teacher can readily observe which students do not understand the concept and give them more help.

Simply having the students use the models will not help them learn the topics. They must learn how to use the models to focus on the important attributes of the lesson. To provide more structure to the lesson so that the class is focusing on the same idea at the same time, the model could be demonstrated as the teacher leads a class discussion. As the discussion progresses, one of the students could demonstrate the model as the teacher asks questions. When individual students are using the models during the discussion part of the lesson, the teacher should structure their work so that the students are focusing on the same idea.

This can be done with explicit questions and directions on how to use the materials. Students should not be allowed to play with the materials during this part of the lesson.

By introducing the numerical problem in a place-value table, the teacher can guide the students to the written form of the algorithm. In the specific example cited from the teacher's notes, the children added to obtain 13 ones, regrouped them to 1 ten and 3 ones, and then recorded this step in the place-value table. Then the tens were combined and the information recorded. Too often linking the model to the written algorithm is omitted. Simply working with the models is not sufficient. If teachers do not help the students relate their actions on the models to the written form, the students may consider the two activities unrelated.

The last substage of the dynamic principle is the formalization of the concept being learned. The mathematical concept is stated, discussed, and applied in similar situations. By working through the lesson, children will gradually realize that they can do this type of addition without models. They can simply add the numbers in the ones column, regroup when necessary, and then add the numbers in the tens column.

The formalization of mathematical concepts should not be rushed. Structured activities with models may occur for a few *days* prior to symbolic work. Students should make oral generalizations about their work prior to written generalizations. Too often, we are overly concerned with having students recording and doing written work. This is often done at the expense of their conceptual development. Part of this is a function of textbooks as they are written materials, not oral activities. In such cases teachers should be encouraged to ignore the textbook and supplement the unit with activities involving models and oral language.

As children practice the new procedure, it becomes the play stage for developing another new procedure. For example, in this case the children may try their new procedure or algorithm on addition problems containing more than two numbers or on addition problems with three-digit numbers with regrouping. The pattern is cyclic, as shown in Figure 3-10. Learning is dynamic; solving one problem leads to new questions and investigations.

Another way of approaching the process of developing new concepts is Piaget's idea of equilibrium. Piaget's theories are similar to Dienes' in that he believes children build new concepts on what they already know. Piaget regards equilibrium as the most important factor that affects development. Equilibrium is the process through which an individual maintains balanced thought processes. Equilibrium is composed of two cyclic processes: assimilation and accommodation. Children take in or assimilate information from their environment. If this information is contrary to what they already know—their mental structure—it may upset their equilibrium. In order to regain equilibrium, their present structure must be adapted or changed by the new information. This process of adapting the present structure is called accommodation.

As children approach new problems, they study the situation and organize the new content in terms of what they already know and what fits into their perception of the world. This process is called assimilation. If the information is very different from their past experiences, they will need first to assimilate the information and then to accommodate to the situation to achieve equilibrium. The children's new experiences are assimilated into their existing mental structures. They must then adjust or accommodate to the demands of the problems by revising their perceptions of the situations. New mental structures are formed during the process of accommodation.

Piaget's theory of equilibrium, like Dienes' dynamic principle, can be related to addition of two-digit whole numbers with regrouping. The addition chapters cited began by reviewing the concept of addition of two-digit numbers with no regrouping and the concept of regrouping 10 or more ones into tens and ones. This knowledge should be part of the children's existing structure. When a problem such as 23 + 18 is introduced, the children's equilibrium would be upset. They would recognize the problem as being similar to their previous experience, but they may be uncertain of how to record 11 ones. By working with the counting sticks and being guided by the teacher's questions and directions, they will discover that 11 ones can be renamed as 1 ten and 1 one and written accordingly. Through accommodation the children will develop a new structure that they can use to add any two-digit numbers.

PRACTICING/MASTERY OF THE NEW TOPIC

As noted in the preceding section, the majority of class time should be spent developing the topic. Research studies indicate that to optimize learning, practice *must* be preceded by instruction that builds mean-

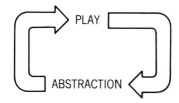

FIGURE 3-10.
Dienes' dynamic principle.

ings or understandings. As students learn at different rates, the amount of time individuals need to develop the topic will vary. Students will set aside the models as they gain confidence in their ability to use the algorithm to solve problems. During the same time period, some students will still be using counting sticks to obtain the answer to problems such as 28 + 17 (Figure 3-11a); other students will be using counting sticks and relating the process to the algorithm with place-value tables (Figure 3-11b); still others will have progressed to using the written

form of the algorithm only (Figure 3-11c). When certain students appear not to be making progress in developing the written algorithm, the teacher should encourage them and ask guiding questions to help them progress to the written form.

When students are practicing the written form of the algorithm, the design of the practice should vary to maintain their interest. Examples of some variations of assignments on two-digit addition problems are shown (Figure 3-12). Note that three of these activities (a, c, and d) are self-checking. Just as the

FIGURE 3-11.
Developing the addition algorithm.

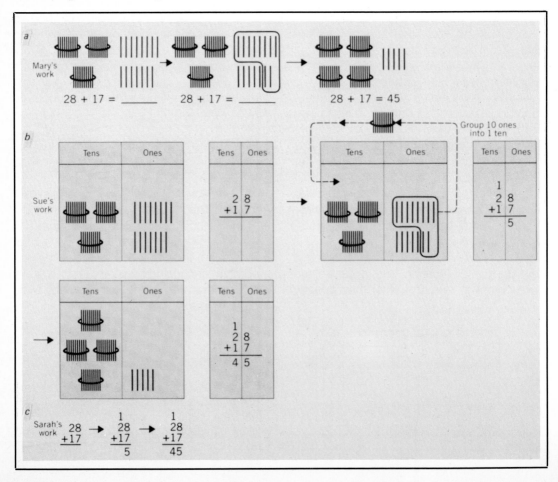

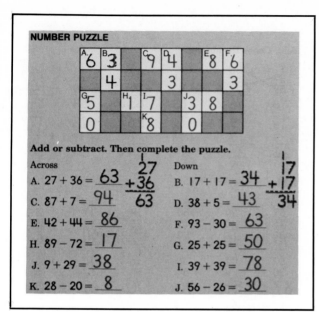

NUMBER PUZZLE

Add or subtract. Then complete the puzzle.

Across
A. 27 + 36 = 63
C. 87 + 7 = 94
E. 42 + 44 = 86
H. 89 − 72 = 17
J. 9 + 29 = 38
K. 28 − 20 = 8

Down
B. 17 + 17 = 34
D. 38 + 5 = 43
F. 93 − 30 = 63
G. 25 + 25 = 50
I. 39 + 39 = 78
J. 56 − 26 = 30

FIGURE 3-12.
Practice pages from second-grade textbooks.
(a) From A.V. Buffington, A.R. Garr, J. Graening, P.P. Halloran, M.L. Mahaffey, M. O'Neal, **Merrill Mathematics: Grade 2,** Merrill Publishing Company, 1985, p. 214. Copyright © Merrill Publishing Company.

FIGURE 3-12.
(b) From Robert Eicholz, Phares O'Daffer, Charles' Fleenor, Randall Charles, Sharon Young, Carne Barnett, **Addison-Wesley Mathematics Book 2,** p. 166. Copyright © 1985, Addison-Wesley Publishing Co., Inc.

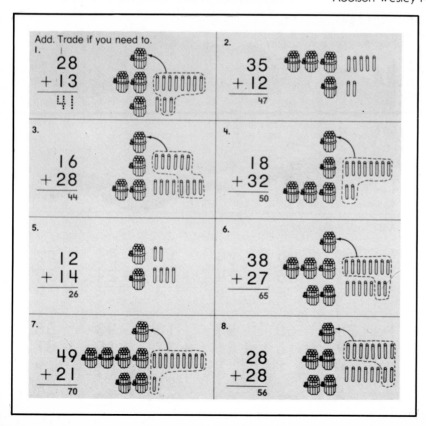

Add. Trade if you need to.

1. 28 + 13 = 41
2. 35 + 12 = 47
3. 16 + 28 = 44
4. 18 + 32 = 50
5. 12 + 14 = 26
6. 38 + 27 = 65
7. 49 + 21 = 70
8. 28 + 28 = 56

FIGURE 3-12.
(c) From C.A. Dilley, D.W. Lowry, W.E. Rucker, **Heath Mathematics**, D.C. Heath & Company, 1985, Grade 2, p. 151. Reprinted by permission of D.C. Heath & Company.

amount of time individual students need to develop topics varies, the practice time and the number of practice exercises needed to obtain mastery will vary. No matter how interesting the worksheet appears, if students have mastered the skill, additional practice lessons will probably be regarded as boring, repetitious drill. Since distributed practice is important, the teacher may decide to limit the number of problems on any given assignment, depending on the individual students.

As children work with either models or the written algorithm, errors should be noted and corrected as they occur. Samples of various children's errors are shown in Figure 3-13. In Mike's case, his two errors involve a basic fact, namely 8 + 7 = 15. The teacher will need to determine whether this error was the result of carelessness or whether Mike does not know this basic fact. Kari has ignored place value. It would be helpful for her to use counting sticks or base-ten blocks to represent the problem. After she realizes

Add. Write the letter of the problem above the answer.

Knock, Knock

who is There?

Lettuce

Lettuce who?

L 55 +28 83	I 24 +17 41	S 36 +32 68	U 26 +24 50	O 27 +35 62
T 48 + 6 54	N 41 +54 95	E 16 +26 42	D 64 +27 91	C 35 +16 51

L E T T U C E   I N .
83 42 54 54 50 51 42   41 95

I T   I S   C O L D
41 54   41 68   51 62 83 91

O U T S I D E .
62 50 54 68 41 91 42

FIGURE 3-12.
(d) From Robert Eicholz, Phares O'Daffer, Charles Fleenir, Randall Charles, Sharon Young, Carne Bennett, **Addison-Wesley** Book 2, p. 170. Copyright © 1985, Addison-Wesley Publishing Co., Inc.

Mike's Work

38	46	13	27	34
+17	+37	+35	+48	+13
53	83	48	73	47

Kari's Work

38	46	13	27	34
+17	+37	+35	+48	+13
415	713	48	615	47

Jeremy's Work

38	46	13	27	34
+17	+37	+35	+48	+13
55	83	58	75	57

FIGURE 3-13.
Errors in addition of whole numbers.

that 411 is not a reasonable answer, she should put the 11 counting sticks in the ones column together, regroup 10 ones into 1 ten, and add the tens in the tens column, recording the appropriate part of the algorithm after each step.

Jeremy's error is that he has learned to "carry the 1" most efficiently. He does so for all problems whether or not any regrouping is needed. Perhaps the assignments he has worked included only problems involving regrouping. He has not learned to discriminate which addition problems require regrouping. Jeremy—and his classmates—should have practice pages that contain addition problems that do not require regrouping mixed in with those that do (Figure 3-14). The purpose of one lesson could simply be to discriminate which problems need regrouping rather than to actually solve the problems.

In the overview to the unit or in individual lessons some textbooks include suggestions for diagnosing student errors. In some texts topics that have been found to be difficult for students have been noted. A description of how to teach to minimize the probability of

students making errors is included. Some textbooks give examples of possible student errors and discuss how to remediate these errors. Analysis of students' errors is one aspect of formative evaluation which is discussed later in this section.

After children have learned to work problems accurately and have developed confidence in their ability, the rate at which they work the problems should be considered. Just as students comprehend topics at different rates, so they will also work the problems at different rates. There will always be those students who will have the seatwork correctly completed in less than the allotted time and others who will never finish within that time period.

For many assignments, speed is not an important variable. For other assignments, such as mastering the basic facts, speed should be considered. If students are given unlimited time to solve twenty basic-fact problems, they may solve all of them by counting. Even though they may have the correct answers for all the problems, it would be incorrect to assume that they have the facts mastered. Whenever speed and accuracy are to be considered, students should be given timed practice and encouraged to improve their own time and accuracy scores. The emphasis should be on individual improvement, not on doing better than other students.

REVIEW OF PREVIOUSLY STUDIED TOPICS

Throughout various chapters in any elementary textbook, problems will be encountered that are *not related to the topic being developed* in the particular chapter. These problems are designed as review. Although students may have shown mastery on cer-

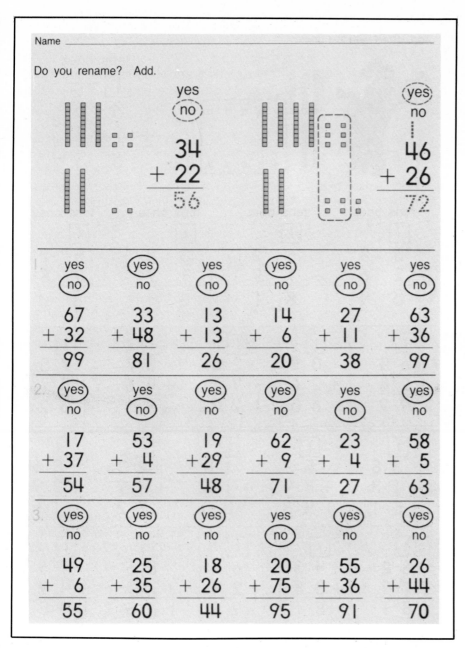

Name _____

Do you rename? Add.

yes
(no)

$$\begin{array}{r} 34 \\ + 22 \\ \hline 56 \end{array}$$

(yes)
no

$$\begin{array}{r} 46 \\ + 26 \\ \hline 72 \end{array}$$

1. yes / (no)

$$\begin{array}{r} 67 \\ + 32 \\ \hline 99 \end{array}$$

(yes) / no

$$\begin{array}{r} 33 \\ + 48 \\ \hline 81 \end{array}$$

yes / (no)

$$\begin{array}{r} 13 \\ + 13 \\ \hline 26 \end{array}$$

(yes) / no

$$\begin{array}{r} 14 \\ + 6 \\ \hline 20 \end{array}$$

yes / (no)

$$\begin{array}{r} 27 \\ + 11 \\ \hline 38 \end{array}$$

yes / (no)

$$\begin{array}{r} 63 \\ + 36 \\ \hline 99 \end{array}$$

2. (yes) / no

$$\begin{array}{r} 17 \\ + 37 \\ \hline 54 \end{array}$$

yes / (no)

$$\begin{array}{r} 53 \\ + 4 \\ \hline 57 \end{array}$$

(yes) / no

$$\begin{array}{r} 19 \\ + 29 \\ \hline 48 \end{array}$$

(yes) / no

$$\begin{array}{r} 62 \\ + 9 \\ \hline 71 \end{array}$$

yes / (no)

$$\begin{array}{r} 23 \\ + 4 \\ \hline 27 \end{array}$$

(yes) / no

$$\begin{array}{r} 58 \\ + 5 \\ \hline 63 \end{array}$$

3. (yes) / no

$$\begin{array}{r} 49 \\ + 6 \\ \hline 55 \end{array}$$

(yes) / no

$$\begin{array}{r} 25 \\ + 35 \\ \hline 60 \end{array}$$

(yes) / no

$$\begin{array}{r} 18 \\ + 26 \\ \hline 44 \end{array}$$

yes / (no)

$$\begin{array}{r} 20 \\ + 75 \\ \hline 95 \end{array}$$

(yes) / no

$$\begin{array}{r} 55 \\ + 36 \\ \hline 91 \end{array}$$

(yes) / no

$$\begin{array}{r} 26 \\ + 44 \\ \hline 70 \end{array}$$

FIGURE 3-14.
Discriminating whether or not to regroup. (From Joseph Payne et al., **Harper &
Row Mathematics, Grade 2**, p. 227. Copyright © 1985 Macmillan, Inc. Reprinted
with permission of Scribner Educational Publishers, a division of Macmillan, Inc.)

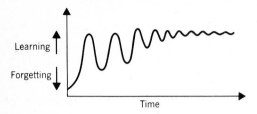

FIGURE 3-15.
Pattern of learning and forgetting.

tain topics, review is necessary for retention over time. The pattern of learning and forgetting illustrated in Figure 3-15 shows why this is needed. After students initially learn a topic, if they do not review it, they will forget a large portion of what they have learned. Each time a topic is encountered and studied, the students are forced to review their previous learning and thinking. With each encounter, the topic becomes more and more familiar to the students, and it is more likely to be retained.

Most chapters in elementary textbooks have sections that review topics previously studied. Some textbooks will have complete pages of review; others will have parts of var-

ious lessons devoted to review. In one elementary text, the chapter on addition with regrouping contains an entire page devoted to review of addition and subtraction basic facts. In the corresponding chapter of another text, one lesson has a short section reviewing one less than and another lesson has a similar section on subtraction facts (Figure 3-16). Some textbooks have review built into the teacher's notes for each lesson (Figure 3-17). These reviews involve the children in ordering numbers, applying calendar skills, doing mental arithmetic, and problem solving. Regardless of the format used, these reviews should not be omitted, as they are designed to provide systematic reinforcement across all curricular topics.

Although textbooks usually provide review pages, elementary teachers may want to include additional review for a particular class. The teacher may perceive that the class as a whole needs more practice on such topics as story problems, mental arithmetic, basic facts, or estimation. The review could be presented via the overhead projector, a ditto sheet, or by oral problems. Some teachers use the first 5 to 10 minutes of every

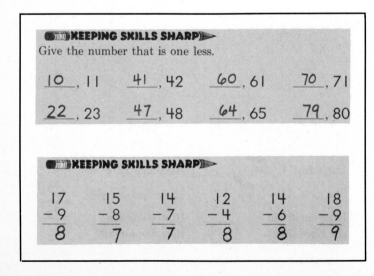

FIGURE 3-16.
Parts of pages used as review.
(From C.A. Dilley, D.W. Lowry, W.E. Rucker, **Heath Mathematics**, D.C. Heath & Company, 1985, Grade 2, pp. 148 and 138. Reprinted with permission of D.C. Heath & Company.)

DAILY MAINTENANCE

Which is greater?

1. 329
   349          $(349) > (329)$

   538
   291          $(538) > (291)$

   772
   776          $(776) > (772)$

2. If Thursday is the 13th, what is next Wednesday's date? *(19th)*
3. If Monday is the 2nd, what is the date Friday? *(6th)*

DAILY MAINTENANCE

Ring the numbers with a 4 in the tens place.

1. (342)   423   324   (42)

2. What number can you add to 26 to get 48? *(22)*
3. What number can you subtract from 58 to get 31? *(27)*

FIGURE 3-17.
Review included in teacher's notes. (From Robert Eicholz, Phares O'Daffer, Charles Fleenor, Randall Charles, Sharon Young, Carne Barnett, **Addision-Wesley Mathematics, Book 2**, pp. 167 and 163. Copyright © 1985, Addison-Wesley Publishing Co., Inc. and Joseph Payne et al., **Harper & Row Mathematics, Grade 2**, pp. 225 and 229. Copyright © 1985 Macmillan, Inc. Reprinted with permission of Scribner Educational Publishers, a division of Macmillan, Inc.)

Quick Review Have students give the number of dimes and pennies for each.

| 25¢ | 13¢ | 54¢ | 60¢ | 41¢ |
| 5¢ | 44¢ | 39¢ | 8¢ | |

Quick Review Ask students to raise their hands if their birthday is in one of the following months. Remind them that January is the first month.

third   fifth   fourth   eleventh   sixth   second   tenth

mathematics period for review. In any case the review should be short and directed at a specific purpose. Depending on individual responses, follow-up work may be needed for some students.

STORY PROBLEMS/APPLICATIONS

It is important for students to compute with whole numbers, common and decimal fractions, and integers; to solve proportions; to read measuring instruments; and to use other similar skills. However, if they do not know *when* to apply such processes, the usefulness of these skills is severely limited. Students must encounter a variety of situations that involve the application of different skills. The applications should be provided frequently instead of only at the end of a chapter. The situations should also be discussed so that the students will note that often there is more than one way to think about and solve a problem.

Story problems can be presented in various forms. Some examples from the addition chapter in a second-grade textbook are shown in Figure 3-18. Notice that these problems offer mixed practice (both addition and subtraction) and that they ask the question in a variety of ways. This lesson focuses on consumer skills, a particularly important application of mathematics.

Solve.

Bear bought a book for 16¢. He bought a horn for 20¢.

$$\begin{array}{r} 16¢ \\ +20¢ \\ \hline 36¢ \end{array}$$

How much did they cost?

Robin had 15¢. She bought a nest for 9¢.

$$\begin{array}{r} 15¢ \\ -9¢ \\ \hline 6¢ \end{array}$$

How much did she have left?

Rabbit bought a dish for 24¢. She bought a book for 16¢.

$$\begin{array}{r} 24¢ \\ +16¢ \\ \hline 40¢ \end{array}$$

How much did she spend?

A book costs 16¢. A nest costs 9¢.

$$\begin{array}{r} 16¢ \\ -9¢ \\ \hline 7¢ \end{array}$$

How much more does a book cost?

A book costs 16¢. Owl bought 2 books.

$$\begin{array}{r} 16¢ \\ +16¢ \\ \hline 32¢ \end{array}$$

How much did Owl spend?

A horn costs 18¢. Fox had 9¢.

$$\begin{array}{r} 18¢ \\ -9¢ \\ \hline 9¢ \end{array}$$

How much more money did Fox need?

FIGURE 3-18.
Story problems for second graders. (From C.A. Dilley, D.W. Lowry, W.E. Rucker, **Heath Mathematics**, D.C. Heath & Company, 1985, Grade 2, p. 148. Reprinted by permission of D.C. Heath & Company.)

Many students are apprehensive about story problems because their previous experiences have been unsuccessful. Part of this failure results from the way in which story problems are presented in elementary textbooks. In reviewing the story problems in chapters on the addition of whole numbers with regrouping in seven second-grade textbooks copyrighted 1983-1985, we can make various observations. The number of pages containing story problems varies from three to nine pages. As the total number of pages in the chapters varies from 15 to 27 pages, only a small percentage of the total pages contain story problems. (One chapter had 33 pages, but it contained both addition *and* subtraction.) Although the main purpose of the chapter is to teach the regrouping algorithm, children should be involved in studying situations that involve addition.

Two of the textbooks used a story problem and picture as a unit opener. The directions for story problems in one text told the children that they were to add. The same text primarily used the questions "How many?" or "How many in all?" Although children need a thorough understanding of the concept of addition, they need a variety of experiences, not the same experience repeated over and over.

Five of the seven textbooks have problems involving subtraction as well as addition problems. In these cases the students need to read the problem carefully to determine whether addition or subtraction is appropriate. If children notice in certain textbooks that the story problems presented involve only the skill currently being studied, they may not bother reading the problems. They may simply skim a problem to find the numbers and apply the operation being studied.

If a particular chapter is lacking in the number of or quality of story problems, the teacher should supplement the work accordingly. In addition to finding other problems in teacher resources, the teacher and the students can write problems as discussed in Chapter 1. To develop confidence and positive attitudes, students must be involved in successfully solving a number of story problems.

PROBLEM SOLVING

Although problem solving has been developed in Chapter 1, it needs to be discussed here in relation to elementary textbooks. In a number of current textbooks a section involving problem solving is provided for each lesson. Problems may be included in the teacher's notes as well as on the student page. Due to the importance of problem solving, a number of publishers provide additional resource books on this topic.

For the purpose of investigating elementary mathematics textbooks, some problem-solving situations involving addition will be discussed. This section will emphasize problem solving as an approach to learning and teaching. In essence, the last few sections have posed situations where the students needed to solve problems. With regard to prerequisite skills and review, if the students did not immediately recognize the topic, they needed to review previous experiences or relearn the topic. In developing the topic, students had to reorganize their thoughts and consider new options in order to solve the problem. With regard to story problems, students needed to consider such factors as what the situation is, what is asked, and what is relevant so that they can construct a situation with which they are familiar, in order to solve the problem.

There is no common agreement on a definition of problem solving. Problem solving is sometimes considered to be just solving textbook story problems. But story problems are only a small part of this broad topic. Any situation in which a solution is not immediately evident and which requires careful thought can be considered a problem-solving situation.

In Chapter 1, problem solving was discussed by examining Polya's four steps and the strategies used by good problem solvers. Problem solving could also be discussed with regard to the different types of thinking people exhibit in solving problems. By studying Benjamin Bloom's taxonomy, which classifies this thinking into categories, the reader can gain increased understanding of problem solving. The categories of Bloom's taxonomy are listed from the simplest to the most complex.

Knowledge

The simplest category includes questions that require the recall of specific facts, definitions, or processes. Factual recall does not imply that the concept or fact is understood. For example, most second graders, when asked to complete the basic fact $3 + 5 =$?, will automatically say 8. This fact is part of their structure. Other children may know the meaning of the plus sign and the number concepts of three and five, but they may not know the sum of three and five. They may have to count out three counters and then five more to solve the problem. After counting all of the counters, they could conclude that the answer was eight. These children did not have the answer of eight as part of their structure, but they were able to employ problem-solving techniques because of their knowledge and understanding of addition and number.

Children may be able to compute two-digit addition problems but be unable to determine what would be a reasonable answer. For example, Sarah and Sue both had per-

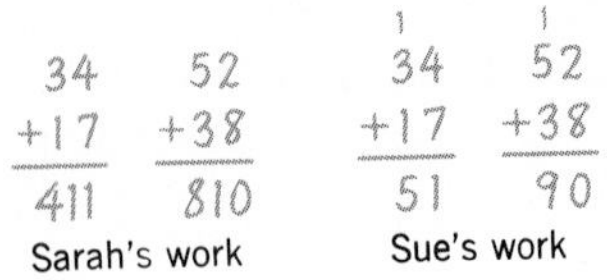

FIGURE 3-19.
Addition problems from Sarah's and Sue's papers.

fect papers for two-digit addition problems with no regrouping. When they compared some of their answers for problems involving regrouping, they found that their answers differed (Figure 3-19). In discussing their answers, Sarah explained that $4 + 7 = 11$ and $3 + 1 = 4$. Sarah treated each problem as two separate basic-fact problems. In doing problems such as $34 + 12$, she had reasoned that $4 + 2 = 6$ and $3 + 1 = 4$, and because she knew her addition basic facts, she had perfect papers as long as regrouping was not required. However, she did not understand the procedure she was using. In order to correct her error, she will need to understand or comprehend the importance of place value.

Comprehension

This category is more complex than the previous one because it involves the ability to interpret given material. In the previous example Sarah obtained an incorrect answer because of her lack of understanding of the concept. Sue, perplexed by the differences between Sarah's and her own answers, looked over the problem $34 + 17$. She studied the digits in the tens column. She knew that the digit 4 was larger than 3, but the 3 represented 3 tens and the 4 represented only 4 ones. In looking at 17, she noted the 1 ten and 7 ones. Since 7 ones were just about 1 group of ten, she rounded 17 to 2 tens. Since 3 tens and 2 tens were 5 tens, she estimated that the correct answer should be around 50. She had an answer of 51 compared to Sarah's answer of 411 so she decided Sarah's answer was definitely wrong. She then checked her work with counting sticks by combining the counting sticks representing ones, regrouping, and then combining the bundles representing tens. In this example, Sue clearly comprehended what was involved in the addition algorithm.

Application

This category involves the ability to use previously learned concepts and principles in new situations. For example, Jody and Jeremy were working on a page of addition and subtraction story problems. Jeremy kept looking for words or phrases such as "more," "sum," or "many in all" to indicate addition and "take away" or "how many left" to indicate subtraction. But the story problems were nonroutine as they contained more numbers than were needed or not enough information. There were such problems as "Diana had picked four apples. Thurza had 20 in her basket and then picked five more. How many more apples did Thurza have than Diana?" Jeremy missed over half of the problems. Jody carefully read each problem thinking about the situation and what type of process was involved. In some cases she drew pictures to illustrate the situation. In each case she was able to use the appropriate operation or operations. Although Jeremy and Jody both knew how to add and subtract two-digit numbers, Jeremy was unable to apply the concepts in appropriate situations. He will need more help on developing the concept of addition and subtraction in various situations.

Notice that the categories are not independent of each other. To solve the previous problem, Jody's *knowledge* of basic facts and her *comprehension* of how to solve addition problems were essential in obtaining the correct solution. She also was able to *apply* addition and subtraction correctly as she understood or comprehended the concept of each operation. The next three categories will be defined separately and discussed through a common example.

Analysis

This category involves the ability to break down material into its component parts. The relationships and organization are studied. Recognizing assumptions and fallacies and distinguishing between facts and inferences are also included in this category.

Synthesis

This category involves forming a new structure by combining ideas and solutions through invention and design.

Evaluation

The most complex category involves the ability to judge the value of materials or ideas for a given purpose. This category requires judgments that are based on valid criteria.

Marta and Augusta were looking ahead at new topics in their mathematics book. They started working problems from the subtraction section as shown in Figure 3-20. After working a few, they looked back at their work. For the first problem they estimated 2 tens minus 1 ten would be 1 ten so 12 appeared to be a reasonable answer. For the second problem Marta reasoned similarly that 3 tens minus 1 ten is 2 tens. Augusta didn't agree. She commented that 19 is just

$$\begin{array}{ccc} 22 & 33 & 32 \\ -14 & -19 & -17 \\ \hline 12 & 26 & 25 \end{array}$$

FIGURE 3-20.
Marta's and Augusta's subtraction problems.

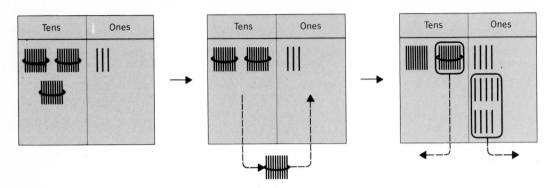

FIGURE 3-21.
Solving a problem using counting sticks.

about 2 tens so 3 tens minus 2 tens was 1 ten. Also, she noted that 19 + 1 is 20 and 13 more is 33. Since 19 + 14 is 33, 33 − 19 must be 14. They were perplexed. They went back and reviewed the problem 33 − 19 by noting 3 − 9 = 6 and 3 − 1 = 2. This was the same answer they had obtained earlier. Augusta was confused. Their work looked right, but the related addition sentence gave them a different answer. To check themselves, Marta suggested that they use counting sticks to work the problem. Marta placed 33 sticks on a place-value table (Figure 3-21). Augusta noted that they needed to take away 9 sticks but there were only 3 sticks in the ones column. Marta suggested regrouping 1 ten to 10 ones. After regrouping 1 ten, Augusta took away 9 ones from the ones column and then 1 ten from the tens column. Since 1 ten and 4 ones were left, they decided that 14 was the correct answer.

Looking back at their written work, Marta muttered "three minus nine is six, three minus nine is six . . . whoops, nine minus three is six! We can't do three minus nine." Augusta observed that with the counting sticks they took away 9 ones by first regrouping 1 ten. Marta suggested that they redo the problem with counting sticks and record each part of their work in algorithmic form on a place-value table. Their work is shown in Figure 3-22. Augusta observed that they had regrouped 1 ten to 10 ones just as in some addition problems they changed 10 ones for 1 ten. They tried this process with other problems on the page and found other errors that they had made.

In the example, Marta and Augusta needed to decide which answers were correct. They needed to *evaluate* their thinking and determine if it was correct. They validated their thinking through the use of counting sticks. To solve the problem, they broke it down—*analyzed* it—into ones and tens and noted the relationship between the 1 ten and 10 ones. They were able to coordinate the counting sticks with their written work to arrive at a new process for them, namely the subtraction algorithm with regrouping. This process of generating the algorithm involved *synthesis*.

All the categories of Bloom's taxonomy are important. In order to develop problem-solving skills, children need experiences with each of these categories. Teachers must make a special effort to design questions in *all* of the categories.

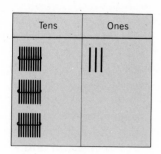

"We need 3 tens and 3 ones."

Tens	Ones
3	3
−1	9

FIGURE 3-22.
Developing the subtraction algorithm with counting sticks.

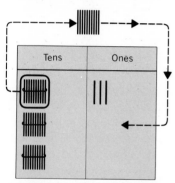

"Since we can't take 9 ones from 3 ones, we'll regroup 1 ten for 10 ones. 2 tens are left in the tens column; 13 ones are in the ones column."

Tens	Ones
2	13
3̸	3̸
−1	9

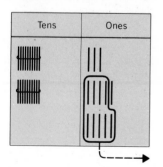

"Now take away 9 ones; 4 ones are left."

Tens	Ones
2	13
3̸	3̸
−1	9
	4

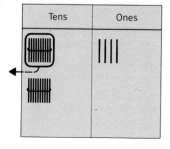

"Take away 1 ten, One ten is left. The answer is 14."

Tens	Ones
2	13
3̸	3̸
−1	9
1	4

ENRICHMENT

Enrichment activities are provided throughout elementary textbooks. Enrichment should take one of two forms. It can be "in-depth" work in a topic covered in the regular course, or it can be a completely new topic, perhaps something that is not appropriate for every elementary student to spend time studying.

Enrichment activities can be used with all students. Any topic that is unfamiliar to students can become a problem-solving activity and a challenge. Students can be motivated by new topics since they do not have previous failures associated with them. Bright students can find new challenges in enrichment activities that can lead to further study. Slower students can find opportunities for success in topics outside the main curriculum. Furthermore, this success can have a good effect on the students' regular work because it will give them a positive attitude toward mathematics and an expectation of further success. All students should be given the opportunity to pursue new topics. However, students should be given appropriate guidance and encouragement so that their success is at a maximum and their failure at a minimum. They should also be encouraged to develop more independent thinking and problem-solving skills.

Most series provide a separate resource booklet that contains an enrichment activity for each lesson. These are usually an extension of the particular topic. The number of enrichment activities that a teacher will choose to include from any particular unit will depend on the students' skill for that topic. If the content has been introduced in a previous level, some students will be ready for more challenging problems.

Enrichment should involve exploration activities and in-depth studies, not drill exercises or memorization of rules. Drill, even when disguised as a game, is still drill, and for the student who has already mastered a topic, more drill—even when it is fun—is not a very profitable way to use the time. Students who finish their work quickly and accurately should be given not more of the same type of problems but enrichment activities to broaden their perception and understanding of mathematics.

EVALUATING STUDENT PROGRESS

Just as students need to evaluate their thinking and work, teachers need to evaluate their students' learning. There are two types of evaluation: summative and formative. Summative evaluation is the testing of the final product of learning. Standardized achievement tests are a form of summative evaluation since they are a means of measuring the student's level of achievement at a particular time. In elementary textbooks, examples of summative evaluation would be the tests at the end of the chapters, units, or book. Students should also be evaluated on their understanding of the model or the procedures with the model. If the text does not provide such testing, the teacher should supplement the testing accordingly.

Formative evaluation takes place before and during the learning process. It includes tests on prerequisite skills to determine review work needed. It also includes observations of students' learning activities to note what successes and failures they are experiencing. By noting the students' weaknesses and difficulties, teachers can design relevant learning activities and ask pertinent guiding questions that will help students correct their errors. Throughout the previous sections, examples of formative evaluation have been noted such as testing prerequisite skills, observing children's actions with models, and studying their papers for error patterns. If only summative evaluation were used, children's misconceptions would not be discovered until after the learning activities were completed.

Some students will need more time for developing a topic than others; some students will need additional practice. The resources with a textbook series usually include a resource book for extra practice that can be used as needed. Some textbook series also include resource books on reteaching the topic. The teacher must evaluate the class and individual student needs to determine whether these resources are appropriate for the particular objective. Often the teacher can evaluate the whole class's progress by a few well-designed questions.

Some textbooks include suggestions for diagnostic interviews as part of the testing program. In order to determine individual progress, a different approach must be taken. The teacher should select a few students to be evaluated each day. Although questions and the discussion will not be limited to these students, the teacher should interact with them sufficiently so that their progress can be determined. When all students have been evaluated by this process, the teacher should start the cycle over. This method provides information about each student, and it also involves all students.

Individual evaluation can also be done through homework. After the papers have been corrected, the teacher should analyze the errors to determine whether there is a pattern in the student's errors or whether the errors are due to carelessness. The students should correct the errors and be encouraged to work more carefully. If the errors are conceptual, the error in thinking should be discussed with the student, and the topic retaught. In some cases peer teaching is appropriate for this.

Student progress should be shared with parents of the children. Most textbook series include a page in each chapter that illustrates current student work. This page is usually in the form of a letter to the parents. Parents should be apprised of student progress and also become aware of the current topics and methods of learning mathematics. Good communication between parents and teachers should result in more encouragement, help, and support for individual students.

QUESTIONS AND ACTIVITIES

1. a. Examine the opening pages of a unit from each of two different elementary mathematics textbooks. What are the various sections that have been designed for helping you plan the units? What is the purpose of each? How are the two series alike? Different?

   b. Examine an individual lesson from each of two different textbook series. What are the various sections that have been designed for helping you plan the lessons? What is the purpose of each? How are the two series alike? Different?

2. The next set of questions focuses on the different parts of a unit. Analyze a unit that introduces subtraction of two-digit numbers with renaming. You may find it helpful to do this problem with another student; by selecting two different series, you can compare the series as well as each other's ideas. Cite the publisher and copyright date. As you analyze the unit, cite the page numbers where you found the answers.

   a. What is the main purpose of the unit? What are the other purposes or objectives of the unit? Is there an opening picture or problem to introduce the unit? Does the introduction appear relevant and motivating?

b. What are the prerequisites to this unit? Are they reviewed in the first lessons? In the preceding chapter? In other earlier chapters? Are pretests available? Are the pretests on the prerequisites or on the unit?

c. What models are suggested to teach this topic? Are models available with the series? Are explicit directions given on how to use the models? How are the models related to the recording?

d. What lessons are used to practice the new concept? Read through the teacher notes for some of these lessons. Are there notes on how to relate the practice to the concept to reinforce understanding? If not, how could this be done? Why is it important to relate the practice to the concept?

e. Is there a daily review built into this textbook? Where is it located? Is it oral or written? About how many minutes would it take to conduct this review? How would you involve all students in this review?

f. What provision is made for story problems in this unit? Is there a variety of situations? Questions?

g. Where is the problem solving located in this unit? Is it included daily? Are supplementary resources available to the teacher? How are they keyed into the textbook? Comment on the quality of problem solving included in the unit.

h. What provisions are made for enrichment? What supplementary resources are available to the teacher? How are they keyed into the textbook?

i. What provisions are made for evaluation? Are there practice tests in the student book? Are the individual items keyed to specific lessons? What supplementary resources are available to the teacher? Are the students evaluated on skills *and* understandings? Are there suggestions for oral interviews to gain further information on individual students?

j. Is there information to be sent to parents that reflects on student work?

k. Are examples of learning centers and/or bulletin boards included? Comment on the quality of the suggestions and the completeness of the descriptions.

3. Students have difficulty with multistep translation problems and find simple translation ones relatively easy.
   a. *For your resource file:* Read "Problem Solving Tips for Teachers" by Leutzinger for suggestions on how to use intermediate questions to help children learn how to solve multistep problems. Add these ideas to your resource file.
   b. Read the teacher notes of "Ideas" by Leutzinger. Work through one of the student activity sheets for helping children analyze story problems. Compare these problems with ones that you experienced as an elementary student. How are they alike? Different?

4. *For your resource file:* Barnett, Sowder, and Vos in "Textbook Problems: Supplementing and Understanding Them," LeBlanc in "Teaching Textbook Story Problems," and Charles in "Get the Most Out of Word Problems" suggest teaching strategies for story problems. Read and copy one of these articles for your resource file. Describe two new ideas that you learned from the article.

5. Define equilibrium with respect to accommodation and assimilation. Use different aspects of the same mathematical example to illustrate these processes.

6. Piaget states that children learn through activity, both physical and mental. Discuss the implications of this for the *classroom teacher*.

7. Describe the implications of each part of Dienes' dynamic principle as to how to use models in your classroom. How do you decide when to start the next substage?

8. Solve the problems below. After working through each problem, decide whether

skills such as knowledge, comprehension, application, analysis, synthesis, or evaluation were needed to solve the problem. Relate these skills to the problem.

a. Give an example of the associative property.

b. Estimate the product of 0.8639 and 5.714.

c. If $x(x - y) = 0$ and if y does not equal zero, which of the following is true? (1) $x = y$; (2) either $x = 0$ or $x = y$; (3) $x = 0$; (4) $x^2 = y$; (5) both $x = 0$ and $x - y = 0$.

d. Given the data on the cost of living, would you make a circle, bar, or line graph to display the results? Defend your answer.

e. Margaret stated that every even number greater than 2 is the sum of two primes. Is she correct? Why or why not?

f. Study the attribute train below; select the next element from the given choices.

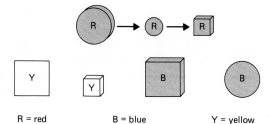

R = red   B = blue   Y = yellow

g. Given the addition problem 3/20 + 7/15, David reasoned as follows:
   (1) 5 is the largest number that will exactly divide both 15 and 20.
   (2) 15 ÷ 5 = 3.
   (3) 3 × 20 = 60, so 60 is the lowest common denominator. Is his reasoning correct? Why or why not?

9. In "10 Essential Ideas for Better Teaching," Suydam states that questioning consumes about 40% of instructional time. In one study, 80% of the questions were of the knowledge and comprehension levels; there were no questions at the higher levels. Why is it important that teachers use all of Bloom's levels when planning lessons and questions for their classes?

10. What guidelines have been developed for planning review work? What types of review have been found to be effective? Read "Research Report: The Role of Review in Mathematics Instruction" by Suydam for answers to these questions.

11. In "Not All Math Texts Are Created Equal," Akers lists eight questions to consider in evaluating math textbooks. What are the questions? How would this help you evaluate textbooks?

12. Read sections of *The Book of Think* or *The I Hate Mathematics Book* by Burns. How could these activities be used for enrichment?

13. A learning center for your students could be set up for enrichment. How would you set up a learning center? How could you get your students involved in maintaining and setting up new centers? How could the students share their special interests with other students? Discuss your organizational ideas with your classmates.

14. In order to evaluate their students' learning, teachers will use procedures to supplement the testing program in their textbooks. In addition to quizzes and teacher-made tests, teachers can evaluate learning through observations and interviews.

a. Read "Using the Individual Interview to Assess Mathematics Learning" by Schoen for suggestions on how to use interviews for diagnosing individual students, for planning class instruction, and for evaluating instruction.

b. Read "Writing an Effective Arithmetic Test" by Long for guidelines and suggestions on test design. Choose a topic and write three good test questions on that topic.

c. Read "Improve Your Evaluation Techniques" by Norton for suggestions on formative evaluation techniques and how to use test results effectively.

DAILY PLAN

In addition to yearly and unit plans, a daily plan is needed. Research has shown that effective teachers of mathematics plan organized lessons and make good use of class time. These two aspects and a third one, knowledge of subject matter and methods, are interrelated factors that have been found in expert teachers (Leinhardt, 1986). Expert teachers have been found to proceed differently from novices in conducting their daily lessons.

It has also been observed that the amount of time that is spent on a particular subject can vary greatly among teachers (Berliner, 1984). Some teachers spend twice as much time as others. A teacher who allots only 15 minutes a day to a subject limits the students' opportunity to learn compared to a teacher who allots 50 minutes.

The time on task also needs to be considered. Two different teachers may both allot 50 minutes for their math instruction, but their use of that time could vary. One may spend 15 minutes correcting homework, the other one less than 3 minutes. One may lose 3 minutes between different activities; the other may have a smooth transition from one activity to the next.

Students need to be on task as soon as class begins. They should immediately become involved in a meaningful activity. Their involvement and the momentum created in the beginning of the class should be maintained throughout the class period. If transitions between activities are not smooth or involve too much time, the momentum can

---

Daily Review (first 8 minutes except Mondays)
1. Review the concepts and skills associated with the homework
2. Collect and deal with homework assignments
3. Ask several mental computation exercises
Development (about 20 minutes)
1. Briefly focus on prerequisite skills and concepts
2. Focus on meaning and promoting student understanding by using lively explanations, demonstrations, process explanations, illustrations, etc.
3. Assess student comprehension
    a. Using process/product questions (active interaction)
    b. Using controlled practice
4. Repeat and elaborate on the meaning portion as necessary
Seatwork (about 15 minutes)
1. Provide uninterrupted successful practice
2. Momentum—keep the ball rolling—get everyone involved, then sustain involvement
3. Alerting—let students know their work will be checked at end of period
4. Accountability—check the students' work
Homework Assignment
1. Assigning on a regular basis at the end of each math class except Fridays
2. Should involve about 15 minutes of work to be done at home
3. Should include one or two review problems
Special Reviews
1. Weekly review/maintenance
    a. Conduct during the first 20 minutes each Monday
    b. Focus on skills and concepts covered during the previous week
2. Monthly review/maintenance
    a. Conduct every fourth Monday
    b. Focus on skills and concepts covered since the last monthly review

FIGURE 3-23. Guide to daily planning. (From T. L. Good, D. A. Grouws, and H. Ebmeier, **Active Mathematics Teaching**, p. 32, Copyright © 1983 by Longman Inc. All rights reserved.)

be lost and the teacher will need to expend more energy getting students motivated and back on task again. (A number of excellent suggestions on management and organization are contained in Johnson's *Every Minute Counts: Making Your Math Class Work*.)

The amount of time on task is related to high achievement. More important, academic learning time, the time when students are engaged in relevant learning tasks at a high rate of success, is highly related to achievement (Caldwell and others, 1982). Consequently, teachers need to learn what new methods of teaching mathematics have been found to be more successful than methods that have been used in the past.

The traditional daily plan of teaching mathematics has been: correct homework, present the day's lesson by working a few examples on the chalkboard, and then give the next day's assignment. This show-and-tell format produces students who may be able to do only rote procedures. Other formats of daily plans have been found to be effective in educating students who not only can do mathematics but also can understand, apply, and enjoy it.

A daily plan devised by Good and Grouws is discussed in this section (Figure 3-23). They found that students whose teachers used this format performed significantly better than students whose teachers taught in their traditional way. As you study this plan, note the emphasis on organization of the lesson and the use of time. This plan is presented as *a* model, not *the* model, for more effective teaching. This model provides for daily review, development, seatwork, homework, and special reviews. Evaluation is included as a part of seatwork, homework, and review. Each of the sections of Good and Grouws' model is defined and discussed below.

DAILY REVIEW

One aspect of the opening minutes of class is mental computation. Mental computation could be used to start the mathematics class as a "warm up." The purpose of this section of the lesson is to get all students actively thinking about mathematics and practicing mental computations. Mental computation also provides review of concepts and operations. Students should be asked to estimate the answers to problems such as $345 - 127$ or $\frac{23}{45} + \frac{2}{19}$, to give the exact answers to problems such as $43 - 19$ or 7×8, or to decide whether $\frac{3}{4}$ or 0.62 is larger. Problems can be shown one at a time on the overhead or written on the chalkboard. Students should be given enough time to think about the problem but not enough time to use pencil and paper to figure the answer. This momentum should be maintained in the transition to reviewing the day's lesson and correcting the homework.

As part of the daily review, homework is to be evaluated. This evaluation is formative; from this information the teacher adjusts plans for individual students, small groups, or the entire class. The correcting should be done efficiently and quickly. The entire assignment does not need to be checked; a sample can suffice. The answers could be read, written on the chalkboard, or shown on the overhead. Those answers that are incorrect should be marked or circled. The teacher can do a quick survey to determine whether or not there were errors and what types of errors were made. If the errors are conceptual, the teacher may need to reteach the lesson to the class or to a particular group of students or modify the lesson for the day. This assignment should be related to the concept being introduced in the development part of the lesson.

DEVELOPMENT

The main part of the lesson is development. Its importance as well as its relationship to prerequisites was discussed in the section on development of the topic in unit planning. In the transition from the first section of the period, the development should be clearly linked to the previous work. The purpose of the lesson should also be explicitly stated so that the students know the goal and the direction of the next activity. It has been found that less effective teachers did not discuss the purpose or were unclear in stating goals to the students (Berliner, 1984).

As discussed earlier, the time needed for development will vary according to the topic and the students. The amount of time depends on the complexity of the topic, whether the topic is new to the students or whether they have had previous difficulty with the topic. The first lessons in a new unit usually need a large block of time devoted to development. In later lessons development should be continued by asking the students to explain and verify; development, like practice, needs reinforcement. Considering that research suggests that 50 to 75 percent of the time should be devoted to development, 20 minutes should be considered a minimal average.

One of the aspects that Good and Grouws included in their format was assessing student comprehension. As discussed earlier, formative evaluation should be used to evaluate learning on a day-to-day basis. By appropriate questions and observations the teacher can decide whether the class understands the prerequisites and is ready to start the new topic, whether they need more examples at a particular level, or whether they are ready for more sophisticated examples. Although the teacher has the lesson planned, the lesson will be modified as the teacher assesses the students' understanding.

The use of models, examples, and active questioning is also recommended by Good and Grouws. Active teaching with student involvement with models and examples guided by teacher questions is desired, not teaching with the students as a passive audience who receive rules to be memorized. The class session should be a dialogue between the teacher and the students and among the students; there should be no long periods of teacher lecture where the communication is one way. When presenting explanations and examples, the teacher should ask questions to assure that the students are on task and are understanding the discussion.

All students should be expected to answer mentally any question asked. There are a number of strategies that teachers can use to maximize participation. When asking a question to the class, the teacher should pause, giving students time to think about the question. This is called wait time. This procedure directs the question to the entire class. Depending on the situation, the teacher may ask all students to write down their responses, ask for a class response, hold up a paper or slate showing the answer, or call on a particular student to give the answer. Other students should be asked if they agree with a given response so that the students learn to listen to each other and evaluate each other's thinking. Incorrect answers are part of learning; they should be discussed in a positive atmosphere so that students will realize that participation is for all students, not just the top three students in the class.

The amount of wait time needed will vary depending on the purpose of the questions. A number of questions involve only brief answers or explanations. Such questions can be used to determine possession of prerequisite skills, to conduct reviews, to determine the correct completion of homework answers, or to determine whether students are following the current discussion. These questions are often at the knowledge and comprehension levels of Bloom's taxonomy. These types of questions do not require as much wait time as higher-level questions.

It has been found that most teacher questions involve the lower levels of Bloom's taxonomy. In order for students to acquire higher levels of thinking that involve such skills as analysis, synthesis, and evaluation, teachers need to pose questions that require such responses. It has also been found that higher-level questions do facilitate learning. There is evidence that students obtain higher test scores when teachers ask higher-level questions than if the same lesson were taught using lower-level questions (Berliner, 1984).

For questions at any level, more wait time is needed than is usually given. The average wait time is 1 second. When teachers increase their wait time to 3 or more seconds, several results have been noted. Student responses were more appropriate; students were more confident in answering; student responses were more varied; and a higher level of student thinking was observed.

In the first part of the development, the teacher and the class are often working together as problems are introduced, explored, and discussed. The first problems are often solved as an entire group; the teacher should use models or examples that illustrate the process or concept being developed. Gradually, as the students learn more about the topic, the teacher will not need to ask as many guiding questions. The students will start to use the models to solve the problems without as many teacher ques-

tions to guide them through the process or to help them focus on the attributes of the concept. The process of the class and of individual students should be evaluated through class discussion. If the teacher simply calls on those students who indicate that they know the answer, the teacher will only be receiving feedback from a small portion of the class. Also the information will be misleading if only the best students are interacting with the teacher.

As the students become more confident about the topic, they will be working more independently of the teacher, either in small groups or as individuals. As the students work through different problems, the teacher can circulate among them, observing their work and helping individual students or groups as needed. Gradually, the lesson has moved from "formal development" to controlled practice.

Controlled practice does not necessarily mean that the students are working problems with paper and pencil. Consider the situations described earlier regarding the addition algorithm with regrouping. In the first lessons the controlled practice may involve students individually solving problems with counting sticks. In another lesson controlled practice may involve pairs of students with one working the problems with models and the other recording the process in written form. In another lesson they may be working in groups of four, with the responsibility of determining which addition problems from a particular set would need to be regrouped. In controlled practice, if the class appears to have difficulties, the teacher may go back to whole-class instruction.

SEATWORK

Seatwork is a continuation of controlled practice. Earlier the teacher had been presenting problems for the students to practice. Now the students may be working on select problems from their textbook, a worksheet, or problems written on the board. The purpose and directions for the activity should be concise so that the students know how to proceed. The purpose and the format of the page may be evident to the teacher, but that is not necessarily true for the students. A specific set of problems should be assigned for this section of the lesson. Because their work rates vary, not all students will complete the designated problems within class time. The purpose of this seatwork is to give all students an opportunity to complete sample problems successfully under a teacher's supervision. The teacher should continue to monitor student work and to keep students on task. The completed problems should be checked at the end of this time. Any misconceptions should be corrected so that the students should be able to work successfully the homework assigned.

HOMEWORK

Homework is part of learning. It is essential because *distributed* practice is needed for retention. It should be viewed positively as an opportunity to reinforce and extend one's learning. Negative attitudes toward study and learning are fostered by using no homework as a reward for students if they do good work during the class period.

The topics that were discussed and introduced during class time should be reinforced by further practice. Since the students have been working on similar problems during the seatwork section of the lesson, they should be able to complete their homework successfully. The probability for student errors on homework should be greatly reduced. Also due to the seatwork portion of the lesson, the students should be familiar with the format and expectations of the assignments.

In their study, Good and Grouws recommended 15 minutes of homework Monday through Thursday. As with other recommendations, this is a suggested average. This would be modified depending on the grade level and on the lesson studied. No homework was given on Friday, as Monday was a special review day.

SPECIAL REVIEW

Good and Grouws recommend weekly and monthly reviews. When children restudy various topics over time, long-term learning is enhanced (Figure 3-15). The weekly review every Monday focuses on the previous week's work. Each month there is a review of the month's work. These sessions should include reviews of development and story problems as well as review of procedures. As discussed earlier, some textbooks have daily review built into each lesson. By having regular reinforcement, the students are more likely to be able to retain and transfer what they have learned.

SUMMARY

Organizing instruction and various sections of elementary mathematics textbooks have been introduced. The teacher's edition should be regarded as a valuable resource that teachers can use as a basic structure in planning learning activities for their class. Textbooks can be extremely helpful when used appropriately, but the textbook will not have all the answers. The development of topics in different textbook series varies in both quality and quantity. Teachers need to know when to use, supplement, or ignore this resource.

To be effective, teachers must know how to implement effectively what is currently known about teaching different topics. Throughout this text methods that have been found to be effective for teaching elementary school mathematics are described. Teachers who know appropriate teaching methods and who have good textbooks in their classrooms will find it easier to become effective teachers. But these conditions are not sufficient to becoming an effective teacher. Teachers who have been found to be highly effective are those who know how to use time wisely and have organized lessons as well as knowing the content and methods of teaching elementary school mathematics.

At the center of planning and organizing for instruction are the students' needs. Teachers must tailor the lessons to their students. By carefully observing the students' learning and their needs, teachers will note when to modify their lessons. Ultimately, the teacher is the person who will structure the learning environment in an individual classroom. The desirable classroom environment can best be described by Dienes: "It is suggested that we shift the emphasis from teaching to learning, from our experience to the children's, in fact, from our world to their world."

QUESTIONS AND ACTIVITIES

1. From their research, Good and Grouws proposed and tested a schedule that includes key instructional behaviors.

   a. What were the five instructional behaviors and the rationale for each?

   b. What was the time allocation for each? The time allocations will vary depending on the topic and the part of the unit. If this is the case, why are time periods given?

2. The questions below relate to Good and Grouws' five major points.

   a. What are the different aspects of the section called the daily review? Why should the concepts or skills related to the homework be reviewed? List three ways that homework can be dealt with efficiently.

   b. Why is focusing on prerequisite skills the first part of the development section? What were the four ways listed to help develop the topic? Part of the development portion of the lesson was formative evaluation. Why do teachers need to evaluate during the development? What is meant by using process questions to assess student comprehension? Product questions? Controlled practice?

   c. What is the difference between seatwork and controlled practice? Between seatwork and homework? What is the purpose of each? What is meant by "momentum," "alerting," and "accountability," and why is each important?

   d. Why is homework essential? Why was Friday considered a possible exception for homework?

   e. What special reviews were recommended? What was the purpose?

3. *For your resource file:* West raises (and answers) a number of questions in "Teaching: Using a Textbook Effectively." Read the article; it will help you gain a perception of the role of the textbook. Add these ideas to your resource file.

4. *For your resource file:* For your professional development, read and add some of these ideas to your resource file. Trafton

discusses effective teaching in "Toward More Effective, Efficient Instruction in Mathematics." Johnson discusses organizing your class in *Every Minute Counts: Making Your Math Class Work*. Suydam presents current research on direct instruction in "Research Report: Direct Instruction."

5. *For your resource file:* Guidelines for learning to ask good questions are presented in "Teaching: How to Ask Effective Questions" by McCullough and Findley and "The Role of Questioning" by Burns. Read one of these articles and add the ideas to your resource file.

6. It is important to get students immediately on task. Some educators use the opening few minutes for warm-ups—math activities where the class is actively involved. Read "Warm-Ups—Keys to Effective Mathematics Lessons" by Williams for the rationale on warm-ups and some examples to use in class.

7. Review, practice, and problem-solving activities can be found in the IDEAS section of the *Arithmetic Teacher* each month. Suggestions for teaching a particular topic and appropriate worksheets for grades 1–6 (sometimes K–6) are included. Refer to "Ideas, Ideas, Ideas from IDEAS: An Annotated Bibliography" by Hirsch and Meyer for a description of each article. Select one reference for each of two different topics. Look up the appropriate *Arithmetic Teacher* and read through the IDEAS section. What are the common features of each article? How could you use these in your future classroom for review, practice, or problem solving?

8. a. Practice activities should follow activities designed to develop concepts and procedures. Guidelines on practice are included in "How to Use, Not Abuse, Those Practice Exercises" by McKillip and Aviv. Read the article and summarize the main points.

b. In "Research Report: Homework: Yes or No?" Suydam reports what is currently known about homework. Comment on the validity of the following statements: "Homework is always beneficial" and "Elementary school children are too young to benefit from homework."

9. Should calculators be banned from the classroom? Read "Calculators in the Elementary Classroom: How Can We Go Wrong!" by Reys. Summarize the main points presented in the article.

10. Read the recommendations for school mathematics in the 1980s as presented in the NCTM's *An Agenda for Action*. [If unavailable, the main points are given in "President's Address 58th Annual Meeting" by Shirley Hill in *Arithmetic Teacher 28* (September 1980): 49–54.] Choose two or three recommendations that you consider the most important. Give the reasons why you selected them and what you could do to implement these recommendations in your classroom. Further information on implementing the agenda is contained in the 1983 yearbook, *The Agenda in Action* (Shufelt and Smart, 1983).

11. When are games appropriate? To gain a perspective of the uses of games, read one or more of the following articles.
a. Nelson and Whitaker discuss maintenance games and teaching games in "Teaching Games: More Than Practice."
b. In "Fitting Games into a Mathematics Curriculum," Jones discusses the advantages of games for teachers and students, how to construct games, and how to incorporate them into the curriculum.
c. Harvey and Bright argue that games can be used for higher-level thought processes in "Mathematical Games: Antithesis or Assistance." To gain an appreciation of their arguments, play one of the games in the article.

TEACHER RESOURCES

Akers, Joan. "Not All Math Texts Are Created Equal." *Learning 12* (January 1984): 34–35.

Barnett, Jeffrey C., Larry Sowder, and Kenneth E. Vos. "Textbook Problems: Supplementing and Understanding Them." In *Problem Solving in School Mathematics,* 1980 Yearbook of the National Council of Teachers of Mathematics, pp. 92–103. Reston, VA: The Council, 1980.

"Basic Skills: Position Papers from NCTM and NCSM." *Arithmetic Teacher 25* (October 1977): 18–22.

Berliner, David C. "The Half-Full Glass: A Review of Research on Teaching." In *Using What We Know About Teaching,* pp. 51–77. Alexandria, VA: Association for Supervision and Curriculum Development, 1984.

Biggs, Edith E., and James R. MacLean. *Freedom to Learn: An Active Approach to Mathematics.* Don Mills, Ontario: Addison-Wesley (Canada), 1969.

Brownell, William A. "Psychological Considerations in the Learning and Teaching of Arithmetic." In *Readings in the History of Mathematics.* Reston, VA: National Council of Teachers of Mathematics, 1970.

Burns, Marilyn. "Does Math Make Good Homework?" *Instructor 96* (September 1986): 92–97.

———. "Groups of Four: Solving the Management Problem." *Learning 10* (September 1981): 46–51.

———. "The Role of Questioning." *Arithmetic Teacher 32* (February 1985): 14–16.

Burns, Paul C. "Development of Elementary School Mathematics Teaching in the United States." *Arithmetic Teacher 17* (May 1970): 428–437.

Caldwell, Janet H., William G. Huitt, and Anna O. Graeber. "Time Spent in Learning: Implications from Research." *Elementary School Journal 82* (May 1982): 470–480.

Campbell, Patricia F. "What Do Children See in Mathematics Textbook Pictures?" *Arithmetic Teacher 28* (January 1981): 12–16.

Carpenter, Thomas P., Mary Kay Corbitt, Henry Kepner, Jr., Mary Montgomery Lindquist, and Robert E. Reys. "Students' Affective Responses to Mathematics: Results and Implications from National Assessment." *Arithmetic Teacher 28* (October 1980): 34–37, 52–53.

Carpenter, Thomas P., Westina Matthews, Mary Montgomery Lindquist, and Edward A. Silver. "Achievement in Mathematics: Results from the National Assessment." *The Elementary School Journal 84* (May 1984): 485–496.

Charles, Randall I. "Get the Most Out of Word Problems." *Arithmetic Teacher 29* (November 1981): 39–40.

Clark, H. Clifford. "How to Check Elementary Mathematics Papers." *Arithmetic Teacher 34* (September 1986): 37–38.

Dirkes, M. Ann. "Say It with Pictures." *Arithmetic Teacher 28* (November 1980): 10–12.

Driscoll, Mark. "Research Report: Effective Teaching." *Arithmetic Teacher 33* (May 1986): 19. 48.

Gilbert-Macmillan, Kathleen, and Steven J. Leitz. "Cooperative Small Groups: A Method for Teaching Problem Solving." *Arithmetic Teacher 33* (March 1986): 9–11.

Good, Thomas L., Douglas A. Grouws, and Howard Ebmeier. *Active Mathematics Teaching.* New York: Longman, 1983.

Hamrick, Kathy B. "Are We Introducing Mathematical Symbols Too Soon?" *Arithmetic Teacher 28* (November 1980): 14–15.

Harvey, John G., and George W. Bright. "Mathematical Games: Antithesis or Assistance." *Arithmetic Teacher 32* (February 1985): 23–26.

Hirsch, Christian R., and Ruth A. Meyer. "Ideas, Ideas, Ideas from IDEAS: An Annotated Bibliography." *Arithmetic Teacher* 28 (January 1981): 52–57.

Johnson, David R. *Every Minute Counts: Making Your Math Class Work.* Palo Alto, CA: Dale Seymour Publications, 1982.

Jones, Sue M. "Fitting Games into a Mathematics Curriculum." *Arithmetic Teacher* 30 (December 1982): 35–36.

Kane, Robert, Mary Ann Byrne, and Mary Ann Hater. *Helping Children Read Mathematics.* New York: American Book Co., 1974.

Kurtz, V. Ray. "Kindergarten Mathematics—A Survey." *Arithmetic Teacher* 25 (May 1978): 51–53.

Larson, Carol Novillis. "Organizing for Mathematics Instruction." *Arithmetic Teacher* 31 (September 1983): 16–20.

LeBlanc, John F. "Teaching Textbook Story Problems." *Arithmetic Teacher* 29 (February 1982): 52–54.

Leinhardt, Gaea. *Cognitive Skill of Teaching on Expertise in Math Teaching.* Pittsburgh, PA: Learning Research and Developmment Center, 1986.

Leutzinger, Larry P. "Ideas." *Arithmetic Teacher* 34 (January 1987): 19–24.

———. "Problem Solving Tips for Teachers," edited by Phares G. O'Daffer. *Arithmetic Teacher* 33 (October 1985): 34–35.

Lindquist, Mary Montgomery. "The Elementary School Mathematics Curriculum: Issues for Today." *The Elementary School Journal* 84 (May 1984): 595–608.

Long, Lynette. "Writing an Effective Arithmetic Test." *Arithmetic Teacher* 29 (May 1982): 16–18.

McCullough, Dorothy, and Edye Findley. "Teaching: How to Ask Effective Questions." *Arithmetic Teacher* 30 (March 1983): 8–9.

McKillip, William D., and Cherie Adler Aviv. "How to Use, Not Abuse, Those Practice Exercises." *Arithmetic Teacher* 26 (April 1979): 10–12.

National Council of Teachers of Mathematics. *An Agenda for Action: Recommendations for School Mathematics of the 1980s.* Reston, VA: The Council, 1980.

National Council of Teachers of Mathematics. *How to Evaluate Mathematics Textbooks.* Reston, VA: The Council, 1982.

Nelson, Rebecca S., and Donald R. Whitaker. "Teaching Games: More Than Practice." *Arithmetic Teacher* 31 (October 1983): 25–27.

Nicely, Robert F., Helen R. Fiber, and Janet C. Bobango. "Research Report: The Cognitive Content of Elementary School Mathematics Textbooks." *Arithmetic Teacher* 34 (October 1986): 60–61.

Norton, Mary Ann. "Improve Your Evaluation Techniques." *Arithmetic Teacher* 30 (May 1983): 6–7.

Poage, Melvin, and Esther G. Poage. "Is One Picture Worth One Thousand Words?" *Arithmetic Teacher* 24 (May 1977): 408–414.

Reys, Robert E. "Calculators in the Elementary Classroom: How Can We Go Wrong!" *Arithmetic Teacher* 28 (November 1980): 38–40.

———. "Mental Computation and Estimation: Past, Present, and Future." *The Elementary School Journal* 84 (May 1984): 547–557.

Reys, Robert E., and Thomas R. Post. *The Mathematics Laboratory: Theory to Practice.* Boston: Prindle, Weber & Schmidt, 1973.

Schoen, Harold L. "Using the Individual Interview to Assess Mathematics Learning." *Arithmetic Teacher* 27 (November 1979): 34–37.

Shufelt, Gwen, and James R. Smart (Eds.). *The Agenda in Action,* 1983 Yearbook of the National Council of Teachers of Mathematics. Reston, VA: The Council, 1983.

Skypek, Dora Helen. "One Point of View: Girls Need Mathematics, Too." *Arithmetic Teacher* 27 (February 1980): 5–7.

Stevenson, Harold W. "Learning and Cognition." In *Mathematics Learning in Early Childhood,* Thirty-seventh Yearbook of the National Council of Teachers of Mathematics, pp. 1–14. Reston, VA: The Council, 1975.

Suydam, Marilyn N. "Research Report: Direct Instruction." *Arithmetic Teacher 32* (May 1985): 37.

———. "Research Report: Homework: Yes or No?" *Arithmetic Teacher 32* (January 1985): 56.

———. "Research Report: Individualized or Cooperative Learning." *Arithmetic Teacher 32* (April 1985): 39.

———. "Research Report: Manipulative Materials." *Arithmetic Teacher 31* (January 1984): 27.

———. "Research Report: The Role of Review in Mathematics Instruction." *Arithmetic Teacher 33* (September 1985): 26.

———. "10 Essential Ideas for Better Teaching." *The Iowa Council of Teachers of Mathematics Journal 12* (Spring 1984): 10–18.

Suydam, Marilyn N., and J. Fred Weaver. "Research on Mathematics Learning." In *Mathematics Learning in Early Childhood,* Thirty-seventh Yearbook of the National Council of Teachers of Mathematics, pp. 43–67. Reston, VA: The Council, 1975.

Trafton, Paul R. "The Curriculum." In *Mathematics Learning in Early Childhood,* Thirty-seventh Yearbook of the National Council of Teachers of Mathematics, pp. 15–41. Reston, VA: The Council, 1975.

———. "Toward More Effective, Efficient Instruction in Mathematics." *The Elementary School Journal 84* (May 1984): 514–528.

West, Tommie A. "Teaching: Using a Textbook Effectively." *Arithmetic Teacher 30* (October 1982): 8–9.

Williams, David E. "Warm-Ups—Keys to Effective Mathematics Lessons." *Arithmetic Teacher 32* (September 1984): 40–43.

CHILDREN'S LITERATURE

Burns, Marilyn. *The Book of Think (Or How to Solve a Problem Twice Your Size).* Illustrated by Martha Weston. Boston: Little, Brown, 1976.

———. *The I Hate Mathematics Book.* Illustrated by Martha Hairston. Boston: Little, Brown, 1975.

Charosh, Mannis. *Mathematical Games for One or Two.* Illustrated by Lois Ehlert. New York: Crowell, 1972.

Frédérique and Papy. *Graph Games.* Illustrated by Susan Holding. New York: Crowell, 1971.

4
TEACHING NUMERATION OF WHOLE NUMBERS

Holding up three bundles of ten counting sticks, Mr. Rathmell asked, "How many tens?" One first grader responded "thirty." How would you respond to the child?

"I don't use manipulatives in my classroom; the kids think they are babyish." How would you respond if this teacher were one of your colleagues?

PRENUMBER ACTIVITIES

Long before children use any numbers, they begin *doing* mathematics. Even very young children classify their toys into sets by putting all the plastic bottle caps into a box or all the alphabet blocks in the wagon. Thus they are beginning to develop the concept of sets. As these children mature, their classifications become more sophisticated. A 3-year-old may separate the bottle caps into subsets according to color (Figure 4-1a). An older child may separate all the alphabet blocks with the letter E (Figure 4-1b). Whereas at first children formed simple sets of objects, now they can separate these sets into subsets.

However, as Piaget's studies have shown, children may still be unable to see any relationship between the set and its subsets. For example, there are 10 green bottle caps and 5 red ones in a box (Figure 4-1a). Young children can probably recognize that there are more green caps than red ones. However, when asked whether there are more green bottle caps or more bottle caps, they will probably say that there are more green bottle caps. Although the children are able to compare correctly the numbers of two subsets, they cannot see the relationship between the larger subset and the entire set. They are unable to see that the larger subset is a part of the entire set and, therefore, is smaller than the entire set. Instead they continue to compare the larger subset to the smaller subset.

Children and adults continue to use classification both in everyday life and in mathematics. When shoppers walk into a grocery store, they know that carrots and onions will be found with the other vegetables in the produce section, whereas milk and butter will not be found in that section. Carrots and onions belong to the set of vegetables, but milk and butter are not elements of that set.

In mathematics classes students observe that certain story situations are addition problems even though some may involve whole numbers and others fractions or integers. Since these situations had similar characteristics, they all belong to the set of problems that can be solved using addition. When students extend their study of the set of whole numbers to integers and rational numbers, they will see that these are sets of which whole numbers are a subset. When you were working on problem-solving situations in Chapter 1, you may have observed that certain problems could be solved using tables or finding number patterns. You were classifying problems by strategy.

In analyzing sets, adults and children often focus on the size of the set. As preschool children's awareness of number

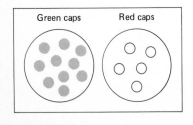

a

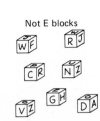

b

FIGURE 4-1.
Simple classification.

grows, they begin to distinguish one from more than one. Next they distinguish groups of one, two, and perhaps three from groups of more than two or three. In looking at larger sets, they begin making comparisons between the numbers of these sets. Ideas of less than and greater than become part of their conceptual framework. They begin to use the idea of one-to-one correspondence of the objects in one set with the objects in another set to determine the relative sizes of the two sets.

It is interesting to note that early civilizations probably used one-to-one correspondence even before counting was developed. A person could carry in a pouch a pebble for each sheep owned. Before the sheep were put in the pen at night, the pouch could be emptied. As the sheep entered the pen, a pebble was put back into the pouch each time a sheep went through the gate. If the last sheep matched with the last pebble, all of the sheep were in the pen.

Although children acquire many of these early number concepts before they start school, they may still need help in classifying their ideas. Models are particularly important for developing classification concepts because young children are in the concrete stage of learning. Commercially available attribute blocks can be used in classification activities.

One commercial set of attribute blocks consists of 32 wooden pieces in four colors, four shapes, and two sizes. Another type of attribute blocks, also called logic blocks, is a set of 60 plastic pieces. These pieces come in five shapes (circle, hexagon, rectangle, square, triangle) and each shape has three colors (red, yellow, blue), two sizes, and two thicknesses. The blocks can then be sorted by any of these four attributes (shape, color, size, thickness). Appropriate problems would include the following:

Make a set containing all the red pieces.

Find all of the small thick pieces.

Are there more triangles or more red triangles?

Are there more squares or more blue pieces?

Here is a large, thin, blue circle. Make a set of all the pieces that go with it.

Notice that the last problem has many "right" answers. One child might select all the large thin pieces, another all the blue circles, and so on. Two more possible answers are shown in Figure 4-2. Each student should give the rule for the set that was chosen. Students should be encouraged to find as many different sets, each containing the given piece, as they can.

Many noncommercial items can and should also be used for classification activities. For example, young children could group themselves into sets according to the shoes they are wearing. They could classify themselves by shoe type—tennis, sandals, and so on; by shoe fastening—tie, slip-on, Velcro, zip; or by shoe color. The children should be encouraged to find other attributes by which their shoes could be classified. They could also group themselves into

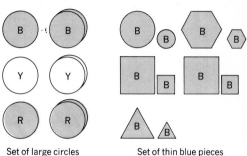

Set of large circles   Set of thin blue pieces

FIGURE 4-2.
Attribute subsets.

sets according to other clothes they are wearing—blue jeans, other slacks, skirts; or T-shirts versus button shirts.

Small items available in the classroom or brought from home can also be used for classification activities. Plastic milk bottle caps, blocks, pens and pencils, books, or lids such as yogurt, peanut butter, and cottage cheese all offer opportunities for classification. Sets such as these can be used for a wide variety of classification activities from simple to complex. Some of the classification activities will occur as specifically planned lessons, whereas others, such as putting away toys after a play period, will occur incidentally. For example, the toys in Figure 4-3 could be classified by considering whether or not they roll, whether they are soft or hard, whether they have legs or wheels, or whether they are noisy or quiet.

In addition to classification activities, the idea of one-to-one correspondence is basic to mathematics. Without it even such a simple process as counting is not possible. There are many opportunities for developing the idea of one-to-one correspondence. Passing out one paper to each child, having each child in group A find a partner in group B to play a game, or putting each coat on a separate hook with a name over it are just a few of the possible activities. Unifix pattern blocks are an appropriate commercial model for the concept of one-to-one correspondence (Figure 4-4). Blocks are put in one-to-one correspondence with the depressions on each board. For later work each pattern board can be associated with its corresponding numeral.

With the development of the concept of one-to-one correspondence, the ideas of less than, greater than, and equal to become more sophisticated. Children can see that if two sets can be put in one-to-one correspondence, they have the same number of elements. If not, the one that has one or more elements left over is the larger of the two sets. Initially, children can indicate which of the two sets is larger or smaller by pointing to the appropriate set.

After children have developed the less-than/greater-than concept, they are ready for the idea of one set having just one more element than another. Thus quantities can be ordered such that each has just one more than the one before it. Any kind of counters put in sets can be used for developing this idea. Unifix pattern boards that go from 1 to 10 are an appropriate model.

FIGURE 4-3.
Set of toys.

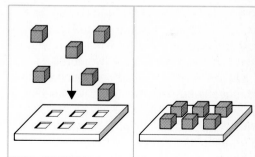

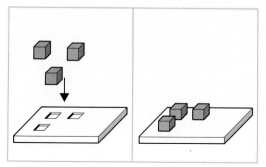

FIGURE 4-4.
Unifix pattern blocks.

Another particularly useful model for this concept is Cuisenaire rods (Figure 4-5). These are colored wooden rods each having a base of one square centimeter. The lengths of these rods, ranging from 1 to 10 centimeters, correspond to the whole numbers represented. The rods are color keyed, that is, the yellow rod always represents five and is 5 centimeters long. The white rods (units) can be used to demonstrate the length of each of the other rods. The entire group of rods can be arranged in a stairstep fashion. Then the white rod can be used to show that each rod is exactly one unit longer than the previous rod.

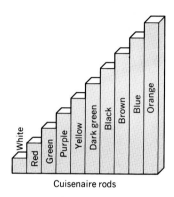

Cuisenaire rods

FIGURE 4-5.
One-more-than concept.

COUNTING

One of the first number skills that children need to acquire is counting. Unfortunately, language does not help them in their development of counting. It would be easier if languages did not contain so many adjectives that can be used to quantify objects. For example, people usually speak of *a* book rather than *one* book, *the* elephant rather than *one* elephant, a *pair* of dogs rather than *two* dogs, and a *dozen* eggs rather than *twelve* eggs. They may also call 8 people a *group,* 15 birds a *flock,* or 5 minutes a *few* minutes. Nonnumeral quantifiers, both definite and indefinite, are used for convenience. However, because there are so many different quantifiers, children may be slowed in the early development of number concepts.

ROTE AND RATIONAL COUNTING

In spite of the language, many children will arrive in the kindergarten class with some counting ability. The first level of ability in counting that is generally recognized is that of rote counting. Rote counting is the ability to say the oral names for the numbers in sequence, that is, to say one, two, three, and so on. Some students will not have a stable order for numbers. A child may count, "one, two, . . . , nine, ten, eleven, thirteen, sixteen, seventeen, twelve, twenty." The next day the same child may count, "one, two, three, . . . , ten, eleven, twelve, sixteen, thirteen, fourteen, seventeen, twenty." Two weeks later this child may count, "one, two, . . . , ten, eleven, twelve, thirteen, fourteen, seventeen, sixteen, nineteen, twenty."

Along with rote counting the teacher should introduce the skill of rational counting. Children who can count rationally are able to count a set of objects or to count a subset of objects from a larger set. For example, when given the set of objects shown in Figure 4-3, children would be able not only to say the number names in order, but also to point to a different object each time they say a different number. This is another example of one-to-one correspondence, as each time they say an oral name it is related to an object. Thus, when finished, they would be able to say that there are nine objects in the set. Or, given the same set of toys, they should be able to count three trucks or two stuffed animals.

In practice, the teaching of rote counting usually does not need a great deal of emphasis in the school curriculum. Most students start school already familiar with rhymes such as "One little, two little, three little Indians" and "One, two, buckle my shoe." For some students who still do need assistance with rote counting skills, these and other counting rhymes may be useful tools. Others will acquire these rote counting skills through class activities in rational counting or activities with the sequence of numerals through 20.

Another technique for rote counting instruction is for students to count in order when organizing for various activities. For example, when the students leave the room for lunch, each student could count when walking through the doorway. That is, the first student says "one," the second student says "two," and so forth. This technique also helps lay a foundation for rational counting because, in effect, the students collectively are counting the number of children in the class.

A later counting skill that is often overlooked is the ability to count starting from numbers other than one. It is surprising how many children can count from 1 to 20 but if asked to count from 12 to 20 are unable to do so. To help students practice this technique the teacher might ask, "Mary, what number comes after seven?" or "Susan, what number comes before ten?" or "George, please count from eight to fourteen." This kind of practice helps reinforce learning the order of the numbers and also provides a foundation for beginning addition that can be done by counting one set onto another. For example, when adding six blocks and two blocks, instead of counting "one, two, three, four, five, six, seven, eight," the children can count merely "SIX, . . . , seven, eight" (Figure 4-6).

Rational counting will probably require more teaching effort than rote counting. Many proud parents will tell how Johnny can "count" to 20, or 30, or 100. However, when Johnny is faced with a set of objects, such as shown in Figure 4-3, he has no clear idea of how to find out how many objects he has. He may count some objects twice and/or others not at all. He may possibly arrive at

FIGURE 4-6.
Counting from a number other than one.

the right number for the total, but this would be purely accidental rather than from any real understanding of counting. To count rationally, children must form a concept of number and must realize that oral names for numbers can be put in one-to-one correspondence with objects to answer the question, "How many?"

The first skill of rational counting, correctly counting a set of objects, can be observed by giving students a set of objects and asking, "How many are there?" The teacher should evaluate the students' counting processes to be sure that they are not just getting the right number from a combination of complementary mistakes. There are ample counting materials available in any classroom and the teacher can easily bring in others. Sets of counting sticks, cubes, rocks, books, windows, bottle caps, desks, or classmates are all useful for practice in rational counting.

The second skill of rational counting is for children to be able to correctly count a subset from a set. For this activity the students are asked to get nine sticks from a set of sticks greater than or equal to nine. Or, given a set of alphabet blocks, they may be asked to count just those blocks with the letter E on them.

Some of the commercial aids for counting are Cuisenaire rods, counting frames, and interlocking cubes. One type of interlocking cubes are 1-centimeter plastic cubes that each have a small plastic extension on one face that can be pushed into a hole on the face of another cube to "lock" the cubes together. These cubes can be fastened together to form rods similar to Cuisenaire rods (Figure 4-7). The rods can be made into any length. A single rod can be all one color or may be made of several colors so that the individual units can be easily seen. Larger interlocking cubes and in-

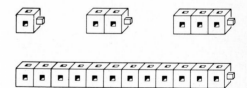

FIGURE 4-7.
Interlocking cubes.

terlocking links are also available as counting aids.

Counting frames usually consist of one hundred beads grouped equally on ten wires (Figure 4-8). As each bead is counted the child slides the bead to the other side of the frame. Since each wire only contains ten beads, the concepts of grouping by tens and the patterns of the decades are informally introduced. A modification of this model has one hundred disks on a string with a color change for each ten counters.

Games can be devised to help children learn rational counting. For example, teams can be selected, and they can give each other problems involving the counting of objects. Many commercially available board games require counting skill for moving from one space to another. While playing these games, children can help each other to reinforce counting skills.

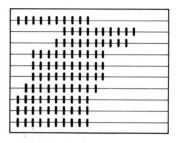

FIGURE 4-8.
Counting frame.

Other counting skills that need practice are counting backward and counting by various multiples. Relating counting backward to the countdown for a space launch can help reinforce counting-backward skills and can link mathematics skills to the "real" world. Counting backward rationally also lays a foundation for later work in subtraction. As a foundation for multiplication, counting by twos, threes, fives, or tens is helpful for the child. Counting by tens and hundreds can also be valuable for reinforcing place-value concepts and developing an understanding of the structure of the number system.

Since there are many levels of counting skill, counting is more than just a primary-grade activity. Practice in various types of counting should be continued at all grade levels. Estimation skills and number sense can be enhanced by asking children to estimate the size of a set and then count it. Counting activities should not be restricted to the mathematics classroom. Teachers should continually make use of the many counting opportunities that arise throughout the day in other classes and on the playground.

CARDINAL AND ORDINAL USE OF NUMBERS

As children are learning to count, they should also learn the two uses of numbers: cardinal and ordinal. Cardinal numbers are used to tell how many. Ordinal numbers are used to tell which one; that is, they give the order or sequence of an object in a set. For example, in the statement "There are thirty-three students in this room," the thirty-three is used as a cardinal number. The statement, "The third student in the fourth row in Room 202 is wearing blue jeans," contains three ordinal numbers.

When children count various sets of objects, they are using numbers in the cardinal sense; that is, they are finding out how many. At the same time they can easily be led to discover that numbers are used for purposes other than counting. There is probably a room number on the door that indicates something other than the number of rooms in the building. Starting with this observation the teacher should lead the students to realize that numbers are commonly used for identification purposes. Other examples of ordinal numbers can be given by the children, and eventually the use of numbers to denote position will enter into the discussion.

Sometimes cardinal and ordinal uses of numbers overlap. For example, in the rote counting activity mentioned earlier, the students counted off as they left the room for lunch. When Jane says, "Five," she is using a cardinal number in the sense that five students have now left the room and an ordinal number in the sense that she is the fifth child to leave. Children should also discuss this type of double usage for numbers.

MODEL—ORAL NAME—NUMERAL ASSOCIATION

As children gain skill in rational counting, they should learn both the numerals and the written words that are associated with the models and oral names of numbers. First they should learn to recognize the numerals and words. Later they should learn to write the numerals. As in all other topics to be learned, there will be a wide diversity in what

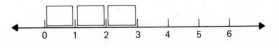

FIGURE 4-9.
Number line.

FIGURE 4-10.
Number track.

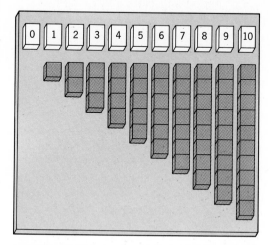

FIGURE 4-11.
Counting stair.

movable counters, can be constructed to accommodate different situations.

A special type of number line is the number track that is included in the Unifix materials (Figure 4-10). An extension of the track is possible by adding units of ten. Other Unifix materials that may be helpful in teaching early number concepts are the pattern boards and the counting stair. The counting stair requires the children to place the rods and the numeral blocks in the appropriate places (Figure 4-11). Similar to the counting stair is a number chart showing both the numeral and the pictorial representation of the number (Figure 4-12).

Numerals can also be studied using a hundred chart (Figure 4-13). Initially, the chart can be used to reinforce the model–numeral relationship. One of the class members can point to the appropriate numerals as another student places counters, one at a time, on a table. The oral name–numeral association can be shown by having the class count orally as one individual points to the numerals on the board. As the children say the oral names and look at the numerals, they will soon discover that the ones digit follows the same pattern in each decade. This same pattern will be further extended when children learn to consider numbers such as 36 as 3 tens 6 ones rather than as

the children already know. Some children will already be able to write all the digits 0 to 9, and others will not be able to identify any of the digits.

The model–numeral association can be illustrated with the number line. Since this model is conceptually relatively abstract, counters can be placed beside the number line as the child counts (Figure 4-9). This activity helps the child to focus on the intervals rather than on the marks for each numeral. Various kinds of number lines, such as floor number lines, chalkboard lines, or lines with

0	1	2	3	4	5	6	7	8	9	10
	•	• •	• • •	• • • •	• • • • •	• • • • • •	• • • • • • •	• • • • • • • •	• • • • • • • • •	• • • • • • • • • •

FIGURE 4-12.
Number chart.

0	1	2	3	4	5	6	7	8	9
10	11	12	13	14	15	16	17	18	19
20	21	22	23	24	25	26	27	28	29
30	31	32	33	34	35	36	37	38	39
40	41	42	43	44	45	46	47	48	49
50	51	52	53	54	55	56	57	58	59
60	61	62	63	64	65	66	67	68	69
70	71	72	73	74	75	76	77	78	79
80	81	82	83	84	85	86	87	88	89
90	91	92	93	94	95	96	97	98	99

FIGURE 4-13.
Hundred chart.

36 ones. The hundred chart can also be used for counting on from a number other than one, for counting backward, and for skip counting, such as by twos, fives, or tens.

To reinforce the model–numeral association, the teacher or children can make a set of cards. Ten cards can be made with the digits 0 to 9 on them, ten with the pictorial representation of the numbers, and ten with the words "Zero" through "Nine." This packet of 30 cards can then be used in various games. For example, children could play a simple "rummy" game in which players must get a sequence such as (2 3 4) or (★ ★★ ★★★) or one in which they must get three of a kind such as the cards (2 ★★ two) or a combination of the two. They could also play a concentration-type game in which the cards are placed face down and the children take turns turning up any two cards and keeping them if they are a match. In both of these games the association of the proper oral names can be reinforced by having the children say the oral names for the cards they play.

The teacher could also use this packet of cards on an individual basis. The cards could be shuffled and a child could arrange them in order by groups of three. The same cards could be used in a sorting box (Figure 4-14). A groove in the back of the sorting box holds some of the cards in an upright position. The other cards are dropped through the corresponding slots into compartments inside the box. Thus the teacher or another child can quickly check a child's sorting ability. This sorting box has the advantage of allowing the key cards to be placed in any order. Also any of the three types of cards, or a combination of any two or of all three, can be used as the key cards.

As children become skilled in numeral recognition, they should begin writing the numerals. Each of the ten digits has a recommended form for writing which should be taught. Figure 4-15 shows the recommended form for writing the digits 0 to 9. Children who have already been taught other forms of writing should not be forced to change as long as their numerals can be easily read. Only "4" and "5" require lifting the pencil from the paper. All other figures are written without lifting the pencil.

Not all teachers' manuals will give detailed instructions for teaching the writing of digits. Figure 4-16 shows one teaching technique. The children begin by tracing the digit and are then given progressively less and less guidance in writing. By the time children reach the last few boxes, they are writing the numerals entirely on their own. Another ap-

FIGURE 4-14.
Sorting box.

FIGURE 4-15.
Writing figures.

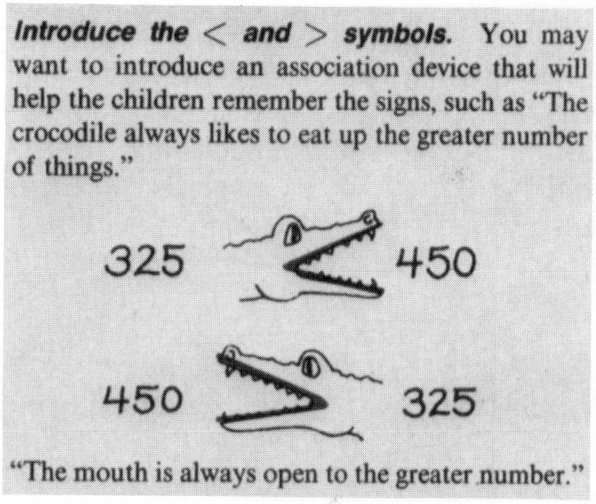

proach that can be used concurrently is to give the children sandpaper digits that they can trace with their fingers. This tactile approach can help develop their feel for how the digits should be written.

When children are given a mimeographed sheet on which to practice writing digits, they should also be asked to draw the appropriate number of objects beside the numeral. In this way they are relating the digit being practiced to the correct number of objects (numeral–model association). The children should also be given the corresponding manuscript word to look at although they are probably not ready to print the word at this stage.

The children should continue their study of comparisons and begin learning the relation symbols $=$, $<$, and $>$. Meanings for these symbols should be taught just as meanings for numerals and the operation symbols are studied. To introduce the symbols for greater than and less than, some textbooks suggest using characters such as alligators, ducks, crocodiles, or goldfish (Figure 4-17). (*Note:* Figure 4-17 shows an

Introduce the $<$ and $>$ symbols. You may want to introduce an association device that will help the children remember the signs, such as "The crocodile always likes to eat up the greater number of things."

325 ⤳ 450

450 ⤳ 325

"The mouth is always open to the greater number."

FIGURE 4-17.
Less than/greater than symbol. (From C.A. Dilley, D.W. Lowry, W.E. Rucker, **Heath Mathematics**, D.C. Heath & Company, 1985, Grade 2, p. 263. Reprinted by permission of D.C. Heath & Company.)

example of three-digit numbers from a second-grade textbook; for younger children objects arranged in sets to represent numbers such as eight and twelve would be

FIGURE 4-16.
Practice writing 4.

used instead of numerals.) In each situation, the character always gobbles up the larger of the two sets. Thus the animal's mouth, in the shape of the less-than/greater-than symbol, is always open toward the greater quantity.

Comparison situations such as the following can be posed to and acted out by the children. "We have 6 chairs and 4 students. Do we have more chairs or students? If we take three chairs away, do we have more chairs or students?" "Sue has two books and Ted has five. Does Ted or Sue have more? Chuck gives three more books to Sue. Now who has more?" These symbols should be used in number sentences paired with groups of objects (Figure 4-18). Gradually, the objects themselves should be omitted with only the symbolic representations being retained.

Four is less than six

4　　<　　6

Three equals three

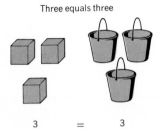

3　　=　　3

FIGURE 4-18.
Relation symbols.

QUESTIONS AND ACTIVITIES

1. Read the scope-and-sequence charts of at least two elementary mathematics textbook series to determine when the following concepts are introduced.
   a. greater than/less than
   b. one through ten
   c. zero
   d. one through twenty
   e. place value through 99
   f. place value through 999
   g. place value through 9999
   h. place value to millions
   i. cardinal numbers
   j. ordinal numbers

2. a. Distinguish between rational and rote counting.
   b. Why is one-to-one correspondence basic to rational counting?
   c. Read "Rational Counting" by Liedtke for a discussion of classification and beginning number concepts. Outline the main ideas. Describe as briefly as possible an activity for each of the main ideas.

3. a. Rote counting should occasionally start at 14, 35, or 107, for example, instead of always beginning with 1. Design a classroom activity in which it is logical to start counting from a number other than 1.
   b. List at least five ways to implement counting in other subjects taught in the curriculum.
   c. Devise an activity for the classroom that introduces the concept of ordinal numbers.

4. How can a child who does not know how to count rationally decide which of the two sets at the top of the next page is smaller?

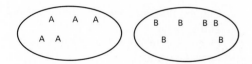

5. In counting a set a child picked up one of the counters and said "This is three." What two uses of number is the child confusing?

6. Write a story situation that children can solve with counters and that involves each of the following concepts.
   a. comparing thirteen and seven
   b. deciding whether twelve is smaller or larger than nine
   c. finding a number two more than eight
   d. finding a number one less than ten
   e. finding a number four more than twenty-one
   f. finding a number three less than twenty-one

7. Using materials similar to those shown in Figure 4-11, 4-12, or 4-14, design an activity that reinforces the numeral → model and model → numeral tasks. How could you adapt your activity to include oral names for number?

8. Practice writing the numerals as shown in Figure 4-15. Did you write them correctly? If not, adapt your style to one that is appropriate for young children.

9. Consult a teacher's edition of a kindergarten or first-grade textbook. What teaching suggestions are given to help children link models to the oral names? To the written names?

10. To gain an appreciation of how to help children learn about number lines, line up cubes or linked paper clips along a line as shown in Figure 4-9. Label the first mark 0 and then mark off each interval and label with appropriate numerals.

11. Spread out six counters on a piece of paper divided into two sections. How many different ways can you rearrange the whole of six so that part of the counters are on one side and part on the other side? How many ways if the part on either side can be zero counters? How many ways if you used seven counters? Why could this be considered a pre-addition or pre-subtraction experience?

12. Counting frames and one hundred charts can be used for helping children count. To gain an appreciation of children's experiences use these models to count as indicated below. Reflect on why these different experiences are needed.
   a. by twos through thirty
   b. by ones from fifty-three to thirty-eight
   c. by twos from forty-five to thirty-one
   d. by threes through thirty
   e. by fives from thirty-five to sixty
   f. by tens to one hundred
   g. by tens from one hundred to sixty
   h. by tens from forty-two to seventy-two
   i. by fives from thirty-five to fifty-five then by ones to fifty-eight

13. Devise calculator codes to do the counting exercises in Problem 12.

14. In other rote experiences such as memorizing nursery rhymes or the alphabet, we do not say that *"little is larger than Mary"* or *"b is smaller than e."*
   a. How could you use a counting frame to help a child develop the concept that ten is more than seven as it comes after seven? That forty-three is larger than thirty-one as it comes after thirty-one.
   b. How could you use a hundred board to help a child develop the concept that 43 is more than 31? 26 is less than 52?

15. Use a counting frame to count forward and backward by ones, twos, fives, and tens.

16. How would you help a child who counts "95, 96, 97, 98, 99, 100, 200, 300"?

17. Read a selection of children's counting books. Several are listed in the section Children's Literature.

a. How could counting books be used to help a child who does not have a stable order list for counting.

b. Six tasks involving models, oral names, and numerals were defined for number. How could counting books be used to help children with the following translations?
(1) oral name → model
(2) model → numeral
(3) numeral → oral name
(4) model → oral name
(5) numeral → model
(6) oral name → numeral

18. Some counting books, such as *Anno's Counting Book,* have several sets to count on any two-page spread. Other counting books, such as Hoban's *1, 2, 3,* contain only one set to count. Discuss the differences among the various types of counting books that you have read with regard to the reader's prerequisite skills. What classification skills are required in order to do the counting?

19. *Materials needed:* Cuisenaire rods. Charbonneau's *Hidden Rods/Hidden Numbers* is a collection of riddles that explore various number concepts. Solve at least six of them. What concepts are being developed?

20. Create or collect some activities that could be used to help children with early number concepts. Some good resources for counting activities that are listed in Teacher Resources include those by Leutzinger and Nelson, Baratta-Lorton, and Clements and Callahan.

21. a. The accompanying figure shows one- and two-difference attribute trains made with the 60-piece attribute set described earlier. What could be the next two pieces in train A? In train B? Are these answers unique?

b. How is this activity like order in numbers?

c. *For your resource file:* Read and copy some of the classification, ordering, and patterning activities for prenumber and number in "Let's Do It: 'Button Bag' Mathematics" by Horak and Horak.

22. *For your resource file:* Lindquist and Dana describe counting applications for first and second graders that would involve collecting and representing data, problem solving, and measurement across various subject areas.

23. Read Suydam's "Research Report: The Process of Counting" for further information on what is known about counting and how it is extended to pre-addition and pre-subtraction concepts.

WHOLE-NUMBER NUMERATION

PLACE VALUE

In children's counting experiences, they learned oral names and numerals for an appropriate number of objects. Similar tasks must be designed for developing the concept of place value. There are six tasks or translations children should master in their study of number (Figure 4-19). Their first experience should include the oral ↔ objects translation. They should be able to tell how many objects, given a set of objects, (ob-

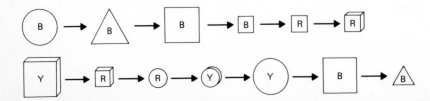

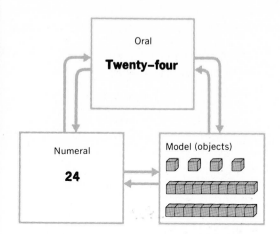

FIGURE 4-19.

Tasks for numeration.

jects → oral) as well as to show a specific set of objects after being asked to represent a certain number (oral → objects). It should not be assumed that just because children can name a number that is represented with objects, they can also do the reverse task. Throughout this section various activities involving these tasks will be described. (Consult "Number and Numeration" by Payne and Rathmell for further explanation and other activities for developing these concepts.)

Some mathematics educators recommend that after children have learned to count to ten, they should be taught to count *by* tens, that is, ten, twenty, thirty, and so on. Next they should be taught counting within the twenties, such as 21, 22, 23, and so on. Later the teen numbers can be taught. The rationale for this approach to counting is that it reinforces the structure of the number system. Because the teen number names do not follow the regular pattern found in other decades, some children have difficulty with them. Learning some of the regular decades first can help children see the number pattern. They will realize that the teen *numerals*

follow the same pattern and only the oral names are irregular.

According to a survey by Rea and Reys (1970), 75 percent of children entering kindergarten could count rationally beyond ten, but only 40 percent could count rationally to 20. Since more than half of the children do not know the teen numbers, an emphasis on the pattern of numeration is appropriate before learning the teen numbers. As discussed earlier, a hundred chart can be used for counting as well as to discover numeration patterns. For example, a child should observe the similar pattern when counting from twenty to thirty or seventy to eighty. Activities that require counting from one decade into the next such as counting from thirty-five to forty-five are particularly needed since many children initially have difficulty remembering what comes after numbers such as 39, 89, or 49.

The children who have learned counting through or beyond the teens in the traditional way will also profit from counting by tens, as this reinforces their understanding of the structure of the number system. Although these children can rationally count out thirty-five objects, they probably do not know that thirty-five means 3 tens and 5 ones.

Children who can count rationally are ready to develop the concepts of grouping and place value. Models are critically important for developing these concepts. One of the common models for teaching grouping is a large number of sticks such as popsicle sticks, tongue depressors, drinking straws, or the like. Children can count the sticks individually and then group 10 ones into 1 ten. Whenever another group of 10 ones is reached in counting, the sticks can be fastened together with a rubber band to form 1 more set of ten. The children should count the sets of ten that they have bundled in two different ways. They should learn to count the sets as 1 ten, 2 tens, 3 tens, and so on; and they should also count these sets as ten, twenty, thirty, and so on.

To count groups of tens and ones such as twenty-four, children will need to recognize the number as 2 tens and 4 ones (Figure 4-20). They will need to be able to count by tens and count on by ones, for example, "ten, twenty, twenty-one, twenty-two, twenty-three, twenty-four." Also, children should be asked to compare a set of 24 ones and a set of 2 tens, 4 ones. They should realize that the two representations are equivalent. In addition to model → oral tasks, oral → model tasks should be included. Thus, children should be asked to use counting sticks to represent such numbers as forty-five or 6 tens, 7 ones.

To emphasize the repetitive factor of our numeration system, students can start counting sticks one at a time from twenty. As one more stick is added to the set, the stu-

dent can count "twenty, twenty-one, twenty-two, . . . twenty-nine, thirty." This activity should be continued by starting with thirty, forty, and so on. Thus students will find the same regular pattern of number names being repeated in each decade.

In addition to representing numbers with models and learning their oral names, children need to relate this to the numerals. At first the children record in a form such as "3 tens 5 ones." Place-value tables can be used very effectively for the transition to the standard form for writing numerals.

In Figure 4-21 the number thirty-five has been represented using counting sticks. To help organize the children's work, a sheet of paper was folded in half and labeled tens and ones. The counting sticks were placed in the appropriate columns. As the teacher asks guiding questions, the students can record the numbers of tens and ones in a similar table on their assignment sheet (Figure 4-21a). This form is more concise than "3 tens, 5 ones" because the digits 3 and 5 are placed in the appropriate spatial relationship to each other. The representation looks like the standard numeral 35.

Through these activities, students will also discover the importance of zero as a place holder. Zero should not be described as "nothing" or as a "number with no value." Rather zero has a particular value; it is the number of the empty set. Its value becomes clear when it is needed in numerals of two or more digits. In Figure 4-21b, there are 5 tens and no ones. Zero is needed in recording this numeral to indicate that there are no ones or that the number of ones is zero. Without the zero, this numeral would be incorrectly shown as 5. Similarly, in writing numerals such as 203 or 3.04, zero is needed to represent "zero tens" and "zero tenths" and to keep the other digits in their correct places.

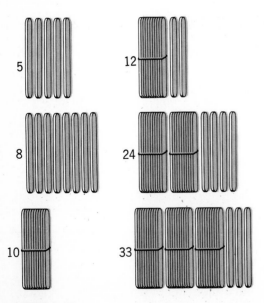

FIGURE 4-20.
Stick representation of numerals.

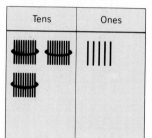

How many tens? (3)
How many ones? (5)
What number is this?
(thirty-five)

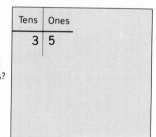

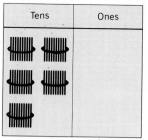

How many tens? (5)
How many ones? (0)
What number is this?
(fifty)

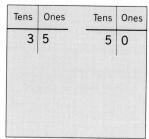

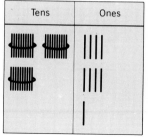

How many tens? (3)
How many ones? (9)
What number is this?
(thirty-nine)

FIGURE 4-21.
Place-value tables.

The teacher should ask guiding questions to help the children discover that a digit changes its meaning according to its position in the numeral. For example, the digit 5 occurs in both 35 and 50, but the two 5's do not represent equal values. In the first case the 5 represents 5 ones, whereas in the second case it represents 5 tens.

In teaching concepts such as grouping and place value, the teacher should never depend on just one model. Counting sticks which can be physically grouped into tens are a good beginning model for developing these concepts. Used with the place-value table, they can help children begin to abstract the concept of place value. A good transitional model for teaching place value is base-ten blocks. Generally, these blocks are in four sizes: units that are small cubes, longs that are rods of 10 units, flats that are 10 × 10 squares of 100 units, and blocks that are large 10 × 10 × 10 cubes of 1000 units. These pieces and their use in representing numerals are shown in Figure 4-22.

The base blocks are slightly more abstract conceptually than counting sticks because whenever 10 units are collected the child must trade them for one long instead

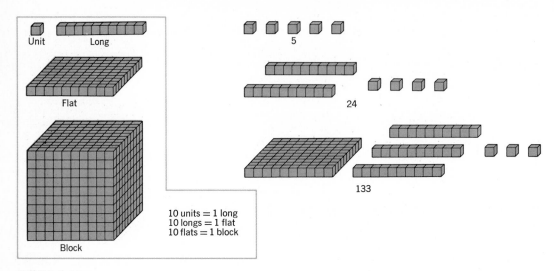

10 units = 1 long
10 longs = 1 flat
10 flats = 1 block

FIGURE 4-22.
Base-ten blocks.

of fastening those same units together as is done with the sticks. However, base-ten blocks are a superior model for representations of large numbers. Although 10 bundles of ten sticks can be grouped to represent 1 hundred, representing numbers larger than one hundred with counting sticks is cumbersome.

No discussion of teaching place-value concepts would be complete without mention of the abacus. This mathematical tool, used from ancient times to now, is the most conceptually abstract of the place-value models discussed in this text. Therefore,

children should be reasonably secure with simple place-value concepts before the abacus is introduced.

To help the children make a transition from the base-ten blocks to the abacus, the teacher could have them place the appropriate size block beside the corresponding wire on the abacus. They could also represent various numbers using the base-ten blocks and show the corresponding representation on the abacus. Thus the abacus could be used to reinforce and extend prior learning. Figure 4-23 shows the abacus representation of several numbers.

FIGURE 4-23.
Abacus representation of numerals.

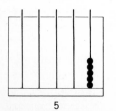

5

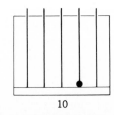

10

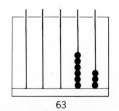

63

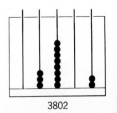

3802

As children learn to associate the proper numeral with its physical representation, they should also extend the repetitive pattern of the digits that make up the numerals. As they count "twenty, twenty-one, twenty-two, . . . , twenty-nine," the ones digits occur in the sequence 0, 1, 2, . . . , 9. As they progress to larger numbers, the children will note this same sequence occurring for the tens digit, the hundreds digit, and so on.

As children are developing the concept of grouping, they should also be learning the place-value names. They begin by grouping 10 ones into one group of ten. Next, one hundred should be introduced as the name for 10 groups of ten. Again children should be helped to discover the pattern developing so that they will realize immediately that the next place value, thousand, must be equal to 10 hundreds. They should observe that each place value will be 10 times larger than the one to the immediate right.

In learning how to read large numbers, the place-value table is helpful (Figure 3-4f and g). Children should observe that each period of three digits has a different name, such as ones, thousands, millions, billions, and so on. Within each period the names ones, tens, and hundreds are repeated.

To help children learn to read and write large numerals, the teacher could provide individual place-value tables. As the teacher reads numbers such as "two hundred three million, twenty-four thousand, one hundred sixty-eight," the children can write the numeral in their charts. To help the children learn how to read numerals correctly, different numerals could be written in a place-value chart and then the children could read

them. Common errors, such as writing four-thousand eight as 40008, could be corrected by having children write the digits in the appropriate columns on their place-value tables. After writing the numeral correctly, the children should also read it.

As the students become proficient with this concept, first the labels and later the entire place-value chart can be eliminated. Children who are having difficulties with this concept should be allowed to continue using place-value charts as needed.

For students who are ready for that level of abstraction, expanded notation could be helpful in reinforcing place-value concepts. Four forms of expanded notation for the same number are shown in Figure 4-24. The third form of expanded notation particularly emphasizes the fact that as one moves to the left each place value is 10 times greater than the one before. These four expanded notation forms are shown in the correct learning sequence. As students mature mathematically they are introduced, over various grade levels to increasingly complex forms.

Students should be given a large number of experiences grouping counting sticks, base blocks, and other models since these concept-building activities are essential for understanding place value in whole and decimal numbers. Furthermore, students must have a good understanding of place value before they are ready to learn algorithms for the various operations. By planning appropriate activities and asking good questions, teachers can guide students to construct and to discover these concepts. Research indicates that students under-

$$
\begin{aligned}
2356 &= 2000 + 300 + 50 + 6 \\
&= (2 \times 1000) + (3 \times 100) + (5 \times 10) + (6 \times 1) \\
&= [2 \times (10 \times 10 \times 10)] + [3 \times (10 \times 10)] + [5 \times 10] + [6 \times 1] \\
&= (2 \times 10^3) + (3 \times 10^2) + (5 \times 10^1) + (6 \times 10^0)
\end{aligned}
$$

FIGURE 4-24.
Expanded notation forms.

stand a concept better and retain the concept longer when they have developed it meaningfully.

COMPARING AND ORDERING WHOLE NUMBERS

In the discussion of rational counting, comparing numbers was considered with regard to whether one number was greater than or less than another number. Initially, children solve this problem by one-to-one correspondence or counting in sequence. More sophisticated thinking strategies are soon needed as numbers become larger. When children are comparing two numbers to determine which number is the smaller or larger, they must consider a number of factors that involve place value. For example, when comparing 4236 to 673 the child considers that since hundreds are less than thousands, 673 is smaller than 4236 even though 4 is less than 6. To determine which is smaller of 436 or 628, John used base-ten blocks to represent the numbers (Figure 4-25). He observed that the flats were the largest unit when compared to tens and ones; the tens and ones were so small when compared to the hundreds that they could be ignored. Since 4 hundreds is smaller than 6 hundreds, 436 is smaller than 628.

Ordering is an extension of comparing. It involves sequencing two or more numbers from largest to smallest or smallest to largest. To order three numbers, children simplify the problem. They compare two of the numbers and place them in order. Through one or two more comparisons, they determine where the third number fits into the sequence.

For example, to order 11, 7, and 16, Jeremy first compared eleven and seven. Since he knew that seven is smaller than ten and eleven is larger than ten, he reasoned that seven must be smaller than eleven. By the same thinking he knew that sixteen is also larger than seven. Then he compared eleven and sixteen. He counted from ten to determine that sixteen is larger than eleven. By making a series of comparisons, children can extend this process to ordering more than three numbers.

In ordering large numbers, the place values of each digit must be considered. For example, in ordering the numbers 35, 50, and 39, a student may think 39 is the largest number as 9 is the largest digit. This student has disregarded place value. In looking at the counting sticks that represent the numbers (Figure 4-21), the student should note that fifty is the largest as it is made up of 5 tens. Since 35 and 39 each contain 3 tens,

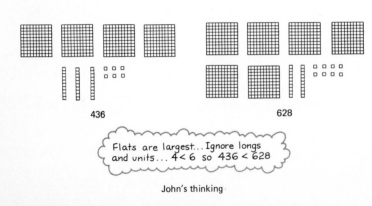

436   628

FIGURE 4-25.
Ordering numbers using base-ten blocks.

Flats are largest... Ignore longs and units... 4 < 6 so 436 < 628

John's thinking

the digit in the ones' place must be considered. Since 9 ones is larger than 5 ones, 39 is larger than 35.

ROUNDING AND ESTIMATING WHOLE NUMBERS

We often read news accounts that 15 000 people attended the concert or that over 400 people were at the presentation. We realize that some other number such as 14 734 or 15 030 people really attended the concert and that these are simply approximations to give us an indication of the size of the event. The exact number is not important in these cases.

Rounding

Children's first experiences with approximation can include rounding numbers to the nearest ten. For example, after counting and bundling 23 sticks, the class could be asked, "Is 23 closer to twenty or thirty?" The class discussion should involve the children in determining that 2 bundles of ten and 3 more ones is 3 more than 2 tens or twenty. They should also determine how many more ones are needed to obtain thirty. The class could estimate the number and then check their estimation by counting on from twenty-three. This discussion should be repeated with numbers such as 24, 38, 56, and 45.

A number line marked in multiples of ten centimeters and used with Cuisenaire rods is also a good model to develop these concepts (Figure 4-26). After the children place the rods along the number line, they should be asked questions such as "Thirty-four lies between which tens? Is thirty-four closer to 3 tens or 4 tens?" In the situation where the number is midway in the interval such as forty-five, the children should note that it is neither closer to forty nor closer to fifty. They should discuss real-life situations in which they would need to round up or round down. It should be discussed that in general when the number is midway in the interval we round up, simply so that our results are all the same. However, children should realize that in real-life situations rounding up is not always appropriate.

The hundred chart can also be used to develop and to reinforce rounding concepts. The children could use the chart to answer such questions such as "Sixty-three is in which row? What is the number of tens right before sixty-three? After sixty-three? What numbers are between forty and fifty? Which are closer to forty? Closer to fifty? Midway between forty and fifty?"

As the children become more familiar with these concepts, less structure should be given to them in the original problem. They should determine the interval in which the number is contained. The teacher could pose questions such as "If we are counting by tens, how many tens is a little less than forty-three? What is the next group of tens

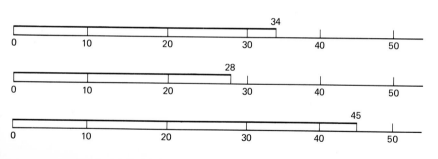

FIGURE 4-26.
Rounding numbers.

after forty-three? If we are counting by tens, seventy-two is between which two groups of ten?" The children should form a generalization as to when they round down and when they round up.

These concepts are extended in later grades to rounding three-digit and four-digit numbers to the nearest hundred and thousand. Most children find this extension relatively easy as long as they are rounding to the largest place value in the given number. Examples for various levels are shown in Figure 4-27. Once children have mastered the type of problems shown in Figure 4-27a and b, they do not need a great deal of practice to extend this skill to the type of problems in parts (c) and (d).

However, rounding numbers to something other than the largest place value—round 356 to the nearest ten or round 13 364 to the nearest thousand—is more difficult for most children. Teacher questions can guide children to consider the place value to which they are rounding and the one to its right. For example, to help children round 356 to the nearest ten, the teacher might ask, "How many tens in 356? 356 lies between what tens? How many ones are there? Is this number more or less than halfway between 35 tens and 36 tens? Should we round up or down? What is the rounded number?" Similar questions can be used to help children

Round to the nearest ten

47   582   1039   698   7341

Round to the nearest thousand

8342   10 682   439 728   63 482   838

FIGURE 4-28.
Rounding to various place values.

round 64 835 to the nearest hundred or 534 682 to the nearest ten thousand. Various levels of practice exercises to help children develop this skill are shown in Figure 4-28.

Special attention needs to be given to exercises such as "round 97 to the nearest ten" or "round 4982 to the nearest hundred." Often children assume that if they are rounding to the nearest hundred, the hundreds digit cannot be zero. Again teacher questions are needed to help children see that since "82" dictates rounding up 1 hundred, then 49 hundreds and 1 more hundred will be 50 hundreds or 5000. Similarly, because 7 ones is more than halfway to another ten, 9 tens and 1 more ten makes 10 tens or 100.

Estimating

Rounded numbers are used for simplicity in situations where we may know the exact number but where that degree of precision is not necessary. In other situations where knowing the exact number is not important, we often use estimation. When the number of objects in a set is small, estimation skills are unnecessary. If a set contains five or fewer objects, students can take in the entire set at a glance and know exactly how many objects are in it without consciously counting. In somewhat larger sets, if the objects are arranged in a pattern such as three rows of four or three sets of four, students can quickly name the exact number of objects in the set without realizing that they have

a. Round to the nearest hundred

436   372   684

b. Round to the nearest thousand

9764   2378   4236

c. Round to the nearest ten thousand

62 408   57 349   83 704

d. Round to the nearest million

1 683 421   5 384 623   7 902 236

FIGURE 4-27.
Rounding larger numbers.

added or multiplied. They are not estimating in these cases; they have simply applied their knowledge about number and its operations to determine an exact answer.

ARRAYS FOR ESTIMATION.   These strategies can be extended to estimating larger numbers. For example, to estimate the number of seats in a theater, stadium, or classroom, a good strategy is to use the array. The students can estimate the number of seats in any one row, estimate the number of rows, and then multiply. If the numbers to be estimated are large, students can estimate a group such as five, ten, or twenty-five and mentally mark off similar-sized groups.

A more difficult problem is to estimate the number of people in the space when the seats are not all filled. In these cases the estimators will have to find an average. They may observe that the seats in front are all filled but that there are very few people in the back rows. They may decide to mentally shift some of the people in the front to the back and then decide that each row has about forty people in it. Another strategy would be to estimate the total number of seats and then estimate what fractional part of the total is filled.

PARTITIONING FOR ESTIMATION.   Partitioning can be used to estimate in some situations such as estimating the number of people in a lunchroom or a restaurant, the number of children on a playground, or the number of cows in a field. When estimating the number of students in a lunchroom, the estimators may note that each group is approximately the same size, so they would estimate the size of one group and the number of groups and then multiply. In a cafe the number of people per table will vary. A person may estimate the average number at each table and

then multiply by the number of tables. Alternatively, a series of additions could be used. The estimator may note there are about six tables with four people . . . about 25, ten tables with three . . . so a total of 55, about 11 tables with two, so . . . around 75 and less than ten people dining individually, so about 80 to 85 people are in the cafe. Notice that at times the estimator compensated overestimating by underestimating, and rounding was used to keep additions simple.

SAMPLING FOR ESTIMATION.   A similar estimation strategy is sampling. In this situation the person considers a small part or sample of the whole. If this sample is about one tenth of the set, the estimate of the sample would be multiplied by ten. Sometimes the sample can be measured. For example, in estimating the number of dried beans in a jar, students could count the number of dried beans in a handful and then estimate the number of handfuls in the jar and multiply (Figure 4-29).

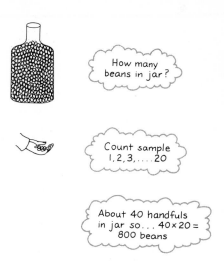

FIGURE 4-29.
Sampling for estimation.

HALVING FOR ESTIMATION. Halving is another good estimation strategy. For example, Penny was estimating the number of geese that had stopped at the game reserve on their way south for the winter. The number to be estimated was very large, so Penny mentally divided the set in half, that half in half, and so on until the set was small enough that she felt comfortable estimating it. She then doubled her estimate of that portion as many times as she had halved the original set to obtain her estimate of the whole flock.

COMPARISONS FOR ESTIMATION. Another effective estimation strategy is the use of comparisons. If students know that a particular room will seat 30 students, and they are in a room twice as large, they simply double thirty to determine the seating capacity. If Jerome knows that he lives seven blocks from school and it takes 10 minutes to walk to school, he may estimate that it would take 15 minutes to walk to the store that is 3 blocks beyond the school.

Becoming good estimators requires many experiences over time. Throughout the school year, students should be given many opportunities to make estimates. They need to have a variety of experiences in which they solve problems by estimating the number of elements in a set, such as people in a room, books on the shelves, cars in the parking lot, or counting sticks on the table. In addition to estimating sets, students should have experiences estimating measures such as lengths, areas, volumes, times, angles, and temperatures. They should write down their estimates and compare results. When everyone has made an estimation of the same quantity, they should note the range of different estimates within the class. They should share their estimation strategies and discuss how to use different strategies effectively.

POSITIONAL AND NONPOSITIONAL NUMERATION SYSTEMS

Our base-ten numeration system is a positional system. A positional system is one that uses place value as discussed in an earlier section. The value of any particular digit depends on its position in the numeral. Thus in Figure 4-30, the digit 2 represents, successively, quantities of two, twenty, two hundred, two thousand, twenty thousand, two hundred thousand, and two million. This is a convenient system because with only ten digits, 0 to 9, any numeral can be written.

Our numeration system is based on groups of ten, but a positional numeration system with some other base (grouping by fours, fives, or sixes) works just as well. In fact other bases are commonly used in certain contexts. The U.S. monetary system is based on ten. However, if a particular selection of coins—pennies, nickels, and quarters—is considered, this is a base-five system. Many items are sold as single units, by the dozen, and by the gross—a base-twelve system.

Young children (and adults too) often group objects by fours or fives to make counting easier. These smaller groups are

Millions	Thousands			Ones		
Ones	Hundreds	Tens	Ones	Hundreds	Tens	Ones
1,	3	6	7,	4	5	2
1,	4	8	9,	3	2	5
1,	6	8	7,	2	3	6
1,	4	9	2,	8	1	0
1,	3	2	0,	5	6	3
1,	2	6	1,	4	8	7
2,	3	0	4,	5	7	1

FIGURE 4-30.
Base-ten numeration.

often easier to use than groups of ten be-cause children can see four objects at a glance, whereas groups of ten must be counted. Using a model such as counting sticks, children can make groups of five each and then group five groups. With money they can see that five pennies make a nickel and five nickels make a quarter. Thus students are learning that there are many different ways of grouping objects, and they are gaining a good foundation for later work with multiplication and division with fives and tens.

Intermediate elementary students can also study bases other than ten to extend their understanding of the base-ten system. The underlying concepts and structure of a positional base-five system are the same as those of our base-ten system. Most students should be able to grasp the basic ideas and to do such things as simple counting in a base other than ten.

Although work with another base system is not a necessary part of the elementary cur-riculum, it is a topic that many students enjoy just because it is new and different or be-cause they can use it to mystify their friends and parents. Also, working with the same ideas of structure, but in another base sys-tem, can cause the student to realize sud-

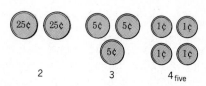

FIGURE 4-31.
Base-five representation of 69¢.

denly that it doesn't matter what number we use as a base; the positional system still has the same structure.

If other base systems are to be taught to elementary students, models are essen-tial. Base five can be easily introduced using money since students are already familiar with the values of coins. To express a num-ber in base five, the students would first find the simplest way to show the number using only quarters, nickels, and pennies. Then they could write the base-five numeral by counting how many of each coin was used. The base-five representation of 69¢ is shown in Figure 4-31.

Other useful models for teaching bases are multibase blocks and interlocking cubes. The same kind of pieces—units, longs, flats, and blocks—are available in other bases or can be built using interlocking cubes. By

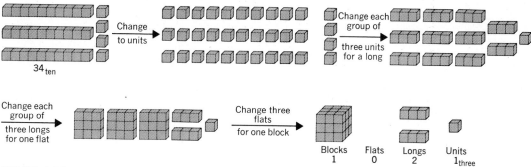

FIGURE 4-32.
Process of changing 34_{ten} to base three.

changing a base-ten number representation all to units and then regrouping the units in another base, students can easily change a base-ten numeral to a numeral in another base. Figure 4-32 shows the process of changing 34_{ten} to base three. This same general process can be used for changing a number from its representation in any one base to its equivalent representation in any other base. Figure 4-33 shows the representation of 34_{ten} in base four, base five, and base six using multibase blocks.

When students are ready to represent numbers with numerals in other bases, they can invent their own new symbols instead of using the same symbols that they use for base ten. A possible set of symbols for base five is shown in Figure 4-34. Students can also invent their own oral names for the numbers. Inventing numerals and oral names for their base-five system will help students avoid confusing these numerals and oral

Numerical symbol	Number of apples represented by symbol
φ	
\	
X	
X̄	
X̲	
\φ	

FIGURE 4-34.
Symbols for base five.

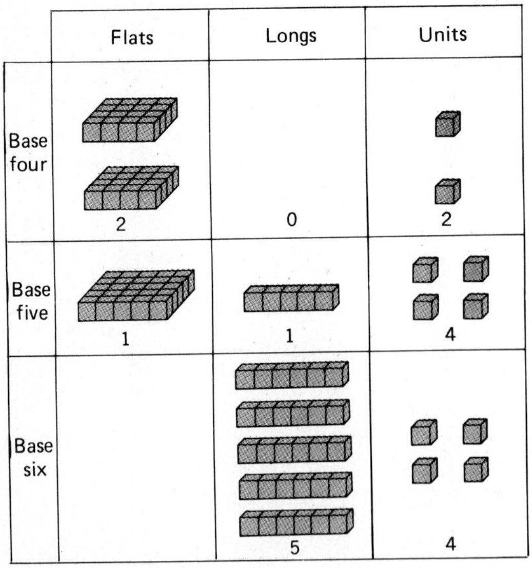

names with those for base ten. The activity should include creating a pattern with the oral names similar to the base-ten system. A discussion could also include renaming the base-ten teen numbers so that the pattern is consistent.

Teachers and students alike will benefit from studying bases other than base ten. It will help them better understand the structure of a positional number system, hence of our own base-ten system. Study of other bases is an excellent enrichment topic. Particularly for primary-grade teachers, the study of an unfamiliar base system is a good activity to help them understand what the beginning student encounters in learning the base-ten system.

Since everyday operations are done with a positional base-ten system, this system seems only natural. However, this is not the only numeration system that has been used. When primitive people first began us-

	Flats	Longs	Units
Base four	2	0	2
Base five	1	1	4
Base six		5	4

FIGURE 4-33.
Multibase blocks.

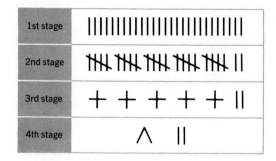

1st stage	‖‖‖‖‖‖‖‖‖‖‖‖‖‖‖‖‖‖‖‖‖‖
2nd stage	𝍫𝍫 𝍫𝍫 𝍫𝍫 𝍫𝍫 𝍫𝍫 ‖
3rd stage	+ + + + + ‖
4th stage	∧ ‖

FIGURE 4-35.
Numeration progression.

ing written symbols to represent numbers, they probably used some sort of tally system; that is, they simply made as many marks as they had sheep or whatever.

Later they probably realized that some type of grouping would make it easier to see at a glance how many tally marks they had. Still later they began using a separate single symbol to represent these groups and then another symbol for groups of groups. This progression is shown in Figure 4-35. This system is nonpositional. A symbol ∧ means 25 or 5 groups of five no matter what position it occupies. The fourth stage shown would represent the same number if it were written ‖∧ or |∧|. The symbols have only face value, not place value.

Many ancient people used nonpositional systems. These systems were employed strictly for recording, not for computation. Computation was all done with models, usually some form of an abacus.

Some students may be interested in studying the historical uses of the abacus as a computation tool. They will find that several different types of abacuses have been used (Figure 4-36). Considering the advantages and disadvantages of each type can help reinforce place-value concepts. These students may also want to compare the abacus

to today's hand-held calculator as a computational aid.

Eventually, someone studied the procedures that were used with the abacus and realized that the same process could be done in writing. A symbol was used to represent the quantity on each wire of the abacus. Before this, a zero symbol was never needed because zero was not used in counting. But if the written system were to be positional like the abacus computational system, a zero symbol would be needed to represent an empty wire on the abacus.

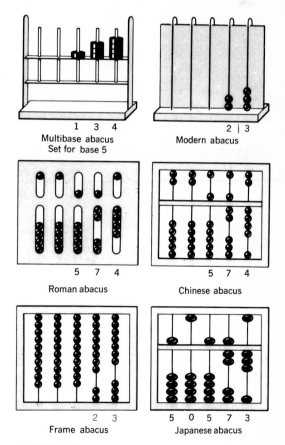

FIGURE 4-36.
Types of abacuses.

One ancient numeration system that is still used for some things, such as to express a certain year, and is therefore usually taught in the elementary school, is the Roman numeral system. While this system is not positional in the sense that our Hindu-Arabic system is, neither is it a strictly nonpositional system. If a symbol for a small value came after a symbol for a large value, the two values were added. Thus, when the symbol for 1 (I) was written after the symbol for 10 (X), the value represented was 11 (XI). But if the symbol for the smaller value was written before the symbol for the larger value, the smaller value was subtracted from the larger value. Thus IX represented ten minus one, or nine. It is interesting to note that this system has separate symbols for 5 (V), 50 (L), and 500 (D), as well as the symbols for 1 (I), 10 (X), 100 (C), and 1000 (M).

QUESTIONS AND ACTIVITIES

1. Why is it essential that a child be given experiences counting by tens? By hundreds?

2. Most counting books represent the numbers one through ten. Read Tana Hoban's *Count and See* and describe how she introduces the multiples of ten.

3. At first a child determines "how many" through rational counting. What are two different ways that a child who has been introduced to grouping and place value should be able to "count" the following sets?
   a. 3 bundles of ten
   b. bundles showing 42
   c. base-ten blocks showing 57
   d. base-ten blocks showing 135
   e. base-ten blocks showing 307

4. Represent the following numbers using counting sticks and base-ten blocks: 37, 52, 40, 123. How would you use each model to help children with the oral names for the representations? How would you use each model to help children learn to write the numerals for the representations?

5. Represent the following numbers using base-ten blocks and an abacus: 72, 325, 106, 1235, 3402. How would you help children with the transition from base-ten blocks to the abacus? How would you use each model to help children with the oral names for the representations? How would you use each model to help children learn to write the numerals for the representations?

6. For each of the following concepts, write a story situation that children can solve with models.
   a. three more than two hundred
   b. five less than twenty
   c. comparing 34 and 52
   d. deciding whether 225 or 252 is larger
   e. finding a number halfway between 60 and 70

7. Solve the following riddles using a hundred chart. What concepts are being taught?
   a. I am a number that contains an eight and I am in the twenties. Who am I?
   b. I am more than seventy but less than eighty. One of my digits is also in sixty. Who am I?
   c. I have the same digits as 25 but I have a different value. Who am I.
   d. I am halfway between fifty and sixty. Who am I?
   e. Both of my digits are the same and I am close to thirty. Who am I?
   f. I am halfway between thirty and fifty. Who am I?
   g. I am more than sixty but closer to seventy than sixty. Who could I be?
   h. Create two riddles of your own.

8. Use base-ten blocks to find another name for each number.

a. 12 tens
b. 12 hundreds
c. 42 using only 3 tens
d. 103 using only 9 tens
e. 1034 using only 9 hundreds

9. Use only the ⬚1, ⬚0, and ⬚+ keys on your calculator to display the numeral 3048. What is the minimum number of entries needed to solve the problem? List the code you used to solve the problem.

10. a. Consult a beginning numeration unit in the teacher's edition of an elementary textbook. What models are used? What teaching suggestions are given to help children link models to oral language? To numerals?

    b. *For your resource file:* Beattie describes how to make a booklet that would help children reinforce the connections among models, oral names, numerals, and place value.

    c. *For your resource file:* Copy and read "Developing Numeration Concepts and Skills" by Harrison and Harrison for activities involving place value, ordering, and rounding for two-digit and larger numbers.

11. a. Draw and label a place-value chart similar to the one shown in Figure 4-30. Write the numeral for each of the following numbers in your chart.
      (1) thirty-five thousand three hundred eight
      (2) eight hundred thousand seventy-eight
      (3) thirteen billion six hundred
      (4) seven hundred million thirteen thousand six

    b. Read the numerals in Figure 4-30 reflecting on how the chart can be used to help students use the correct oral names.

    c. *For your resource file:* In "Let's Do It: Some Aids for Teaching Place Value" O'Neil and Jensen suggest some activities for reading and writing larger numbers.

12. List step by step the thinking a student needs to develop to be able to order the following pairs of numbers: 123 and 97, 48 and 63, 483 and 435.

13. a. Devise an activity using models that would help children develop the appropriate thinking for ordering 483 and 435. Include appropriate teacher questions that would guide your students in developing this thinking.

    b. *For your resource file:* "Ideas" by Bright contains some activity sheets on ordering one-, two-, and three-digit numbers. In "Ideas" (1975) Burns includes some problem-solving activities and games for numeration.

14. A game for teaching the concept of bases is called chip trading. The equipment is shown below. Each of the colors—yellow, blue, green, red, and black—represents a different place value. To play, the children roll a single die and are given that number of yellow chips. They then trade whatever chips they can, at the rate specified, for chips of greater value. The first child to acquire a black chip is the winner.

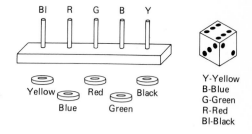

a. Play this game with a classmate.
b. If the trading rule is 3 for 1, regroup the chips in the accompanying diagram so that the same number is represented in simplest form.

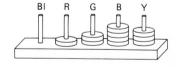

c. A child has the chips shown here and rolls a six. If the trading rule is 4 for 1, show step by step all the trades the child can make. Write the base-four numeral for the final number shown on the chip board.

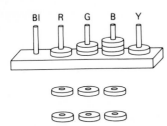

d. *For your resource file:* Copy and read the article on grouping by Bruni and Silverman.

15. a. Adapt the chip-trading game described in Problem 14 to a base-ten game. For larger goals you may want to use two or three dice. Since children need an organized work space, each player should partition a sheet of paper to form a playing board like the one shown in Figure 4-21. Adapt the board as the situations change. With one to three others, play the game using the following guidelines.
(1) Use counting sticks with a goal of 34. A goal of 100.
(2) Use base-ten blocks with a goal of 100. A goal of 175 starting with 103. A goal of 23 starting with 85.
(3) Use chip trading or an abacus with a goal of 206.
b. Reflect on these variations. How did they differ conceptually? What was the purpose of each? Did you provide a penalty if a player neglected to regroup? By using guidelines such as "the person who notes the error receives 5 units from the person who made the error," children will become involved in everyone's turn, not just their own turns.
c. This game involves models only. Adapt it to focus on model → oral tasks. To focus on model → numeral tasks.
d. Modify this game to extend the place-value pattern. For example, use base-ten blocks to play to a goal of 1000. Similarly, use chip trading or an abacus to play to a goal of 2001; to a goal of 540 starting with 700.

16. Use the symbols given in the chart to answer the following questions.

0	0
1	1
2	∧
3	△

a. Using only these symbols, write a nonpositional numeral equivalent to 11.
b. Assuming that these are all the symbols you have, write a positional numeral equivalent to 11.

17. Donald Duck encountered the number system in this chart while touring Mathemagic Land.

Base-ten equivalent	New system
1	1
2	X
3	X̄
4	X̲
5	Ⓧ
6	10
7	11
8	1X
9	1X̄
10	1X̲

a. What is the base of this system?

b. Is it a positional or a nonpositional numeration system? Explain.

18. Use base-ten blocks to represent each of the following numbers, and then round as directed. Devise questions that would help students focus on what interval the given number is in and how they would decide on the answer.

a. Round 42 to the nearest ten.

b. Round 37 to the nearest ten.

c. Round 75 to the nearest ten.

d. Round 103 to the nearest ten.

e. Round 324 to the nearest ten.

f. Round 324 to the nearest hundred.

19. a. Describe how you could use a hundred chart to round 42 to the nearest ten. 76 to the nearest ten.

b. *For your resource file:* Copy one of the following articles. In "Let's Do It: The Versatile Hundred Board," Horak and Horak describe activities involving counting, number, addition, subtraction, and multiplication using the hundred board. In "Ideas," Burns (1974) includes activity sheets on problem solving and pattern boards.

20. *Materials needed:* Container of Cuisenaire rods. Given that the white rod has a value of one, estimate the total value of the rods in the container. Write down your estimate. Devise an efficient plan to find the actual total. Carry out the plan and compare this total with your estimate.

21. a. List the strategies that were discussed for estimating number. Define them in your own words.

b. Use an appropriate strategy for estimating each of the situations below. Write your estimate and the strategy that you used for each situation.

(1) the number of people in your mathematics methods class

(2) the number of chairs in the room of your mathematics methods class

(3) the number of people having lunch at the main cafeteria in the student union

(4) the number of chairs in the main cafeteria in the student union

(5) the number of people on the main floor in the library in the evening

(6) the numer of people who use one of the copying machines in the library each hour

(7) the number of people at the parade (volleyball, basketball, or football game)

(8) the number of windows in one of the big dorms on campus

22. Name three situations in which an approximation is appropriate. Describe two real-life situations in which you would round down.

23. Master Mind is a popular commercial strategy game. A similar game can be played with whole numbers. One player would write down a four-digit number. The other player would try to figure out what the number is within ten turns. The second player would write down a four-digit number and then ask the other player if this number is correct. The first player would respond with such information as "two of the digits are correct and one place value is correct." Based on this information the second player would venture a second guess, and so on until either the number is discovered or ten turns have passed. Variations of this game would be to change the number of digits involved, the number of place values involved, or the number of turns allowed. For example, younger children (K-2) might play this game using two-digit numbers with only the digits 1 through 5.

24. In "Computer Corner," Ryoti includes a program called Guess, a game for two people. One player enters a number; the other player tries to guess it. Players receive only information as to whether the number entered is greater than or less than the current guess. Copy the program and play the game with another student.

25. *For your resource file:* Create or collect some activities that could be used to help children learn the following concepts.
    a. counting by tens and hundreds
    b. grouping and place value
    c. the six tasks involving models, oral names, and numerals
    d. renamings
    e. comparing and ordering
    f. rounding
    g. estimating

    A resource that would be helpful is "Number and Numeration." Payne and Rathmell describe the rationale and sequence of number. Activities for number, one-digit through three-digit, are included throughout the article.

26. *For your resource file:* Read and copy the ideas from one of the following articles. All of the articles include information on making or collecting materials for manipulatives and activities for using these manipulatives. Dana and Lindquist describe how to use graph paper to make base-ten materials. Van de Walle and Thompson (1981) describe how to make bean sticks. Burton describes a variety of models for number and numeration.

27. Children are intrigued with large numbers and also need to get a sense of these numbers. Read and write an evaluation of one of the following resources. In the children's book, *How Much Is a Million?*, Schwartz cleverly introduces a million, a billion, and a trillion. In "How to Make a Million," Harrison describes how the class made a cubic meter and related it to a million cubic centimeters.

28. Two children's books that introduce bases other than ten are *Base Five* by Adler and *Binary Numbers* by Watson. Read one of these books and describe how it could be used to introduce base five or base two.

29. Read the children's book *How to Count Like a Martian* by St. John. This book could readily be used by students to develop their own numeration system. What would be the purpose of such an activity?

30. Various activities are described in the children's book *Roman Numerals* by Adler. Work through the activities described in this book.

31. *For your resource file:* In "Developing Problem-Solving Ability with Multiple-Condition Problems," Greenes and Schulman present problems involving place value and operations for students in grades three through eight. Explicit activities are described using Polya's steps as the framework for problem solving. Read this article and add it to your resource file.

32. *For your resource file:* Read Van de Walle and Thompson (1985) for estimation activities involving sets, lengths, and areas.

33. *For your resource file:* A variety of games utilize dice or cards. Horak and Horak describe various games involving early number concepts, addition, subtraction, and place value in "Let's Do It: Dice Have Many Uses." Lund describes a variety of card games in "Tricks of the Trade with Cards." Add one of these articles to your resource file.

TEACHER RESOURCES

Baratta-Lorton, Mary. *Mathematics Their Way.* Reading, MA: Addison-Wesley, 1973.

Beattie, Ian D. "The Number Namer: An Aid to Understanding Place Value." *Arithmetic Teacher* 33 (January 1986): 24–28.

Bright, George W. "Ideas." *Arithmetic Teacher* 25 (April 1978): 28–32.

Bruni, James V., and Helene Silverman. "Let's Do It: Developing the Concept of Grouping." *Arithmetic Teacher* 21 (October 1974): 474–479.

Burns, Marilyn. "Ideas." *Arithmetic Teacher* 21 (November 1974): 601–610.

———. "Ideas." *Arithmetic Teacher 22* (October 1975): 477–484.

Burton, Grace M. "Teaching the Most Basic Basic." *Arithmetic Teacher 32* (September 1984): 20–25.

Charbonneau, Manon. *Hidden Rods/Hidden Numbers.* New Rochelle, NY: Cuisenaire, 1975.

Clements, Douglas H., and Leroy G. Callahan. "Number or Prenumber Foundational Experiences for Young Children: Must We Choose?" *Arithmetic Teacher 31* (November 1983): 34–37.

Dana, Marcia E., and Mary Montgomery Lindquist. "Let's Do It: Let Squares Do Their Thing." *Arithmetic Teacher 26* (October 1978): 6–10.

Gibb, E. Glenadine, and Alberta M. Castaneda. "Experiences for Young Children." In *Mathematics Learning in Early Childhood,* Thirty-seventh Yearbook of the National Council of Teachers of Mathematics, pp. 95–104. Reston, VA: The Council, 1975.

Greenes, Carole E., and Linda Schulman. "Developing Problem-Solving Ability with Multiple-Condition Problems." *Arithmetic Teacher 30* (October 1982): 18–21.

Harrison, Marilyn, and Bruce Harrison. "Developing Numeration Concepts and Skills." *Arithmetic Teacher 33* (February 1986) 18–21, 60.

Harrison, William B. "How to Make a Million." *Arithmetic Teacher 33* (September 1985): 46–47.

Hendrickson, A. Dean. "A Psychologically Sound Primary School Mathematics Curriculum." *Arithmetic Teacher 30* (January 1983): 42–47.

Horak, Virginia K., and Willis J. Horak. "Let's Do It: 'Button Bag' Mathematics." *Arithmetic Teacher 30* (March 1983): 10–16.

———. "Let's Do It: Dice Have Many Uses." *Arithmetic Teacher 30* (February 1983): 8–11, 52.

———. "Let's Do It: The Versatile Hundred Board." *Arithmetic Teacher 30* (October 1982): 10–16.

Leutzinger, Larry, and Glenn Nelson. "Let's Do It: Positive Patterning." *Arithmetic Teacher 27* (September 1979): 8–13.

Liedtke, W. "Rational Counting." *Arithmetic Teacher 26* (October 1978): 20–26.

———. "Young Chldren—Small Numbers: Making Numbers Come Alive." *Arithmetic Teacher 31* (September 1983): 34–36.

Lindquist, Mary Montgomery, and Marcia E. Dana. "Let's Do It: Make Counting Really Count." *Arithmetic Teacher 25* (May 1978): 4–11.

Lund, Charles H. "Tricks of the Trade with Cards." *Arithmetic Teacher 24* (February 1977): 104–111.

O'Neil, David R., and Rosalie S. Jensen. "Let's Do It: Some Aids for Teaching Place Value." *Arithmetic Teacher 29* (November 1981): 6–9.

Payne, Joseph N., and Edward C. Rathmell. "Number and Numeration." In *Mathematics Learning in Early Childhood,* Thirty-seventh Yearbook of the National Council of Teachers of Mathematics, pp. 125–160. Reston, VA: The Council, 1975.

Ryoti, Don E. "Computer Corner." *Arithmetic Teacher 34* (September 1986) 46–47.

Suydam, Marilyn N. "Research Report: The Process of Counting." *Arithmetic Teacher 33* (January 1986): 29.

Van de Walle, John, and Charles S. Thompson. "Let's Do It: Estimate How Much." *Arithmetic Teacher 32* (May 1985): 4–8.

———. "Let's Do It: Give Bean Sticks a New Look." *Arithmetic Teacher 28* (March 1981): 6–12.

CHILDREN'S LITERATURE

Adler, David A. *Base Five.* Illustrated by Larry Ross. New York: Crowell, 1975.

————. *Roman Numerals*. Illustrated by Byron Barton. New York: Crowell, 1977.

Anno, Mitsumasa. *Anno's Counting Book*. Illustrated by the author. New York: Crowell, 1975.

————. *Anno's Counting House*. Illustrated by the author. New York: Philomel Books, 1982.

Berenstain, Stanley, and Janice Berenstain. *Bears on Wheels*. Illustrated by the authors. New York: Random House, 1969.

Burningham, John. *Count Up: Learning Sets*. New York: Viking Press, 1983.

————. *Five Down: Numbers as Signs*. New York: Viking Press, 1983.

————. *Just Cats: Learning Groups*. New York: Viking Press, 1983.

————. *Read One: Numbers as Words*. New York: Viking Press, 1983.

Charosh, Mannis, and Dorothy Bloomfield (Eds.). *Number Ideas Through Pictures*. Illustrated by Giulio Maestro. New York: Crowell, 1974.

Feelings, Muriel. *Moja Means One: The Swahili Counting Book*. Illustrated by Tom Feelings. New York: Dial Books, 1971.

Froman, Robert. *Venn Diagrams*. Illustrated by Jan Pyk. New York: Crowell, 1972.

Gerstein, Mordicai. *Roll Over*. Illustrated by the author. New York: Crown Publishers, 1984.

Hoban, Russell, and Sylvie Selig. *Ten What? A Mystery Counting Book*. Illustrated by Sylvie Selig. New York: Scribner, 1975.

Hoban, Tana. *Count and See*. New York: Macmillan, 1974.

————. *1, 2, 3*. Illustrated by the author. New York: Greenwillow Books, 1985.

Kingsley, Emily Perl, Jeffery Moss, Norman Stiles, and Daniel Wilcox. *The Sesame Street 1, 2, 3 Storybook*. Illustrated by Joseph Mathieu, Kelly Oechsli, Mel Crawford, and Bob Taylor. New York: Random House, 1973.

Kredenser, Gail. *One Dancing Drum*. Illustrated by Stanley Mack. New York: Phillips, 1971.

Leighton, Ralph, and Carl Feynman. *How to Count Sheep Without Falling Asleep*. Illustrated by George Ulrich. Englewood Cliffs, NJ: Prentice-Hall, 1976.

Lewin, Betsy. *Cat Count*. Illustrated by the author. New York: Dodd, Mead, 1981.

Loots, Barbara. *Fun on the Farm with Numbers*. Illustrated by Ellen Sloan. Kansas City, MO: Hallmark.

Pienkowski, Jan. *Numbers*. New York: Harvey House, 1975.

St. John, Glory. *How to Count Like a Martian*. New York: Henry Z. Walck, 1975.

Schwartz, David M. *How Much Is a Million?* Illustrated by Steven Kellogg. New York: Lothrop, Lee and Shepard, 1985.

Sitomer, Mindel, and Harry Sitomer. *How Did Numbers Begin?* Illustrated by Richard Cuffari. New York: Crowell, 1976.

————. *Zero Is Not Nothing*. Illustrated by Richard Cuffari. New York: Crowell, 1978.

Watson, Clyde. *Binary Numbers*. Illustrated by Wendy Watson. New York: Crowell, 1977.

Yeoman, John. *Sixes and Sevens*. Illustrated by Blake Quentin. New York: Macmillan, 1974.

5
TEACHING NUMERATION OF COMMON AND DECIMAL FRACTIONS

"Our district doesn't have the money to buy models."

"Calculators? Our parent association bought three classroom sets—each set has a calculator for every two students."

"I had some cardboard base-ten materials and fraction bars run off on the ditto machine. Ms. Whalen's students made fraction bars in class."

"Three of the other teachers from my building were also interested in ordering models, so we pooled our requests. We realized that we were always spending our supply money on workbooks or ditto masters that needed to be replaced yearly."

"I'm a first-year teacher. The school I teach in doesn't have models. The other teachers seem to manage without, so. . . . Everyone says they are so expensive."

Discuss with classmates the statements above. What materials do you anticipate will be available in your first classroom? How will you handle this situation?

COMMON FRACTIONS

In Chapter 4 in the discussion of teaching numeration, only whole numbers were considered. Often it is necessary to express parts of something, and for this purpose fractions are needed. Most children already have some beginning fraction concepts when they enter school. The fact that these fraction concepts are often rather vague is shown by such statements as, "I want the bigger half." On the other hand, when Shawn says, "That's not fair; Kari's half is bigger than mine," he is forming a clearer idea of half as being one of two equal parts.

CONCEPT OF COMMON FRACTIONS

The concept of equal-sized parts is just one of the ideas that children encounter in their study of fractions. Four principal ideas must be exemplified in the models and diagrams used to develop the concept of fractions. They are:

1. The size and shape of the whole unit.
2. Whether the whole is divided into equal-sized parts.
3. The number of equal-sized parts in the whole.
4. The number of parts being considered.

These ideas, as well as the sequence of developing the concepts, are discussed in the examples that follow. (The activities illustrating common fractions and equivalent fractions are based on "A Teaching Sequence from Initial Fraction Concepts Through the Addition of Unlike Fractions" by Ellerbruch and Payne.)

As with the development of whole numbers, models of fractions and their oral names are developed before the number names for fractions are introduced. The oral names and models for developing the concepts of one half, one third, and one fourth are usually introduced at the end of kindergarten or at the beginning of first grade. Most textbooks introduce these fractions as "parts of a whole" or measurement models. This approach is easily understood and many different models can be used for needed explanation. There are few classrooms that do not have circular models divided into pie-shaped pieces to represent halves, thirds, fourths, and so on, to demonstrate fractions. But if only pie-shaped pieces are used, the children's concept of fractions might be limited to regions of circles. Fractions should be expressed as parts of other figures whose sizes and shapes vary (Figure 5-1).

The diagrams in this figure also show wholes that are not divided into equal-sized parts. Children need to discriminate whether or not wholes are divided into equal-sized parts. They should have many activities that involve folding, coloring, or cutting figures into equal parts. One activity could be folding a worksheet into two equal-sized parts. The teacher should encourage each child to fold the paper in several different ways. To check whether a solution is correct, the child can cut along the folded line and then see if one part will fit exactly on top of the other.

A similar activity could be done using rectangles of various sizes or figures of various shapes. A class discussion on the "size" of one half should follow this experiment. With activities of this sort children can discover that the size of one half is dependent on the size of the whole. They can then notice that although one half must always be equal to the other half of the same whole, two halves taken from different wholes are not necessarily equal. These activities

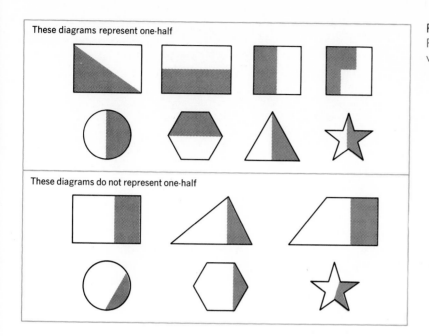

FIGURE 5-1.
Fractions as part of a whole.

should be extended to other fractions such as thirds and fourths.

Another essential idea of fractions and their models that needs to be considered is the total number of equal-sized parts in the whole—the denominator. As mentioned earlier, the first fractions children are introduced to are one half, one third, and one fourth. The teacher should introduce different sheets of the same-sized papers divided into 2, 3, and 4 equal-sized parts and relate the names of halves, thirds, and fourths respectively. The question should be posed to the class that if they were offered one of the parts, would they choose a part from the halves, the thirds, or the fourths if they wanted the smallest part? The biggest part? The class should develop the generalization that the greater the number of equal-sized parts the smaller each part will be.

The last idea is the number of parts being considered—the numerator. As chil-dren are first introduced to unit fractions, fractions whose numerators are one, the emphasis is on one concept—the number of equal-sized pieces. Children can be introduced to other fractions, such as three fourths or three fifths, by having them shade, respectively, three of four parts or three of five parts.

After the children are familiar with the models and the oral names for fractions, the symbolic form of the fractions can be introduced (Figure 5-2). Since the parts being considered are usually shaded, the numer-

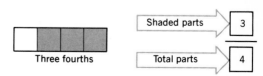

FIGURE 5-2.
Model—Oral name—Number name.

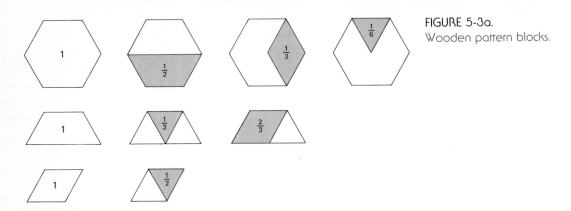

FIGURE 5-3a.
Wooden pattern blocks.

ator and denominator of the fraction can be labeled as shown.

Another useful model for developing the concept of fractions is wooden pattern blocks (Figure 5-3a). The hexagon can be defined as one, making the trapezoid equal to one half, the rhombus equal to one third, and the triangle equal to one sixth. Or the trapezoid can be defined as one, making the triangle equal to one third and the rhombus equal to two thirds. Or if the rhombus is defined as one, the triangle is then equal to one half. Some children may have difficulty visualizing the total number of parts. For example, in the case of the hexagon, they may need to cover the hexagon with the triangular pieces to determine that each triangle represents one sixth. This problem-solving activity helps emphasize that before children know the size of one half or one third, they must know the size of one whole.

All the measurement models described above were region models. Another type of measurement model is the number line. This conceptually more abstract model should be introduced by using a region model such as fraction bars, as shown in Figure 5-3b. After a line is drawn, a student can use a fraction bar to mark off equal-sized parts. These parts should then be labeled. Using the fraction bar with the number line will help em-

phasize that the entire interval rather than the labeled mark represents the number.

A second type of model that is necessary for a complete understanding of fractions is the concept of a fraction as "part of a set" (Figure 5-4). This approach is usually introduced after region models because it seems to be harder to understand. Children may look at the diagram representing three fourths and see only that there are four objects rather than considering *one group* of four objects. Another problem in interpreting these models is that children often look at the set as two separate parts. They would read Figure 5-4c as "one fifth" because they

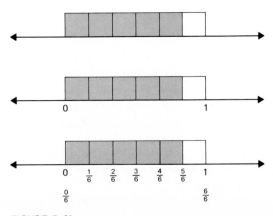

FIGURE 5-3b.
Fraction number line.

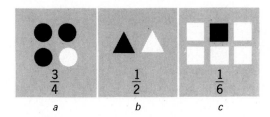

$\dfrac{3}{4}$

a

$\dfrac{1}{2}$

b

$\dfrac{1}{6}$

c

FIGURE 5-4.
Fractions as part of a set.

are comparing the black objects to the white objects instead of comparing the black objects to the entire set.

With this set model, the denominator represents the total number in the set while the numerator represents the number in the subset being considered. In teaching this concept of fractions, an egg carton could be used to present a set. Children could then place objects in the different sections to represent various fractions. Egg cartons could also be cut into smaller sections for working

with sets other than 12 (Figure 5-5). Here, too, the student should be helped to realize that the size of the fraction is dependent on the size of the set.

As children explore and extend fraction concepts, they should relate these ideas to division of whole numbers. Models and real-life situations are needed to help them relate fractions such as $\frac{3}{4}$ to 3 ÷ 4. To exemplify 3 ÷ 4, "Marta, Don, Cathy, and Kim ordered three different kinds of pizza to share equally among themselves. Each of them would like to try each kind; what part of a pizza would each person get?" (Figure 5-6b). If these parts were rearranged, each person's share would be 3 fourths of a pizza (Figure 5-6c). This is similar to the situation, "Marta ordered a pizza and ate three of the four slices. What part of the pizza did she eat?" as in either case Marta eats the same amount of pizza.

A good activity to help reinforce children's understanding of the part-whole relationship would be to give them a certain

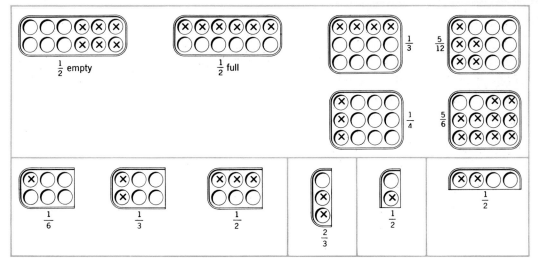

FIGURE 5-5.
Egg carton fractions.

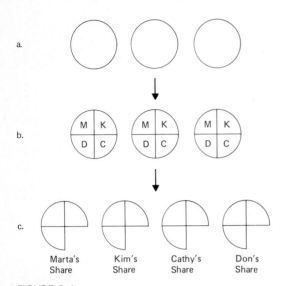

Complete the whole		Complete the set	
□	⊟	••• •••	✕ ✕ ✕
$\frac{1}{2}$	$\frac{2}{4}$	$\frac{1}{3}$	$\frac{3}{4}$

FIGURE 5-7.
Part—whole relationship of a fraction.

FIGURE 5-6.
Relating division to fractions.

fractional part of a region and ask them to complete the region (Figure 5-7). Teacher questions to motivate the discussion should include: "How many parts of the whole are shown? How many parts in the whole? How many more parts do you need to draw?" This

activity should be extended using set models.

Fractions equal to or greater than one should now be introduced using both region and set models (Figure 5-8). These fractions have been called improper fractions, but most texts are now deleting the term "improper." Two different forms of writing these fractions are commonly used, the fraction form and the mixed-number form. These forms are simply two different names for the same fraction concept. In some cases one form may more clearly represent the concept than the other form even though the numbers are equivalent.

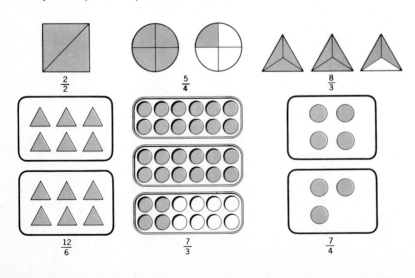

FIGURE 5-8.
Fractions equal to or greater than one.

Consider the following example. "How much pie is needed if we wish to serve one sixth of a pie to each of seven people?" The person serving the pie will be working with 7 pieces (7 sixths); whereas the cook may be planning on baking one pie and serving that and the one piece left over from the luncheon (one and one sixth). Thus either $\frac{7}{6}$ or $1\frac{1}{6}$ is a correct answer to the original question. Depending on the situation, students may sometimes be allowed to choose either form and other times be required to use one form or the other. In either case students need to know that both forms name the same fractional number.

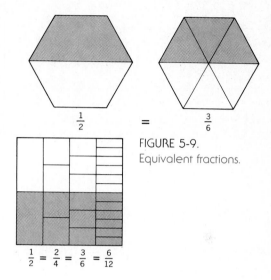

FIGURE 5-9.
Equivalent fractions.

$$\frac{1}{2} = \frac{2}{4} = \frac{3}{6} = \frac{6}{12}$$

EQUIVALENT FRACTIONS

As students become comfortable with the meanings of fractions, they should be introduced to the concept of equivalent fractions. Again models should be used. Figure 5-9 illustrates equivalent fractions using pattern blocks and fraction bars.

Paperfolding is an excellent activity in which children can represent fractions and equivalent fractions. Folding papers in halves is easy. This process can be extended to represent fourths, eighths, and sixteenths. Later, this thinking is helpful in renaming fractions since halves can readily be transformed to fourths or eighths.

Other fractions, such as thirds and sixths, are similarly related. For example, children learn to fold thirds because letters are commonly folded in thirds before mailing. This skill can be extended to represent sixths, ninths, and twelfths. Note that sixths required foldings for halves and thirds. Halves and thirds can both be renamed as sixths.

Fifths and tenths should also be introduced early as students encounter tenths in many situations both in and out of the elementary classroom. Fifths can be folded after children can estimate thirds. Figure 5-10 shows a procedure for folding fifths. Students can then adapt this procedure to represent tenths.

When children are introduced to this activity, the emphasis should not be on equivalent fractions but simply on how denominators are related. Later, these same activities can be extended for learning about equivalent fractions.

Another model for representing equivalent fractions is Cuisenaire rods. If the red

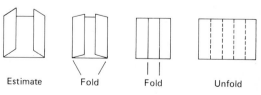

| Estimate | Fold | Fold | Unfold |

FIGURE 5-10.
Folding fifths.

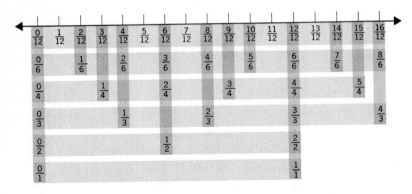

FIGURE 5-11.
Fractional family number line.

rod is the unit of one, the white rod is one half since two white rods are the same length as one red rod. Similarly, if the orange rod is one, the yellow rod is one half; or if the purple rod is one, then the red rod is one half. The students also know other names for the rods, so they could name the various models $\frac{1}{2}$, $\frac{5}{10}$, and $\frac{2}{4}$, respectively. If the blue rod were defined as one, a light green rod would represent one third, as three light green rods are the same length as one blue rod. Another name for the light green rod would be three ninths. Two light green rods would represent $\frac{2}{3}$ or $\frac{6}{9}$.

Fraction bars are another model that can be used to represent equivalent fractions. First children can sort the bars into sets that each have the same amount of shading. The results for each set can be recorded to show various names for the same amount (Figure 5-9). These results could also be recorded on a number line. In this case, the students could draw number lines for twelfths and then record all the names they found for each number of twelfths (Figure 5-11). The class should observe and discuss the fact that some fractions have a number of equivalent names, whereas others, such as $\frac{7}{12}$, do not have equivalent names with the denominators represented. At a glance the children can see that $\frac{1}{2}$, $\frac{2}{4}$, $\frac{3}{6}$, and $\frac{6}{12}$ are all names for the same number

or that $\frac{3}{4}$ is larger than $\frac{2}{3}$. Extending this number line beyond 1 is a good way to reinforce the idea that there are fractional numbers equal to or greater than 1 and that these fractions, too, can be written in many different forms.

Often the emphasis in these activities is placed on renaming fractions in higher terms. Children also need to practice renaming fractions such as $\frac{6}{8}$, $\frac{3}{9}$, or $\frac{6}{12}$ in lower terms. National Assessment results show that children are able to represent a fraction when given a diagram divided into the same number of parts as the denominator. If the diagram has more parts, the students have difficulty. Examples of these two different types of problems are shown in Figure 5-12. In the second problem, children *see* twelfths. They need to be able to reinterpret the diagram in terms of thirds.

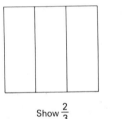

Show $\frac{2}{3}$ Show $\frac{2}{3}$

FIGURE 5-12.
Representing fractions.

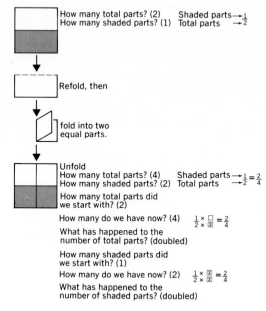

How many total parts? (2)   Shaded parts $\rightarrow \frac{1}{2}$
How many shaded parts? (1)   Total parts $\rightarrow \frac{1}{2}$

Refold, then

fold into two
equal parts.

Unfold
How many total parts? (4)   Shaded parts $\rightarrow \frac{1}{2} = \frac{2}{4}$
How many shaded parts? (2)   Total parts $\rightarrow \frac{1}{2}$ $\frac{4}{}$

How many total parts did
we start with? (2)

How many do we have now? (4) $\frac{1}{2} \times \frac{\square}{\boxed{2}} = \frac{2}{4}$

What has happened to the
number of total parts? (doubled)

How many shaded parts did
we start with? (1)

How many do we have now? (2) $\frac{1}{2} \times \frac{\boxed{2}}{\boxed{2}} = \frac{2}{4}$

What has happened to the
number of shaded parts? (doubled)

FIGURE 5-13.
Algorithm for equivalent fractions.

After children have had experiences renaming fractions with models, they should be introduced to the algorithm for this renaming. Paperfolding is again an appropriate activity. For example, one half could be folded, shaded, and recorded numerically (Figure 5-13). The paper should then be refolded and this section folded once more. Before unfolding the paper, the children should be asked to guess how many total parts the paper will now be folded into and how many parts will be shaded. They should then unfold the paper to check their guesses.

After the children have recorded the number of total and shaded parts, the teacher should direct their attention to the total parts. The children should compare the number of total parts that they started with to the final number of total parts. They

should observe that the number of parts doubled or that the number of parts is two times more. They then record that the original number of total parts has been multiplied by two. Then the class should compare the original number of shaded parts and the final number of shaded parts. They should conclude and record that the number of shaded parts has also doubled or has been multiplied by two. This activity should be repeated with other fractions.

When children were learning to rename fractions informally with models, they should also have been learning that these fractions can be renamed in either higher or lower terms. Just as they saw from models that $\frac{1}{2}$ could be renamed as $\frac{3}{6}$, they also saw that $\frac{3}{6}$ can be renamed as $\frac{1}{2}$. When they were first introduced to the algorithm, children were renaming fractions to others whose numerators and denominators were a multiple of the original numerator and denominator (Figure 5-14a).

They also need to learn the *algorithm* for renaming a fraction to simpler form. When the numerator and the denominator have a common factor, they may both be divided by that factor to rename the fraction in simpler form (Figure 5-14b). These two procedures are inversely related. One procedure "undoes" the other procedure.

Although a fraction can be written with many different names, sometimes it is desir-

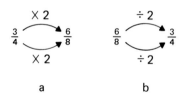

a   b

FIGURE 5-14.
Algorithm for renaming fractions.

able to use the simplest name. The simplest name is the one having the smallest possible numerator and denominator or in which the numerator and denominator have no common factors. However, in some real-life situations the simplest name is not the most useful name. Using the pie example again, if one sixth of a pie is to be given to each of eight people, the logical way to express the amount of pie needed is $\frac{8}{6}$ rather than $\frac{4}{3}$ or $1\frac{1}{3}$. However, when children encounter fractions like $\frac{51}{68}$ or $\frac{39}{52}$, they will probably find it easier to conceptualize the simplest name, $\frac{3}{4}$.

An extension of renaming is needed when students are adding fractions. To be added, fractions must have the same name or denominator. Thus, to add $\frac{3}{4}$ and $\frac{1}{3}$, students must not only be able to find other names for each of these fractions, but they must also be able to find names such that both equivalent fractions have the *same* denominator. These concepts will be developed further in the sections on adding and subtracting fractions.

COMPARING AND ORDERING COMMON FRACTIONS

Just as children compared and ordered whole numbers, they will need to compare and order fractions. At first they look at the models used to represent two fractions to determine which is more or which is less. When the size of the whole is the same, the children simply need to compare which of the two models has the larger amount shaded (Figure 5-15). This thinking is an extension of comparing two whole numbers by placing them in one-to-one correspondence.

A popular fraction-bar game for two players teaches and reinforces comparison of fractions. The same number of fraction bars are dealt to each student. They each

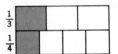 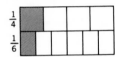

FIGURE 5-15.
Fraction bars.

place their fraction bars in a pile face down on the table. For each turn the students set their top fraction bars on the table face up and compare the two models. The student who has the larger (or smaller) amount shaded wins both fraction bars. If the models represent equivalent fractions, the winner of the next pair of fractions will win all four fraction bars.

Variations of and discussions about this game can extend children's thinking about fractions. As the models are placed on the table, the children could say (or write) the fraction name and state (or write) the inequalities such as $\frac{3}{4}$ is greater than $\frac{5}{12}$. The teacher could ask questions such as "Which ones were equivalent to one whole? To zero? To one half? Which ones were close to one whole? To one half? To zero? Which ones are greater than one half but less than one? Greater than zero but less than one half?" By posing such questions the teacher is helping the students estimate numbers and decide in which interval these numbers are contained.

Another more abstract model which is useful for comparing fractions is the number line. Just as whole numbers correspond to specific lengths on a number line, common fractions can be ordered on the number line. With a number line like the one in Figure 5-11, students can easily see that $\frac{3}{4}$ is larger than $\frac{2}{3}$.

Similarly, comparisons should be made of unit fractions that are parts of sets. For some students this comparison may be easier than with fractions as parts of regions because the fraction that is part of a set is a countable quantity. In Figure 5-5 the whole egg cartons show the comparison of $\frac{1}{2}$, $\frac{1}{3}$, and $\frac{1}{4}$ and the comparison of $\frac{5}{6}$ and $\frac{5}{12}$. The half cartons show the comparison of $\frac{1}{2}$, $\frac{1}{3}$, and $\frac{1}{6}$.

There are many different strategies for ordering fractions that can be explored over various grade levels. Fraction bars or other paper models can be used to order families of fractions. A family of fractions will be defined as those fractions with the same denominator. With fraction bars a different color differentiates each family so that the children can conveniently find all of the members of one family. If they are ordering twelfths, they would order all of the orange bars from 0 twelfths to 12 twelfths.

To order the fourths family using a paperfolding model, the children could fold the same-sized sheets of paper to show four equal parts. Each group of children should then shade in any number of parts from zero parts to all four parts so that each fraction in the fourths family is represented. Each group should order their fraction models. The results should be recorded and discussed. Other fraction families should be similarly modeled, ordered, and recorded. The children should form a generalization as to how to order fractions if all of the denominators are the same.

In the examples above, the children were comparing and ordering fractions strictly using models. As children extend their understanding of fractions, they can use models to develop generalizations for comparing fractions numerically. One of the first strategies for comparing fractions is comparing numerators when the denominators are the same. As the children played the fraction-bar game described earlier, they probably turned up such combinations as $\frac{3}{4}$ and $\frac{1}{4}$, $\frac{1}{2}$ and $\frac{2}{2}$, or $\frac{5}{6}$ and $\frac{3}{6}$. Teacher questions

can help them find a pattern. "When you turned up $\frac{5}{6}$ and $\frac{3}{6}$, what did you notice about the total number of parts in each fraction? How did the number of shaded parts compare? How did the size of the fractions compare? Answer these questions for $\frac{3}{4}$ and $\frac{1}{4}$. Do you see a pattern? What pattern? Will this pattern work for other pairs of fractions? What generalization have you discovered? How can we use this strategy for comparing $\frac{23}{78}$ and $\frac{17}{78}$ or $\frac{75}{103}$ and $\frac{92}{103}$? How can you extend this strategy for ordering fractions such as $\frac{22}{47}$, $\frac{16}{47}$, and $\frac{43}{47}$?"

Another strategy that children can develop for comparing and ordering fractions is to compare denominators if the numerators are the same. This concept should first be explored with unit fractions. Children could fold the same-sized sheets of paper into different numbers of equal-sized pieces and shade in one of the parts for each model. They should then compare their results to see which paper has the larger amount of shading. If the numbers they represented were one third and one fourth, they should observe that one fourth is smaller or that $\frac{1}{4} < \frac{1}{3}$. Other examples should follow until children can form the generalization that if the numerators are both one, then the larger the number of total parts (denominator) the smaller the fraction.

This activity should be extended beyond unit fractions to comparing other fractions whose numerators are both the same such as $\frac{2}{5}$ and $\frac{2}{6}$. A variation of this activity is to have the students order more than two fractions. Fraction bars are also an appropriate model for the activities described above.

An extension of this strategy involves the complement of a set. When ordering $\frac{7}{8}$ and $\frac{5}{6}$, Steve observed that both numbers were close to one. Then he noticed that $\frac{7}{8}$ was exactly $\frac{1}{8}$ less than one while $\frac{5}{6}$ was exactly $\frac{1}{6}$ less than one. Since he knew that $\frac{1}{6}$ was larger than $\frac{1}{8}$, he reasoned that $\frac{7}{8}$ must be larger than $\frac{5}{6}$ because it was closer to one.

Susan extended this same strategy for ordering $\frac{49}{57}$, $\frac{37}{45}$, and $\frac{55}{63}$. She reasoned, "$\frac{49}{57}$ is $\frac{8}{57}$ from one, $\frac{37}{45}$ is $\frac{8}{45}$ from one, and $\frac{55}{63}$ is $\frac{8}{63}$ from one. I already know how to order these complementary fractions because they all have 8 for a numerator, so the order is $\frac{8}{63}$, $\frac{8}{57}$, and $\frac{8}{45}$ from smallest to largest. Since the complements tell me how far away from one the original fractions are, I can now order them correctly from smallest to largest as $\frac{37}{45}$ is farthest from one, $\frac{49}{57}$ next, and $\frac{55}{63}$ closest to one."

Two strategies for comparing and ordering fractions that students develop in the upper grades are finding equivalent fractions and applying cross products. Both of these strategies are based on common denominators. For example, after students have studied equivalent fractions, they often use this strategy to rename the fractions being considered so that all of the denominators are the same. Then they can simply compare numerators as they did in one of the first strategies that they learned.

To compare two fractions using cross products, the students multiply each denominator times the numerator in the other fraction. For example, when comparing $\frac{2}{3}$ with $\frac{5}{7}$, the student would multiply 7 times 2 and 3 times 5 (Figure 5-16a). Since 14 is less than 15, $\frac{2}{3}$ is less than $\frac{5}{7}$. Common denominators are being applied, although it is not as immediately obvious to the student. In our example $\frac{2}{3}$ is multiplied by $\frac{7}{7}$ and $\frac{5}{7}$ by $\frac{3}{3}$. Since $\frac{7}{7}$ and $\frac{3}{3}$ are simply other names for one, $\frac{2}{3}$ and $\frac{5}{7}$ have been renamed to a common denominator of 21, and then the numerators can be compared (Figure 5-16b).

Another strategy introduced in upper grades is changing the fractions to their dec-

a	b
Which is larger	Which is larger?
$\frac{2}{3}$ or $\frac{5}{7}$	$\frac{2}{3}$ or $\frac{5}{7}$
7 × 2 or 3 × 5	$\frac{7}{7} \times \frac{2}{3}$ or $\frac{3}{3} \times \frac{5}{7}$
14 or 15	$\frac{14}{21}$ or $\frac{15}{21}$
14 < 15	$\frac{14}{21} < \frac{15}{21}$
so $\frac{2}{3} < \frac{5}{7}$	so $\frac{2}{3} < \frac{5}{7}$

FIGURE 5-16.
Cross products to compare fractions.

imal form. This can be done readily with a calculator; the students can then compare the numbers using place-value concepts. Comparing and ordering decimal fractions is discussed later in this chapter.

Although the last three strategies can be used in any situation, no *one* strategy will be the most appropriate for all students. The students should use strategies that are appropriate for the numbers being considered. Also, other strategies, such as estimation, are often more efficient for ordering numbers such as $\frac{3}{7}$ and $\frac{1}{15}$ or $\frac{2}{10}$, $\frac{7}{10}$, and $\frac{1}{2}$. As students develop their number sense, they should learn to recognize fractions as being close to 0, $\frac{1}{2}$, or 1 and to use this knowledge for ordering fractions. By developing a variety of strategies, students will be extending their concepts of common fractions.

ROUNDING AND ESTIMATING COMMON FRACTIONS

Rounding

As with whole numbers, an approximation is often appropriate with common fractions. Sometimes answers are rounded to the near-

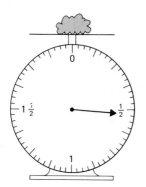

FIGURE 5-17.
Rounding fractions.

est whole number or half unit because an exact answer is not needed. For example, Fred was not sure how much hamburger was left in the package, so he put it on the scale (Figure 5-17). Although Fred could have read the measurement shown as $\frac{17}{32}$, this degree of precision was not necessary. Instead, he rounded this fraction and thought, "I have about $\frac{1}{2}$ a pound of hamburger— enough to serve two people."

FRACTIONS CLOSE TO ZERO.   In the preceding section, a game with fraction bars was described. As students in Mr. Bartels class compared fractions, they were asked to consider which fractions were close to one, one half, or zero. At first students were observing that the shadings were either about one half or close to one. Questions were directed so that the students made appropriate generalizations. For example, Sarah observed that the numbers $\frac{1}{5}$, $\frac{2}{7}$, and $\frac{4}{15}$ were close to zero,

and she also noticed that the numerator was very small in comparison to the denominator. She concluded that numbers like $\frac{2}{64}$, $\frac{5}{100}$, and $\frac{13}{89}$ would also be close to zero.

FRACTIONS CLOSE TO ONE.   Jill extended this idea to fractions such as $\frac{7}{8}$, $\frac{5}{6}$, and $\frac{7}{10}$; she noted that they were all close to one. At first she was looking only at the numerators, but then she observed that $\frac{5}{10}$ was one half and $\frac{7}{100}$ was very small. She concluded that if the numerator and denominator were relatively the same size, the fraction was close to one. She also observed that the number was less than one if the numerator was smaller than the denominator or greater than one if the numerator was larger.

FRACTIONS CLOSE TO ONE HALF.   Mr. Bartels asked the class if they could determine which numbers were close to one half. First they wrote various names for one half—$\frac{3}{6}$, $\frac{5}{10}$, $\frac{6}{12}$. Ted observed that the denominators were always twice as large as the numerators. Based on that statement, Shawn wrote the numbers $\frac{34}{68}$, $\frac{30}{60}$, and $\frac{345}{690}$ and stated that these were all names for one half. The teacher then wrote a series of numbers on the board and asked the students to copy them and circle the ones that were about one half (Figure 5-18a).

Todd noted that he not only knew which ones were about one half, but he also had made comparisons to determine which were greater than or less than one half. Todd marked the numbers with a greater-than or

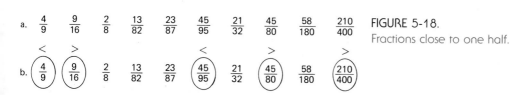

FIGURE 5-18.
Fractions close to one half.

less-than sign to indicate this. He put his results on the board (Figure 5-18b) and asked the rest of the class if they could figure out his thinking. The class then discussed his strategy. This type of estimation, in which students decide whether fractions are close to 0, $\frac{1}{2}$, or 1, is very important later for estimating answers to fractional computations. This thinking strategy should also be used in comparing or ordering fractions.

Estimating

Sometimes we must estimate a fractional part of something. For example, "Jackie's mother said that she could have $\frac{1}{3}$ of the orange juice in the refrigerator but she must leave a fair share for her brother and sister." Jackie must look at the total amount of juice and then estimate $\frac{1}{3}$.

We also use the set model of fractions in estimating whole numbers. "Ms. Lambert's P.E. class had 22 students. When Ms. Lambert arrived on Thursday, she saw immediately that about $\frac{1}{2}$ the class was absent. She decided that with such a small class left, they could not play an actual game of baseball so they spent the period practicing pitching and batting." In this example, Ms. Lambert has estimated a fractional part of the class and adjusted her lesson plan accordingly.

In order to become good estimators, children need experience in estimating. One type of activity is to give them a reference length and then ask them to estimate things in the room which are half that length or $\frac{1}{3}$ of that length. After they have made their estimates, they should check by measuring to see how close they came. They should discuss which of their estimates were closest and what techniques they used in making those estimates.

QUESTIONS AND ACTIVITIES

1. a. Use paperfolding to determine how many different ways you can fold a sheet of paper into four equal-sized pieces.
   b. Do the parts have to be the same shape? The same size?

2. Penny offered to trade $\frac{1}{3}$ of her pastrami sandwich for $\frac{1}{3}$ of Betsy's submarine sandwich. Although Betsy liked pastrami, she looked at Penny's sandwich and refused the offer, as she was very hungry. When does "$\frac{1}{3}$" not equal "$\frac{1}{3}$"?

3. a. Fold a paper into four equal-sized parts. Shade in one of them. How would you teach children the oral name for this number? How would you teach them the numeral name for this model?
   b. Shade in two more parts. How would you teach children the oral name for this number? How would you teach them the numeral name for this model?
   c. Why should children be introduced to unit fractions before fractions whose numerators are other than one.

4. Six translations were discussed in Figure 4-19. Design a series of six activities, one for each task, that could be used to introduce common fractions.

5. The two types of fraction models are set and measurement. Paperfolding and fraction bars are both region or area models, a form of measurement model. Measurement models can also be linear. Cuisenaire rods and number lines are two examples.
   a. With Cuisenaire rods, let the orange rod be the whole or one. Give the fractional name of each of the other rods.
   b. Let the blue rod be the whole or one. Represent the following fractions: 1 third, 2 thirds, 3 thirds, and 5 ninths.

c. Let the brown rod be the whole. Represent the following fractions: 1 half, 1 fourth, 2 fourths, 3 fourths, 4 fourths.

d. Let the dark green rod be the whole. Represent the following counting series: 1 sixth, 2 sixths, 3 sixths . . . ; 1 third, 2 thirds, 3 thirds, . . . ; 1 half, 2 halves. . . .

e. Let the yellow rod be the whole. What is the fractional name of each of the other rods?

f. Let the purple rod be the whole. What is the fractional name of each of the other rods?

g. Let the dark green rod be the whole. What is the fractional name of each of the other rods?

h. *For your resource file:* In "Let's Do It: Fractions with Fraction Strips," Van de Walle and Thompson describe activities for developing fraction concepts with Cuisenaire rods and/or paper strips.

6. To understand the fractional number line, students need to be involved in activities that link their understanding of the region model to the number line. For this activity, cut two strips of paper between 10 and 20 centimeters long and about 2 to 3 centimeters wide.

a. To make a number line marked in fourths, first draw a line on a sheet of paper longer than the paper strip. Fold the strip into fourths so that all of the folds are parallel to each other. Lay the strip along the line and mark the two ends of the strip on the line. Label these points 0 and 1. Starting at 0, move along the strip marking at each fold and labeling each mark appropriately.

b. Adapt part (a) to make a number line marked in tenths.

c. *For your resource file:* Chiosi describes activities to develop meanings for fractions on the number line.

7. a. Use a set model to represent 3 fourths, 2 fifths, 9 twelfths, 1 and 2 thirds.

b. A common error is naming set fractions by comparing the two parts of the set. For example, the first fraction represented in Figure 5-4 would be named one third and the last fraction one fifth. Describe how you would use part/whole concepts to help students develop appropriate oral names.

c. Describe how you could use counters and egg cartons or region models (that have been cut apart) to help children identify the set as the whole.

d. *For your resource file:* Peck and Jencks describe lessons to develop meaning for denominators.

8. Consult a fourth-grade textbook and analyze the various types of models that are used to represent fractions. Briefly describe the different diagrams (use a word or phrase such as circles, rectangles, a group of animals) and classify the models as parts of a set or parts of a unit.

9. a. In what grades do you think the following topics are introduced? Write down your guesses.
   (1) common fractions
   (2) decimal fractions
   (3) equivalent fractions
   (4) multiplying fractions
   (5) adding fractions
   (6) algorithm for renaming fractions

b. Consult a scope-and-sequence chart from an elementary textbook series to find the actual grade levels. Include the publisher of the series and the copyright date.

10. a. Use fraction bars to find other names for 2 thirds. For 3 fourths.

b. Use paperfolding to change 3 fourths to eighths. 2 fifths to tenths. 2 thirds to twelfths.

c. Students should have a number of experiences finding equivalent fractions with models before being taught the related algorithm. Consider changing 2 thirds to sixths and 3 fourths to twelfths.

Devise teacher questions that link the models to the algorithm. Write out the appropriate algorithm for each step in renaming a fraction.

d. Explain how you would use this activity to help students generalize that:

$$\frac{a}{b} = \frac{a \times n}{b \times n}$$

e. *For your resource file:* In "Let's Do It: Using Rectangles and Squares to Develop Fraction Concepts," Bruni and Silverman describe a number of beginning activities for basic fraction concepts and equivalent fractions.

11. Discuss why "renaming fractions" should be used rather than "reducing fractions."

12. *Materials needed:* Fraction bars. Sort the fraction bars from the largest to the smallest. Place all equivalent fractions in the same row. Record your results.

13. *Materials needed:* Pattern blocks. From the pattern blocks, select appropriate blocks and show why $\frac{3}{6} = \frac{1}{2}$. Use diagrams to show what was done.

14. Use a calculator to determine which of the following is another name for $\frac{3}{4}$.

$$\frac{21}{28} \qquad \frac{15}{20} \qquad \frac{39}{52}$$

15. Students sometimes develop their own algorithms. The elementary teacher must be able to analyze the student's reasoning. If the student is incorrect, the teacher should devise activities to help the student discover the error.

a. To find the lowest common denominator for $\frac{7}{20}$ and $\frac{5}{24}$, Steve reasoned that 4 is the largest number that divides both 20 and 24. 20 divided by 4 is 5. 5 times 24 is 120 so 120 is the lowest common denominator. Is this reasoning correct? Explain.

b. After watching Steve, Loretta, to find the least common denominator for $\frac{7}{18}$ and $\frac{5}{24}$, reasoned that 3 divides both 18 and

24. 18 divided by 3 is 6; 6 times 24 is 144, so the lowest common denominator is 144. Is she correct? Explain.

16. Explain how you would use models to help students form the generalization that $n/n = 1$.

17. a. $0/0 = 1$. This was a student's answer on a recent test. The student stated the rule "any number divided by itself is 1" in discussing why this was a correct answer. Give an example that would help the student understand his or her error.

b. Read "A Uniform Approach to Fractions" by Ettline for some suggestions on symbolic notations for renaming fractions to simpler terms.

18. a. Diagrams of several fractions are shown below. For each fraction, draw the whole or unit of one.

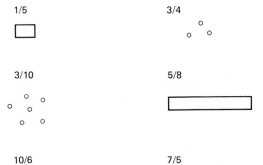

1/5

3/4

3/10

5/8

10/6

7/5

b. *For your resource file:* For student activity sheets and lesson plans, read "Ideas" by Zawojewski. Add this article to your resource file.

19. a. Use paperfolding to find the fraction name for 1 and $\frac{3}{5}$. For $2\frac{1}{3}$. Use fraction bars to find the fraction name for $1\frac{3}{4}$. What generalization should students form from activities of this type?

b. Use paperfolding to find the mixed

number name for $\frac{7}{6}$. For $\frac{9}{4}$. Use fraction bars to find the mixed number name for $\frac{15}{12}$. What generalization should students form from activities of this type?

20. Write a real-life situation and draw diagrams to show 4 divided by 5. Rearrange the model to show that 4 divided by 5 is equivalent to $\frac{4}{5}$.

21. Explain how you would help students realize that another name for $\frac{3}{1}$ is 3. It is helpful to discuss $\frac{3}{3}$ and $\frac{3}{2}$ before discussing $\frac{3}{1}$.

22. a. Find a fraction bar that represents 2 thirds. Find the other members of the thirds family. Order them from smallest to largest. Write their oral names in order using a form like "2 thirds" to emphasize the family name. What pattern do you observe? Write their number names in order. What pattern do you observe?

b. Find the sixths family. Which of these are equivalent to members of the thirds family? Order them from smallest to largest. Is the pattern that you predicted for part (a) also true?

c. Repeat parts (a) and (b) using paperfolding.

23. a. Paperfolding can be used to model numerous common fractions. Consider denominators with the numbers 2 through 15. Use paperfolding to determine which of these could readily be represented. Give the family name for each model. Note that the family name is the same as the ordinal name for that number of parts. Which of these are commonly used families?

b. Shade in one of the parts of each model. Order them from smallest to largest. What pattern can you observe? Write their oral names and number names in order. What pattern can you observe?

c. As you folded various fractions, you obtained sixths by folding thirds and

halves. Thirds and sixths are called "unlike related fractions," as thirds can readily be changed to sixths. What other unlike related fractions did you note from *folding*?

24. Ms. Jones and her students used a paperfolding activity to order $\frac{3}{10}$, $\frac{3}{5}$, $\frac{3}{6}$, and $\frac{3}{8}$. What is the order of the numbers from smallest to largest? What generalization should they make from this activity?

25. Circle the larger number in each pair below. Name or briefly describe an appropriate but different strategy for each pair.

a. $\frac{7}{35}$ or $\frac{9}{35}$ b. $\frac{12}{23}$ or $\frac{8}{17}$

c. $\frac{2}{17}$ or $\frac{2}{19}$ d. $\frac{32}{35}$ or $\frac{20}{23}$

26. Use cross products to decide which of the numbers below is larger. How would you explain this procedure to your class so that they understood why it works?

$$\frac{7}{23} \qquad \frac{15}{49}$$

27. Of the models for common fractions, paperfolding and fraction bars are conceptually more concrete than the number line. Describe how to use a region model to introduce a fractional number for sixths.

28. Draw a number line like the one shown below. On your number line, mark an appropriate position that is a reasonable estimate of each given number. Label these positions as a, b, c, and d.

(a) $\frac{21}{67}$
(b) $\frac{2}{36}$
(c) $\frac{17}{35}$
(d) $\frac{27}{13}$

29. Name three situations in which an approximation is appropriate. Describe two real-life situations in which you would round down.

30. In the section, "Comparing and Ordering Common Fractions," a game is described for comparing fractions. Redesign the game so that it involves ordering fractions and can be played by three or more people. Write the rules and then play the game. Redesign if necessary.

31. Both fraction and mixed-number forms are used for numbers greater than one. Use *both* forms to order the numbers below. For comparing and ordering, do you consistently prefer one form over the other, or does your preference vary from example to example?

    a. $\frac{9}{8}$, $1\frac{3}{8}$
    b. $3\frac{1}{5}$, $\frac{33}{10}$, $\frac{52}{15}$
    c. $2\frac{4}{7}$, $\frac{15}{7}$
    d. $\frac{11}{4}$, $2\frac{3}{5}$
    e. $2\frac{1}{3}$, $\frac{8}{3}$, $\frac{5}{3}$
    f. $14\frac{2}{3}$, $\frac{72}{5}$

32. In the section "Rounding and Estimating Common Fractions," Todd devised a strategy to determine numbers greater than or less than one half. Analyze his results shown in Figure 5-18b. Describe one or more strategies that he may be using.

33. Read "A Teaching Sequence from Initial Fraction Concepts Through the Addition of Unlike Fractions" by Ellerbruch and Payne. Outline the teaching sequence for the initial fraction concept and equivalent fractions. Briefly describe activities that can be used to illustrate these concepts.

34. *For your resource file:* The articles below focus on how to use specific models to help children develop fraction concepts. Read and copy those for which you want further information. In "Fractions Taught by Folding Paper Strips," Scott describes folding paper strips, a model similar to fraction bars. Leutzinger and Nelson focus on circular models in "Let's Do It: Fractions with Models." Jensen and O'Neil describe how to introduce set models using egg cartons in "Let's Do It: That's Eggzactly Right!" Van de Walle and Thompson describe using grids with counters to make a transition to the set model in "Let's Do It: Fractions with Counters."

35. What do children know about fractions? Read Suydam's "Research Report: Fractions" to answer this question.

36. With another student, work through some of the activities described in "Estimation and Children's Concept of Rational Number Size" by Behr, Post, and Wachsmuth.

DECIMAL FRACTIONS

In the past, common fractions and all the operations with them were taught before decimals were introduced. However, with increasing use of the metric system and hand-held calculators, decimals and fractions with denominators of 10 will need to be introduced earlier in the elementary curriculum. For this, the student should have a thorough understanding of two main concepts: place value and common fractions.

CONCEPT OF DECIMAL FRACTIONS

Common fractions are usually taught before decimal fractions in the elementary school. Most children come to school with beginning ideas of halves, thirds, and fourths, but few have any idea of what tenths mean. In children's early work with common fractions, many examples having a denominator of ten should be included. This will serve as a basis for introducing decimal fractions later. As students mature, they can also be given work with common fractions with denominators of one hundred.

Many teachers assume that by the time students are introduced to decimal fractions, they have reached a level of abstraction at which they no longer need models. Research shows that although models are often

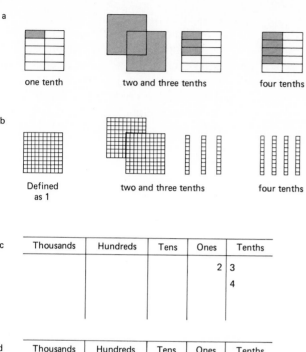

a

one tenth   two and three tenths   four tenths

b

Defined   two and three tenths   four tenths
as 1

FIGURE 5-19.
Introducing tenths.

c

Thousands	Hundreds	Tens	Ones	Tenths
			2	3
				4

d

Thousands	Hundreds	Tens	Ones	Tenths
			2.	3
			0.	4

not used after third grade, students in the middle grades and junior high would benefit if teachers used models to develop and to illustrate concepts. In fact, even adults benefit from working with models when they are introduced to any concept for the first time.

To introduce decimal fractions, work with common fractions in tenths should be reviewed orally with models. As with common fractions, paperfolding is a good model. Students can be asked to represent numbers such as one tenth, two and three tenths, or four tenths, as shown in Figure 5-19a. Note that this is strictly an activity involving models and oral names. It is no different from their activities representing common fractions.

Another model for this activity is base-ten blocks. When flats are defined as representing ones, numbers in tenths can be represented (Figure 5-19b). Since it takes ten longs to equal one flat, one long would be one tenth, two longs would be two tenths, and so on.

After students have reviewed models of tenths, a place-value table should be introduced for recording the numerals. The notation for decimal fractions is a simple extension of place value. The oral names for 0.3 and $\frac{3}{10}$ are the same. The only new idea is writing the decimal fraction. In extending place value to the left, students discovered the pattern that each time a digit is moved

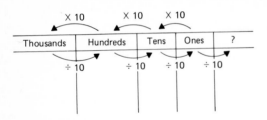

FIGURE 5-20.
Place-value patterns.

to the left one place, its value is multiplied by 10 (Figure 4-30). Now students need to observe that the reverse is also true—that each time a digit is moved to the right one place, its value is divided by 10. To move from the thousands place to the hundreds place, students must divide by 10. Similarly, they must divide by 10 to move from the hundreds place to the tens place, and from the tens place to the ones place (Figure 5-20). As students notice this pattern of dividing by 10, they will realize that the same idea can be extended beyond the ones place to the right, giving tenths.

To help students make the transition from models to numerals, the teacher should make a place-value table with appropriate headings. The numbers represented by the paperfoldings or the base-ten blocks are then recorded in the table (Figure 5-19a through c). For example, the number two and three tenths would be recorded with the 2 in the ones column and the 3 in the tenths column. Members of the class may note that the numeral 23 in the table could be confused with the whole number twenty-three if it were removed from the table. The teacher can then introduce the decimal point to separate the whole numbers from the fractional numbers and can place it accordingly in the ones column in the table (Figure 5-19d).

To facilitate reading, a zero is placed in the ones column of a numeral that has only a fractional part. It should be pointed out that $\frac{4}{10}$ and 0.4 are both read as four tenths. For numbers greater than one, the decimal point is read as "and"; for example, 2.3 is read as two and three tenths.

This is not the students' first introduction to decimal points. They have encountered them previously in working with money. However, although they read the decimal point in numbers representing money as "and," they do not treat the numbers to the right of the decimal point as fractions. For example, they would read $3.18 as three dollars and eighteen cents, not three and eighteen hundredths dollars. In considering the value of the digits 3, 1, and 8, they are more likely to discuss 3 dollars, 1 dime, and 8 pennies than 3 dollars, 1 tenth of a dollar, and 8 hundredths of a dollar.

Children are first introduced only to the concept of tenths. Later, these concepts are extended in a similar lesson to include hundredths. Again the base-ten flat could be defined as one and the long would be one tenth. The pattern of dividing by ten that was observed in the place-value table should be extended. If the long were divided into ten equal-sized pieces, units would be obtained. Since it takes 100 units to equal one flat, one unit would be one hundredth, two units, two hundredths, and so on. Representations of various numbers and their numerals are shown in Figure 5-21.

With whole numbers and common fractions, six translations among the oral name, model, and numeral must be mastered by the students. The same translations must be included in the students' introductory work with decimal fractions. One special concern is reading the numerals correctly. A rationale must be built for reading 0.23 as twenty-

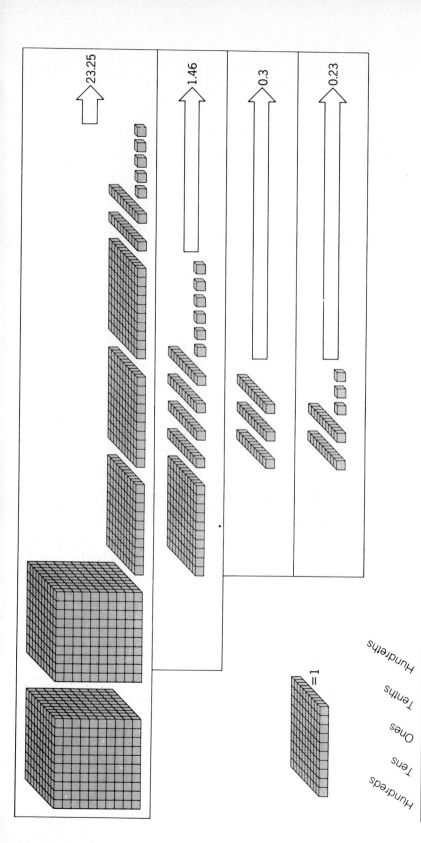

FIGURE 5-21.
Base-ten block representation of decimals and corresponding numerals in place-value table.

Hundreds	Tens	Ones	Tenths	Hundredths
	2	3.	2	5
		1.	4	6
		0.	3	
		0.	2	3

three hundredths rather than two tenths, three hundredths (Figure 5-21). By trading the two tenths for their equivalent in unit blocks or hundredths, the students will discover that another name for 2 tenths is 20 hundredths. The 20 hundredths together with the 3 hundredths is a total of 23 hundredths. The students should have a variety of these experiences, such as finding other names for 14 tenths, 30 tenths, 18 hundredths, or 32 hundredths. The students should observe that this is the same renaming that they experienced with whole numbers and common fractions.

A common error that students make is reading 0.003 as three hundredths. They are thinking of the fact that hundreds is in the third place to the left of the decimal point. Instead, they should think of the decimal point as being located in the ones place rather than between the ones and the tenths. Therefore, they can discover how the system is symmetric around the ones place. To the left of the ones place can be found the tens place; to the right, the tenths place; to the left of the tens place, hundreds; to the right of the tenths place, hundredths (Figure 5-22).

After working with base-ten blocks, students can use 10 × 10 graph paper to give a pictorial representation of what they have done with the blocks. This pictorial representation provides a good intermediate step between the concrete and the abstract (Figure 5-23).

Another model for teaching place value involving decimal fractions is the abacus. By defining one of the middle rods as ones, students can demonstrate place value in both directions from the ones. The decimal point can be marked on the abacus in the ones column with a piece of tape. As stated in Chapter 3, the abacus is a more abstract model than base-ten blocks because a disk on the abacus in one column is not physically different, except perhaps for color, from a disk in any other column. Figure 5-24 shows the abacus representations for the same numbers shown with base-ten blocks in Figure 5-21. Three of these numbers are also represented with graph paper in Figure 5-23.

Students should also learn the place-value names and the power-of-10 concept for fractional place values. By using the symmetry of the place value system, students

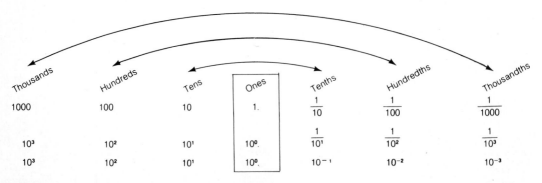

FIGURE 5-22.
Symmetry of place values around the ones place.

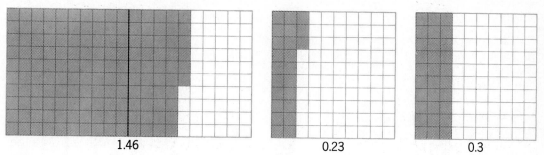

1.46

0.23

0.3

FIGURE 5-23.
Pictorial representation of decimals.

can easily build on what they have already learned. Expanded notation can again be used in teaching this concept (Figure 5-25).

The symmetry of numeration around the ones place is another example of the patterns that are so prevalent in mathematics and the decimal numeration system. This pattern should be emphasized and examined; students should be guided in discovering patterns and the structure of the decimal numeration system. These patterns will help their understanding of the numeration system and will aid their learning when problem-solving situations are encountered.

FIGURE 5-24.
Abacus representation of decimals.

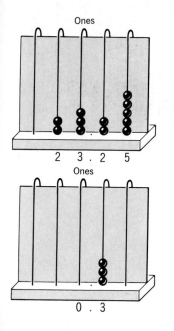

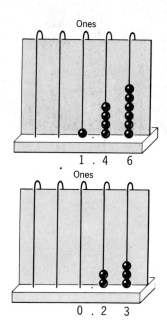

$$423.68 = 400 + 20 + 3 + 0.6 + 0.08$$
$$= 4 \text{ hundreds} + 2 \text{ tens} + 3 \text{ ones} + 6 \text{ tenths} + 8 \text{ hundredths}$$
$$= (4 \times 100) + (2 \times 10) + (3 \times 1) + (6 \times \tfrac{1}{10}) + (8 \times \tfrac{1}{100})$$
$$= (4 \times 10 \times 10) + (2 \times 10) + (3 \times 1) + (6 \times \tfrac{1}{10}) + (8 \times \tfrac{1}{10 \times 10})$$
$$= (4 \times 10^2) + (2 \times 10^1) + (3 \times 10^0) + (6 \times \tfrac{1}{10^1}) + (8 \times \tfrac{1}{10^2})$$
$$= (4 \times 10^2) + (2 \times 10^1) + (3 \times 10^0) + (6 \times 10^{-1}) + (8 \times 10^{-2})$$

FIGURE 5-25.
Expanded notation.

COMPARING AND ORDERING DECIMAL FRACTIONS

It is often assumed that since students can order whole numbers, they can also order decimal fractions. Students often have difficulties, as they have not thoroughly developed the concept of decimal fractions. The exercises in some textbooks are limited to comparing tenths to tenths or hundredths to hundredths: for example, 0.2 to 0.6 or 0.45 to 0.38. The students can correctly answer these problems simply by making whole-number comparisons and without considering place values of less than one. In such cases the students should explain what place values are being compared and the lessons should be supplemented accordingly.

Students often argue that 0.23 is larger than 0.3 as "twenty-three is larger than three" or because "hundreds" are larger than "tens." Either argument is based on a misunderstanding of decimal fractions. To help students correct their thinking, the numbers 0.23 and 0.3 could be represented by base-ten blocks. The students should note that 3 longs or 3 tenths is the same as 30 units or 30 hundredths or $\tfrac{3}{10} = \tfrac{30}{100}$. Then it becomes obvious that 0.30 or $\tfrac{30}{100}$ is larger than 0.23 or $\tfrac{23}{100}$. Just as with common fractions, it is easier to compare two decimal fractions when they have the same denominator.

a Jill's work

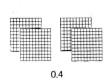
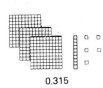

Defined as 1   0.4   0.315   0.06

b Lois's work

Ones	Tenths	Hundredths	Thousandths
0.	4	○	○
0.	3	1	5
0.	0	6	○

c Ginny's work

Ones	Tenths	Hundredths	Thousandths
0.	4		
0.	3	1	5
0.	0	6	

FIGURE 5-26.
Place-value tables for comparing decimal fractions.

The place-value approach to solving this misconception should also be discussed. In representing 0.23 as two longs and three units and 0.3 as three longs, students should note that longs represent the larger place value, tenths. Since 3 tenths is more than 2 tenths, 0.3 is greater than 0.23. Thus ordering of decimal fractions is simply an extension of ordering of whole numbers.

Students should apply similar strategies when ordering more than two numbers. For example, when ordering 0.4, 0.06, and 0.315, Ginny, Lois, and Jill used three different strategies. Jill represented the three numbers with base-ten blocks using the large block to represent one (Figure 5-26a). Since flats were the largest pieces needed to represent the numbers, Jill observed, "4 flats or 4 tenths is more than 3 flats or 3 tenths, so 0.4 is greater than 0.315. Since 0.06 has zero flats, it is the smallest number."

Lois and Ginny both wrote the numerals in place-value tables to determine the order of the numbers (Figure 5-26b and c). Lois reasoned, "0.4 means 4 tenths, 0 hundredths, 0 thousandths, so I'll write in the zeros accordingly for 0.4 and 0.06." She then observed, "Since all of the decimal fractions are now in terms of thousandths, I can simply compare the numerators and order them as 0.400, 0.315, 0.060." Ginny stated, "Since tenths is the largest place value represented, I will compare the digits in the tenths column and order the numbers accordingly."

ROUNDING AND ESTIMATING DECIMAL FRACTIONS

Rounding

Most of the situations in which we use rounded decimal fractions involve measure. For example, if Susan is measuring a window, she may find that the measure is between 1.34 and 1.35 meters. She will round up or down depending either on which measure is closer or on how the measure is to be used. Other situations could involve reading a scale that indicates a measure between 3.45 and 3.50 kilograms or a measure between 0.75 and 0.80 liter.

There are other aspects of rounding decimals that we encounter in our lives. For example, Iris was shopping at the natural food co-op store. She needed some Colby cheese for a new recipe. She cut off a piece of cheese that she thought would be enough. When she put it on the digital scale, the scale registered 0.27 pound. She thought, "That's close enough to a quarter of a pound. I'll just take the whole piece." She has rounded a decimal fraction to a common fraction.

The cheese cost $2.95 per pound. To find out how much the piece cost, the clerk punched in the numbers 2, 9, and 5 on the scale. The scale showed a cost of $0.80. At the same time, Iris figured the cost with her calculator. She found that 2.95×0.27 was 0.7965. The scale had rounded this four-place decimal to a two-place decimal.

Rounding skills are also needed in order to use calculators effectively. For instance, Troy had exactly five dollars to spend on a Mother's Day present. After much shopping, he selected a glass bowl that cost $4.81. As he started for the checkout counter, he realized that he would need money for sales tax. Since he was unsure whether he had enough, he used his calculator to figure the 4% sales tax. His calculator display was 0.1924. He rounded this figure to hundredths to determine that he should pay 19¢ sales tax. He thought, "Aha! I have enough to get the bowl." Suddenly he realized that stores almost always round the amount of tax up. So before checking out, he found his sister,

Jody, and borrowed another penny just to be sure that he had enough.

Another "rounding" example that students will encounter on the calculator is with repeating decimals. Jeremy entered 1 ÷ 3 and then multiplied that result by 3. The display showed 0.9999999. He wrote the sentence 1 ÷ 3 × 3 and realized that he should have obtained 1 since $\frac{1}{3} \times 3$ is 1. He redid the problem on his calculator with the same results. He then borrowed his brother Troy's calculator, which gave a display of 1.

Calculations like these need to be explained to students. Jeremy's calculator "rounded" the result of 1 ÷ 3 from $0.\overline{3}$ to 0.3333333. Consequently, when this was multiplied by three, 0.9999999 was the result. If Jeremy had tried 2 ÷ 3 × 3, he would have obtained 1.9999998 rather than 2. His calculator does not round numbers; it simply drops the extra digits. Troy's scientific calculator "remembered" the repeating decimal and so returned to the whole number.

Another decimal rounding skill involves rounding a given decimal to a certain place value. This is similar to the rounding described with whole numbers. Given the decimal 0.473982, students should be able to round it to a specific place value, such as the nearest tenth, the nearest thousandth, and so on. As with whole numbers, some of these roundings will be easier than others. Also as with whole numbers, students need to learn to focus on the place value they are rounding to and on the next smaller place value. If asked to round this decimal to the nearest ten-thousandth, students would focus on the 9 ten-thousandths and the 8 hundred-thousandths. However, since 8 is more than halfway through the interval, the 9 will need to be rounded up, making it 10. Thus the rounded number would be 0.4740 to the nearest ten-thousandth. In this case the 0 in the ten-thousandths column is nec-essary, and the number should not be reported as 0.474. If asked to round this decimal to the nearest whole number, students should recognize that it is closer to 0 than to 1. However, they should also see that it is very close to $\frac{1}{2}$, as that will be a more useful rounding for computation.

Estimating

When we estimate fractional parts, we usually estimate with common fractions rather than with decimal fractions. When John says, "I have five tenths of a liter of milk," he is probably reporting a measurement. When he says, "I have half a liter of milk," he is probably reporting an estimate.

Similarly, to estimate for computations we are more likely to use common fractions than decimal fractions even when we are given the decimal fraction. Replacing decimal fractions with estimates of the equivalent common fractions can simplify computations. For example, to determine 78% of 358, Erika thought, "78% is 0.78 or about $\frac{3}{4}$, so $\frac{3}{4}$ of 360 is about 270." To estimate the answer to 0.27 + 8.87 + 1.4, students could estimate "9 + $1\frac{1}{2}$ is $10\frac{1}{2}$; $10\frac{1}{2}$ plus $\frac{1}{4}$ more is $10\frac{3}{4}$." Such activities will extend students' concepts of fractions, both decimal and common.

RELATING COMMON AND DECIMAL FRACTIONS

In the introduction of decimal fractions, decimals were related to place value and common fractions. The relationship that decimal fractions and common fractions are simply different *forms* for the same concept needs to be reinforced. Because they are just different *forms,* decimal fractions can be renamed as common fractions and common fractions can be renamed as decimal fractions.

To change most of our commonly used decimals to common fractions, we simply need to know the oral names of common and decimal fractions. To rewrite 0.4, we use the oral name 4 tenths, so we write $\frac{4}{10}$. To rewrite 0.023, the oral name twenty-three thousandths is then written as $\frac{23}{1000}$. Similarly, common fractions whose denominators are powers of ten (10, 100, 1000, . . .) are easily written as decimals. The fractions $\frac{34}{100}$ and $\frac{23}{10}$ become 0.34 and 2.3. In the latter case the students should recognize that $\frac{23}{10}$ can be renamed as $2\frac{3}{10}$ or 2.3. They should also recognize that 20 tenths is 2 so 23 tenths is 2 and 3 tenths.

It is easy to change common fractions whose denominators are 2, 4, 5, 20, 25, or 50 to the decimal form, as these numbers divide 10 or 100. These renamings should be included in mental computation activities. Students should be able to do them without paper and pencil (Figure 5-27). These mental computations are often needed in everyday situations. Students should learn to recognize that "$\frac{1}{4}$ off" and "25% off" are equivalent expressions.

Previously, students have studied the relationship between fractions and division of whole numbers. They have learned that $\frac{3}{4}$ can be rewritten as $3 \div 4$, and so on. They can use this knowledge to change common fractions to decimals by dividing the numerator by the denominator. Students will use this method for rewriting fractions whose denominators may include such numbers as 3,

$$\frac{1}{3} = 1 \div 3 \qquad \frac{5}{8} = 5 \div 8 \qquad \frac{5}{12} = 5 \div 12$$

$$
\begin{array}{r}
0.33\overline{3} \\
3\overline{)1.000} \\
9 \\
\hline
10 \\
9 \\
\hline
10 \\
9 \\
\hline
\end{array}
\qquad
\begin{array}{r}
0.625 \\
8\overline{)5.000} \\
4\,8 \\
\hline
20 \\
16 \\
\hline
40 \\
40 \\
\hline
\end{array}
\qquad
\begin{array}{r}
0.416\overline{6} \\
12\overline{)5.0000} \\
4\,8 \\
\hline
20 \\
12 \\
\hline
80 \\
72 \\
\hline
80 \\
72 \\
\hline
\end{array}
$$

FIGURE 5-28.
Common fractions to decimals by dividing.

12, 9, 8, 15, or 365 (Figure 5-28). Some of these fractions, such as $\frac{1}{3}$, $\frac{2}{3}$, or $\frac{1}{8}$, are commonly used, and students will memorize the decimal equivalents after experiences with these numbers.

Other decimal fractions can be found by using a calculator. However, students should first explore some of these problems using pencil and paper to do the division because the list contains some fractions which terminate in their decimal form and others which are nonterminating. Students should be involved in class discussions regarding remainders and rounding. These results should be related to calculators, so that the students understand the calculator results. These types of problems and changing decimals to fractions are explored further in the problem set.

$$\frac{1}{2} = \frac{5}{10} = 0.5 \qquad \frac{3}{4} = \frac{75}{100} = 0.75$$

$$\frac{7}{20} = \frac{35}{100} = 0.35 \qquad \frac{37}{50} = \frac{74}{100} = 0.74$$

FIGURE 5-27.
Easy common fractions to decimal fractions.

QUESTIONS AND ACTIVITIES

1. Use paperfolding to represent 4 tenths. Relate this model to the oral name and numeral for *common* fractions. Relate this model to the oral name and numeral for *decimal* fractions. How are the six different

tasks involving models, oral names, and number names alike between decimal fractions and common fractions? How are they different? Why should they be similar?

2. Use base-ten blocks to represent each of the following fractions. Use the flat as your unit of one.
   a. 3 tenths
   b. 0.65
   c. 2 and 16 hundredths

3. Use base-ten blocks to represent each of the following fractions. Use the block as your unit of one.
   a. 0.004
   b. 3 tenths
   c. 0.65
   d. 2 and 16 hundredths

4. Use an abacus to represent each of the following fractions. Redefine the place-value wires.
   a. 0.004
   b. 3 tenths
   c. 0.65
   d. 2 and 16 hundredths

5. a. To explain why $\frac{4}{10}$ is written as the decimal 0.4, the place-value pattern must be explained. With another student, devise a lesson extending place values to tenths. Start with whole-number place values, devise appropriate teacher questions, and use models to explain this concept. Practice the lesson by having one student assume the role of teacher, the other of student. Discuss questioning and revise after the lesson.
   b. Reverse teacher–student roles and work through the lesson extending the place values to hundredths.

6. The common oral name for 0.26 is not 2 tenths 6 hundredths but 26 hundredths. Use models to explain why the two terms are equivalent. Why do we read it as 26 hundredths rather than 2 tenths 6 hundredths?

7. Mary Ann consistently reads 0.004 as "four hundredths" and 400 as "four hundred." Are the "hundredths" and the "hundreds" place values symmetrical around the units place or the decimal point? Design an activity to help her discover her error.

8. Kim said she changed 0.4 to 0.40 by adding a zero. Why is this language inappropriate? Use a 10-by-10 grid to explain why 0.4 and 0.40 are equivalent.

9. Use base-ten materials to rename 16 tenths. To rename 20 tenths.

10. Finish the following sequences. Check your results by using the constant function on your calculator. Orally count, predicting the next number before depressing the equal key.
    a. 0.1, 0.2, ——, ——, ——, ——, ——, ——, ——
    b. 0.95, 0.96, ——, ——, ——, ——, ——, ——, ——
    c. 0.25, 0.30, ——, ——, ——, ——, ——, ——, ——
    d. 0.85, 0.90, ——, ——, ——, ——, ——, ——, ——
    e. 6.5, 6.25, ——, ——, ——, ——, ——, ——, ——
    f. 0.14, 0.15, ——, ——, ——, ——, ——, ——, ——

11. a. Consult an elementary textbook series. At what grade level is the decimal form for tenths introduced? Analyze the introductory lessons. How are these decimals related to common fractions? How is the oral name emphasized? How is it related to the place values of whole numbers? If needed, how could these lessons be supplemented?
    b. At what grade level are decimal fractions in hundredths introduced? Analyze the introductory lessons? How is this concept related to common fractions? How is the oral name emphasized? How are decimals in hundredths related to the place values of whole numbers? If needed, how could these lessons be supplemented?

12. Should decimal fractions be taught before common fractions? Read "Curricular Issues: Teaching Rational Numbers" by Payne. Do you agree with his arguments? Why or why not?

13. In "Let's Do It: From Halves to Hundredths," Dana and Lindquist describe a number of sequenced activities for introducing decimal fractions. Read the article and briefly describe the activities on ordering.

14. The next activity can be used to extend place values to the right of the decimal point. Use a large ten-by-ten grid as your whole.

a. Shade in one row. What fractional part of the whole is the row? Write this as a common fraction and as a decimal fraction.

b. Shade in one square. What fractional part of the row is the small square? What fractional part of the whole is the small square? Write this as a common fraction and as a decimal fraction.

c. Shade in one tenth of one small square. What fractional part of the row is this part? What fractional part of the whole is this part? Write this as a common fraction and as a decimal fraction.

15. *Materials needed:* Graph paper cut into 10-by-10 squares. Show how students could find the decimal fraction equivalent for the common fractions listed below. Use the graph-paper model.

a. $\frac{3}{10}$ b. $\frac{1}{4}$ c. $\frac{3}{4}$ d. $\frac{3}{8}$
e. $\frac{7}{100}$ f. $\frac{70}{100}$

16. To change common fractions to decimal fractions, a ten-by-ten grid can be folded. Fold and shade grids to illustrate each of the fractions below. Do the shading on the unlined side. Flip the grid to the lined side to determine each common fraction's decimal equivalent.

a. $\frac{1}{2}$ b. $\frac{3}{4}$ c. $\frac{1}{8}$ d. $\frac{3}{8}$ e. $\frac{1}{3}$ f. $\frac{1}{6}$

17. Use the models explored in Problems 15 and 16 to help interpret the results obtained when a calculator is used to change a fraction from its common to its decimal form.

18. Penny used her calculator to find the decimal fraction equivalents of $\frac{1}{5}$, $\frac{2}{5}$, and $\frac{3}{5}$. She then predicted the next three decimals in the sequence and recorded all of her results: 0.2, 0.4, 0.6, 0.8, 1.0, 1.2. What are some of the patterns your students would discover when they used a calculator and prediction to find the decimal equivalents of the following sequences.

a. $\frac{1}{10}, \frac{2}{10}, \frac{3}{10}, \frac{4}{10} \ldots$
b. $\frac{1}{100}, \frac{2}{100}, \frac{3}{100}, \frac{4}{100} \ldots$
c. $\frac{1}{3}, \frac{2}{3}, \frac{3}{3}, \frac{4}{3} \ldots$
d. $\frac{1}{9}, \frac{2}{9}, \frac{3}{9}, \frac{4}{9} \ldots$ (Caution on $\frac{9}{9}$.)
e. $\frac{1}{7}, \frac{2}{7}, \frac{3}{7}, \frac{4}{7} \ldots$
f. $\frac{1}{8}, \frac{2}{8}, \frac{3}{8}, \frac{4}{8} \ldots$

19. On the number lines below, estimate the location of each given decimal.

a.

0	$\frac{1}{4}$	$\frac{1}{2}$	$\frac{3}{4}$	1

0.1   0.6   0.08   0.333   0.48
0.005   0.0038   0.78   0.23
0.66666   0.875   0.125

b.

0   1

0.1   0.6   0.08   0.333   0.48
0.005   0.0038   0.78   0.23
0.66666   0.875   0.125

20. On the decimal number line, estimate the location of each given common fraction. Check your estimates by changing the common fractions to decimal fractions on your calculator.

0 0.1 0.2 0.3 0.4 0.5 0.6 0.7 0.8 0.9 1.0 1.1 1.2

$\frac{1}{5}$ $\frac{1}{3}$ $\frac{1}{4}$ $\frac{1}{6}$ $\frac{1}{8}$ $\frac{1}{9}$ $\frac{1}{10}$ $\frac{2}{5}$

$\frac{3}{5}$ $\frac{2}{3}$ $\frac{17}{17}$ $\frac{3}{4}$ $\frac{3}{8}$ $\frac{0}{20}$ $\frac{6}{5}$ $\frac{1}{20}$

$\frac{3}{100}$ $\frac{234}{230}$ $\frac{7}{25}$ $\frac{3}{50}$ $\frac{7}{1000}$ $\frac{3}{200}$

21. a. As quickly as you can, write the decimal equivalent for each of the fractions below. Time yourself to see how long it takes.

$$\frac{1}{2} \quad \frac{3}{4} \quad \frac{1}{3} \quad \frac{2}{10} \quad \frac{3}{100} \quad \frac{45}{1000} \quad \frac{3}{50}$$
$$\frac{6}{25} \quad \frac{7}{20} \quad \frac{39}{100} \quad \frac{45}{1000} \quad \frac{345}{1000}$$
$$\frac{7}{10} \quad \frac{2}{3} \quad \frac{3}{5} \quad \frac{3}{50}$$

b. Using a calculator and recording your answers, again quickly change each fraction to its decimal equivalent. Time yourself again.

c. Compare your accuracy for the two methods. Was it the same or similar? Compare your times. Were they the same? If not, which method was faster? Which method was more accurate?

22. What are two different strategies a student could use to order the following numbers?

0.324   0.304   0.342   0.3   0.34
0.234

23. Patty and Sarah were arranging the fractions $\frac{70}{99}, \frac{7}{10}, \frac{7}{9}, \frac{7}{100}, \frac{77}{100}$, and $\frac{707}{100}$ from smallest to largest. Patty started to find a common denominator for the fractions. Sarah suggested that they use their calculator to change the common fractions to decimal fractions. Patty agreed that that would be faster, but she was confused by her results of 0.7070707, 0.7, 0.7777777, 0.07, 0.77,, and 7.07. She thought 0.7777777 was the largest number. Sarah suggested that they list the results in a place-value table. What concept was she trying to help Patty focus on?

24. *For your resource file:* What are some of the problem areas in teaching decimal concepts? What suggestions are given to minimize these difficulties? Read "Initial Decimal Concepts: Are They Really So Easy?" by Zawojewski or "Decimals: Results and Implications from National Assessment" by Carpenter, Corbitt, Kepner, Lindquist, and Reys to answer these questions. Add these recommendations to your resource file.

25. *For your resource file:* In "Teaching Rational Numbers—Intermediate Grades," Jacobson describes region, number line, and value (money) models for the teaching of decimal fraction concepts. Read this article and add it to your resource file.

26. *For your resource file:* Ockenga in "Chalk Up Some Calculator Activities for Rational Numbers" and Judd in "Instructional Games with Calculators" both describe excellent activities using the calculator. Do three of the activities from either article and write an evaluation of them. Add these ideas to your resource file.

27. a. George knows that one dollar can be divided into four parts and that $\frac{1}{4}$ of a dollar is equivalent to $0.25, that is, $1.00 \div 4 = \$0.25$. From this, he reasons that any fraction can be rewritten as a decimal by dividing the numerator by the denominator. Using this method, change the following fractions to decimals:

$$\frac{1}{2}, \quad \frac{2}{3}, \quad \frac{4}{5}, \quad \frac{3}{8}, \quad \frac{5}{12}, \quad \frac{7}{20}, \quad \frac{3}{1000}, \quad \frac{2}{35}$$

b. Notice that some of the divisions have remainders of zero (terminating decimals) while others continue to have nonzero remainders (repeating decimals). Explain why $\frac{7}{20}$ is a terminating decimal and why $\frac{2}{35}$ is a nonterminating decimal by discussion of the factors in the denominator.

c. Given the following base-ten fractions:

$$\frac{1}{2}, \quad \frac{1}{3}, \quad \frac{1}{4}, \quad \frac{1}{5}, \quad \frac{1}{6}, \quad \frac{1}{8}, \quad \frac{1}{9}, \quad \frac{1}{10}$$

By examining the factors of the denominators, list the fractions which are terminating decimals in base-twelve system of numeration. Explain how you arrived at your answer.

28. *For your resource file:* Add one of the following to your resource file. Pereira-Mendoza describes games involving a variety of topics in "Using Dice: From Place Value to Probability." In "Let's Do It: Roll 'n' Spin," Shaw includes activities using spinners and dice for such topics as place value, fractions, and probabilities. The activities are appropriate for children in primary through sixth grades.

TEACHER RESOURCES

Behr, Merlyn J., Thomas R. Post, and Ipke Wachsmuth. "Estimation and Children's Concept of Rational Number Size." In *Estimation and Mental Computation,* 1986 Yearbook of the National Council of Teachers of Mathematics, pp. 103–111. Reston, VA: The Council, 1986.

Bohan, Harry. "Paper Folding and Equivalent Fractions—Bridging a Gap." *Arithmetic Teacher 18* (April 1971): 245–249.

Bruni, James V., and Helene J. Silverman. "Let's Do It: Using Rectangles and Squares to Develop Fraction Concepts." *Arithmetic Teacher 24* (February 1977): 96–102.

Carpenter, Thomas P., Mary Kay Corbitt, Henry S. Kepner, Jr., Mary Montgomery Lindquist, and Robert E. Reys. "Decimals: Results and Implications from National Assessment." *Arithmetic Teacher 28* (April 1981): 34–37.

Chiosi, Lou. "Fractions Revisited." *Arithmetic Teacher 31* (April 1984): 46–47.

Coxford, Arthur F., and Lawrence W. Ellerbruch. "Fractional Numbers." In *Mathematics Learning in Early Childhood,* Thirty-seventh Yearbook of the National Council of Teachers of Mathematics, pp. 191–203. Reston, VA: The Council, 1975.

Dana, Marcia E., and Mary Montgomery Lindquist. "Let's Do It: From Halves to Hundredths." *Arithmetic Teacher 26* (November 1978): 4–8.

Ellerbruch, Larry W., and Joseph N. Payne. "A Teaching Sequence from Initial Fraction Concepts Through the Addition of Unlike Fractions." In *Developing Computational Skills,* 1978 Yearbook of the National Council of Teachers of Mathematics, pp. 129–147. Reston, VA: The Council, 1978.

Ettline, J. Fred. "A Uniform Approach to Fractions." *Arithmetic Teacher 32* (March 1985): 42–43.

Jacobson, Marilyn Hall. "Teaching Rational Numbers—Intermediate Grades." *Arithmetic Teacher 31* (February 1984): 40–42.

Jensen, Rosalie, and David R. O'Neil. "Let's Do It: That's Eggzactly Right!" *Arithmetic Teacher 29* (March 1982): 8–13.

Judd, Wallace. "Instructional Games with Calculators." *Arithmetic Teacher 23* (November 1976): 516–518.

Leutzinger, Larry P., and Glenn Nelson. Let's Do It: Fractions with Models." *Arithmetic Teacher 27* (May 1980): 6–11.

Minnesota State Department of Education and Minnesota Council of Teachers of Mathematics. *Fractions in the Mathematics Curriculum.* St. Paul, MN: Department of Education, September 1976.

Ockenga, Earl. "Chalk Up Some Calculator Activities for Rational Numbers." *Arithmetic Teacher 31* (February 1984): 51–53.

Payne, Joseph N. "Curricular Issues: Teaching Rational Numbers." *Arithmetic Teacher 31* (February 1984): 14–17.

Peck, Donald M., and Stanley M. Jencks. "Share and Cover." *Arithmetic Teacher 28* (March 1981): 38–41.

Pereira-Mendoza "Using Dice: From Place Value to Probability." *Arithmetic Teacher 28* (April 1981): 10–11.

Scott, Wayne R. "Fractions Taught by Folding Paper Strips." *Arithmetic Teacher 28* (January 1981): 18–21.

Shaw, Jean M. "Let's Do It: Roll 'n' Spin." *Arithmetic Teacher 31* (February 1984): 6–9.

Suydam, Marilyn N. "Research Report: Fractions." *Arithmetic Teacher 31* (March 1984): 64.

Van de Walle, John, and Charles S. Thompson. "Let's Do It: Fractions with Counters." *Arithmetic Teacher 28* (October 1980): 6–11.

———. "Let's Do It: Fractions with Fraction Strips." *Arithmetic Teacher 32* (December 1984): 4–9.

Zawojewski, Judith S. "Ideas." *Arithmetic Teacher 34* (December 1986): 18–25.

———. "Initial Decimal Concepts: Are They Really So Easy?" *Arithmetic Teacher 30* (March 1983): 52–56.

CHILDREN'S LITERATURE

Dennis, J. Richard. *Fractions Are Parts of Things.* Illustrated by Donald Crews. New York: Crowell, 1973.

Matthews, Louise. *Gator Pie.* Illustrated by Jeni Bassett. New York: Dodd, Mead, 1979.

6

TEACHING ADDITION AND SUBTRACTION OF WHOLE NUMBERS

"Homework? I don't think elementary children should have homework."

"I always assign all of the problems in the book."

"I never collect homework."

"My students think homework is an option not a requirement."

"It takes so much time to grade homework whether we grade it in class or whether I take it home."

"We only check parts of their homework the next day in class."

"If you come in quietly from lunch, there will be no homework tonight."

Evaluate these teacher comments with regard to each teacher's beliefs and practices. What effect will these practices have on their students?

CONCEPT OF ADDITION AND SUBTRACTION

Addition and subtraction are generally defined by mathematicians as binary operations; that is, they combine two elements of a set of numbers to yield a unique third element of the set. However, this type of formal approach is not very useful for the elementary classroom. Instead, the teacher should introduce the concept of addition through problem situations such as the following. "Jerome has 2 blocks. Lisa has 3 blocks. How many blocks in all?" To solve this problem, children should make a set of two blocks and a set of three blocks, combine these sets, and count the number of blocks in the new set to find the answer (Figure 6-1).

Through many similar activities in solving problems, children develop the concept of addition and learn to recognize addition situations. After many play activities in joining sets, children can, through discussion, formulate their own definition of addition. As they are developing a concept for the operation, they should be introduced to the term "addition" as the name of this operation. They should learn that the symbol "+,"

called a plus sign, is used to represent addition and that the symbolic form "3 + 2 = 5" is read "three plus two equals five."

The concept of subtraction, the inverse operation, should be introduced soon after the concept of addition and related to addition so that children will not view it as a completely new topic. By relating subtraction to addition the teacher is simply applying Piaget's theory of learning, which states that individuals build from their present structures. The teacher should build on the children's previous experiences in which they have encountered the concept of subtraction. For example, as Michelle eats dinner, she notices the amount of food on her plate become smaller and smaller until nothing is left. She observes pieces of bread being removed from the loaf, one slice at a time, until the wrapper is empty. If her new slacks are too long, she sees her mother turning them up to a shorter length.

As noted above, children must be involved in situations exemplifying the concepts of addition and subtraction when the operations are introduced. Addition is usually developed as a process of joining sets. Two sets or parts are combined or considered together to form a whole. This language of part/part/whole can be extended to subtraction concepts.

Subtraction is developed through three different situations: take-away, missing addend, and comparison. The first two subtraction situations can be related to the part/part/whole (subset/subset/set) concept of addition. It has been found that using the language of part/part/whole has helped children in solving word problems. In developing the concepts of addition and subtraction, children were asked to identify the given information as parts or wholes. They also identified what is to be found as a part or a whole.

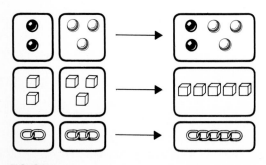

FIGURE 6-1.
Combining sets.

If they had a part and a whole and they needed to find a part, they knew it was a subtraction situation.

The third subtraction situation is a comparison between two sets or wholes. Even in this situation, one set is considered in one-to-one correspondence with a *part* of the other set. Thus the children know the *whole* set and the *part* that can be placed in one-to-one correspondence, and they are trying to determine the *part* that cannot be put in one-to-one correspondence.

As with addition, as children are developing a beginning concept of subtraction, they should be introduced to the word "subtraction" as the name for this operation. They should learn that the symbol " − ," called a minus sign and read "minus," is used to represent subtraction. Particularly since the take-away concept of subtraction is usually introduced first, care should be taken that when children read a number sentence such as "4 − 3 = 1," they say "four minus three equals one" and not "four take-away three equals one."

JOINING SETS—CONCEPT OF ADDITION

Most of the addition situations that children first encounter are *active* ones that involve joining two parts to form a whole. For example, "Three children were playing on the playground. They were joined by two other children. How many children are playing together now?" Some addition situations are *inactive* in that the two parts are separate and are not actually joined. For example, "The group of children on one team had three blondes and two brunettes. How many children?" or "Susan has three books on her desk. David has two books on his. How many books altogether?" No action is implied; in the first situation the whole has been partitioned into two parts—blondes and brunettes. The students can count both parts to determine the whole. In the second situation, Susan's and David's books may remain on their separate desks, but the children can count them all to determine the total.

In all the situations above, children can apply the problem-solving strategy "using models" with the *actual* objects to solve the problems. In other cases, the children will need to use models to represent the situation; for example, "One of the exhibits at the zoo contains three white sheep. Another one contains a family of four black sheep. How many sheep in all?" In this situation the students cannot physically combine the groups nor even see both groups at the same time in order to count a total. Instead, they must use other objects such as popsicle sticks, poker chips, plastic bottle caps, pebbles, or other small, readily available items to represent the sheep.

One useful set of counters is our set of fingers. Although a variety of other counters should also be used, there is nothing wrong with teaching the lower addition facts using the fingers as one model. Students will abandon finger counting whenever they find it unnecessary and time consuming.

Both set and measurement models should be used to illustrate these situations. The examples of counters above are all used to illustrate the set model for addition. Measurement models should also be illustrated. Addition with sets of objects can be extended to addition of lengths. Links, interlocking cubes, or paper clips can be joined together to represent various addition problems.

Whereas sets consist of separate, countable objects, measurement is continuous. Models such as paper clips and interlocking cubes make a good transition from

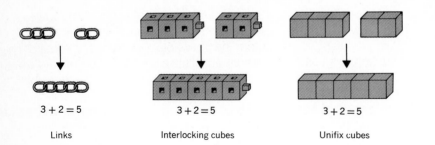

FIGURE 6-2.
Addition with lengths.

$3 + 2 = 5$

Links

$3 + 2 = 5$

Interlocking cubes

$3 + 2 = 5$

Unifix cubes

set models to measurement models. Although length is an attribute of these models, they can also be seen as set models.

In the models shown in Figure 6-2, two sets or parts have been combined to form a whole. Children should also analyze the parts that make up the whole. By comparing a chain of 3 blue links and 4 red links with a chain of 5 blue links and 2 red links, children will find that the two chains are the same length. By comparing and combining various lengths or parts and counting the units that form the whole, children will be acquiring measurement skills as well as learning about addition.

Children can also use Cuisenaire rods as a measurement model for addition. To solve the problem "Eric gave the geranium three tablespoons of water. Ivy gave it another five tablespoons of water. How many tablespoons of water did the plant get?" children place the green rod end to end with the

yellow rod (Figure 6-3). They then search for a rod that is equivalent to the combined length of the green and yellow rods. It is also very useful to combine the Cuisenaire rods with a centimeter number line. In this way the children do not have to search for the corresponding answer rod; instead the correct answer is found on the number line (Figure 6-4).

The teacher can draw arrows under a number line attached to the chalkboard to demonstrate various addition combinations. On a floor number line, the children could walk three steps and then four steps to demonstrate the addition sentence $3 + 4 = 7$ (Figure 6-5).

Children can also solve problems using individual number lines to represent the problem and its solution. This is a more abstract model than counters, so care should be taken that in using the number line the children start at zero, not at one. Sometimes instead of correctly counting the spaces between the numerals, the children count the marks beside the numerals. One way of cor-

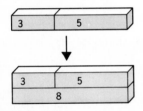

FIGURE 6-3.
Cuisenaire-rod addition.

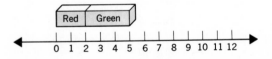

FIGURE 6-4.
Cuisenaire rods used with number line.

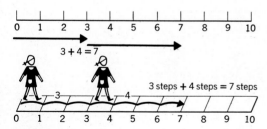

FIGURE 6-5.
Number line addition.

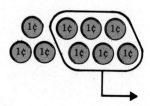

FIGURE 6-6.
Take-away subtraction.

recting this error is by using some type of counting rod that exactly fits the spaces on the number line. When these models are used together, the children will readily notice why they need to start at zero (Figure 6-4). This concept of counting spaces is directly related to measurement. In order to use any measurement scale correctly, the children must learn that the reference point is always zero and that each *space* represents a given quantity.

TAKE AWAY—CONCEPT OF SUBTRACTION

The concept of subtraction is usually introduced with the take-away situation. Beginning subtraction can be introduced in a rational counting exercise. For example, the take-away subtraction situation, "Elizabeth brought 9 cents to school. She payed Michelle the 6 cents she owed her. How much money does Elizabeth still have?", can be represented using the pennies as counters (Figure 6-6). The children can act out the problem by starting with a set of nine pennies and rationally counting six pennies from the set. They can observe that there are three pennies left. In this manner, subtraction is related to counting in much the same way that addition is related to counting.

The part/part/whole language can be

readily extended to the take-away situation. To solve the problem "Tamara, after being sick for a week, had 9 pages of makeup work in mathematics. She completed 6 pages during the school day. How many pages did she have to do at home?", children should identify that the whole is the nine pages, the six pages is a part, and the unknown is the other part. The children can use nine counters to represent the whole and then remove six counters, the part that Tamara had completed. The remaining part (three counters) represents the answer to the situation. Figure 6-7 shows a textbook page of subtraction situations. The children are asked to tell a story, identify the whole, and write a number story. As with addition, sometimes the students can use the actual objects to solve a problem, and other times they must use a representation. In either case when the take-away concept of subtraction is involved, the children can physically "take away" the appropriate number of objects.

COMPARATIVE—CONCEPT OF SUBTRACTION

The concept of subtraction as a comparison can be related to children's conceptions of comparing two sets or wholes to determine which is greater or which is less. For example, to solve the problem "Kyle has five cats.

FIGURE 6-7.
Subtraction—take-away situations. (From Joseph Payne et al., **Harper Row Mathematics**, Grade 1, p. 91. Copyright © 1985, Macmillan, Inc. Reprinted with permission of Scribner Educational Publishers, a division of Macmillan, Inc.)

His brother Ryan has three. How many more cats does Kyle have?'', children can be given two sets of counters to represent Kyle's and Ryan's cats (Figure 6-8). First they must determine whether there are more white counters or more black counters. After matching each white counter with a black one. they have black counters left over. Then they can determine that there are two more black counters than white counters. Since black counters represent Kyle's cats, they can conclude that Kyle has two more cats than Ryan.

The children's experiences should also include comparisons of measurements. Measurement concepts of longer than and shorter than are similar to set concepts of greater than and less than. For example, Jason and Jill both brought trucks for show and tell. To compare the lengths of their toy trucks, the children can use interlocking links (Figure 6-9). To determine how much shorter Jason's truck is than Jill's truck, the links representing the measures of the two trucks are matched one to one. This is similar to the example using counters (set model) as sev-

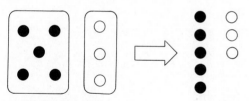

FIGURE 6-8.
Comparison using counters.

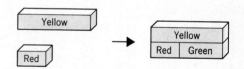

FIGURE 6-10.
Comparison using Cuisenaire rods.

eral distinct objects (links) are used. However, these links are fastened together to form a continuous length (measurement model).

Children should be encouraged to express their solution in a variety of ways. Some children may conclude that three more links need to be added to the shorter chain so that the two chains are of equal length. Others may want to remove three links from the longer chain.

A similar comparison can be made using Cuisenaire rods. Children can determine how the length of the yellow rod compares to the length of the red rod (Figure 6-10). They can demonstrate how much longer the yellow rod is by placing the green rod beside the red rod. The following problem situation can be solved using Cuisenaire rods. "Steve and Carol bought new pencils at the same time. At the end of a month Carol's pencil was considerably shorter than Steve's pencil. How much shorter was it?" Cuisenaire rods were used to measure the lengths of

the pencils. The rods that represent the pencils' lengths were then compared (Figure 6-11). The difference between their lengths was the brown rod, which has a length of eight units. In subtraction situations involving the comparison concept, the students need to compare two quantities to find the difference between them.

MISSING ADDEND—CONCEPT OF SUBTRACTION

Counting can also be used to introduce the missing-addend (additive) concept of subtraction. Missing-addend subtraction cannot be solved by the one-to-one correspondence approach since only one set is given.

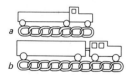

FIGURE 6-9.
Comparison using links.

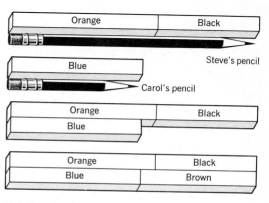

FIGURE 6-11.
Comparison situation using Cuisenaire rods.

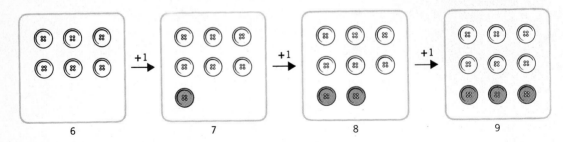

FIGURE 6-12.
Additive subtraction by counting.

An illustration of this concept is "If Steve has six buttons, how many more does he need to have the nine buttons he needs for the new shirt his mother just made?" This can be solved by counting (Figure 6-12). Since there are six buttons, the children start counting from six. As each button is added to the group, it is counted, "seven, eight, nine." The children stop at the number nine and examine how many buttons have been added to the group to find that Steve needed three more buttons.

The missing-addend concept relates subtraction to addition, a previously learned concept. The desired whole and one part are known; the unknown is the other part. In the situation described above, the whole is the nine buttons and one part is the six buttons. The children found the missing part by counting on from one part.

Cuisenaire rods are another model for representing missing-addend subtraction situations. They can be used alone, but a more appropriate method is to combine them with a centimeter number line. For example, to solve the problem, "Carol and Steve were walking to the store to buy new pencils for Carol. The store was fifteen blocks away. After walking six blocks, they became hot and tired, so they stopped for ice cream cones. How much farther did they have to walk?", Cuisenaire rods and a centimeter ruler were used to represent the situation (Figure 6-13).

A number line instead of the ruler can be used similarly to solve the same problem. Children can also use either the ruler or the number line without the Cuisenaire rods when they are ready for a greater level of abstraction. For example, "At the yard sale,

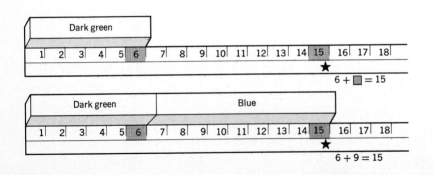

FIGURE 6-13.
Additive subtraction using Cuisenaire rods and a metric ruler.

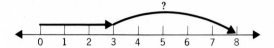

FIGURE 6-14.
Number line subtraction.

Elizabeth would like to buy a toy truck that costs eight cents. She has three cents. How much more money does she need?" The number line is a good model for solving this problem (Figure 6-14). If the children draw an arrow from 0 to 3 on the number line, they must then determmine how much farther they need to go to get to position 8.

Again, this relates subtraction to counting but also introduces the idea of difference as being the concept of moving from one number to another. That is, the difference

between 3 and 8 is the distance from 3 to 8 on the number line. An appropriate number sentence for this story problem would be $3 + \square = 8$. The square represents the missing quantity. This type of equation will relate missing-addend subtraction to addition. By using this format, the child will be able to relate a new concept, subtraction, to a concept already known, addition.

As illustrated in these examples, the use of models is important for developing the concepts of subtraction and for introducing the basic facts. The children are still at the concrete and pictorial stages of learning. The three types of subtraction situations are illustrated, using pictures of peaches for the solution. A take-away subtraction situation is, "Sarah picked 12 peaches but gave 5 of them to Susan. How many peaches does she have left?" (Figure 6-15a) A comparative

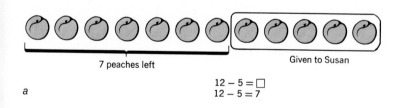

FIGURE 6-15a.
Take-away subtraction.

7 peaches left

Given to Susan

$12 - 5 = \square$
$12 - 5 = 7$

a

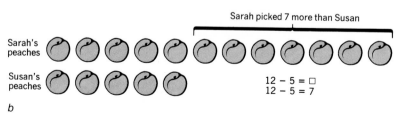

FIGURE 6-15b.
Comparative subtraction.

Sarah picked 7 more than Susan

Sarah's peaches

Susan's peaches

$12 - 5 = \square$
$12 - 5 = 7$

b

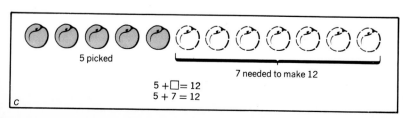

FIGURE 6-15c.
Missing addend subtraction.

5 picked

7 needed to make 12

$5 + \square = 12$
$5 + 7 = 12$

c

subtraction situation is, "Sarah picked 12 peaches and Susan picked 5 peaches. How many more peaches did Sarah pick than Susan?" (Figure 6-15b) A missing-addend subtraction situation is, "Sarah picked 5 peaches, but she needs 12 peaches to make a pie. How many more peaches does she need to pick?" (Figure 6-15c)

Students need to understand all three situations. In some problems individuals will perceive the situations differently. For example, "Ruth had prepared for six luncheon guests but ended up with ten guests. How many more people came than were expected?" Penny represented the six guests with white counters and then added on red counters until she had ten. She then counted the red counters. She used a missing-addend strategy. Ira used ten sheets of paper to represent place mats for the larger group. She placed one counter on one each of six papers to represent place settings for the original guests. She then counted the place mats that did not have a setting. She used a comparison strategy. Jan got out ten water glasses. She put six of them on the table to represent the six guests that were expected. Then she counted the glasses that were left in the kitchen. She used a take-away strategy. Children should be encouraged to solve problems in more than one way and to share their thinking with others.

QUESTIONS AND ACTIVITIES

1. In developing the concept of an operation, children need to be introduced to a variety of *situations* and *vocabulary* so that they will develop the *concept of the operation*. Children should recognize that vocabulary such as "total," "sum," and "How many in all?" usually indicate addition, just as "take away" and "How many are left?" usually indicate subtraction.

   a. Write six addition situations none of which involve the "key words" mentioned above and that illustrate different situations in which we apply the addition concept. Use the lower basic facts.

   b. List the three different types of subtraction situations. Write two situations to illustrate each of the different types. None of these should involve the "key words" mentioned above, and they should illustrate different situations in which we apply the subtraction concept. Use the subtraction facts related to the lower basic addition facts.

2. Consider two of the addition problems and all of the subtraction problems that you wrote in Problem 1. What is missing—the part or the whole? What is given—parts or part and whole? Show how children would solve each situation using counters. How would they find the answer?

3. Consult a subtraction chapter in an elementary textbook for any grade level from two through six. Count the number of story problems. Classify the subtraction problems as take-away, comparison, or missing-addend. List the grade level, publisher, and publication date.

4. In the section "Concept of Addition and Subtraction," an activity was described in which children separated a number of counters into different parts. Put seven counters on a sheet of paper divided into two parts. How many different ways can you separate the counters into two parts? Record your results. Repeat using ten counters. Why is this considered a pre-addition and pre-subtraction activity? How can it be used as an addition and subtraction activity? What types of questions could you ask the children to relate this to part/part and part/whole concepts?

5. a. The concept of union of sets is used in teaching beginning addition. Relate this to part/whole language.

  b. Consult two different elementary textbooks for examples of how the concept of addition is introduced. List the publishers and publication dates. What types of models or diagrams are used? How are the examples alike? Different?

  c. If you add the number of elements in two different sets, will this be the same as the number of elements in the union of these two sets? Give an example to justify your reasoning.

6. Analyze the introduction to the concept of equality in two different textbooks. How is the concept introduced? How and when is the symbol introduced?

7. Read Van de Walle and Thompson's "Let's Do It! A Poster Board Balance Helps Write Equations." Describe how each of the following is introduced.

  a. equality and inequality concepts
  b. equality symbol
  c. inequality symbols
  d. equations involving addition and subtraction

8. a. The diagram given shows how, over a series of lessons, one elementary school textbook introduces the children to the written expressions and gradually the equation. How will this help children better understand the operation concepts? The writing of the operation symbol? The equals symbol?

  b. *For your resource file:* Read "Let's Do It: Modeling Subtraction Situations." In the article, Thompson and Van de Walle describe activities on connecting models to abstractions.

9. Analyze the introduction to the addition concept in two different textbooks. How is the concept introduced? How and when is the operation symbol introduced? How

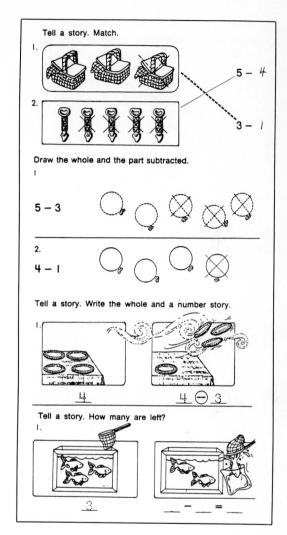

(From Joseph Payne et al., **Harper & Row Mathematics**, Grade 1, pp. 89, 90, 91, 93. Copyright © 1985, Macmillan, Inc. Reprinted with permission of Scribner Educational Publishers, a division of Macmillan, Inc.)

and when is the situation linked to an equation? If needed, how could these lessons be adapted or supplemented to delay symbol work?

10. Analyze the introduction to the subtraction concept in two different textbooks. How is the concept introduced? How and when is the operation symbol introduced? How and when is the situation linked to an equation? If needed, how could these lessons be adapted or supplemented to delay symbol work?

11. Use a set model to illustrate the following problems. Simply set up the expression; do not solve. For example, 3 + 4 can be represented by 3 counters and 4 counters.
    a. three joined with two more
    b. five plus one more
    c. seven minus two
    d. 6 is how much more than 4?
    e. 3 + 5
    f. 6 − 1

12. In working through addition and subtraction story problems, Lee solved some of the problems using the wrong operation. If the teacher tells Lee which ones she has wrong, she could change to the opposite operation and compute the correct answers, but this will not help her in future situations. What are some ways that the teacher could handle this situation?

13. a. Both set and measurement models should be used in modeling concepts. Use a model such as paper clips, interlocking cubes, or links which can be a set model *and* can readily be made into a measurement model. Represent the problems below using the set model. Use counting to find an equivalent name for these expressions, just as a child would need to use counting to find the answer.
    (1) four joined with three more
    (2) three plus two more
    (3) six minus two
    (4) four is how much more than three?
    (5) 3 + 4
    (6) 5 − 2
    b. Re-solve part (a) using the model as a measurement model. Reflect on the differences between the two types of models.

14. Marta used the number line to solve 2 + 3 = □ as shown. *Telling* Marta that she is wrong or *showing* her what is correct will not aid her understanding. Describe an activity that will lead her to discover the error and correct it herself.

15. Why should 13 − 9 not be read as "thirteen take away nine"? How should it be read?

16. Read through six pages of addition and subtraction story problems in a second-grade textbook. As you read through the problems, think in terms of part/whole language. Reflect on how this will help children decide which operation to use.

17. Read through two different lessons of mixed addition and subtraction story problems in a third- or fourth-grade textbook. Do any of the problems contain too much information? Too little information? As you read through the problems, think in terms of part/whole language.

18. Describe how you would have the children write their own addition and subtraction problems. How would this further their concepts of those operations?

19. What is known about how children solve addition and subtraction problems? To answer this question, read "Research Report: Addition and Subtraction—Processes and Problems" by Suydam (1985).

20. *For your resource file:* After reading one of the following articles, describe how these ideas should influence how we teach addition and subtraction. In "Young Children Are Good Problem Solvers," Moser and Carpenter describe children's strategies for solving addition and subtraction verbal problems. Campbell

describes how to help children analyze verbal problems in "Using a Problem-Solving Approach in the Primary Grades."

21. Are symbols introduced too early? Read "Learning Difficulties: Helping Young Children with Mathematics: Subtraction" by Liedtke. What recommendations are made for increasing children's understanding of subtraction?

PROPERTIES OF ADDITION

As the concepts of the operations are introduced, children should begin discovering the properties of addition. As children combine two sets to form a new set, they will observe that each of these sets can be represented by a familiar counting number or zero (whole numbers). Thus, adding any two whole numbers yields a unique whole number, or more formally, addition of whole numbers is closed.

The commutative law or order principle of addition should be introduced while children are developing the concept of addition. Children can represent the commutative law by using such models as buttons, blocks, plastic shapes, Cuisenaire rods, or the number line (Figure 6-16). They will quickly realize that the order of addends can be changed with no effect on the answer. Application of the commutative law is very helpful when children are learning the basic facts of addition (all the combinations of a one-digit number with another one-digit number) because it reduces the number of facts to be learned by about half.

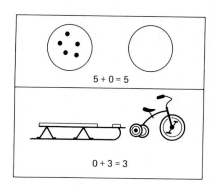

FIGURE 6-17.
Additive identity property of zero.

The additive identity, zero, should be introduced after children have learned the counting-on strategy for 1, 2, and 3. Models should be used to represent addition combinations where one of the addends is zero. If children solve problems using models such as counters, they will soon be able to generalize a rule for adding zero (Figure 6-17). Questions such as "How many wheels are there on your tricycle and your sled?" will also help to develop the concept that zero plus any number or any number plus zero is that number. Once the generalization is formed, it can aid students in learning the basic facts since now all 19 facts with zero as an addend can be learned by one concept.

Another property—the associative law or grouping property for addition—can also be helpful in learning basic facts. The strategy of finding the sums for the near-doubles is based on the associative property. For example, to solve $7 + 8$, students think,

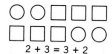

$2 + 3 = 3 + 2$

$2 + 3 = 3 + 2$

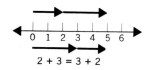

$2 + 3 = 3 + 2$

FIGURE 6-16.
Commutative law of addition.

$$7 + 8 = 7 + (7 + 1)$$ Closure — addition of whole numbers

$$= (7 + 7) + 1$$ Associative property of addition

$$= (14) + 1$$ Closure — addition of whole numbers (Doubles fact)

$$= 15$$ Closure — addition of whole numbers

FIGURE 6-18.

Rationale for near-doubles strategy.

"7 + 7 is 14, 7 + 8 is one more so 7 + 8 is 15." Figure 6-18 shows the mathematical reasoning for this strategy.

Knowledge of the partitions of ten can also be helpful in learning the basic facts or in doing mental computation. This strategy is also based on the associative property. For example, given the problem 9 + 4, students may think "9 + (1 + 3), which can be grouped as (9 + 1) + 3 or 10 + 3, is 13." To mentally add 97 + 5, students may think "97 + 3 is 100 plus 2 more is 102."

Mathematically, addition is a binary operation, so only two numbers can be added at a time. The associative and commutative laws are especially important when the given problem requires the addition of three or more numbers because most students find that some combinations of numbers are easier to add than others. An example of a column addition problem is explained using the laws as justification for each step (Figure 6-19). The first column of addends was reordered by applying the commutative law. The second column was regrouped by applying the associative law as shown in the third column.

The process of adding by groups of ten is an important skill that should be developed for mental and column addition. This is a situation where the importance of the emphasis given the tens facts becomes apparent. When first using this approach, students will probably find it easier to rewrite the problem applying the commutative and associative laws so that the groups of ten are physically together. Some students may continue to do this rewriting in order to have a written record to help them avoid mistakes such as leaving a number out or adding a number twice. Others will progress to simply searching for the groups of ten and near-ten and physically or mentally marking them off without rewriting (Figure 6-20). In the second example, three different thought patterns all lead quickly and efficiently to the right answer. In this way, students can first add the easy combinations of ten and other combinations that are simpler for them personally.

Some books will suggest the procedure of adding from the top down and then checking by adding from the bottom up for any problem in column addition. This often makes a problem more difficult. When this procedure is applied to the previous example, there is no step that results in an exact number of tens (Figure 6-21). Therefore, students must jump from one decade into the next, for example, from 15 to 22, from 29 to 38, and so on. This is a difficult process for many students and hence a common source of error. By using the commutative and associative laws, students can search out easy combinations first and thus simplify the problem. At the same time their understandings of concepts and of the structure of the numeration system are being reinforced.

The use of mathematics terminology such as "identity law of addition" or "com-

8		8		8	> 10
4		2		2	
5	Reorder	4	Regroup	4	> 10
6	→	6	→	6	
+ 2		5		5 5	

FIGURE 6-19.

Column addition (grouping by tens).

FIGURE 6-20.
Using the associative law.

mutative law" depends on the language sophistication of the students, and generally such terminology should not be introduced until the higher grades. Students themselves are the best judge of when they are ready for such terms. Some students will immediately incorporate these mathematical terms into their vocabulary while others will continue to say "zero rule for addition" or "order rule." As the laws are discussed in class, it is good practice for the students to develop their own ways of expressing the concepts. These definitions formed through class discussion are generally easier for students to understand than a formal rule given in the text or stated by the teacher.

PROPERTIES OF SUBTRACTION

As the various concepts of subtraction are introduced, so are the special properties of subtraction. In studying addition, children found that any combination of two whole numbers yielded a unique whole number answer, in other words, that addition of whole numbers is closed. As they explore whether the commutative or order principle holds for subtraction, children will discover that some subtraction combinations do *not* yield a whole-number answer. Therefore, subtraction of whole numbers is not closed.

Just as children need to learn that addition is commutative, they should discover that subtraction is not. For example, if children have eight counters and take away six counters, two counters are left (Figure 6-22a). When the order of the numbers is changed, the children discover that eight counters cannot be taken away (Figure 6-22b). Therefore 8 − 6 is not equivalent to 6 − 8.

Some children may question what happens when a larger number is taken from a smaller number. They may have already encountered negative numbers by trying such problems as 6 − 8 or 43 − 65 on their calculators. If their interest and questions indicate an early introduction to negative numbers, the teacher should give them an example suitable for their maturity. If the children have encountered temperatures below zero, temperature could be used as an example. An illustration using money is "If the child has 6 cents and owes another child 8 cents, can the debt be paid?" The questions involving negative numbers should be an-

FIGURE 6-21.
Add down—add up to check.

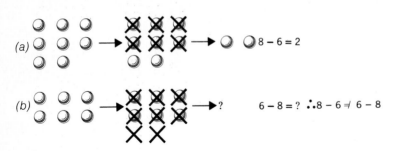

FIGURE 6-22.
Subtraction is not commutative.

swered. It is not sufficient nor correct to say that a larger number cannot be subtracted from a smaller number. The answer will simply be a negative number.

Some textbooks circumvent this problem by stating that only whole numbers are to be used (Figure 6-23). The students are not to solve the problems but merely to decide which problems can be solved using whole numbers. This skill is extremely important later for subtraction problems that will require regrouping, such as 62 − 17. If students recognize that 2 − 7 will not yield a whole number, they can quickly see the need for regrouping.

The associative property should also be explored in relation to subtraction. Figure 6-24a shows the process when three balls are taken from nine balls to leave six balls. Two balls are subtracted from the remaining six balls to leave four balls. In Figure 6-24b the children know that three minus two is one. Then they subtract one ball from the nine balls to leave eight balls. Since 4 is not equivalent to 8, $(9 − 3) − 2 \neq 9 − (3 − 2)$ or the associative law is not true for subtraction.

Since zero is the identity element for addition, it is also a special element for subtraction. Thus if zero is subtracted from any

FIGURE 6-23.
Subtraction of whole numbers—not closed. (From **SRA Mathematics Learning System**, Teacher's Guide, Level 2 by M. V. DeVault, H. Frehmeyer, H. J. Greenberg, and S. J. Bezuska. © 1974, Science Research Associates, Inc. Reprinted by permission.)

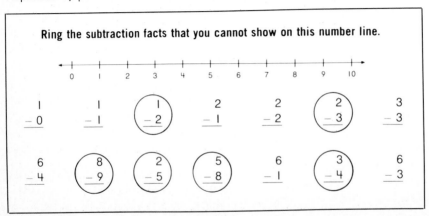

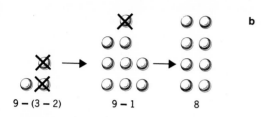

a

$(9 - 3) - 2$ $6 - 2$ 4

$(9 - 3) - 2 \neq 9 - (3 - 2)$

b

$9 - (3 - 2)$ $9 - 1$ 8

FIGURE 6-24.
Subtraction is not associative.

number, that same number is the result. However, zero is not a true identity for subtraction because zero minus any number is not that number. Instead, if any number is subtracted from itself, the result is zero.

LEARNING THE BASIC FACTS OF ADDITION AND SUBTRACTION

In any academic area there is certain information that must be learned for instant recall. The basic facts of addition and subtraction fall into this category. The importance of learning the basic facts can best be stated by saying that little success in arithmetic is possible without understanding and immediate recall of the basic facts.

The basic facts of addition, as mentioned earlier, are all the different combinations of a one-digit number with another one-digit number. Thus $3 + 6 = 9$, $0 + 3 = 3$, $8 + 7 = 15$, and $7 + 8 = 15$ are all basic

facts; $12 + 3 = 15$ is not a basic fact. A chart of all one hundred basic addition facts is shown (Figure 6-25). The basic addition facts can be classified into three categories: (1) the lower basic facts, those which have sums less than 10; (2) the tens basic facts, those which have sums equal to 10; and (3) the higher basic facts, those which have sums greater than 10. Children learn many of the lower basic facts while studying the concept of addition.

The subtraction basic facts are the inverses of the addition basic facts. Thus $3 + 6 = 9$ is a basic addition fact, so $9 - 6 = 3$ is a basic subtraction fact. To read the basic subtraction facts from the addition chart (Figure 6-25), first a number within the chart is selected. That number lies in a particular row and a particular column in the chart. The chosen number minus the number at the far left of its row equals the number at the top of its column.

+	0	1	2	3	4	5	6	7	8	9
0	0	1	2	3	4	5	6	7	8	9
1	1	2	3	4	5	6	7	8	9	10
2	2	3	4	5	6	7	8	9	10	11
3	3	4	5	6	7	8	9	10	11	12
4	4	5	6	7	8	9	10	11	12	13
5	5	6	7	8	9	10	11	12	13	14
6	6	7	8	9	10	11	12	13	14	15
7	7	8	9	10	11	12	13	14	15	16
8	8	9	10	11	12	13	14	15	16	17
9	9	10	11	12	13	14	15	16	17	18

FIGURE 6-25.
Chart of basic addition facts.

STRATEGIES FOR ADDITION

After being introduced to the concepts of the operations, children should be introduced to strategies for learning the basic facts. There are several useful strategies for teaching the basic addition facts. These strategies give children a method other than counting or rote memorization for learning the basic facts, and the strategies also help children to develop their concepts of number. Although there is some overlap as to which strategies are appropriate for specific facts, all strategies should be taught because there are also important differences among them. (Consult "Using Thinking Strategies to Teach the Basic Facts" by Rathmell for further explanation and other activities on thinking strategies.) If the children's textbook does not have the learning of basic facts organized in clusters appropriate to these strategies, the teacher will need to supplement it.

Counting On

One strategy used in the early teaching of basic facts is counting on. When one of the addends is one, two, or three, this strategy is appropriate. At first when children are learning the concept of addition, they usually count the entire combined set. For example, to solve 4 + 1, they combine the sets and count, "one, two, three, four, five." To use the counting-on strategy, the children would first identify the larger of the two addends and then count on from there; that is, to solve 4 + 1 = ?, they would say "FOUR . . . five." Similarly, to solve 2 + 7, the children would count "SEVEN . . . eight, nine" (Figure 6-26). The child's voice inflection should differentiate between the starting point and the numbers counted on.

Adding Zero

After learning the strategy of counting on, children can extend this to adding zero. Adding zero is another strategy children easily learn. To teach this special property of zero, the teacher can form two different loops on the overhead projector: A certain number of counters can be placed in one loop and zero counters in the second loop. By observing the total number of counters in the two sets, the children should generalize that any number plus zero or zero plus any number will always be that number.

Practice lessons for this strategy should not be limited to only combinations with zero as one of the addends. The problems should be designed so that in each combination one of the addends is zero, one, or two. As children develop this generalization for zero, it will facilitate their learning of the basic facts.

Partitions

Another strategy for teaching basic facts of addition uses addition fact partitions. In this strategy the addition facts are separated into sets of facts with each fact in a given set having the same sum. Learning the various combinations of parts that make up any whole will help children in learning the addition and subtraction facts. As children use counters to find the different partitions of a whole, they can record their results (Figure 6-27). They should discover that in some pairs of combinations the parts are the same but the order is different. For example, in the fives partitions, the combination 2 + 3 and the combination 3 + 2 both yield five. The fives partitions are shown in Figure 6-28 along with the pictures of the appropriate sets of black and white counters. In using this part/part/whole strategy, the tens parti-

FIGURE 6-26.
Counting on for addition. (From Robert Eicholz, Phares O'Daffer, Charles Fleenor, Randall Charles, Sharon Young, Carne Barnett, **Addison-Wesley Mathematics: Book 1**, p. 75. Copyright © 1985, Addison-Wesley Publishing Co. Inc.)

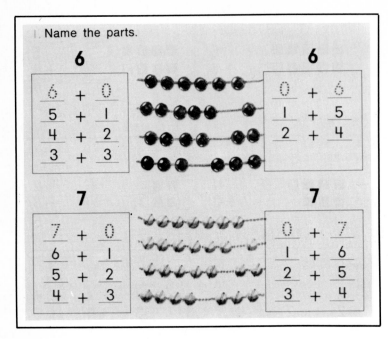

FIGURE 6-27.
Partitions for addition. (From Joseph Payne et al., **Harper & Row Mathematics**, Grade 1, p. 195. Copyright © 1985, Macmillan, Inc. Reprinted with permission of Scribner Educational Publishers, a division of Macmillan, Inc.)

tions are of particular importance. They should be given extra emphasis because later they are needed for applying more complex strategies and because they are extremely useful in mental arithmetic.

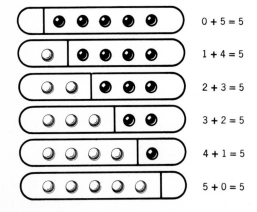

FIGURE 6-28.
The fives partitions.

Doubles

The doubles facts are those facts in which a number is added to itself. These facts are easily learned by most children. Not only do children find them inherently interesting, but some doubles occur in everyday life. Examples include 2 threes or 2 fours—pop cartons, 2 fives—fingers, 2 sixes—egg cartons, and 2 sevens—days in two weeks (Figure 6-29).

Near Doubles

The doubles facts are a prerequisite for the near doubles. Near doubles are those facts that differ from the doubles by plus or minus one or plus or minus two. Examples include 5 + 6, 8 + 7, 6 + 8, or 9 + 7. When first using this strategy, children are introduced only to the doubles-plus-one concept. To solve 6 + 7, the children should be guided to think "6 + 6 is 12 and 6 + 7 is one more, so 6 + 7 is 13." In beginning work they are

FIGURE 6-29.
Doubles for addition. (From Robert Eicholz, Phares O'Daffer, Charles Fleenor, Randall Charles, Sharon Young, Carne Barnett, **Addison-Wesley Mathematics: Book 1**, p. 175. Copyright © 1985, Addison-Wesley Publishing Co. Inc.)

given both the near-doubles combination *and* a related doubles combination (Figure 6-30). Giving the doubles combination is gradually phased out as the children learn to associate an appropriate doubles fact.

As they become familiar with this strategy, children can extend it to doubles-plus-two. To solve 6 + 8, children can be guided to think "6 + 6 is 12 and 6 + 8 is two more, so 6 + 8 is 14" (Figure 6-31a). A further extension to doubles-minus-one-or-two allows children to choose the doubles facts they find easiest. For example, to solve 8 + 7, they may think "8 + 8 is 16 . . . 8 + 7 is one less, so 8 + 7 is 15." Another child may solve this same problem using a dou-

FIGURE 6-30.
Doubles plus one. (From Robert Eicholz, Phares O'Daffer, Charles Fleenor, Randall Charles, Sharon Young, Carne Barnett, **Addison-Wesley Mathematics: Book 1**, p. 177. Copyright © 1985, Addison-Wesley Publishing Co. Inc.)

a.
$$\begin{array}{r} 6 \\ +8 \\ \hline \end{array}$$
6 + 6 is 12
6 + 8 is two more
so 6 + 8 is 14.

b.
$$\begin{array}{r} 8 \\ +7 \\ \hline \end{array}$$
8 + 8 is 16
8 + 7 is one less
so 8 + 7 is 15.

FIGURE 6-31.
Doubles plus or minus one or two.

bles-plus-one strategy. This strategy uses an application of the associative property.

Adding Nine

Another strategy is based on the fact that adding ten is easy; for example, 10 + 3 is 13 or 6 + 10 is 16. This concept is used to develop a strategy for adding nine. For example, to solve 9 + 6, the children may think "10 + 6 is 16 . . . 9 + 6 is one less, so 9 + 6 is 15." This thinking is similar to that used in the doubles-minus-one strategy (Figure 6-32). This strategy is also an application of the associative property.

FIGURE 6-32.
Adding nine. (From Robert Eicholz, Phares O'Daffer, Charles Fleenor, Randall Charles, Sharon Young, Carne Barnett, **Addison-Wesley Mathematics: Book 2**, p. 77. Copyright © 1985, Addison-Wesley Publishing Co. Inc.)

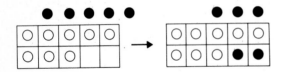

$$8 + 5 = 8 + (2 + 3) = (8 + 2) + 3 = 10 + 3 = 13$$

FIGURE 6-33.
Using a grid for compensation.

Compensation

The partitions of ten are a prerequisite for this strategy. In adding 8 + 5 a child may reason, "8 + . . . 2 more is 10 . . . 10 plus the 3 more is 13, so 8 + 5 is 13." To develop this thinking, a grid as shown in Figure 6-33 is helpful. Counters representing 8 are placed on the grid and those representing 5 beside it. The students can clearly see that if two more counters were added to eight, they would have ten. Two counters are transferred onto the grid so that 8 + 5 or 8 + (2 + 3) becomes (8 + 2) + 3 or 10 + 3 is 13. To solve 9 + 6 Bob used compensation rather than the strategy of adding nine. Bob stated, "9 + 1 more is 10; 10 + 5 more is 15, so 9 + 6 is 15." This strategy is another application of the associative property.

STRATEGIES FOR SUBTRACTION

Knowing the addition basic facts is a prerequisite skill to learning the related subtraction basic facts. However, children should not wait until they have learned all the addition facts before they begin to study subtraction.

Counting On and Counting Patterns

After learning the basic facts that can be solved using counting on, children can learn the related subtraction facts. These related subtraction facts can be learned by counting back. To solve 5 − 1, students may count back saying "FIVE . . . four" (Figure 6-34). Similarly, to solve 7 − 2, they may count back by saying, "SEVEN . . . six, five." As with counting on in addition, the first number

FIGURE 6-34.
Counting back. (From Joseph Payne et al., **Harper & Row Mathematics**, Grade 1, p. 109. Copyright © 1985, Macmillan Inc. Reprinted with permission of Scribner Educational Publishers, a division of Macmillan, Inc.)

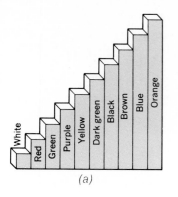
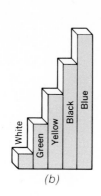
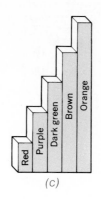

FIGURE 6-35.
Stairsteps using Cuisenaire rods.

(a)   (b)   (c)

should be said in a different tone of voice to distinguish the starting point from the "one" or "two" taken away. Through experiences with this strategy and through other counting experiences, children may form generalizations such as "any number minus one is the preceding number" or "any number minus the preceding number is one." They can form similar generalizations for problems in which the difference is two. Their experience in counting even- or odd-number sequences will help them recognize combinations that are exactly two apart, such as $7 - 5$, $6 - 4$, and so on.

The generalizations relating to differences of one or two can be taught using Cuisenaire rods as a model. The Cuisenaire rods can be lined up as stairsteps (Figure 6-35a). As children place each rod in order from left to right, they can observe that each rod is one unit longer than the previous one. When progressing from right to left, each rod is one unit less than the previous rod. Other stairsteps can be built based on two units more than or less than the previous rod (Figure 6-35b and c). These stairsteps can be related to counting backward. When counting "down" the stairsteps, children count 10, 9, 8, 7 . . . or 9, 7, 5 . . . or 10, 8, 6. . . . Counting backward by ones or twos with relation to the Cuisenaire rods helps develop the

generalizations of "one less than" or "two less than."

Addition and Subtraction Fact Families

Another strategy for learning basic subtraction facts is to use addition and subtraction fact families. Each family contains the four basic facts that relate three numbers through addition and subtraction. Such a family for the numbers 3, 4, and 7 is shown in Figure 6-36. Children can be led to discover the relations within this family. For example, Tim counted each of the three white counters as he placed them one by one into a container. He then counted four more black counters and added them to find a total of seven counters, or $3 + 4 = 7$ (Figure 6-37). As he removed the four black counters, he obtained his original three white counters, or $7 - 4 = 3$.

If Tim understands the order (commutative) law, he should realize that $4 + 3 = 7$ is equivalent to $3 + 4 = 7$. The equation $7 - 3 = 4$ can be generated by removing

$$3 + 4 = 7$$
$$4 + 3 = 7$$
$$7 - 4 = 3$$
$$7 - 3 = 4$$

FIGURE 6-36.
Addition and subtraction fact family for 3, 4, and 7.

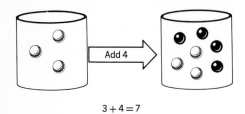

3 + 4 = 7   7 − 4 = 3

FIGURE 6-37.
Counters used for fact family.

three objects in part *b* instead of the four objects. When subtraction is related to addition, the addition facts are reinforced and the concept that subtraction is the inverse operation of addition is clearly illustrated.

Another way that subtraction facts can be related to the corresponding addition facts is through partitions. For example, Figure 6-28 showed all the partitions of the fives family. These partitions of five can be related to all the addition–subtraction fact families for which the sum is five. By using counters or Cuisenaire rods, children can find all the partitions of various other families. They should find the different *parts* that make up the *whole*. For example, each combination

of parts—4 and 3, 5 and 2, 6 and 1, or 7 and 0—makes up the whole—seven. For each combination the children should state or write the four related addition and subtraction facts—that is, for 7, 5, and 2 they should write 5 + 2 = 7, 7 − 2 = 5, 7 − 5 = 2, and 2 + 5 = 7—before considering another combination, such as 3, 4, and 7. Part of a lesson on this topic from an elementary textbook is shown in Figure 6-38.

Zero Patterns for Subtraction

As with addition, zero facts should be introduced with concrete examples. "There are five people in the Meidinger family. On Monday night all of them go out to meetings. How

FIGURE 6-38.
Addition-subtraction fact families. (From Robert Eicholz, Phares O'Daffer, Chalres Fleenor, Randall Charles, Sharon Young, Carne Barnett, **Addison-Wesley: Book 1**, p. 293. Copyright © 1985, Addison-Wesley Publishing Co. Inc.)

many are at home on Monday night?" "On Tuesday night nobody in the family goes out for anything. How many are at home on Tuesday night?" Through representing problems of this type with counters and through thinking about and discussing them, children can generalize about subtraction facts with zero. They will discover that any number minus itself is zero and any number minus zero is itself.

Missing Addend

Another way of relating subtraction to addition is through the missing-addend concept. To illustrate this idea, the teacher could place seven counters on the overhead projector. After the class recognizes that there are seven counters in the set, the entire set should be covered by a sheet of paper. Three of the counters can then be pulled out from under the paper. Since the class can see three of the counters, they should be encouraged to think, "three and *what* are seven." (Note that the counters are not taken away. Part of the set is covered up.) By using the vocabulary "3 plus what is 7?," children are encouraged to think of addition or the missing addend. The children should write down their answers and *then* discuss the appropriate answer after uncovering the hidden counters. Since each child writes down a response, *all* students must make a decision; this way a few students do not dominate the class discussion. This activity should be repeated for other partitions of seven and for other fact families. As the problems are presented, the teacher can observe individual responses noting which students may need extra help.

After activities with counters, paper and pencil activities could include problems such as 6 + 7 = ☐. The children should fill in the sum and then rewrite the sentence into appropriate subtraction sentences such as

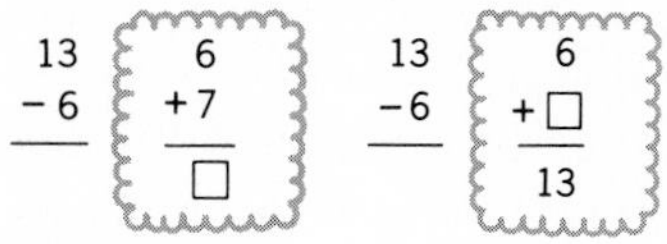

FIGURE 6-39.
Relating subtraction to addition.

13 − 7 = 6 or 13 − 6 = 7. Also, subtraction problems could be written on the board, and the children could write down which addition basic fact would help them solve the problem. Other problems that relate addition to subtraction are shown in Figure 6-39. Since the first "think cloud" shows the answer to the subtraction problem, it should be used only initially. After the children have become confident of their abilities to think addition, the addition think clouds can be phased out.

Note that the teaching sequence for these basic facts goes back and forth between addition and subtraction. The easier addition facts are taught first, and then the related subtraction facts are taught. Then the addition facts which require more sophisticated learning strategies are taught, followed by their related subtraction facts.

MEMORIZING THE BASIC FACTS OF ADDITION AND SUBTRACTION

In using the strategies to teach basic facts to children, we must consider several factors. The focus of instruction should be on just one strategy at a time. As a particular strategy is being developed, only those facts for which it is appropriate should be used. The strategy should be practiced for short intervals (5 to 10 minutes each day) for a period of 2 to 3 weeks. (In "Suggestions for Teaching the Basic Facts of Arithmetic" by Edward Davis in *Developing Computational Skills,* ten guidelines are presented to help teachers plan effective practice.)

The number balance can be used for practicing basic facts as it is self-checking. The number balance uses the concept of mass to represent number. The balance arm rests in a horizontal position until a standard mass is placed on any peg of either side. The pegs are numbered 1 through 10, and the children should discover that a mass placed on any peg assumes the value of the peg's number. After placing standard masses to represent a basic addition combination on one side of the balance, the child places a standard mass or masses to represent the correct answer on the other side of the balance. The horizontal position of the balance arm will reinforce the child's correct solutions.

Thus Figure 6-40 shows the correct solution for $8 + 7$ as $8 + 7 = 15$. As an extension, children can explore the relationship between combinations in partitions. By balancing a combination such as $6 + 5$ with another member of the elevens partitions such as $3 + 8$, they can see that $6 + 5 = 3 + 8$.

Subtraction facts can also be practiced as missing-addend combinations. Since 12 on one side and 7 on the other will not balance, the child must place another mass in the correct location to make the arm balance. By the position of the horizontal arm, the child can check whether or not the answer is correct.

Calculators can be used to practice the basic facts of addition and subtraction. The child could punch in the basic fact combination, "guess" the answer, and then check that answer by pushing the "=" key. Children can use the constant function to practice the strategy counting on. One of the addends appropriate for this strategy can be entered into the calculator as a constant. The child should enter the other addend, give the answer, and then check it. The strategy adding nine and its prerequisite adding ten can be practiced similarly.

A calculator subtraction game for two players also involves problem solving. One player selects a two-digit number and enters it on the calculator. The players take turns subtracting any one-digit number except zero. The child to reach zero first is the loser. To develop a winning strategy, children must *find a pattern*. If the numbers that the children are allowed to subtract are restricted, they will have to find a different pattern.

Some special calculators are also designed for drill and practice activities. Such calculators as the Little Professor and the Dataman present various combinations of any one of the four operations in random order. As well as selecting the operation to practice, the child can select an appropriate level of difficulty. These calculators re-present the problem when an error is made, display the correct answer after a certain number of incorrect trials, and give the number of correct answers at the end of a practice set. However, in comparing regular calculators with preprogrammed calculators such as the Little Professor or Dataman, it was found that students using regular calculators or paper and pencil outperformed those children using special calculators. Since the regular calculator can also be used for a variety of problems, it is a better

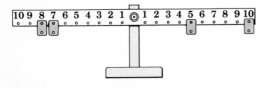

FIGURE 6-40.
Number balance addition.

purchase for both schools and individuals (Suydam, 1982).

Many computer programs for practicing the basic facts of addition and subtraction are also available. These programs present basic-fact combinations in random order, and the child must punch in the answer. Most programs give the child immediate feedback on whether or not the answer is correct. Some programs will re-present the problem if the child has made a mistake. After a designated number of incorrect guesses or when the correct response is given, the computer will present the next combination. Some programs will also give the correct answer if the child has not found it. At the end of the session, most programs will give the child feedback on the total number of correct responses.

An important feature of computers is record keeping. Some programs provide information on the amount of time used and the specific difficulties encountered by an individual student on any one practice set. The teacher can plan future activities for the individual and for the class accordingly.

Simple programs for practicing basic facts are fairly easy to write (see Appendix I). By writing his or her own program, the teacher can give students extra practice on selected facts. Some programs allow children to choose which operations they wish to practice. Others will give mixed practice on two or more operations. Since most students are excited about a chance to work with the computer, it is also a good motivational tool. Although much computer practice for children on basic facts is not significantly different from the old-fashioned flash cards, if the children see it as exciting, they will probably practice longer and thus learn more.

Many games and contests can be organized using flash cards. They can be used for a class activity with students writing the answers on paper. Pairs of students can use them, with one student acting as the tutor. They can also be used by individual students who need extra practice while learning the basic facts. Each student can make his or her own flash cards of the basic facts to be learned. Students can be encouraged to study the basic facts independently.

Special number cubes with numerals instead of dots on the sides can be made from inexpensive wooden cubes (Figure 6-41). Students practicing addition can roll the number cubes and name the sums. These number cubes can be used by groups of students during class time, or the students can be encouraged to use them during their free periods and play time. Spinners can be used in much the same manner as the number cubes (Figure 6-42). Similar equipment can be used to practice basic subtraction facts. For these games, the students would name the differences.

Activity sheets can be designed to reinforce addition and subtraction concepts (Figure 6-43). ○'s, □'s, and △'s are place-

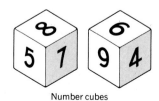

Number cubes

Flash cards

FIGURE 6-41.
Learning aids.

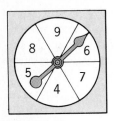

FIGURE 6-42.
Spinners.

holders representing various numbers. The children are to determine the rule by which the three numbers are related. For the example shown in Figure 6-43a, one child may guess the rule as $\bigcirc + \square = \triangle$ since 6 + 3 = 9 and 5 + 2 = 7. Another child may guess the rule as $\triangle - \square = \bigcirc$, which would also be correct. The rule for the third table is that $\triangle + \square = 10$ or $10 - \triangle = \square$ or $10 - \square = \triangle$. Such activities give practice with the basic facts. They also provide problem-solving situations in which the child must determine what operation to use.

Card games can also be developed that

reinforce the learning of the basic addition facts. For example, a card game to aid the children's learning of the basic addition facts would include cards labeled with appropriate addends and sums. The cards should be designed so that they give the most practice with those facts that the students find difficult. A rummy game could then be played with a sequence being any three cards that form an addition fact. The cards $\boxed{5}$, $\boxed{6}$, $\boxed{11}$ would be considered a sequence since 5 + 6 = 11. Obviously, the same set of cards could be used for subtraction as 11 − 6 = 5.

A board game based on the number line and designed especially for subtraction is shown in Figure 6-44. This game uses a number cube and markers and is designed for two or more players. When the number cube is tossed, it determines how many spaces the player should move a marker. Before the student moves the marker, she or he should predict the space on which it will land. For example, if the student's marker is on 13 and a 5 turns up on the number cube, the prediction may be that the marker will land on 9 or that 13 − 5 = 9. After making the move, the student should see the mistake for 13 − 5 = 8. The marker will be moved back to 13 since the prediction was incorrect. The first player whose marker passes 1 wins the game.

Variations of this game are practically unlimited. A wooden cube with the numerals 4, 5, 6, 7, 8, and 9 on it can replace the standard die or number cube. Various spaces on the board can direct the player to pick up a card from a stack on the game board. These cards can dictate various moves such as "move back five spaces" or "move ahead two spaces, then back three spaces." The cards should be written so that they reinforce the particular skills the stu-

●	■	▲
6	3	9
5	2	7
4		7
2		8
	6	
5	3	

(a)

●	■	▲
9	4	5
8	7	1
7		2
6	1	
	4	3
	9	8

(b)

■	▲
7	3
5	5
4	
	8
9	
	2
7	
	4

(c)

FIGURE 6-43.
What's my rule? Activity to reinforce addition and subtraction basic facts.

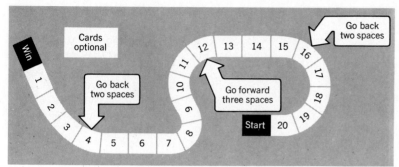

FIGURE 6-44.
Board game using number line.

dents need to practice. The cards may vary from day to day and from one group of students to another. New cards can be added as new concepts are developed.

The Arithmetic Teacher, the elementary-level journal of the National Council of Teachers of Mathematics (NCTM), has numerous articles on games that can be used to reinforce concepts. Various articles explain card games, contests, and board games. The objectives, the directions for making the game, and the rules for playing the game are included in each article. Any game should be freely adapted to meet the needs of an individual classroom. Students can be encouraged to create their own games. (Guidelines on the role of games and suggestions on how to use and create games for learning basic facts are discussed in "Games: Practice Activities for the Basic Facts" by Robert Ashlock and Carolynn Washbon in *Developing Computational Skills*.)

Care must be taken to select games wisely. The type of play involved must be considered. A good game should keep everyone involved, make the waiting time between turns as short as possible, and give all students opportunities for success. Some games such as the old-fashioned spelldown type should be avoided as these give the most practice to the students who need it least and leave many students sitting in their seats doing nothing for most of the game time. Good games also include those that are easily made by the students and/or the teacher and that can be used many times over. A game that can be made in five minutes but used only once might have similar value to one that takes three hours for construction but can be used over and over. Some games should be designed for practicing particular learning strategies and others for general practice in random recall of facts.

As is implied by the learning activities for the basic facts, all of the work is mental. Unfortunately, for most students, learning the basic facts is all the mental computation they will be required to do. This should not be the case as mental computation activities should be used throughout the elementary curriculum. Another skill that should also be used throughout the curriculum is estimation. Children should be encouraged to use estimation when developing addition and subtraction concepts. For example, after children have studied the lower basic facts but before they learn the higher basic facts, they should be able to estimate that the answer for 8 + 7 is between ten and twenty or the answer to 12 − 5 would be less than ten.

QUESTIONS AND ACTIVITIES

1. What is the difference between the concept of addition and strategies of addition? Between strategies of addition and memorizing the basic facts of addition?

2. a. A child can count by twos (2, 4, 6, . . . and 1, 3, 5, 7, . . .). How will this help in his or her addition skills?
   b. A child can count 20, 19, 18, 17, . . . and 10, 8, 6, . . . and 11, 9, 7, ... How will this help in his or her subtraction skills? Consider with regard to combinations like 7 − 5 as well as 7 − 2.
   c. Devise a calculator code to count as shown in parts (a) and (b).
   d. *For your resource file:* Read "Let's Do It: Counting with a Purpose" by Leutzinger and Nelson. Write up at least four activities that you could use to teach "counting on." Add these to your resource file.

3. Note how the equation 8 + 7 = 15 can be written from the results shown in Figure 6-40. How could the number balance be used for teaching the meanings of equals and helping children write equations?

4. Name an appropriate strategy for teaching each of the basic facts below. Write out the student's thinking.
   a. 6 + 7   b. 0 + 8
   c. 9 + 5   d. 7 + 2
   e. 8 + 6   f. 3 + 5

5. a. Build an addition table for the basic facts. Name and describe at least four generalizations that children could discover when building their own addition table.
   b. List and describe, in your own words, the strategies for learning the basic facts. On the addition table, shade in which facts are appropriate for each strategy.

6. Describe how you would use models and appropriate questions to teach "counting on" one or two. Consider that part of the process is learning how to use the strategy for 9 + 2 and 2 + 9. Collect or devise some oral activities that involve this strategy. How and when would you adapt these activities to extend the children's thinking to counting on three or counting back for subtraction?

7. Describe how you would use models and appropriate questions to teach the doubles. How would you adapt this activity to extend the children's thinking to the doubles-plus-one? How and when would you adapt these activities to extend the children's thinking to doubles-plus-two? Doubles-minus-one or -two?

8. Describe how you would use models and appropriate questions to teach adding ten. How would you adapt this activity to extend the children's thinking to adding nine?

9. a. Illustrate the partitions of 6 using Cuisenaire rods. Write the corresponding number sentences.
   b. Describe how you would use counters and appropriate questions to teach the partitions of ten. How would you help children extend this thinking to solve addition facts using compensation? Describe how to solve 8 + 6 using this strategy.
   c. *For your resource file:* Read "Let's Do It: The Power of 10." In the article Thompson and Van de Walle describe how to develop this strategy and how to extend it to mental computation.

10. a. Give a numerical example of an addition and subtraction fact family. Explain why this fact family is a useful teaching tool.
    b. How is this related to part/part/whole concepts?

11. a. Read and summarize the article "A Successful Strategy for Teaching Missing Addends" by Thompson and Babcock.

b. Several sequenced activities for teaching subtraction facts are described in "Let's Do It: Using Addition Facts to Learn Subtraction Facts" by Leutzinger and Nelson. Read the article and write up sample activities from each sequenced lesson.

12. Create or collect a number of activities that could be used to teach the strategies for learning addition and subtraction facts.

13. Create or collect a number of games that could be used to practice the strategies for learning addition and subtraction facts or to practice basic facts. Use materials such as number cubes, spinners, cards, calculators, or game boards. Chance and skill should be designed into the format of the game. When the game is being used to practice a particular strategy, include only those facts that are appropriate for that strategy or perhaps sometimes for previously learned strategies. The articles listed in the Teacher's Resources contain numerous helpful ideas.

14. Why is adding zero considered a strategy *and* a property? Use counters and appropriate questions to teach this concept to another student.

15. Describe how Cuisenaire rods could be used to illustrate the associative property of addition.

16. a. The concept of commutativity can be explored in nonnumerical ways. For example, children could be asked whether the action of putting on a sweater and a shirt is commutative. Write at least six nonnumerical actions that can be classified as either commutative or not commutative (three of each).
    b. Give a numerical or practical example of the commutative property. Name an appropriate teaching aid and explain how this aid can be used to develop this concept.

c. Why is it important for children to be able to use the order (commutative) property?

17. Write a calculator code that could be used for a child practicing the facts appropriate for counting on with 2. For counting back.

18. How can a calculator be used to help a child learn the strategy "think addition" for solving basic subtraction combinations?

19. How can a calculator code be used for a child practicing addition or subtraction basic facts?

20. Play "Target 25" as described in "Calculator Games: Combining Skills and Problem Solving" by Fisher. How could you use this game with your students? What skills are being practiced as the game is played?

21. Analyze the presentation of basic facts in two different textbook series.
    a. What strategies are introduced to the students? If strategies are not introduced, how are the children expected to find the answer? How could you supplement the text?
    b. How is drill work presented? Is accuracy emphasized in the lesson? Accuracy and speed? Are there any time guidelines for the teacher?

22. When should children start drilling on basic facts?

23. a. What is the place of drill in the elementary classroom for teaching basic addition and subtraction facts?
    b. Read "Suggestions for Teaching the Basic Facts of Arithmetic" by Davis. List the principles that should be considered in teaching basic facts.

24. *For your resource file:* For further information on addition strategies, read at least one of the following articles. In "Mastering Basic Facts of Addition: An Alternate Strategy," Lazerick describes activities to teach a number of the strategies. In "72 Addition Facts Can Be

Mastered by Mid-grade 1," Rightsel and Thornton describe methods of teaching strategies to first graders. In "Doubles Up—Easy!" Thornton gives a number of examples that children can use for learning their doubles. She describes activities for teaching strategies to special children in "Helping the Special Child Measure Up in Basic Fact Skills."

25. *For your resource file:* For information on strategies for subtraction facts, consider the following articles. In "Children's Difficulties in Subtraction: Some Causes and Cures," Baroody describes how to help children remediate difficulties as they develop strategies. In "Young Children's Strategies for Solving Subtraction-Fact Combinations," Beattie describes children's strategies; some of which are inefficient and lead tc errors. In "Mrs. Weill's Hill: A Successful Subtraction Method for Use with the Learning-Disabled Child," Weill describes how to teach strategies using compensation to get ten. Add the ideas from at least one of these articles to your file.

26. *For your resource file:* Read and add at least one of the following to your file: The articles "All Hands on Deck" by Lent and "Variations on Concentration" by Tucker describe card games for the basic facts and other topics. Schroeder describes a basic fact game in "Capture: A Game of Practice, a Game of Strategy."

ALGORITHM FOR ADDITION OF WHOLE NUMBERS

In real life, children encounter a variety of situations that will require addition such as:

Dewey school was collecting soup labels to earn playground equipment. On Monday Chad brought 20 labels. On Wednesday Grace brought thirty labels. Lars brought 50 labels on Thursday, and Karol brought 60 on Friday. How many labels did the boys bring to school that week? The girls?

Lydia and Jerome were participating in Jump Rope for Heart. Lydia jumped 300 times before she needed to stop for a rest. Jerome jumped 400 times on his first turn. How many times had they both jumped after their first turn?"

To solve these problems, children must learn procedures or algorithms. Children's first experiences with the addition algorithm involve problems in which exact multiples of ten or one hundred must be added. Problems of this type form the basis for developing the addition algorithm with no regrouping and later the algorithm with regrouping.

When children begin developing the addition algorithm for two- and three-digit numbers, models such as counting sticks, base-ten blocks, or the abacus should be used to illustrate the problems and to reinforce place-value concepts. For example, Cuisenaire rods could be used to illustrate 40 + 20. The children would combine 4 tens and 2 tens into a set of 6 tens or sixty. The problem should be recorded as 4 tens + 2 tens = 6 tens and 40 + 20 = 60 to relate the model to the written algorithm and to reinforce place-value concepts. Similarly, examples involving hundreds should be illustrated before extending the written algorithm to three-digit numbers (Figure 6-45). The problem represented on the abacus is more abstract since the abacus is a conceptually more abstract model than the Cuisenaire rods and because the sum requires regrouping.

The next step in using the algorithm is to add tens and ones to tens and ones with-

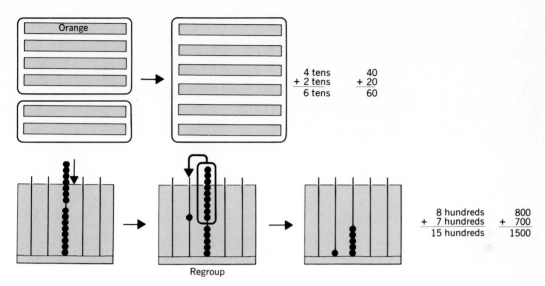

$$\begin{array}{rr} 4 \text{ tens} & 40 \\ + 2 \text{ tens} & + 20 \\ \hline 6 \text{ tens} & 60 \end{array}$$

$$\begin{array}{rr} 8 \text{ hundreds} & 800 \\ + 7 \text{ hundreds} & + 700 \\ \hline 15 \text{ hundreds} & 1500 \end{array}$$

Regroup

FIGURE 6-45.
Cuisenaire rods and abacus to add tens and hundreds.

out regrouping. As part of children's experiences with algorithms, verbal problems can be used to motivate the topic and extend their concepts as to the *uses* of addition. After students have solved several addition problems with models, the teacher should guide them in relating the model to the algorithm. A possible dialogue with appropriate questions is given below.

Ms. Schurrer: We have twenty-three boys and thirty-four girls in the first grade. If each child is to have a popcorn ball at our Halloween party, how many popcorn balls will we need?

Mike: Lots!

Ms. Schurrer: But exactly how many? How can we find out?

Judy: You have to add how many boys to how many girls.

Ms. Schurrer: Good. Can someone state that as a number sentence?

Karl: Twenty-three plus thirty-four.

Ms. Schurrer: Okay! Let's solve twenty-three plus thirty-four with our base-ten blocks. What will you do first?

Teresa: We'll need longs and units— 2 longs 3 units and 3 longs 4 units.

Ms. Schurrer: Use your blocks to form the two sets. (Walks around checking children's representations; Figure 6-46.) . . . What do we do next?

Mike: Push them together to form one large set.

Ms. Schurrer: Okay, let's look at the ones first. How many ones do we have?

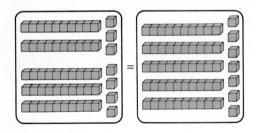

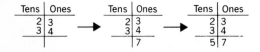

FIGURE 6-46.
Addition—no regrouping.

Laura:	7 ones. 3 ones and 4 more.
Ms. Schurrer:	Let's record that in the ones column. (Writes 7 in the ones column on the chalkboard.) 3 ones plus 4 ones is 7 ones. Now how many tens do we have?
Judy:	I have 5 longs . . . 5 tens.
Ms. Schurrer:	We'll record that in the tens column. (Writes 5 in the tens column on the chalkboard.) 2 tens plus 3 tens is 5 tens. Our answer is 5 tens 7 ones or . . . Karl?
Karl:	Fifty-seven.

Through further class discussion, the children should gradually become more involved in recording the algorithm and less dependent on teacher questions to guide them. An example of an introductory lesson from a first-grade textbook is shown in Figure 6-47. Pictures of base-ten blocks were used to represent 32 and 57. First the ones were grouped for a total of 9 ones; the result was

recorded in the ones column. The tens were then added to obtain 8 tens, and this was recorded appropriately. The sum was 8 tens 9 ones or 89. The textbook has clear illustrations of models for tens and ones and shows the step-by-step process.

However, children often do not link these illustrations to the class activity, so the teacher should discuss such examples with the children. This written exercise should follow a class activity similar to the one described above so that children will think through such procedures and learn to solve problems. After supervised seatwork on various examples, the children can work appropriate problems from their textbooks to practice the concept.

The addition algorithm with regrouping was discussed in detail in Chapter 3, but a brief summary is included in this section. The prerequisite skills for this algorithm are: (1) regrouping ten or more ones to the corresponding number of tens and ones and (2) the addition algorithm with no regrouping. After reviewing these skills, the children can be introduced to addition problems involving regrouping. They should begin this new step by first working several sample problems with models. Through class discussion, the process used with the models should be related to the algorithmic process. Figure 6-48 clearly illustrates the step-by-step procedures of adding ones, regrouping, and adding tens. Each diagram relates the appropriate recording of the written algorithm to the model.

Adding a two-digit number to a one-digit number with regrouping is often included in a different lesson from adding a two-digit number to a two-digit number with regrouping (Figure 6-48). In one case, after regrouping the ones the students will add one more ten to the single tens digit in the problem. In

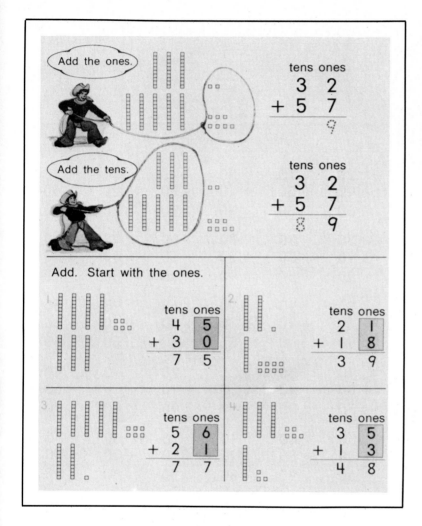

FIGURE 6-47.
Two-digit addition—no regrouping. (From Joseph Payne et al., **Harper & Row Mathematics**, Grade 1, p. 213. Copyright © 1985, Macmillan, Inc. Reprinted with permission of Scribner Educational Publishers, a division of Macmillan, Inc.)

the other case, after regrouping the ones, the students will need to add three digits that represent tens.

Usually, the next type of addition problems that are introduced involve three-digit addends with no regrouping; these are followed by three-digit addends with one regrouping. The addition algorithm for three-digit numbers is simply an extension of the algorithm for two-digit numbers. The algorithm is extended to problems with more than

two addends as well as to addends with more digits.

A further extension of the algorithm is to problems that require more than one regrouping. Children are usually introduced to addition problems that have two regroupings in third grade. For example, to solve 57 + 68, students must rename 15 ones as one 1 ten 5 ones and rename 12 tens as 1 hundred 2 tens (Figure 6-49). A place-value table was extended to hundreds to record the algo-

FIGURE 6-48.
Two-digit addition with regrouuping. (From J. J. Bezdek, C. Tobin, A.P. Troutman, **Using Mathematics: Grade 2**, Laidlaw Brothers, 1984, p. 114. By permission of Laidlaw Brothers, a division of Doubleday & Company, Inc.)

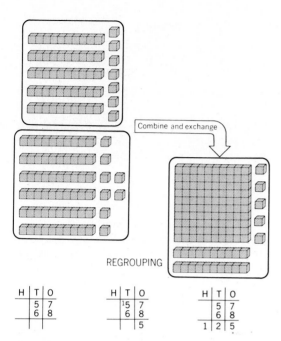

Combine and exchange

REGROUPING

H	T	O
	5	7
	6	8

H	T	O
	¹5	7
	6	8
		5

H	T	O
	5	7
	6	8
1	2	5

FIGURE 6-49.
Addition—two regroupings.

rithm step by step. When students encounter three-digit addends such as 354 + 197, they will need to adapt their use of the algorithm.

For a better understanding of the addition algorithm, a few problems could be analyzed using expanded notation (Figure 6-50). As can be seen from the figure, 23 + 34 is the same as 20 + 30 and 3 + 4. These last two addition problems exemplify prerequisite skills for the algorithm needed to solve 23 + 34. This is an explanation of addition, not a procedure for addition that children should be expected to practice. When applying the addition algorithm, we add the ones first (3 + 4) and then the tens (2 + 3).

The same place-value concepts used for expanded notation can help children in making estimates and doing mental computations. Some people, using place value

$$\begin{array}{r} 23 \\ +34 \end{array} \longrightarrow \begin{array}{r} 20+3 \\ 30+4 \\ \hline 50+7 \end{array} \longrightarrow 57$$

FIGURE 6-50.
Rationale for addition.

for estimation, will think, "The answer will be about 5 tens or 50 as the addends contain 2 tens and 3 tens." Others, using an expanded form, will think, "The answer will be at least in the 50s as the addends are in the 20s and 30s." Estimation and mental computation will be explored further in a later section.

ALGORITHM FOR SUBTRACTION OF WHOLE NUMBERS

The sequence for developing the subtraction algorithm is parallel to the sequence for developing the addition algorithm. As in addition, subtraction of multiples of ten comes first, followed by the algorithm with no regrouping and then by the algorithm with regrouping. Also, as with addition, after the children are familiar with solving problems using models, this process should be related to the written algorithm.

SUBTRACTION WITHOUT REGROUPING

First, children should solve problems such as 30 − 20 or 50 − 30. Subtracting these decade numbers is actually easier for many children than some of the basic facts such as 17 − 9 or 13 − 6. Even so, they should begin by solving these problems with appropriate models such as base-ten blocks or counting sticks. In the example of 50 − 30, they should represent fifty as 5 tens. Then

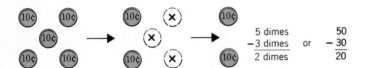

FIGURE 6-51.
Subtraction of decade numbers.

they should take away thirty or 3 tens to obtain an answer of 2 tens or twenty.

Money can also be used to solve subtraction problems involving decade numbers (Figure 6-51). Children can use their well-developed counting skills for the multiples of ten to solve the problem. As they take away the three dimes, the children count, "10 cents, 20 cents, 30 cents" and then observe that "10 cents, 20 cents are left." After several examples, these activities can be related to the algorithm by writing the problem in a place-value table.

Subtraction with no regrouping involving a two-digit number minus a one-digit number is usually introduced in textbooks before subtraction of a two-digit number minus a two-digit number. By first subtracting one-

digit numbers, children must focus on subtracting in the ones place. Then, when they are introduced to a two-digit number minus a two-digit number, they are using the same procedure—first subtracting the ones, then the tens. A subtraction problem with no regrouping is represented with models in Figure 6-52. After the children can solve the problems using the models, the algorithm should be related to the model.

SUBTRACTION WITH REGROUPING

This same procedure, using the model first and then relating it to the algorithm, should be utilized in teaching subtraction with regrouping. In order to solve subtraction problems that require regrouping, children must

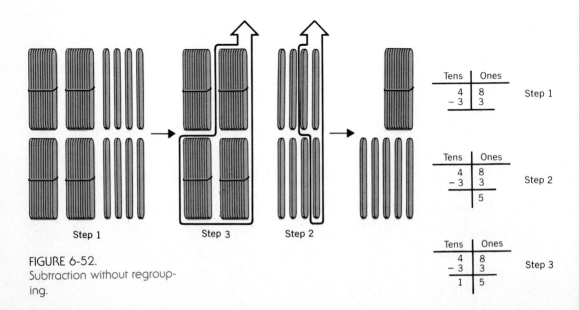

FIGURE 6-52.
Subtraction without regrouping.

possess the prerequisite skills of knowledge of the basic subtraction facts, ability to rename 1 ten as 10 ones, and ability to use the subtraction algorithm with no regrouping. Children should review renaming numbers such as 5 tens 3 ones to 4 tens 13 ones with models and in written form.

After reviewing problems using the subtraction algorithm with no regrouping, a problem with regrouping should be introduced. Again, two-digit minus one-digit problems usually precede two-digit minus two-digit problems. The children should use models such as counting sticks or base-ten blocks to solve the problems. After gaining facility with this process, the children should be taught how to relate the model to the algorithm. The problem 63 − 27 can be solved by using similar procedures to those described in Figure 6-52. The process where regrouping is required is illustrated with base-ten blocks and with the abacus (Figure 6-53a). The following dialogue is a possible discussion in which the teacher is guiding the class in solving the problem 63 − 27.

Mr. Pascal: "The Jean Shop had 63 pairs of beige corduroy jeans in stock. During the first day of a special sale, they sold 27 pairs of the beige jeans. How many pairs were still on hand?" How would we solve this problem?

Ted: It's subtraction because 27 were taken away.

Amy: It's sixty-three minus twenty-seven.

Mr. Pascal: How can we solve sixty-three minus twenty-seven using our base-ten blocks?

Charles: We need to start with sixty-three blocks.

Mr. Pascal: Please show that number. (Walks around observing students' work.) What base blocks did you use?

Joan: 6 tens, 3 ones, or 6 longs, 3 units.

Mr. Pascal: Good. What number are we going to subtract?

Ted: Twenty-seven.

Mr. Pascal: What do we subtract first?

Amy: 7 ones.

Nancy: But we only have 3 ones.

Jimmy: Can't we use one of the longs?

Mr. Pascal: How?

Charles: The long is 1 ten—we could trade it for 10 ones.

Mr. Pascal: Let's try that. (Again observes students as they work.) Now how many ones do we have?

Ted: 13 ones.

Amy: But we only have 5 tens left.

Mr. Pascal: Is 5 tens and 13 ones the same as 6 tens and 3 ones?

Nancy: Yes, we just traded. Now we can take away 7 ones.

Mr. Pascal: Then do so . . . How many ones do you have left?

Ronnie: 6 ones.

Mr. Pascal: So 13 ones minus 7 ones is 6 ones. What do we do next?

Jimmy: Take away 2 tens, which would give us 3 tens.

Mr. Pascal: So 5 tens minus 3 tens is 2 tens. Is that the answer to our problem?

Joan: Yes, 3 tens, 6 ones.

Marilyn: That's thirty-six.

Amy: So they had thirty-six pairs of jeans left.

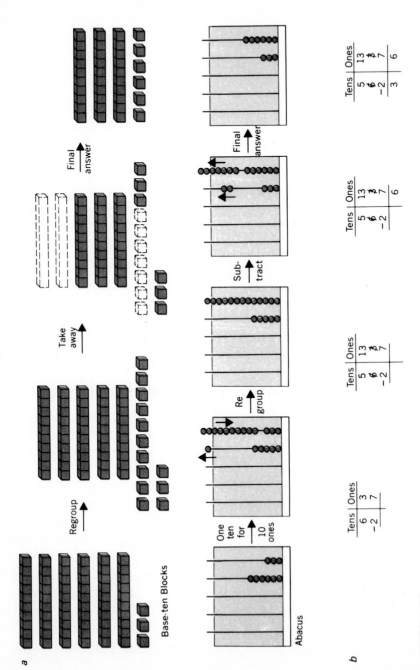

FIGURE 6-53.
Subtraction with regrouping.

Charles: That sounds right as they had 63 pairs and sold almost 30 pairs so a few more than 30 pairs should be left.

To relate this situation to the algorithm, the teacher needs to incorporate recording the algorithm as the work with the model proceeds, as shown in Figure 6-53. Models are intended for initial discovery and algorithmic development to allow students to better understand the concepts underlying the algorithm. Children will set aside the model when they are ready since the algorithm is more convenient and faster to use. As children solve the problem through the use of models, they should record the steps of their process in a place-value table. This process can be used to develop the subtraction algorithm.

Gradually, the place-value table should be phased out. In the example in Figure 6-53b, the child crossed out the 3 ones and wrote 13 ones. Later, children will start writing only a 1 beside the ones digit to indicate the regrouped ten. Whether or not they progress to a form in which the renaming is done mentally is an individual matter. Each child will adopt whichever form or forms work best for him or her as a permanent algorithm.

More complex problems can be solved using the same techniques as those developed for the last examples. In the case of multiple renaming, children will discover that they simply need to apply skills that they already know. Since every place value in our system is a power of 10, the same idea or technique is employed whether the student is regrouping tens to ones or hundred millions to ten millions.

If the subtraction algorithm is carefully developed so that children comprehend the underlying concepts, common errors can be avoided. After children have developed the concepts for subtraction both without renaming and with renaming, they need practice in using the algorithm. Practice exercises should include both types of problems so that children will learn to discriminate between the two.

If, after the concept of subtraction with renaming is developed, children are given only problems that require renaming, they may conclude that subtraction always requires renaming. For example, in solving 46 − 23, Jim automatically renamed 6 as 16 and "4" as "3." He then thought "3 from 6 is 3 and 2 from 3 is 1," and thus obtained an answer of 13 (Figure 6-54a). Jeanine followed a similar procedure for renaming. However, when she subtracted, she thought, "16 minus 3 is 13 and 3 minus 2 is 1," and obtained an answer of 113 (Figure 6-54b).

On the other hand, if students are given insufficient practice with problems that involve renaming, they may not recognize when it is required. Another common error pattern results from this misconception. In subtracting 54 − 17, Julie failed to recognize that renaming was needed. However, she knew that seven could not be subtracted from four. She thought, "7 minus 4 is 3 and 5 minus 1 is 4," and obtained an answer of 43 (Figure 6-54c).

Another common error occurs in subtraction computation of the type shown in Figure 6-54d. Instead of renaming 1 hundred as 10 tens, Hilary has renamed 1 hundred as 10 ones. The teacher can help Hilary discover her error by having her work the same problem using base-ten blocks. By using the blocks, Hilary can easily see that 1 hundred is not equivalent to 10 ones. Instead 1 hundred must be exchanged for 10 tens, and then 1 ten exchanged for 10 ones (Figure 6-55). By working several examples of this type, Hilary should be able to correct the algorithmic error.

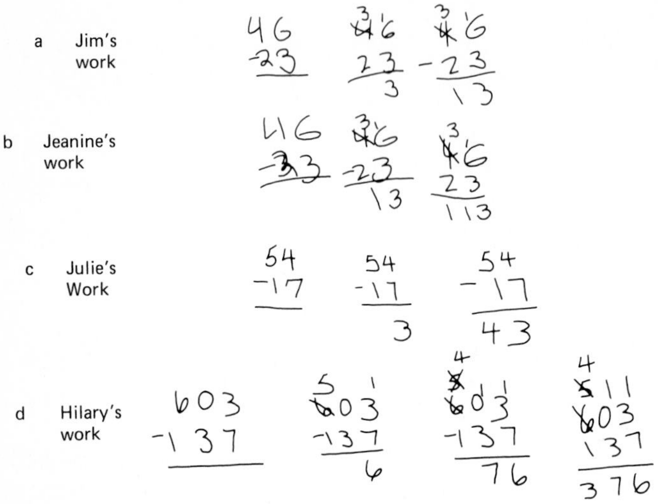

FIGURE 6-54.
Error patterns.

a   Jim's work

$$\begin{array}{r} 46 \\ -23 \\ \hline \end{array} \qquad \begin{array}{r} \overset{3}{\cancel{4}}6 \\ 23 \\ \hline 3 \end{array} \qquad \begin{array}{r} \overset{3}{\cancel{4}}6 \\ -23 \\ \hline 13 \end{array}$$

b   Jeanine's work

$$\begin{array}{r} 46 \\ -33 \\ \hline \end{array} \qquad \begin{array}{r} \overset{3}{\cancel{4}}6 \\ -23 \\ \hline 13 \end{array} \qquad \begin{array}{r} \overset{3}{\cancel{4}}6 \\ 23 \\ \hline 113 \end{array}$$

c   Julie's Work

$$\begin{array}{r} 54 \\ -17 \\ \hline \end{array} \qquad \begin{array}{r} 54 \\ -17 \\ \hline 3 \end{array} \qquad \begin{array}{r} 54 \\ -17 \\ \hline 43 \end{array}$$

d   Hilary's work

$$\begin{array}{r} 603 \\ -137 \\ \hline \end{array} \qquad \begin{array}{r} \overset{5}{6}\overset{1}{0}3 \\ -137 \\ \hline \end{array} \qquad \begin{array}{r} \overset{4}{\cancel{5}}\overset{1}{\cancel{0}}3 \\ -137 \\ \hline 76 \end{array} \qquad \begin{array}{r} \overset{4}{\cancel{5}}\overset{1}{\cancel{0}}\overset{1}{3} \\ 603 \\ 137 \\ \hline 376 \end{array}$$

Another method of correcting this error is to focus on place value by having the student consider 603 as 60 tens and 3 ones. The 60 tens is renamed as 59 tens and 10 ones. When this approach is used, the problem is easily understood (Figure 6-56). These approaches (base-ten blocks and place-value names) are also appropriate for correcting the other error patterns discussed above. By examining students' homework and by observing their work in class, the teacher should be able to determine the kinds of errors they are making and to design activities that will help the students correct their work.

After the students have progressed through the modeling stage and the paper-and-pencil stage of algorithms, the use of calculators for problem solving will be reintroduced. Research has found that children achieve higher scores on addition and subtraction number sentences when they use calculators. However, if the sentences are written in nontraditional forms such as 23 + _____ = 45, students still have difficulty with the problems. Using a calculator to compute answers is not a substitute for conceptual development. Students need to develop the concepts of operations and relationships between them in order to use the calculator effectively (Suydam, 1982).

Children are sometimes told that they can not subtract a larger number from a smaller number. Some children will soon discover that their calculator can do such problems but that a "minus" sign appears with the display. This is an opportunity to introduce children to negative numbers. Their questions should be answered informally and completely in terms and with situations

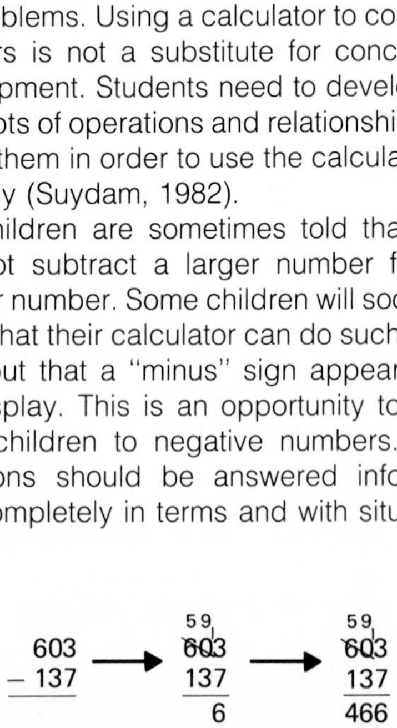

$$\begin{array}{r} 603 \\ -137 \\ \hline \end{array} \longrightarrow \begin{array}{r} \overset{59}{\cancel{6}}\overset{}{0}3 \\ 137 \\ \hline 6 \end{array} \longrightarrow \begin{array}{r} \overset{59}{\cancel{6}}\overset{}{0}3 \\ 137 \\ \hline 466 \end{array}$$

FIGURE 6-56.
Regrouping across zero.

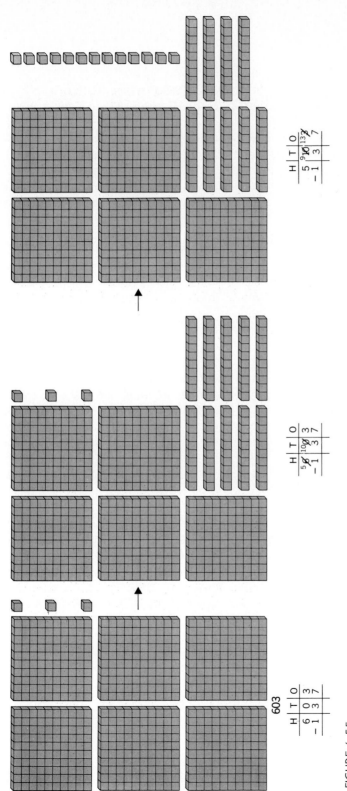

FIGURE 6-55.
Regrouping with base-ten blocks.

that they can understand such as temperatures below zero, owing money, or card scores that are in the hole.

Kurtz describes a calculator game using addition or subtraction that also reinforces place-value concepts. The game is for two players. One player enters a three-digit number and tells the other player to use subtraction to take away all the tens. If this is done correctly, the second player scores one point. The second player enters a new number and tells the other player to take away all the ones, tens, or hundreds. Play continues. This game can be modified using addition. In this case the players must add a certain number of tens, ones, or hundreds to obtain a zero in a particular place value. Other objectives could be obtaining a different digit such as 2 in a certain place value or having the place value in the hundreds place decrease by subtracting a minimum number of tens. The game could also be extended to larger or smaller numbers, including decimal fractions.

ALTERNATIVE ALGORITHMS FOR SUBTRACTION

Some children will develop their own algorithms. The additive method of subtraction can be applied in the algorithm form. For example, to solve 83 − 28, after Mike renamed 83 as 7 tens and 13 ones, he changed his thinking from 13 − 8 = □ to 8 + □ = 13. He reasoned that 8 + 2 more is 10 and 3 more is 13; therefore, 8 + 5 = 13. Mike

could also reason that 28 + 2 more is 30. Since 83 minus 30 is 53, 28 + 2 + 53 = 83 or 28 + 55 = 83 (Figure 6-57). This type of compensation strategy is particularly useful for mental computation.

One aspect of subtraction that is generally overlooked is that the same number can be added to both numbers of the subtraction problem without changing the answer. The equal-additions method of subtraction is the basis for certain algorithms and for explaining shortcuts in computations. Understanding this method is also an important concept for mental computation.

Children can use Cuisenaire rods and the number line (Figure 6-58a) to show the difference between 123 and 97. By moving the rods three spaces to the right, which is equivalent to adding 3 to both 123 and 97, the children can see that the difference between 123 and 97 is the same as the difference between 126 and 100. Figure 6-58b shows the process in algorithmic form as 3 is added to both 123 and 97. This equal-additions method can be used to simplify a problem so that renaming is unnecessary.

In many areas of the world our standard algorithm of subtraction by renaming is not the predominant form. The form generally adopted is the equal-additions algorithm. In this method when children solve a problem requiring renaming such as 64 − 38, they add *1 group of ten* to the 38 and *10 ones* to the 64. Thus the problem changes from (60 + 4) − (30 + 8) to (60 + 14) − (40 + 8). As shown in Figure 6-59, children are subtracting 4 tens and 8 ones from 6 tens and 14 ones.

Any of the algorithms shown is an acceptable method of subtracting. Once children master a satisfactory algorithm for an operation, there is no need for them to learn another unless it will further develop their concept understanding without disrupting

$$83 \quad \longrightarrow \quad \overset{7}{\cancel{8}}3 \qquad 8 + \square = 13$$
$$-\,28 \qquad\qquad \cancel{2}8$$

FIGURE 6-57.
Finding the missing addend.

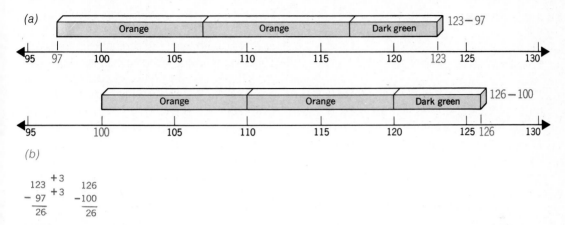

FIGURE 6-58.
Subtraction by equal additions.

their skill with the primary algorithm. Regardless of the algorithm used, practice is necessary for children to acquire skill in using it.

ESTIMATION AND MENTAL COMPUTATION FOR ADDITION OF WHOLE NUMBERS

In the ways that mathematics is usually used by most adults, estimation is a very important skill. Many times, an exact sum is not necessary for answering a question. For example, "Jane has been out shopping for clothes. She has found two blouses that she really likes, but she also needs a pair of jeans. One blouse costs $8.95. The other blouse is only $6.22 this week during the Washington's Birthday Sale. The only pair of

jeans she likes cost $23.85. She has $40.00 to spend. Can she purchase all three items? Any combination of two?" She does not need the exact sum to answer her question. She only needs to know if the total is greater than or less than $40.00. However, if her estimate is close to $40.00, she may need to consider sales tax and make another, more refined estimation.

Throughout this text, the ideas described in *Computational Estimation Instructional Materials* by Reys, Trafton, Reys, and Zawojewski have been used. This is an excellent resource that describes specific teaching lessons for developing estimation skill. Also included in this resource are materials that can be used to make transparencies or student practice sheets.

Good estimations have some important characteristics. They can be done quickly; several different estimations can be used in one short shopping trip. All the work is done mentally; since no tools (pencil and paper, calculator) are needed, estimations can be done anywhere and anytime. They produce reasonable results; in many situations they provide sufficient information for decision making, and they are useful as a check on

$$
\begin{array}{cc}
64 & \xrightarrow{+\ 10\ \text{ones}} & 6\overset{1}{4} \\
-\ 38 & \xrightarrow{+\ 1\ \text{ten}} & -\ ^4\!38 \\
& & \overline{26}
\end{array}
$$

FIGURE 6-59.
Subtraction by equal additions.

pencil-and-paper computations or calculator results.

ESTIMATING SUMS

As children are learning the addition algorithm, they also need to be developing estimation skills for addition. When they were learning the basic facts, children were also extending their number sense through class discussions. Thus they should recognize totally unreasonable answers such as 8 + 7 is 35. Teacher-directed discussions should help the children to realize that in adding 2 one-digit numbers their answer was always either another one-digit number or a two-digit number in the teens decade. This concept can be extended for estimating the sum of any combination of a two-digit number and a one-digit number. Through examples, children can discover that this answer will always be in the same decade as the two-digit number or in the next higher decade. Thus, if with the algorithm they find that 47 + 8 = 65, they know immediately from estimation that something is wrong. Later this place-value concept can be extended to help children see that the sum of any 2 two-digit numbers will always be a two-digit or a three-digit number, and so on. However, this place-value consideration provides only an extremely rough estimation for addition. It is helpful but certainly not sufficient to help Jane make the decision about what clothes she can buy.

Front-End Estimation

To develop their estimation skills, children's concept of number needs to be extended so that they are able to predict what would be a reasonable sum or to decide whether their answer, obtained from using an algorithm, is a reasonable result. Models such as base-ten blocks can be used to develop estima-

tion skills. In the discussion of the addition of 23 and 34, the students represented the numbers with longs and units (Figure 6-46). The students know that the longs represent the greater place value. From their knowledge of place value and rounding, they can estimate their answer by simply noting that 2 tens plus 3 tens equals 5 tens. Since 23 and 34 are greater than 2 tens and 3 tens, their answer will be more than 5 tens. This technique for estimation is often called "front-end" estimation; that is, the students look at the front-end (largest place value) of each number and add just these digits. Extending this same technique to larger numbers, an estimate of 234 + 316 would be 2 hundreds + 3 hundreds or 5 hundreds, an estimate of 234 + 378 would be 2 hundreds + 3 hundreds or 5 hundreds, and an estimate of 672 + 863 would be 6 hundreds + 8 hundreds or 14 hundreds. (A good discussion of this strategy can be found in "Estimation and Mental Arithmetic: Important Components of Computation" by Paul Trafton in *Developing Computational Skills*.)

This same front-end technique is particularly useful when three or more numbers are to be added (Figure 6-60a and b). Finding the sum of three or four single digits is much easier to compute mentally than trying to consider the entire number. Care must be

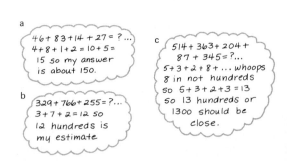

a
$46 + 83 + 14 + 27 = ?...$
$4 + 8 + 1 + 2 = 10 + 5 =$
15 so my answer
is about 150.

b
$329 + 766 + 255 = ?...$
$3 + 7 + 2 = 12$ so
12 hundreds is
my estimate

c
$514 + 363 + 204 + 87 + 345 = ?...$
$5 + 3 + 2 + 8 + ...$ whoops
8 in not hundreds
so $5 + 3 + 2 + 3 = 13$
so 13 hundreds or
1300 should be
close.

FIGURE 6-60.
Front-end estimation.

taken in using front-end estimation for multi-addend problems that all the "front" digits that are added have the same place value. For the example in Figure 6-60c, the students should think "5 + 3 + 2 + 3 = 13 hundreds," not "5 + 3 + 2 + 8 + 3 = 21 hundreds." The "8" is in the tens column and thus is not part of the "front end" of this problem.

Rounding for Estimation

An estimation technique similar to, but somewhat more refined than, front-end estimation uses an extension of students' already known skill of rounding numbers. With this technique addends are rounded to the highest place value (tens for two-digit numbers, hundreds for three-digit numbers, and so on), and then these numbers are added. In this way the estimation for 234 + 316 would still be 200 + 300 = 500, but the estimate for 234 + 378 would now be 200 + 400 = 600, and an estimate for 124 + 268 + 453 would be 100 + 300 + 500 = 900. These estimates, although more refined than some of those obtained with the front-end technique, are still only rough estimates.

Refined Front-End Estimation

After students have learned to obtain a rough estimate of sums, they should be taught to refine these skills further. By introducing appropriate examples and asking leading questions, the teacher can help the students build their own generalizations. When the students estimated that 23 and 34 would have a sum of more than 5 tens, the teacher could ask if the answer would be more than 6 tens. Students should be able to explain that the sum of three and four is less than ten, so the ones column would not need to be renamed, so the sum would be more than 5 tens but less than 6 tens. Now the students are again using a front-end es-

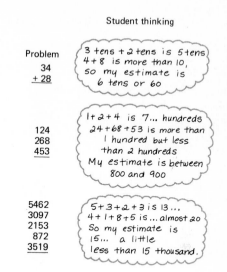

Student thinking

Problem
34
+ 28

> 3 tens + 2 tens is 5 tens
> 4 + 8 is more than 10,
> so my estimate is
> 6 tens or 60

124
268
453

> 1 + 2 + 4 is 7... hundreds
> 24 + 68 + 53 is more than
> 1 hundred but less
> than 2 hundreds
> My estimate is between
> 800 and 900

5462
3097
2153
872
3519

> 5 + 3 + 2 + 3 is 13...,
> 4 + 1 + 8 + 5 is... almost 20
> So my estimate is
> 15... a little
> less than 15 thousand.

FIGURE 6-61.
Refined front-end estimation.

timation strategy but with greater refinement. Now the digits in the largest place values are added, and then the result is adjusted depending on the value of the rest of each addend. To add 34 and 28, the students should reason that 3 tens plus 2 tens is 5 tens and since 8 plus 4 is more than ten, the sum would be more than 6 tens (Figure 6-61).

This is similar to the rounding strategy as in the example 234 + 378 students would now think "34 + 78 is more than 100 so 2 hundreds plus 3 hundreds plus 1 more hundred is 6 hundreds." This is the same estimate obtained by rounding, a closer estimate than the one obtained with front-end estimation using only the largest place value. However, in the example of 124 + 268 + 453 the students could determine that 24 + 68 + 53 is more than 1 hundred but less than 2 hundred so an estimate of the sum is more than 8 hundreds (1 + 2 + 4 + 1) but less than 9 hundreds. This gives a closer estimate than did simple rounding. Not only do these activities develop estimation skills,

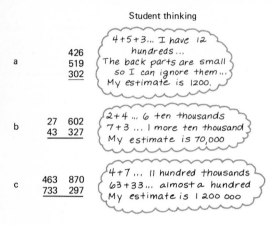

a
426
519
302

b
27 602
43 327

c
463 870
733 297

FIGURE 6-62.
Front-end estimation for larger numbers.

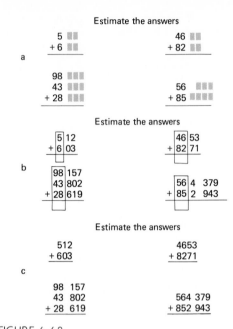

FIGURE 6-63.
Practice exercises for front-end estimation

but they also reinforce the students' under-standings of regrouping and the addition algorithm.

As students develop skill with front-end estimation, they need to extend this tech-nique to larger numbers (Figure 6-62a). They should discover that as the numbers get larger they can ignore much of the back part without significantly affecting their estimate. To estimate the sum of two numbers in the ten-thousands, students may simply add the front digits (ten-thousands) and adjust that sum in relation to the second digits (thou-sands); they may completely ignore the dig-its in the hundreds, tens, and ones places (Figure 6-62b). Alternatively, they may con-sider the front digits and the next two in mak-ing their estimate (Figure 6-62c). To help stu-dents develop this skill, the teacher might give them exercises like the one shown in Figure 6-63a. Since they are not given the back parts but only the indication of digits, students will be better able to focus on the front end. As their skills increase, they can be given exercises like Figure 6-63b and, later, ones like Figure 6-63c with no helps at all.

Compatible Numbers for Estimation

Compatible numbers for addition are those whose sums are easy to add. Compatible numbers are particularly useful when a sum for several addends must be found. Using compatible numbers simplifies the problem by creating addends that can be combined mentally to give an estimate. Figure 6-64 shows how compatible numbers can be used to estimate the sum of five numbers.

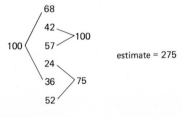

FIGURE 6-64.
Using compatible numbers.

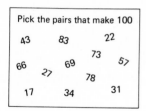

FIGURE 6-65.
Finding compatible numbers.

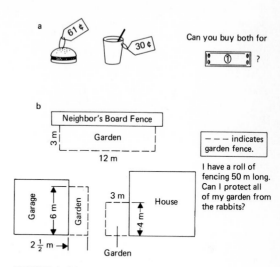

FIGURE 6-66.
Estimating with a reference point.

Usually, compatible numbers are considered to be those whose sum is 10 or 100 or 1000. However, some people might call 23 and 24 compatible as their sum is almost 50 and that is easy to add to other numbers. Which numbers are "compatible" will depend both on the situation and on personal preference. Children can be given worksheets designed to help them learn to look for compatible numbers (Figure 6-65). When using compatible numbers to estimate sums, children should be encouraged to compare and discuss their results.

Reference Points for Estimation

Sometimes a rough estimate will be sufficient. Often we make estimations only in relation to a reference point. For Jane's clothing purchases, the reference point is $40.00. If the blouses cost $22.44 and $25.97, respectively, she could see at a glance that it would be impossible to buy any two items. Likewise, if the cost of the blouses were as given in the original problem but the jeans were on a half-price sale and now cost only $11.93, even a very rough estimate would tell her that she could easily buy all three items for her $40.00. Other examples of using a reference point in estimation are given in Figure 6-66. Having a reference point often simplifies the estimation, as students do not necessarily need a close estimate but

only one that will identify the sum as greater than or less than the reference point.

Use of a reference point is also helpful in teaching estimation skills. Students can be given exercises like those shown in Figure 6-67a. In these examples, they are not actually asked to estimate the sum, only to tell whether it will be greater than or less than the reference sum. As their estimation skills increase, these exercises in using a reference point can become more sophisticated (Figure 6-67b).

Range Estimation

For some estimations it is important to establish a range within which the exact answer will fall. To do this students will need to make two estimations, one that is certain to be low and another that is certain to be high. The following is one example of a student's thinking. "I need to add 387 and 523. If I use 'front-end' estimation, I get 3 hundreds + 5 hundreds = 8 hundreds. Since 300 and 500 are both smaller than the actual numbers, I

40 + 50 = 90   so   42 + 53 is _____ (greater/less) than 90.

70 + 30 = 100   68 + 24 is _____ (greater/less) than 100.

300 + 500 = 800   Tell whether the following
                     are greater than or less
                     than 800.

                     321 + 518 _____
                     300 + 532 _____
                     297 + 500 _____
                     301 + 505 _____
a   285 + 496 _____

---

25 + 60 = 85   so   23 + 59 _____ (< >) 85

25 + 62 _____ (< >) 85

300 + 500 = 800   Tell whether the following are
                     less than, equal to, or greater than 800.

                     513 + 302 _____
                     297 + 522 _____
                     290 + 510 _____
                     275 + 510 _____
                     286 + 505 _____
                     515 + 285 _____
                     540 + 250 _____
b   330 + 480 _____

FIGURE 6-67.

Practice exercises for estimating with a reference point.

know that my actual answer must be more than 800. If I round both numbers up, I get 4 hundreds + 6 hundreds = 10 hundreds. Since these rounded numbers are both larger than the actual numbers, I know that my answer will be less than 1000. My answer should be between 800 and 1000."

Another student might use similar, but more refined, techniques to establish the range. "387 + 523 . . . First, I'll compare the 'back parts' of the two addends. 87 > 23. Now I'll round down the addend containing the smaller back part. My new problem is 387 + 500, which I can do in my head. That makes 887 which must be smaller than the actual answer. Then I'll round the other number up. 400 + 523 = 923, so my answer must be smaller than 923. The answer to 387

+ 523 must be between 887 and 923." This type of estimation in which a range is established is particularly useful for checking the reasonableness of an answer obtained through computation with an algorithm.

Practicing Estimation in Addition

In order to develop estimation skills, students need many opportunities to practice them. Estimation activities should be included throughout the year and throughout the curriculum. To provide practice in these skills, teachers may find it helpful to include estimation problems in a warm-up exercise for the first few minutes of the period. A large portion of this practice in estimation should be done orally so that students have neither the time nor the inclination to do a written computation instead of estimating.

While students should be introduced to a variety of estimation strategies, they should be encouraged to *use* whatever strategy best fits the particular problem and their own particular style of thinking. Several students' estimations of 25 + 47 are shown in Figure 6-68. Although the thinking patterns vary, all of these estimations use valid strategies and give the estimator useful information about the answer.

In class discussions, students should not only report their estimations but also share their thinking in arriving at those estimations. Discussion should include questions such as "What strategies were used? Which ones give a closer estimate? Why might a particular strategy work well for a specific problem but not be good for another problem? Might an estimate that is certain to be high or low sometimes be more useful than one that is closer, and if so, why?"

Some written practice in estimation can also be included. Worksheets like Figure 6-66 or Figure 6-67 can be used for practicing estimation skills. Another example for

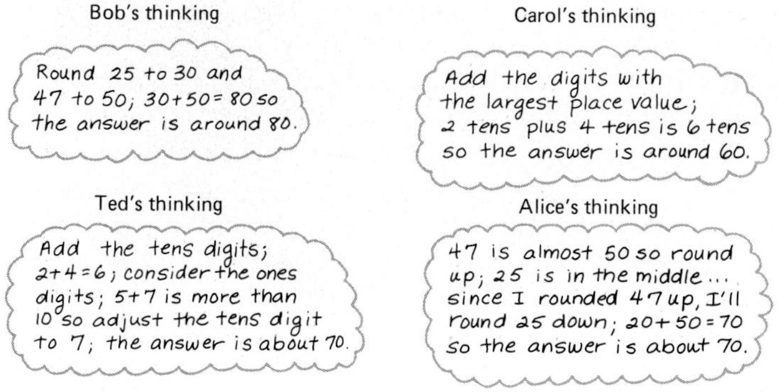

Bob's thinking

Round 25 to 30 and
47 to 50; 30+50 = 80 so
the answer is around 80.

Carol's thinking

Add the digits with
the largest place value;
2 tens plus 4 tens is 6 tens
so the answer is around 60.

Ted's thinking

Add the tens digits;
2+4=6; consider the ones
digits; 5+7 is more than
10 so adjust the tens digit
to 7; the answer is about 70.

Alice's thinking

47 is almost 50 so round
up; 25 is in the middle...
since I rounded 47 up, I'll
round 25 down; 20+50=70
so the answer is about 70.

FIGURE 6-68.
Varied thinking patterns for estimation.

practice in finding the range is shown in Figure 6-69. The teacher must be aware that in many estimation exercises more than one answer may be acceptable. In Figure 6-69, one student may say "89 + 42 is between 120 and 140 because 80 + 40 = 120 and 90 + 50 = 140." Another may say, "89 + 42 is between 129 and 132 because 89 + 40 = 129 and 90 + 42 = 132." Both students have used acceptable estimation techniques and both are correct.

To help students develop, improve, and apply estimation skills, the teacher could give them five to ten problems and ask them to estimate the answers. After everyone has made their estimations, the class should discuss their estimates and strategies. Students should be encouraged to try each other's strategies. For some lessons, the students might also use calculators to find the exact sums and check their estimates.

When students are working on a practice page of addition problems, estimation could easily be added to the assignment. Before computing a problem, the students could write their estimate to the left of the problem and circle that estimate. The students should then compare the results of their computations to their estimates to determine whether their computational results are reasonable. Care should be taken not to

overuse this technique, as students may feel that they are being required to do every problem twice. They may decide that a shortcut is to compute the problem, round that answer, and write this result as their estimate. To prevent this, class discussions before such written assignments should focus on the usefulness of estimation as an aid to achieving correct results in computation.

Obviously, estimations done along with written computations are useful as a check on the computations. Also, as students prac-

Estimate to locate each sum between two points.
The first one is done for you.

43 + 38 is between 70 and 90
because 40 + 30 = 70 and 50 + 40 = 90

25 + 42 is between _____

because _____

89 + 74 is between _____

because _____

246 + 592 is between _____

because _____

415 + 523 is between _____

because _____

FIGURE 6-69.
Estimating the range.

tice estimating, computing, and comparing, they can refine their estimation skills so that their estimations will be closer to the actual answer. At the same time they will be developing a better concept of number.

MENTAL COMPUTATION IN ADDITION

Sometimes, even a close estimate is not adequate. For example, "Fred is doing his Christmas shopping. He has just $5.00 to spend, and he knows that he must allow about 25 cents of that for sales tax. For his little brother, Jerome, he has chosen a toy truck for $1.78. A belt his big sister has admired costs $2.99." From estimation, Fred figures that these two items will cost about $4.75, but he can't be sure whether the actual amount will be a little more or a little less. An estimate is not sufficient; he needs to know the exact cost of these two items.

Estimation skills can be extended further when an exact answer is desired. Mental computation skills require many similar thought processes. Children have already learned some of the techniques useful for mental computation in their study of the basic facts. Just as adding 9 was easy to do

by adding 10 and subtracting 1, so adding 19, 29, 39, and so on, is similarly easy. Compensation—looking for ways to make 10—is also helpful in mentally adding larger numbers. To add 27 and 5 the student may think "27 plus 3 more makes 30 and 30 plus the other 2 left from the 5 makes 32, so 27 + 5 = 32."

As with estimation, the teacher must allow for and encourage flexibility and a variety of thinking procedures for mental computation. Several thinking procedures for mentally calculating an exact answer to 25 + 47 are shown in Figure 6-70. Each of these approaches is slightly different, and different students will find different procedures easiest to use. Still other thinking patterns may be more useful for other types of problems. Again, students should be encouraged to share their thinking procedures with their classmates.

Children should be given opportunities for oral practice in mental computation. As they learn the addition algorithm for a one-digit number plus a two-digit number, they can also be given oral practice in computing these sums mentally. These are relatively simple since the only decision that must be

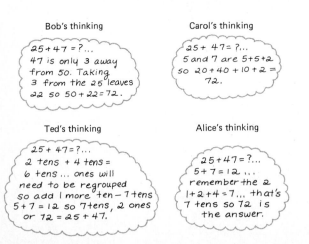

Bob's thinking

25 + 47 = ?...
47 is only 3 away
from 50. Taking
3 from the 25 leaves
22 so 50 + 22 = 72.

Carol's thinking

25 + 47 = ?...
5 and 7 are 5+5+2
so 20 + 40 + 10 + 2 =
72.

Ted's thinking

25 + 47 = ?...
2 tens + 4 tens =
6 tens ... ones will
need to be regrouped
so add 1 more ten — 7 tens
5 + 7 = 12 so 7 tens, 2 ones
or 72 = 25 + 47.

Alice's thinking

25 + 47 = ?...
5 + 7 = 12 ...
remember the 2
1 + 2 + 4 = 7 ... that's
7 tens so 72 is
the answer.

FIGURE 6-70.
Variety of thinking for mental computation.

		34 + 22	35 + 46
Step 1	Do ones need renaming	4 + 2 ⋯ no	5 + 6 ⋯ yes
Step 2	Add tens	30 + 20 = 50	30 + 40 = 70
Step 3	Adjust tens if necessary	no, so still 50	yes, so 80
Step 4	Add ones	4 + 2 = 6 so 56	5 + 6 = 11 so 81

FIGURE 6-71.

Front-end computation.

made about renaming is whether the answer will be in the same decade as the two-digit addend or in the next higher decade.

When children are ready to mentally compute exact sums for 2 two-digit addends (usually, after the corresponding algorithm has been developed), they may find that a "front-end" approach like that used in estimation is helpful. In this approach the digit with the largest place value is computed first. Thus the addition is done from left to right instead of from right to left as in the standard algorithm. The steps to compute such combinations as 34 + 22 or 35 + 46 are shown in Figure 6-71. Students must first check the ones digits to see whether or not the sum will need to be renamed (Step 1). Then they add the tens (Step 2), adjust that sum if regrouping ones is necessary (Step 3), and add the ones digits to determine the ones digit of the answer (Step 4).

This "front-end" algorithm works well for practicing mental computation with a special calculator, such as Little Professor or Dataman. When the student chooses the program on two-digit addition, the calculator will display a randomly selected series of two-digit addition problems. In answering these problems, the student must enter the digit

with the largest place value first. Thus for the problem 64 + 28, the correct answer code is ⑨ ② . If the child tries to enter the digits in the same order as for written computation (2 ones first, and then 9 tens), the calculator will read "29," an incorrect answer.

With the "front-end" algorithm, the student finds the tens digit first and then the ones digit which makes it easy to say the answer in its proper order. If they use the same form for mental computation that they do for the written algorithm, they must complete one more step of reversing the digits to the correct order for speaking before giving the answer. For two-digit problems this last step is not particularly difficult, but as mental computation is extended to larger numbers, the "front-end" strategy becomes definitely easier. An example of this extension is shown in Figure 6-72.

Computer programs can also be used for practicing mental computations. As with

FIGURE 6-72.

Front-end computation with larger numbers.

oral activities, often the digits of an answer are entered into the computer in the same order in which they would be spoken. The program could be designed so that when the solution is incorrect, the student is given another chance. A time limit can be built in making it difficult for the student to resort to pencil-and-paper algorithms instead of using mental computation. As with basic facts, the program can be designed to give both the student and the teacher feedback which will be useful for designing future practice activities.

ESTIMATION AND MENTAL COMPUTATION FOR SUBTRACTION OF WHOLE NUMBERS

ESTIMATING DIFFERENCES

The procedures for estimating differences are similar to those for estimating sums. One distinction is that in subtraction the student is never dealing with more than two numbers at a time. However, the same techniques described for estimating sums are also used in estimating differences.

Rounding

If a "rough" estimate is desired for problems like 83 − 51 or 467 − 207, the student may simply reason 8 tens minus 5 tens is 3 tens or 5 hundreds minus 2 hundreds is 3 hundreds. However, if the students simply round the numbers to the largest place value and then subtract, their results may be misleading. For each of the following examples: 467 − 209, 457 − 241, 503 − 226, and 544 − 157, the student would obtain 5 hundreds minus 2 hundreds is 3 hundreds. The actual differences in these cases vary from 213 to 387. These estimations should be refined to

give better approximations. In the example 457 − 241, the students should observe that the numbers are approximately halfway between hundreds. Since 57 and 41 are similar in magnitude, the students should simply estimate 4 hundreds minus 2 hundreds. For the example 544 − 157, they would similarly reason "5 hundreds minus 1 hundred or 4 hundreds."

Compatible Numbers for Estimation

For addition, compatible numbers were those which could be combined to make easy-to-add intermediate sums. For subtraction, compatible numbers are those that are close to the original numbers but easier to subtract. Figure 6-73 shows three different students' thinking to estimate 84 976 − 36 237. Addie, using simple rounding, has obtained an estimate but not a very close one. Joseph, using compatible numbers for

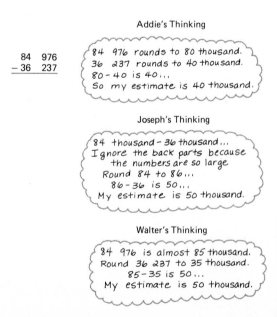

FIGURE 6-73.
Compatible numbers for subtraction.

the same problem, has obtained a much closer estimate. Walter, using a different set of compatible numbers, has obtained this same close estimate.

Refined Front-End Estimation

Front-end estimation could also be used to obtain a better approximation. To consider 457 − 241, Kari thought "4 hundreds minus 2 hundreds is 2 hundred; 57 − 41 is about 15, so my answer will be a little more than 2 hundred." For the example 544 − 157, she reasoned "5 hundreds minus 1 hundred is 4 hundreds; 44 and 57 are similar in size but this subtraction will require renaming, so the answer is a little less than 4 hundred." To solve 467 − 209 she reasoned "67 − 9 is about 50 and 400 − 200 is 200, so the answer is around 250." Each of these estimations is closer to the exact answer than those obtained with rounding.

Reference Points and Range for Estimation

Reference points are used in subtraction in much the same way they were used in addition. Figure 6-74 shows some examples of subtraction estimation in relation to a reference point. In each case the important question is how the estimate compares to the reference point. It does not matter whether the answer will be close to the reference point or far from it as long as the estimate is sufficient to place the answer as *above* or *below* the reference point.

As with addition, sometimes it is necessary to establish a range within which the difference will fall. To establish a range for 523 − 364, Elida reasoned, "5 − 3 is 2 . . . that gives me an estimate of 200, but since 64 is more than 23, I know 200 will be too much. I will have to regroup one of the hundreds so that I can subtract 64 from 123. That will leave 4 hundreds minus 3 hundreds, which is 1 hundred . . . but my answer

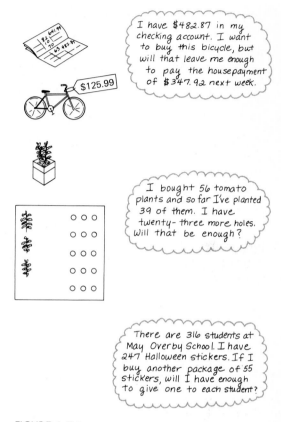

FIGURE 6-74.

Subtraction with a reference point.

will be something more than that. My answer has to be between 100 and 200." This process of establishing a range is particularly helpful when estimation is used to check reasonableness of results.

Estimation skill is useful not only when an approximation is all that is desired but also as a check on algorithmic work. Had the students whose work is shown in Figure 6-54 used estimation to check their answers, they would almost certainly have discovered that their answers were incorrect. Jim and Jeanine could both have estimated by thinking 40 − 20 is 20. Jim would then have seen

Which problem is easier to solve?

136 − 128 or 138 − 130

236 − 17 or 239 − 20

306 − 244 or 312 − 250 or 366 − 304

FIGURE 6-75.

Equal additions for mental computation.

that his answer of 13 was too small, and Jeanine that her answer of 113 was much too large. Julie could have estimated that 50 − 20 = 30, which would have shown 43 to be too large. Hilary would have thought "600 − 100 = 500, but since 37 is more than 3, my answer will be a little less than 500." In this last case Hilary might not have been able to correct her mistake without using the base-ten blocks or having the teacher's help

to focus on place value, but at least she would have recognized that she had a problem with which she needed help.

MENTAL COMPUTATION FOR SUBTRACTION

Some of the strategies for mental computation were mentioned in the section on alternative algorithms. Students will find a number of situations where the additive method of subtraction is convenient. To solve 324 − 180, Marty reasoned, "180 + 20 is 200; 324 − 200 is 124. My answer is 124 + 20 or 144." When Mike was buying an item costing $3.72, he reasoned "3 more cents is 75 cents, plus a quarter is 4 dollars, so 1 dollar plus 28 cents is my change from a $5 bill."

Students should experiment with the equal-additions method. They could be given worksheets with problems like those

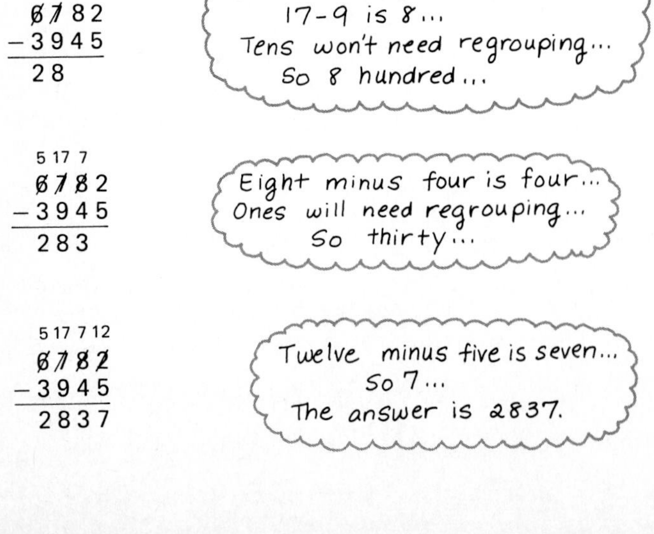

FIGURE 6-76.

Front-end subtraction.

```
    5
    6̸7 8 2
 − 3 9 4 5
        2
```

Six minus three is three...
Hundreds will need regrouping...
So 2 thousand...

```
    5 17
    6̸7̸ 8 2
 − 3 9 4 5
       2 8
```

Seven hundreds plus 10 hundreds ... 17
17−9 is 8...
Tens won't need regrouping...
So 8 hundred...

```
    5 17 7
    6̸7̸8̸ 2
 − 3 9 4 5
     2 8 3
```

Eight minus four is four...
Ones will need regrouping...
So thirty...

```
    5 17 7 12
    6̸7̸8̸2̸
 − 3 9 4 5
   2 8 3 7
```

Twelve minus five is seven...
So 7...
The answer is 2837.

shown in Figure 6-75. Students should discuss how the problems are alike and how they could be' solved mentally. Some students may find the subtraction algorithm used in other parts of the world very efficient in mental arithmetic. The difference of 56 and 27 could be found by noting that 16 − 7 is 9 and 5 tens − 3 tens is 2 tens. The difference is 29.

The front-end strategy is also useful for mental computation in subtraction. As with addition, the student starts with the digit in the largest place value, computes that difference, and adjusts if regrouping will be necessary for the subtraction in the next place value. An example of student thinking in front-end subtraction is shown in Figure 6-76.

Computations—whether done mentally or with paper and pencil or with a calculator—and estimations are important subtraction procedures. None of these should be taught in isolation. As children learn about one of the procedures, these understandings should reinforce and extend their comprehension of the other procedures. In helping children learn *how* to use them, teachers need to focus on the most important aspect of subtraction—*when* to use these procedures.

QUESTIONS AND ACTIVITIES

1. a. Consult a scope-and-sequence chart to construct a hierarchy of addition of whole numbers from the concept of addition to multiplace algorithms. Name the publisher and the publication date. List all the new topics that are introduced at each grade level. Give an example of a typical arithmetic problem for each topic. List any models that

are described in the teacher's notes or shown on the student page.

b. Construct a second list that shows a hierarchy of subtraction of whole numbers from the concept of subtraction to multiplace algorithms. Are parallel topics introduced at the same grade level? In the same chapters or in consecutive chapters? For example, is addition of two-digit numbers with regrouping introduced before, at the same time as, or after two-digit subtraction with regrouping?

2. *Materials needed:* Counting sticks or base-ten blocks, place-value table (paper folded in halves and labeled "tens" and "ones").

a. Set up and solve the following problems on your place-value table. After solving each section, analyze the processes. How do they differ?

(1) 20 + 30	(2) 31 + 45
(3) 34 + 8	(4) 27 + 18
(5) 43 + 17	(6) 234 + 325
(7) 346 + 162	(8) 276 + 147

b. After children have learned to solve problems with the models, this process should be linked to the algorithm. Work through at least four of the problems again with another student. For each problem one student should play the role of a teacher; the other student should play the role of an elementary school student who is being introduced to the algorithm. Re-solve each problem step by step with the models, devising for each step appropriate teacher questions that link the action on the model to the written form of the algorithm.

3. Weaver in "Big Dividends from Little Interviews" describes how to use interviews to determine children's thinking on basic facts. Read this article and then explicitly describe what oral questions you could ask to determine whether your students had the prerequisite skills for studying addition of whole numbers with regrouping.

4. What is the advantage of using "regrouping" or "renaming" rather than "carrying" and "borrowing"?

5. a. Given the models—base-ten blocks, number line, abacus, and number balance—and the problem 43 − 19 = ?, select the appropriate models for demonstrating the concept of regrouping. Choose one of these models and explain how a child could use it to develop the concept of regrouping.

   b. *For your resource file:* Read "Give and Take: Getting Ready to Regroup." Tucker describes activities using various models to help children learn the concept of regrouping. He also gives examples of student thinking that show a lack of understanding of the process.

6. Read one or both of the articles "Let's Do It: Transition Boards: Moving from Materials to Symbols in Addition" and "Let's Do It: Transition Boards: Moving from Materials to Symbols in Subtraction" by Thompson and Van de Walle on the transition from models to the written form of the algorithm. Reflect on your questions and procedures for Problem 2. How could you revise your teaching in consideration of their recommendations? Incorporate these suggestions into your work on the next problem.

7. *Materials needed:* Counting sticks or base-ten blocks, place-value table (paper folded in thirds and labeled "hundreds," "tens," and "ones").

   a. Set up and solve the following problems on your place-value table. After solving each one, analyze the processes.

(1) 50 − 30	(2) 87 − 63
(3) 92 − 45	(4) 500 − 200
(5) 640 − 230	(6) 936 − 412
(7) 583 − 366	(8) 438 − 276
(9) 972 − 685	(10) 604 − 338
(11) 527 − 483	(12) 762 − 555

   b. After children have learned to solve problems with the models, this process should be linked to the algorithm. Work through at least four of the problems again with another student. For each problem, one student should play the role of a teacher; the other student should play the role of an elementary school student who is being introduced to the algorithm. Re-solve each problem step by step with the models, devising for each step appropriate teacher questions that link the action on the model with the written form of the algorithm.

8. a. How can you tell by estimation that 362 + 456 must be larger than 7 hundred?

   b. How can you tell by estimation that 562 − 373 must be smaller than 2 hundred?

9. Bill is very insecure with estimation and mental computation. When he is sent to the store with a five-dollar bill to purchase three items, he will go through the checkout three times—once for each item. This is the only way he is able to be sure that he has enough money for all three items. Design a lesson plan that will help Bill with his estimation skills and save him time at the store.

10. *For your resource file:* For additional materials on estimation and mental computation, consult other resources: teaching suggestions are given in "Let's Teach Mental Algorithms for Addition and Subtraction" by Musser or in "Estimation and Mental Arithmetic: Important Components of Computation" by Trafton; classroom activities are included in the works by Trafton, and in "Estimation and Mental Computation: Patterns on a Hundred Chart" by Reys and Reys.

11. Analyze two different textbooks at either the third- or fourth-grade level. What teaching suggestions have been included for estimation in addition and subtraction? Find at least four different suggestions from each text. Write up your favorite three.

12. In the section "Mental Computation in Addition," the calculators Dataman and Little Professor were discussed with regard to mental arithmetic. For example, if 43 + 15 is displayed, to obtain the correct answer the code ⑤ ⑧ is entered. In mental computation, the answer "fifty-eight"—not "8 (ones), 5 (tens)"—is also desirable. If one of these calculators is available, practice mental computation of two-digit numbers on one of them. If they are not available, mentally do the following problems.

$$32 + 14$$

$$\begin{array}{r} 86 \\ -35 \\ \hline \end{array} \qquad \begin{array}{r} 512 \\ -204 \\ \hline \end{array}$$

$$53 + 28$$

$$\begin{array}{r} 57 \\ -19 \\ \hline \end{array}$$

$$68 - 32 \qquad \begin{array}{r} 57 \\ -19 \\ \hline \end{array} \qquad 50 - 35$$

13. Some common addition errors are given below. Analyze each set to determine the error pattern. "Solve" the fourth problem in the set using that error. How would you remediate each case?

a. $$\begin{array}{r} 2\,4 \\ +3\,7 \\ \hline 1\,6 \end{array} \qquad \begin{array}{r} 3\,1\,4 \\ +1\,5 \\ \hline 1\,4 \end{array} \qquad \begin{array}{r} 1\,7\,9 \\ +2\,6 \\ \hline 2\,5 \end{array} \qquad \begin{array}{r} 4\,6 \\ +3\,2 \\ \hline \end{array}$$

b. $$\begin{array}{r} 3\,2 \\ +\ 7 \\ \hline 1\,0\,9 \end{array} \qquad \begin{array}{r} 4\,5 \\ +\ 3 \\ \hline 7\,8 \end{array} \qquad \begin{array}{r} 5\,1 \\ +\ 8 \\ \hline 1\,3\,9 \end{array} \qquad \begin{array}{r} 6\,3 \\ +\ 4 \\ \hline \end{array}$$

c. $$\begin{array}{r} 3\,8\,7 \\ +\ 2\,8 \\ \hline 8\,1\,1 \end{array} \qquad \begin{array}{r} 5\,3\,8 \\ +\ 9\,4 \\ \hline 9\,1\,1 \end{array} \qquad \begin{array}{r} 1\,4\,3 \\ +7\,8 \\ \hline 3\,1\,1 \end{array} \qquad \begin{array}{r} 1\,2\,7 \\ +8\,5 \\ \hline \end{array}$$

d. $$\begin{array}{r} 3\,5 \\ +\ 7 \\ \hline 3\,1\,2 \end{array} \qquad \begin{array}{r} 4\,5 \\ +\ 6 \\ \hline 4\,1\,1 \end{array} \qquad \begin{array}{r} 8\,3 \\ +\ 9 \\ \hline 8\,1\,2 \end{array} \qquad \begin{array}{r} 7\,4 \\ +\ 8 \\ \hline \end{array}$$

14. a. This is a sample of Josh's work:

$$\begin{array}{r} 2\,3 \\ -1\,1 \\ \hline 1\,2 \end{array} \qquad \begin{array}{r} 1\,5 \\ -\ 3 \\ \hline 1\,2 \end{array} \qquad \begin{array}{r} 2\,8 \\ -1\,9 \\ \hline 1\,1 \end{array} \qquad \begin{array}{r} 2\,5 \\ -1\,7 \\ \hline 1\,2 \end{array} \qquad \begin{array}{r} 3\,7 \\ -1\,4 \\ \hline 2\,3 \end{array}$$

What is he doing wrong? Design an activity to help Josh correct his difficulties.

b. The following example shows how Nancy "solved" 302 − 87.

$$\begin{array}{r} 3\,0\,2 \\ -8\,7 \\ \hline \end{array} \qquad \begin{array}{r} {\scriptstyle 2}\ {\scriptstyle 1} \\ 3\,0\,2 \\ -\ 8\,7 \\ \hline 5 \end{array} \qquad \begin{array}{r} {\scriptstyle 1} \\ \not{3}\,0\,2 \\ -\ 8\,7 \\ \hline 2\,5 \end{array} \qquad \begin{array}{r} {\scriptstyle 1} \\ \not{3}\,0\,2 \\ -\ 8\,7 \\ \hline 1\,2\,5 \end{array}$$

Explain what Nancy's mistake is. Develop an activity, using at least one model, to help her correct her mistake.

15. Analyze the subtraction errors in Table 1 in the article, "Diagnosing and Remediating Systematic Errors in Addition and Subtraction Computation" by Cox. Read the article and check your answers. How would you remediate each of the errors?

16. In an elementary textbook, read through the entire chapter that introduces subtraction with renaming. Carefully read the introduction to the chapter and the teacher's notes. Also read additional resources provided by the publisher.

a. Are the prerequisites reviewed? Subtraction basic facts? Renaming tens? Addition with regrouping? To answer this question you may need to check the review in the previous chapter.

b. What models are used? Are there teacher notes or diagrams and instructions on student pages that link the model to the algorithm?

c. Do the practice pages include mixed problems so that students will need to decide when to regroup?

d. Although the main purpose of the chapter is to teach the subtraction algorithm, are there story problems? One-step or multistep? Routine or nonroutine, such as including extra or not enough information?

e. List the different topics included in the daily maintenance or review sections.

f. What problem-solving activities have been included throughout the chapter? What special helps for the teacher?

17. In Chapter 1 the following statement was made: "Computational procedures can be taught through a problem-solving process that will help children understand the procedures. Also, children will gain in their problem-solving abilities if they are *actively involved in developing* the algorithm rather than being *told* what steps to follow."

   a. Reflect on this statement with regard to your experiences as an elementary school student. Write your reactions.

   b. Reflect on this statement with regard to your studies in this chapter. Write your reactions.

   c. If as an elementary child you were taught via a rule rather than a meaningful approach, what are the advantages of using a meaningful approach with your students? The disadvantages?

   d. If as an elementary child you were taught via a rule rather than a meaningful approach, what are the advantages of using a rule approach with your students? The disadvantages?

18. *For your resource file:* Read "Ensuring That Practice Makes Perfect: Implications for Children with Learning Disabilities." In the article, Moyer and Moyer describe step by step the type of thinking that children must develop to solve problems involving the subtraction algorithm.

19. Do at least two of the activities using calculators described in "Let's Do It: Let's Use Calculators" by O'Neil and Jensen.

20. Brumfield and Moore in "Problems with the Basic Facts May Not Be the Problem," Engelhardt in "Using Computational Errors in Diagnostic Teaching," and Swart in "Some Findings on Conceptual Development of Computational Skills" discuss how to diagnose and remediate student errors. Read one of the articles.

What implications does this have for analyzing errors on students' papers and listening to student explanations in class?

21. *For your resource file:* "Ideas" by Tucker and Bazik includes activity sheets for estimating sums and differences (products and quotients are also included). Write an evaluation of one of the activities.

22. *For your resource file:* In "Sticks and Bones," Hagan describes the game "sticks and bones." Ockenga and Duea in "Ideas" use the game tic-tac-toe for various experiences in the four operations.

23. *For your resource file:* Read and copy "Estimation and Mental Computation: Patterns on a Hundred Chart" by Reys and Reys. What place-value patterns are involved? What addition and subtraction patterns are involved?

24. *For your resource file:* Copy and read one of the following for your resource file: "Estimation and Mental Computation: It's 'About' Time," by Reys or "Estimation and Mental Computation—Their Time Has Come" by Reys and Reys.

25. *For your resource file:* For a detailed description of estimation strategies, read "Teaching Computational Estimation: Concepts and Strategies" by Reys.

TEACHER'S RESOURCES

Ashlock, Robert, and Carolyn Washbon. "Games: Practice Activities for the Basic Facts." In *Developing Computational Skills,* 1978 Yearbook of the National Council of Teachers of Mathematics. Reston, VA: The Council, 1978.

Backman, Carl A. "Analyzing Children's Work Procedures." In *Developing Computational Skills,* 1978 Yearbook of the National Council of Teachers of Mathematics, pp. 177–195. Reston, VA: The Council, 1978.

Baroody, Arthur J. "Children's Difficulties in Subtraction: Some Causes and Cures." *Arithmetic Teacher 32* (November 1984): 14–19.

Beardslee, Edward C. "Teaching Computational Skills with a Calculator." In *Developing Computational Skills,* 1978 Yearbook of the National Council of Teachers of Mathematics, pp. 226–241. Reston, VA: The Council, 1978.

Beattie, Ian D. "Young Children's Strategies for Solving Subtraction-Fact Combinations." *Arithmetic Teacher 27* (September 1979): 14–15.

Brumfield, Robert D., and Bobby D. Moore. "Problems with the Basic Facts May Not Be the Problem." *Arithmetic Teacher 33* (November 1985): 17–18.

Campbell, Patricia F. "Using a Problem-Solving Approach in the Primary Grades." *Arithmetic Teacher 32* (December 1984): 11–14.

Cox, L. S. "Diagnosing and Remediating Systematic Errors in Addition and Subtraction Computation." *Arithmetic Teacher 22* (February 1975): 151–157.

Davis, Edward J. "Suggestions for Teaching the Basic Facts of Arithmetic." In *Developing Computational Skills,* 1978 Yearbook of the National Council of Teachers of Mathematics, pp. 51–60. Reston, VA: The Council, 1978.

Engelhardt, Jon M. "Using Computational Errors in Diagnostic Teaching." *Arithmetic Teacher 29* (April 1982): 16–19.

Fisher, Bill. "Calculator Games: Combining Skills and Problem Solving." *Arithmetic Teacher 27* (December 1979): 40–41.

Hagan, Michael. "Sticks and Bones." *Arithmetic Teacher 33* (September 1985): 44–45.

Inskeep, James E., Jr. "Diagnosing Computational Difficulty in the Classroom." In *Developing Computational Skills,* 1978 Yearbook of the National Council of Teachers of Mathematics, pp. 163–176. Reston, VA: The Council, 1978.

Kurtz, Ray. "Teaching Place Value with the Calculator." *The Agenda in Action,* 1983 Yearbook of the National Council of Teachers of Mathematics, pp.. 128–130. Reston, VA: The Council, 1983.

Lazerick, Beth E. "Mastering Basic Facts of Addition: An Alternate Strategy." *Arithmetic Teacher 28* (March 1981): 20–24.

Lent, Barbara C. "All Hands on Deck!" *Arithmetic Teacher 30* (December 1982): 39–40.

Leutzinger, Larry P., and Glenn Nelson. "Let's Do It: Counting with a Purpose." *Arithmetic Teacher 27* (October 1979): 6–9.

———. "Let's Do It: Using Addition Facts to Learn Subtraction Facts." *Arithmetic Teacher 27* (December 1979): 8–13.

Liedtke, Werner. "Learning Difficulties: Helping Young Children with Mathematics: Subtraction." *Arithmetic Teacher 29* (April 1982): 40–42.

Merseth, Katherine Klippert. "Using Materials and Activities in Teaching Addition and Subtraction Algorithms." In *Developing Computational Skills,* 1978 Yearbook of the National Council of Teachers of Mathematics, pp. 61–77. Reston, VA: The Council, 1978.

Moser, James M., and Thomas P. Carpenter. "Young Children Are Good Problem Solvers." *Arithmetic Teacher 30* (November 1982): 24–26.

Moyer, Margaret B., and John C. Moyer. "Ensuring That Practice Makes Perfect: Implications for Children with Learning Disabilities." *Arithmetic Teacher 33* (September 1985): 40–42.

Musser, Gary L. "Let's Teach Mental Algorithms for Addition and Subtraction." *Arithmetic Teacher 29* (April 1982): 40–42.

Ockenga, Earl, and Joan Duea. "Ideas." *Arithmetic Teacher 26* (November 1979): 28–32.

O'Neil, David R., and Rosalie Jensen. "Let's Do It: Let's Use Calculators." *Arithmetic Teacher 29* (February 1982): 6–9.

Rathmell, Edward C. "Using Thinking Strategies to Teach the Basic Facts." In *Developing Computational Skills,* 1978 Yearbook of the National Council of Teachers of Mathematics, pp. 13–38. Reston, VA: The Council, 1978.

Reys, Barbara J. "Estimation and Mental Computation: It's 'About' Time." *Arithmetic Teacher 34* (September, 1986): 22–23.

———. "Teaching Computational Estimation: Concepts and Strategies." In *Estimation and Mental Computation,* 1986 Yearbook of the National Council of Teachers of Mathematics, pp. 31–44. Reston, VA: The Council, 1986.

Reys, Barbara J., and Robert E. Reys. "Estimation and Mental Computation—Their Time Has Come." *Arithmetic Teacher 33* (March 1986): 4–5.

———. *GUESS.* Palo Alto, CA: Dale Seymour Publications, 1983.

Reys, Robert E., Barbara J. Bestgen, Terrence G. Coburn, Harold L. Schoen, Richard J. Shumway, Charlotte L. Wheatley, Grayson H. Wheatley, and Arthur L. White. *Keystrokes: Calculator Activities for Young Students: Addition and Subtraction.* Palo Alto, CA: Creative Publications, 1979.

Reys, Robert E., and Barbara J. Reys. "Estimation and Mental Computation: Patterns on a Hundred Chart." *Arithmetic Teacher 34* (September 1986): 24–25.

Reys, Robert E., Paul R. Trafton, Barbara Reys, and Judy Zawojewski. *Computational Estimation Instructional Materials,* Grades 6, 7, and 8. Palo Alto, CA: Dale Seymour Publications, 1986.

Rightsel, Pamela S., and Carol A. Thornton. "72 Addition Facts Can Be Mastered by Mid-grade 1." *Arithmetic Teacher 33* (November 1985): 8–10.

Schroeder, Thomas L. "Capture: A Game of Practice, a Game of Strategy." *Arithmetic Teacher 31* (December 1983): 30–31.

Suydam, Marilyn N. "Research Report: Addition and Subtraction—Processes and Problems." *Arithmetic Teacher 33* (December 1985): 20.

———. "Research Report: Learning the Basic Facts." *Arithmetic Teacher 32* (September 1984): 15.

———. "The Use of Calculators in Pre-college Education." Columbus, OH: Calculator Information Center, August 1982.

Swart, William L. "Some Findings on Conceptual Development of Computational Skills." *Arithmetic Teacher 32* (January 1985): 36–38.

Thompson, Charles, and Judith Babcock. "A Successful Strategy for Teaching Missing Addends." *Arithmetic Teacher 26* (December 1978): 38–41.

Thompson, Charles S., and A. Dean Hendrickson. "Verbal Addition and Subtraction Problems: Some Difficulties and Some Solutions." *Arithmetic Teacher 33* (March 1986): 21–25.

Thompson, Charles S., and John Van de Walle. "Let's Do It: Modeling Subtraction Situations." *Arithmetic Teacher 32* (October 1984): 8–12.

———. "Let's Do It: The Power of 10." *Arithmetic Teacher 32* (November 1984): 6–11.

———. "Let's Do It: Transition Boards: Moving from Materials to Symbols in Addition." *Arithmetic Teacher 28* (December 1980): 4–8.

———. "Let's Do It: Transition Boards: Moving from Materials to Symbols in Subtraction." *Arithmetic Teacher 28* (January 1981): 4–8.

Thornton, Carol A. "Doubles Up—Easy!" *Arithmetic Teacher 29* (April 1982): 20.

———. "Helping the Special Child Measure Up in Basic Fact Skills." *Teaching Exceptional Children 9* (Winter 1977): 54–55.

Thornton, Carol A., and Margaret A. Toohey. *A Matter of Facts—Addition.* Palo Alto, CA: Creative Publications, 1985.

———. *A Matter of Facts—Subtraction.* Palo Alto, CA: Creative Publications, 1985.

Trafton, Paul R. "Estimation and Mental Arithmetic: Important Components of Computation." In *Developing Computational Skills,* 1978 Yearbook of the National Council of Teachers of Mathematics, pp. 196–213. Reston, VA: The Council, 1978.

Tucker, Benny F. "Give and Take: Getting Ready to Regroup." *Arithmetic Teacher 28* (April 1981): 24–26.

———. "Variations on Concentration." *Arithmetic Teacher 29* (November 1981): 22–23.

Tucker, Benny F., and Edna F. Bazik. "Ideas." *Arithmetic Teacher 30* (December 1982): 25–30.

Van de Walle, John, and Charles S. Thompson. "Let's Do It: A Poster Board Balance Helps Write Equations." *Arithmetic Teacher 28* (May 1981): 4–8.

Weaver, J. Fred. "Big Dividends from Little Interviews." *Arithmetic Teacher 2* (April 1955): 40–47.

Weill, Bernice F. "Mrs. Weill's Hill: A Successful Subtraction Method for Use with the Learning-Disabled Child." *Arithmetic Teacher 26* (October 1978): 34–35.

Adler, David A. *Calculator Fun.* Illustrated by Arline and Marvin Oberman. New York: Franklin Watts, 1981.

Anno, Mitsumasa. *Anno's Counting House.* New York: Philomel Books, 1982.

Burningham, John. *Pigs Plus.* New York: Viking Press, 1983.

———. *Ride Off.* New York: Viking Press, 1983.

Gerstein, Mordicai. *Roll Over.* New York: Crown Publishers, 1984.

Hawkins, Colin. *Take Away Monsters.* Illustrated by the author. New York: Putnam, 1984.

Mathews, Louise. *The Great Take-Away.* Illustrated by Jeni Bassett. New York: Dodd, Mead, 1980.

7

TEACHING MULTIPLICATION AND DIVISION OF WHOLE NUMBERS

One teacher to another: "What do you mean, don't bother teaching division with three-digit divisors? It's in the book!" How would you respond?

Calculator? Paper and pencil? Mental computation? Estimation? Which process should I decide to use on a problem? On any one assignment should I let the students determine which process to use? What guidelines do I give them?

CONCEPT OF MULTIPLICATION

The concept of multiplication is closely related to the concept of addition. Both, in the physical representation, are processes of combining sets to make a new set. Multiplication differs from addition in that the sets being combined must be equal in size. There are three different situations we use to represent the concept of multiplication: repeated addition, arrays, and Cartesian products. Each of these will be discussed.

REPEATED ADDITION

Children's first introduction to the multiplication concept should be through verbal problems. Solving these problems requires joining sets which all have the same number

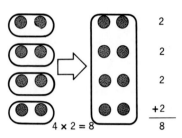

FIGURE 7-1.
Repeated addition and multiplication sentences.

of objects. They can solve these problems by repeated addition. For example, "Alicia wants to give 2 cookies apiece to herself, Martha, Julie, and Sarah. How many cookies should Alicia get from the cookie jar?" To solve the problem, the children placed counters in 4 sets of 2 each. Figure 7-1 shows the repeated addition sentence and

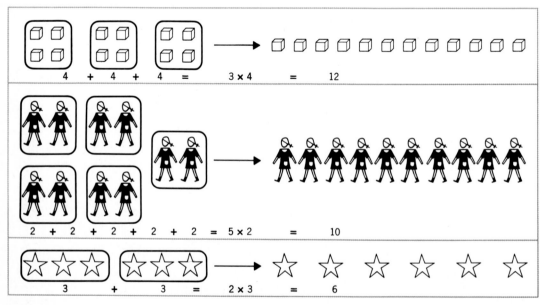

FIGURE 7-2.
Union of sets.

the related multiplication sentence for this problem.

Since multiplication can be represented as repeated addition, some children may wonder why they need to learn a new operation. A few problems should soon convince them that repeated addition is inadequate as a permanent algorithm. For example, "There are fifteen children in the club. Each member sells 7 tickets. How many tickets did they sell in all?"

In the children's first experiences, they will be counting the number of sets and the number of counters in each set. When this information is initially recorded, it should be in the form of "4 sets of two" as well as in a repeated addition sentence. The numeral (4) represents the number *of* sets and the oral name (two) represents the number *in* each set.

Nonexamples of the multiplication concept should also be included in these first lessons. Children should observe that if there are 3 sets of four and 1 set of five it cannot be written as 4 sets of four or 4 sets of five. These activities will reinforce that the sets must be equal-sized.

Counters of many kinds can be used as models to represent the concept of multiplication. As in addition, the lower basic facts should be used for beginning concept work. As shown in Figure 7-2, this allows children to count to find the answer to the problem. It is obvious that this approach is not as useful for higher multiplication facts, such as 7×9, 8×9, and so on, because the children would waste too much time counting.

In addition to set models, measurement situations and their models are also used to illustrate multiplication. In set models the *number of each set* is the same. In measurement models the *measure of each object* is the same. In each case repeated addition can be used.

Measurement situations can be solved with models such as Cuisenaire rods, interlocking cubes, and the number line. Consider the following situation.

Fred and Jerome were going to walk to the store with their mother. It's a long walk so they decided to take the wagon. Fred said, 'I'll pull you in the wagon some of the time if you'll take a turn pulling me.' Jerome answered, 'Okay, let's take turns for three

Multiplication using counting rods.

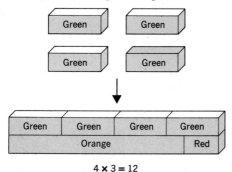

$4 \times 3 = 12$
Cuisenaire rods

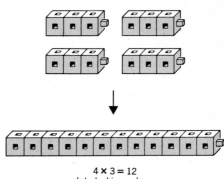

$4 \times 3 = 12$
Interlocking cubes

FIGURE 7-3.

Multiplication using counting rods.

blocks at a time.' When they arrived at the store, Fred said, 'That worked out well. I had two full turns to pull and two full turns to ride.' Since there were four turns in all, how far did the boys have to go to get to the store?

To solve this problem, the class represented each turn with a three-rod. They lined up four of the three-rods and matched their combined length to the ten- and two-rods (Figure 7-3). Thus the children could see that 4 lengths of three is 12.

The children could have used the rods with a number line of equal spacing (Figure 7-4). Each space on the number line equals one unit of the counting rods. This has the advantage of allowing the children to read the answer directly from the number line instead of having to search for the corresponding rods.

Another multiplication situation involving measurement is "In measuring one side of the house, Mr. Calhoun used a three-meter length of twine. He repeated this unit four times. How long is the side of his house?" To solve this problem, Alex decided to use only a number line. He counted and marked off three units. After he did this a total of four times, he determined that his answer was twelve.

The number line alone is a somewhat more abstract model than the counting rods used with a number line. To help children consider spaces along the line, the teacher

could have them visualize hopping bugs. In the example above, Alex could visualize a three-hopping bug (one that always hops three spaces at a time) starting at zero and making four hops. As shown in Figure 7-5, the bug lands on twelve. From this, Alex can see that 4 lengths of three is 12. This relates multiplication to previous activities in counting by twos, threes, and so on as well as to repeated addition.

A useful number line would be a paper number line, marked in centimeters, that could be fastened directly onto the children's desks. The children simply make the necessary hops with their fingers to find the answer. If a record of what was done is desired, a piece of paper could be placed directly above the number line and arrows drawn on this paper.

Examples of many types of problems should be used with the repeated addition concept until children realize that an addition problem such as 3 sets of four objects or 3 fours can be represented as a multiplication problem. After many concept-exploration activities, children can be introduced to a symbolic replacement for "sets of." The symbol "×," read "times," is the form used in early multiplication work and commonly in everyday life. Later, students will encounter other ways to represent multiplication symbolically: parentheses, "3(5)"; a dot "6·4"; or the algebraic form of no symbol at all, "ab."

The relationship between multiplication and addition can be reinforced using the calculator. The children can use the calculator to solve $4 + 4 + 4 + 4 + 4 = ?$. Then they can be challenged to write a shorter calculator code using the multiplication symbol. Later this can be extended to writing shorter codes for expressions such as $4 + 6 + 6 + 6$ or $3 + 7 + 7 + 7 + 7 + 15$.

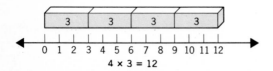

FIGURE 7-4.
Rods on number line.

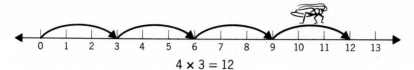

$$4 \times 3 = 12$$

FIGURE 7-5.
The three bug.

ARRAYS

As children encounter larger factors, they will find it is convenient to arrange the objects in rows rather than in sets. Thus 4 sets of six can be arranged to form 4 rows of six. Figure 7-6 shows 4 sets and their rearrangement as an array on a pegboard. Multiplication facts (except zero facts) can be represented easily as arrays. An array is an orderly rectangular arrangement of objects in rows. Arrays are convenient because children can observe at a glance that there are the same number of objects in each row. Since this model is new to children, they must be explicitly taught to count the number of rows and the number in each row. Previously they have been counting the number of sets and the number in each set.

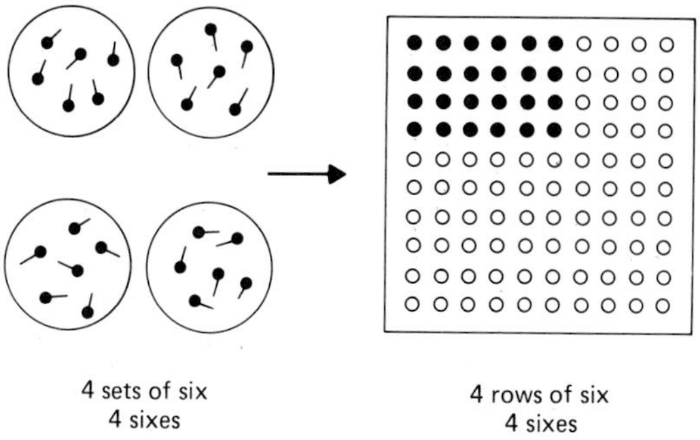

Some situations in which we naturally use arrays are given below.

Andrew observed in his classroom that the desks were arranged in 5 rows and there were five desks in each row.

Jo was watching the homecoming parade. When the school band marched by, she noticed that there were 7 rows with six players in each row.

Angie was grocery shopping with her dad. She noticed that the egg cartons had 2 rows with six eggs in each row. She watched a man stocking shelves. When he opened a box of soup cans, she saw that there were 4 rows of cans with six cans in each row. In the bakery section the doughnuts were boxed in 4 rows with two in each row.

Tim was installing carpet squares in the utility room. Six tiles fit along one wall. He found that nine tiles could be laid along the adjacent wall.

Jane saw that the black keys on her calculator were placed in 4 rows with five keys in each row.

Susan observed the pattern of 8 rows with eight squares in each row on the checkerboard.

In the flat of tomato plants Fred bought, the plants were arranged in 2 rows of three plants each. When he set them out in his garden, he made 1 row with all six plants.

4 sets of six
4 sixes

4 rows of six
4 sixes

FIGURE 7-6.
Sets as arrays.

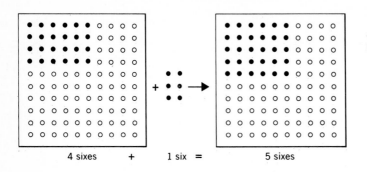

FIGURE 7-7.
Adding one more group on hundred pegboard.

4 sixes   +   1 six   =   5 sixes

All of these examples use arrays because that arrangement is functional. This also makes it possible to use multiplication to find out how many people in the band, eggs in the carton, desks in the classroom, and so on.

Children can use models of arrays to represent multiplication situations. Small 10 × 10 pegboards can be bought or made inexpensively so that each student could have a pegboard to work on. With these pegboards, the children can relate the set model of multiplication to the array model (Figure 7-7). They can see that arrays are composed of equal-sized sets arranged neatly in rows. Pictorial representations of arrays are included in children's textbooks (Figure 7-8).

The children should also draw arrays. Similarly, they can use graph paper to represent arrays (Figure 7-9).

CARTESIAN PRODUCTS

Another approach to the introduction and explanation of multiplication is the concept of Cartesian products of sets. In some texts Cartesian product of sets is referred to as cross product of sets. Since cross product can also refer to other concepts in mathematics, the term Cartesian products will be used here. Children may first encounter Cartesian products when classifying attribute blocks. For example, if children place the appropriate wooden attribute pieces in

4 × 3 = 12

FIGURE 7-8.
Pictorial array.

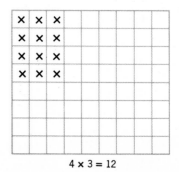

4 × 3 = 12

FIGURE 7-9.
Graph paper as an array.

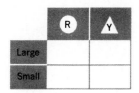

FIGURE 7-10.
Cartesian product using attribute blocks.

the chart shown in Figure 7-10, they have formed a Cartesian product model for the multiplication sentence $2 \times 2 = 4$.

Another way to introduce Cartesian products as a multiplication concept is through a problem situation. For example, "Joe's Carry Out has three kinds of cones (wafer, nut, and sugar), and it has four kinds of ice cream (vanilla, chocolate chip, peanut butter, and banana). If you are going to have an ice cream cone, what are all the different combinations you can choose from?" The students should be given time to find the various combinations, and then the problem should be analyzed. The students can discover a pattern for answering all problems of this type by organizing the information in a table. One pattern that can be developed

is closely related to arrays (Figure 7-11). There are 12 intersection points in the figure, each representing a different combination. The intersection marked "A" represents the combination of nut cone and chocolate-chip ice cream.

Although the diagram is in an array format, each element in the Cartesian product is unique or ordered. The element "sugar, vanilla" is not the same as the element "wafer, banana." In an array the elements are not ordered or unique. Each element in the array represents one object, and any two of them could change places without changing the array.

Another difference between arrays and Cartesian products is that Cartesian products can be used to represent the zero facts. For example, "If Joe's Carry Out has four flavors of ice cream but has used up its supply of cones, how many different combinations do you have to choose from?" This problem can be represented as a Cartesian product of sets (Figure 7-12). There are no intersections; therefore, $0 \times 4 = 0$.

Cartesian products can also be expressed as tree diagrams. In the first example above, the person must first decide what type of cone to order. Those three choices represent three branches of the tree

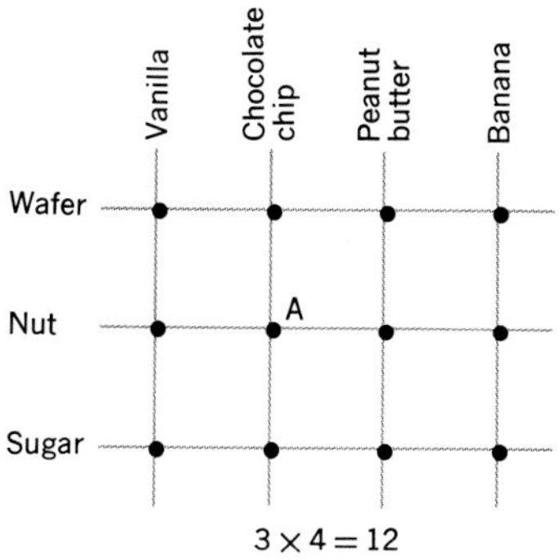

FIGURE 7-11.
Cartesian product of sets.

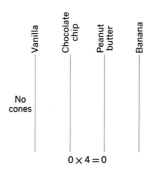

FIGURE 7-12.
Cartesian product of sets with zero multiplier.

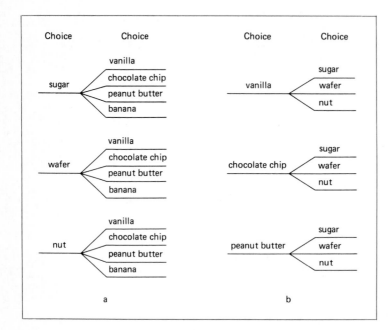

FIGURE 7-13.
Tree diagrams for Cartesian products.

(Figure 7-13a). The next choice is what type of ice cream, which is represented by four branches at the end of each of the three main branches. The twelve branches indicate the 12 different solutions. By tracing the paths students can readily see that the path which represents choosing a wafer cone and then chocolate ice cream leads them to a different choice from the path for a sugar cone and banana ice cream.

After children have seen many models and understand the concept of Cartesian products, then a pattern for their solution can be developed using multiplication as a way of finding the total number of combinations. These concepts of Cartesian products will be extended further as students study elementary concepts of probability. Students should explore other situations that involve this concept. Examples might include the different choices one has when selecting an outfit from a wardrobe of five pairs of slacks,

six shirts, and three pairs of shoes or when choosing a seat in an auditorium with rows A through X and 50 seats in each row.

As with addition and subtraction, models and story problems should be used to explore the concept of multiplication. All three multiplication situations—repeated addition, arrays, and Cartesian products—should be used. Once children understand the concept of multiplication, they will be able to apply multiplication to everyday situations.

CONCEPT OF DIVISION

The concepts of division are studied after multiplication concepts since division is the inverse operation of multiplication. Just as multiplication is a process of combining equal-sized sets, division, the inverse operation, is a process of separating a set into equal-sized subsets. Since the division process deals with parts, it is also closely related to fraction concepts. Both multiplication and division concepts require a higher level of mathematical maturity than addition or subtraction concepts.

Before formal instruction in division, children have many experiences with division problems that occur in everyday situations. For example, the children in Ms. Fryman's second grade class have decided to clean up the school playground. Since the playground is sectioned into four different areas, four equal-sized groups of children are needed. Susan counts and finds that there are 24 children in the class. Ms. Fryman asks the class to predict how many children will be in each group. After the class divides into four groups, they discover that there are six children in each group. Billy says, "Twenty-four children, divided into four groups, makes six children in each group."

At lunch time, Billy finds that his mother has put 16 carrot sticks in his lunchbox so that he can share with his friends. Since he usually eats three carrot sticks, he takes out three for himself and begins giving three to each of his friends. He gives away as many sets of three as he can and then finds he has one carrot left. Billy observes that from his 16 carrot sticks he was able to give three carrot sticks each to five people with one carrot stick left over which he gives to Ms. Fryman.

By solving such problems, children will develop division concepts. They will be able to explore the concept of division by discovering patterns of groups. Among these everyday problems children will encounter two types of division situations: measurement division and partitive or sharing division.

MEASUREMENT DIVISION

One concept of division that elementary school children will experience is known as subtractive or measurement division. This first type of division can be illustrated by the following problem. "Ann has twelve apples to share, and she wants to give two apples to each of her friends and keep two for herself. How many people will get apples?" Ann removed sets of two apples at a time until the apples were all passed out. Then she counted how many people received apples (Figure 7-14). The process Ann used to solve this division problem was repeated subtraction.

This type of division is called subtractive or measurement division because an amount is subtracted or measured out in equal-sized sets until there is not enough left to take away another set. The answer is the number of sets that were subtracted or measured out.

The relationship between subtraction and division can also be explored using the calculator. Problems such as how many threes can be subtracted from 21 can first be solved using repeated subtraction. The problems can then be re-solved using the division key.

Examples should not be limited to those which have an exact number of sets to be measured off and no objects left over. For example, "Allen brought his collection of 27 small toy cars to school. At recess, he wanted to give as many friends as possible four cars each to play with. How many friends can he give cars to?" Allen can pass out four cars at a time until he runs out or has fewer than four cars left. After measuring out his cars, Allen can conclude that with 27 cars, 6 friends can play with 4 cars each and there will be three cars left over.

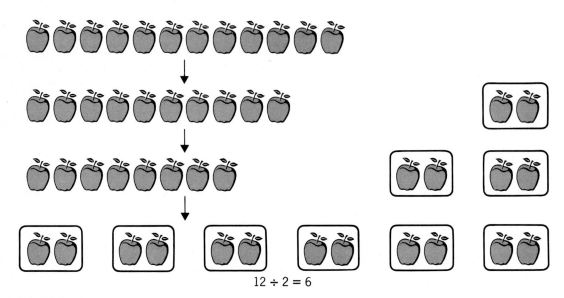

$$12 \div 2 = 6$$

FIGURE 7-14.
Measurement division.

Subtractive or measurement division can also be illustrated using measurement models instead of set models. For example, "Jeff is making little dolls for the church bazaar. Each doll needs to have two eight-centimeter hair ribbons. He has on hand a suitable piece of red ribbon 60 centimeters long. How many red hair ribbons can he make?" To solve this problem, Jeff can measure off or subtract eight-centimeter pieces until there is not enough ribbon left to cut another piece. He can then conclude that 60 centimeters of ribbon will make 7 hair ribbons which are each eight centimeters long and there will be four centimeters of ribbon remaining unused. In another case, Edna encountered a measurement division situation when she was deciding how many 25-cent items she could buy with three dollars.

Just as multiplication is introduced in elementary textbooks by repeated addition, division is introduced by repeated subtraction. Just as models were used to develop the concepts of addition, subtraction, and multiplication, they should be used in developing the concept of division. For example, David was building block towers. He had 30 blocks altogether, and he wanted to make each tower 6 blocks tall. How many towers can he build? David solved this problem by building towers until he had used all the blocks (Figure 7-15a). His older sister, Malinda, used paper and pencil (Figure 7-15b). David used a model to solve 30 divided by 6. Malinda worked the same problem using repeated subtraction. Although David used a model and Malinda used an algorithm, they both solved the problem by the same process—subtracting or measuring off equal-sized sets.

Just as children encounter multiplication situations in the form of arrays, they also encounter division situations in the array form.

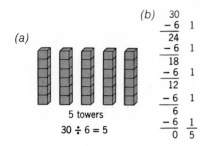

(a)

5 towers

30 ÷ 6 = 5

(b)
```
   30
 - 6   1
 ─────
   24
 - 6   1
 ─────
   18
 - 6   1
 ─────
   12
 - 6   1
 ─────
    6
 - 6   1
 ─────   ─
    0   5
```

FIGURE 7-15.
Division as repeated subtraction.

For example, Freddy's little wooden wagon holds exactly one layer of twenty blocks. By placing the blocks into the wagon, Freddy discovered that 20 blocks, divided into rows of 5 blocks each, made four rows. Figure 7-16 shows the array that Freddy formed in solving this problem. In this situation, Freddy knew the total number of blocks and the number of blocks in one row. If this situation is related to multiplication, he knew the product and one of the factors, the size of each set. The other factor, the number of sets, was unknown. This model is very appropriate for relating division to multiplication.

As with the other operations, the division symbol "÷" should be introduced only after the children have developed a concept of division. The form 15 is 3 sets of 5 or 15 divided by 3 equals 5 is changed to the form

15 ÷ 3 = 5. Again, language is also important. The symbolic form "30 ÷ 5 = 6" is read as "thirty divided by five equals six." Still later, children will be introduced to other forms for writing division, the fraction forms $\frac{15}{3}$ and 15/3 and the algorithmic form $3\overline{)15}$.

PARTITIVE OR SHARING DIVISION

The other type of division that must be developed is the concept of sharing or partitive division. Elementary children will have had some encounters with this concept in everyday situations also. For example, "There were eight ears of corn in the bowl and four members of Billy's family were sitting at the table. If they shared the corn equally, how many ears was each person allowed to eat?" To solve this problem, Billy suggested that they pass the bowl of corn around the table with each person taking one ear of corn at a time until all the corn was gone. Billy then counted the ears of corn on his plate to conclude that 8 ÷ 4 = 2 (Figure 7-17). This type of division is called sharing or partitive division because the amount to be divided is shared or partitioned on a one-to-one basis until there is not enough left for another round.

In this situation Billy knew the total number of objects and the number of sets among which the objects were to be equally shared.

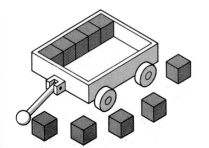

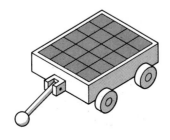

FIGURE 7-16.
Showing division with an array.

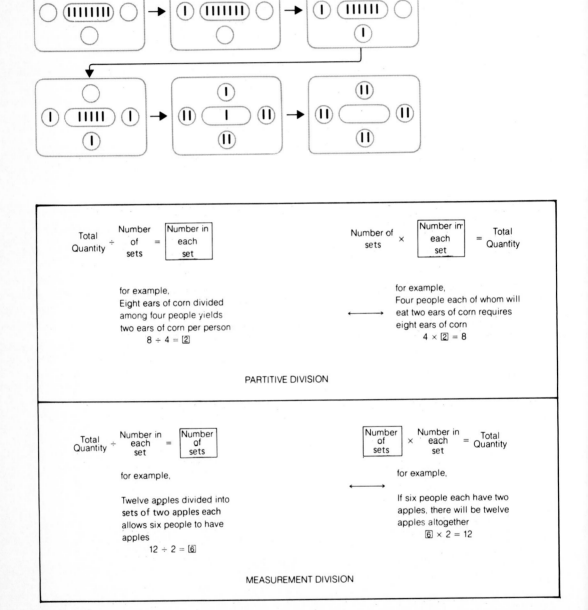

FIGURE 7-17.
Partitive division.

FIGURE 7-18.
Division related to multiplication.

If this situation is related to multiplication, Billy knew the product and one of the factors, the number of the sets. He was trying to find the other factor, the number in each of the equal-sized sets.

To solve simple division situations with set models, children could use countable objects and empty boxes. To determine how many objects would be contained in each of two boxes if ten objects were distributed equally, children could share all the objects between the two boxes. They would alternately place the objects one-by-one into the two boxes. The result would be a set of five objects in each box, so ten divided by two is five or $10 \div 2 = 5$.

Partitive division situations also occur in real life with measurement models. For example, "Daniel has a one-liter bottle of pop and five thirsty people. How much pop can he give to each person?" In this example, Daniel knows the total amount of pop and the number of sets into which it is to be divided. He must find the size of each set.

In comparing the two types of division, it should be noted that in partitive division children are given the quantity to be divided and the *number of sets* into which it is to be divided. In measurement division they are given the quantity to be divided and the *number of objects* in each set. With both types of division situations children should relate division to the inverse operation, multiplication, which they have studied previously (Figure 7-18). It is not necessary for elementary students to learn the names of these two types of division or to be able to label a problem as being partitive or measurement division. However, they should be given sufficient experience with both types of division situations that they will develop a meaningful concept of division and be able to recognize both types as division situations.

QUESTIONS AND ACTIVITIES

1. A variety of situations and language should be introduced to children so that they develop the concept of an operation.
   a. Write four multiplication problems that involve a variety of situations and questions. Two of them should suggest an array model and two a set model.
   b. Write four division problems that involve different situations. Two should involve partitive situations and two measurement situations.

2. Consider the multiplication and division situations that you wrote for Problem 1. What is missing—the size of the set (number in each row), the number of sets (number of rows), or the total number of objects? What is given—the size of the set (number in each row), the number of sets (number of rows), and/or the total number of objects? Show how children would solve the different situations using counters. How would they find the answer?

3. a. Write word sentences for the situations that you wrote in Problem 1. The sentence should reflect the sets or rows. For example, "Ted arranged five sandwiches on each of the four plates. How many sandwiches had been prepared?" would be written as "4 sets of 5 sandwiches is how many sandwiches?"
   b. Rewrite each word sentence into a number sentence.

4. Write a story problem involving Cartesian products for the factors below.
   a. $3 \times 5 = ?$ Diagram the result using an array or chart.
   b. $2 \times 4 \times 3 = ?$ Use a tree diagram to illustrate the solution.

5. a. Given the problem $4 \times 6 = 24$, illustrate how multiplication is repeated addition.

b. Draw arrays that show all the basic facts of multiplication whose products are 6, 12, and 7.

c. Bruni and Silverman, in "Let's Do It!: The Multiplication Facts: Once More with Understanding," describe activities involving multiplication as repeated addition and arrays. Read the article and play two of the games or activities described. What concepts are being developed in the games or activities?

6. Children often state that when you multiply you get more. What is wrong with this statement?

7. Use the constant key on a calculator to activate repeated addition to determine the following products.
   a. 8 twos
   b. 7 threes
   c. 6 fives
   d. 5 sixes

8. Use the constant key on a calculator to activate repeated subtraction to determine the following quotients.
   a. the number of threes in 21
   b. how many sets of 8 are in 48
   c. how many sets of 12 are in 63

9. Write a simple division story problem to match each model below.

a.

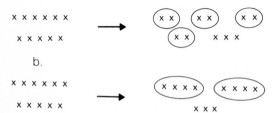

b.

10. a. Use a set or measurement model to illustrate the following problems. Simply set up the situations; do not solve.
   (1) an array that measures 3 by 5
   (2) 3 sets of five
   (3) 14 objects arranged in 7 rows
   (4) 15 objects shared among 5 sets

   (5) 7 lengths of two
   (6) 2 lengths of seven
   (7) 12 meters cut into 4 strips
   (8) 12 meters cut into lengths of 4 meters

   b. Write a division or a multiplication situation that could be depicted by each model in part (a).

11. Analyze the introduction to the multiplication concept in two different textbooks. Are sets or arrays used? Is multiplication related to addition? How are students to determine the answer? Are story situations or pictures to depict story situations given? How and when is the operation symbol introduced? How and when are situations linked to equations? If needed, how could these lessons be adapted or supplemented to delay symbol work? Cite publisher, copyright date, and grade level. When appropriate also cite page numbers with examples.

12. Analyze the introduction to the division concept in two different textbooks. Is partitive or measurement division used? When is the other situation introduced? What type of models are used—set or measurement? Is division related to subtraction? How are students to determine answers? Are story situations given? How and when is the operation symbol introduced? How and when are situations linked to equations? If needed, how could these lessons be adapted or supplemented to delay symbol work? Cite publisher, copyright date, and grade level. When appropriate also cite page numbers with examples.

13. When is the algorithm *form* for division introduced? How is it related to the division symbol? (14/2 versus 14 ÷ 2)

14. Why should $3\overline{)15}$ be read as "fifteen divided by three," not "three goes into fifteen"?

15. Given the following two story problems, what should be done with the remainder in each case? Write appropriate number sentences.

a. A land developer wants to divide 17 acres of land into 5 estates. How much land will be in each estate?

b. The 17 children in Ms. Brosz's kindergarten class are going to the zoo. How many students will ride in each car if there are 5 cars?

16. a. When are remainders introduced? How are they introduced?

b. Write a partitive situation and a measurement situation for 17 ÷ 5. Draw a picture of each situation using counters. Discuss the meaning of the remainder with respect to the divisor and the situation for each case.

17. a. National Assessment Results show that children do well with one-step story problems but have difficulty with nonroutine story problems. Write a multistep story problem for each of the conditions below. Include fantasy as well as real-life situations.

(1) multiplication and division
(2) subtraction and then division
(3) division and then subtraction
(4) addition and multiplication
(5) division and addition
(6) multiplication and then subtraction
(7) subtraction and then multiplication
(8) addition, multiplication, and division

b. In addition to the need for more multistep situations, students need work with problems with too much information or not enough information. Rewrite three of the problems above so that they contain too much information or insufficient information.

18. Read the children's book *The Greatest Guessing Game: A Book About Dividing* by Froman; it contains several examples of partitive and measurement division. How could students use this book to generate story problems? How could you use this to introduce a topic?

19. Analyze the division and multiplication story problems from two textbook series at the fourth- or fifth-grade level. Count the number of story problems. Classify the division problems as partitive or measurement. How many nonroutine problems have been included? What types were included? If needed, how would you supplement these textbooks? List the publisher, grade level, and publication date.

20. *For your resource file:* In "Understanding Word Problems," Knifong and Burton describe a variety of explanations to model situations involving all four operations. Multiplication examples are highlighted in the article. Read this article and add it to your resource file.

21. a. One method of determining children's thinking is to have them draw pictures of problems. Quintero, in "Conceptual Understanding of Multiplication: Problems Involving Combination," uses this technique to observe children's interpretations of combination problems. In "Children's Conceptual Understanding of Situations Involving Multiplication," Quintero describes activities where the children match pictures with multiplication situations. Read one of these articles. Did you understand the children's thinking from the examples?

b. How could you use this technique with your students?

c. *For your resource file:* Duea and Ockenga describe how to generate story problems and then use calculators to solve the problems in "Classroom Problem Solving with Calculators."

22. Read "Productive Pieces: Exploring Multiplication on the Overhead" by Stuart and Bestgen. How did they use arrays to build a multiplication table? Evaluate the teacher questions included in the article. Consider how you can use this with your class.

23. What story does Smith use to motivate a class in "Tiger-Bite Cards and Blank Arrays"? Evaluate this method of introducing division.

24. *For your resource file:* Read and copy one of the articles below about how to assess children's understandings of the concepts of different operations. In "Diagnosing a Student's Understanding of Operation," Sowder, Threadgill-Sowder, Moyer, and Moyer describe and give examples of questions to assess student understanding and modeling of operation concepts. Katterns and Carr describe how they used oral interviews to assess children's understanding in "Talking with Young Children About Multiplication."

PROPERTIES OF MULTIPLICATION

The properties of multiplication should be explored and discussed along with the concept of multiplication and the basic facts. These properties are important as they are necessary for children's understanding of multiplication concepts. The properties are used in the strategies children apply for learning the basic facts (the one hundred combinations of a one-digit number times another one-digit number—Figure 7-33) and are also needed for the multiplication algo-

rithm. They can also greatly facilitate the child's memorization of the basic facts.

As children are developing multiplication concepts, they should observe that multiplying any two whole numbers yields a unique, whole-number answer or that multiplication of whole numbers is closed. Discussion should also help relate addition to multiplication; that is, since addition of whole numbers is closed and multiplication is repeated addition, multiplication of whole numbers must also be closed.

The order property or commutative law is one that can particularly help children in learning the basic facts. This property can easily be demonstrated with arrays on a pegboard. An array consisting of 3 rows of five pegs each (3 × 5) is shown in Figure 7-19. Without changing the array, the pegboard can be rotated one fourth of a turn to show an array of 5 rows of three pegs each (5 × 3).

A geoboard and the concept of area can be used similarly. In Figure 7-20 the rubber band shows a 2-by-4 area. This area is rotated to form a 4-by-2 area.

With set models, children may think that 4 sets of two is not the same as 2 sets of four as the physical representation is different. However, by rearranging the same eight objects, they can see that the total number

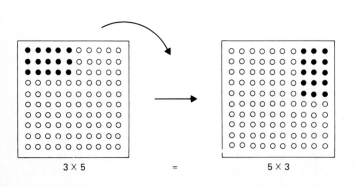

3 × 5   =   5 × 3

FIGURE 7-19.

Commutative law of multiplication on a pegboard.

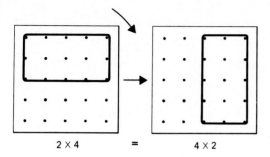

FIGURE 7-20.
Commutative law of multiplication on a geoboard.

of objects is unchanged or that mathematically, 4 × 2 = 2 × 4.

Cartesian product situations should also be used to extend the commutative property. Children may think that the order of their choices affects the total number of alternatives. By using tree diagrams in the problem about Joe's Carry Out, children can see that they will have the same number of combinations to choose from regardless of whether they choose the cone first and then the ice cream or the ice cream first and then the cone (Figure 7-13).

Many examples of the commutative property using various models and situations

should be used to reinforce and generalize this concept. As the commutative law of multiplication is explored, the same law for addition should be reviewed.

The associative law or grouping principle for multiplication can be discovered in a manner similar to that used for the commutative law. In this case a three-dimensional array made of interlocking cubes could be used (Figure 7-21). To show the first form of the problem given, children could build an array four cubes high and two cubes wide. To multiply this by three they could build two more identical arrays and fasten the three arrays together. The answer to the multiplication problem could then be found by counting the cubes. For the second form of the problem, children would first build an array two cubes wide and three cubes long and then stack four such arrays together. By counting the cubes and by looking at the finished three-dimensional arrays, children could easily see that multiplication is associative as (4 × 2) × 3 = 4 × (2 × 3).

Alternatively, a Cartesian product example and tree diagrams could be used. In choosing an outfit from a wardrobe of 4 shirts, 2 skirts, and 3 pairs of shoes, children could first consider deciding on a shirt–skirt

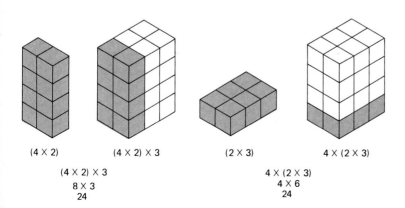

(4 × 2)   (4 × 2) × 3   (2 × 3)   4 × (2 × 3)

(4 × 2) × 3   4 × (2 × 3)
8 × 3   4 × 6
24   24

FIGURE 7-21.

Associative law of multiplication.

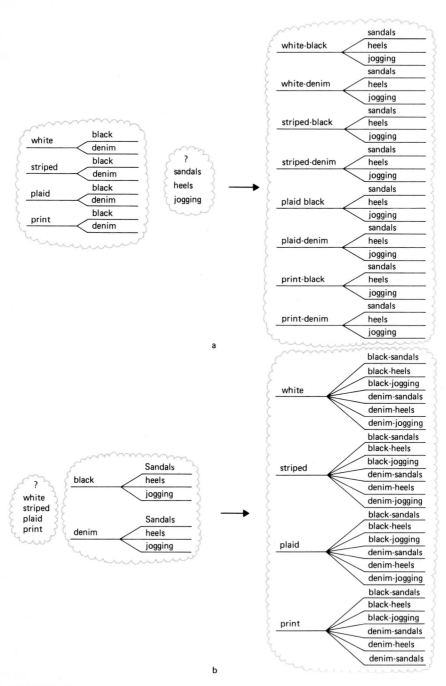

FIGURE 7-22.

Associative law with Cartesian products.

$3 \times (8 \times 3) \longrightarrow$	$3 \times (3 \times 8)$	by the commutative law
	$(3 \times 3) \times 8$	by the associative law
	9×8	
	72	
$(25 \times 7) \times 4 \longrightarrow$	$(7 \times 25) \times 4$	by the commutative law
	$7 \times (25 \times 4)$	by the associative law
	7×100	
	700	

FIGURE 7-23.

Applying the associative and commutative laws.

combination and then picking shoes to go with that (Figure 7-22a). Then they could consider looking at skirt–shoes combinations first, then picking a shirt and a good skirt–shoes combination to go with it (Figure 7-22b). From this they could see that either way they have the same number of choices or $(4 \times 2) \times 3 = 4 \times (2 \times 3)$.

After both the associative law and the commutative law are developed, they should be used in doing the operations. The teacher can introduce special problems that allow the students to apply these principles (Figure 7-23). In these examples the students should discover that by applying these laws appropriately the computation can be easily done mentally. The properties should be learned and applied when doing operations, not just studied in isolation.

Just as addition has an identity element, so does multiplication. The multiplicative identity property of one is easy to discover. Proper development of this important generalization will be discussed in the sections on strategies and memorizing the basic facts. This property reduces the number of separate basic facts to be memorized and is also important later for the development of the multiplication algorithm.

The number zero also has a special role to play in multiplication. Multiplication with zero can be developed using patterns that start with larger numbers. Appropriate questions to develop the concept of multiplication of zero by some other number (Figure 7-24) might include:

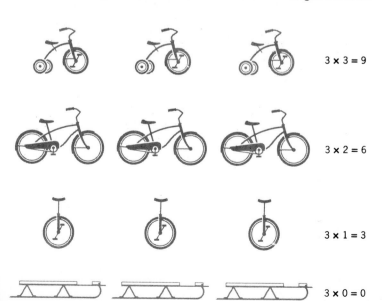

FIGURE 7-24.

Development of multiplication of zero.

$3 \times 3 = 9$

$3 \times 2 = 6$

$3 \times 1 = 3$

$3 \times 0 = 0$

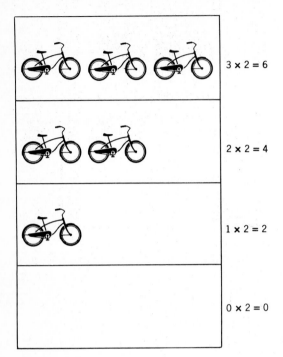

FIGURE 7-25.
Development of multiplication by zero.

How many wheels on three tricycles?

How many wheels on three bicycles?

How many wheels on three unicycles?

How many wheels on three sleds?

Appropriate questions to develop the concept of multiplication by zero (Figure 7-25) could include:

John has three bicycles. How many tires does he need?

Crystal has two bicycles. How many tires does she need?

Jessica has one bicycle. How many tires does she need?

Sam has no bicycles. How many tires does he need?

By studying these patterns and working with sets, children can see that multiplication of and by zero is reasonable, and they can learn the zero facts as one generalization.

Since zero is a special element for both addition and multiplication, it is appropriate to have class discussion on zero's differing roles in the two operations. Although the multiplication facts related to zero and one appear easy, they should be given special emphasis to avoid confusion. These numbers behave uniquely in the four operations, and these uniquenesses should be emphasized.

Another property that children will encounter is the distributive property. This is an extremely powerful property that they can apply in various situations. For example, children might want to find out how many plates they need if they are going to put four plates each on seven tables (7×4). If the children already know 5×4 and 2×4, they may think, "Five tables will need $5 \times 4 = 20$ plates and two tables will need $2 \times 4 = 8$ plates. Altogether $20 + 8$ or 28 plates will be needed to set seven tables." This thinking process is shown in pictures and in an abstract form in Figures 7-26 and 7-27, respectively. This form of the distributive law is the same principle introduced later as the "splitting the array" strategy for learning the basic facts as 7 fours is 5 fours plus 2 fours (7 fours = (5 + 2) fours = 5 fours + 2 fours).

The form of the distributive law that splits 7 fours into 5 fours and 2 fours is the only form used for strategies. However, a second form that considers 4 sets of 7 as 4 sets of 5 and 4 sets of 2 is needed for developing the standard algorithm for multiplication of whole numbers. Figure 7-28 shows a 4×7 array split two different ways. The corresponding calculations are also shown.

Another facet of the distributive law that is too often overlooked is that multiplication

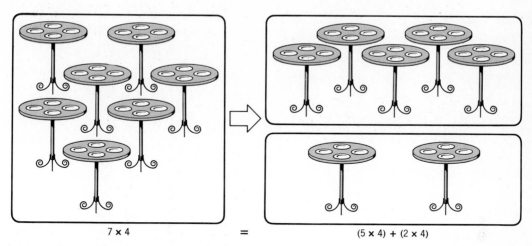

FIGURE 7-26.
Distributive law as repeated addition.

is distributive over subtraction. This form of the distributive law can also help children learn basic facts. An example is given in the strategy section "Splitting the Array." To find 4 sevens the child reasoned, "4 sevens is 5 sevens minus 1 seven or 35 − 7 is 28." Mathematically, this is $4 \times 7 = (5 - 1) 7 = (5 \times 7) - (1 \times 7)$.

cation of whole numbers is closed, children will find that division is not since some combinations, such as $3 \div 9$, $7 \div 3$, and $14 \div 28$, do not yield whole numbers.

To test whether division is commutative, children could consider the following situations.

PROPERTIES OF DIVISION

When children were studying addition and subtraction, they found that although addition of whole numbers is closed, some subtraction combinations did not yield a whole-number answer. Likewise, although multipli-

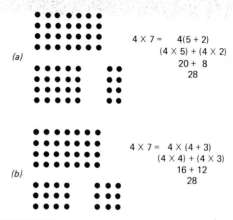

(a)

$$4 \times 7 = \quad 4(5 + 2)$$
$$(4 \times 5) + (4 \times 2)$$
$$20 + 8$$
$$28$$

(b)

$$4 \times 7 = \quad 4 \times (4 + 3)$$
$$(4 \times 4) + (4 \times 3)$$
$$16 + 12$$
$$28$$

$$7 \times 4$$
$$(5 + 2) \times 4$$
$$(5 \times 4) + (2 \times 4)$$
$$20 + 8$$
$$28$$

FIGURE 7-27.
Distributive law.

FIGURE 7-28.
Distributive law using arrays.

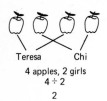 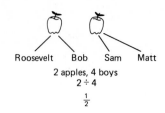

FIGURE 7-29.
Division not commutative.

Teresa   Chi   Roosevelt   Bob   Sam   Matt

4 apples, 2 girls   2 apples, 4 boys

$4 \div 2$ $\neq$ $2 \div 4$

2 $\neq$ $\frac{1}{2}$

Teresa and Chi have 4 apples to share. How many apples can each girl have?

Roosevelt, Bob, Sam, and Matt have 2 apples to share. How many apples can each boy have?

In exploring these situations through discussion and models, children will find that division is not commutative because $4 \div 2 \neq 2 \div 4$ as $2 \neq \frac{1}{2}$ (Figure 7-29).

To explore the associative property with division, examples can be used. Ms. Wolfe's class was exploring division concepts and calculator codes. She had given them $16 \div 8 \div 2$, $16 \div (8 \div 2)$, and $(16 \div 8) \div 2$ to solve. When they obtained different results, they wondered why. To guide their thinking Ms. Wolfe presented the following problems.

16 apples, 8 couples; how many apples per person?

16 apples, 8 people; how many apples per couple?

She told the class that both these problems could be solved by the number sentence $16 \div 8 \div 2$ with the appropriate parentheses. After some thinking time, Lee explained, "Well, in the first problem there were 16 apples and 8 couples, so I divided 16 by 8 to find that each couple got 2 apples. Then I divided that answer by 2 and found that each person got 1 apple" (Figure 7-30a). Jennie said, "In the second problem the question is different. Since it asks how many apples per couple, I first divided 8 by 2 to find that there were 4 couples. Then I

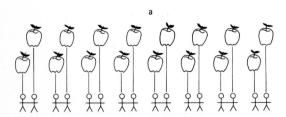

a

16 apples, 8 couples, 1 apple per person
$(16 \div 8) \div 2$
$2 \div 2 = 1$

b

16 apples, 8 people, 4 apples per couple
$16 \div (8 \div 2)$
$4 = 14 \div 4$

FIGURE 7-30.
Division not associative.

divided 16 by 4 so each couple gets 4 apples" (Figure 7-30b). Through further discussion the class decided that the situations *are* different, so the number sentences and their results *must* be different. $(16 \div 8) \div 2 = 1$, $16 \div (8 \div 2) = 4$, and $1 \neq 4$. Since $(16 \div 8) \div 2 \neq 16 \div (8 \div 2)$, division is not associative.

It is important for students to realize that division by one does not change the number being divided. To develop the identity property of one, children could put eight blocks into one set and tell how many blocks are in the set. Also, they could put eight blocks into sets of one block each and tell how many sets they have. In either case, they can easily see that the answer is eight, that is, that the original number is unchanged when dividing by one. However, since division is not commutative, one is considered only a partial identity element for division.

Since zero is a special element for multiplication, children should investigate the role of zero in division. They should first consider division of zero by some other number. This could be introduced with a problem. "Jane has invited Rob, Linda, Paul, and Mary to come over for dessert. She plans to serve cookies, but when she looks in the cookie jar, she finds it empty. How many cookies will each person get?" To children as well as adults, it is immediately obvious that $0 \div 5 = 0$.

This type of problem can also be related to multiplication. If $0 \div 5 = \square$, it follows that $\square \times 5 = 0$. Since zero correctly completes the multiplication sentence, it is also the answer to the division problem. Other examples can soon lead children to the generalization that zero divided by any other number is still zero.

To explore division by zero, students can try some examples by relating division to its inverse, multiplication. For example, the division problem $6 \div 0 = \square$ can be rewritten as the corresponding multiplication sentence, $\square \times 0 = 6$. Whatever number is tried for $\square$, the product will always be zero. Since zero does not equal six, there is no number that will make the multiplication sentence true. Therefore, there is no number that will make the corresponding division sentence true.

In investigating division by zero, students will probably try the special case of $0 \div 0 = \square$. When they write the corresponding multiplication sentence, $\square \times 0 = 0$, they find that any number substituted for $\square$ makes a true statement. Since division is defined as an operation on two numbers that yields a *unique* third number, it can not be true that $0 \div 0 = 2$ and also that $0 \div 0 = 6$. Therefore, students can conclude that division by zero is undefined.

Another property of division that should be explored is that multiplying both terms of a division problem by the same number does not change the answer. Students can use this concept to transform the original problem into an easier problem that can be done without paper and pencil. For example, for $245 \div 5$, it is easier to reason that 245×2 is 490 and $490 \div 10$ is 49, so $245 \div 5$ is 49.

The mathematical rationale for this is shown in Figure 7-31. Students already know that a division problem can be rewritten as a fraction (Figure 7-31, Step 1). They also know how to use multiplication by the identity to find equivalent fractions (Figure 7-31a). Each of these steps in fraction form can be rewritten in an equivalent division form (Figure 7-31b). By studying these and other examples, students will see that they have rewritten a division problem as a simpler, equivalent problem by multiplying both

	a		b
	$245 \div 5$ ↓		
Step 1	$\frac{245}{5}$		$245 \div 5$
Step 2	$\frac{245}{5} \times \frac{2}{2}$	⟶	$(245 \div 5) \times (2 \div 2)$
Step 3	$\frac{245 \times 2}{5 \times 2}$	⟶	$(245 \times 2) \div (5 \times 2)$
Step 4	$\frac{490}{10}$	⟶	$490 \div 10$
Step 5	49	⟶	49

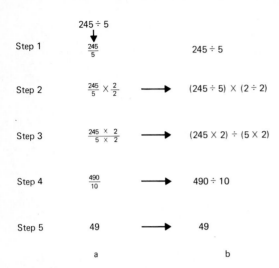

FIGURE 7-31.
Multiplying division problem by identity.

terms (dividend and divisor) by the same number.

Since multiplication is distributive, students should explore whether division is also distributive. They can test this informally by using numerical examples. From working examples, students will discover that division is only partially distributive. For the example $24 \div 6$, they will find that when 24 (the dividend) is renamed as a sum or a difference, the distributive law does apply. However, when six (the divisor) is renamed as a sum or a difference, the distributive law does not apply.

As with multiplication, the distributive law for division can be used to simplify mental computation. For example, "If tomato soup is on sale at 5 cans for 95 cents, how much will one can cost?" Students will probably solve this problem by dividing $1.00 by 5 to get 20 cents and then subtracting 1¢(5 ÷ 5) from 20 cents to obtain an answer of 19 cents per can (Figure 7-32).

$$\$0.95 \div 5 = (\$1.00 - \$0.05) \div 5 =$$

$$(\$1.00 \div 5) - (\$0.05 \div 5) = \$0.20 - \$0.01 = \$0.19$$

FIGURE 7-32.
Using the distributive law in division.

LEARNING THE BASIC FACTS OF MULTIPLICATION AND DIVISION

As children use models to develop the concepts and the properties of multiplication and division, they will also be learning some of the basic facts. Knowledge of all the basic facts is necessary for success in the study of arithmetic. This knowledge is essential for mental computation as well as for use of a written algorithm.

STRATEGIES FOR MULTIPLICATION

In Figure 7-33 the one hundred basic facts of multiplication are shown. Those written in boldface type are generally the most difficult facts for children to learn. Although approximately half of the facts can be related by the order or commutative property, simply memorizing the remaining 55 facts is still a large undertaking. Representing the facts by sets or arrays and then adding or counting the objects is time consuming and not mathematically productive.

Strategies for learning the basic facts are discussed in "Using Thinking Strategies to Teach Basic Facts" by Edward Rathmell in the NCTM yearbook *Developing Computational Skills*. The outline given below is based on this article and on work by Larry Leutzinger, Carol Thornton, and Margaret Toohey. As discussed in Chapter 6, strategies are helpful because they give children a way to find the answer besides counting.

×	0	1	2	3	4	5	6	7	8	9
0	0	0	0	0	0	0	0	0	0	0
1	0	1	2	3	4	5	6	7	8	9
2	0	2	4	6	8	10	12	14	16	18
3	0	3	6	9	12	15	18	21	24	27
4	0	4	8	12	16	20	24	28	32	36
5	0	5	10	15	20	25	30	35	40	45
6	0	6	12	18	24	30	36	**42**	**48**	**54**
7	0	7	14	21	28	35	**42**	49	**56**	**63**
8	0	8	16	24	32	40	**48**	**56**	64	**72**
9	0	9	18	27	36	45	**54**	**63**	**72**	81

FIGURE 7-33.
The basic facts of multiplication.

Since the strategies use concepts such as the commutative and distributive laws and other number patterns, children will be de-veloping specific number concepts as well as gaining a better number sense. These same concepts will be extended in algo-rithmic development and mental computa-tion. The strategies for multiplication are or-ganized by families.

Twos Family

The first family to be introduced is the twos family. Since the children know their addition doubles combinations, such as 6 + 6, 3 + 3, and so on, these pairs should be related to the corresponding multiplication facts. For example, when children encounter 2 × 4, they should think, "2 fours or 4 + 4 = 8, so 2 × 4 = 8." In the case of 6 × 2, they should recognize that this is equivalent to 2 × 6. Therefore, they should think, "2 sixes or 6 + 6 = 12, so 6 × 2 = 12."

Another way to introduce the twos family is through counting by twos. This approach as presented in one elementary textbook is shown in Figure 7-34. Both these strategies will help children learn the twos facts.

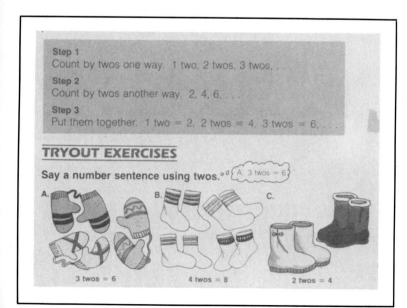

Step 1
Count by twos one way. 1 two, 2 twos, 3 twos, . . .
Step 2
Count by twos another way. 2, 4, 6, . . .
Step 3
Put them together. 1 two = 2, 2 twos = 4, 3 twos = 6, . . .

TRYOUT EXERCISES

Say a number sentence using twos. A. 3 twos = 6

A. B. C.

3 twos = 6   4 twos = 8   2 twos = 4

FIGURE 7-34.
Twos family. (From Jseph Payne et al., **Harper & Row Mathematics**, Grade 3, p. 188. Copyright © 1985, Macmillan, Inc. Reprinted with permission of Scribner Educational Publishers, a division of Macmillan, Inc.)

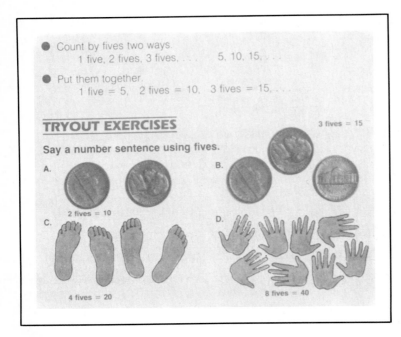

FIGURE 7-35.
Fives family. (From Joseph Payne et al., **Harper & Row Mathematics**, Grade 3, p. 196. Copyright © 1985, Macmillan, Inc. Reprinted with permission of Scribner Educational Publishers, a division of Macmillan, Inc.)

Fives Family

The fives family is also easy for children to learn. As they begin learning the fives, they will soon notice that each product ends in a five or a zero. This pattern can be reinforced by counting by fives. This skill is also needed for counting money and telling time. The clock shown in Figure 7-35 helps develop the fives family. When children first learn to tell time to 5-minute intervals, the outer ring is used. After preliminary counting by fives around the clock, the outer ring should be phased out. When the minute hand points to 3, the children should think, "3 fives is 15, or $3 \times 5 = 15$." Other examples for this strategy are shown in Figure 7-35.

Ones and Zeros Families

The ones and zeros families should be learned by generalizations. For example, to show 6 ones, six loops can be arranged on the overhead projector. Then one counter should be placed in each loop. When asked, "How many counters in all?" the students should observe 6 ones or 6, so $6 \times 1 = 6$ (Figure 7-36a). After repeating with different numbers of loops, the children should be able to generalize that any number times one

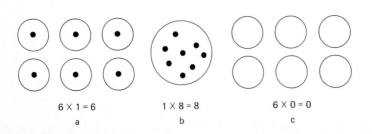

$6 \times 1 = 6$
a

$1 \times 8 = 8$
b

$6 \times 0 = 0$
c

FIGURE 7-36.
Ones and zeros families.

is that number. To illustrate that one times any number equals the number, the order property can be used. Some difficulties arise in showing one group of any number. For example, in illustrating 1 × 8 (Figure 7-36b), children simply see eight counters in a loop. They think "eight" not "1 × 8." To encourage them to think multiplication, the discussion should center on *one set of eight,* which can be written "1 × 8."

The zeros family is introduced similarly. For example, to illustrate 6 × 0, six loops can be placed on the overhead projector. Then the teacher can state that zero counters will be placed in the loops and follow that with the question, "How many counters in all?" Since there are zero counters, 6 sets of 0 is zero or 6 × 0 = 0 (Figure 7-36c). After repeating with different numbers of loops, the children should generalize that any number times zero is zero. The order property can be used to show that zero times any number is zero. With sets, zero times any number is difficult to show

because if the class considers zero sets of six, they will probably be thinking of six and be more likely to end up with a product of six than zero. The Cartesian product example as shown in Figure 7-12 would be an appropriate model for 0 × 4 = 0.

Just as practice on addition of zero should not be done in isolation, multiplication of zero and one should not be practiced in isolation either. Practice lessons and pages should include other previously learned combinations as well as combinations with factors of zero and one.

Nines Family

One strategy for the nines family is based on multiplication by ten. To solve 7 × 9, the child would think, "7 tens is 70 . . . but one is missing from each set, so subtract 7. . . . 70 − 7 = 63, so 7 × 9 = 63 (Figure 7-37). Similarly, to solve 9 × 6, a child would think, "10 sixes is 60 . . . 9 sixes is 1 six less so 9 sixes is 60 minus 6 or 54." For a problem like 4 × 9 the child would think, "4 × 9 . . . that

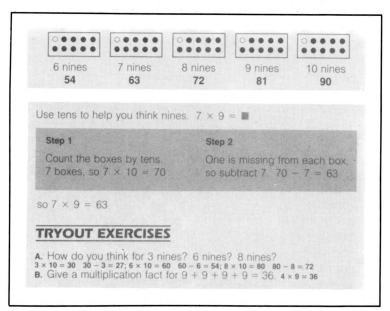

FIGURE 7-37.
Nines family based on ten.
(From Joseph Payne et al.,
Harper & Row Mathematics,
Grade 3, p. 250. Copyright
© 1985, Macmillan, Inc.
Reprinted with permission of
Scribner Educational Publishers, a division of Macmillan
Inc.)

6 tens = ___ 6 nines = □4 7 tens = ___ 7 nines = □3 4 tens = ___ 4 nines = □6	5 + ___ = 9 8 + ___ = 9 ___ + 4 = 9 6 + ___ = 9 ___ + 2 = 9	1 × 9 = 9 2 × 9 = 18 3 × 9 = 27 4 × 9 = 36 5 × 9 = 45 6 × 9 = 54 7 × 9 = 63 8 × 9 = 72 9 × 9 = 81	6 × 9 = 5___ 4 × 9 = 3___ 9 × 2 = 1___ 9 × 5 = 4___	9 × 3 = _____ 6 × 9 = _____ 4 × 9 = _____ 9 × 8 = _____ 9 × 9 = _____
a	b	c	d	e

FIGURE 7-38.
Nines family.

is the same as 9 × 4, so I can use the multiply-by-ten strategy. 10 fours is 40, so 9 fours is 40 − 4 or 36."

Another strategy for the nines can be based on the pattern that the sum of the digits of any product in the nines is nine. For example, 2 × 9 is 18; the digits 1 and 8 add up to 9. First the children should be taught to estimate the tens digit. Since 3 tens equal thirty, then 3 nines is less than thirty or 3 nines is in the twenties. The children should observe that the number in the tens place is always one less than the number of nines. After the children have learned to correctly estimate the tens digit, they should review the partitions of nine. The next step is to have them discover the pattern of the sum of the digits in the product. Then they should practice writing the ones digit in the product when the tens digit is given. The last step would be to write the product when given the factors. An example of these activities is given sequentially in Figure 7-38.

Splitting the Array
The threes, sixes, and fours facts are all presented with an add-on strategy. This thinking is the most sophisticated so these facts are presented last. The prerequisite skill for the threes facts and the fours facts is the twos

facts. The fives facts are prerequisite to learning the sixes facts. In all these cases the array is a helpful model. For example, for 3 × 7, children need to think 3 sevens, which can be shown as 3 rows of seven (Figure 7-39). Since 3 sevens is 2 sevens plus 1 more seven, children can reason that 2 sevens is 14, so one more seven is 14 + 7 or 21. In preliminary work on this strategy, children should be given practice splitting the array into facts that they know.

Other preliminary work for this strategy includes mental computation. For the sixes and threes families, children need to be able to mentally add two-digit numbers to one-digit numbers, such as 30 + 6, 18 + 9, or 12 + 6. To mentally add these sums, the children should observe whether the ones column will need to be renamed, then adjust the tens digit if needed, and add the ones column. For example, to add 16 + 8 a student would think, "6 + 8 is more than ten,

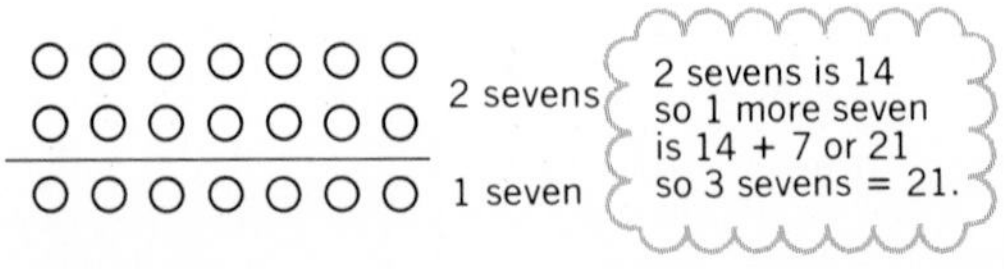

2 sevens

1 seven

2 sevens is 14
so 1 more seven
is 14 + 7 or 21
so 3 sevens = 21.

FIGURE 7-39.
Learning the threes facts.

so the answer will be in the next decade, so twenty . . . four, as 6 + 8 ends with 4."

The teacher should note that this add-on strategy is based on the distributive property, as in the example 2 sevens plus 1 seven is (2 + 1) sevens or 3 sevens. When using this strategy, all written work should use the word names for the number of members in the set. If, in the example discussed above, the numerical form 3 × 7 is used, the student may think 3 × 6 is 18 and then try to add 7, 6, or 3 to 18 to obtain the answer. Instead, 3 sevens was broken down into 2 sevens plus one more seven. This type of language clearly emphasizes sevens.

The fours family is also based on the twos family. For example, an array of 4 sevens can be split into 2 sevens plus 2 sevens. Since 2 sevens is 14, 4 sevens is twice as much or 14 + 14 = 28.

A prerequisite for the fours family is mentally adding a two-digit number to itself. Examples could include 14 + 14, 16 + 16, 18 + 18, or 12 + 12. The thinking for this computation is similar to that used for adding a one-digit number to a two-digit number. For example, the child may think, "16 + 16 . . . ten plus ten would be twenty, but 6 + 6 is more than ten so . . . thirty . . . 6 + 6 is 12, so . . . thirty-two."

An alternative for the fours family is to base it on the fives family. Thus 4 sevens is seen as 5 sevens − 1 seven or 4 sevens is 35 − 7 or 28. This is also using the distributive law.

The sixes family is based on adding one more group to the fives family (Figure 7-40). For exercise 31 a child might think, "5 sevens is 35, so 1 more seven or 6 sevens is 35 + 7 or 42, so 6 sevens or 6 × 7 is 42."

Other Facts

A few facts (7 × 7, 7 × 8, 8 × 7, 8 × 8) were not included in any of the above strate-

gies. Just as children usually find addition doubles easy to learn, they also learn easily the product of a number times itself. For 7 × 8, the children could use splitting the array or add-on strategy. They could think, "7 eights . . . well, 5 eights is 40 and 2 more eights is 16, so 7 eights is 5 eights plus 2 eights or 40 + 16 or 56, so 7 × 8 = 56." Then 8 × 7 could be learned by applying the order principle or 7 × 8 = 8 × 7.

Or a child might consider 8 × 7 first and think, "8 sevens . . . that's 4 sevens and 4 sevens . . . 28 + 28 = 56, so 8 × 7 = 56." This follows the thinking pattern used in generating the fours facts from the twos facts. The same prerequisite skills plus a knowledge of the fours facts are required.

Children should use and extend these strategies. Many combinations can be solved with more than one strategy. Since 2 × 9 is equivalent to 9 × 2, children can think of this using either the twos strategy or the nines strategy. Thus by applying the strategies and engaging in adequate practice using the strategies, children will efficiently master all the basic facts of multiplication.

STRATEGIES FOR DIVISION

Just as subtraction is the inverse of addition, division is the inverse of multiplication. Thus the subtraction basic facts were related to the addition basic facts, and the division basic facts can be related to the multiplication basic facts. However, although there are 100 basic multiplication facts, there are only 90 basic division facts, since division by zero is impossible (Figure 7-41). As with the other operations, children should develop immediate recall of the basic division facts.

Multiplication-Division Fact Families

Division basic facts can be taught after the children have learned the related multipli-

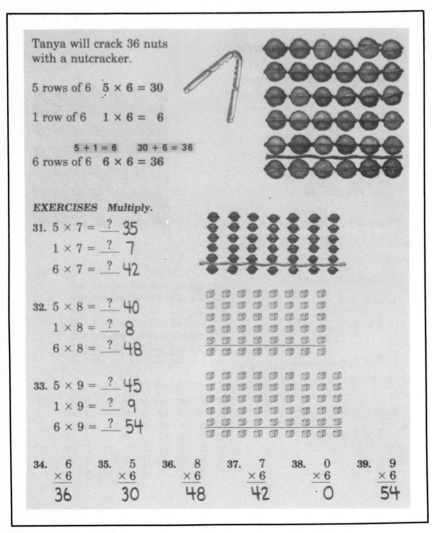

Tanya will crack 36 nuts
with a nutcracker.

5 rows of 6   **5 × 6 = 30**

1 row of 6   **1 × 6 = 6**

       5 + 1 = 6   **30 + 6 = 36**
6 rows of 6   **6 × 6 = 36**

EXERCISES *Multiply.*

31. 5 × 7 = _?_ 35

    1 × 7 = _?_ 7

    6 × 7 = _?_ 42

32. 5 × 8 = _?_ 40

    1 × 8 = _?_ 8

    6 × 8 = _?_ 48

33. 5 × 9 = _?_ 45

    1 × 9 = _?_ 9

    6 × 9 = _?_ 54

34.	35.	36.	37.	38.	39.
6	5	8	7	0	9
×6	×6	×6	×6	×6	×6
36	30	48	42	0	54

FIGURE 7-40.
Learning the sixes facts. (From A. V. Buffington, A.R. Garr, J. Graening,
P.P. Halloran, M.L. Mahaffey, M. O'Neal, **Merrill Mathematics: Grade 3.**
Merrill Publishing Company, 1985, p. 191.)

cation facts. The array can be used to relate the division facts to the previously learned multiplication facts. For example, in one third-grade textbook, the children are asked to consider 12 objects arranged in 4 rows of three (Figure 7-42). This is the same format that was used to introduce multiplication facts. Not only is the concept of division clearly illustrated, but it is also related to the concept of multiplication. When the multiplication facts already learned are related to the new division combinations, learning the division facts is greatly facilitated.

Another third-grade textbook uses sets

$$\frac{0}{1\overline{)0}} \quad \frac{1}{1\overline{)1}} \quad \frac{2}{1\overline{)2}} \quad \frac{3}{1\overline{)3}} \quad \frac{4}{1\overline{)4}} \quad \frac{5}{1\overline{)5}} \quad \frac{6}{1\overline{)6}} \quad \frac{7}{1\overline{)7}} \quad \frac{8}{1\overline{)8}} \quad \frac{9}{1\overline{)9}}$$

$$\frac{0}{2\overline{)0}} \quad \frac{1}{2\overline{)2}} \quad \frac{2}{2\overline{)4}} \quad \frac{3}{2\overline{)6}} \quad \frac{4}{2\overline{)8}} \quad \frac{5}{2\overline{)10}} \quad \frac{6}{2\overline{)12}} \quad \frac{7}{2\overline{)14}} \quad \frac{8}{2\overline{)16}} \quad \frac{9}{2\overline{)18}}$$

$$\frac{0}{3\overline{)0}} \quad \frac{1}{3\overline{)3}} \quad \frac{2}{3\overline{)6}} \quad \frac{3}{3\overline{)9}} \quad \frac{4}{3\overline{)12}} \quad \frac{5}{3\overline{)15}} \quad \frac{6}{3\overline{)18}} \quad \frac{7}{3\overline{)21}} \quad \frac{8}{3\overline{)24}} \quad \frac{9}{3\overline{)27}}$$

$$\frac{0}{4\overline{)0}} \quad \frac{1}{4\overline{)4}} \quad \frac{2}{4\overline{)8}} \quad \frac{3}{4\overline{)12}} \quad \frac{4}{4\overline{)16}} \quad \frac{5}{4\overline{)20}} \quad \frac{6}{4\overline{)24}} \quad \frac{7}{4\overline{)28}} \quad \frac{8}{4\overline{)32}} \quad \frac{9}{4\overline{)36}}$$

$$\frac{0}{5\overline{)0}} \quad \frac{1}{5\overline{)5}} \quad \frac{2}{5\overline{)10}} \quad \frac{3}{5\overline{)15}} \quad \frac{4}{5\overline{)20}} \quad \frac{5}{5\overline{)25}} \quad \frac{6}{5\overline{)30}} \quad \frac{7}{5\overline{)35}} \quad \frac{8}{5\overline{)40}} \quad \frac{9}{5\overline{)45}}$$

$$\frac{0}{6\overline{)0}} \quad \frac{1}{6\overline{)6}} \quad \frac{2}{6\overline{)12}} \quad \frac{3}{6\overline{)18}} \quad \frac{4}{6\overline{)24}} \quad \frac{5}{6\overline{)30}} \quad \frac{6}{6\overline{)36}} \quad \frac{7}{6\overline{)42}} \quad \frac{8}{6\overline{)48}} \quad \frac{9}{6\overline{)54}}$$

$$\frac{0}{7\overline{)0}} \quad \frac{1}{7\overline{)7}} \quad \frac{2}{7\overline{)14}} \quad \frac{3}{7\overline{)21}} \quad \frac{4}{7\overline{)28}} \quad \frac{5}{7\overline{)35}} \quad \frac{6}{7\overline{)42}} \quad \frac{7}{7\overline{)49}} \quad \frac{8}{7\overline{)56}} \quad \frac{9}{7\overline{)63}}$$

$$\frac{0}{8\overline{)0}} \quad \frac{1}{8\overline{)8}} \quad \frac{2}{8\overline{)16}} \quad \frac{3}{8\overline{)24}} \quad \frac{4}{8\overline{)32}} \quad \frac{5}{8\overline{)40}} \quad \frac{6}{8\overline{)48}} \quad \frac{7}{8\overline{)56}} \quad \frac{8}{8\overline{)64}} \quad \frac{9}{8\overline{)72}}$$

$$\frac{0}{9\overline{)0}} \quad \frac{1}{9\overline{)9}} \quad \frac{2}{9\overline{)18}} \quad \frac{3}{9\overline{)27}} \quad \frac{4}{9\overline{)36}} \quad \frac{5}{9\overline{)45}} \quad \frac{6}{9\overline{)54}} \quad \frac{7}{9\overline{)63}} \quad \frac{8}{9\overline{)72}} \quad \frac{9}{9\overline{)81}}$$

FIGURE 7-41.
Basic division facts.

FIGURE 7-42.
Multiplication and division related with arrays. (From Charles E. Allen et al: **Houghton Mifflin Mathematics (Teacher's Edition), Grade 3**, p. 198. Copyright © 1985 by Houghton Mifflin Company. Used by permission.)

Multiplication helps you learn division.

Dave planted 4 rows of trees with 3 trees in each row. How many trees did Dave plant in all?

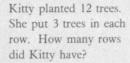

$$4 \times 3 = 12$$

David planted 12 trees in all.

Kitty planted 12 trees. She put 3 trees in each row. How many rows did Kitty have?

$$12 \div 3 = 4$$

Kitty had 4 rows of trees.

Exercises

Complete.

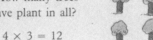

1. An orchard has five rows of trees. Each row has two trees. How many trees are there in all?

$$5 \times 2 = \underline{?\,10}$$

2. An orchard has ten trees. Each row has two trees in it. How many rows of trees are there?

$$10 \div 2 = \underline{?\,5}$$

3. $2 \times 3 = \underline{?\,6}$

  $6 \div 3 = \underline{?\,2}$

4. $2 \times 2 = \underline{?\,4}$

  $4 \div 2 = \underline{?\,2}$

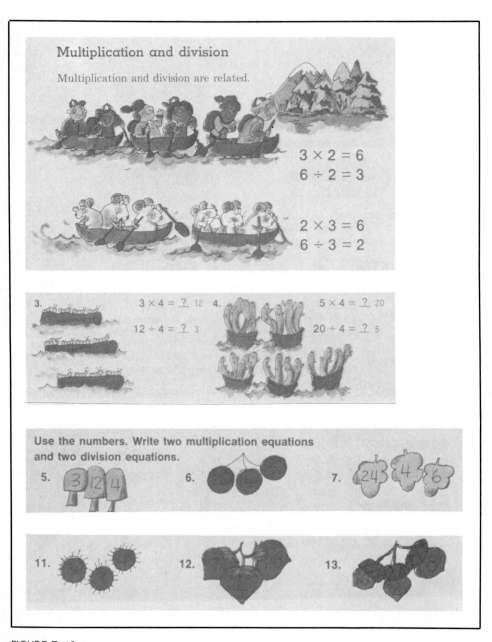

FIGURE 7-43.
Relating multiplication and division. (From C.A. Dilley, D.W. Lowry, W.E. Rucker,
Heath Mathematics. D.C. Heath & Company, 1985, Grade 3, pp. 202–203.
Reprinted by permission of D.C. Heath & Company.)

to relate the division facts to the multiplication facts (Figure 7-43a). In each example, the sets clearly illustrate the facts to be recorded. This exercise is followed by writing multiplication and division fact families (Figure 7-43b). For problem 5, the children would write the multiplication sentences $3 \times 4 = 12$ and $4 \times 3 = 12$ and the related division sentences $12 \div 3 = 4$ and $12 \div 4 = 3$.

Missing Factors

Multiplication-division fact families can be extended to introduce the missing-factor strategy of division. This idea as developed in one third-grade textbook is shown in Figure 7-44. The example emphasizes the fact family—"If you know this multiplication fact, you know another multiplication fact and two division facts" (Figure 7-44a). This example is followed by practice in giving the answers

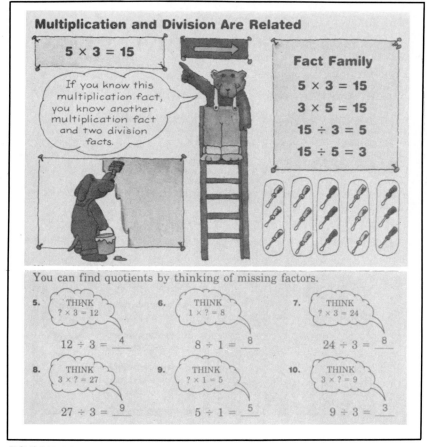

FIGURE 7-44.
Fact families to introduce missing-factor strategy (From Robert Eicholz, Phares O'Daffer, Charles Fleenor, Randall Charles, Sharon Young, Carne Barnett, **Addison-Wesley Mathematics: Book 3**, p. 232. Copyright © 1985, Addison-Wesley Publishing.)

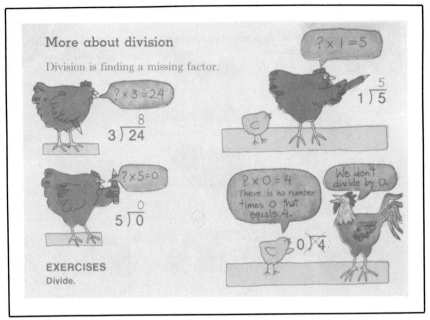

FIGURE 7-45.

Missing-factor strategy for division. (From C.A. Dilley, D.W. Lowry, W.E. Rucker, **Heath Mathematics**, D.C. Heath & Company, 1985, Grade 3, p. 204. Reprinted by permission of D.C. Heath & Company.)

to all combinations in several multiplication and division fact families (not shown). Finally, the children are asked to solve division equations by thinking of the related multiplication fact (Figure 7-44b). Figure 7-45 shows the missing-factor strategy as presented in another third-grade text. Note that this example introduces the rationale for not dividing by zero.

Partial arrays can be used as a learning strategy to relate division combinations to missing-factor sentences (Figure 7-46). Since part of the array is hidden, the number of counters in the array must be given. The children must be able to see the number of rows but not the number of counters in each row. They can observe that in this example there are three rows, but they must determine the number of counters in each row. To

relate the problem to multiplication, the teacher should ask such questions as, "What number times three is fifteen?" Since one of the factors is missing, this is called the missing-factor approach. Just as the missing-addend approach was used to help children learn the subtraction basic facts, the missing factor approach can help them learn the division basic facts. Wilson Goodwin suggests drawing bold lines along the edges of the array and placing the dividend

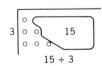

FIGURE 7-46.

Partial arrays.

and divisor as shown. This relates the written form 15 ÷ 3 to the form used for algorithms (3)15).

Patterns

A number of facts can be learned by finding patterns. Counters should be used to help the children act out the following situations (Figure 7-47a).

6 counters, 3 people; how many counters for each?

6 counters, 6 people; how many counters for each?

3 counters, 3 people; how many counters for each?

7 counters, 7 people; how many counters for each?

The children should discuss the pattern and then extend their discussion to problems like 203 counters, 203 people or 897 counters, 897 people. After many examples and appropriate discussion, the children should form the generalization that any number divided by itself is one.

Similarly, another pattern can be developed for division by one. Again, children should act out the situations using counters (Figure 7-47b).

6 counters, 3 people; how many counters for each?

6 counters, 2 people; how many counters for each?

6 counters, 1 person; how many counters for each?

8 counters, 1 person; how many counters for each?

2 counters, 1 person; how many counters for each?

5 counters, 1 person; how many counters for each?

Again, the children should discuss this pattern and then extend to problems with a larger dividend such as 46 counters, 1 person or 245 counters, 1 person. This time they

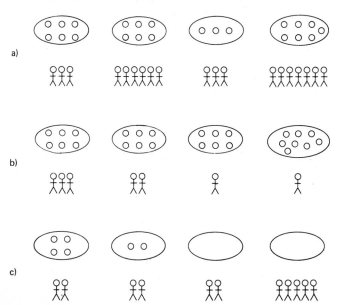

FIGURE 7-47.
Patterns for division.

should form the generalization that any number divided by one is itself.

Another group of facts that can be learned by a single generalization are those in which zero is divided by any *other* number such as 0 ÷ 3 or 0 ÷ 9. To help children discover this generalization, the teacher should ask such questions as:

4 counters to share between 2 people; how many to each?

2 counters to share between 2 people; how many to each?

0 counters to share between 2 people; how many to each?

0 counters to share among 5 people; how many to each?

0 counters to share among 8 people; how many to each?

In each case the children should act out the situation with models (Figure 7-47c). After sufficient discussion of the pattern, children can extend this to problems with larger divisors such as 0 counters, 100 people or 0 counters, 478 people. Then they can form the generalization that zero divided by any *other* number is still zero.

MEMORIZING THE BASIC FACTS OF MULTIPLICATION AND DIVISION

For each of the multiplication and division strategies, sets or arrays were used to develop the thinking needed to use that strategy. After the children understand the thinking for a specific strategy, they should be given short (5 to 10 minute), daily practice periods for a few weeks to apply that particular strategy. Only those facts for which that strategy is appropriate should be studied at that time.

After children have learned and practiced the different strategies separately, ad-

ditional practice exercises should include a variety of basic fact combinations. The children will need to apply different strategies for different facts. Their goal is to be able to recall any fact at random.

A table of basic multiplication facts can be a very useful teaching tool if the students construct their own table. As they work through the table, they should consider patterns. One pattern they should notice is the multiplication properties of zero and one. They should note symmetry along the diagonal of the table resulting from the commutative property. They should also note the patterns in each individual row or column. For example, in the sevens row the pattern 0, 7, 14, 21 . . . 63 is generated by adding seven. Using this same chart, children can explore the relationship of the division basic facts to the multiplication basic facts.

Materials are available to aid in the memorization of basic multiplication facts. Phonograph records that rely on the order of the facts and teach by rhythm and repetition are listed in many educational catalogues. These records have only limited value because the facts are learned as part of a sequence and not in isolation. If basic facts are studied only in order, students may not be able to respond to 4 × 8 until they have gone through the entire 4 list. That is, students mentally recall 4 × 1 = 4, 4 × 2 = 8, 4 × 3 = 12, and so on until they reach the desired problem, 4 × 8. Instead they must learn to recall the facts at random since this is how they occur in everyday problem situations.

The constant function on the calculator can be used to practice families of facts. To practice the fours facts, 4 is entered as a multiplication constant. Then the other factor is entered. The child should "guess" the answer before pushing the equals key to obtain the answer. This process should be repeated for other combinations in the fours family. This use of the calculator allows random practice of any particular fact family.

Calculators can also be used for the type of random practice described in Chapter 6 in the section "Memorizing the Basic Facts of Addition and Subtraction." In this case the child would enter any basic multiplication or division fact, "guess" the answer, and then check by pressing the " = " key.

A technique used by many teachers is to have the students complete a random chart of the basic facts (Figure 7-48). The numbers are arranged at random across the top of the page and down the left side. Then the students are given time to put the products in the proper spaces. This is a simple technique, emphasizes the random recall of facts that is desired, is not very time consuming, and can be corrected in class by having one of the students put the answers on the chalkboard.

Another variation of this chart is one that does not have all the numbers across the top and down the side but does have some of the products filled in. The student should then complete the chart (Figure 7-49). In this form the students are practicing division facts as well as multiplication facts. Since these are both only partial charts, they can

FIGURE 7-49.
Basic fact practice.

be designed to give students the greatest amount of practice with those facts that they find most difficult.

As with addition and subtraction, many computer programs are available for practice of basic facts of multiplication and division. Again, these programs give the student immediate feedback, and some also keep a record of the student's performance for the teacher. Thus the teacher has additional information on which to base future practice sessions.

Computers and one special calculator, the Dataman, can also be used for practicing missing-factor sentences. The computer presents problems in which either the first or the second factor is missing, such as $3 \times [\ ] = 18$ or $[\ ] \times 2 = 14$. If the student punches in the correct factor, the computer will give positive reinforcement and then present the next problem. If the student punches in the wrong factor, the computer may either repeat the problem, give the correct answer, or simply go on to the next problem, depending on the particular program.

Another method of using the calculator will help children learn division facts and will reinforce the relationship between multiplication and division. The products of the multiplication facts can be written on individual

FIGURE 7-48.
Basic fact practice.

36	40	48	30
56	63	64	35
49	42	25	45
32	54	72	28

    8   7   6
    5   9   4

FIGURE 7-50.
Practicing multiplication facts.

cards. As cards are displayed, the students think of factors that can be used to obtain that product. These multiplication combinations are then tried on the calculator to see if the correct product is obtained. This activity is suitable for individuals or small groups as it is self-checking.

A variation of this game is to write products in a 4-by-4 grid and the factors in a list below (Figure 7-50). Students could play in pairs; the winner is the first student to initial three products in a row. One student selects a product and two factors that will yield that product. With a calculator, the student then finds the product of the two selected factors, and if correct, initials that product on the grid. Factors may be used more than once. If an error is made or the product is already initialed, the student loses that turn. This game can be individualized by selecting factors and products for which different individuals need further practice. For older students a larger grid could be used and the

factors and products could be other than basic facts. In order to select appropriate factors students will need to use estimation and number properties.

In the section "Memorizing the Basic Facts of Addition and Subtraction" in Chapter 6, practice activities using number cubes, spinners, flash cards, and card games were described. Any of these activities can be adapted for multiplication or division.

Games such as Contig and Krypto can be played with combinations of any two operations or all operations. The rules for the game can be redefined according to the objective for the practice. These games are also helpful for teaching order of operations. Contig is described in *The Arithmetic Teacher,* May 1972. Krypto is briefly described below.

Krypto is played with a deck of 52 cards including three cards each with numerals 1 to 10, two each with numerals 11 to 17, and one each with numerals 18 to 25. Five cards are dealt to each player (from two to eight players) and one objective card is turned face up. Each player uses their five cards and any combination of the four operations of addition, subtraction, multiplication, or division to try to match the number shown on the objective card. The player must use each of the five cards once and only once. Figure 7-51 shows two possible ways to play one hand. The first player to call Krypto, if correct, is the winner of the round. The winner's score is found by adding the numbers on the

24
Object card

$15 + 7 + 4 - (3 - 1) = 24$
Step 1 $15 + 7 + 4 = 26$
Step 2 $3 - 1 = 2$
Step 3 $26 - 2 = 24$

1   3   15   7   4
Players hand

$[15 \div (1 + 4)] \times 7 + 3 = 24$
Step 1 $1 + 4 = 5$
Step 2 $15 \div 5 = 3$
Step 3 $3 \times 7 = 21$
Step 4 $21 + 3 = 24$

FIGURE 7-51.
Krypto.

cards and on the Krypto card (in this case 1 + 3 + 15 + 7 + 4 + 24 = 54). If the player is incorrect, this same sum is subtracted.

Regardless of the time and effort spent and the multitude of manipulative aids used, some students will still not know all the basic facts when algorithms are introduced. These students should be allowed to construct and use a chart that contains those basic facts which they have not yet memorized. Repeated use of the chart will help them memorize these basic facts. Besides this, they should continue to practice these basic facts using the multiplication and division strategies.

Finger computations, including finger multiplication, are sometimes taught as a panacea for learning the basic facts and for other computations. These finger computations are interesting tricks but should never be taught as a complete computational method. The student who is having real difficulty with multiplication is as likely to be confused as to be helped by these methods. Learning the procedure for finger computation is at least as difficult as simply memorizing the basic facts. Besides, finger computation does nothing to increase the child's understanding of the multiplication process. For the bright students, finger multiplication can be given as an enrichment activity. They can be challenged to figure out why these "tricks" work.

QUESTIONS AND ACTIVITIES

1. a. How would you use arrays to help children discover the order (commutative) property for multiplication?
   b. How would you use sets?

2. What is the strategy for learning the twos family? Write out the child's thinking for 2 × 6 and 9 × 2.

3. a. What pattern should the children detect with regard to the fives family?
   b. Describe how you would use the clock to help children with the fives family. When do children learn to tell time in 5-minute intervals? When do they learn their fives facts?
   c. How could their knowledge of money be used to help them with the fives family?

4. Two different strategies were described for the nines family. Write out the child's thinking in these two different ways for 6 × 9. Which way is easier for you? Is the same method easier for all of your classmates? Do you think all of your students will develop the same thinking patterns?

5. a. Describe activities to help children develop the concept of multiplication by zero. By one.
   b. Why are the zeros and ones families taught after other facts instead of first? What errors could occur between problems like 0 × 4 and 0 + 4? 1 + 6 and 1 × 6? How could errors like this be avoided or minimized?

6. a. Draw diagrams to indicate how to split the array 6 × 7 and write out the differences in thinking for:
   (1)   6 × (5 + 2)
   (2)   (5 + 1) × 7
   b. Which is easier to think about (5 + 1) × 7 = 5 × 7 + 1 × 7 or 6 sevens is 5 sevens plus 1 more seven? Why?

7. Draw an array for each of the following. Assume that the child does not know the fact. Decide how to split the array based on an easier fact. Write out the child's thinking for each fact.
   a. 6 × 8   d. 8 × 3
   b. 3 × 7   e. 9 × 4
   c. 4 × 7   f. 7 × 6

8. Read the children's book *Building Tables on Tables: A Book About Multiplication* by Trivett. How could these ideas be used as a lesson plan for a class? As an enrichment activity for some students?

9. Devise an activity that uses the missing-factor approach for teaching the division basic facts.

10. What results would be obtained if the problems below were tried on a calculator? Why?
    a. 0 ÷ 5
    b. 7 ÷ 0
    c. 0 ÷ 0

11. How do the activities below help children relate division facts to multiplication facts?
    a. Write all basic multiplication combinations whose product is in the 40s. In the 50s.
    b. Name a pair of factors for each of the following products: 35, 16, 36, 54, 64, 72.

12. Write up an example that you could use with your students to show that:
    a. multiplication is associative.
    b. division is not commutative.
    c. division is not associative.

13. a. Division is only partially distributive. In the problems below, 24 ÷ 6 has been written in various forms. In which cases is the distributive property appropriately applied?
    (1) Is (12 + 12) ÷ 6 equivalent to (12 ÷ 6) + (12 ÷ 6)?
    (2) Is (30 − 6) ÷ 6 equivalent to (30 ÷ 6) − (6 ÷ 6)?
    (3) Is 24 ÷ (2 + 4) equivalent to (24 ÷ 2) + (24 ÷ 4)?
    (4) Is 24 ÷ (8 − 2) equivalent to (24 ÷ 8) − (24 ÷ 2)?
    b. What special problems would students encounter when they solved the foregoing problems with a calculator?

14. *For your resource file:* Sequenced activities to teach multiplication facts are developed in "Using Thinking Strategies to Teach the Basic Facts" by Rathmell. Read the article, summarize the types of activities, and outline the suggested sequence. Read and summarize "Multiply Successes When Introducing Basic Multiplication Ideas to Visually Handicapped Children" by Dodd. Read "The Learning Disabled Child—Learning the Basic Facts" by Myers and Thornton.

15. In "How Students Do Their Division Facts," Kalin describes how he tested and interviewed students to determine their knowledge of the division basic facts. Read the article. What is your evaluation of his diagnostic and remediation techniques? How could you adapt this to your students' work?

16. *For your resource file:* The following articles all focus on games. Read and evaluate at least one of them. "Ideas" by Ockenga and Duea includes game boards for multiplication, addition, and number. In "Multiplication Games That Every Child Can Play," Nelson describes games that combine representation with number facts. In "Variations on Rummy," Nelson describes how to modify a card game to reinforce different topics.

ALGORITHM FOR MULTIPLICATION OF WHOLE NUMBERS

As discussed earlier in this chapter, the basic facts of multiplication involve a one-digit number being multiplied by another one-digit number, such as 8 × 7 = 56. These facts are learned for immediate recall. Although students may memorize multiplication combinations for elevens and twelves, they will also need to learn a process or algorithm for multiplying larger numbers. Although they can use calculators to determine answers, they need to be able to

3 × 24	34 × 58
24	58
× 3	× 34

FIGURE 7-52.
Reading multiplication statements.

decide whether those answers are reasonable. As they learn about algorithms and understand how these algorithms work, they should become better estimators. As students learn about estimation, this should reinforce their algorithmic skills and improve their mental computation skills.

When children were first introduced to the multiplication symbol, they were taught how to read multiplication sentences. They also need to be introduced to the form that is used for written computation. Both problems in Figure 7-52a are read "three times twenty-four." Care must be taken not to switch order and read the vertical form of the problem as "twenty-four times three." Although children know that multiplication is commutative, it is still confusing to them if when working and reading this problem, statements such as "four times three" or "2 tens times 3" are intermixed with "three times four" and "three times 2 tens" for the same problem. Similarly in Figure 7-52b, the problem should be read as "thirty-four times fifty-eight" and the partial combinations read in the same order such as "four times 5 tens" or 3 tens times 5 tens," not as "5 tens times four" or "5 tens times 3 tens."

The first step in the development of the multiplication algorithm involves multiplying a multidigit number by a one-digit number. This process is broken down into several small steps. The sequencing of the multiplication algorithm varies slightly from one elementary textbook series to another. Most textbooks develop the algorithm conceptually through models, place value, and patterns, but a few series still use solely a rule approach and so need more supplementation. The sequence described here is based on Donald Hazekamp's article "Teaching Multiplication and Division Algorithms" in *Developing Computational Skills*.

ONE-DIGIT NUMBER TIMES A MULTIPLE OF TEN OR ONE HUNDRED

The first step encountered in learning the multiplication algorithm is multiplying a single-digit number times ten and then a single-digit number times one hundred. Models such as counting sticks and base-ten blocks should be used to develop this concept. This is simply reviewing place value since 6 × 10 is represented as 6 sets of 1 ten or 6 tens or 60.

The written form or number sentence should emphasize the pattern developed with models. The first recordings should be 6 × 1 ten and 6 × 10, where the tens place is written in boldface or a different color. Similarly, 3 × 100 is 3 sets of 1 hundred or 3 × 1 hundred or 3 hundreds or 300. The written form should include this pattern of 3 × 1 hundred and 3 × 100.

The children's next experiences should involve multiplying a one-digit number times a multiple of ten or one hundred. Problems of this type vary in difficulty. One of the simpler problems, 3 × 20, can be represented as 3 sets of 2 tens (Figure 7-53). The children may count "twenty, forty, sixty" or "2 tens, 4 tens, 6 tens" to solve this problem. This process gives them the correct answer, but they also need to observe the pattern of 3 × 2 tens is 6 tens or 60. This can be facilitated by asking the children guiding questions such as the following:

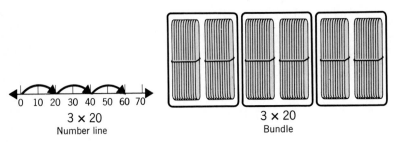

FIGURE 7-53.

Multiplying tens number by single-digit multiplier.

3 × 20
Number line

3 × 20
Bundle

How many sets do we have? (3)

How many bundles are in each set? (2 bundles)

How many bundles in all? (6)

Can you say that mathematically? (3 × 2 bundles is 6 bundles)

Since each bundle contains ten sticks, how many tens do we have in all? (6 tens)

So the mathematical statement for what we have done is 3 × 2 tens is 6 tens or 3 × 20 = 60.

Similar questioning patterns can be used with multiples of one hundred. For example, base-ten blocks could be used to represent 2 × 400. The children should observe that 2 sets of 4 flats are 8 flats. Since a flat is 1 hundred, 2 sets of 4 hundreds are 8 hundreds or 800, so 2 × 4 hundred or 2 × 400 = 800.

It is important to relate the written form to the children's work with models. Also, as

the children are developing this concept, they should be given problems to solve mentally such as 2 × 3 hundred or 4 × 2 tens and 2 × 300 or 4 × 20 presented orally or written on the chalkboard or flashed on the overhead.

When working problems of this type, children will be reviewing other place-value concepts. Problems such as renaming 6 tens as 60 and 8 hundreds as 800 are easier than problems in renaming 56 tens as 560 or 20 tens as 200. These place-value ideas are prerequisite to successfully solving problems such as 8 × 7 tens and 4 × 5 tens. Base-ten blocks are used in Figure 7-54 to represent the problem 4 × 5 tens and relate the two names. In this case children recognize that 20 tens is another name for 200.

Models should also be used to review renaming hundreds before children start multiplying a one-digit number times a multiple of one hundred. For example, to show 5 × 700 the children should use base-ten

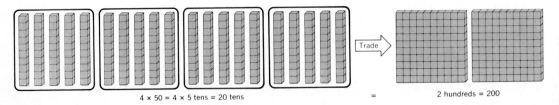

4 × 50 = 4 × 5 tens = 20 tens

Trade

=

2 hundreds = 200

FIGURE 7-54.

Multiplying single-digit and multiples of ten.

5 × 7 ones	= 35 ones	or	35	so 5 × 7	=	35
5 × 7 tens	= 35 tens	or	350	so 5 × 70	=	350
5 × 7 hundreds	= 35 hundreds	or	3500	so 5 × 700	=	3500

FIGURE 7-55.
Patterns in multiples of ten and hundred.

blocks to represent 5 sets of 7 hundreds. They should observe that part of the 35 hundreds can be traded for 3 blocks and the set renamed as 3 thousand 5 hundred. Another method to help children develop this concept is the study of patterns (Figure 7-55). The children should note in each case that the next problem is ten times larger so one more zero is annexed.

The children could also observe these patterns by solving these problems on a calculator. They could start out with a problem such as 4 × 10 and then multiply that result by ten, that product by ten, and so on. They could also work a series of problems such as 8 × 6, 8 × 60, 8 × 600, 8 × 6000, 8 × 60 000, and so on until the calculator overloads. Discussion should follow such activities so that children will make an appropriate generalization about the total number of zeros used as placeholders in the product.

This work should also be complemented with mental arithmetic. As a warm-up the teacher can orally give problems such as "six times three hundred, seven times four hundred, and three times six thousand." Warm-ups with mental arithmetic should also include displaying problems one at a time on the overhead. Examples should include problems such as 6 × 300, 7 × 400, 3 × 6000, and 5 × 400.

ONE-DIGIT NUMBER TIMES A TWO-DIGIT OR THREE-DIGIT NUMBER

The next step in developing the multiplication algorithm involves multiplying a one-digit number times a two-digit number without renaming. In analyzing the problem shown in Figure 7-56, it should be noted that 2 × 23 is broken down into two problems: 2 × 3 and 2 × 20. Thus we see that basic facts of multiplication and multiplying a one-digit number times a multiple of ten are prerequisite skills. The distributive law is being used to show that 2 × 23 = 2(20 + 3) = 2(20) + 2(3).

Another form of expanded notation is shown in Figure 7-57. In class discussion, a student stated, "3 × 2 ones is 6 ones or 6; then 3 times 5 tens is 15 tens or 150." The teacher recorded each step on the board. This form is helpful for explaining the algorithm and for developing mental computation. For mental computation, the student will think "3 × 5 tens is 150 . . . 3 × 2 is 6, so 156."

Although expanded notation is useful for explaining multidigit multiplication, this form does not lead to the more condensed form of the algorithm as efficiently as the use of a place-value table does. This can be intro-

$$
\begin{array}{c}
52 \\
\times\ 3 \\
\hline
6 \\
150 \\
\hline
156
\end{array}
\quad
\begin{array}{l}
\longleftarrow\ 3 \times 2 \text{ ones or } 3 \times 2 \\
\longleftarrow\ 3 \times 5 \text{ tens or } 3 \times 50
\end{array}
$$

FIGURE 7-56.
Multiplication by expanded notation.

FIGURE 7-57.
Multiplication using partial products.

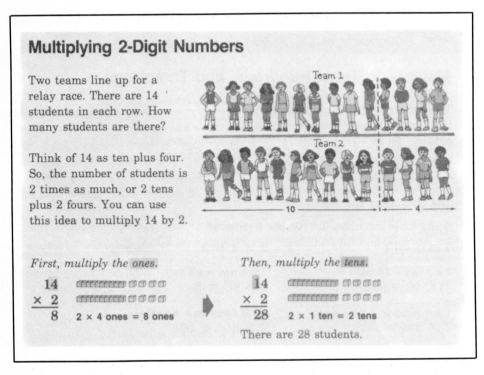

FIGURE 7-58.
Multiplying ones and tens by a single digit. (From A.V. Buffington, A.R. Garr, J. Graening, P.P. Halloran, M.L. Mahaffey, M. O'Neal, **Merrill Mathematics: Grade 4**, Merrill Publishing Company, 1985, p. 150.)

duced through a problem situation such as "Sharon and Janet were each returning twenty-four books to the library. How many books did they return in all?" The students could use base-ten blocks to represent the 2 sets of 24 books. Each set would contain 2 longs and 4 units. The teacher could then ask the following questions: "How many ones in all?" (8) "How many tens in all?" (4) "What number is 4 tens and 8 ones?" (forty-eight). After the students have worked through several examples using models and pictures of models, they should be introduced to the algorithm. A place-value table can be used very effectively to relate the model to the algorithm (Figure 7-58). In this example taken from a fourth-grade textbook,

the model is related step by step to the algorithm. First the ones are considered: 2 sets of 4 ones or 2 × 4 ones is 8 ones. The result is recorded. Next the student thinks, "2 sets of 1 ten is 2 × 1 ten or 2 tens," and this is also recorded.

Figure 7-58 also shows multiplication represented as an array. The two teams of 14 are shown as 2 rows of 14. The array was split to show 2 rows of ten and 2 rows of four. The problem 2(10 + 4) is solved by considering 2(10) + 2(4). Splitting the array was also used as one of the thinking strategies for learning the basic facts of multiplication. This example clearly shows the situation and the order of thinking that relates the array to the algorithm.

The next concept to be introduced is multiplying a one-digit number times a two-digit number with regrouping. Again, the students should use models to illustrate and solve the problems. Then this process should be related to the algorithm. Figure 7-59 shows a page from a third-grade textbook where the algorithm is related to the model. After the problem is represented, the 3 sets of 8 ones or 24 ones are regrouped to 2 tens and 4 ones. Then the model is related to the written form of 3 times 8 ones is 24 ones or 2 tens, 4 ones. The 4 ones and 2 tens are recorded in the appropriate columns. Originally, there were 3 sets of 1 ten or 3 tens. Also, there were 20 ones regrouped to 2 tens, so 3 tens plus 2 tens is 5 tens. This is related to 3×1 ten to obtain 3 tens plus the 2 tens, so 5 tens is recorded. Thus 3×18 is 5 tens 4 ones or fifty-four.

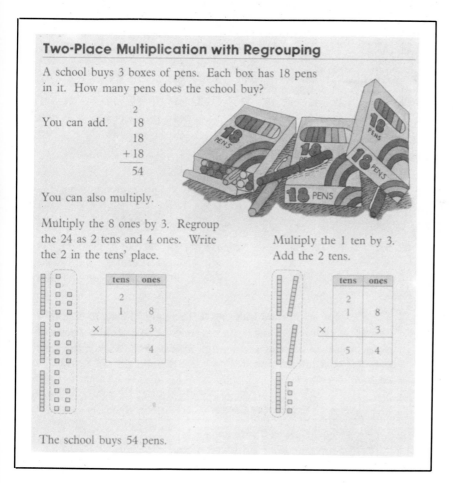

Two-Place Multiplication with Regrouping

A school buys 3 boxes of pens. Each box has 18 pens in it. How many pens does the school buy?

You can add.

$$\begin{array}{r} 2 \\ 18 \\ 18 \\ + 18 \\ \hline 54 \end{array}$$

You can also multiply.

Multiply the 8 ones by 3. Regroup the 24 as 2 tens and 4 ones. Write the 2 in the tens' place.

	tens	ones
	2	
	1	8
×		3
		4

Multiply the 1 ten by 3. Add the 2 tens.

	tens	ones
	2	
	1	8
×		3
	5	4

The school buys 54 pens.

FIGURE 7-59.
Developing multiplication algorithm using base-ten blocks. (From Charles E. Allen et al: **Houghton Mifflin Mathematics (Teacher's Edition), Grade 3**, p. 270. Copyright © 1985 by Houghton Mifflin Company. Used by permission.)

Appropriate questions should be used with the class to guide them through the process.

Figure 7-60a shows a similar example but involves two renamings. A dialogue that could occur between a teacher and the class to relate the algorithm to the model follows.

Ms. Stubben: Let's try this problem. Yesterday we talked about bringing our favorite books to school to share with the rest of the class. Each student is bringing one book each day for the rest of the week. How many extra books will we have by Friday?

Rick: There are twenty-seven in our class, so today we have 27 books.

Sharon: Tuesday, Wednesday . . . we'll be bringing books for four days, so that's four times twenty-seven, which is . . . big.

Ms. Stubben: Could we use our base-ten blocks to help us solve the problem?

Sharon: Sure, we need four sets.

Dave: With twenty-seven in each set.

Wade: Twenty-seven is 2 tens and 7 ones. That's easy to set up.

Ms. Stubben: (Walks around class—helps students when needed.). . . Let's write our problem in a place-value table (see Figure 7-60b). Let's put the four sets of 7 ones together. How many ones do we have?

Jean: A lot. Let's see 2, 4, 6, 8 . . . a lot . . . more than ten.

Debbie: There should be 28 ones as $4 \times 7 = 28$.

Rachelle: Let's trade some for tens.

Bernie: 28 ones would be . . . 2 tens and 8 ones. Right?

Ms. Stubben: (Waits for the class to trade the 28 ones.). . . We had 4 sets of 7 ones or 28 ones which we traded for 2 tens and 8 ones. So we'll record the 8 ones in the ones column and save the 2 tens at the top of the tens column. So 4×7 is 28 or 8 ones and 2 tens (Figure 7-60c). What do we do next?

Nancy: We have 4 sets of 2 tens or 8 tens.

Rita: 8 tens and 2 more tens is 10 tens.

Bernie: 10 tens is 1 hundred.

Ted: I traded the 10 longs for 1 flat, so I have 1 hundred and 8 ones as my answer.

Nancy: One hundred eight books! That's a lot. Where will we put them all?

Ms. Stubben: Sounds like we'll need to clear an extra shelf. Let's see, we had 4 sets of 2 tens or 8 tens plus 2 more tens. Let's look at our written problem. We need to multiply 4×2 tens, which is 8 tens plus the 2 tens we saved is 10 tens, which we'll record in the tens column (Figure 7-60d), so our answer is . .

Sue: One hundred eight.

This problem could also be illustrated as an array. In multiplying with the Cuisenaire

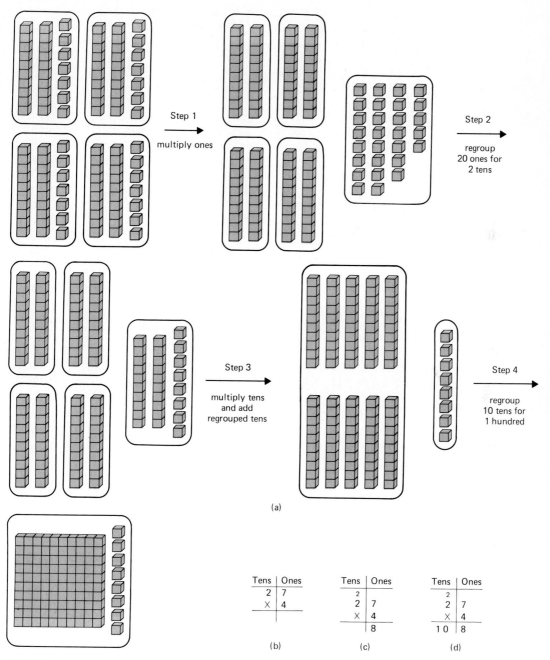

(a)

(b)

Tens	Ones
2	7
×	4

(c)

Tens	Ones
2	
2	7
×	4
	8

(d)

Tens	Ones
2	
2	7
×	4
1 0	8

FIGURE 7-60.
Multiplication with base-ten blocks.

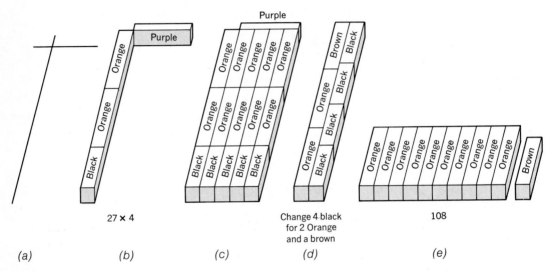

FIGURE 7-61.

Multiplication with Cuisenaire rods.

rods, Loretta first drew perpendicular line segments on a paper (Figure 7-61a). Next she placed the Cuisenaire rods representing the two numbers to be multiplied along the two line segments. Then she filled in the region delineated by the rods from the top (Figure 7-61c). This region represents the product of 4 and 27. The region Loretta has formed is a 27 × 4 array. To read this product more efficiently, she exchanged the black rods for two orange rods and one brown rod. Then she grouped the orange rods to form a square. Thus she could see that the answer is 108 (Figure 7-61e).

The sequence for teaching problems involving one-digit multipliers is not rigid. For example, one textbook series teaches multiplying a one-digit number times a two-digit number and times a three-digit number without renaming before teaching any problems with renaming. Another series follows multiplying a one-digit number times a two-digit number without renaming by similar prob-

lems with one renaming and later teaches a one-digit number times a three-digit number without renaming followed by similar problems with one renaming. One recommended sequence is shown in Figure 7-62.

The models will also vary from one textbook series to another. Whereas it was important to use various models when representing the concept of a number, it is probably not as important to show various models when representing algorithms. When teaching algorithms the model is being used to teach a procedure. The teacher should select a model that she or he is most comfortable with and that the students readily understand. Although you (the teacher) may select the base-ten blocks in sets for teaching a one-digit number times a two-digit number, you will need to change to an array model for a two-digit number times a two-digit number. Since these procedures are developed in different grade levels, this should not be a problem.

10	100	20	300	32	121	27	314	48
× 4	× 6	× 3	× 3	× 2	× 3	× 3	× 3	× 6
40	600	60	900	64	363	81	942	288

FIGURE 7-62.
Single-digit multipliers.

Figure 7-63 shows a type of problem that is a common source of error. Too often the student ignores the zero. Jim, who made this error, should first be asked to do the problem with a model such as base-ten blocks or an abacus. Then he could write the algorithmic form as a record of what he has done with the model. Next, Jim could be asked to use the partial product forms of computation (Figure 7-63b and c). This would help reinforce the concept that zero is a number and cannot be ignored. Thus Jim would see that when the problem of 6 × 403 is worked by the multiplication algorithm, the second step of 6 × 0 tens is an essential part of the algorithm.

In addition to these two steps, Jim should be reminded to use estimation. He should look at the original problem (6 × 403) and think, "I am multiplying a number a little larger than 400 by 6, so the answer must be larger than 6 × 400 or 2400." If Jim then looks at his original answer, he can see that it is obviously too small. When Jim first moves to the condensed form of the algorithm, he should think as a second step, "6 × 0 tens = 0 tens, 0 tens + 1 ten = 1 ten." As he gains skill in using the algorithm, he may essentially omit this step, thinking instead, "6 × 3 = 18 and 6 × 400 = 2400." This error of ignoring a zero is one that also often occurs when students are using a division algorithm. This could probably be avoided if sufficient emphasis were given to place-value concepts in the study of multiplication.

MULTIPLE OF TEN TIMES A TWO-DIGIT NUMBER

In fourth grade, children are usually introduced to multiplying a two-digit number by a two-digit number. The sequence is similar to the sequence for multiplying a one-digit number times a two-digit number. At first only exact multiples of ten are introduced as factors. Children know from their previous experience that 10 tens can be traded for 1 hundred. They also recognize that the flat in the base-ten blocks has 10 rows and 10 units in each row or 1 ten times 1 ten is 1 hundred. This pattern can be extended to problems like 30 × 40 or 3 tens times 4 tens. The array in Figure 7-64 is 3 tens by 4 tens or 12 hundreds or 1200.

Sets should be used to develop this concept also. For example, "Whenever the school store ran out of pencils, Becky, the

```
    1
   403        403        403        403
  × 6        × 6        × 6        × 6
  ────       ────       ────       ────
   258         18         18       2418
                00       2400
              2400       2418
              ────
              2418

    a          b          c          d
```

FIGURE 7-63.
Zero in multiplication.

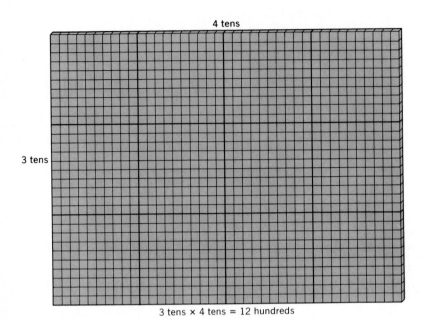

4 tens

3 tens

3 tens × 4 tens = 12 hundreds

FIGURE 7-64.
Multiplying multiples of ten.

manager, would order 10 boxes of pencils. Each box contained 40 pencils. On each of the following dates she ordered ten boxes of pencils: September 15 and 25, October 8, and November 5 and 21. Becky kept a cumulative record of how many boxes she had ordered during the course of the semester so that next semester she could make one large order at the beginning of the semester. Her records are shown in Figure 7-65. How many boxes should she order next semes-

ter? How many pencils were purchased last semester?''

The class could solve this problem by multiplying 10 × 40 to obtain 400 and then adding another 400 for each order. The pattern shown in Figure 7-66 should be discussed. The children should generalize that they need to find the product of the tens digits and then annex two zeros to indicate hundreds. The students should be given various opportunities to use mental computation

FIGURE 7-65.
Becky's records.

Date	No. of Boxes	Total Number of Boxes	No. of Pencils Per Box	Total Number of Pencils
Sept. 5	10	10	40	10 × 40 = 400
Sept. 25	10	20	40	20 × 40 = 800
Oct. 8	10	30	40	30 × 40 = 1200
Nov. 5	10	40	40	40 × 40 = 1600
Nov. 21	10	50	40	50 × 40 = 2000

1 ten	×	4 tens	=	4 hundreds	$10 \times 40 = 400$
2 tens	×	4 tens	=	8 hundreds	$20 \times 40 = 800$
3 tens	×	4 tens	=	12 hundreds	$30 \times 40 = 1200$
4 tens	×	4 tens	=	16 hundreds	$40 \times 40 = 1600$
5 tens	×	4 tens	=	20 hundreds	$50 \times 40 = 2000$

FIGURE 7-66.
Patterns: multiples of ten.

to answer problems such as 3 tens × 2 tens, 6 tens × 4 tens, 20 × 30, and 30 × 40. This pattern can be extended with calculators by trying such problems as 30 × 400, 500 × 60, or 800 × 7000. The class should generalize the pattern "find the product of the digits in the largest place value and then annex the appropriate number of zeros." Once students have generalized the pattern they will find that using mental computation, they can solve these problems much faster than they can using a calculator.

In multiplying ten times any two-digit number such as 10 × 24, students obtain that number of tens, or in this case 24 tens. This is a renaming that relates to the students' earlier experiences with place value. Multiplying a multiple of ten times any two-digit number is introduced in a fourth-grade text as shown in Figure 7-67. The students are led to consider 3 × 12 first and then ten times that product. This pattern can also be related by discussing the following sequence of problems: 3 × 12 = 36, 3 tens × 12 = 36 tens, 30 × 12 = 360.

TWO-DIGIT NUMBER TIMES A TWO-DIGIT NUMBER

After sufficient practice with multiplying by multiples of ten, students will have all the prerequisite skills needed for multiplying a two-digit number times a two-digit number.

One fourth-grade textbook introduces this idea by starting with the following problem.

Emiko, Beth, Don, and Tak are working in Mr. Ogata's garden.

Don said, "We need enough fertilizer to cover the garden. How many bags of fertilizer is that?"

"The garden is 57 meters long," said Beth.

"And it's 36 meters wide," added Tak.

Emiko said, "Each bag of fertilizer covers 100 square meters."

The children begin to solve their problem as shown in Figure 7-68. They find that, after splitting the array, they now know how to find the area for each section separately. Then these areas can be added to give the total area of the garden.

This thinking is then related step by step to an expanded form of the standard algorithm. These steps are shown in Figure 7-69a. Later, students will progress to the standard algorithm (Figure 7-69b).

Both of these forms are based on the distributive law. In the standard form (36)57 is seen as (30 + 6)57 or (30 × 57) + (6 × 57). In using the algorithm 57 is first multiplied by 6 and then by 30. The two partial products are then added to obtain the complete product.

To help students concentrate on the order of multiplication, have them prepare a card that is blank on one side and has the word "tens" written on the other side. They can use the blank side of this card to cover the tens digit while multiplying by the ones digit (Figure 7-70). When they are multiplying by the digit in the tens place, they can turn the card over covering the ones digit and revealing the word "tens." This will remind the students that they are now multiplying by tens.

FIGURE 7-67.
Multiplying by tens. (From C.A. Dilley, D.W. Lowry, W.E. Rucker, **Heath Mathematics**, D.C. Heath & Company, 1985, Grade 4, p. 256. Reprinted by permission of D.C. Heath & Company.)

"First we need to find the area of the garden," said Beth.

So the children drew a picture of the garden. It didn't seem to help.

"We don't know how to multiply 57 × 36," they said.

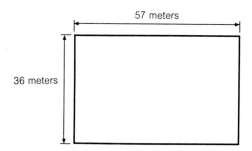

"I have an idea," Emiko said suddenly. "Let's draw lines to make a few sections, like this."

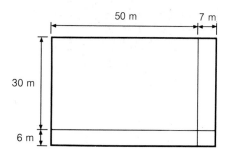

"Then we can figure out the area of each section and add them up."

FIGURE 7-68.
Multiplying two-digit numbers using arrays. (From **Real Math: Level 4** by Carl Bereiter et al., copyright © 1985, 1981, Open Court Publishing Company. Reprinted by permission.)

```
        57
      X 36
   a    42    6 X 7            Step 1
       300    6 X 5 tens       Step 2
       210    3 tens X 7       Step 3
      1500    3 tens X 5 tens  Step 4
      2052    42 + 300 + 210 + 1500   Step 5
```

```
        57
      X 36
   b   342    6 X 57
      1710    30 X 57
      2052
```

FIGURE 7-69.
Developing algorithm for two-digit multiplication.

Base-ten blocks can also be used to build arrays representing multiplication problems with two-digit factors. To represent 45 × 72, the appropriate flats, longs, and units are set up in a rectangle that is 45 units in one direction and 72 units in the other (Figure 7-71). This model can also be related to the multiplication algorithm. Regions A and B in the rectangle represent 5 × 72 or the first partial product 360, and regions C and D represent 40 × 72 or the second partial

FIGURE 7-70.
Multiplying 2 two-digit numbers.

product 2880. Thus the distributive law is being used in a manner similar to the preceding example.

As students continue to use the multiplication algorithm, they may begin to omit certain steps. For example, at first, Liane continued to write the zero in the ones place in the second partial product. She also wrote the numerals indicating the renaming above the problem (Figure 7-72a). Later she no longer needed these written reminders. She placed the second partial product correctly from her knowledge of place value and she did the renaming mentally (Figure 7-72b). This shortened form of the multidigit algorithm may not be developed by all students. The continued use of written reminders can help students to avoid minor errors while doing multiplication problems. Students should never be forced to use the short form of an algorithm before they are ready for it.

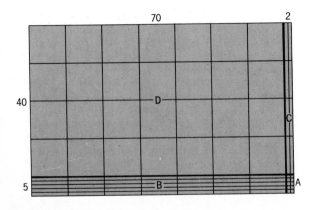

```
        72
      × 45
       360
       288
      3240
```

FIGURE 7-71.
Array multiplication with base-ten blocks.

```
  2 4
  1 2
  536            536
× 74           × 74

 2144           2144
37520           3752

39664          39664
 (a)            (b)
```

FIGURE 7-72.
Algorithm for multiplication.

The development of more complex multiplication problems becomes a task of applying the principles of place value and extending the basic algorithm. Special emphasis must be given to those problems that have a zero in the multiplier since they are a common source of error. One way to solve this problem is to have students write out the multiplication by zero as a complete partial product (Figure 7-73a). As their understanding of place value increases, most students will progress to a short form for writing the algorithm (Figure 7-73b or c).

OTHER MULTIPLICATION ALGORITHMS

The traditional multiplication algorithm is the one that should be generally taught because it is the easiest algorithm to teach rationally. That is, students can more readily grasp the underlying concepts, the "why it works," with the traditional algorithm. However, other mul-

tiplication algorithms may sometimes be taught for enrichment.

One such algorithm is called lattice multiplication. This is done on a rectangular lattice as shown in Figure 7-74. One factor is written along the top of the lattice, and the other is written down the right side. Each pair of digits is multiplied and the answer (partial product) placed in the appropriate box with the tens digit above the diagonal and the ones digit below it. When all spaces have been filled, the numbers are added along the diagonals starting in the lower right-hand corner.

By comparing this method to the form using individual partial products, the brighter students can explain why it works and how the place values are arranged along the diagonals. A discussion might be developed about whether it makes any difference which partial product is written first, second, and so on. This could then be compared to the traditional algorithm and the question of whether the order of finding partial products matters in the traditional algorithm. The slower students might also use the lattice algorithm since it gives them practice in the basic facts in a different form. However, since it is more difficult to understand the underlying concepts of lattice multiplication, it should not be substituted for the traditional algorithm as a permanent method of computation.

```
  1
 1 1
 436      436      436
 203      203      203

1308     1308     1308
000      8720      872
872      88508    88508

88508
 (a)      (b)      (c)
```

FIGURE 7-73.
Multiplying by zero.

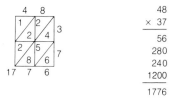

```
          48
        × 37

          56
         280
         240
        1200

        1776
```

FIGURE 7-74.
Lattice multiplication.

```
47 × 26          47 × 26
94 × 13          94 × 13              94
188 × 6          188 × 6             376
376 × 3          376 × 3             752
752 × 1          752 × 1
                                    1222
Step 1           Step 2           Step 3
```

FIGURE 7-75.
Russian peasant multiplication.

```
A    B                      A    B
─    ─                      ─    ─
1    47                     1    47
2    94                    ②    94  →   94
4    188    →              4    188     376
8    376                  ⑧    376  →   752
16   752                 ⑯    752      1222 = 47 × 26
```

FIGURE 7-77.
Egyptian multiplication.

Another interesting multiplication algorithm is known as the Russian peasant method of multiplication (Figure 7-75). In this algorithm, the problem is written horizontally. Then one factor is multiplied by 2 and the other is divided by 2 to form the next pair of factors, but on the division side remainders are ignored. This halving and doubling process continues until the number on the halving side is 1. The next step is to cross out all even numbers on the halving side and the corresponding numbers on the doubling side. Finally, the numbers remaining on the doubling side are added. This sum is the same as the product of the original two numbers. As an enrichment activity, students can be taught this algorithm and then challenged to figure out why it works. If they need assistance, they can be given special problems in a developmental order (Figure 7-76).

A third enrichment algorithm that also involves doubling is sometimes called the Egyptian form of multiplication. As shown in Figure 7-77, to multiply 47 × 26, Cindy chose one of the two numbers, in this case 47, and wrote successive doubles of it as shown in column B. She also wrote the series 1, 2, 4, 8, . . . as shown in column A. Notice

```
47 ×      26 = 1222
①        26 →    26
②        52 →    52
④       104 →   104
⑧       208 →   208
16       416     832
㉜       832    1222
47
```

```
11 ×      23 = 253
①        23 →    23
②        46 →    46
4        92      184
⑧       184      253
11
```

```
141 ×    324 = 45684
①        324
2        648      324
④       1296 →  1296
⑧       2592 →  2592
16       5184    41472
32      10368    45684
64      20736
⑫8      41472
141
```

FIGURE 7-78.
Examples of Egyptian multiplication.

```
(a)  23 × 8   =   184      (b)  23 × 9   =      23
     46 × 4                     46 × 4        + 184
     92 × 2                     92 × 2          207
     184 × 1                    184 × 1

(c)  23 × 10  =    46      (d)  23 × 11  =      23
     46 × 5       184            46 × 5          46
     92 × 2       230            92 × 2         184
     184 × 1                     184 × 1         253
```

FIGURE 7-76.
Russian peasant multiplication: development of underlying concepts.

that if 47 is multiplied by a number in column A the product is the corresponding number in column B, that is, $1 \times 47 = 47$, $2 \times 47 = 94$, $4 \times 47 = 2 \times 94 = 188$, and so on. Then from column A, Cindy selected those numbers whose sum is the other factor, in this case 26. Finally, she added the corresponding multiples of 47 from column B. This gave her the answer for 47×26, namely 1222. Of course, since multiplication is commutative, she could have doubled the 26 instead of the 47. This process and other examples are shown in Figure 7-78. Again, the students should try to figure out why this system works. Study of this algorithm might be particularly appropriate along with work in a base-two numeration system.

```
5)33
  - 5   1
   28
  - 5   1
   23
  - 5   1
   18
  - 5   1
   13
  - 5   1
    8
  - 5   1
    3   6
(a)
```

```
5)33
   15   3
   18
   15   3
    3   6
(b)
```

```
5)33
   10   2
   23
   20   4
    3   6
(c)
```

FIGURE 7-79.

Introducing the division algorithm.

ALGORITHM FOR DIVISION OF WHOLE NUMBERS

The form for the division algorithm is introduced while students are learning the basic facts (Figure 7-45). When students are introduced to this notation, the teacher should read it in a consistent manner. For example, $24 \div 6$ and $6\overline{)24}$ are both read "twenty-four divided by six." The expression "six goes into twenty-four" is inappropriate since it is not consistent with the concept of division or the form $24 \div 6$.

Again, as with the other operations, division problems should be introduced using story problems and the problems should be solved using models before the algorithm is introduced. For example, "Beth has decided to make her valentines this year. She thinks she can make five valentines each night. If there are 34 students in Beth's class, how many nights will it take her to make enough valentines for all her classmates?"

The students could solve this problem by subtracting sets of 5 objects from a set of 33 objects. They would obtain 6 sets of five objects and 1 set of three objects. They could record this procedure as a series of repeated subtractions (Figure 7-79). As students develop a better understanding of the written algorithm, they may use methods similar to the ones shown in Figure 7-79b and c. At this more sophisticated level, they realize immediately that there are several fives in 33, so they do not need to subtract them one at a time. In Figure 7-79b, for example, they subtracted 3 fives from 33 and then another 3 fives. Then these were added to find that a total of 6 fives are contained in 33.

Although this example uses measurement division, the same subtractive algorithm could be used for a partitive division situation. If Beth had wanted to make her 33 valentines in five nights, she would need to know how many valentines she had to make each night. In using the form shown in Figure 7-79a to solve the measurement problem, the students would think, "Beth needed to make thirty-three valentines and wanted to make five valentines each night. If she worked one night, she would need to make twenty-eight more valentines; if she worked two nights, she would need to make twenty-three more valentines, and so on. It will take her six nights and part of one more night to make all the valentines." Using the same form to solve the partitive problem, the students would think, "Beth needed to make thirty-three valentines and wanted to make them all in five nights. If she made one valentine each night, she would need twenty-eight more valentines; if she made two valentines each night, she would need twenty-three more valentines, and so on. Beth will need to make at least six valentines each night and seven on each of three nights to make all the valentines in five nights."

Although a measurement division situation leads naturally to a subtractive algorithm, a partitive division situation can also be solved with this algorithm. Similarly, a partitive division situation leads naturally to a distributive algorithm, but a measurement situation can also be solved with the distributive algorithm.

REMAINDERS

One common difficulty in the division of whole numbers is the question of what to do with a remainder. "Can the remainder be ignored? Do I need to finish the division to consider fractional parts? Should the quotient be rounded up or down? Or does the situation dictate that rounding is inappropriate?"

When students are just doing practice computations, the decision of what to do with the remainder is purely arbitrary. When they are solving story problems, the *situation* determines what should be done with the remainder. The following story problems illustrate this.

1. Four children from Ms. Jennings' class are cleaning up after a party. There are 22 doughnuts left, and they decide to share them equally. There are also 3 liters of punch that they give to Ms. Jennings. How many doughnuts will each child get?
2. Out on the playground 22 children are going to run relay races. They have decided to split into four teams for the first seven races. If they make the teams as equal in size as possible without leaving anyone out, how many children will be on each team?
3. Mary and Jane are making long skirts for the girls in their octet. If each skirt requires 4 yards of material, how many skirts can they make from 22 yards?
4. Twenty-two boys in Mr. Lawless' boy scout troop are going on a camping trip for six days. Each car can carry four boys and their camping equipment. How many cars will be needed to take all the boys to their campsite?

Each of these problems can be solved by dividing 22 by 4, but the remainder of 2 will be treated differently in each situation (Figure 7-80). In problem 1, the two doughnuts can each be cut in half and one half will be given to each student. In problem 2, it would not make sense to have $5\frac{1}{2}$ children on each team. Instead the remainder would be distributed as far as it would go. Thus, there would be two teams of six players each and two teams of five players each. In problem 3, it is not reasonable to make half a skirt or to make each skirt a little bigger or to make some of the skirts bigger. Instead the 2 yards would simply be left over. It could be put away and used to make something else later on. For problem 4, none of the above solutions is reasonable. Instead, an extra car would be needed to transport the

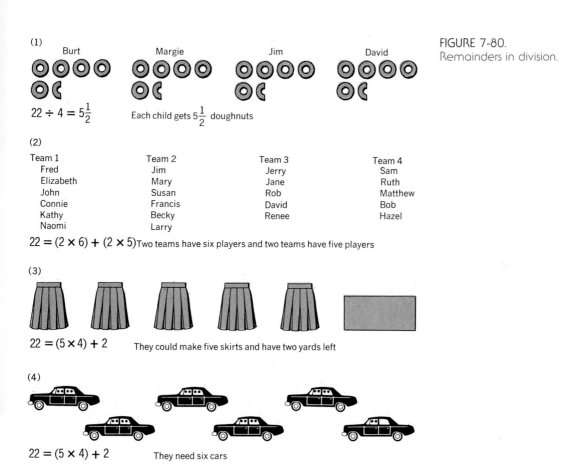

FIGURE 7-80.
Remainders in division.

(1)

Burt   Margie   Jim   David

$22 \div 4 = 5\frac{1}{2}$ Each child gets $5\frac{1}{2}$ doughnuts

(2)

Team 1
  Fred
  Elizabeth
  John
  Connie
  Kathy
  Naomi

Team 2
  Jim
  Mary
  Susan
  Francis
  Becky
  Larry

Team 3
  Jerry
  Jane
  Rob
  David
  Renee

Team 4
  Sam
  Ruth
  Matthew
  Bob
  Hazel

$22 = (2 \times 6) + (2 \times 5)$ Two teams have six players and two teams have five players

(3)

$22 = (5 \times 4) + 2$ They could make five skirts and have two yards left

(4)

$22 = (5 \times 4) + 2$ They need six cars

two remaining boys. In this case, five cars would carry four boys each and one more car would carry the remaining two boys. Figure 7-80 shows a diagrammatic sketch of what was done, an appropriate number sentence, and an answer to the question for each problem. In each case the *situation* determines what *must* be done with the remainder.

Sometimes students will develop one computational procedure for handling remainders and will follow this procedure all of the time. If the remainders in the examples above had all been rounded or had all been ignored, some of the answers would have been incorrect. Some students may always round up if they note that the remainder is one half or more of the divisor. They have *overgeneralized* a rule. They need to consider the situation.

For example, if in problem 3 Mary and Jane had had 23 yards of material, students who simply rounded the answer to the nearest whole number would say that they can make 6 skirts. However, although 3 yards is almost enough, it will not make another skirt. The *situation* dictates rounding down. Similarly, in problem 4 even if there had only

$$
\begin{array}{r}
8 \\
7\overline{)58} \\
56 \\
\hline \boxed{2}
\end{array}
\qquad (a)
$$

$$
\begin{array}{r}
8 \;\boxed{R2} \\
7\overline{)58} \\
56 \\
\hline 2
\end{array}
\qquad (b)
$$

$$
\begin{array}{r}
8 \;\boxed{\tfrac{2}{7}} \\
7\overline{)58} \\
56 \\
\hline 2
\end{array}
\qquad (c)
$$

$58 = (7 \times 8) + \boxed{2}$

(d)

FIGURE 7-81.
Expressing the remainder.

been 21 boys, the trip would still have required 6 cars. The *situation* dictates rounding up.

When students are merely doing computations with numbers, there are several commonly used formats for expressing remainders (Figure 7-81). For computation, it does not matter greatly which form is used as long as it is mathematically correct. However, it should be noted that the form shown in Figure 7-81b may be confusing to students. When the remainder is written right beside the quotient, they may think the two numbers represent the same kind of quantities. Actually the 8 represents 8 sevens, and the 2 represents 2 ones that have not been divided. Certainly the answer should

not be written as "8 and 2" or "8 and 2 remaining" since these forms look as if the 8 and the 2 could be added. The equation form $58 \div 7 = 8R2$ should also be avoided because it leads to confusion and false concepts.

In Figure 7-81a, the remainder has simply been left at the bottom as an undivided portion of the dividend. More mathematically mature students may complete the division by dividing the two remaining by seven and expressing the answer as a fraction (Figure 7-81c). An equation reinforces the fact that division and multiplication are inverse operations and this form should be used some of the time with all grade levels (Figure 7-81d). The form to be used in computation can be

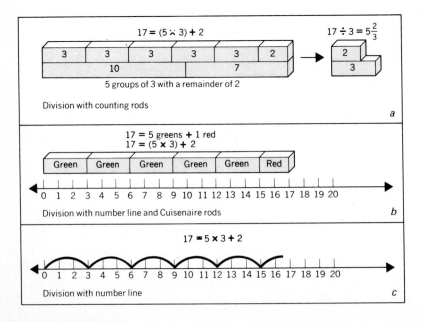

FIGURE 7-82.
Division with number lines.

chosen by the teacher based on what form the students need to practice, or sometimes the students may be allowed to decide individually which form they prefer.

To develop students' concepts for computations involving remainders, models should be used. Counting rods can be used by children in beginning division experiences (Figure 7-82a). The 10 rod and the 7 rod are used to represent the number 17. The quantity is then divided by three by placing rods representing three end to end alongside the rods representing 17. By counting the rods, students find that there are 5 groups of three and that 2 ones out of the original 17 remain undivided. Some students may complete the division by comparing the remainder of 2 with the three that they are dividing by to find that it is two-thirds of another three. Thus, $17 \div 3 = 5\frac{2}{3}$. The same division concepts can be developed with counting rods and a number line of equal spacing or with the number line alone (Figure 7-82b and c).

ONE-DIGIT AND TWO-DIGIT DIVISORS

As with the other operations, types of division problems are sequenced according to their difficulty. Hazekamp in "Teaching Multiplication and Division Algorithms" in *Developing Computational Skills* outlines sequentially a set of activities for teaching division with one-digit and two-digit divisors. Each task is carefully described and appropriate prerequisite skills reinforced. Problems with one-digit divisors are introduced first to students. Partitive division can be effectively used to teach this procedure. To introduce one-digit divisors, the children first are asked to solve such problems as 80 $\div$ 4 or 90 $\div$ 3 using base-ten blocks. In the first example, they should share the 8 tens

FIGURE 7-83.
Dividing tens by one-digit divisor.

among 4 sets equally. After partitioning the tens, they will find 2 tens in each set. The written form of the algorithm can be expressed as shown in Figure 7-83. The first case can be used as an explanatory form. The form using a place-value table is slightly more abstract. To help children use this form appropriately, the teacher can guide them with such questions as the following. "How many tens in each set?" (2) "So let's record the 2 in the tens column. How many ones do we have?" (0) "Let's record zero in the ones column, so 8 tens divided by 4 is 2 or twenty."

Division by one-digit divisors with no regrouping is introduced in one third-grade textbook with base-ten blocks (Figure 7-84). The first paragraph of the "Teaching Suggestions" describes appropriate activities to *precede the page* in the textbook. The problems suggested are similar in their level of difficulty. After the students have worked some examples with their tens strips and ones squares, they are ready to work through the page from the text as described in the "Teaching Suggestions." Two pages later the written algorithm is introduced (Figure 7-85). Several examples should be worked as a class so that the students become comfortable with the process.

In introducing the concept by *using this page* in the textbook, the teacher should discuss each step with the students. It may be helpful to refer to each step of the problem as it is being worked out with base-ten blocks and loops on an overhead projector.

6 DIVIDE TENS AND ONES

Enzio, Sam, and Angie divide 126 blocks equally. How many does each get?

There are 3 equal parts.

So, 126 ÷ 3 = ▓

Think of 126 as 12 tens 6 ones.

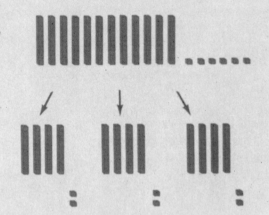

1. Divide the tens.

12 tens ÷ 3 = 4 tens

2. Divide the ones.

6 ÷ 3 = 2

3. Put the tens and ones together.

126 ÷ 3 = 4 tens 2 ones
126 ÷ 3 = 42

Each receives 42 blocks.

TRYOUT EXERCISES
Either two- or three-dimensional drawings are acceptable. See right.

1. 84 ÷ 2 = ▓ **42**

Make 2 equal parts.

Make a drawing to show equal parts when you divide.

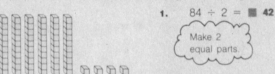

2. 129 ÷ 3 = ▓ **43** **3.** 84 ÷ 4 = ▓ **21** **4.** 108 ÷ 2 = ▓ **54** **5.** 84 ÷ 3 = ▓ **28**

12 tens 9 ones   8 tens 4 ones   10 tens 8 ones   8 tens 4 ones

FIGURE 7-84.

Introducing division of 2- or 3-digit number by a 1-digit number. (From Joseph Payne et al., **Harper & Row Mathematics**, Grade 4, p. 192. Copyrght © 1985, Macmillan, Inc. Reprinted with permission of Scribner Educational Publishers, a division of Macmillan, Inc.)

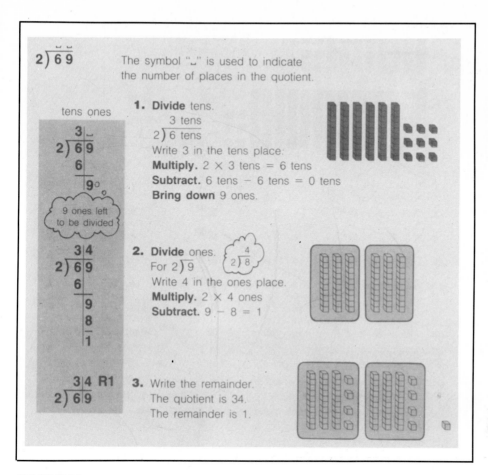

FIGURE 7-85.

Long-division algorithm. (From Joseph Payne et al, **Harper & Row Mathematics**, Grade 4, p. 194. Copyright © 1985, Macmillan, Inc. Reprinted with permission of Scribner Educational Publishers, a division of Macmillan, Inc.)

This will focus the class's attention on each individual step. Note that a place-value table is used to mark the tens and ones. As the students divide 69 into 2 groups, they find that each group contains 3 tens and 4 ones with a remainder of 1 from the 69 that is left undivided. The 3 tens and 4 ones and the remainder are recorded in the appropriate places of the place-value table as each step is worked out with the base-ten blocks.

Next the students can be introduced to dividing by a one-digit number *with* regrouping. A sample lesson from one third-grade textbook uses money to represent tens and ones (Figure 7-86). In this case, 52 was represented by 5 dimes and 2 pennies. After the dimes (tens) were shared, there was 1 ten in each set and 1 ten left to be shared among the 4 sets. In the second step, the 1 ten was exchanged for 10 ones to obtain a total of 12 ones. The 12 ones were then shared equally among the 4 sets. Since 3

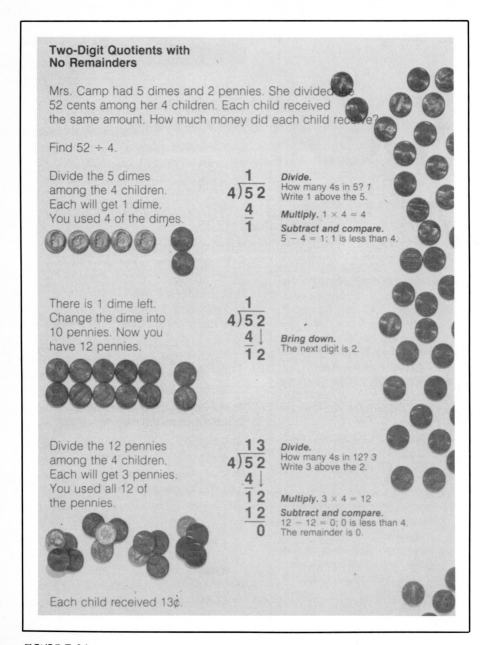

Two-Digit Quotients with No Remainders

Mrs. Camp had 5 dimes and 2 pennies. She divided the 52 cents among her 4 children. Each child received the same amount. How much money did each child receive?

Find 52 ÷ 4.

Divide the 5 dimes among the 4 children. Each will get 1 dime. You used 4 of the dimes.

$$\begin{array}{r} 1 \\ 4\overline{)52} \\ 4 \\ \hline 1 \end{array}$$

Divide.
How many 4s in 5? *1*
Write 1 above the 5.

Multiply. 1 × 4 = 4

Subtract and compare.
5 − 4 = 1; 1 is less than 4.

There is 1 dime left. Change the dime into 10 pennies. Now you have 12 pennies.

$$\begin{array}{r} 1 \\ 4\overline{)52} \\ 4\downarrow \\ \hline 12 \end{array}$$

Bring down.
The next digit is 2.

Divide the 12 pennies among the 4 children. Each will get 3 pennies. You used all 12 of the pennies.

$$\begin{array}{r} 13 \\ 4\overline{)52} \\ 4\downarrow \\ \hline 12 \\ 12 \\ \hline 0 \end{array}$$

Divide.
How many 4s in 12? *3*
Write 3 above the 2.

Multiply. 3 × 4 = 12

Subtract and compare.
12 − 12 = 0; 0 is less than 4.
The remainder is 0.

Each child received 13¢.

FIGURE 7-86.
Dividing by a one-digit divisor with regrouping. (From L. Carey Bolster et al., **Invitation to Mathematics: Grade 3, Teacher's Edition**, copyright © 1985, Scott Foresman and Company. Used by permission.)

[13]	
3	
10	
4)52	
40	10 x 4
12	
12	3 x 4
0	

FIGURE 7-87.
Amy's work—subtractive division.

Susan's work

7)346	
210	30
136	
70	10
66	
63	9
3	49

Wade's work

49
9
40
7)346
280
66
63
3

49 Regular tables – one small table

FIGURE 7-88.
Subtractive division.

ones were contained in each set and 12 ones were used, the 3 and the 12 are recorded appropriately. Base-ten blocks or counting sticks could be used similarly to solve this problem.

The subtractive form of division could also be used to solve this problem and to extend students' understanding of the division algorithm (Figure 7-87). In this case, Amy recognized that 10 × 4 is less than 52 and 20 × 4 would be too large, so she recorded 10 × 4 = 40. After subtracting 40 from 52, she divided the 12 ones by 4. Since she knew that 12 ÷ 4 = 3, she recorded 3 in the quotient and 3 × 4 = 12 below in the problem. She subtracted and obtained a remainder of 0. Finally, she added the 10 and the 3 to obtain an answer of 13.

As students progress, they can use this algorithmic form to solve problems such as the following. "Bobby and Matthew are setting up tables for the banquet. There are going to be 346 people attending. If each table seats 7 people, how many tables must they set up?" Two different computations are shown in Figure 7-88. Both students used subtractive division and both found the same answer. Susan began by estimating that there are 30 sevens in 346. After subtracting 30 sevens, she found that she still needed to subtract another 10 sevens. Then 9 more sevens were subtracted and there was a remainder of three. Wade was able to estimate 40 sevens in his first step. Also, he is writing his partial quotients above the division problem, a more sophisticated form of the algorithm. Although in this problem the dividend is a three-digit number, the quotient is only a two-digit number.

Another approach to this problem is shown in Figure 7-89. Since 3 hundreds are not enough to place at least 1 hundred in each of 7 sets, Tom considered 34 tens. Since 7 × 4 = 28 and 7 × 5 = 35, he realized that 7 × 5 tens was too large and considered 7 × 4 tens or 28 tens. Tom recorded the 4 tens and 28 tens and then sub-

	H	T	O
7)	3	4	6

	H	T	O
		4	
7)	3	4	6
	2	8	
		6	

	H	T	O
		4	
7)	3	4	6
	2	8	
		6	6

	H	T	O
		4	9
7)	3	4	6
	2	8	
		6	6
		6	3
			3

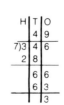

FIGURE 7-89.
Tom's work.

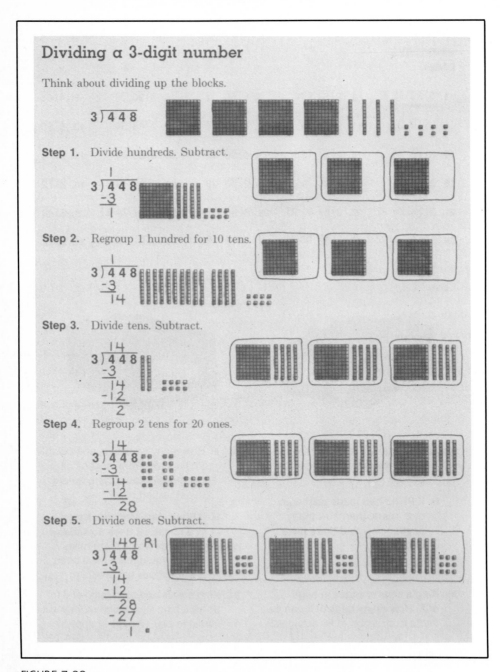

FIGURE 7-90.

Developing the division algorithm. (From C.A. Dilley, D.W. Lowry, W.E. Rucker, **Heath Mathematics**, D.C. Heath & Company, 1985, Grade 4, p. 298. Reprinted by permission of D.C. Heath & Company.)

tracted 34 tens minus 28 tens. He then renamed 6 tens as 60 ones, combined the 60 ones with the 6 ones from the original dividend, and considered 66 ones. The next question he asked himself was, "7 times what number is close to but less than 66?" Since 7 × 9 is 63, he recorded the 9 and the 63 and subtracted to obtain a remainder of 3. This is the distributive division algorithm, as Tom was *sharing* 346 among 7 sets.

Some problems that involve three-digit dividends divided by one-digit divisors will have three-digit quotients (Figure 7-90). In working through such problems, the teacher should carefully guide the students as they record the algorithm. One series of appropriate questions and statements for each step follows.

Step 1: "Our problem is to divide 448 by 3. What do we divide first?" (Hundreds.) "Share the hundreds among the 3 loops. How many hundreds in each loop?" (1 hundred.) "Record the 1 in the hundreds column. How many hundreds were shared?" (3.) "Record 3 as 3 × 1 hundred equals 3 hundred. How many hundreds do we have left?" (1 hundred, as 4 hundreds minus 3 hundreds is 1 hundred.)

Step 2: "Can we share the 1 hundred among the 3 sets?" (No, we need to regroup.) "Let's regroup 1 hundred as 10 tens. How many tens do we have in all?" (14 tens since 10 tens plus 4 tens is 14 tens.) "Write the 4 tens down beside the 10 tens to show 14 tens.

Step 3: "Share the 14 tens. How many tens in each set?" (4 tens.) "Record the

4 in the tens column. How many tens were shared?" (12 tens.) "Record 12 as 3 × 4 tens equals 12 tens. How many tens are left?" (2 tens, as 14 tens minus 12 tens is 2 tens.)

Step 4: "Can we share the 2 tens among the 3 sets?" (No, we need to regroup tens for ones.) "Let's regroup the tens. ... How many ones in all?" (28 ones as 20 ones plus 8 ones is 28 ones.) "Write the 8 ones down beside the 20 ones to indicate the 28 ones."

Step 5: "Share the 28 ones. ... How many in each set?" (9 ones.) "Record the 9 in the ones column. How many ones were shared?" (27 ones.) "Record 27 as 3 × 9 is 27. How many ones left?" (1, as 28 minus 27 is 1.)

By solving problems with models using the partitive approach and linking these actions to the written algorithm with appropriate language, students will develop an understanding of the distributive algorithm and a facility in carrying out each step. Throughout the development of the division algorithm, there should be an emphasis on place value. Marking the hundreds, tens, and ones columns can guide the students in this process. As they focus attention on place value, the students' understanding of the algorithm will be enhanced. This will also help them to avoid many common errors in division.

Some common errors involving place value are shown in Figure 7-91. These errors result from a combination of improper recording, lack of understanding of place value, and failure to check the reasonableness of the answer. In the first example, Gale did not finish the division. As soon as the subtraction step yielded a zero and since the

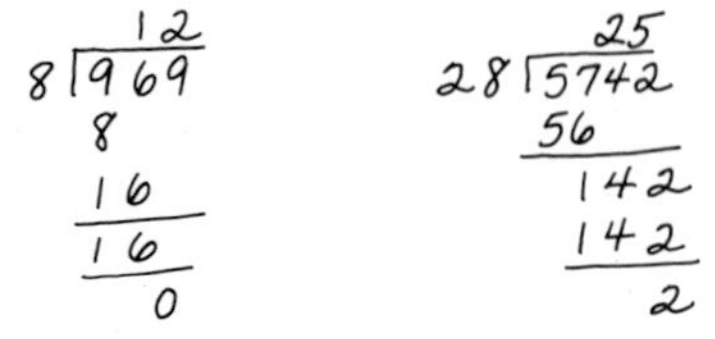

$$
\begin{array}{r}
12 \\
8\overline{)969} \\
8 \\
\overline{16} \\
16 \\
\overline{0}
\end{array}
\qquad
\begin{array}{r}
25 \\
28\overline{)5742} \\
56 \\
\overline{142} \\
142 \\
\overline{2}
\end{array}
$$

Gale's work   Ron's work

FIGURE 7-91.

Common errors in division.

numbers were not recorded neatly in their proper places, she assumed the problem was finished.

One way to help Gale correct her error would be to have her do a complete subtraction each time she uses the subtraction step. This technique is shown in Figure 7-92. By doing this, she would not obtain a 0 remainder until she had actually completed all the division.

In the second example, when 14 was obtained, Ron reasoned that, "28 does not divide 14 so I bring down the 2 to get 142 ÷ 28." However, he failed to record the 0 tens in the quotient. Completing the subtraction each time which was suggested for Gale would probably not help Ron and might even make him more likely to make this mistake. Instead, he needs to use a thinking pattern that helps him focus better on place value. In the second division step, he could be encouraged to think, "14 tens to share among

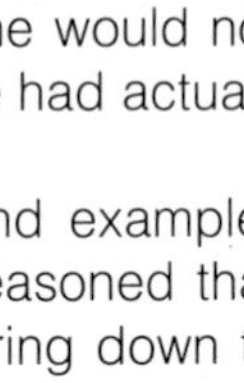

$$
\begin{array}{r}
121 \\
8\overline{)969} \\
800 \\
\overline{169} \\
160 \\
\overline{09} \\
8 \\
\overline{1}
\end{array}
$$

FIGURE 7-92.

Correcting division errors.

28 sets . . . not enough for each set to have 1 ten, so record 0 tens in the quotient. Then rename 14 tens as 140 ones and consider sharing 142 ones among 28 sets." These types of errors commonly occur with both one-digit and two-digit divisors.

If either of these students had used estimation to predict their answers or to check the reasonableness of their results, they would have found that these answers were obviously wrong. Gale could have reasoned that since 800 ÷ 8 = 100, then 969 ÷ 8 must be more than 100. Similarly, Ron could have reasoned that 6000 ÷ 30 = 200, so 5742 ÷ 28 should be somewhere near 200. Even these very rough estimations would have shown the answers they obtained to be unreasonable.

As students develop a greater understanding of the division process and the division algorithm, they can be introduced to problems with two-digit divisors. The first of these problems would involve only exact groups of tens. Such problems should be related to students' previous experiences with multiplication. For example, the problems 80 ÷ 20, 800 ÷ 20 and 1500 ÷ 30 should be written as shown in Figure 7-93. These written forms should help students conceptualize the place-value concepts involved in division. These forms should then be related to the numeral form of the algorithm.

The more complex the division problem, the more important good estimation becomes. In working with two-digit divisors, students must use both rounding and estimating skills. Figure 7-94 shows three different students' computations for 789 ÷ 18. The first two students, Troy and Jody, are not using refined estimation skills. Troy made too low a first estimate and so had an extra step in his computation. Jody made too large a first estimate and so had to start over. Jer-

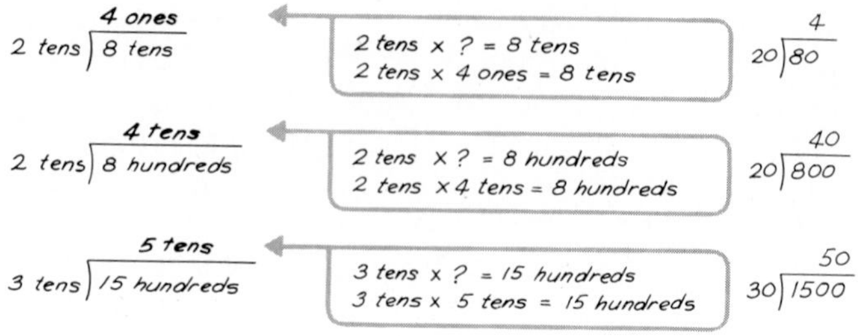
4 ones
2 tens ⟌ 8 tens
2 tens x ? = 8 tens
2 tens x 4 ones = 8 tens
20⟌80 = 4
4 tens
2 tens ⟌ 8 hundreds
2 tens x ? = 8 hundreds
2 tens x 4 tens = 8 hundreds
20⟌800 = 40
5 tens
3 tens ⟌ 15 hundreds
3 tens x ? = 15 hundreds
3 tens x 5 tens = 15 hundreds
30⟌1500 = 50

FIGURE 7-93.
Division by multiples of ten.

emy thought, "18 is close to 20 and 789 is close to 800. 800 ÷ 20 = 40, so I'll try 40." A similar thought process gave him a second partial quotient of 3. All three students have done correct computations and found the right answer. However, Jeremy has done it most efficiently.

All students should be encouraged to work toward an efficient method of computation. The teacher can aid the students' development of rounding and estimating skills by selecting appropriate problems. For example, Figure 7-95 shows a problem and four possible ways of rounding it. Most students will immediately realize that the first two forms are not reasonable because 18 is much closer to 20 than to 10. In choosing between the second two forms, students will get a close estimate by rounding both divisor and dividend in the same direction. Thus 20⟌80 would be used to estimate 18⟌73.

However, in working with other examples, students will discover that a close estimate is sometimes too large. For example, if the preceding problem had been 18⟌71, the closest estimate of the answer would still be found by using 20⟌80. However, since this estimate, 4, is slightly too large, they would have to erase their work and begin again. By practicing with many appropriate examples, students can discover that if they always round the divisor up and the dividend down, they may sometimes find a trial quotient that is too small but never one that is too large.

Thus in Figure 7-94, Troy, whose estimate was too small, needed to write an extra step. However, he did not have to start over as did Jody, whose first estimate was too large. As they learn to make *good* estimates, students may need to adjust an estimate by

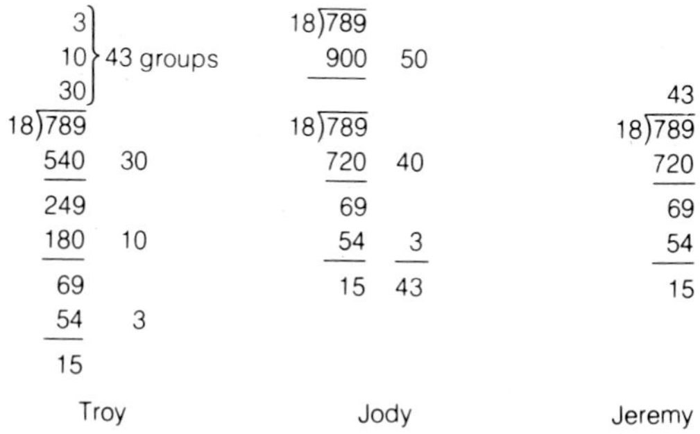
3
10 43 groups
30
18⟌789
540 30
249
180 10
69
54 3
15
18⟌789
900 50
18⟌789
720 40
69
54 3
15 43
43
18⟌789
720
69
54
15
Troy
Jody
Jeremy

FIGURE 7-94.
Three students' division work.

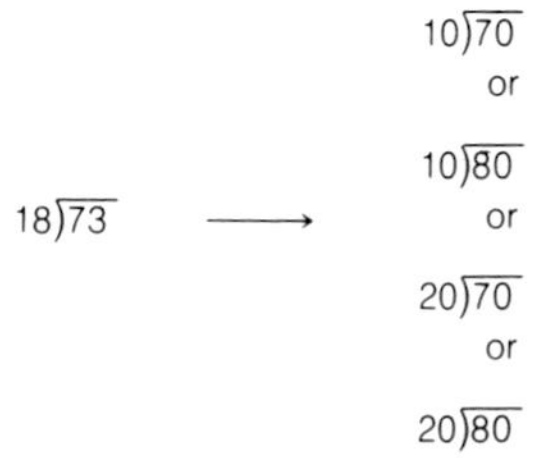
18⟌73
10⟌70
or
10⟌80
or
20⟌70
or
20⟌80

FIGURE 7-95.
Rounding in division.

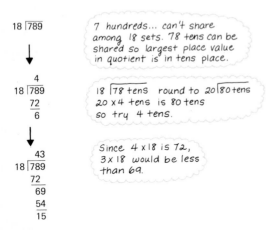

```
18 ⟌789
```
7 hundreds... can't share among 18 sets. 78 tens can be shared so largest place value in quotient is in tens place.

```
     4
18 ⟌789
    72
     6
```
18 ⟌78 tens round to 20⟌80 tens
20 x 4 tens is 80 tens
so try 4 tens.

```
    43
18 ⟌789
    72
    69
    54
    15
```
Since 4 x 18 is 72, 3 x 18 would be less than 69.

FIGURE 7-96.
Estimating the quotient.

one, but they will not need to make a second estimate for this place value.

As individual students develop estimation skills, they will find their own shortcuts that make computation easier. For example, to solve 789 ÷ 18, Don did several estimations (Figure 7-96). First he visualized the base-ten blocks and thought, "7 hundreds to share ... I can't put 1 flat in each of 18 sets, so I'll consider 78 tens. My first quotient digit will be in the tens place." To decide *how many* tens, Don rounded 18 to 20 and 78 tens to 80 tens. Since 80 tens ÷ 20 is 4 tens, he recorded a 4 in the tens place. He then multiplied 4 tens × 18 to obtain 72 tens. He subtracted 78 tens minus 72 tens to find he still had 6 tens. His estimate was correct because 6 is less than 18 so no more tens can be shared. By "bringing down the 9," Don renamed 6 tens plus 9 ones as 69 ones. He reasoned that since 4 × 18 was 72, which was 3 more than 69, the ones digit would be 3. He finished the division as shown.

Linda used another form of estimation to

determine whether the quotient was in the 1000s, 100s, or 10s place (Figure 7-97). First she considered place value. Since the dividend was in the thousands, she thought, "56 × 1000 ... much too large! 56 × 100 is 5600 ... still too large. 56 × 10 is 560 ... that is smaller than 4138, so the quotient will start in the tens place. She then rounded the problem to 40 hundreds ÷ 6 tens and tried a quotient of 6 tens. Since 77, the remainder in this first step, is larger than 56, 6 tens was too small an estimate. Linda noted that 77 was enough to share one more ten with each of the 56 sets. She crossed out the 6 in the tens place and wrote 7 above it. Then she subtracted 56 more tens.

Linda then considered 218 ÷ 56. She

```
56 ⟌4138
```
56 x 1000 = 56000 too large
56 x 100 = 5600 too large
56 x 10   = 560 so
quotient is a multiple
of ten as
10 < quotient < 100

```
      6
56 ⟌4138
   336
    77
     7
```
6 tens   40 hundred
6 tens × 6 tens = 36 hundred
so I'll try 6 tens

```
      7̸
56 ⟌4138
   336
    77
    56
    21
     7
```
77 is larger than 56. Since 77−56 is 21, the quotient is in the 70's. I'll change the 6 to 7 and subtract one more group of 56 tens.

```
     7̸3
56 ⟌4138
   336
    77
    56
   218
   168
    50
```
4(50+6) = 4(50) + 4(6) =
200+24 which is too
large so the next digit
will be 3, not 4.

FIGURE 7-97.
Linda's estimations.

reasoned, "There are 4 fifty-cent pieces in 2 dollars, so 4 × 50 = 200, but 4 × 6 ones is 24 and 200 + 24 is more than 218." Therefore, she wrote a 3 in the ones column and finished the division.

As with the other operations, it is also important to remember that students do not progress at the same rate in developing the division algorithm. As they are learning, students should be encouraged to share and discuss their thinking processes. Through these discussions, they will gain a better understanding of the division algorithm.

After students have learned to divide, should they be expected to master problems with two- and three-digit divisors? What level of expertise is desirable and realistic? The National Council of Teachers of Mathematics has recommended that students' work with division include "mental facility with simple basic computations, paper-and-pencil algorithms for simple problems done easily and rapidly, and the use of the calculator for more complex problems."* It has been found that students are more accurate when they use calculators for solving various problems, especially division problems. Also, low-achievers performed more accurately when they used calculators rather than multiplication tables to aid their division work (Suydam, 1982).

Division problems with divisors that have more than two digits could be solved by extending the concepts used with one-digit and two-digit divisors. However, when such problems are actually encountered in everyday life, most people will solve them with a calculator or by making a rough estimation instead of using the division algo-

rithm. It is not necessary for students to *practice* solving problems with multidigit divisors. However, they do need to realize that these problems simply require an extension of already known concepts.

In spite of the time we spend teaching the division algorithm, many students do not master the procedure. As stated before, when the division is complicated enough to require paper-and-pencil calculations, most people will use an estimate, use a calculator, or transform the problem into one that can be solved mentally. For these reasons, some mathematics educators recommend removing division with two-digit divisors from the elementary curriculum. Eliminating this topic would provide more time for developing concepts and for including other topics, such as problem solving.

ESTIMATION AND MENTAL COMPUTATION FOR MULTIPLICATION OF WHOLE NUMBERS

Since most adults do most calculations either mentally or with calculators, activities with mental computations and reasonable estimates are more important than traditional algorithms with larger numbers (factors of three and four digits). Instead of more practice for students who have difficulty learning how to use the algorithm to multiply two-digit factors, time would be better spent teaching them estimations, applications, and how to use the calculator for exact answers. In this section some activities that were included in the section on the multiplication algorithm will be rediscussed. These ideas are basic to estimations and mental arithmetic as well as essential to the development of the algorithm.

*An Agenda for Action: Recommendations for School Mathematics for the 1980s. Reston, VA: National Council of Teachers of Mathematics, 1980.

ESTIMATING PRODUCTS

Before students are introduced to 3 × 58, they need to develop the concept that 3 × 5 tens is 15 tens. This same strategy needs to be reinforced in estimation procedures. Additionally in discussing this example, the students should realize that 15 tens would be smaller than the actual answer. An estimate of 3 × 6 tens is too large, but it would be a better estimate because 58 is closer to 6 tens than to 5 tens. These two estimates give a range within which the answer should fall. In estimating the product of 6 × 52, the students should discuss whether to multiply 6 × 5 tens or 6 × 6 tens. They should note that the product is between 300 and 360 but closer to 300.

Patterns for Estimating Products

In a previous section on the development of the multiplication algorithm, patterns of multiplying tens by tens or hundreds by tens were discussed. These concepts are necessary for students to understand the multiplication algorithm, to test the reasonableness of their answers, and to estimate products. Mental work with multiples of tens, hundreds, and thousands should be included at various times throughout the year as well as with work on the multiplication algorithm.

Working with patterns for "how many places?" can help improve students' estimating skills (Figure 7-98). As described in the section on algorithms, students can use calculators to generate these patterns. The patterns should be related to estimation with larger numbers.

Practice work should be for a brief period of time; the problems can be shown one at a time on the overhead or students could be given a number of problems to answer

$$1 \times 1 = 1$$
$$1 \times 10 = 10$$
$$1 \times 100 = 100$$
$$1 \times 1000 = 1000$$

$$10 \times 1 = 10$$
$$10 \times 10 = 100$$
$$10 \times 100 = 1000$$
$$10 \times 1000 = 10\ 000$$

$$100 \times 1 = 100$$
$$100 \times 10 = 1000$$
$$100 \times 1000 = 10\ 000$$
$$100 \times 1000 = 100\ 000$$

$$1000 \times 1 = 1000$$
$$1000 \times 10 = 10\ 000$$
$$1000 \times 100 = 100\ 000$$
$$1000 \times 1000 = 1\ 000\ 000$$

a

$$4 \times 1 = 4$$
$$4 \times 10 = 40$$
$$4 \times 100 = 400$$

$$40 \times 1 = 40$$
$$40 \times 10 = 400$$
$$40 \times 100 = 4000$$

b

$$2 \times 3 = 6$$
$$2 \times 30 = 60$$
$$2 \times 300 = 600$$

$$20 \times 3 = 60$$
$$20 \times 30 = 600$$
$$20 \times 300 = 6000$$

c

FIGURE 7-98.
Patterns for multiplication.

on a worksheet. Since the goal of these assignments is mental computation it is not desirable to present these problems in algorithmic form. The students should be able to explain that tens time tens is hundreds as 10 longs or 10 tens is one flat or one hundred. Similarly, tens times hundreds is thousands as 10 flats is 10 hundreds or one block or one thousand. For the first few problems it would be helpful for the students to explain their thinking such as "70 × 40 . . . 7 × 4 is 28. Tens times tens is hundreds, so the answer is 28 hundred or 2 thousand 8 hundred." For 40 × 600 the students may reason "4 × 6 is 24 and 10 hundreds are one thousand, so the answer is 24 thousand."

When students are studying this type of multiplication, a good practice game involves racing against the calculator. Ten problems could be displayed on the overhead. Some of the students or the teacher could work the problems on a calculator while the other students do them mentally. In order to check their results, both groups should record answers only. Both speed and accuracy are goals of this practice. In this game students are computing exact answers rather than estimating, but the skills they are developing are the same ones they will use later for estimation.

Refined Front-End Estimation

The type of problems in the section above should precede estimating products for problems such as 28 × 34 or 42 × 376. For 28 × 34, some students will estimate 6 hundreds after multiplying 2 tens times 3 tens (front-end estimation). They should also discuss that the exact answer is greater than 600. Some students will round 28 to 30 and then multiply 3 tens times 3 tens for an estimate of 900. Is their estimate closer than the estimate of 600? Is the estimate of 900 more or less than the exact answer? That is a harder question to answer and the answer will vary depending on the factors. The students should all realize that 1200, an estimate obtained by multiplying 3 tens times 4 tens, would be too large. In estimating products for 42 × 376, students should observe that 40 × 300 will give an estimate that is too small and that an estimate of 40 times 400 will be too large.

When estimating products of larger numbers, some students have difficulty with getting the significant digits in the proper place values. Through practice with patterns, they can eventually generalize that to estimate the product of two large numbers,

Estimate 5762 × 341

> Round 5762 to 6000 and 341 to 300
> 6 × 3 = 18

> I rounded one factor up and one down... Don't know whether estimate is high or low so I won't try to make any adjustment.

> 3 digits in the "back part of 5762 and 2 in 341. My estimate is 18 with 5 zeros or 1 800 000.

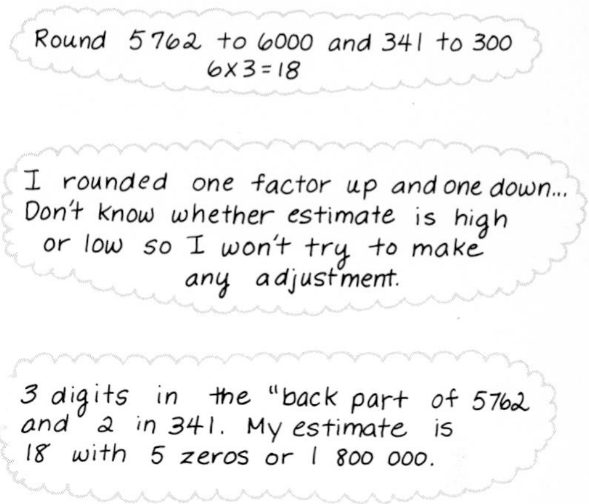

FIGURE 7-99.
Tanya's estimation.

round to the largest place value, multiply those rounded digits, adjust the answer if necessary, and annex as many zeros as there are digits in the "back parts" of both factors (Figure 7-99).

Later, Tanya wanted an exact answer. She used her calculator and obtained an answer of 196416. She knew immediately that either her estimation or her calculation had to be wrong. She checked her estimation again but could find no mistake in her thinking, so she redid the calculation. This time the calculator display read 1964842, a reasonable result. Curious about what had gone wrong the first time, Tanya played around with the calculator until she discovered that apparently when she thought she entered 5762, for some reason the "2" had not registered on the calculator. Thus her first result was the answer to 576 × 341.

After students have been introduced to these procedures, they should be encouraged to discuss whatever estimating procedures they have found to be most useful. Those procedures that are found to be helpful should be shared and practiced with the class. Other procedures are presented in *Computational Estimation Instructional Materials* by Reys, Trafton, Reys, and Zawojewski. They suggest a three-step process that is appropriate for any operation on any system of numbers.

Round: The numbers should be rounded to numbers that can easily be computed mentally. With whole numbers, rounding to the nearest five should be considered as an alternative.

Multiply: Mentally compute the rounded numbers.

Adjust: Depending on the rounding, is the estimate larger or smaller than the exact answer?

To obtain a better estimate of 28 × 34, Josh rounded 28 to 30 and 34 to 35. In order to do this problem mentally, Josh must be able to multiply 3 × 35 in his head. 3 × 35 is 105, so his answer is 1050. For problems like 45 × 65, Linda rounded 45 down and 65 up to obtain 40 × 70, so her estimate was 2800. To multiply 5 × $7.34, Shawn reasoned, "5 × $7 is $35. 5 × 30 cents is $1.50. Since there was 34 cents, my total will be more than $36.50."

When considering the cost of 3 items which each cost $4.77, Ted reasoned "3 × $4 is $12. Seventy-seven can be rounded to 80; 3 × 80 cents is $2.40, so $12 + $2.40 is $14.40." Ted estimated that the items would be slightly less than $14.40, but tax at 5 cents on the dollar would add another 70 cents. A little more than 15 dollars is needed. Ted has obtained a very close estimate.

MENTAL COMPUTATION IN MULTIPLICATION

As with addition and subtraction, sometimes an exact mental multiplication is needed. The strategy of "front-end" computation is again appropriate. For example, to multiply 3 × 36, the student can think 3 × 3 tens is 9 tens. A renaming is required for 3 × 6, so 1 more ten will make 10 tens or 100. Since 3 × 6 is 18, the ones digit is 8; the product is 108. For multiplying 4 × 67, the student thinking would be "4 × 6 tens is 24 tens or 240. Two more tens would be obtained when multiplying 4 and 7, so 260. The ones digit is 8, so the product is 268." Note an important difference here; whereas in combining two addends the regrouped part was never more than 1 ten, 1 hundred, and so on, with multiplication the regrouped part may be anything from 1 to 9 tens, 1 to 9 hundreds, and so on.

Another strategy for exact mental multiplication uses the properties of multiplication. Multiplication is distributive over subtraction, so 3 × 148 can be mentally renamed as 3 × (150 − 2) or (3 × 150) − (3 × 2). This change creates a mentally manageable problem.

Since multiplication and division are inverse operations, students know that they can multiply one factor by a number and divide the other factor by the same number to obtain an equivalent problem. Thus 5 × 345 can be mentally renamed as (5 × 2) × (345 ÷ 2) or 10 × 172.5. This kind of thinking allows people to solve many problems mentally instead of resorting to either a written algorithm or a calculator.

In practical situations, mental computation for multiplication is usually done only when one of the factors is either a single digit or an exact multiple of some power of ten such as 4, 40, 400, and the like. Occasionally, to solve a problem like 25 × 475, a student may think, "Twenty-five times four is 1 hundred, so to multiply 475 by 25 I can multiply by 100 and divide by 4." This thinking has simplified the original problem by making two computations. Instead of multiplying by a two-digit number, this student is multiplying by a power of ten and dividing by a one-digit number. When an exact answer for a problem like 37 × 813 is needed, most people will use a calculator.

ESTIMATION AND MENTAL COMPUTATION FOR DIVISION OF WHOLE NUMBERS

When division problems are encountered in everyday life, estimation or mental computation are much more likely to be needed skills than is facility with the division algorithm. For example, "Usually, the king-size box of detergent at 84 oz. for $3.77 is more economical than the giant-size box at 49 oz. for $2.27. However, the store is currently honoring manufacturer's discounts of $1.00 on king size and 50 cents on giant size. Does this change their relative value? I also have a coupon for 50 cents off any size. What effect does this have?" Few people will use pencil and paper to solve this problem. They will either make an estimate, use a calculator, or decide that it is too complicated and

get the same size as always. If we want students to become comfortable about making estimations, they must be given useful strategies and sufficient practice.

ESTIMATING QUOTIENTS

Unlike the other operations, in division, estimation skills are essential for efficient use of the standard algorithm as well as for determining approximate answers. Patterns with powers of 10 are particularly important for estimating in division (Figures 7-100 and 7-98). Through their knowledge of basic facts and through other beginning work in dividing by a one-digit number, students will realize that while a two-digit number divided by a one-digit number may yield a two-digit answer—for example 26 ÷ 2 = 13—in other cases the answer will only have one digit— 72 ÷ 8 = 9. This same pattern can be extended to larger numbers (Figure 7-101).

This understanding of place value is very important in correctly estimating division problems. In considering a problem such as 54)8762, students should easily see that since 87 hundreds can be shared among 54 sets, the answer will be in the hundreds. This thinking is essential for checking reasonableness of answers. If the students were to do this division and obtain an answer either in the thousands or in the tens, they would know immediately that they had made a mistake. Had they used this type of estimation, neither Gale nor Ron (Figure 7-91) would have been satisfied with the answers they obtained.

1 ÷ 1 = 1	10 ÷ 10 = 1	100 ÷ 100 = 1
10 ÷ 1 = 10	100 ÷ 10 = 10	1000 ÷ 100 = 10
100 ÷ 1 = 100	1000 ÷ 10 = 100	10 000 ÷ 100 = 100
1000 ÷ 1 = 1000	10000 ÷ 10 = 1000	100 000 ÷ 100 = 1000

FIGURE 7-100.

Patterns for dividing by powers of 10.

1 digit ÷ 1 digit = 1 digit
2 digits ÷ 1 digit = 1 or 2 digits
3 digits ÷ 1 digit = 2 or 3 digits
4 digits ÷ 1 digit = 3 or 4 digits

2 digits ÷ 2 digits = 1 digit
3 digits ÷ 2 digits = 1 or 2 digits
4 digits ÷ 2 digits = 2 or 3 digits
5 digits ÷ 2 digits = 3 or 4 digits

FIGURE 7-101.

Digit patterns for whole-number division. (*Note:* Only the whole-number portion of a quotient is being considered in this pattern.)

Rounding for Estimation

Computing with rounded numbers is probably the most commonly taught estimation skill in division. This is used both for estimation when only an approximate answer is needed and also for estimation in computing an exact answer with the algorithm. In applying this estimation strategy for a problem such as 3)726, a student might think, "726 is about 700. Since 7 hundred is a little more than 2 hundred × 3, my answer should be something more than 200." In applying this same strategy to the algorithm, the student could think, "7 hundreds ... can they be shared 3 ways? .. yes, each set will get 2, so record a 2 in the hundreds place."

Compatible Numbers for Estimation

Another strategy that is particularly useful for estimating division is using compatible numbers. Compatible numbers for division are any pair in which one will exactly divide the other. This strategy is similar to rounding but more refined. Scott's thinking using simple rounding techniques and Susan's thinking using compatible numbers for the same problem are shown in Figure 7-102.

As with addition and subtraction, different students will choose different combinations of compatible numbers (Figure 7-103). All of these students are using the strategy of compatible numbers to make estimation easier. With larger or more difficult numbers, students can simply extend this technique (Figure 7-103b and c). Problems of this type are used in studying place-value patterns, not for computations.

Although the students in the example above have all used different pairs of compatible numbers, they have all obtained the same estimate. In some cases, students will arrive at *different* estimates depending on what pair of compatible numbers they decide to use (Figure 7-104). Obviously Daniel's estimate will be closer than Linda's. To improve their estimating skills, students need to compare their results and discuss their various thinking processes in obtaining those results. To help them refine their estimation skills with compatible numbers, the teacher could give them practice in deciding which of two possible compatible numbers will give a better estimate (Figure 7-105).

In using the idea of compatible numbers on an earlier problem (3)726), Teresa said, "I'm dividing by 3 ... 700 is between 600

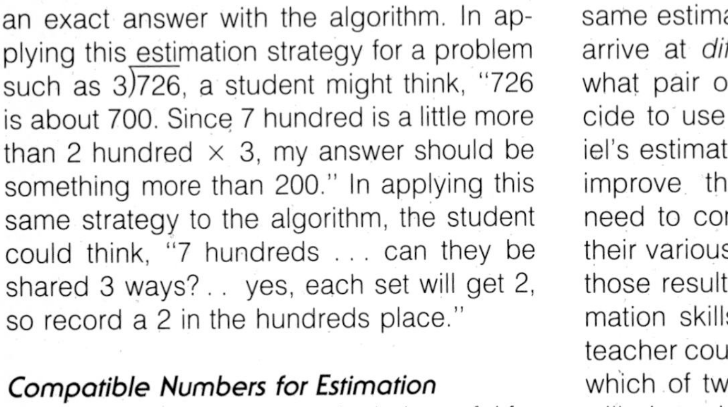

8)337

Scott's Thinking

3 hundreds ... can't be
shared 8 ways...
I'll consider 30 tens...
Share these among 8 sets
and each set gets at least
3 tens...
So 30 is my estimate.

Susan's Thinking

32 ÷ 8 is 4 so round
337 to 320...
320 ÷ 8 will be 40
So 40 is my estimate.

FIGURE 7-102.

Using compatible numbers to estimate division.

a

Estimate $13\overline{)22}$

Dennis's thinking	Marlys's Thinking	Marv's Thinking
22 is close to 26 $13\overline{)26}$ is 2.	13 is close to 11 $11\overline{)22}$ is 2.	13 is close to 12 and 22 is close to 24 $12\overline{)24}$ is 2.

Estimate $13\overline{)2286}$

Dennis's thinking	Marlys's Thinking	Marv's Thinking
2286 is close to 2600 $13\overline{)2600}$ is 200.	13 is close to 11 and 2286 is close to 2200 $11\overline{)2200}$ is 200.	13 is close to 12 and 2286 is close to 2400 $12\overline{)2400}$ is 200.

Estimate $136\overline{)22\ 753}$

Dennis's Thinking	Marlys's Thinking	Marv's Thinking
136... round to 130 22 753... round to 26 000 $130\overline{)26\ 000}$ is 200	136... round to 110 22 753... round to 22 000 $110\overline{)22\ 000}$ is 200	136... round to 120 22 753... round to 24 000 $120\overline{)24\ 000}$ is 200.

FIGURE 7-103.
Rounding to compatible numbers.

Estimate $8\overline{)4576}$

Linda's Thinking	Daniel's Thinking
8 divides 40 so... 4000 ÷ 8 is 500... my answer will be near 500.	5 x 8 = 40 and 6 x 8 = 48... 45 is closer to 48 ... so $8\overline{)4576}$ will be close to but less than 600.

FIGURE 7-104.
Using compatible numbers to estimate division.

$9\overline{)7923}$ $9\overline{)8100}$
        $9\overline{)7200}$

closer _____

$4\overline{)2187}$ $4\overline{)2400}$
        $4\overline{)2000}$

closer _____

$3\overline{)2513}$ $3\overline{)2700}$
        $3\overline{)2400}$

closer _____

$8\overline{)5287}$ $8\overline{)5600}$
        $8\overline{)4800}$

closer _____

FIGURE 7-105.
Practice with compatible numbers for division.

and 900 but closer to 600, so my estimate is something more than 200." Eric replied, "But $3 \times 25 = 75$, so $3 \times 250 = 750$. Since 720 is close to 750, my estimate is 250. That's a little too much, but it's closer than your estimate." "Wait a minute," Jennie said. "72 is $75 - 3$, so if $75 \div 3$ is 25, then $72 \div 3$ is exactly 24. Since $6 \div 3$ is 2, the answer is exactly 242, and I did it all in my head!"

MENTAL COMPUTATION IN DIVISION

Mental computations use many of the same strategies as estimation. The difference is that in mental computation an exact answer is desired. Again a good grasp of place value, knowledge of the basic facts, and understanding of the properties of the operation are important for mental computation. However, adults seldom do *exact* mental computations for division. Occasionally, the problem just happens to be composed of numbers that fit together nicely. For example, if a dozen doughnuts cost $2.40, Karon will probably think, "$24 \div 12$ is 2, so $240 \div 12$ is 20 . . . that's twenty cents a doughnut."

More often a problem for which we need to use division is like the following. "My children would like to try a different kind of breakfast cereal, but I usually don't get it because it's so expensive. The brand I usually buy is $1.99 for 15 ounces. However, the kind they want to try is on sale this week at $1.39 for 9 ounces. I wonder if this price makes it cost less than my regular brand? I wouldn't want to pay much extra because everyone in the family likes the kind I get now and they might not like the new one." Randy's thinking in solving this problem is shown in Figure 7-106. Randy did not use an exact mental computation to answer this question as $139 \div 9$ is not exactly 15 but $15\frac{4}{9}$. She used a combination of mental computation and rounding to find an answer that was close enough to the exact answer that it is sufficient for answering her question.

Another technique in mental computation is to use the properties of division to change a problem into an easier equivalent problem. For example, Samarade and Max needed pencils for school. They were trying to decide which package to buy. One pack-

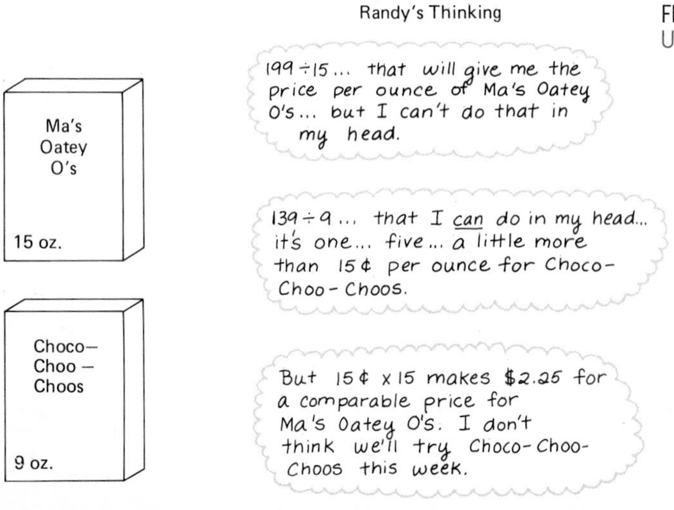

Randy's Thinking

Ma's Oatey O's

15 oz.

Choco— Choo — Choos

9 oz.

$199 \div 15 \dots$ that will give me the price per ounce of Ma's Oatey O's . . . but I can't do that in my head.

$139 \div 9 \dots$ that I *can* do in my head . . . it's one . . . five . . . a little more than 15¢ per ounce for Choco-Choo-Choos.

But 15¢ × 15 makes $2.25 for a comparable price for Ma's Oatey O's. I don't think we'll try Choco-Choo-Choos this week.

FIGURE 7-106.
Using estimation.

age had 5 pencils for 42 cents, another was 25 pencils for $1.85, and a third was 14 pencils for $1.06. Samarade said, "Well, the package with 5 pencils costs a little more than 8 cents per pencil. 25 times 8 would be $2.00, so the biggest package costs less per pencil than the smallest. But how do we compare the other two?" Max replied, "14 pencils for $1.06 would be the same as 7 for $0.53 . . . that I can do in my head. It's a little less than 8 . . . it's $7\frac{4}{7}$ cents per pencil. That's cheaper than the small package, but the big one is more than 7 cents per pencil. We still

need a closer answer." "Well," said Samarade, "Let's try the same kind of strategy. $1.85 and 25 can both be divided by 5 to make a problem with a one-digit divisor. That makes $37 \div 5$ . . . which is $7\frac{2}{5}$. Since $\frac{2}{5}$ is less than half a cent and $\frac{4}{7}$ is more, the biggest package is the lowest cost per pencil." These students have used the properties of multiplication and division to make problems that could be solved mentally.

The thinking Larry used to solve the problem at the beginning of this section is shown in Figure 7-107. In solving this prob-

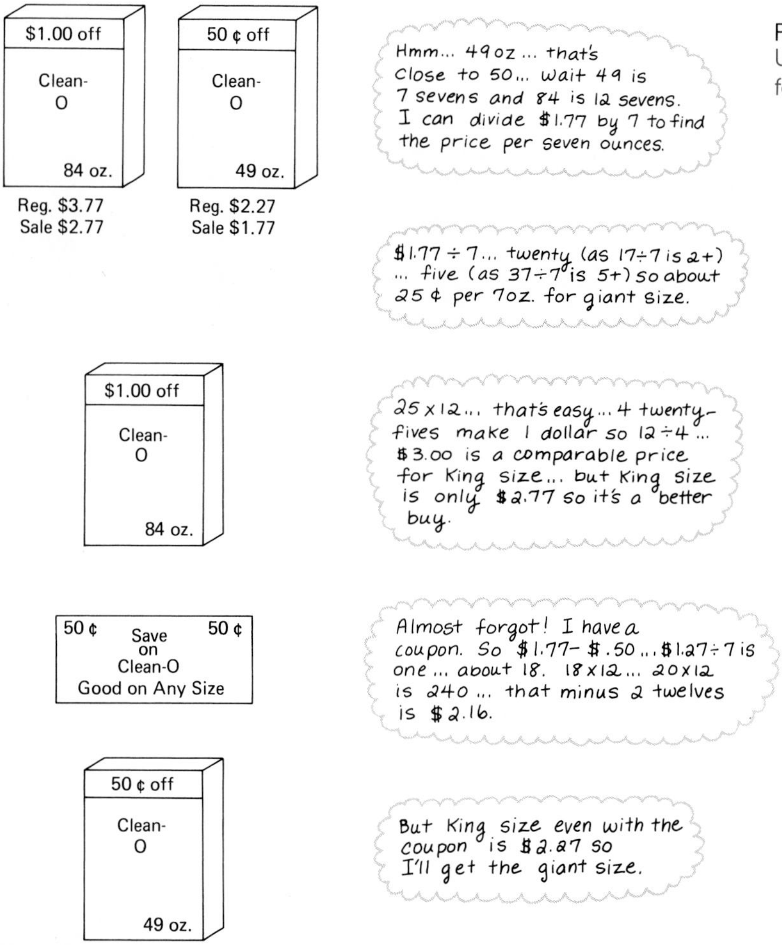

FIGURE 7-107.
Using properties of division for mental computation.

$1.00 off
Clean-O
84 oz.
Reg. $3.77
Sale $2.77

50 ¢ off
Clean-O
49 oz.
Reg. $2.27
Sale $1.77

Hmm... 49 oz ... that's close to 50... wait 49 is 7 sevens and 84 is 12 sevens. I can divide $1.77 by 7 to find the price per seven ounces.

$1.77 ÷ 7... twenty (as 17÷7 is 2+) ... five (as 37÷7 is 5+) so about 25 ¢ per 7oz. for giant size.

$1.00 off
Clean-O
84 oz.

25 × 12... that's easy... 4 twenty-fives make 1 dollar so 12÷4 ... $3.00 is a comparable price for King size... but King size is only $2.77 so it's a better buy.

50 ¢   Save on   50 ¢
Clean-O
Good on Any Size

Almost forgot! I have a coupon. So $1.77 – $.50 ... $1.27 ÷ 7 is one ... about 18. 18 × 12... 20 × 12 is 240 ... that minus 2 twelves is $2.16.

50 ¢ off
Clean-O
49 oz.

But King size even with the coupon is $2.27 so I'll get the giant size.

lem, Larry used a combination of rounding and mental computation with compatible numbers. Rather than dividing by either 49 or 84 to find a price per ounce, he divided the price of the smaller box by 7 (a one-digit divisor) to find the price per seven ounces. Instead of dividing the price of the larger box by 12 (a two-digit divisor), he multiplied his other answer by 12 (easier to do mentally) to find what price the larger box should be at the same price per seven ounces. He also did some rounding as $1.27 \div 7$ is actually $18\frac{1}{7}$ cents. However, the fraction was small enough compared to the rest of the number that he just ignored it.

In practical situations people will rarely try to mentally compute an exact answer to a problem with more than one nonzero digit in the divisor. Instead, they will use an estimate or use properties of division to change the problem to a simpler form. When a division problem cannot be easily changed to one that can be computed mentally, and when an estimate is not sufficient, most people will use a calculator to obtain an exact answer.

Even with this handy tool, good estimation and mental computation skills are still important. Often a person will hit a wrong key or not push a key hard enough to register the number. When this happens, it is important to be able to recognize when an answer is "way off base." When a calculator does division, it will carry the division out to as many decimal places as it has available. If the answer is needed in the form of a whole number and a remainder, obtaining this with the calculator will require a somewhat different technique. The calculator will do the computation correctly. However, to use it effectively the person will need to have a good understanding of the concepts of operations.

QUESTIONS AND ACTIVITIES

1. Represent and solve the following problems using base-ten blocks in set form. Compare the problems noting how they differ conceptually.

   a. $\begin{array}{r} 40 \\ \times\ 2 \\ \hline \end{array}$ b. $\begin{array}{r} 50 \\ \times\ 3 \\ \hline \end{array}$ c. $\begin{array}{r} 50 \\ \times\ 4 \\ \hline \end{array}$

   d. $\begin{array}{r} 200 \\ \times\ 3 \\ \hline \end{array}$ e. $\begin{array}{r} 700 \\ \times\ 4 \\ \hline \end{array}$ f. $\begin{array}{r} 23 \\ \times\ 3 \\ \hline \end{array}$

   g. $\begin{array}{r} 34 \\ \times\ 4 \\ \hline \end{array}$ h. $\begin{array}{r} 24 \\ \times\ 6 \\ \hline \end{array}$ i. $\begin{array}{r} 35 \\ \times\ 6 \\ \hline \end{array}$

2. Work through at least four of the examples from Problem 1 with another student. For each problem, one student should play the role of a teacher; the other student should play the role of an elementary student who is being introduced to the algorithm. Re-solve each problem step by step with the models, devising for each step appropriate teacher questions that link the action on the model to the written form of the algorithm.

3. Explain how to use patterns to develop the process for multiplying a multiple of ten times a two-digit number from the process for a one-digit number times a two-digit number.

4. a. Represent and solve the following problems using base-ten blocks in array form.

   (1) $\begin{array}{r} 10 \\ \times\ 10 \\ \hline \end{array}$ (2) $\begin{array}{r} 12 \\ \times\ 10 \\ \hline \end{array}$ (3) $\begin{array}{r} 12 \\ \times\ 13 \\ \hline \end{array}$

   (4) $\begin{array}{r} 23 \\ \times\ 14 \\ \hline \end{array}$ (5) $\begin{array}{r} 34 \\ \times\ 21 \\ \hline \end{array}$

   b. Re-solve the problems in part (a) relating them to the multiplication algorithm step by step with appropriate teacher questions.

c. *For your resource file:* Examples from basic facts to the algorithm are shown in "Grid Arrays for Multiplication" by Robold.

5. Use base-ten blocks to solve the following problems.

a. $3\overline{)60}$ b. $3\overline{)96}$ c. $4\overline{)86}$

d. $5\overline{)73}$ e. $3\overline{)407}$ f. $3\overline{)619}$

6. a. Work through at least four of the examples from Problem 5 with another student. For each problem, one student should play the role of a teacher; the other student should play the role of an elementary student who is being introduced to the algorithm. Re-solve each problem step by step with the models, devising for each step appropriate teacher questions that link the action on the model to the written form of the algorithm.

b. *For your resource file:* The articles by Irons, Hall, and Peterson all focus on the sharing approach to the division algorithm and all include teacher questions. In "The Division Algorithm: Using an Alternative Approach" by Irons, bundling sticks are used as the model; Hall describes the process with base-ten blocks in "Division with Base-Ten Blocks," and Peterson uses money in "Sharing the Wealth: Dividing with Meaning."

7. Evaluate the method used for this problem.

Answer: 122 with a remainder of 2

Is it correct? Does it yield the correct solution? Is it logically defensible? If so, do the sample problem using the same method.

8. Two questions on the Second and Third National Assessment of Educational Progress were as follows.

A man has 1310 baseballs to pack in boxes which hold 24 baseballs each. How many baseballs will be left over after the man has filled as many boxes as he can?

An army bus holds 36 soldiers. If 1128 soldiers are being bused to their training site, how many buses are needed?

a. Students who did not have access to calculators did better on these problems than students with calculators. For each problem, what calculator display do you think the students who made errors with the calculators obtained? How did they interpret the display?

b. For the first problem, write a calculator code using the whole-number part of the display to describe what they should have done to obtain the answer.

c. For the first problem, write a calculator code using the remainder in its decimal form to find the remainder as a whole number.

9. a. Read "Let's Do It!: Without Paper and Pencil" by Nelson and Leutzinger. Practice these strategies until you are able to apply them readily.

b. It is easier to solve mentally $4 \times 200 - 4 \times 6$ than to multiply mentally 4×194. Use the associative, distributive, and commutative properties to rewrite the following problems into problems that can easily be done without paper and pencil.

(1) 3×56 (4) $82 \times 50 \times 2$

(2) 16×25 (5) $8 \times 16 \times 25$

(3) 11×92

10. Use a calculator, estimation, and number properties to answer the following questions. Think carefully before trying your guesses. Try to find the answers with a minimum of trial and error.
    a. What number times 36 is 540?
    b. What number times 48 is 2688?

11. Use a calculator to find what number divides 760, 12 times with a remainder of 4. How does this problem reinforce or extend a child's concept of division?

12. a. Read "Teaching Multiplication and Division Algorithms" by Hazekamp.
    b. Outline the sequence for multiplication. Cite an activity that can be used to develop each subtopic in the sequence.
    c. Outline the division sequence. Briefly describe an activity for each topic in your outline.

13. a. *For your resource file:* Read "Mental Computation" by Reys. After solving each of the six activities in the article, write a one-sentence evaluation of the activity. Add these ideas to your resource file.
    b. How do you evaluate students' mental computation skills? What guidelines does Reys give in "Testing Mental-Computation Skills"?
    c. Read and think through the mental computation activities in "Components of Mental Multiplying" by Hazekamp.

14. a. Read "Teaching Estimation and Reasonableness of Results." What teaching strategies does Johnson recommend for teaching estimation? What aspects are considered for reasonableness of results?
    b. With another student, play the game described in "A Calculator Activity That Teaches Mathematics" by Lappan and Winter. How is estimation used in the game?
    c. Read "Estimate and Calculate" by Ockenga and Duea. Work through one of the activities. What is your reaction to the activity?

15. a. What does research say with regard to learning multiplication concepts, strategies, and the algorithm? Read Suydam's "Research Report: Improving Multiplication Skills."
    b. Read "Computational Skill in Division: Results and Implications from National Assessment." by McKillip for the National Assessment Test results with respect to division. What were the results? What recommendations were made for improving instruction?

16. Read "Errors That Are Common in Multiplication" by Kilian, Cahill, Ryan, Sutherland, and Taccetta. What errors are cited? How could these be prevented or corrected?

17. *For your resource file:* Read and copy "Let's Do It: Partitioning Sets for Number Concepts, Place Value and Long Division." Van de Walle and Thompson explain how to use models to represent concepts and how to link these ideas to symbolic work.

18. a. Read "Calculators in the Classroom: A Proposal for Curricular Change." What are Wheatley's recommendations for curricular change? Do you agree with them? Why or why not?
    b. As you read and do the activities that are described in "A Calculator Estimation Activity" by Wheatley and Hersberger, use your calculator to check your estimations.

19. *For your resource file:* Starting in 1986, the column "Estimation and Mental Computation" appeared in the *Arithmetic Teacher.* Read one of these articles and add it to your resource file.

TEACHER RESOURCES

Beattie, Ian D. "Modeling Operations and Algorithms." *Arithmetic Teacher* 33 (February 1986): 23–28.

Bruni, James V., and Helene Silverman. "Let's Do It!: The Multiplication Facts: Once More with Understanding." *Arithmetic Teacher 23* (October 1976): 402–409.

Dodd, Carol Ann. "Multiply Successes When Introducing Basic Multiplication Ideas to Visually Handicapped Children." *Education of the Visually Handicapped 7* (May 1975): 53–56.

Duea, Joan, and Earl Ockenga. "Classroom Problem Solving with Calculators." *Arithmetic Teacher 29* (February 1982): 50–51.

Hall, William D. "Division with Base-Ten Blocks." *Arithmetic Teacher 31* (November 1983): 21–23.

Hazekamp, Donald W. "Components of Mental Multiplying." In *Estimation and Mental Computation,* 1986 Yearbook of the National Council of Teachers of Mathematics, pp. 116–126. Reston, VA: The Council, 1986.

———. "Teaching Multiplication and Division Algorithms." In *Developing Computational Skills,* 1978 Yearbook of the National Council of Teachers of Mathematics, pp. 96–128. Reston, VA: The Council, 1978.

Hendrickson, A. Dean. "Verbal Multiplication and Division Problems: Some Difficulties and Some Solutions." *Arithmetic Teacher 33* (April 1986): 26–33.

Irons, Calvin J. "The Division Algorithm: Using an Alternative Approach." *Arithmetic Teacher 28* (January 1981): 46–48.

Johnson, David C. "Teaching Estimation and Reasonableness of Results." *Arithmetic Teacher 27* (September 1979): 34–35.

Kalin, Robert. "How Students Do Their Division Facts." *Arithmetic Teacher 31* (November 1983): 16–19.

Katterns, Bob, and Ken Carr. "Talking with Young Children About Multiplication." *Arithmetic Teacher 33* (April 1986): 18–21.

Kilian, Lawrence, Edna Cahill, Carolann Ryan, Deborah Sutherland, and Diane Taccetta. "Errors That Are Common in Multiplication." *Arithmetic Teacher 27* (January 1980): 22–25.

Knifong, J. Dan, and Grace M. Burton. "Understanding Word Problems." *Arithmetic Teacher 32* (January 1985): 13–17.

Lappan, Glenda, and Mary Jean Winter. "A Calculator Activity That Teaches Mathematics." *Arithmetic Teacher 25* (April 1978): 21–23.

Lindquist, Mary Montgomery, Thomas P. Carpenter, Edward A. Silver, and Westina Matthews. "The Third National Assessment: Results and Implications for Elementary and Middle Schools." *Arithmetic Teacher 31* (December 1983): 14–19.

McKillip, William D. "Computational Skill in Division: Results and Implications from National Assessment." *Arithmetic Teacher 28* (March 1981): 34–37.

Myers, Ann C., and Carol A. Thornton. "The Learning Disabled Child—Learning the Basic Facts." *Arithmetic Teacher 25* (December 1977): 46–50.

National Assessment of Educational Progress. *The Second Assessment of Mathematics, 1977-78: Released Exercise Set.* Denver, CO: Education Commission of the States, 1979.

Nelson, Glenn, and Larry Leutzinger. "Let's Do It: Without Paper and Pencil." *Arithmetic Teacher 27* (January 1980): 8–12.

Nelson, Rebecca S. "Multiplication Games That Every Child Can Play." *Arithmetic Teacher 27* (October 1979): 34–35.

———. "Variations on Rummy." *Arithmetic Teacher 26* (September 1978): 40–41.

Ockenga, Earl, and Joan Duea. "Estimate and Calculate." *Mathematics Teacher 78* (April 1985): 272–276.

———. "Ideas." *Arithmetic Teacher 26* (September 1978): 28–32.

Peterson, Wayne. "Sharing the Wealth: Dividing with Meaning." *Arithmetic Teacher 30* (November 1982): 40–43.

Quintero, Ana Helvia. "Children's Conceptual Understanding of Situations Involving Multiplication." *Arithmetic Teacher 33* (January 1986): 34–37.

———. "Conceptual Understanding of Multiplication: Problems Involving Combination." *Arithmetic Teacher 33* (November 1985): 36–39.

Rathmell, Edward C. "Concepts of the Fundamental Operations: Results and Implications from National Assessment." *Arithmetic Teacher* 28 (November 1980): 34–37.

———. "Using Thinking Strategies to Teach the Basic Facts." In *Developing Computational Skills,* 1978 Yearbook of the National Council of Teachers of Mathematics, pp. 13–38. Reston, VA: The Council, 1978.

Reys, Barbara J. "Mental Computation." *Arithmetic Teacher* 32 (February 1985): 43–46.

Reys, Barbara, and Robert Reys. *GUESS.* Palo Alto, CA: Dale Seymour Publications, 1983.

Reys, Robert E. "Testing Mental-Computation Skills." *Arithmetic Teacher* 33 (November 1985): 14–16.

Reys, Robert E., Barbara J. Bestgen, Terrence G. Coburn, Harold L. Schoen, Richard J. Shumway, Charlotte L. Wheatley, Grayson H. Wheatley, and Arthur L. White. *Keystrokes: Calculator Activities for Young Students: Multiplication and Division.* Palo Alto, CA: Creative Publications, 1979.

Reys, Robert E., Paul R. Trafton, Barbara Reys, and Judy Zawojewski. *Computational Estimation Instructional Materials,* Grades 6, 7, and 8. Palo Alto, CA: Dale Seymour Publications, 1986.

Robold, Alice I. "Grid Arrays for Multiplication." *Arithmetic Teacher* 30 (January 1983): 14–17.

Smith, C. Winston, Jr. "Tiger-Bite Cards and Blank Arrays." *Arithmetic Teacher* 21 (December 1974): 679–682.

Sowder, Larry, Judith Threadgill-Sowder, Margaret B. Moyer, and John C. Moyer. "Diagnosing a Student's Understanding of Operation." *Arithmetic Teacher* 33 (May 1986): 22–25.

Stuart, Maureen, and Barbara Bestgen. "Productive Pieces: Exploring Multiplication on the Overhead." *Arithmetic Teacher* 29 (January 1982): 22–23.

Suydam, Marilyn N. "Research Report: Improving Multiplication Skills." *Arithmetic Teacher* 32 (March 1985): 52.

———. "The Use of Calculators in Pre-college Education." Columbus, OH: Calculator Information Center, August 1982.

Thornton, Carol A., and Margaret A. Toohey. *A Matter of Facts—Division.* Palo Alto, CA: Creative Publications, 1985.

———. *A Matter of Facts—Multiplication.* Palo Alto, CA: Creative Publications, 1985.

Van de Walle, John, and Charles S. Thompson. "Let's Do It: Partitioning Sets for Number Concepts, Place Value and Long Division." *Arithmetic Teacher* 32 (January 1985): 6–11.

Wheatley, Grayson H. "Calculators in the Classroom: A Proposal for Curricular Change." *Arithmetic Teacher* 28 (December 1980): 37–39.

Wheatley, Grayson H., and James Hersberger. "A Calculator Estimation Activity." In *Estimation and Mental Computation,* 1986 Yearbook of the National Council of Teachers of Mathematics, pp. 182–185. Reston, VA: The Council, 1986.

CHILDREN'S LITERATURE

Adler, David A. *Calculator Fun.* Illustrated by Arline and Marvin Oberman. New York: Franklin Watts, 1981.

Anno, Masaichiro, and Mitsumasa Anno. *Anno's Mysterious Multiplying Jar.* New York: Philomel Books, 1983.

Froman, Robert. *The Greatest Guessing Game: A Book About Dividing.* Illustrated by Gioia Fiammenghi. New York: Crowell, 1978.

Srivastava, Jane Jonas. *Number Families.* Illustrated by Lois Ehlert. New York: Crowell, 1979.

Trivett, John V. *Building Tables on Tables: A Book About Multiplication.* Illustrated by Giulio Maestro. New York: Crowell, 1975.

8

TEACHING ADDITION AND SUBTRACTION OF COMMON AND DECIMAL FRACTIONS

"I tried to use paperfolding for teaching addition of fractions, but the kids just didn't get it. They couldn't even figure out how to show three eighths with the paper. After I showed them how to represent three eighths and one fourth, they said the answer was four twelfths. Anyway, I just gave up and showed them how to do the problems. They did just fine. Practically all of the students did their homework right. You just don't need that model stuff."

Consider this teacher statement. What do you think the students could do? What level of understanding would you anticipate? Do you think they could estimate an answer for $\frac{7}{8} + \frac{6}{13}$? Consider the first time you will use models with your students. If your plan doesn't go smoothly or the students don't get it immediately, should you assume that models don't work?

In this chapter the operations of addition and subtraction for common and decimal fractions will be explored. The concepts of common and decimal fractions which were introduced in the chapter on numeration are essential for understanding the operations. To apply and use these operations successfully, the fraction number concepts and operations must be related to the *concepts of each operation*.

ADDITION OF COMMON FRACTIONS

By the time students are introduced to the addition of fractions, they should understand the meaning of fractions both as "part of a whole" and as "part of a set." Also, students will have had some experiences with equivalent fractions and fractions greater than one. In fourth grade, addition of like fractions is introduced. Like fractions are fractions with the same denominator, such as $\frac{1}{3}$ and $\frac{2}{3}$, $\frac{3}{8}$ and $\frac{1}{8}$, or $\frac{1}{10}$ and $\frac{7}{10}$. Fractions with ten as the denominator should be introduced to lay a foundation for the introduction of decimals. Some of the same models used to develop the concept of fractions can be employed to

illustrate addition of fractions (Figure 8-1). Activities with fraction bars or paperfolding can be used to introduce addition of fractions.

ADDITION OF LIKE FRACTIONS

Ken used paperfolding to represent the following situation involving unit fractions. "Jim cut the sandwich into fourths. He ate one fourth of it, and his brother John ate another fourth. What part of the sandwich did they eat?" Ken first folded fourths, then shaded in one fourth to represent Jim's portion. Next he shaded in another fourth to represent John's portion. He observed that he had 2 fourths in all. By using a unit fraction first, Ken's attention is focused on the total number of parts—four.

The next type of problem that Ken encountered involved numerators other than one. "Jim mowed 2 fourths of the back lawn before lunch and another one fourth later in the afternoon. What part of the back yard did he mow?" Ken used two different shadings to represent the parts (Figure 8-2a).

To solve a different situation, Kathy folded a sheet into six equal-sized parts. She shaded in 5 sixths plus one more sixth. She

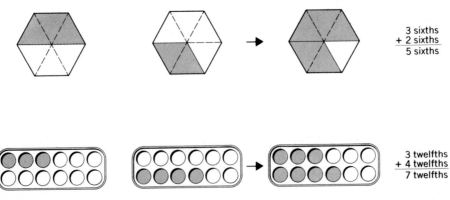

3 sixths
+ 2 sixths
5 sixths

3 twelfths
+ 4 twelfths
7 twelfths

FIGURE 8-1.
Models for adding fractions.

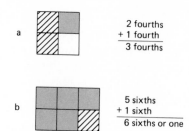

a)   2 fourths
   + 1 fourth
   3 fourths

b)   5 sixths
   + 1 sixth
   6 sixths or one

FIGURE 8-2.

Using paperfolding to add fractions.

had shaded in the whole sheet so "5 sixths plus 1 sixth is 6 sixths or one" (Figure 8-2b).

Fraction bars can also be used to illustrate addition of fractions. To represent 2 fourths plus 1 fourth, children should find fraction bars representing these numbers (Figure 8-3a). The combined number of shaded parts should be observed and a fraction bar found that represents that number. A class discussion should focus on how many total equal-sized parts are represented and how many shaded parts are being considered. The children are adding 2 fourths to 1 fourth just as they previously added 2 tens to 1 ten, 2 centimeters to 1 centimeter, or 2 units to 1 unit.

The numerical statement should be written as a record of what has already been done with the model. If a written form is desired for early work in addition of fractions, the one shown in Figure 8-3b should be used. This form emphasizes the "naming" function of the denominator. Through dis-

cussing the process and writing the appropriate oral names, the children's concepts of units and fractions will be enhanced.

The word form helps to prevent a common error in the addition of fractions. When adding fractions in numerical form, children may add numerator to numerator and denominator to denominator. When the denominators are written in words, there is no temptation to add them. Once children comprehend the concept of adding fractions from sufficient experiences using models, they can easily transfer to the numerical algorithm for computation. Labeling the numerator and the denominator as part and whole can help children with the transition to the written algorithm (Figure 8-3c).

Both paperfolding and fraction bars can be used to represent sums greater than one. To solve 4 fifths plus 2 fifths with paperfolding, the two addends can be shown on separate sheets of paper. The children should observe that 4 fifths plus 2 fifths is 6 fifths (Figure 8-4a). After discussing the problem, the children should re-solve it by representing 4 fifths on a sheet of paper (Figure 8-4b). The class could then discuss that only 1 more fifth can be shaded. A second sheet representing fifths will be needed for shad-

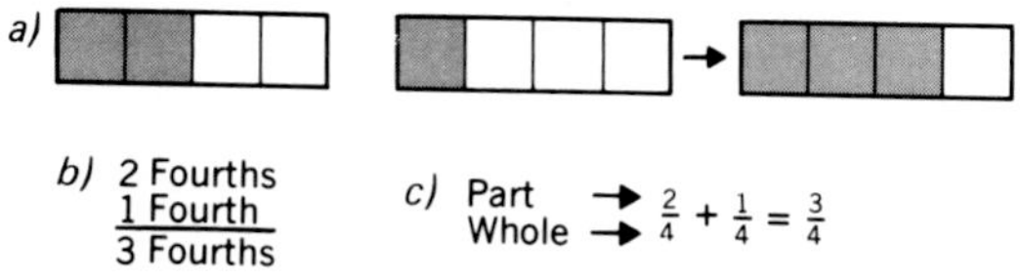

a) [diagram of fraction bars]

b) 2 Fourths
   1 Fourth
   3 Fourths   *c)* Part → $\frac{2}{4}$ + $\frac{1}{4}$ = $\frac{3}{4}$
            Whole →

FIGURE 8-3.

Fraction bars to add like fractions.

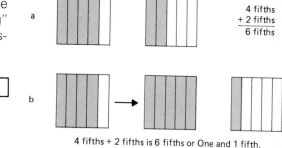

a   4 fifths
     + 2 fifths
     6 fifths

b

4 fifths + 2 fifths is 6 fifths or One and 1 fifth.

FIGURE 8-4.

Adding fifths.

ing in the other fifth. The class should compare and contrast these procedures and results.

Another model for representing the addition of like fractions is the fractional number line. The process used is the same as the process for adding whole numbers on the number line. As with number lines for whole numbers, children need to focus on the intervals not the marks. A good transition is to use fraction bars *with* the number line

(Figure 8-5). To solve $\frac{5}{12} + \frac{2}{12}$ the children first use a twelfths fraction bar to draw and label a number line. The intervals each represent one twelfth, not one as with whole numbers. The whole or one is the entire length of the fraction bar. The region $\frac{5}{12}$ should then be indicated (Figure 8-5b). The 2 twelfths bar can then be placed next to the shaded part of 5 twelfths and indicated. The total shaded is 7 twelfths which can be read from the number line (Figure 8-5c). The frac-

FIGURE 8-5.
Fraction bars with number line.

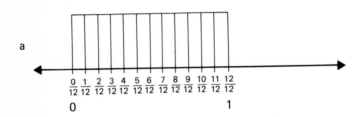
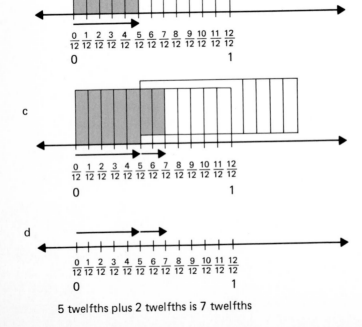

5 twelfths plus 2 twelfths is 7 twelfths

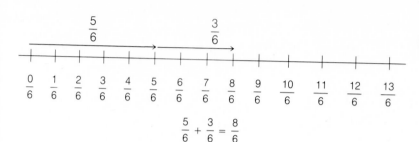

FIGURE 8-6.
Fractional number line.

$$\frac{5}{6} + \frac{3}{6} = \frac{8}{6}$$

tion bars help to emphasize the entire inter-val rather than the end points. After the students understand the process and the model, the number line can be used alone.

A second example representing sums greater than one is shown in Figure 8-6. In this case, each interval is 1 sixth. Since this number line is labeled with fractions and extends beyond $\frac{6}{6}$ or 1, it will also enhance children's understanding of fraction sums greater than one.

Like fractions can also be added using a Cuisenaire-rod model. Again, values are represented by length. To add $\frac{3}{10}$ and $\frac{4}{10}$, children would first find a rod to represent the whole (orange) and then rods to represent the two parts—three (light green) and four (purple). Next, they would combine the two parts and find a single rod that matches this combined length. Thus the sum of $\frac{3}{10}$ and $\frac{4}{10}$ can be seen to be 7 (part) out of 10 (whole) or $\frac{7}{10}$ (Figure 8-7). Note, too, the emphasis on tenths, which forms a good foundation for later work with decimals.

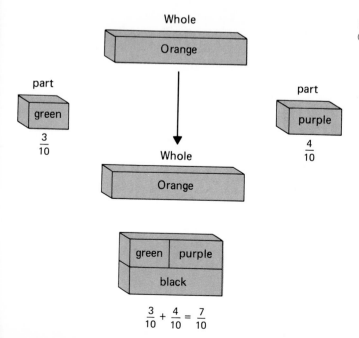

FIGURE 8-7.
Cuisenaire rods for like fractions.

$$\frac{3}{10} + \frac{4}{10} = \frac{7}{10}$$

ADDITION OF UNLIKE RELATED FRACTIONS

After students have learned to add like fractions, they are introduced to the addition of unlike fractions. Unlike related fractions are pairs of fractions that have different denominators but for which one denominator is a factor of the other, for example, $\frac{1}{2}$ and $\frac{1}{4}$ or $\frac{1}{3}$ and $\frac{5}{6}$. Just as students have already learned that they cannot add unlike units such as feet and inches without first renaming them, they can easily see that they cannot add thirds and sixths until they both have the same name. Prerequisites for adding unlike fractions are adding like fractions *and* renaming fractions.

For example, when planning supper Linda observed that there was one half of a mulberry pie left and one piece of peach pie left. If she considered only the number of pieces and not the size of the pieces, she would say, "I have two pieces of pie," an unreasonable statement, as there was more than enough pie for two people. She thought, "I usually cut pies into sixths, so I can cut the half into sixths to get three pieces so that we have four pieces left." Linda was indirectly using addition of fractions. Together the two parts represented $\frac{1}{2} + \frac{1}{6}$ and were recut (renamed) to represent $\frac{3}{6} + \frac{1}{6}$, for a total of $\frac{4}{6}$ or 4 sixths of a pie (Figure 8-8).

Paperfolding activities help children explore and devise extended procedures for adding fractions. To solve $\frac{2}{5} + \frac{3}{10}$, they will

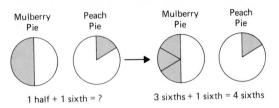

1 half + 1 sixth = ?   3 sixths + 1 sixth = 4 sixths

FIGURE 8-8.
Adding unlike related fractions.

first need to represent each fraction (Figure 8-9). They can see that fifths will need to be folded into smaller pieces. When showing 3 tenths, they had to decide to fold fifths *and* halves. Since they had already solved this problem, the renaming of 2 fifths to tenths should be more evident. Only one fraction needed to be renamed and the renaming was in the same units as the other fraction.

In using fraction bars to add $\frac{1}{3} + \frac{5}{6}$, the students will need to rename thirds as sixths (Figure 8-10). A fraction bar representing 2 sixths can be matched with the bar representing 1 third. The students can then add 2 sixths and 5 sixths for a total of 7 sixths or one and 1 sixth. The original problem ($\frac{1}{3} + \frac{5}{6}$) was changed to a problem involving adding like fractions, a process the students have already learned. At first children simply record the results of renaming that they are doing with models (Figure 8-9). Eventually they will need to combine their written procedure for renaming fractions with adding fractions.

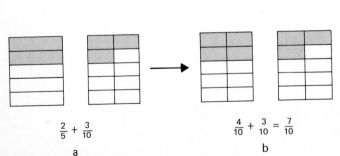

$\frac{2}{5} + \frac{3}{10}$

a

$\frac{4}{10} + \frac{3}{10} = \frac{7}{10}$

b

FIGURE 8-9.
Paperfolding to add fifths to tenths.

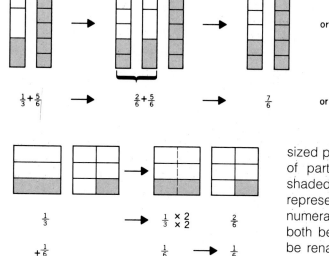

FIGURE 8-10.
Adding unlike related fractions with fraction bars.

$\frac{1}{3} + \frac{5}{6}$ → $\frac{2}{6} + \frac{5}{6}$ → $\frac{7}{6}$ or $1\frac{1}{6}$

$\frac{1}{3}$ → $\frac{1}{3} \times \frac{2}{2}$ $\frac{2}{6}$

$+\frac{1}{6}$ → $\frac{1}{6}$ → $\frac{1}{6}$

$\frac{3}{6}$

FIGURE 8-11.
Adding related fractions by paperfolding.

Paperfolding can be used to reinforce the algorithm for renaming fractions. For example, when Judy was adding $\frac{1}{3} + \frac{1}{6}$, she first folded and shaded sheets of paper to represent these fractions (Figure 8-11). To fold sixths, Judy folded the paper into thirds and then folded it once more in the other direction. She observed that the paper divided into thirds could also be folded again so that it, too, would be divided into 6 equal-sized parts. She noted that the total number of parts doubled as did the number of shaded parts when she folded the paper representing 1 third. Judy recorded that the numerator and the denominator of $\frac{1}{3}$ had both been doubled or multiplied by two to be renamed as $\frac{2}{6}$. She then added $\frac{2}{6}$ and $\frac{1}{6}$ for a sum of $\frac{3}{6}$. In this case, Judy has applied a previously learned skill—renaming fractions—as part of her algorithm for adding unlike related fractions. This procedure leads to the type of thinking shown in Figure 8-12.

Thus adding related fractions is a two-step process. The first step is to rewrite the fraction with the smaller denominator so that it has the same denominator as the other fraction. The problem is now changed so that the second step is simply to add like fractions, a process already known.

As an alternative transition between using models to find the renamed fraction and using the algorithm for renaming fractions, one textbook gives lists of equivalent frac-

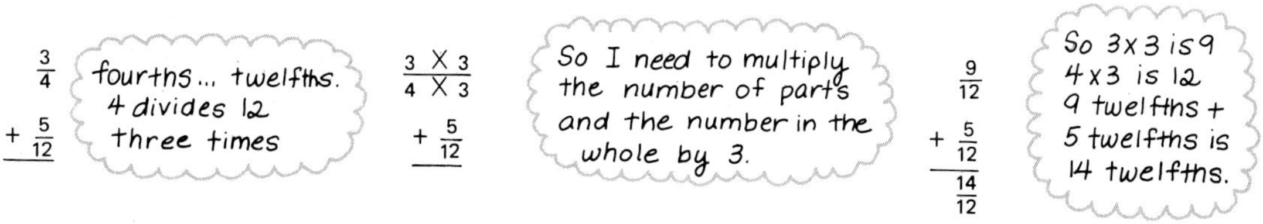

$\frac{3}{4}$ *fourths... twelfths.* $\frac{3 \times 3}{4 \times 3}$ *So I need to multiply* $\frac{9}{12}$ *So 3×3 is 9*
4 divides 12 *the number of parts* *4×3 is 12*
$+\frac{5}{12}$ *three times* $+\frac{5}{12}$ *and the number in the* $+\frac{5}{12}$ *9 twelfths +*
whole by 3. *5 twelfths is*
$\frac{14}{12}$ *14 twelfths.*

FIGURE 8-12.
Renaming fractions.

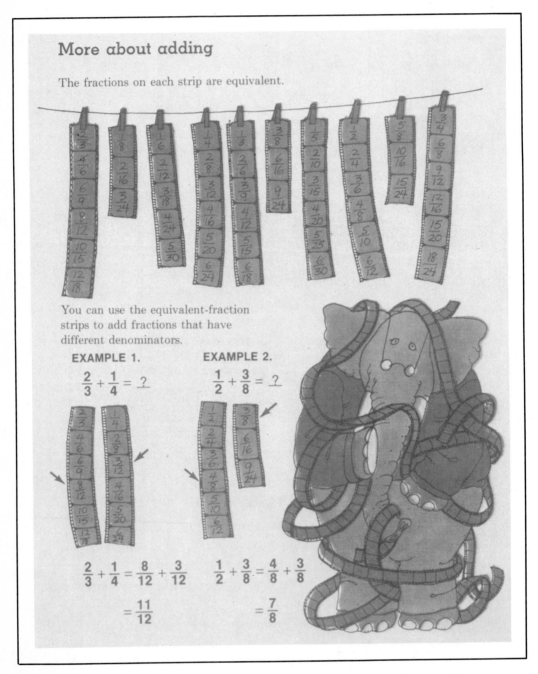

More about adding

The fractions on each strip are equivalent.

You can use the equivalent-fraction strips to add fractions that have different denominators.

EXAMPLE 1.

$$\frac{2}{3} + \frac{1}{4} = \underline{?}$$

$$\frac{2}{3} + \frac{1}{4} = \frac{8}{12} + \frac{3}{12}$$

$$= \frac{11}{12}$$

EXAMPLE 2.

$$\frac{1}{2} + \frac{3}{8} = \underline{?}$$

$$\frac{1}{2} + \frac{3}{8} = \frac{4}{8} + \frac{3}{8}$$

$$= \frac{7}{8}$$

FIGURE 8-13.
Equivalent fraction strips. (From C.A. Dilley, D.W. Lowry, W.E. Rucker, **Heath Mathematics**, 1985, Grade 4, p. 196. Reprinted by permission of D.C. Heath & Company.)

$$\frac{1}{2} = \frac{2}{4} = \frac{3}{6} = \frac{4}{8} = \frac{32}{64} = \frac{100}{200} = \frac{1 \cdot N}{2 \cdot N}$$

$$\frac{3}{4} = \frac{6}{8} = \frac{12}{16} = \frac{30}{40} = \frac{90}{120} = \frac{3 \cdot N}{4 \cdot N}$$

FIGURE 8-14.
Families of fractions.

1. Finding a common denominator.
2. Rewriting the fractions so they have this common denominator.
3. Adding like fractions.

tions that the student can use as a reference (Figure 8-13). Each list shown has been generated by multiplying the original fraction by $\frac{2}{2}$, $\frac{3}{3}$, $\frac{4}{4}$, and so on.

To solve the second example, students must rename one of the addends. One fraction's denominator is a factor of the other fraction's denominator. In the example $\frac{1}{2}$ + $\frac{3}{8}$, halves must be renamed as eighths. To solve such problems independently, students must learn to write their own lists of equivalent fractions (Figure 8-14).

ADDITION OF UNLIKE UNRELATED FRACTIONS

In adding unlike related fractions, children had to rename only one fraction in terms of the other fraction's denominator. All addends must be renamed in adding unlike unrelated fractions. Unlike unrelated fractions are fractions that have different denominators and for which neither denominator is a factor of the other such as $\frac{1}{3}$ and $\frac{3}{4}$ or $\frac{2}{3}$ and $\frac{5}{8}$. Sometimes, however, the denominators may contain common factors as with $\frac{1}{6}$ and $\frac{5}{8}$ or $\frac{3}{4}$ and $\frac{7}{10}$. Through appropriate concept-building activities with models, students will discover that the algorithm for the addition of unlike unrelated fractions really combines three distinct steps—each of which is easily understood when studied in isolation. The three steps are:

The second and third steps of this algorithm are a duplication of the algorithm for adding unlike related fractions. Instead of using a new technique to solve complex problems, the problem is simplified to one for which a method for solution is already known.

Finding an appropriate common denominator is the only new step. There are several techniques for finding a common denominator for a set of fractions. Some techniques are easier than others, but an easy method may not always be practical for a particular set of numbers. One method is to use lists of equivalent fractions to solve problems such as $\frac{2}{3}$ + $\frac{1}{4}$ (Figure 8-13). Students could examine these lists until they find the first pair of fractions that are equivalent to $\frac{2}{3}$ and $\frac{1}{4}$ but have the same denominator. In this case they are merely recognizing fractions with common denominators.

Another technique for finding a common denominator is to select the larger of the two denominators. The multiples of this denominator are generated in order until one is found which is also a multiple of the other denominator. The teacher can help students understand this procedure by discussing specific examples. For example, Ms. Lubinski represented $\frac{1}{6}$ and $\frac{1}{4}$ using paperfolding and discussed the process with her class. "We will need at least how many total parts? (6) Does 4 divide 6? (No) Let's look at our model. (Re-folds the sixths) If we folded the sixths once more, how many parts would we have? (Twelfths) Can we change fourths into twelfths? (Yes)" So students changed both $\frac{1}{6}$ and $\frac{1}{4}$ into twelfths and added the twelfths.

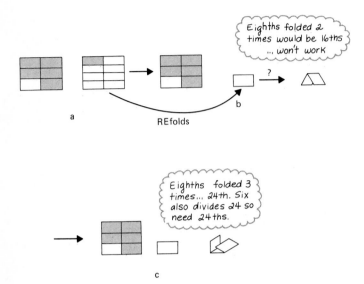

FIGURE 8-15.
Developing addition algorithm.

In a second example, Ms. Lubinski used $\frac{5}{6}$ and $\frac{1}{8}$ (Figure 8-15a). "Since 6 does not divide 8, which one should we start renaming? (Eighths, as we have more total parts.) We'll re-fold the eighths. Now *if* we folded the eighths again, how many parts? (16, but 6 does not divide 16; Figure 8-15b) Okay, *if* we folded the eighths into three parts, we would have how many parts? (24) Good, 6 divides 24, so we can use 24 (Figure 8-15c). Since 24 divided by 8 is 3, we'll multiply $\frac{3}{3}$ times $\frac{1}{8}$ to get $\frac{3}{24}$. 24 divided by 6 is 4, so multiply $\frac{4}{4}$ times $\frac{5}{6}$ for $\frac{20}{24}$."

After this conceptual development with models, children may use this technique simply by listing the multiples of the larger denominator. For example, given the denominators 2 and 7, students would list the multiples of 7 until a number is found that is also a multiple of 2 (Figure 8-16a). A common denominator can be found similarly for $\frac{1}{6}$ and $\frac{3}{8}$ (Figure 8-16b).

This technique is appropriate for the examples given, and for most problems with two addends. It can become very cumber-some in some situations. If students tried to use this technique for finding the common denominator for the set of denominators 8, 9, and 15, they would have to check 24 multiples of 15 before obtaining a common denominator of 360.

Another beginning technique is simply to multiply all the denominators together to find a common denominator. Thus the common denominator for 2 and 7 would be found

a) $\frac{1}{2} + \frac{3}{7}$

Multiples of seven

$1 \times 7 = 7$--not divisible by 2
$2 \times 7 = 14$—divisible by 2
So LCD is 14.

b) $\frac{1}{6} + \frac{3}{8}$

Multiples of eight

$1 \times 8 = 8$—not divisible by 6
$2 \times 8 = 16$—not divisible by 6
$3 \times 8 = 24$—divisible by 6
So LCD is 24.

FIGURE 8-16.
Using multiples to find lowest common denominator.

by multiplying 2 × 7, yielding a common denominator of 14. For 9 and 15 students would multiply 9 × 15 obtaining a common denominator of 135. Although this technique will always yield *a* common denominator, it will not always yield the *lowest* common denominator. Although any common denominator can be used successfully, most students make fewer errors when working with smaller numbers, and consequently the lowest common denominator is desirable. However, because of the simplicity of this technique, some students may adopt it as a permanent algorithm.

In teaching fractions, commonly used denominators such as 2, 3, 4, 5, 6, 8, 10, and 12 should be emphasized. As children develop number sense, they will be able to easily find common multiples for these numbers. Other denominators such as 25, 20, 50, and 100 need to be included prior to work on decimal fractions and percents. These numbers can also be used to introduce children to other procedures for determining common denominators.

In addition to these commonly used denominators, other denominators should also be studied to help children develop more sophisticated procedures such as prime factoring and the concept of the least common multiple. Figure 8-17 shows how this technique can be used to find the lowest common denominator for $\frac{2}{9}$ and $\frac{7}{15}$. This method is discussed in detail in the chapter on number theory. Once students master the skills of factorization, the factoring technique for

finding a common denominator is quick and efficient. It always yields the lowest common denorninator and is the form used later in adding algebraic fractions. For commonly used fractions, this technique is usually unnecessary. Students can immediately "see" a common denominator because of their well-developed number sense.

ADDITION OF MIXED NUMBERS

The addition of mixed numbers is not a new topic but is an extension of adding whole numbers and adding fractions. These situations should also be introduced with models. To add $2\frac{2}{5}$ and $1\frac{4}{5}$, students can first represent the fractions with models (Figure 8-18). First the students consider the fractional parts $\frac{2}{5} + \frac{4}{5}$. Since the sum of 6 fifths is more than 1, the fraction is renamed as $1\frac{1}{5}$. The

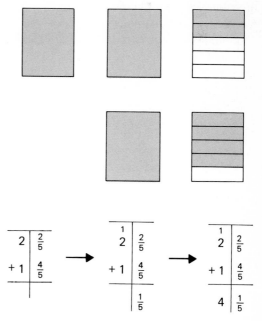

$$\frac{2}{9} \times \frac{5}{5} = \frac{10}{45}$$

$$\frac{7}{15} \times \frac{3}{3} = \frac{21}{45}$$

$$\frac{31}{45}$$

FIGURE 8-17.

Finding the common denominator.

FIGURE 8-18.

Adding mixed numbers.

one fifth is recorded in the fraction column and the one in the ones column for whole numbers. The whole numbers can then be added.

Once the prerequisite skill of addition of like fractions has been taught, the addition of mixed numbers that contain *only* like fractions can be introduced. Similarly, the addition of mixed numbers containing unlike related fractions can follow the prerequisite skill, adding unlike related fractions. By the time students have learned to add unlike unrelated fractions, the addition of this type of mixed numbers should be a simple extension of known skills.

ESTIMATION FOR ADDITION OF COMMON FRACTIONS

National Assessment results have included questions on estimating sums of fractions. In the Second Assessment, about $\frac{1}{4}$ of the 13-year-olds and slightly more than $\frac{1}{3}$ of the 17-year-olds correctly selected the answer of 2 for the estimate of $\frac{12}{13} + \frac{7}{8}$. Over $\frac{1}{2}$ of the 13-year-olds and about $\frac{1}{3}$ of the 17-year-olds selected answers of 19 and 21. These answers indicate that students are just memorizing rules which they neither understand nor apply correctly. Instead, they should be developing the concepts for adding fractions.

In the preceding section, models were

Sums Greater than = 1	Sums Less than 1
$\frac{1}{2} + \frac{}{30}$	$\frac{1}{2} + \frac{}{30}$
$\frac{1}{2} + \frac{}{7}$	$\frac{1}{2} + \frac{}{7}$
$\frac{1}{2} + \frac{}{16}$	$\frac{1}{2} + \frac{}{16}$

FIGURE 8-19.
Estimating approximately one half.

used to illustrate the addition of fractions. Through language these models and the action on the models were related to the written form of the algorithm. Estimation skills will also help students understand these addition and fraction concepts. Some of the fractions used in estimation activities, such as $\frac{29}{56}$ or $\frac{13}{87}$, are not ones that we commonly encounter. This type of number should be selected so that the students do not compute the answers and then round to find an estimate.

ESTIMATING FRACTIONAL SUMS WITH 0, $\frac{1}{2}$, AND 1

In the examples from National Assessment, the students should have considered that both $\frac{12}{13}$ and $\frac{7}{8}$ were about 1, so their sum is around 2. They should also realize that since the numbers were both less than one, their

Sums Close to One		Sums Greater than 2	
$1 + \frac{2}{}$	$1 + \frac{}{10}$	$1 + \frac{2}{}$	$1 + \frac{}{10}$
$1 + \frac{15}{}$	$1 + \frac{}{25}$	$1 + \frac{15}{}$	$1 + \frac{}{25}$

FIGURE 8-20.
Estimating zero and one.

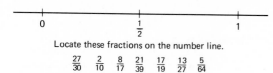

FIGURE 8-21.
Estimating fractions on a number line.

sum should be less than 2. Even this rough estimate would have prevented students from choosing answers of 19 or 21 in the example above.

In the section "Rounding and Estimating Common Fractions" in Chapter 5, strategies for estimating whether numbers were close to 0, $\frac{1}{2}$, or 1 were discussed. These skills are prerequisite for estimation of fraction sums. A number of excellent activities are found in *Computational Estimation Instructional Materials* by Reys, Trafton, Reys, and Zawojewski.

One type of activity that focuses on one half is shown in Figure 8-19. To solve these problems the students know that $\frac{1}{2} + \frac{1}{2} = 1$. Then the second $\frac{1}{2}$ must be adjusted to make sums greater than or less than one. For the third example students will probably think,

"16 . . . 8 sixteenths is one half, so 9 sixteenths for a sum greater than one." The students should discuss other answers, such as 10, 11, or 20 sixteenths. They should also discuss which addends give sums closer to one. Similar exercises can be designed to have the students focus on zero or one as the other addend (Figure 8-20).

A number line can be helpful in teaching students to estimate fractions as near zero, one half, or one (Figure 8-21). When given the line with zero, one half, and one marked on it, the students should then place other fractions in their approximate locations. To place these fractions correctly, students must focus on how they are related to the given points. Addition of fractions can also be explored with this number line. Students should observe such general results as "adding two fractions which are both near one half produces an answer close to one," "adding two fractions near one produces a sum near two," or "adding a fraction near one and a fraction near zero produces a sum close to one."

Another activity to help students improve estimation skills is to have them determine which numbers are near 0, $\frac{1}{2}$, or 1

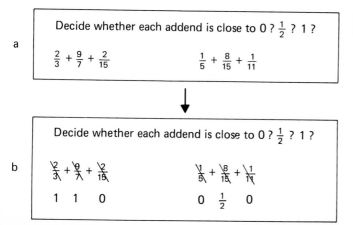

FIGURE 8-22.
Estimating sums.

Circle the best choice

$\frac{2}{3} + \frac{9}{10}$ about $\frac{1}{2}$ about 1   about 2

$\frac{1}{4} + \frac{3}{11}$ about $\frac{1}{2}$ about 1   about 2

$\frac{9}{16} + \frac{3}{8}$ about $\frac{1}{2}$ about 1   about 2

$\frac{11}{9} + \frac{1}{5}$ about $\frac{1}{2}$ about 1   about 2

FIGURE 8-23.
Refined estimating of sums.

(Figure 8-22a). Rather than finding the sum, the focus of the activity should be on estimating whether each addend is closest to 0, $\frac{1}{2}$, or 1. Later these same problems can be used for estimating the sum. At first some students may want to write in their estimates as shown (Figure 8-22b). As the students' estimation skills improve they should be able to estimate sums more accurately. Figure 8-23 shows this type of exercise.

FRONT-END ESTIMATION AND ROUNDING

Reys, Trafton, Reys, and Zawojewski suggest three strategies for estimating the sum of mixed numbers: front-end addition, rounding, and using nice numbers. With mixed numbers we commonly use a combination of these strategies. Front-end addition is recommended for numbers such as $5\frac{7}{8} + 14\frac{5}{9}$. After mentally adding the whole numbers, the result is adjusted by rounding the fractions to 0, $\frac{1}{2}$, or 1. For this example the student would think "5 + 14 is 19. $\frac{7}{8}$ is about 1 and $\frac{5}{9}$ is a little more than $\frac{1}{2}$, so my estimate is $20\frac{1}{2}$."

For some problems rounding one number is suggested. The number is rounded so that it has no fractional part but only a front end. Then this rounded front end is added

$$12\frac{4}{5} + 2\frac{3}{10}$$

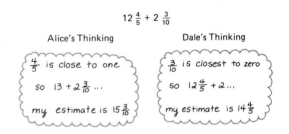

Alice's Thinking

$\frac{4}{5}$ is close to one

so $13 + 2\frac{3}{10}$ ...

my estimate is $15\frac{3}{10}$

Dale's Thinking

$\frac{3}{10}$ is closest to zero

so $12\frac{4}{5} + 2$ ...

my estimate is $14\frac{4}{5}$

FIGURE 8-24.
Rounding one mixed number and not the other.

to the other entire number for an estimate of the sum. In a problem like $2\frac{15}{16} + 21\frac{3}{5}$, the student may round $2\frac{15}{16}$ to 3 and say $3 + 21\frac{3}{5}$ is $24\frac{3}{5}$. Figure 8-24 shows two different samples of student thinking in using this strategy to estimate $12\frac{4}{5} + 2\frac{3}{10}$. When rounding, the relative sizes of all the fractional parts can also be considered. In class discussion, students should compare these estimations and should see that Alice's estimate will be a little large and Dale's will be a little small.

For some situations the fractional parts should be ignored. For larger numbers such as $28\frac{3}{5} + 15\frac{1}{6} + 51\frac{3}{4}$, the fractional parts are insignificant when compared to the whole numbers. In this case the student may estimate by thinking "30 + 50 is 80. 80 + 15 more is 95." Practice exercises can be designed to help students focus on just the digits needed for making an appropriate estimate (Figure 8-25).

All of these activities should extend the students' understanding of fractional num-

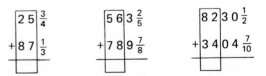

FIGURE 8-25.
Estimating sums of large mixed numbers.

bers. These activities should reinforce students' comprehension of the addition algorithm. They also provide a means of checking for reasonableness of results when doing computations with fractions.

ADDITION OF DECIMAL FRACTIONS

Although addition and subtraction of common fractions are studied together in elementary school, this text will develop addition of decimal fractions next in order to show the parallels between addition of common and decimal fractions—the same numbers, but different forms. Both addition of decimal fractions and addition of common fractions are introduced in the fourth grade. Although the sequence of these topics may vary among elementary textbook series, usually addition of common fractions is introduced first. Since decimal fractions are based on common fractions and place value, the lessons should be carefully developed so that students will conceptualize the process.

The addition of decimals involves few new concepts. By this time, students have studied the meaning of decimal fractions, how to add common fractions—including those with denominators of 10 or 100—and how to add whole numbers. However, National Assessment results show that students do have difficulties in estimating answers for problems requiring addition of decimal fractions. They also do not do well on decimal problems that are written horizontally. These results indicate that more work on place value and understanding of decimal concepts is needed. Consequently, the prerequisite skills of place value and addition of fractional numbers should be reviewed and

reinforced to help students develop an algorithm for adding decimals.

ADDITION OF "LIKE" DECIMAL FRACTIONS

From their previous experiences in adding whole numbers, students know that they must add ones to ones, tens to tens, and so on. Since decimal fractions involve extensions of place value to the right to represent parts of whole numbers, tenths will be added to tenths, hundredths to hundredths, and so on. A common false assumption in teaching the addition of decimals is the idea that students no longer need models such as paperfolding, grids, base-ten blocks, or an abacus. However, models are still needed for developing the new concepts found in this topic.

Grids, which are similar to base-ten blocks but are easily made, are particularly helpful for developing decimal concepts. Grids are ten-by-ten squares cut from graph paper or copied onto paper or transparencies. The ten-by-ten square is defined as one. The grids can be flipped over to show an undivided "one." Paper grids can be plastic laminated for durability. In this way the students can write on them to solve one problem and then wipe them clean for doing the next problem. Figure 8-26a shows the grid representations of some decimal fractions.

Some of the grids can be cut into one-by-ten strips to represent tenths. Like the large squares, these strips can be flipped over to show undivided "tenths." These strips can be used separately or they can be used on the grid so that students can see that they exactly cover a row of ten squares. Small squares can be used to cover the hundredths (Figure 8-26b and c). This can help facilitate student thinking as one tenth (a strip) covers 10 hundredths (10 squares).

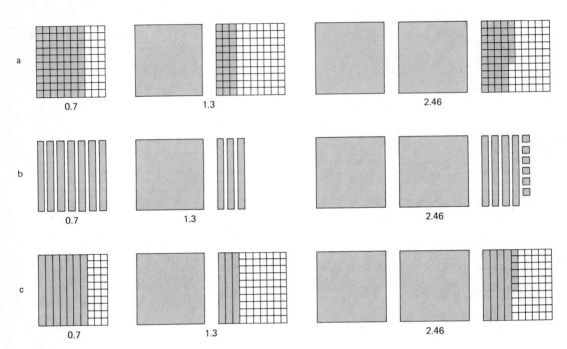

FIGURE 8-26.
Grids to represent decimal fractions.

This form is particularly good for concept building in addition and subtraction when hundredths or tenths must be renamed. (*Note:* When the 10-by-10 grid is made from centimeter paper, the students and teacher may find it easier to use centimeter cubes for hundredths instead of the small paper squares.)

Students' first experiences with adding decimal fractions should be in adding tenths to tenths. This concept should be related to their previous experiences with adding fractions and to real-life situations. These situations should be used to extend students' understanding of how decimals are applied.

The National Weather Service reported that Plainfield had received 1.6 inches of rain on Tuesday, 2.3 inches on Wednesday, and none the rest of the week. What was the total rainfall in Plainfield that week?

Paperfolding could be used as a model to represent one and six tenths plus two and three tenths (Figure 8-27a). After the students have represented the numbers, they should discuss adding like units as tenths to tenths and ones to ones. These results should then be recorded in word, common fraction, and decimal fraction forms (Figure 8-27b). The similarities and differences should be discussed. The students should observe that the decimal form is the same as the whole number addition form since place values are lined up and added.

Grids and base-ten blocks can also be used to introduce problems such as 2.3 + 1.4. To show 2.3, three grid squares are needed. Two whole squares and 3 tenths of the third square would be shaded. The representations of both 2.3 and 1.4 are shown in Figure 8-28. The models should be related

This problem also involves regrouping. Regrouping tenths to ones is an extension of the regrouping students learned with whole numbers and with common fractions. Renaming 10 tenths as 1 one should be related to renaming 10 ones as 1 ten, 10 hundreds as 1 thousand, and $\frac{10}{10}$ as 1. Consequently, 12 tenths is 1 and 2 tenths. The results should be recorded step by step in a place-value table.

These same models can be used to introduce addends in the hundredths. The problem 1.04 + 0.35 has been represented with base-ten blocks and on an abacus (Figure 8-29). In order to represent these numbers the students need to consider 35 hundredths in place-value terms. It is represented as 3 tenths, 5 hundredths. Again the students should discuss adding like units and the pattern of adding like place values. Hundredths should be added to hundredths, tenths to tenths, and ones to ones. They should also relate this to addition of fractions where hundredths were added to hundredths and ones to ones. These examples should be extended to problems with one or more renamings.

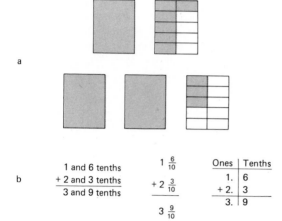

a

b

		Ones	Tenths
1 and 6 tenths	$1\frac{6}{10}$	1.	6
+ 2 and 3 tenths	$+2\frac{3}{10}$	+ 2.	3
3 and 9 tenths		3.	9
	$3\frac{9}{10}$		

FIGURE 8-27.

Adding "like" decimals.

to the written form of the algorithm by first joining and then recording the tenths and then joining and recording the ones.

Base-ten materials are used similarly. The flat should be redefined as "the whole" or "one." For the problem 2.7 + 1.5, the numbers could be represented on the overhead as 2 flats 7 longs and 1 flat 5 longs.

FIGURE 8-28.

Using grids to add decimals.

2 and 3 tenths

1 and 4 tenths

Ones	Tenths
2.	3
+ 1.	4
3.	7

2.3
+ 1.4
3.7

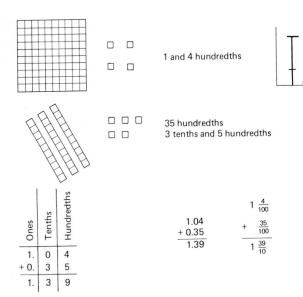

FIGURE 8-29.

Base-ten blocks and abacus representing addition of "like" decimals.

1 and 4 hundredths

35 hundredths
3 tenths and 5 hundredths

Ones	Tenths	Hundredths
1.	0	4
+ 0.	3	5
1.	3	9

$$\begin{array}{r} 1.04 \\ + 0.35 \\ \hline 1.39 \end{array}$$

$$\begin{array}{r} 1\frac{4}{100} \\ + \frac{35}{100} \\ \hline 1\frac{39}{10} \end{array}$$

Money is often suggested as a model for adding decimals as children usually develop skill in using numbers representing money before developing the same skills with decimal numbers. However, as discussed in Chapter 5, the children perceive the decimal point as separating dollars and cents, not dollars and fractional parts of dollars. Since the numbers representing money are always written with two places to the right of the decimal point ("like" decimals), the digits always "line up" correctly. Thus the problems children encounter will not be substantially different from those found in addition of whole numbers.

In adding decimal fractions, problems should be presented in both the horizontal and vertical forms. If all the problems are presented in the vertical form, the students are not being given the opportunity to decide how the problem needs to be written for computational purposes. This is a particularly important skill needed for adding and subtracting "unlike" decimal fractions.

ADDITION OF "UNLIKE" DECIMAL FRACTIONS

Adding "unlike" decimal fractions refers to problems such as 0.4 + 1.23, where one addend is expressed in tenths and the other in hundredths. In addition of *unlike* common fractions such as $\frac{1}{4} + \frac{3}{8}$, the addends were renamed to *like* fractions $\frac{2}{8}$ and $\frac{3}{8}$. Similarly, "unlike" decimals 0.4 and 1.23 are often renamed to "like" decimals, 0.40 and 1.23. Although it is not necessary to rename in *addition* of decimal fractions, it is needed in subtraction for problems like 3.2 − 1.84.

Grids were used to represent the problem 1.3 + 0.27 (Figure 8-30a). In working through the problem, the students observed, "We need to add tenths to tenths and hundredths to hundredths. We have 7 hundredths, but there are no hundredths in the other number . . . so we have 7 hundredths altogether. 3 tenths and 2 tenths are 5 tenths . . . so 1 one, 5 tenths, and 7 hundredths or one and fifty-seven hundredths (1.57)." To

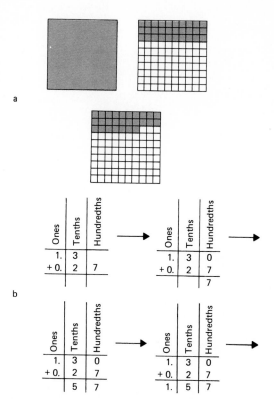

a

b

FIGURE 8-30.
Adding "unlike" decimals using grids.

solved the problem (Figure 8-30b). "7 hundredths plus . . . 1.3 has no hundredths, but that is really 0 hundredths. If we write in 0, it shows 1.30. Since 3 rows are 30 small squares, 1 and 30 hundredths is another name for 1 and 3 tenths. So 7 hundredths and 0 hundredths is 7 hundredths. (Record) Then 3 tenths and 2 more tenths is 5 tenths. (Record) . . . And one. (Record)"

This algorithm should also be related to the common fraction form (Figure 8-31). The problem 1.3 + 0.27 is renamed to common fraction form. The addend $1\frac{3}{10}$ is then renamed to hundredths and then added. The fraction form for 1.30 + 0.27 is $1\frac{30}{100} + \frac{27}{100}$, a problem involving addition of like fractions.

A common error in the addition of decimals results from overgeneralization of a concept for addition of whole numbers. When students were given whole-number addition problems in horizontal form, they may have learned to write the vertical form for computation by "lining up the last digit on the right." Sometimes students will try to use this same rule for the addition of decimals.

When the decimals to be added are "like," this "rule" still works (Figure 8-32a). However, when "unlike" decimals are added, results such as shown in Figure 8-32b are obtained. Students need to realize why the "rule" worked for whole numbers. Since the "last place to the right" in a whole number is always the ones column, the "rule" resulted in lining up all place values—ones with ones, tens with tens, and so on.

relate the process of using the model to the written form, the class went back and re-

$$
\begin{array}{l}
1.3 \\
+\,0.27
\end{array}
\longrightarrow
\begin{array}{r}
1\frac{3}{10} = 1\frac{30}{100} \\
+\frac{27}{100} = +\frac{27}{100} \\
\hline
1\frac{57}{100}
\end{array}
$$

$$
\begin{array}{l}
1.30 \\
+\,0.27
\end{array}
\longrightarrow
\begin{array}{r}
1\frac{30}{100} \\
+\ \frac{27}{100} \\
\hline
1\frac{57}{100}
\end{array}
$$

FIGURE 8-31.
Relating addition of "unlike" decimal fractions to common fractions.

$$
\begin{array}{r}
6.47 \\
12.23 \\
+\ 0.86 \\
\hline
19.56
\end{array}
\qquad
\begin{array}{r}
2.4 \\
32.46 \\
+\ \ 3.8 \\
\hline
33.08
\end{array}
\qquad
\begin{array}{r}
2.4 \\
32.46 \\
+3.8 \\
\hline
38.66
\end{array}
$$

a　　　　　　b　　　　　　c

FIGURE 8-32.
Decimal addition.

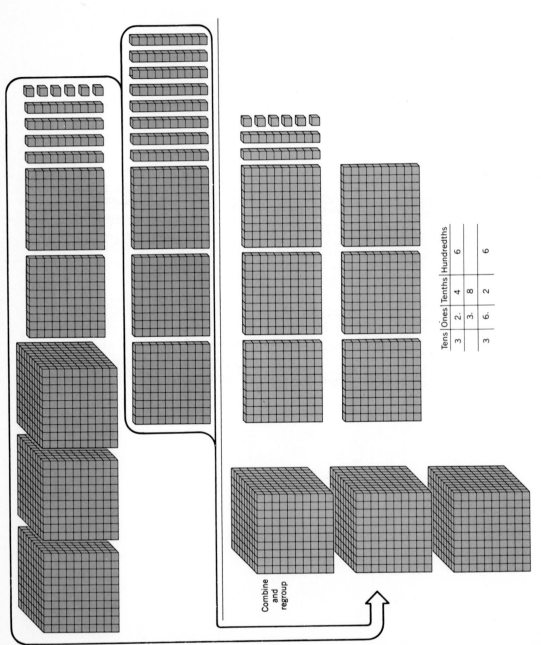

Tens	Ones	Tenths	Hundredths
3	2.	4	6
	3.	8	
	2		
3	6.	2	6

Combine
and
regroup

FIGURE 8-33.
Decimal addition with base-ten blocks.

Similarly, they need to generalize that to add decimals they must "line up place values"—ones with ones, tenths with tenths, hundredths with hundredths (Figure 8-32c).

Models are helpful for students who are having this kind of problem. If the problem 32.46 + 3.8 were solved using base-ten blocks (the flat is redefined as equal to one), students would automatically add hundredths to hundredths, tenths to tenths, and so on, as the physical representation of each is different (Figure 8-33). When the numerals are recorded in the appropriate columns of a place-value table, the students will find that the place values are lined up and so are the decimal points. These activities can help them generalize the appropriate rule that "to add decimals, line up the place values."

Use of a place-value table simplifies the addition of "unlike" decimals. It was not necessary to place the zero in the hundredths column (Figure 8-30b), but it helped the students understand that the space represented 0 hundredths. In the students' beginning work they should record and practice the algorithm on a page that has place-value tables. Some students may continue placing the zero in an empty column, especially when place-value charts are no longer needed for recording.

In planning lessons and in evaluating students' learning, the teacher needs to be aware that many students who can correctly solve a decimal addition problem presented in correct vertical form cannot solve the same problem presented in horizontal form. When problems are presented in vertical form, the addition is not significantly different from whole-number addition. Thus students do not need a great deal of practice in *computation* with decimals. What is needed is careful *concept development*. Discussions and evaluations should include questions on determining what answers are reasonable,

estimating answers, drawing appropriate representations to explain problems, and applying decimal concepts to real-life situations.

ESTIMATION FOR ADDITION OF DECIMAL FRACTIONS

Just as students began the addition of decimal fractions with adding tenths to tenths, they should also begin estimating these sums. Estimation for addition of decimal fractions is closely related to the same kind of estimation with whole numbers. The only real difference is the place value of the front end. Exercises for estimation should help students focus on the appropriate front end (Figure 8-34). The same estimation techniques described in the section "Estimation and Mental Computation for Addition of Whole Numbers" in Chapter 6 are also appropriate for addition of decimal fractions.

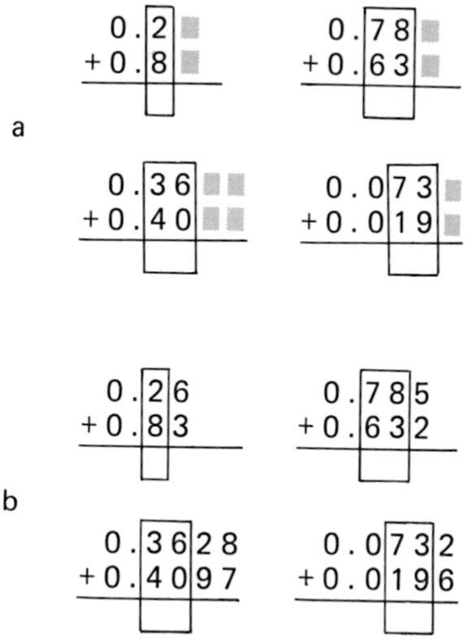

FIGURE 8-34.
Estimating sums of "like" decimal fractions.

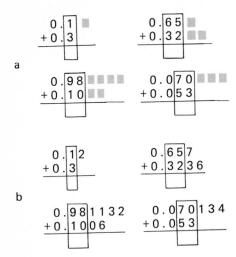

a

b

FIGURE 8-35.
Estimating sums of "unlike" decimal fractions.

$$\begin{array}{r} 2\,1.5 \\ 1.8\,1\,3 \\ 4.1\,4 \\ \hline 3\,4.4\,2 \end{array}$$

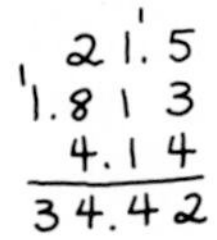

FIGURE 8-36.
Estimating to catch errors in decimal addition.

After students have had experience with estimating sums for "like" decimal fractions, they should extend these skills to "unlike" decimals (Figure 8-35). In part (a), the students are forced to concentrate on the front end because the rest of the digits are not given but only indicated. Part (b) shows a transitional exercise. Later students should be given estimation exercises without these "crutches." Problems should sometimes be given in horizontal form and estimation skills should be extended to include mixed numbers.

Some students, when given the problem 21.5 + 1.813 + 4.14 in horizontal form, will add as shown in Figure 8-36. They may have memorized a rule such as "line up the last digit" instead of developing the concept of adding the digits within each place value. One way to correct this problem is to help students be aware of the reasonableness of their answers. Proper questioning can lead students to observe that they are adding the whole numbers 21, 1, and 4 and some decimal fractions. By looking back at the original problem, they can see that 34.42 is an unreasonable answer. Since 21 + 1 + 4 is 26, any answer less than 26 is unreasonable. Since the three parts not considered in this estimate are all fractions less than one, their total cannot be more than 3. Thus the answer to the original problem cannot be more than 29 or less than 26.

In the above problem, a form of the front-end addition strategy was used to estimate the range of the answer. The front-end strategy can be applied to obtain a more exact estimate. After mentally adding the whole numbers, the parts are considered. In this case a student could think, "0.813 and 0.14 . . . 8 tenths and 2 tenths is 1. So 26 . . . 27, so my answer will be more than 27 or 27 plus 5 more tenths for an estimate of 27 and 5 tenths." Notice that this student rounded 0.14 to 0.2, although it is closer to 0.1. Because 0.8 and 0.2 have a sum of 1, they are compatible numbers.

Rounding to whole numbers is another strategy that could have been used. In the example 21.5 + 1.813 + 4.14, the numbers would be rounded to 22 + 2 + 4. An estimate of 28 would be obtained.

As was the case with adding larger mixed common fractions, in adding larger mixed decimal fractions the fractional parts become insignificant. For example, 23.8 + 53.067 + 38.5 could be rounded to 20 + 50 + 40 or to 24 + 53 + 40, depending on the skill of the student.

In estimating larger numbers students should also consider numbers that are compatible, that is, ones that make combinations which are easy to add. For example, to add 23.8 + 53.067 + 81.256 a student may think "20 plus 80 is 100. Since I rounded both 23.8 and 81.256 down, I will round 53.067 up to 55. So my estimate is 155."

In addition of whole numbers, some students had difficulty in estimating a sum for 546 + 309 + 215 + 87 + 351 because they did not notice that the digit 8, although it was the front digit of 87, was not part of the front end of the problem. The front end of the problem was in the hundreds not the tens. The same problem occurs in estimating decimal sums (Figure 8-37).

In this example, Lindy looked only at the front nonzero digit in each number. She failed to consider what was the front *place value* for the whole problem. Louie did con-

sider the place values. For each problem he added only those digits that were in the largest place value of the problem and adjusted this sum based on the second largest place value. In the first example Lindy and Louie have the same estimate because all the addends had the same place values. In the third example, Lindy has not realized that when she is adding 65 hundredths and 8 hundredths, the third addend of 2 thousandths will have very little effect on the sum. Lindy needs more practice with the type of estimating shown in Figure 8-35.

This practice should also include some problems in which the addends do not all have their first nonzero digit in the same place value (Figure 8-38). These exercises are arranged in developmental sequence both from left to right and from top to bottom.

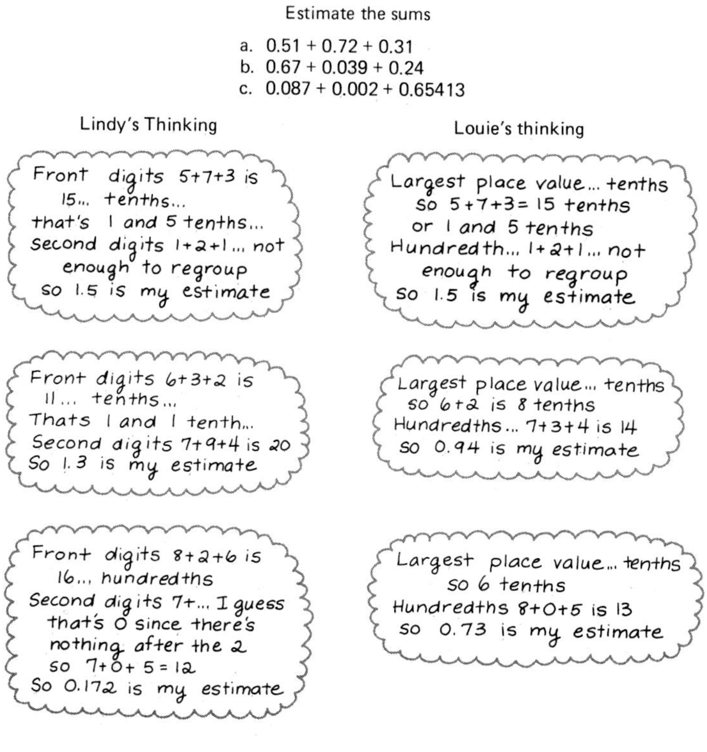

Estimate the sums

a. 0.51 + 0.72 + 0.31
b. 0.67 + 0.039 + 0.24
c. 0.087 + 0.002 + 0.65413

FIGURE 8-37.

Estimating decimal sums.

Lindy's Thinking

Front digits 5+7+3 is
  15... tenths...
that's 1 and 5 tenths...
Second digits 1+2+1... not
  enough to regroup
so 1.5 is my estimate

Louie's thinking

Largest place value... tenths
  so 5+7+3= 15 tenths
  or 1 and 5 tenths
Hundredth... 1+2+1... not
  enough to regroup
so 1.5 is my estimate

Front digits 6+3+2 is
  11... tenths...
Thats 1 and 1 tenth...
Second digits 7+9+4 is 20
So 1.3 is my estimate

Largest place value... tenths
  so 6+2 is 8 tenths
Hundredths... 7+3+4 is 14
so 0.94 is my estimate

Front digits 8+2+6 is
  16..., hundredths
Second digits 7+... I guess
  that's 0 since there's
  nothing after the 2
  so 7+0+ 5 = 12
So 0.172 is my estimate

Largest place value... tenths
  so 6 tenths
Hundredths 8+0+5 is 13
so 0.73 is my estimate

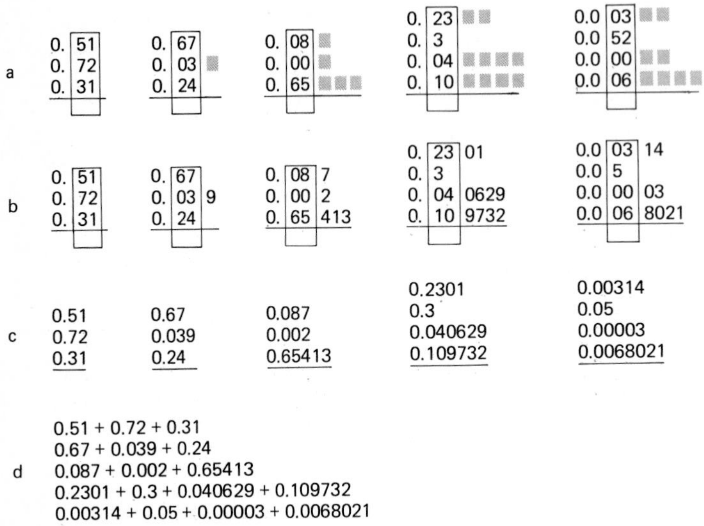

FIGURE 8-38.

Developmental levels for estimating sums of decimal fractions.

a
0. 51	0. 67	0. 08	0. 23 ▪▪	0.0 03 ▪▪
0. 72	0. 03 ▪	0. 00 ▪	0. 3	0.0 52
0. 31	0. 24	0. 65 ▪▪▪	0. 04 ▪▪▪▪	0.0 00 ▪▪
			0. 10 ▪▪▪▪	0.0 06 ▪▪▪▪

b
0. 51	0. 67	0. 08 7	0. 23 01	0.0 03 14
0. 72	0. 03 9	0. 00 2	0. 3	0.0 5
0. 31	0. 24	0. 65 413	0. 04 0629	0.0 00 03
			0. 10 9732	0.0 06 8021

c
0.51	0.67	0.087	0.2301	0.00314
0.72	0.039	0.002	0.3	0.05
0.31	0.24	0.65413	0.040629	0.00003
			0.109732	0.0068021

d
0.51 + 0.72 + 0.31
0.67 + 0.039 + 0.24
0.087 + 0.002 + 0.65413
0.2301 + 0.3 + 0.040629 + 0.109732
0.00314 + 0.05 + 0.00003 + 0.0068021

These various levels would not all be presented in the same practice lesson. Rather, as students' skills increased, they would gradually be given more difficult estimation tasks.

Since students' skills in estimating vary, their estimates will also vary. Their thinking should be shared with the class. As a result of such discussions, students should broaden their repertoire of estimation strategies and consequently become better estimators.

QUESTIONS AND ACTIVITIES

1. Use a sheet of paper to solve each of the following problems.
   a. Shade in 2 eighths. Shade in 3 more eighths. How many eighths in all?
   b. Fold a paper into fourths. Shade in one fourth, then another fourth, . . . ,
   counting as you are considering one more part.
   c. 2 sixths plus 1 more sixth. How many sixths?

2. *Materials needed:* Fraction bars. Illustrate how to use fraction bars to solve the problems listed below. Record the appropriate algorithms. Record parts (a) through (c) using the oral names. Reflect on this format as compared to writing simply the number names. For the questions involving unlike fractions, write the renamed fractions as well as the original expression.
   a. One twelfth + 4 twelfths is?
   b. $\frac{1}{6} + \frac{5}{6} = \square$
   c. $\frac{5}{6} + \frac{2}{6} = \underline{\hspace{1cm}}$
   d. $\frac{3}{8} + \frac{1}{4} = \underline{\hspace{1cm}}$
   e. $\frac{1}{2} + \frac{1}{3} = \triangle$
   f. $\square = 1\frac{1}{3} + 2\frac{1}{2}$

3. For students who do not understand fractions a common error is to solve problems as follows $\frac{3}{4} + \frac{1}{7} = \frac{4}{11}$. How could the procedure of writing the oral names help prevent this type of thinking? How could it be used as a transition between

oral activities with models and the numerical form?

4. a. Use the procedure shown in Figure 8-5 to construct and solve the following problems on a number line.
(1) $\frac{2}{6} + \frac{1}{6}$
(2) $\frac{3}{4} + \frac{2}{4}$
(3) $\frac{1}{4} + \frac{1}{2}$
(4) $\frac{2}{3} + \frac{5}{12}$

b. *For your resource file:* Procedures that incorporate number lines and regions are described in "Fun with Fractions for Special Education" by Jacobson. How could you use these ideas to teach addition of fractions?

c. *For your resource file:* In "Ideas" by Ockenga and Duea, the game tic-tac-toe is combined with fraction models. Experiences for fraction concepts and addition and multiplication of fractions are included.

5. Use paperfolding to solve the following problems. Record the appropriate algorithms.
a. $\frac{1}{4} + \frac{2}{4}$
b. $\frac{3}{8} + \frac{7}{8}$
c. $\frac{2}{5} + \frac{3}{10}$
d. $\frac{1}{3} + \frac{5}{6}$
e. $\frac{1}{4} + \frac{2}{3}$
f. $\frac{3}{5} + \frac{1}{2}$
g. $1\frac{1}{2} + 2\frac{1}{3}$
h. $2\frac{1}{3} + 1\frac{5}{6}$

6. In Problem 5 you used models to add the fractional parts. Work through at least four of the problems with another student; at least one problem should be unlike related; another unlike unrelated; another should involve renaming a fraction to a whole number. For each problem one student should play the role of a teacher; the other student should play the role of an elementary student who is being introduced to the algorithm. Give a story situation to introduce and motivate each problem. Resolve the problems step by step with the models devising for each step appropriate

teacher questions that link the action on the model with the written form of the algorithm. Why is it helpful to record in a vertical format as opposed to a horizontal format? Discuss renamings and how they should be recorded.

7. Mary solved $2\frac{1}{3} + 5\frac{2}{5}$ as shown below. Although her procedure is not incorrect, it is inefficient and she is more likely to make errors due to the number of extra steps. Explain how you would help her develop more efficient procedures.

$$2\frac{1}{3} + 5\frac{2}{5}$$
$$\frac{7}{3} + \frac{27}{5}$$
$$\frac{35}{15} + \frac{81}{15}$$
$$\frac{116}{15}$$
$$7\frac{11}{15}$$

8. Use paperfolding to solve parts (a) and (b). Use a ten-by-ten grid to solve parts (c) and (d); define the grid as one whole. Record your results.
a. $\frac{3}{10} + \frac{2}{10}$
b. $\frac{5}{10} + \frac{7}{10}$
c. $\frac{6}{100} + \frac{3}{100}$
d. $\frac{23}{100} + \frac{7}{100}$

9. Reconsider Problem 8. Compare the processes and the solutions for Problem 8 with the processes and solutions for solving the problems below. Record in a place-value table.
a. $0.3 + 0.2$
b. $0.5 + 0.7$
c. $0.06 + 0.03$
d. $0.23 + 0.07$

10. Use base-ten blocks or a ten-by-ten grid to solve the following problems. Define the flat as one whole. Record the decimal fractions in a place-value table.
a. $\frac{3}{10} + \frac{14}{100}$
b. $0.3 + 0.14$
c. $\frac{23}{100} + \frac{9}{10}$
d. $0.23 + 0.9$
e. $1\frac{7}{10} + 3\frac{53}{100}$
f. $1.7 + 3.53$

11. Compare the problems within each set. How are they all alike?
- a. $23 + 15$ $3\frac{1}{4} + 2\frac{2}{4}$ $2.3 + 1.5$
- b. $23 + 18$ $3\frac{3}{4} + 2\frac{2}{4}$ $2.3 + 1.8$
- c. $200 + 8$ $\frac{1}{5} + \frac{3}{4}$ 2 tenths $+$ 16 hundredths $0.2 + 1.008$

12. a. Use Cuisenaire rods to solve the following problems. Define the orange rod as one whole.
- (1) blue rod = _____ dm
- (2) red rod and purple rod = _____ dm
- (3) orange rod and red rod = _____ dm
- (4) brown rod and dark green rod = _____ dm
- (5) $\frac{7}{10} + \frac{2}{10}$
- (6) $0.7 + 0.2$
- (7) $0.5 + 0.2$
- (8) $\frac{1}{2} + \frac{2}{10}$

b. Use Cuisenaire rods and a meter stick to solve the following problems; define the meter as one whole.
- (1) blue = _____ m
- (2) red rod and purple rod = _____ m
- (3) orange rod and red rod = _____ m
- (4) brown rod and dark green rod = _____ m
- (5) $\frac{7}{10} + \frac{2}{10}$
- (6) $0.7 + 0.2$
- (7) $\frac{3}{10} + \frac{17}{100}$
- (8) $0.3 + 0.17$
- (9) $0.5 + 0.2$
- (10) $\frac{1}{2} + \frac{2}{10}$

13. The problems below were done on a calculator, but the decimal point was not recorded. Use estimation to place the decimal point. A calculator could be used to check your answers.
- a. $2.3 + 1.45 = 375$
- b. $2.34 + 31.3 = 3364$
- c. $2.37 + 1.33 = 37$
- d. $0.34 + 0.26 = 6$
- e. $0.64 + 0.36 = 1$
- f. $12.6 + 1.2006 = 138006$

14. Solve the problems below using your calculator. Compare your procedures with other students. Reflect on any special

problems your students may have in solving the problems or in interpreting the sums. What guidelines could you give them?
- a. $\frac{2}{10} + \frac{16}{100}$
- b. 8 hundredths plus 62 hundredths
- c. $\frac{1}{5} + \frac{3}{10}$
- d. $\frac{1}{4} + \frac{2}{5}$
- e. $\frac{1}{3} + \frac{1}{2}$
- f. $\frac{1}{9} + \frac{2}{3} + \frac{2}{9}$

15. In Chapter 6 at the end of the section "Algorithm for the Subtraction of Whole Numbers," a calculator game by Kurtz was described. Modify that game for decimal fractions and play the game with a friend.

16. Consult scope-and-sequence charts from at least two elementary mathematics textbook series to determine at what grade level the following concepts are introduced; if the grade level is the same, check page numbers to determine which concept is introduced first. List the publishers and publication dates.
- a. word names and pictorial representations of one fourth, one third, and one half
- b. symbolic form and pictorial representations of $\frac{1}{4}$, $\frac{1}{3}$, and $\frac{1}{2}$
- c. decimal fraction for $\frac{1}{10}$
- d. decimal fraction for $\frac{1}{100}$
- e. decimal fraction for $\frac{1}{1000}$
- f. equivalent fractions
- g. addition of like fractions
- h. addition of unlike fractions
- i. addition of decimals
- j. subtraction of like fractions
- k. subtraction of unlike fractions
- l. subtraction of decimals
- m. multiplication of fractions
- n. multiplication of decimals
- o. division of fractions
- p. division of decimals

Why do you think so much time is spent on naming fractions?

17. Consider the estimation activities presented in Figures 8-19 through 8-25. Use these problems to evaluate another person's thinking. Interview an elementary student or a peer who is not taking this course.

a. Present the problems one at a time to the person being tested. Have them explain how they arrived at their estimates. Write a one-sentence description of their thinking for each task.

b. If they do not know any strategies, teach them appropriate strategies as you proceed through each task and help them apply them to new problems.

18. Consider the problems in Figures 8-34, 8-35, and 8-38.

a. How does each problem in part (a) differ from the other ones; that is, how does the content vary?

b. As a set, how do the problems in part (a) differ from those in part (b); that is, how does the pedagogy vary? In Figure 8-38 extend this question to parts (c) and (d).

SUBTRACTION OF COMMON FRACTIONS

The subtraction of fractions is closely related to addition of fractions. The same procedures that were developed for addition of fractions should be used with their subtraction. Since the concept of subtraction is not new to the students, the algorithm for subtraction of fractions can be introduced at the same time as the algorithm for addition of fractions.

In some textbooks renaming and addition of like and unlike fractions are introduced before subtraction of like and unlike fractions. In other textbooks renaming fractions and addition and subtraction of like fractions are introduced prior to addition and subtraction of unlike fractions. One advantage of the second sequence is that students

learn that *like* units are needed in order to add or subtract common fractions. When they begin work with unlike related fractions for either operation, the only new procedure is to obtain like units by renaming one of the fractions. Students need practice with this new renaming procedure. Whether the practice is with addition or subtraction is not as relevant as whether the practice is with the new procedure.

Students should become competent with these procedures (subtracting like fractions and renaming unlike related fractions) before beginning work with unlike unrelated fractions. In some textbooks operations with related and unrelated fractions are introduced on the same page. If the students have had many experiences with renaming, this may not be a problem. Otherwise, the teacher may decide to omit those problems with unlike unrelated fractions or use supplementary practice sheets until the students gain confidence in their ability to change unlike related addition and subtraction problems into like addition and subtraction problems. Learning is more successful if the process is broken into small, well-sequenced steps.

SUBTRACTION OF LIKE FRACTIONS

As with addition of like fractions, real-life situations should be used to motivate the topic and models should be used to develop the algorithm. Also, the emphasis should be on oral language with a gradual transition to the numerical forms. This topic could be introduced with the following story problem.

Five sixths of the garden needs to be weeded. During the evening Sandy finished two more sixths. What part of the garden still needs to be weeded?

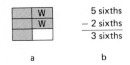

$$\begin{array}{r} 5 \text{ sixths} \\ -\ 2 \text{ sixths} \\ \hline 3 \text{ sixths} \end{array}$$

a   b

FIGURE 8-39.
Introducing subtraction of fractions.

The class could decide to use a piece of paper to represent the garden and then fold it into six equal-sized sections. They could then discuss how to represent how much needed to be weeded originally and how much Sandy did later (Figure 8-39a).

This type of discussion could take place while the children are developing fraction concepts. The discussion and action on the model could lead them to conclude that "Sandy had 5 sixths of the garden to weed. She weeded two more sixths. She had 3 more sixths to weed." Sentences such as these show that the children correctly interpreted and solved the situation. When these situations are introduced informally, no attempt should be made to link them to the algorithm. Later this same type of situation and process can be reintroduced to the children and linked to a written form (Figure 8-39b). These types of situations and the ones described in addition of like fractions should be the basis of the first lessons. Gradually, the numerical form can be introduced. When the oral forms are emphasized, the teacher should find that when children are introduced to the numerical forms

they will understand and master the written forms sooner and with less difficulty than if the numerical forms are introduced too early.

Two-step verbal problems should also be included in children's experiences. For example (Figure 8-40),

> David, who baked a batch of brownies, cut it into 15 pieces. When David came back from the store, he discovered that someone had eaten 3 pieces. David ate two more brownies with a glass of milk. What fractional part of the original cake was left?

The model clearly depicts the subtractions. In both this situation and the first one, the children used a "take-away" process to solve the problems. The teacher can write the word forms on the chalkboard during class discussion to help reinforce the numerical form.

SUBTRACTION OF UNLIKE RELATED FRACTIONS

Just as models were used in addition of unlike related fractions, models such as paperfolding, fraction bars, Cuisenaire rods, and number lines can be used to develop the subtraction algorithm. Whereas the take-away approach was used most often for subtracting whole numbers, the comparative approach is particularly helpful for subtracting fractions. This approach works well when using fraction bars as a model for subtracting

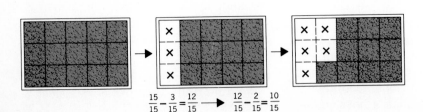

$$\frac{15}{15} - \frac{3}{15} = \frac{12}{15} \longrightarrow \frac{12}{15} - \frac{2}{15} = \frac{10}{15}$$

FIGURE 8-40.
Subtraction of like fractions.

fractions. The thinking is similar to the addition process. Figure 8-10 shows how to *add* $\frac{1}{3}$ and $\frac{5}{6}$. If the problem were changed to $\frac{5}{6} - \frac{1}{3}$, the renaming process would be just the same. The situation changes since the students are now considering how much more $\frac{5}{6}$ is than $\frac{1}{3}$. The process with the bars would be the same. Thirds cannot be compared to sixths, so 1 third is renamed as 2 sixths. The fraction bars for 2 sixths and 5 sixths are compared. Since 5 sixths is 3 sixths longer than 2 sixths, their difference is 3 sixths or $\frac{5}{6} - \frac{2}{6} = \frac{3}{6}$.

Other models from the addition section can be similarly used. The teacher should select models that are appropriate for the topic and that can be extended as the topic develops. After considering the models available and their familiarity with those models, teachers may choose to work exclusively with certain models. Whether or not a variety of models is needed depends on the topic and the students. Careful development with the model is needed for any topic. Students also need time to become familiar with the models. If students do not have prior experiences using a particular model for development of fraction concepts and for addition and subtraction of like fractions, they may have difficulty if the model is first introduced for unlike fractions.

Another model that can be used for either addition or subtraction of fractions is Cuisenaire rods. Comparative subtraction is used to find the difference between $\frac{4}{5}$ and $\frac{7}{10}$. First the students need to select the size of the whole. The five rod could be used for $\frac{4}{5}$ but not for $\frac{7}{10}$ (Figure 8-41a). The ten rod is selected as a possible whole and the black rod is shown as $\frac{7}{10}$, as it is 7 units long as compared to the whole of 10 units long (Figure 8-41b). The next decision is to determine whether the whole can be divided into fifths.

The 5 red rods are the same length as the orange rod, so each red rod represents one fifth (Figure 8-41c). If one red rod is 1 fifth, 4 fifths can be represented by 4 red rods or a length of 8. These four red rods could be exchanged for one brown rod (Figure 8-41d). A comparison should then be made; the difference is $\frac{1}{10}$ (Figure 8-41e).

Paper strips which can be folded are a model similar to both Cuisenaire rods and fraction bars, as they also are based on lengths. Paper strips were used to illustrate the process of solving the following problem (Figure 8-42).

Pat picked up two remnants of matching fabric to make curtains. The remnants were the same width but different lengths. One piece measured $\frac{7}{8}$ of a yard, the other measured $\frac{3}{4}$ of a yard. Since the short piece was the correct length, how much should be cut from the longer piece?

SUBTRACTION OF UNLIKE UNRELATED FRACTIONS

As with addition of unlike unrelated fractions, students need to have developed skills in renaming fractions and in adding and subtracting like fractions before being introduced to subtraction of unlike unrelated fractions. Figure 8-43 shows how the following situation was solved using like fractions on a number line.

Elizabeth's skirt is $\frac{2}{3}$ of a yard long and is presently too short. It needs to be $\frac{3}{4}$ of a yard long. What length of a ruffle needs to be sewn onto the skirt so that it is the desired length?

In this case a number line marked in twelfths, fourths, and thirds was used to solve the problem. From the number line it

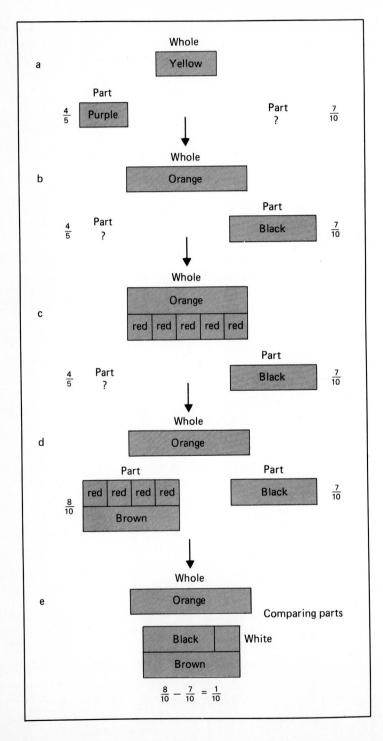

FIGURE 8-41.
Subtraction of related fractions with Cuisenaire rods.

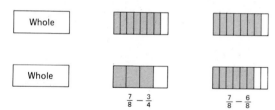

FIGURE 8-42.
Subtraction of unlike fractions—paper strips.

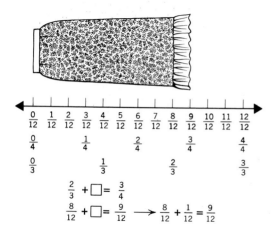

FIGURE 8-43.
Subtraction of unlike unrelated fractions.

both units into like terms—twelfths. The problem has been simplified to one of like fractions—finding the difference between $\frac{9}{12}$ and $\frac{8}{12}$.

A good model to show the renaming is fraction bars. To solve $\frac{3}{4} - \frac{1}{3}$ with fraction bars, the students will note that fourths and thirds are different-sized parts (Figure 8-44). However, fraction bars divided into twelfths will match both the fourths and the thirds as 12 is divisible by both 4 and 3. After renaming both fractions as twelfths by matching them with appropriate fraction bars, the students will observe that $\frac{9}{12}$ is $\frac{5}{12}$ greater than $\frac{4}{12}$ so $\frac{9}{12} - \frac{4}{12} = \frac{5}{12}$.

With paperfolding, the problem can be done similarly. The creases making fourths and thirds should be folded in opposite directions on separate sheets of the same-sized paper (Figure 8-45). Students should observe that the paper representing fourths must also be divided into thirds and the paper representing thirds into fourths. The papers should be folded accordingly. Consequently, $\frac{3}{4}$ has been renamed as $\frac{9}{12}$ and $\frac{1}{3}$ as $\frac{4}{12}$. Also, the first sheet has been folded so there are 3 times as many total parts and shaded parts or $\frac{3 \times 3}{4 \times 3} = \frac{9}{12}$. Similarly, the second sheet has 4 times as many total parts and shaded parts, so $\frac{1 \times 4}{3 \times 4} = \frac{4}{12}$.

As discussed in the section on addition of unlike unrelated fractions, this type of thinking should be extended so that students develop a procedure for finding the lowest

can be seen that another name for $\frac{2}{3}$ is $\frac{8}{12}$ and for $\frac{3}{4}$ is $\frac{9}{12}$. The ruffle of length $\frac{1}{12}$ needs to be added to the skirt to make it the appropriate length of $\frac{3}{4}$ of a yard. The difference between $\frac{3}{4}$ and $\frac{2}{3}$ was found by renaming

FIGURE 8-44.
Subtracting using fraction bars.

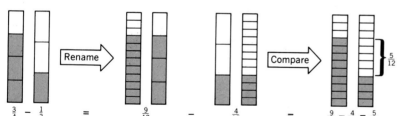

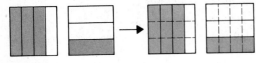

FIGURE 8-45.
Subtracting fractions using paper-folding.

common denominator. In the addition section, Figure 8-15 shows the steps and corresponding thinking for solving $\frac{5}{8} + \frac{1}{8}$. Figure 8-46a shows similar development for $\frac{9}{10} - \frac{5}{6}$ *and* extends this thinking in parts (b), (c), and (d) to a process without models. This is a strategy using multiples. It is an organized list of "try" numbers. Students should be de-

veloping and applying their number sense. In part (d), they should realize that 5 must be a factor and should not need to go through the list shown. This should then lead to a discussion on analyzing the factors to determine the least common multiple or lowest common denominator.

SUBTRACTION OF MIXED NUMBERS

Subtracting mixed numbers is no different from subtracting whole numbers or fractions. In subtracting a two-digit number, the student subtracts the smallest unit—the ones—first. In subtracting mixed numbers, the fractional parts are subtracted first. Paperfolding

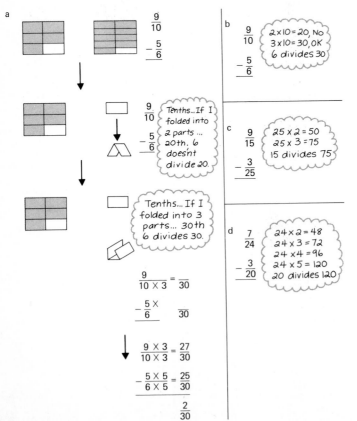

FIGURE 8-46.
Finding the lowest common denominator.

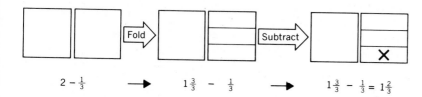

FIGURE 8-47.
Subtracting mixed numbers with paperfolding.

and fraction bars can be used effectively to show this process. For example, to show $2 - \frac{1}{3}$, the student could start with two whole sheets of paper. Since $\frac{1}{3}$ needs to be subtracted, one of the sheets can be folded into thirds or renamed as thirds (Figure 8-47). Now $\frac{1}{3}$ can be subtracted, so $1\frac{3}{3} - \frac{1}{3} = 1\frac{2}{3}$.

To subtract $2\frac{1}{6} - \frac{5}{6}$ with fraction bars, the representation of $2\frac{1}{6}$ should first be found. The fraction bars representing two should be placed face down (Figure 8-48). Since 5 sixths cannot be subtracted from 1 sixth, one of the bars representing two is flipped over to show 6 sixths. Now $2\frac{1}{6}$ has been renamed $1\frac{7}{6}$; consequently, $1\frac{7}{6} - \frac{5}{6} = 1\frac{2}{6}$.

The developmental algorithm for mixed numbers is shown in Figure 8-49. The number 4 is renamed as $3\frac{12}{12}$. The $\frac{12}{12}$ is added to the $\frac{5}{12}$ making $\frac{17}{12}$. Now $\frac{11}{12}$ is subtracted from $\frac{17}{12}$, and then 2 is subtracted from 3.

For subtracting mixed numbers some students change both mixed numbers to fraction form. Although this is an acceptable process, it can lead to incorrect answers as there is more opportunity for error since

more steps are needed to solve the problem. Also, if the problem is one such as $7\frac{7}{12} - 1\frac{11}{12}$, the numbers are awkward as the problem becomes $\frac{91}{12} - \frac{23}{12}$. The forms shown in Figure 8-50 are the ones that should be introduced and taught to the students. Those forms are simply an extension of the renaming algorithm for whole numbers.

Many common error patterns in the subtraction of mixed numbers are similar to those already discussed for whole numbers. Another common error occurs when a problem such as $3 - 1\frac{1}{3}$ is written vertically. Students often obtain an answer of $2\frac{1}{3}$. They are confusing subtraction with addition. If stu-

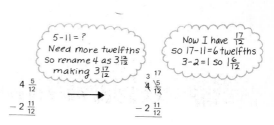

FIGURE 8-49.
Subtraction of mixed numbers with regrouping.

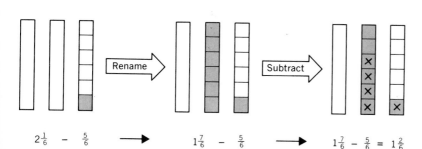

FIGURE 8-48.
Subtracting mixed numbers with fraction bars.

a   b

$$7\frac{7}{12} = \quad 6\frac{19}{12}$$

$$\begin{array}{c} 6 \quad 19 \\ \cancel{7} \quad \cancel{\frac{7}{12}} \end{array}$$

$$-1\frac{11}{12} = -1\frac{11}{12}$$

$$-1\frac{11}{12}$$

FIGURE 8-50.
Subtracting mixed numbers.

$\frac{12}{12} - \frac{11}{12} = \frac{1}{12}$	$\frac{12}{12} - \frac{2}{12} = \frac{10}{12}$	$\frac{12}{12} - \frac{5}{12} = \frac{7}{12}$
$\frac{23}{23} - \frac{21}{23} = \frac{2}{23}$	$\frac{23}{23} - \frac{5}{23} = \frac{18}{23}$	$\frac{23}{23} - \frac{11}{23} = \frac{12}{23}$
$\frac{17}{17} - \frac{16}{17} = \frac{1}{17}$	$\frac{17}{17} - \frac{1}{17} = \frac{16}{17}$	$\frac{17}{17} - \frac{9}{17} = \frac{8}{17}$
$\frac{43}{43} - \frac{40}{43} = \frac{3}{43}$	$\frac{43}{43} - \frac{4}{43} = \frac{39}{43}$	$\frac{43}{43} - \frac{20}{43} = \frac{23}{43}$

FIGURE 8-51.
Patterns in subtracting a fraction from 1.

dents have developed number sense and learned to check their answers for reasonableness of results, they should realize that the answer should be less than two.

In the example $2\frac{1}{6} - \frac{5}{6}$, a common error is to change $2\frac{1}{6}$ to $1\frac{11}{6}$. Instead of understanding the process of renaming, the student is simply "borrowing" according to a memorized rule. Careful conceptual development should help students realize that 1 must be renamed as $\frac{2}{2}, \frac{3}{3}, \frac{4}{4}$, and so on, or in this case as $\frac{6}{6}$.

ESTIMATION FOR SUBTRACTION OF COMMON FRACTIONS

Before children begin trying to estimate answers to problems involving a fraction minus a fraction, they need practice to develop patterns for subtracting a fraction from one (Figure 8-51). From their previous experience with estimating fractions as near 0, $\frac{1}{2}$, or 1, they can form some generalizations about subtracting a fraction from one. They should notice that if the fraction subtracted is near one, the answer will be near zero, and vice versa. They should also notice that when the fraction subtracted is near one half, the answer will also be near one half.

When they begin estimating answers to problems of a fraction minus another frac-

tion, the children need to consider the relative sizes of the two fractions. They will note that when the fractions are relatively close together (both near zero, both near one half, or both near one) the difference between them will be near zero. However, if one fraction is near one and the other is near zero, the difference will be between one half and one.

ROUNDING AND FRONT-END ESTIMATION

After developing patterns for subtracting fractions, students need to extend these to differences of mixed numbers. In the previous section on subtracting mixed numbers, an error pattern involving renaming was discussed. When students subtract a mixed number from a whole number, they often subtract the whole numbers and ignore the fraction. In the example of $5 - 2\frac{1}{6}$ with an incorrect response of $3\frac{1}{6}$, a check of the reasonableness of results would have been helpful. In estimating the answer, a student should realize that 5 minus 2 equals 3. If more than 2 was subtracted, the answer must be less than 3. Consequently, $3\frac{1}{6}$ is an unreasonable answer.

In the section "Estimation for Addition

of Common Fractions," strategies for estimating with 0, $\frac{1}{2}$, and 1 were discussed. These strategies can be extended to discuss problems similar to the example discussed above. Consider the following three problems.

$$7 - 2\frac{1}{8}$$
$$7 - 2\frac{11}{25}$$
$$7 - 2\frac{47}{50}$$

These problems are all the same except for the fractional parts. If the students simply round, they will obtain answers of 5, 5, and 4, respectively. In the first two cases, using this strategy to check for the reasonableness of their answer, they would probably not notice incorrect responses of $5\frac{1}{8}$ and $5\frac{11}{25}$ for the first two problems. By reflecting on the size of the fractions they can improve their estimates.

The first problem is similar to the example of $5 - 2\frac{1}{6}$ discussed before. An estimate of "a little less than 5" would be obtained. In the second problem the student could think "7 minus 2 is 5. $\frac{11}{25}$ is about one half, so my answer should be around $4\frac{1}{2}$." In the third example the student could think "7 − 2 is 5. $\frac{47}{50}$ is about one, so my answer will be about 4 . . . a little more than 4." Alternatively, the student may think "$2\frac{47}{50}$ is about 3. 7 − 3 is 4. Since $2\frac{47}{50}$ is less than 3, my answer is more than 4."

If both of the mixed numbers contain fractions, the size of the fractions relative to each other should be considered (Figure 8-52). In each set, one of the problems contains fractions that are relatively the same size. For problems like $14\frac{14}{35} - 2\frac{11}{25}$, since the fractions are both near one half, the fractions can be ignored and the whole numbers subtracted. For problem (c) in set (1), since the fractions are both close to one, the fractions could have been ignored and the whole numbers subtracted. Alternatively, the same results could have been found by rounding as both numbers are being rounded in the *same* direction. For problems like $14\frac{1}{6} - 2\frac{11}{25}$, the students should note that one fraction is near 0 and the other near $\frac{1}{2}$. A good estimate could be found by considering $14 - 2\frac{1}{2}$ or $14 - 2$ is 12, $12 - \frac{1}{2}$ is $11\frac{1}{2}$.

The examples in Figure 8-52 were all written with fractions near 0, $\frac{1}{2}$, and 1. But some cautions on rounding are needed for other mixed numbers. In the problem $9\frac{1}{3} - 5\frac{2}{3}$ if the rounding strategy were used, a student would estimate "9 − 6 is 3, so the answer should be near 3," but the answer is $3\frac{2}{3}$, which is closer to 4 than to 3. In this case a better estimate could be found by rounding both numbers in the same direction as $10 - 6 = 4$. Similarly, for $9\frac{2}{3} - 5\frac{1}{3}$, rounding both numbers in the same direction to $10 - 6$ is a better estimate of the answer ($4\frac{1}{3}$) than rounding to $10 - 5$.

Students may wonder whether it is always true that both mixed numbers should be rounded in the same direction. A work-

	Set 1	Set 2	Set 3
a.	14 7/8 − 2 1/10	14 1/6 − 2 1/10	14 14/35 − 2 1/10
b.	14 7/8 − 2 11/25	14 1/6 − 2 11/25	14 14/35 − 2 11/25
c.	14 7/8 − 2 8/9	14 1/6 − 2 8/9	14 14/35 − 2 8/9

FIGURE 8-52.
Relative size of fractions.

Problem	Round normally	Round both same direction	Actual answer
$7\frac{2}{3} - 4\frac{1}{3} =$	$8 - 4 = 4$	$8 - 5 = 3$	$3\frac{1}{3}$
$8\frac{1}{3} - 3\frac{2}{3}$	$8 - 4 = 4$	$8 - 3 = 5$	$4\frac{2}{3}$
$6\frac{8}{12} - 4\frac{5}{12}$	$7 - 4 = 3$	$7 - 5 = 2$	$2\frac{3}{12}$
$10\frac{11}{12} - 5\frac{1}{12}$	$11 - 5 = 6$	$11 - 6 = 5$	$5\frac{10}{12}$
$12\frac{1}{5} - 7\frac{4}{5}$	$12 - 8 = 4$	$12 - 7 = 5$	$4\frac{2}{5}$
$12\frac{4}{5} - 7\frac{1}{5}$	$13 - 7 = 6$	$13 - 8 = 5$	$5\frac{3}{5}$
$12\frac{3}{5} - 7\frac{2}{5}$	$13 - 7 = 6$	$13 - 8 = 5$	$5\frac{1}{5}$
$12\frac{2}{5} - 7\frac{3}{5}$	$12 - 8 = 4$	$12 - 7 = 5$	$4\frac{4}{5}$

FIGURE 8-53.
Round normally or same direction?

sheet like the one shown in Figure 8-53 can help them explore this question. After students have completed the worksheet, teacher questions can guide their thinking. "Did you always get a closer estimate when you rounded both numbers in the same direction?" (no) "Did you sometimes get a better estimate by rounding both in the same direction?" (yes) "Look at the pairs of fractions in the problems where you got a better estimate by rounding in the same direction. Do you notice anything about the relative sizes of these fractions?" "Consider the problems where you got a better estimate by rounding normally (up if the fraction was more than one half and down if it was less). Do you notice anything about the relative sizes within those pairs of fractions?" For this part of the discussion, students may need more detailed questions to help them answer the more general questions. It may be necessary to direct their attention to a particular problem and ask them to find the difference between just the fractional parts and then to notice which rounding method gave them

a closer estimate. After studying the examples, they should be able to form the generalization that if the difference between the fractional parts is less than one half, a better estimate will be obtained by rounding both numbers in the same direction; if this difference is more than one half, rounding normally will give a better estimate.

As in estimating sums of common and decimal fractions, if the whole numbers are large, the fractional parts are insignificant. In these cases the numbers should be rounded to numbers that are easy for the students to subtract mentally. These results will simply give *estimates* of answers; they would not be appropriate for catching such errors as $234 - 32\frac{1}{4} = 202\frac{1}{4}$.

SUBTRACTION OF DECIMAL FRACTIONS

As in the addition of decimals, subtraction of decimals can be introduced by relating decimals to the following previously learned concepts: place value, fractions with denominators of ten or one hundred, and money. The algorithm for subtracting decimals is related to the algorithm for subtracting common fractions and the algorithm for subtracting whole numbers. To subtract decimals, the units must be the same as in subtracting like fractions.

To subtract whole numbers, the ones are always subtracted from the ones, the tens from the tens, and so on. By extending place value, students can observe that the tenths are subtracted from the tenths. Often the rule "line up the decimal points" is considered a new concept, but students should realize that by lining up the decimal points they are actually lining up the place values, which is not a new procedure.

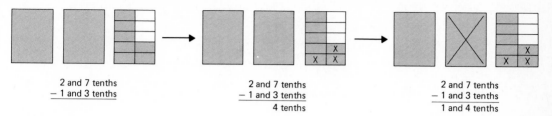

2 and 7 tenths		2 and 7 tenths		2 and 7 tenths
− 1 and 3 tenths		− 1 and 3 tenths		− 1 and 3 tenths
		4 tenths		1 and 4 tenths

FIGURE 8-54.
Subtracting "like" decimals step by step.

SUBTRACTION OF "LIKE" DECIMAL FRACTIONS

The algorithm for subtracting "like" decimal fractions is similar to the algorithm for adding "like" decimal fractions. As with addition of decimal fractions, paperfoldings, grids, base-ten blocks, and abacuses are appropriate models for developing this algorithm. The models would be used similarly but usually only the subtrahend is represented and the take-away approach is used rather than representing both numbers and using comparative subtraction.

Figure 8-54 shows step by step how paperfolding was used to solve 2.7 − 1.3. The model is marked, indicating each step of the process as tenths are subtracted first and then ones. Oral language is used to record each step. In the first lessons *only* the models and the oral language are used.

After experiences with models and oral language, children should be introduced to numerical forms for recording. Just as a relationship was established between addition of decimal fractions and addition of common fractions, subtraction of decimal fractions should be linked to subtraction of common fractions (Figure 8-55).

For both the common fraction and decimal fraction forms, the model is marked to show that tenths are first subtracted from

tenths. After the result is recorded, the ones are then marked to indicate take away and that result is recorded. The paperfolding model and the place-value chart are helpful in linking the concepts of subtracting common and decimal fractions. The appropriate oral language will also help students recognize that these are simply different forms for the same problem.

As with addition of decimal fractions and subtraction of common fractions, students will encounter decimal fractions where renaming is needed. If the problem discussed above were changed to 2.7 − 1.9, the ones would need to be renamed to tenths. In this case the students could fold one of the wholes into ten equal–sized pieces (Figure 8-56). The problem has now become 1 and 17 tenths minus 1 and 9

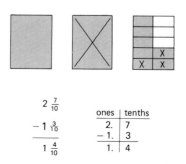

$$2\frac{7}{10}$$
$$-1\frac{3}{10}$$
$$\overline{1\frac{4}{10}}$$

ones	tenths
2.	7
− 1.	3
1.	4

FIGURE 8-55.
Subtracting "like" decimals.

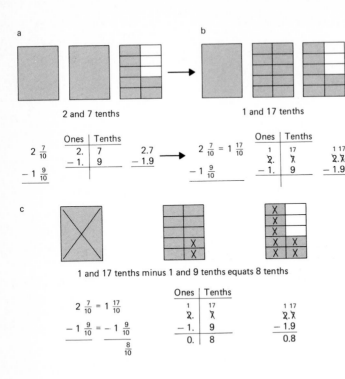

a

2 and 7 tenths

b

1 and 17 tenths

FIGURE 8-56.

Subtracting "like" decimals with regrouping.

$$2\frac{7}{10}$$
$$-1\frac{9}{10}$$

Ones	Tenths
2.	7
− 1.	9

2.7
− 1.9

$$2\frac{7}{10} = 1\frac{17}{10}$$
$$-1\frac{9}{10}$$

Ones	Tenths
1	17
2̶.	7̶
− 1.	9

1 17
2̶.7̶
− 1.9

c

1 and 17 tenths minus 1 and 9 tenths equats 8 tenths

$$2\frac{7}{10} = 1\frac{17}{10}$$
$$-1\frac{9}{10} = -1\frac{9}{10}$$
$$\frac{8}{10}$$

Ones	Tenths
1	17
2̶.	7̶
− 1.	9
0.	8

1 17
2̶.7̶
− 1.9
0.8

tenths and the subtraction can be completed. This subtraction should again be related to the common fraction form. The class should discuss the likenesses and the differences.

Figure 8-57 shows how subtraction of "like" decimal fractions with hundredths is introduced in a fourth-grade textbook. The diagram of grids is similar to a base-block representation of the problem 249 − 113. The only difference is that the flat is defined as one whole and the longs and units are shown as parts of a whole. In the second example, the emphasis is on place value and regrouping.

SUBTRACTION OF "UNLIKE" DECIMAL FRACTIONS

The level of difficulty varies among problems involving subtraction of "unlike" decimal fractions. The problems shown in Figure 8-58 are different as some of them involve renaming. The second problem involves a renaming from ones to tenths, the third involves renaming tenths to hundredths, and the last one involves two renamings. The students may be able to solve the first two problems simply by "bringing down the 7," but this will not help them understand the process of solving the last two problems. The first step in the first problem is not "bring down the 7" or 7 hundredths minus no hundredths. It is 7 hundredths minus 0 hundredths. The first problem has been represented with grids and strips in Figure 8-59a. Some students may think "3 . . . 3 ones . . . 47 hundredths . . . 40 hundredths, so I'll cover 40 squares or 4 rows of squares. Then I need 7 more small squares. Now I need to subtract 2 and 1 tenth. 1 tenth is one row, so I'll remove one strip of 10 squares or 10

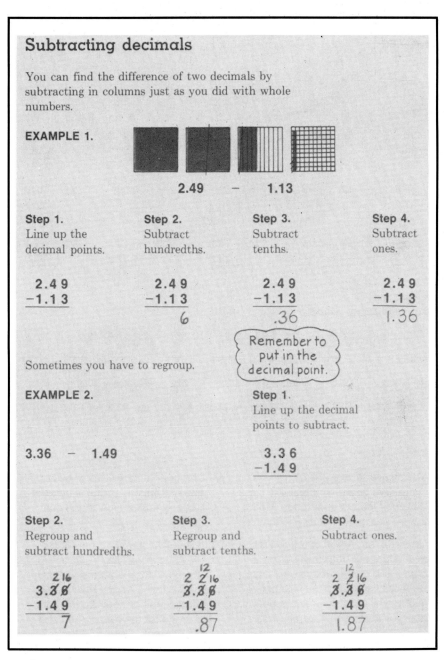

FIGURE 8-57.

Subtracting decimals. (From C.A. Dilley, D.W. Lowry, W.E. Rucker, **Heath Mathematics**, 1985, Grade 4, p. 336. Reprinted by permission of D.C. Heath & Company.)

$$
\begin{array}{cccc}
3.47 & 3.47 & 3.4 & 3.4 \\
-\,2.1 & -\,1.6 & -\,1.27 & -\,1.67 \\
\hline
\end{array}
$$

FIGURE 8-58.
Subtracting "unlike" decimal fractions.

hundredths. Take away 2 wholes and there is one left." This student is primarily considering like fractions (Figure 8-59b).

Other students may think "4 tenths . . . 4 rows, 7 hundredths . . . 7 small squares . . . need to subtract 2.1. Consider the smallest unit. No or zero hundredths to take away, so have 7 hundredths. 1 tenth . . . 1 row, so left with 3 tenths. Take away 2 wholes, so left with 1." These students primarily used place-value concepts to do the subtractions (Figure 8-59c). The thinking illustrated by both groups of students needs to be developed and discussed. The relationships between common fractions and place values for decimal fractions need to be clearly established.

A more sophisticated problem is one that involves renaming. Base-ten blocks were used to represent this process for the problem 3.4 − 1.27. This process is shown step by step in Figure 8-60. The teacher's questions to guide the students are included for each step. Note that in each case the students use the *model* to answer the questions and the results are then recorded. The teacher questions are essential to relate the work with models to the written form. The written form is then related back to the model through teacher statements such as "10 hundredths minus 7 hundredths equals 3 hundredths." These statements are necessary to help students realize that the results obtained from the *model* can also be obtained from the *written form*.

Metric measurement can also be used in subtraction of decimals. For example, "Ken cut 32 centimeters off a 1-meter board. How much of the board is left?" To solve this problem, Ken could convert 1 meter to 100 centimeters and solve the problem using whole numbers (Figure 8-61). Or Ken could have changed the 32 centimeters to meters.

a

FIGURE 8-59.
Subtracting "unlike" decimals using grids.

b

$$
\begin{array}{r}
3.47 \\
-\,2.1 \\
\hline
\end{array}
\qquad
\begin{array}{r}
3\frac{47}{100} \\
-\,2\frac{1}{10} \\
\hline
\end{array}
\qquad
\begin{array}{r}
3\frac{47}{100} \\
-\,2\frac{10}{100} \\
\hline
\end{array}
$$

c

$$
\begin{array}{r}
3.47 \\
-\,2.1 \\
\hline
\end{array}
$$

	1	$\frac{1}{10}$	$\frac{1}{100}$
3.	4	7
− 2.	1	

	3	$\frac{4}{10}$	$\frac{7}{100}$
− 2	$\frac{1}{10}$	$\frac{0}{100}$

Model   Teacher Questions

Show 3 and 4 tenths ⋯

What do we subtract
first? Can we take
away 7 hundredths? ⋯

⋯ How many hundredths
do we have now? ⋯ (Records)

1	$\frac{1}{10}$	$\frac{1}{100}$
3.	4	
− 1.	2	7

Now can we take away
7 hundredths? How can
we get more hundredths
Okay, regroup 1 long. Now
how many hundredths?
⋯ tenths? ⋯ (Records)

1	$\frac{1}{10}$	$\frac{1}{100}$
3.	4	0
− 1.	2	7

Now take away 7 hundredths?
How many hundredths remaining.
(Records) So 10 tenths minus
7 tenths is 3 tenths.

1	$\frac{1}{10}$	$\frac{1}{100}$
3.	3 4	10 0
− 1.	2	7

What do we subtract next?
How many tenths do we take
away? How many are left?
(Records) So 3 tenths minus
2 tenths is 1 tenth.

1	$\frac{1}{10}$	$\frac{1}{100}$
3.	3 4	10 0
− 1.	2	7
	1	3

What to subtract next?
How many ones did you
take away? How many
are left? (Records) So
3 minus 1 is 2. Our
answer is. . . (2 and 13
hundredths)

1	$\frac{1}{10}$	$\frac{1}{100}$
3.	3 4	10 0
− 1.	2	7
2.	1	3

FIGURE 8-60.
Developing subtraction algorithm for decimals.

```
100 centimeters              1.00 meters
–  32 centimeters       OR   – .32 meters
   68 centimeters            .68 meters
```

FIGURE 8-61.

Decimal subtraction using metric measurement.

Since there are 100 centimeters in 1 meter, 32 centimeters is equivalent to $\frac{32}{100}$ or 0.32 meter. Since Ken already knows that the answer is 68 centimeters or 0.68 meter, he can use this information to help discover the correct placement of the decimal points.

In working subtraction problems using money, children are usually given numbers that involve dollars and/or cents (Figure 8-62). In the first two situations the children do not need to use a decimal point. In the third case although decimal points are used, the children can still line up the last digit of each numeral and use the algorithms discussed with whole numbers to obtain a correct answer. As discussed earlier in addition of decimal fractions, children do not see the decimal point as separating whole numbers and fractional numbers but as separating dollars and cents.

Decimal point placement can be introduced by having students make change from dollar bills of various denominations. For example, if $1.32 is owed and a person pays with a five dollar bill ($5), the students can no longer line up the last digits in order to obtain a correct answer.

ESTIMATION FOR SUBTRACTION OF DECIMAL FRACTIONS

As with addition of decimal fractions, some students experience difficulties with problems presented horizontally which do not have the same number of decimal places in both numbers such as 34.2 − 1.16. They often line up the digits rather than the place values (Figure 8-63a). Estimation is a strategy that will help them realize that they made an error. First, both answers of 2.26 and 22.6 are unreasonable. If the students had used what they already know about estimation with whole numbers, they would have realized that the answer should be about 34 − 1 or 33. Estimation will make the students aware of their errors and may help them realize that they did not line up the place values. Procedures such as recording in place-value tables or annexing zeros to make "like" decimals will help them correct their errors. If the errors are conceptual, the algorithm should be redeveloped with models such as base-ten blocks, grids or place-value tables.

FRONT-END SUBTRACTION

Just as front-end estimation was used with addition of whole numbers, common frac-

```
8¢ – 3¢        33¢ – 17¢      $4.52 – $1.73
   8 pennies      33¢             $4.52
–  3 pennies    – 17¢           – 1.73
   5 pennies      16¢            $2.79
```

FIGURE 8-62.

Subtraction problems using money.

```
34.2    34.2
–1.16   –1.16
 2.26   22.6
```
      a

10's	1's	$\frac{1}{10's}$	$\frac{1}{100's}$
3	4.	2	○
–	1.	1	6

      b

FIGURE 8-63.

Correcting decimal errors.

Estimate the answers

a
$$\begin{array}{r} 0.5\boxed{6} \\ -0.1\boxed{3} \\ \hline \boxed{} \end{array}$$

$$\begin{array}{r} 0.7\boxed{0}\ \blacksquare\blacksquare \\ -0.3\boxed{6} \\ \hline \boxed{} \end{array}$$

$$\begin{array}{r} 0.0\boxed{8} \\ -0.0\boxed{6}\ \blacksquare \\ \hline \boxed{} \end{array}$$

b
$$\begin{array}{r} 0.5\boxed{6} \\ -0.1\boxed{3} \\ \hline \boxed{} \end{array}$$

$$\begin{array}{r} 0.7\boxed{0}31 \\ -0.3\boxed{6} \\ \hline \boxed{} \end{array}$$

$$\begin{array}{r} 0.0\boxed{8} \\ -0.0\boxed{6}2 \\ \hline \boxed{} \end{array}$$

FIGURE 8-64.
Estimating decimal subtraction.

tions, and decimal fractions and with subtraction of whole numbers and common fractions, this strategy can be adapted to subtraction of decimal fractions. Students should have some practice with estimating subtractions involving only decimal fractions (Figure 8-64). However, most situations in which they actually need to use decimal estimation will involve mixed numbers.

As discussed in the estimation sections for common and decimal fraction addition and for common fraction subtraction, the fractional part of a mixed number is considered only when the whole numbers are relatively small. First the whole numbers are subtracted, and then the estimate is adjusted by considering the fractional part. Examples applying this strategy are shown in Figure 8-65. The thinking is the same as with estimating subtraction of common fractions; the two fractional parts are compared and the front-end estimate is adjusted accordingly. In the last example, the decimal fraction is rounded to a familiar common fraction for ease in estimation and for obtaining a more exact estimate.

Examples   Student thinking

FIGURE 8-65.
Front-end subtraction with decimals.

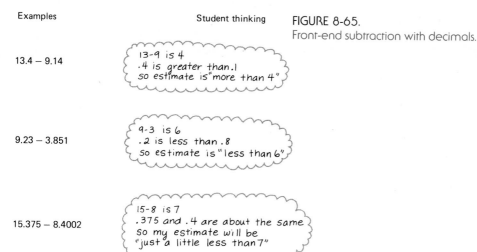

13.4 − 9.14

> 13−9 is 4
> .4 is greater than .1
> so estimate is "more than 4"

9.23 − 3.851

> 9−3 is 6
> .2 is less than .8
> So estimate is "less than 6"

15.375 − 8.4002

> 15−8 is 7
> .375 and .4 are about the same
> so my estimate will be
> "just a little less than 7"

6 − 2.476

> 6−2 is 4
> Still need to subtract about one half
> 4 − ½ is 3½

Example	Student thinking
13.4 − 9.14	13 - 9 is 4
9.23 − 3.851	9 - 4 is 5
15.375 − 8.4002	15 - 8 is 7
6 − 2.376	6 - 2 is 4

FIGURE 8-66.
Rounding to estimate subtraction of decimals.

ROUNDING

Rounding is also an appropriate strategy for estimating mixed decimal subtraction. When rounding, consideration should be given to the relative size of the fractional part as analyzed in the section "Estimation for Subtraction of Common Fractions" in this chapter. Rather than rounding to the nearest whole number, it may sometimes be more appropriate to round in the same direction. The examples that were illustrated in the preced-

ing section have been rounded in Figure 8-66. These estimates are not as accurate as the ones for front-end subtraction. For some problems these less accurate estimates are sufficient. In the last example the rough estimate may be appropriate to give an estimate for a real-life situation. If a student is using this estimate as a check for a computation, it would probably not be helpful.

Both of these strategies can be adapted for larger numbers. (A combination of front-end subtraction and rounding is applied for larger numbers.) In these cases due to the relative size of the numbers, the fractional parts can be ignored. This is similar to the way the digits in the smaller place values are ignored in estimating differences of larger whole numbers. The numbers should be rounded or adjusted so that the subtractions can readily be done mentally. Examples of different students' thinking are shown in Figure 8-67.

Since the fractional parts are ignored, the problems simply require estimating subtraction of whole numbers. Place-value concepts continue to be essential to this process as the students consider tens, hundreds, and so on. As can be seen from

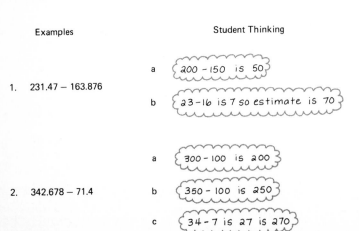

Examples		Student Thinking
1. 231.47 − 163.876	a	200 - 150 is 50
	b	23 - 16 is 7 so estimate is 70
2. 342.678 − 71.4	a	300 - 100 is 200
	b	350 - 100 is 250
	c	34 - 7 is 27 is 270

FIGURE 8-67.
Subtraction estimation with larger numbers.

the examples, the closeness of the students' estimates will depend on their skill with numbers. This is a learned skill which can be enhanced through class discussions. As the students practice estimates, time must be allotted for them to share their thinking.

QUESTIONS AND ACTIVITIES

1. Write a story problem for each of the following conditions.
   a. addition with unlike common fractions
   b. comparative subtraction with like common fractions
   c. missing addend with mixed numbers
   d. take-away with unlike common fractions
   e. multistep involving addition and subtraction of common fractions
   f. two-step involving subtraction of common fractions

2. a. Reconsider Problem 1. Change the term "common fraction" to "decimal fraction." Rewrite the situations; include at least three situations that include too much or not enough information.
   b. How are the situations that you wrote for part (a) and Problem 1 alike? How do they differ from the problems that you wrote in the section on whole numbers?

3. Use a sheet of paper to solve each of the problems below.
   a. Shade in 3 eighths. Cross off 2 eighths to indicate 2 eighths being taken away. How many eighths in all?
   b. Fold a paper into sixths. Shade in one whole or six sixths. Consider one part at a time; count backward from 6 sixths.
   c. 3 tenths minus 1 tenth. How many tenths?

4. *Materials needed:* Fraction bars. Solve the following problems using fraction bars. Record the appropriate algorithms. Record parts (a) through (c) using the oral names.

Reflect on this format as compared simply to writing the number names. For the questions involving unlike fractions, write the renamed fractions as well as the original expression.
   a. 5 twelfths minus 2 twelfths
   b. $\frac{2}{3} - \frac{1}{3}$
   c. $\frac{7}{6} - \frac{2}{6}$
   d. $\frac{5}{6} - \frac{1}{2}$
   e. $2 - \frac{1}{3}$
   f. $\frac{3}{4} - \frac{1}{6}$

5. Use paperfolding to solve the following problems with another student. For each problem, one student should play the role of a teacher; the other student should play the role of an elementary student who is being introduced to subtraction of fractions. Concentrate on the models and the oral language linking the new concepts to the student's prerequisite skills. Give a story situation to introduce and motivate each problem.
   a. $\frac{5}{8} - \frac{2}{8}$
   b. $\frac{12}{10} - \frac{3}{10}$
   c. $\frac{2}{5} - \frac{3}{10}$
   d. $\frac{5}{6} - \frac{1}{3}$
   e. $\frac{2}{3} - \frac{1}{5}$
   f. $\frac{3}{4} - \frac{1}{6}$
   g. $3 - 2\frac{1}{4}$
   h. $2\frac{1}{3} - 1\frac{5}{6}$

6. In Problem 5 you used models to subtract the fractional parts. Work through at least four of the problems with another student; at least one problem should be unlike related; another unlike unrelated; another should involve renaming a whole number to a fraction. Re-solve the problems above step by step with the models devising for each step appropriate teacher questions that link the action on the model with the written form of the algorithm. Why is it helpful to record in a vertical format as opposed to a horizontal format? Discuss renamings and how they should be recorded.

7. Use the procedure shown in Figure 8-5 to construct and solve the following problems on a number line.

a. $\frac{5}{6} - \frac{1}{6}$

b. $\frac{7}{12} - \frac{2}{12}$

c. $\frac{5}{6} - \frac{1}{3}$

d. $\frac{2}{3} - \frac{5}{12}$

8. Use paperfolding to solve parts (a) and (b) below. Use a ten-by-ten grid to solve parts (c) and (d); define the grid as one whole. Record your results.

a. $\frac{5}{10} - \frac{2}{10}$

b. $\frac{10}{10} - \frac{3}{10}$

c. $\frac{16}{100} - \frac{4}{100}$

d. $\frac{23}{100} - \frac{7}{100}$

9. Reconsider Problem 8. Compare the processes and the solutions for Problem 8 with the processes and solutions for solving the following problems. Record in a place-value table.

a. $0.5 - 0.2$

b. $1.0 - 0.3$

c. $0.16 - 0.04$

d. $0.23 - 0.07$

10. Use base-ten blocks or a ten-by-ten grid to solve the following problems. Define the flat as one whole. Record the decimal fractions in a place-value table.

a. $\frac{23}{100} - \frac{9}{10}$

b. $0.23 - 0.9$

c. $\frac{3}{10} - \frac{14}{100}$

d. $0.3 - 0.14$

e. $3\frac{4}{10} - 1\frac{13}{100}$

f. $3.4 - 1.13$

g. $2\frac{3}{10} - \frac{43}{100}$

h. $2.3 - 0.43$

11. Compare the problems within each of the following sets. How are they all alike?

a. $28 - 15 \qquad 3\frac{3}{4} - 2\frac{1}{4} \qquad 2.8 - 1.5$

b. $23 - 18 \qquad 3\frac{1}{4} - 2\frac{3}{4} \qquad 2.3 - 1.8$

c. $23 - 8 \qquad \frac{7}{8} - \frac{3}{4} \qquad 2$ tenths $-$
16 hundredths $\qquad 3.2 - 1.008$

12. a. Use Cuisenaire rods to solve the following problems; define the orange rod as one whole.

(1) How much longer is the dark green rod than the red rod?

(2) Brown rod $-$ dark green rod

(3) $\frac{7}{10} - \frac{2}{10}$

(4) $0.7 - 0.2$

(5) $0.5 - 0.2$

(6) $\frac{1}{2} - \frac{2}{10}$

b. Use Cuisenaire rods and a meter stick to solve the following problems; define the meter as one whole.

(1) How much longer is the dark green rod than the red rod?

(2) Brown rod $-$ dark green rod $=$ _____ m.

(3) $\frac{7}{10} - \frac{2}{10}$

(4) $0.7 - 0.2$

(5) $\frac{3}{10} - \frac{17}{100}$

(6) $0.3 - 0.17$

(7) $0.5 - 0.2$

(8) $\frac{1}{2} - \frac{2}{10}$

13. a. Sylvia solved the problem $4.28 - 1.3$ as shown below. She should realize that her answer is unreasonable. Why?

$$\begin{array}{r} 4.28 \\ -\ 1.3 \\ \hline 4.15 \end{array}$$

b. Describe how you could use base-ten blocks and/or a place-value table to help her correct her error.

14. The following problems were done on a calculator, but the decimal point and some zeros were not recorded. Use estimation to place the decimal point. A calculator could be used to check your answers.

a. $2.37 - 1.33 = 104$

b. $2 - 1.55 = 45$

c. $2.3 - 0.45 = 185$

d. $0.34 - 0.26 = 8$

e. $25.34 - 23.74 = 16$

f. $12 - 0.2006 = 117994$

15. Solve the following problems using your calculator. Compare your procedures with other students. Reflect on any special problems your students may have in solving the problems or in interpreting the sums. What guidelines could you give them?

a. $\frac{2}{10} - \frac{16}{100}$
b. 82 hundredths minus 62 hundredths
c. $\frac{2}{5} - \frac{3}{10}$
d. $\frac{3}{4} - \frac{2}{5}$
e. $\frac{1}{3} - \frac{1}{4}$
f. $\frac{2}{3} - \frac{2}{9}$

16. In "A Teaching Sequence from Initial Fraction Concepts Through the Addition of Unlike Fractions" by Ellerbruch and Payne, what sequence is recommended for the addition of fractions? How does subtraction of fractions fit into this sequence? Add this sequence and related teaching suggestions and activities to your file.

17. a. What are three generalizations that students should make after analyzing problems like those in Figure 8-51?
b. Use these generalizations to estimate the answers for the problems in Figure 8-52.

18. Interview an elementary student or a person who is not taking this course to determine whether he or she has acquired estimation strategies for subtraction of decimal fractions.
a. Present problems one at a time to the person being tested. Have the person explain how she or he arrived at each estimate. Determine whether or not they know both front-end and rounding strategies.
b. If they do not know any strategies, teach them appropriate strategies and help them apply these to new problems.

19. *For your resource file:* For guidelines on an estimation program and the evaluation of estimation, read and add the following to your resource file: "Teaching Computational Estimation: Establishing an Estimation Mind-Set" by Trafton and "Evaluating Computational Estimation" by Reys.

TEACHER RESOURCES

Ellerbruch, Larry W., and Joseph N. Payne. "A Teaching Sequence from Initial Fraction Concepts Through the Addition of Unlike Fractions." In *Developing Computational Skills,* 1978 Yearbook of the National Council of Teachers of Mathematics, pp. 129–147. Reston, VA: The Council, 1978.

Jacobson, Ruth S. "Fun with Fractions for Special Education." *Arithmetic Teacher 18* (October 1971): 417–419.

Ockenga, Earl, and Joan Duea. "Ideas." *Arithmetic Teacher 25* (January 1978): 28–32.

Reys, Robert E. "Evaluating Computational Estimation." In *Estimation and Mental Computation,* 1986 Yearbook of the National Council of Teachers of Mathematics, pp. 225–238. Reston, VA: The Council, 1986.

Reys, Robert E., Paul R. Trafton, Barbara J. Reys, and Judy Zawojewski. *Computational Estimation Instructional Materials,* Grades 6, 7, and 8. Palo Alto, CA: Dale Seymour Publishing, 1986.

Towsley, Ann E. "Ideas." *Arithmetic Teacher 34* (October 1986): 26–32.

Trafton, Paul R. "Teaching Computational Estimation: Establishing an Estimation Mind-Set." In *Estimation and Mental Computation,* 1986 Yearbook of the National Council of Teachers of Mathematics, pp. 16–30. Reston, VA: The Council, 1986.

9

TEACHING MULTIPLICATION AND DIVISION OF COMMON AND DECIMAL FRACTIONS

"$0.8 \div 0.02 = 40.$ $\frac{5}{4} \div \frac{1}{3} = 3\frac{3}{4}.$ I don't understand . . . With division you should get a smaller number." Evaluate this student thinking. How would you respond to such a student?

In a parent–teacher conference one parent stated, "I can understand why Trudy has trouble with math. I never did well in it either." How would you respond to the parents? To Trudy?

The purpose of this chapter is to develop meanings for the multiplication and division algorithms for common and decimal fractions. Situations and models are emphasized in order that students will be able to conceptualize and apply these operations. From these models, procedures for the operations are devised. The generalizations or "rules" for these procedures are secondary in importance. Of primary concern is helping the students develop the concepts. With such development, they are also more likely to be able to do the operations.

The development of the operations of decimal fractions follows the development of the operations of common fractions in this chapter. This is the traditional development found in most textbooks. Over the last years, decimal operations have been introduced earlier in the curriculum than in previous years. This is due primarily to curricular issues concerning the calculator and the metric system. Currently, there is no clear research to show which topic, common fractions or decimal fractions, should be taught first. Since common fractions are easier to conceptualize than decimal fractions, the teaching order of common fractions followed by decimal fractions was selected.

MULTIPLICATION OF COMMON FRACTIONS

WHOLE NUMBER TIMES A FRACTION

Multiplication of fractions can be introduced using the additive concept of multiplication for multiplying a whole number times a fraction. This type of fraction multiplication can be introduced with several of the models already described. Paperfolding could be

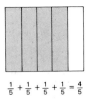

$$\frac{1}{5} + \frac{1}{5} + \frac{1}{5} + \frac{1}{5} = \frac{4}{5}$$

4 sets of 1 fifth is 4 fifths

FIGURE 9-1.
Multiplication as repeated addition.

used to illustrate the problem, "Brad was working on a special project. He completed 1 fifth of the project each evening. How much of the project was completed by the end of the fourth evening?" A paper was folded to represent fifths (Figure 9-1). Four of the one-fifth sections were then shaded. Four shadings of 1 fifth is equivalent to 4 fifths.

The first examples should include unit fractions. This should gradually be extended to fractions with numerators other than one. The repeated addition approach was also used to solve the problem, "Each of the three pillows requires 3 fourths of a yard of fabric. How many yards of fabric are needed for the project?" Donna used fraction bars to solve the problem.

First Donna found three $\frac{3}{4}$ bars (Figure 9-2). She observed that a total of 9 fourths of the whole was shaded. She found two

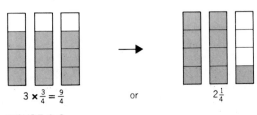

$3 \times \frac{3}{4} = \frac{9}{4}$ or $2\frac{1}{4}$

FIGURE 9-2.
Multiplication with fraction bars.

fraction bars that had four out of four total parts shaded and counted "4 fourths, 8 fourths so I need 1 more fourth." Donna recorded the information in repeated addition form and in multiplication form. She noted that 3 lengths of 3 fourths was a total of 9 fourths.

When students are ready to make the transition from working with a model to using an algorithm, it is important for them to recall that the denominator is the *name* of the fraction. Thus 2 × 3 fourths and 2 × $\frac{3}{4}$ are equivalent expressions. Students should realize that the situation is the same no matter whether the three units that they are doubling are 3 fourths, 3 tens, 3 centimeters, 3 minutes, or 3 books. By working examples of this type, students will soon discover that to multiply a whole number times a fraction, they multiply the whole number times the number of parts being considered. The oral and word forms are used to develop meaning for the numerical form as it is easier for students to conceptualize 2 sets of 3 tenths than 2 × $\frac{3}{10}$. After the students have been introduced to the numerical form, models and oral language should be used to reinforce this thinking.

FRACTION TIMES A WHOLE NUMBER

Since multiplication is commutative, multiplying a fraction times a whole number will give the same result as multiplying a whole number times a fraction. However, knowing that $\frac{1}{4}$ × 2 has the same *answer* as 2 × $\frac{1}{4}$ will not help students *recognize multiplication situations* that involve fractions times whole numbers.

Prerequisites for multiplying a fraction times a whole number are introduced informally in earlier grades as children learn to show fractional parts of sets. A sample les-

son from a fourth-grade textbook is shown in Figure 9-3. To show one fourth of a set, the children must think of fourths—four equal-sized pieces. The children then will need to divide the set of twelve into four equal parts. So the multiplication situation of $\frac{1}{4}$ of a set is solved by dividing the set by 4, a previously learned skill. This also reinforces the idea that a fraction ($\frac{1}{4}$) is simply another way of writing division (1 ÷ 4). Later these examples are extended beyond unit fractions to problems such as 3 fourths of the set. In the case of the objects shown in Figure 9-3, 3 fourths of the set would be 3 of the four equal-sized parts or 9 objects. This concept is encountered in such situations as

$\frac{1}{2}$ of the dozen eggs are left.

$\frac{3}{4}$ of the 24 students in our class passed their swimming test.

The job will take 5 hours and only one half of it is finished.

The present costs $24.36. We have collected two thirds of the money.

This approach is also similar to multiplication of a whole number times a whole number and of a whole number times a fraction. Just as students have found solutions for 2 sets of 3 units or 5 sets of 2 thirds, they can now find a solution for $\frac{1}{2}$ set of 4 units. Just as 2 sets of 6 is 12 and 1 set of 6 is 6, a $\frac{1}{2}$ set of 6 is 3. Since 2 sets of 6 can be written as 2 × 6, a $\frac{1}{2}$ set of 6 is the same as $\frac{1}{2}$ × 6.

The sequence of fraction topics varies slightly among textbook series. A fraction times a whole number may be formally introduced before or after the algorithm for a fraction times a fraction. In this section the multiplication sentences were written in the form $\frac{1}{3}$ × 18 or $\frac{2}{5}$ × 30, not the form $\frac{1}{3}$ × $\frac{18}{1}$ or $\frac{2}{5}$ × $\frac{30}{1}$. The first form is convenient for mental computation as $\frac{1}{3}$ × 18 would become 18

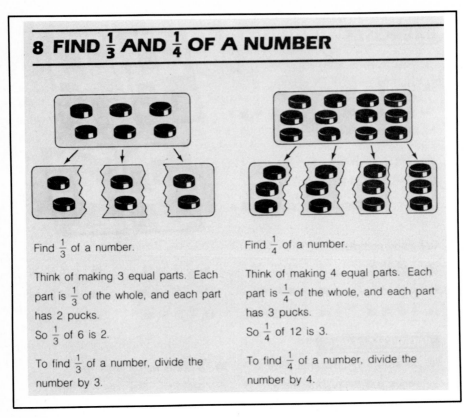

FIGURE 9-3.
Fractional parts of sets. (From Joseph Payne et al., **Harper & Row Mathematics,**
Grade 4, p. 300. Copyright © 1985, Macmillan, Inc. Reprinted with permission
of Scribner Educational Publishers, a division of Macmillan, Inc.)

$\div$ 3 and $\frac{2}{5}$ × 30 would become 30 $\div$ 5 ×
2. Also, the students need to be introduced
to a fraction times a fraction before problems
are written in the second form.

FRACTION TIMES A FRACTION

Both sets and arrays can be used to introduce students to the concept of a fraction
times a fraction. The language of sets that
was extended in the section on a whole number times a fraction can be used (Figure
9-4). To explain the meaning of the sets, an

example illustrating patterns could be used
such as "Several of Sue's friends each offered to bring pizza to the party. They
needed 3 pizzas, so Sue only needed 3 people to volunteer. Sharon brought her share
and Teresa's, as Teresa had to work late. (2
sets of $\frac{1}{3}$ is $\frac{2}{3}$, so Sharon brought $\frac{2}{3}$ of what
was needed; Figure 9-4a.) *But* Mike also
brought a pizza. (1 set of $\frac{1}{3}$ is $\frac{1}{3}$; Figure 9-4b.)
Bob apologized about his share. His
younger sister had helped herself, so he only
brought $\frac{1}{2}$ of his share. ($\frac{1}{2}$ of the $\frac{1}{3}$ that he had
volunteered was $\frac{1}{6}$ of the total amount

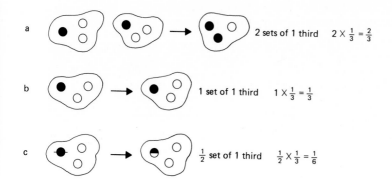

FIGURE 9-4.
Sets for fraction times a fraction.

needed; Figure 9-4c.)" By examining this pattern, students can see that finding $\frac{1}{2}$ set of 1 third is similar to finding 2 sets of 1 third, so $\frac{1}{2}$ of 1 third is the same as $\frac{1}{2} \times \frac{1}{3}$.

Another situation involving multiplication of fractions could be introduced as follows. "After school Mary Jane decided to have a piece of cake. Only one third of the cake was left in the pan. She ate a piece that was one fourth of this strip. What fractional part of the original cake did she eat?" First, one third of a rectangular region is considered. Since only $\frac{1}{4}$ of the 1 third is desired, the 1 third is cut into four equal-sized parts and 1 fourth of the 1 third is considered. To determine what part of the whole is being considered, lines are extended so that the entire region is divided into equal-sized pieces. Therefore, the part being considered can be seen to be one twelfth of the entire region (Figure 9-5).

In another situation, "Debbie and her brother were painting the living room. They were three fourths of the way finished when they stopped for lunch. If they both painted at the same rate, what part of the room did they each paint in two hours?" Debbie could solve this with paperfolding. To solve $\frac{1}{2} \times \frac{3}{4}$, Debbie first folded the paper in fourths in one direction. She opened it up and lightly colored in three of the sections to represent 3 fourths. She folded the paper in half in the other direction. She opened it and colored in one half of the 3 fourths. She noted that her share of the work was $\frac{1}{2}$ of $\frac{3}{4}$ or $\frac{3}{8}$ of the original rectangle (Figure 9-6).

Debbie's rectangular region could also be interpreted as an array. The part that she shaded measured $\frac{1}{2}$ by $\frac{3}{4}$. In one fifth-grade textbook, an array representing multiplication of whole numbers is used to introduce an array presenting multiplication of frac-

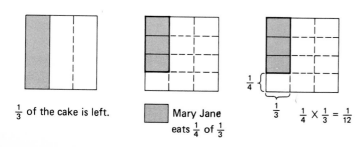

FIGURE 9-5.
Regions for fraction times a fraction.

$\frac{1}{3}$ of the cake is left.

Mary Jane eats $\frac{1}{4}$ of $\frac{1}{3}$

$\frac{1}{4} \times \frac{1}{3} = \frac{1}{12}$

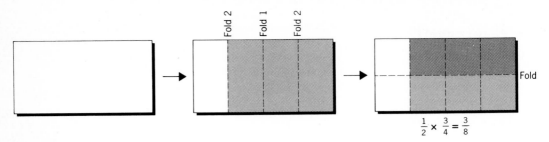

FIGURE 9-6.
Folding and coloring paper.

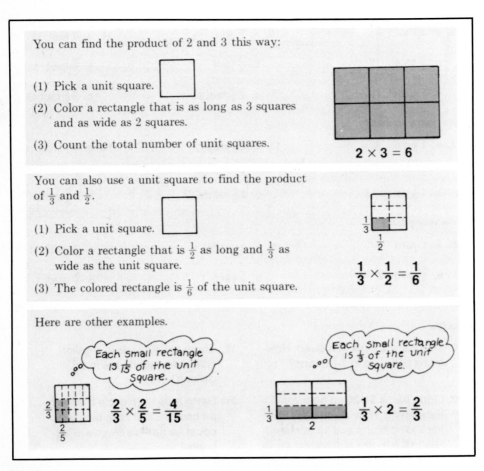

FIGURE 9-7.
Multiplying fractions with arrays. (From C.A. Dilley, D.W. Lowry, W.E. Rucker, **Heath Mathematics**, 1983, Grade 5, p. 212. Reprinted by permission of D.C. Heath & Company.)

tions (Figure 9-7). The lesson on this page is carefully structured so that the students review arrays such as 2 by 3 and 1 by 1. The array for whole numbers is then modified to introduce a fraction times a fraction.

After solving various examples using paperfolding and arrays, the students should record the original problems and their products. By studying their results, they should observe that the product could be obtained by multiplying the numerator times numerator and denominator times denominator.

The similarities among the fraction-times-a-fraction algorithm and the whole-number-times-a-fraction and fraction-times-a-whole-number algorithms should be discussed as they are introduced. The students should recall that any whole number can be written as a fraction with a denominator of 1. Thus $4 \times \frac{1}{3}$ is equivalent to $\frac{4}{1} \times \frac{1}{3}$ and $\frac{1}{2} \times 6$ is equivalent to $\frac{1}{2} \times \frac{6}{1}$. Some practice with problems where the whole-number factor is written in this form will help students realize that they are really using only one algorithm for all three "types" of problems (Figure 9-8).

In doing operations with fractions, sometimes it is desirable to express the fractional answer in simplest form. Along with the operations for the multiplication of fractions, the student should also be introduced to the simplification of fractions as an integral part of any algorithm. At this stage the student would already be familiar with the concept

(1) $\frac{3}{4} \times \frac{16}{15} = \frac{48}{60} = \frac{4\times12}{5\times12} = \frac{4}{5} \times \frac{12}{12} = \frac{4}{5} \times 1 = \frac{4}{5}$

(2) $\frac{3}{4} \times \frac{16}{15} = \frac{3\times16}{4\times15} = \frac{16\times3}{4\times15} = \frac{16}{4} \times \frac{3}{15} = \frac{4\times4}{4\times1} \times \frac{3\times1}{3\times5} =$
$(\frac{4}{4} \times \frac{4}{1}) \times (\frac{3}{3} \times \frac{1}{5}) = (\frac{4}{4} \times 1) \times (1 \times \frac{1}{5}) = \frac{4}{4} \times \frac{1}{5} = \frac{4}{5}$

(3) $\frac{\overset{1}{3}}{4} \times \frac{\overset{4}{16}}{\underset{5}{15}} = \frac{4}{5}$

FIGURE 9-9.

Multiplication and simplification of fractions.

of renaming fractions in simplest form. What needs to be developed is the idea that this simplification can be done before the multiplication as well as after it. By doing the simplification first, the multiplication problem is easier since the student is now operating with smaller numbers. This simplification process is especially useful when more than two fractions are multiplied.

In the example shown in Figure 9-9, Ed who did the first multiplication had to multiply 3×16 and 4×15. Then he had to find the greatest common factor for 48 and 60 and divide to express his answer in simplest form. Julie who did the second multiplication applied what she knows about the structure of the number system. She used the general definition for multiplication of fractions, the commutative law, and the identity property of one. Consequently, she has not had to solve any multiplication or division problem that is not a basic fact. Jeff who did the third multiplication used all the same properties that Julie did. However, he understands the process well enough so that he no longer needs to write out each step. He is using a form that is definitely simpler than Ed's or Julie's forms. All three forms of the algorithm are correct. For a permanent algorithm, each student should adopt individually whichever form works best.

Some students rewrite fraction multiplication problems with common denominators before doing the multiplication. This is not an incorrect procedure as equivalent numbers

Whole number times a fraction	$2 \times \frac{2}{3} = \frac{2}{1} \times \frac{2}{3} = \frac{4}{3}$
Fraction times a whole number	$\frac{3}{4} \times 5 = \frac{3}{4} \times \frac{5}{1} = \frac{15}{4}$
Fraction times a fraction	$\frac{2}{3} \times \frac{4}{5} = \frac{8}{15}$ •

FIGURE 9-8.

Fraction multiplication algorithm.

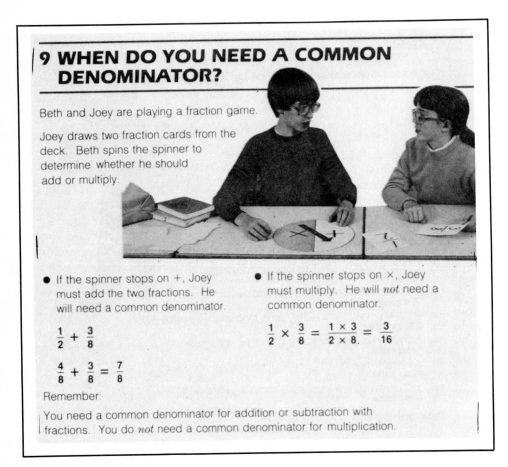

FIGURE 9-10.
Discriminating need for common denominators. (From Joseph Payne et al.,
Harper & Row Mathematics, *Grade 6, p. 266. Copyright © 1985, Macmillan,
Inc. Reprinted with permission of Scribner Educational Publishers, a division of
Macmillan, Inc.)*

are being multiplied, but it is an inappropriate one. (Again, due to the larger factors for the numerator and denominator and the extra steps, students are more likely to make errors.) Students who have developed understandings as to *why* common terms are needed in addition and subtraction are less likely to use inappropriate procedures. One textbook series contains a lesson on discriminating when common denominators are needed (Figure 9-10). This type of lesson helps students to extend their understandings of the operations as they compare different procedures.

MULTIPLYING WITH MIXED NUMBERS

Multiplication of mixed numbers is an extension of multiplication of fractions. The multiplication of mixed numbers does not require

a

(a) $3\frac{1}{2} \times 4\frac{1}{3} = \frac{7}{2} \times \frac{13}{3} = \frac{91}{6} = 15\frac{1}{6}$

(b) $4\frac{1}{2} \times 3\frac{1}{3} = \frac{\overset{3}{\cancel{9}}}{\cancel{2}_{1}} \times \frac{\overset{5}{\cancel{10}}}{\cancel{3}_{1}} = 15$

FIGURE 9-11.
Multiplication of mixed numbers.

b

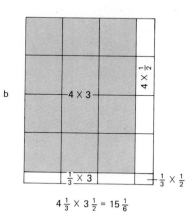

$4\frac{1}{3} \times 3\frac{1}{2} = 15\frac{1}{6}$

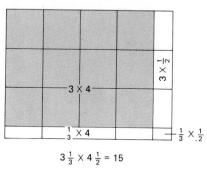

$3\frac{1}{3} \times 4\frac{1}{2} = 15$

c

$$
\begin{array}{r}
3\frac{1}{2} \\
\times\ 4\frac{1}{3} \\
\hline
\end{array}
$$

$\frac{1}{3} \times \frac{1}{2} = \quad \frac{1}{6}$

$\frac{1}{3} \times 3 = \quad 1$

$4 \times \frac{1}{2} = \quad 2$

$4 \times 3 = 12$

$\overline{\qquad}$

$15\frac{1}{6}$

$$
\begin{array}{r}
4\frac{1}{2} \\
\times\ 3\frac{1}{3} \\
\hline
\end{array}
$$

$\frac{1}{3} \times \frac{1}{2} = \quad \frac{1}{6} \longrightarrow \quad \frac{1}{6}$

$\frac{1}{3} \times 4 = \quad 1\frac{1}{3} \longrightarrow \quad 1\frac{2}{6}$

$3 \times \frac{1}{2} = \quad 1\frac{1}{2} \longrightarrow \quad 1\frac{3}{6}$

$3 \times 4 = 12 \longrightarrow \quad 12$

$\overline{\qquad}$

$14\frac{6}{6} = 15$

any new skills. When given such a problem, students change both mixed numbers to fraction form and then multiply the two fractions (Figure 9-11a). Both of these prerequisites have already been studied by the students.

A number of situations involving multiplication of fractions are partially described below. Some problems include whole numbers and dollar amounts.

Don needed to increase the recipe $1\frac{1}{2}$ times. The original recipe called for $2\frac{1}{3}$ cups flour, $\frac{3}{4}$ cup butter . . .

The air fare for children was $\frac{2}{3}$ the price of an adult ticket. Ken and Marilyn planned to take a family trip with their three children. The cost of an adult ticket was $135.

Peaches were priced at 49 cents a pound. Hyo bought $2\frac{3}{16}$ pounds.

The electrician worked for $3\frac{1}{2}$ hours at $35.50 an hour.

The students painted a mural on the wall that was $6\frac{2}{3}$ feet by $9\frac{1}{4}$ feet.

Some of these situations, such as the last one, visually suggest a rectangular region or an array.

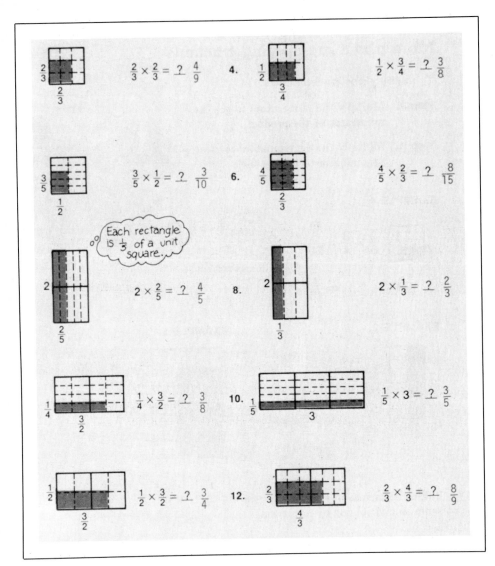

FIGURE 9-12.

Multiplication of fractions greater than one. (From C.A. Dilley, D.W. Lowry, W.E. Rucker, **Heath Mathematics**, 1983, Grade 5, p. 213. Reprinted by permission of D.C. Heath & Company.)

To show multiplication of fractions greater than 1, one fifth-grade textbook uses arrays (Figure 9-12). This is an extension of using arrays to represent multiplication of whole numbers and of fractions less than one. As with whole numbers and other fraction examples, the factors are the lengths of adjacent sides. The grids are marked in the same manner as in paperfolding; the unit of one must first be defined. In each case the

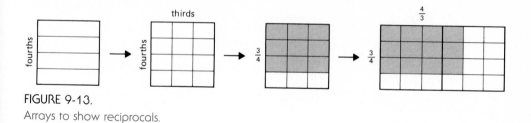

FIGURE 9-13.

Arrays to show reciprocals.

students should compare the shaded parts with the total in the whole or one.

One special array is used in *Harper & Row Mathematics* in division of fractions to introduce the reciprocal or the multiplicative inverse. Reciprocals are numbers that when multiplied have a product of one. In this situation the unit of one is subdivided by fourths and thirds, so it has been divided into twelfths (Figure 9-13). When $\frac{3}{4}$ of the *unit* is considered, we only have $\frac{3}{4}$. If we consider $\frac{3}{4}$ times $\frac{4}{3}$, we have $\frac{12}{12}$ or 1.

Another algorithm for the multiplication of mixed numbers does not require renaming the mixed numbers (Figure 9-11c). This algorithm, too, is a simple extension of what students already know. In multiplying two-digit whole numbers, they multiplied ones times ones, ones times tens and then tens times ones, tens times tens. In multiplying mixed numbers they must multiply fraction times fraction, fraction times whole number, and whole number times fraction, whole number times whole number. In each case, the four partial products are then added to yield the final answer.

As can be seen from the array (Figure 9-11b), the whole number times the whole number contributes the most to the size of the product of two mixed numbers and the fraction times the fraction contributes the least. The relative size of these partial products is the basis of why and how we use the mixed number form in mental computation. The thinking described in the next section is based on the array and the mixed-number form.

ESTIMATION FOR MULTIPLICATION OF COMMON FRACTIONS

As with the other operations, estimations are used to obtain approximate answers when exact ones are not needed or to check on the reasonableness of our computations. An estimation is often sufficient to determine an approximation for the cost of carpeting a room, the amount of seed needed to replace part of the lawn, the weight of $3\frac{1}{2}$ boxes of books, and so on. In most of these situations whole-number answers are sufficient.

ROUNDING MIXED NUMBERS

Most of the situations in which estimations are appropriate involve mixed numbers. If the factors were less than one, an exact answer can usually be quickly computed. In a problem such as $8\frac{1}{3} \times 4\frac{3}{25}$, the problem could be rounded to 8×4. The students should discuss that since they rounded both numbers down, their estimate of 32 is too low. Such discussions will enhance their understandings of fractions and multiplication.

In a problem like $3\frac{2}{3} \times 14\frac{1}{4}$, the problem could be rounded to 4×14 or 4×15, depending on the skills of the students. In either case they may use the doubles strategy to think "$4 \times 14 \ldots 2 \times 14$ is 28, 28 doubled is 56" or "$4 \times 15 \ldots 15, \ldots,$ 30, 60." In the estimate of 4×14, since one factor was rounded up and the other down, the students should know that their estimate will be around 56. For problems with larger numbers such as $32\frac{2}{5} \times 24\frac{3}{10}$, the students should round to numbers that are nice to work with, such as 30×20, 30×25, or 30×24.

REFINED ROUNDING WITH MIXED NUMBERS

Some students may decide to obtain a more refined estimate by rounding only one of the factors. To estimate $4\frac{1}{3} \times 21\frac{2}{5}$, a student may think, "$4\frac{1}{3} \times 21 \ldots 4 \times 21$ is 84. $\frac{1}{3}$ of 21 is 7. $84 + 7$ is 91." This type of thinking is based on applications of the distributive property.

In the example of $8\frac{1}{3} \times 4\frac{3}{25}$, a student may think as follows "$4 \times 8\frac{1}{3} \ldots 4 \times 8$ or 32. $\frac{1}{3}$ of 4 is more than 1, so my estimate is 33, which is a little low." Another student may think "4×8 is 32. $\frac{1}{3}$ of 4 is $\frac{4}{3}$. 32 plus $1\frac{1}{3}$ is $33\frac{1}{3}$, which is still low, as I rounded $4\frac{3}{25}$ down." Again, the estimates will vary among students. Through discussions the students should be encouraged to try more sophisticated strategies suggested by classmates and the teacher.

ESTIMATING WITH A FRACTION TIMES A WHOLE NUMBER

One type of estimating should particularly be emphasized. One of the most frequent ways that we use estimation is determining a percent of a number. Occurrences such as a 15% tip, 25% off the original price, 9% interest, or 5% sales taxes affect us daily. Often we obtain an estimate of these amounts. Since we usually do these calculations mentally, the percents are changed to common fractions rather than to decimal fractions for ease in calculating. Consequently, we will be multiplying a fraction times a whole number. The fractions that have been selected are those that are equivalent to common percents.

At first, student practice exercises should be limited to unit fractions and numbers that are compatible to those fractions. Examples are shown in Figure 9-14a. In each case the students should solve by mentally dividing the whole number by the number of total parts. In each of these cases the students can readily determine an exact answer. These calculations are prerequisites for mentally computing 1%, 10%, 20%, 25%, $33\frac{1}{3}$%, and 50%.

After this strategy is learned, it can be extended to include problems such as shown in Figure 9-14b. For the problem $\frac{2}{3} \times 96$, the student would think "96 divided by 3 is 32. 2×32 is 64." This process again leads to an exact answer. These calculations are prerequisites for mentally computing such percents as 40%, 30%, 75%, 60%, and $66\frac{2}{3}$%.

a	$\frac{1}{4} \times 240$	$\frac{1}{2} \times 24$	$\frac{1}{5} \times 350$
	$\frac{1}{10} \times 320$	$\frac{1}{3} \times 96$	$\frac{1}{100} \times 2400$
b	$\frac{3}{4} \times 240$	$\frac{3}{10} \times 4200$	$\frac{2}{5} \times 350$
	$\frac{7}{10} \times 320$	$\frac{2}{3} \times 96$	$\frac{4}{100} \times 2400$

FIGURE 9-14.
Estimating fraction times a whole number.

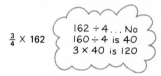 

FIGURE 9-15.
Using compatible numbers.

The numbers in the first two parts were selected so that the numbers were easy to compute mentally. After the students have learned these strategies, they are ready to begin using this strategy with compatible numbers. These strategies may include adapting the fraction, the whole number, or both numbers. Figure 9-15 shows the student thinking for examples where the whole numbers were changed so the numbers were compatible. In some cases the students may choose to round. For the problem $\frac{7}{10} \times 473$, students may think, "470 divided by 10 is 47. $7 \times 47 \ldots$ too hard. 7×50 is 350, so my estimate is 350."

Sometimes fractions will not be easy to work with, such as $\frac{13}{16}, \frac{7}{24}, \frac{27}{30}$. Some of these could be rounded to 0, $\frac{1}{2}$, or 1 or to other familiar fractions. In the examples shown in Figure 9-16a, the students rounded to 1 or $\frac{1}{2}$. In Figure 9-16b these strategies were extended as one student rounded to another familiar fraction, $\frac{1}{3}$. Another student recognized that $\frac{13}{16}$ was close to one but used a

more sophisticated strategy to give a more exact estimate. Students should be given opportunities to share and to explore new strategies in order to become better estimators.

MULTIPLICATION OF DECIMAL FRACTIONS

The multiplication of decimals presents only one new concept to students—that of the placement of the decimal point. Except for this concept, multiplication of decimals is no different from multiplication of whole numbers. It would appear that students who have mastered the multiplication algorithm would have little difficulty with this topic. But this is an important concept that needs further development. In the Second National Assessment about one half of the 13-year-olds and three fourths of the 17-year-olds correctly multiplied decimals or chose the correct

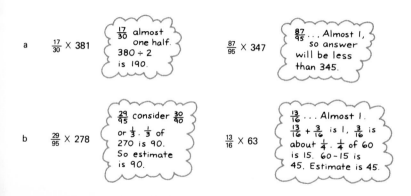

FIGURE 9-16.
Rounding fractions before multiplying.

placement of the decimal point. The results of the Third National Assessment show an improvement of 8 percentage points over all decimal operations since the last assessment. Part of this improvement has been attributed to earlier and increased emphasis on decimal fractions in the curriculum.

The errors on the Second Assessment were about evenly divided between multiplication errors and errors in placement of the decimal point. Students who made errors in computation or in decimal-point placement appeared to ignore or to be unaware of the unreasonableness of their results. On both of these assessments students did poorly on estimation of decimal products. On the Third National Assessment about one fifth of the students were able to select the correct estimate for 3.04×5.3. In addition to "16," the other numerical choices for the estimate were "1.6, 160, and 1600." These choices were selected, respectively, by 28%, 18%, and 23% of the students being tested on this problem. It appears that a large number of students were guessing for all four choices. These results indicate that an emphasis on the *concepts of decimals* must be integrated throughout the development of this topic.

WHOLE NUMBER TIMES A DECIMAL FRACTION

As with common fractions, the first step in multiplication of decimals is to multiply a whole number times a decimal. This can be developed with the idea of repeated addition. Just as the development of addition and subtraction of decimal fractions was related to the addition and subtraction of common fractions, the development of multiplication of decimal fractions needs to be related to the oral language of fractions and the multiplication of common fractions. The situation

described below could be used to introduce these ideas to a class.

> On the night that Jeremy prepared spinach lasagna for his family, they ate six of the ten servings. Jeremy decided to fix the same recipe next week for a surprise party for his mother. Three times as many people have been invited. Assuming that people will eat similar quantities, does he need to triple the recipe?

To solve this problem the class used paperfolding to determine how much food three groups of people would eat. First they represented 3 sets of 6 tenths (Figure 9-17a). One of the students, Jody, thought, "There is a total of 18 tenths, so 3×6 tenths is 18 tenths. She recorded her results (Figure 9-17b). Erica had written her results in common fraction form as shown in Figure 9-17c. She stated "18 tenths is more than 1. Since 10 tenths is 1, we have 1 and 8 tenths." Troy observed, "Since 1.8 is more than 1 but less than 2, two pans will be needed. Two pans is only a doubled recipe." Another student Nicole recorded the results as a repeated

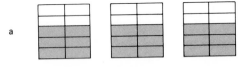

a

b   3 times 6 tenths is 18 tenths

c $3 \times \frac{6}{10} = \frac{18}{10} = 1\frac{8}{10}$

d
$$
\begin{array}{r}
0.6 \\
0.6 \\
+\,0.6 \\
\hline
1.8
\end{array}
$$

FIGURE 9-17.
Paperfolding for representing multiplication of decimals.

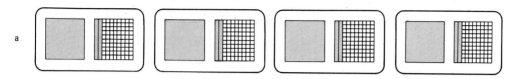

a

b 4 times 1 and 2 tenths is 4 and 8 tenths.

c 1 and 2 tenths
    × 4
   —————
  4 and 8 tenths

d

Ones	Tenths
1.	2
×	4
4.	8

FIGURE 9-18.
Grids for representing a whole number times a mixed number.

addition problem. She also shared her results with the class (Figure 9-17d).

The following situation could be used to discuss a whole number times a mixed number. "How much rain did we receive this month if it rained 1.2 inches four times this month?" Although paperfolding would also be appropriate, grids were used to represent this problem (Figure 9-18). The parts should be considered first. Four sets of 2 tenths is 8 tenths. Then the whole is considered or 4 sets of 1 is 4. First Mr. Christensen had written the statement expressed by the class (Figure 9-18b). Their results could have been recorded as shown in Figure 9-18c. To introduce the class to the algorithm form, he suggested that they write their results in a modified place-value table. Their results are shown in Figure 9-18d. Forms (b) and (c) help the students relate the models to the symbols. Through such experiences, the students' concepts of the numerical form will be reinforced.

The form shown in Figure 9-18d is a modified form of place-value tables. If the lines in the table were extended, the 4 would be incorrectly placed in the tenths column.

This modification is being suggested for those students who need reinforcement that the problem is 4 times 2 *tenths* and 4 times 1 *one*. Some students begin recording their work by insisting that the first step is to "line up the decimal points." This carryover from the addition of decimals is related to finding common denominators for common fractions. The students can generally discover in a class discussion that lining up the decimal points is not an essential step for multiplying decimals, just as finding a common denominator is not essential for multiplying common fractions.

The next situation uses the form with the modified place-value table for recording the process for a problem involving regrouping. Troy swam 1.3 kilometers 4 times this week. He wanted to determine how far he had swum. He wrote the multiplication problem and then represented the problems with base-ten blocks. The flat was redefined as one, so the longs represented tenths (Figure 9-19a). First he grouped the tenths. Since there were 12 tenths, he traded 10 of them for a flat to represent one. Troy then recorded his results as 2 in the tenths column

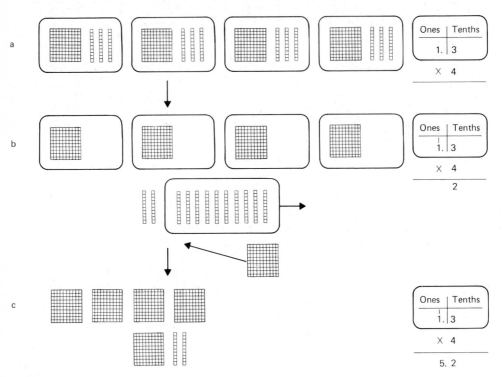

FIGURE 9-19.
Multiplying decimals with regrouping.

and 1 in the ones column (Figure 9-19b). He thought, "4 times 3 tenths is 12 tenths. 12 tenths is 1 and 2 tenths." He then considered the ones, "4 sets of 1 is 4. 4 plus 1 more that I traded is 5 ones." He recorded as shown in Figure 9-19. Studying his written form, Troy reaffirmed his results, "4 times 1 is 4. 4 plus 1 is 5 ones. So my answer is 5 and 2 tenths."

In the problem above, base-ten blocks were used as sets. Arrays are also appropriate. Figure 9-20 shows the block representation of 3.2 and an array that is 2 × 3.2. This array represents multiplication of decimals since one of its dimensions is 3.2 and the other is 2. To find the answer, the students can simply count flats and longs to

discover that 2 × 3.2 = 6.4. The array form is also needed to show multiplication problems when neither of the factors is a whole number.

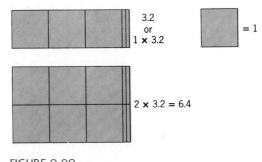

FIGURE 9-20.
Multiplication of decimals using base-ten blocks.

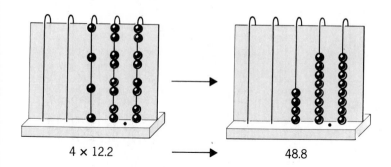

FIGURE 9-21.
Decimal multiplication on abacus.

4 × 12.2   ⟶   48.8

The abacus is appropriate for simple problems involving a one-digit whole number times a decimal. The student simply needs to redefine what each wire represents and use the repeated addition concept of multiplication (Figure 9-21). This problem clearly shows that 4 sets of 12 and 2 tenths is the same as an addition problem with 12 and 2 tenths being used as an addend 4 times. Although the abacus is a convenient model because the place values can be readily changed, it is restricted as to the factors that can be used. For a problem such as 4 times 2.7 there are not enough beads on the tenths rod. It is convenient for representing a one-digit number times hundredths or thousandths such as 3 × 2.14 or 2 × 32.146.

After students have been introduced to a whole number times a number in the tenths, this algorithm is extended to numbers in the hundredths and thousandths. Models such as base-ten blocks, and grids can be modified accordingly. Figure 9-22 shows a representation for the problem 4 × 1.23 using grids.

Since multiplication is commutative, students can write the multiplication algorithm as a whole number times a decimal or as a decimal times a whole number regardless of the verbal situation. Usually, students write the problems such that the factor with the

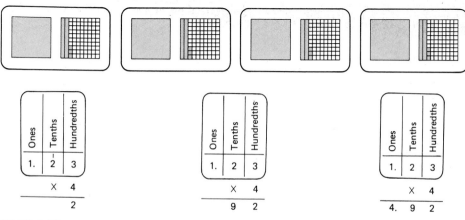

FIGURE 9-22.
Whole number times hundredths.

smaller number of digits is the multiplier. Students can usually recognize situations involving a whole number times a decimal as multiplication situations. However, they may not recognize situations involving a decimal fraction times a whole number as multiplication.

Conceptually, $\frac{3}{10}$ of 6 appears different from 6 sets of $\frac{3}{10}$. The following are examples of situations involving a decimal fraction times a whole number.

> Martha missed 2% or 0.02 of the problems on the final spelling test.
>
> Before lunch Tom finished 0.8 of the seventy pages he needed to type.
>
> Thelma's running time for the race was 23.4 minutes. Her best time for that distance was 0.9 of that.

Students should be given opportunities to discuss various situations involving common and decimal fractions. They should *not solve* these problems but only tell *what operation is needed* for solution.

One computational topic where students encounter difficulties is multiplying a decimal fraction times a power of ten. Examples of such errors are 3.2 × 100 = 3.200 or 1000 × 42.679 is 42.679000. The students are "adding zeros"—an incorrect rule that they memorized. If they had taken time to check the reasonableness of their responses, they would have observed that 100 times a number greater than 3 must be greater than 300. Students should explore problems of this type using calculators. While studying multiplication of whole numbers, students should have had experiences multiplying various numbers by factors such as 10, 10 000, 1000, and 100. Students should have explored these patterns by using the calculator and made appro-

priate generalizations. These generalizations should be extended to decimal fractions greater than one and less than one. The calculator should again be used. These ideas are discussed further in the section "Estimation for Multiplication of Decimal Fractions."

DECIMAL FRACTION TIMES A DECIMAL FRACTION

The concept of a decimal times a decimal can be developed in the same way as for common fractions. When students really understand the concept of multiplication of decimals, developing a technique for the placement of the decimal point is not difficult. Arrays with base-ten blocks can be extended to help the students solve problems such as 2.6 × 3.2. This time they must form an array that is 3.2 in one dimension and 2.6 in the other (Figure 9-23).

Once again, the students can solve the problems simply by counting the pieces and regrouping if necessary. They also have a physical representation of each partial product, including 0.6 × 0.2 = 0.12. This array also corresponds to the arrays they have used previously for the multiplication of two-digit whole numbers and for the multiplica-

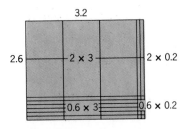

FIGURE 9-23.
Multiplication of decimals using base-ten blocks.

```
  3.4                .782            3
× 2.3      ⟶        7.82    ?      × 2      ∴ 7.82
─────              78.2            ───
 102                                6
  68
─────
 782
```

FIGURE 9-24.

Placing the decimal point.

tion of mixed numbers. When students represent problems with the base-ten blocks, they should have no difficulty with the placement of the decimal point in the answer.

Estimation is another technique that students should use for the placement of the decimal point. As shown in Figure 9-24, Kathy first multiplied the numbers to get the sequence of digits (782) for the answer. She then looked at just the whole number part of the problem. Kathy knew that $2 \times 3 = 6$ and that the numbers she multiplied were just a little more than 2 and 3 respectively. Therefore she knew that 2.3×3.4 would be approximately 7, not 0.7 or 78. Therefore, she placed the decimal point so that the answer was 7.82. For some exercises the students could be given the digits of the answer in sequence and simply asked to place the decimal point correctly.

Some students memorize the rule of "counting the number of decimal places in the factors" without understanding the concepts involved. When such students use calculators to answer problems such as 0.8×2.5 or 17.35×3.02, they may be confused when the display shows 4 (no decimal places) or 52.397 (only three decimal places). They may question their answers as they were expecting answers with 2 or 4 places to the right of the decimal point.

By using all the preceding techniques, students will be able to formulate a consistent procedure for the correct placement

of the decimal point. Practice should be devised so that the emphasis is on this correct placement of the decimal point. Review of multiplication of whole numbers is also appropriate, but it is incidental to the focus of these lessons.

ESTIMATION FOR MULTIPLICATION OF DECIMAL FRACTIONS

In the preceding section, estimation was used to determine the appropriate placement of the decimal point. Although students should learn the generalization regarding the number of place values in order to place the decimal point, in most situations estimation can give them an answer just as quickly. Estimation has the added advantage of helping to determine whether the computations were accurate.

MULTIPLYING BY 1, 10, 100, OR 1000

The prerequisite skill for this activity is being able to multiply by a power of ten. Students should be able to quickly and mentally compute the answers for problems such as "3.24 $\times$ 1000" or "100 $\times$ 27.6845." These skills can then be used for mental computations where one of the factors is near 1, 10, 100, or 1000. Examples of these problems are shown in Figure 9-25a. In these cases the students recognize that one of the factors is near 1, 10, 100, or 1000. In Figure 9-25b this strategy is extended to problems where both factors are decimal fractions.

ROUNDING

Rounding is similar to the strategy above, as one of the factors may conveniently round to

	Problem	Student Thinking
	357 × 1.2873	357 × 1 is 357 So estimate is greater than 357
a	8.976 × 1463	1463 × 10 is 14630 So estimate is less than 14630
	348 × 105.7	348 × 100 is 34800 so estimate is 34800
	3.57 × 1.2873	3.57 × 1 is 3.57 so estimate is more than 3.6
b	8.976 × 1.463	1.463 × 10 is 14.63 so estimate is less than 14
	34.8 × 105.7	34.8 × 100 is 3480 so estimate is greater than 3480

FIGURE 9-25.
Estimating using 1, 10, 100, or 1000.

1, 10, 100, or 1000. It is an extension of the strategy above, as the factors are rounded to other factors that the students can compute readily without paper and pencil. Problems and examples of student thinking are shown in Figure 9-26. As with other problems involving rounding, the accuracy of the rounding will depend on the skills of the students.

FRONT-END ESTIMATION

As with the other operations, front-end estimation requires more than one step, but it provides a better estimate. First the factors are considered. One of the factors may be rounded to the nearest whole number. The other factor will be considered as two entities—the whole number *and* the part which should be rounded to a fractional number that is easy to compute mentally. Examples of problems and student thinking are shown in Figure 9-27. Again student responses will vary depending on their skills and on how they perceive the factors. In all of these situations the students used the distributive property to help with their mental calculations. In one example of student thinking, 3.27 was rounded to 3.25. For doing the calculations, $\frac{1}{4}$, not 0.25, was used. Decimals were rounded to other decimal fractions or familiar common fractions for ease in calculations.

Problems	Student Thinking
83.37 × 112.47	80 × 100 is 8000 estimate more than 8000 80 × 110 is 8800 estimate more than 8800
6.375 × 7.875	6 × 8 is 48 estimate around 48
31.4 × 7.333	30 × 7 is 210 estimate is more than 210 31 × 7 is 217 estimate more than 217

FIGURE 9-26.
Rounding in multiplying decimals.

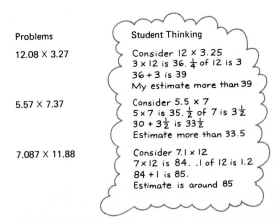

Problems	Student Thinking
12.08 × 3.27	Consider 12 × 3.25 3 × 12 is 36. $\frac{1}{4}$ of 12 is 3 36 + 3 is 39 My estimate more than 39
5.57 × 7.37	Consider 5.5 × 7 5 × 7 is 35. $\frac{1}{2}$ of 7 is 3$\frac{1}{2}$ 30 + 3$\frac{1}{2}$ is 33$\frac{1}{2}$ Estimate more than 33.5
7.087 × 11.88	Consider 7.1 × 12 7 × 12 is 84. .1 of 12 is 1.2 84 + 1 is 85. Estimate is around 85

FIGURE 9-27.
Front-end estimation for multiplying decimals.

QUESTIONS AND ACTIVITIES

1. Write a story problem for each of the following conditions. Include a variety of situations and questions.
   a. multiplication of common fractions
   b. whole number times a common fraction
   c. common fraction times a whole number
   d. multiplication of common fraction times mixed number
   e. two-step with subtraction and multiplication of mixed fractions

2. a. Reconsider Problem 1. Change the terms involving common fractions to decimal fractions. Rewrite the situations. Include at least two situations that contain too little or too much information.
   b. Compare your results to those that you wrote for common fractions and whole numbers. How are they alike? Different?
   c. *For your resource file:* In "Fraction vs. Decimals—The Wrong Issue," Swart argues for teaching the rationale of multiplication of fractions, not just the procedures.

3. Use sets to illustrate each of the following.
   a. 1 third of a set of twelve
   b. 2 thirds of a set of twelve
   c. 3 fourths of a set of twenty
   d. 3 fourths of a set of eighteen
   e. 3 fifths of a package of crackers were left; Jim took 1 third

4. Represent the following using paperfolding or region models.
   a. 3 fifths of a carton of ice cream; Jim served 1 third of it
   b. 2 thirds of a sandwich; Bill ate half of it
   c. Rebecca raked 1 fourth of the remaining 2 thirds of the yard
   d. 2 thirds of 4 fifths
   e. $\frac{1}{2} \times \frac{2}{3}$
   f. $\frac{2}{3}$ of $2\frac{1}{5}$

5. Solve the following using a number line.
   a. 4 jumps of 3 eighths
   b. $2 \times \frac{2}{3}$
   c. $4 \times 1\frac{1}{4}$ (*Hint:* Use the distributive law.)
   d. $3 \times 2\frac{2}{3}$

6. Represent each of the following using the model indicated. Write a common fraction and a decimal fraction number sentence for each.
   a. four sets of 3 tenths (set)
   b. two times 3 tenths (paperfolding)
   c. 4 sets of 2 and 1 tenth (sets using base-ten blocks)
   d. 3 sets of 1 and 6 tenths (sets using base-ten blocks)
   e. 3 × 1.34 (sets using base-ten blocks)
   f. 3 tenths times 7 tenths (array)
   g. 4 tenths times 2 and 3 tenths (array)

7. Consider the models and your procedures for Problem 6. For each part below, compare the problems and the models and procedures that would be used for solving them.
   a. four sets of three—four sets of 3 tenths (sets)
   b. 4 sets of 21—4 sets of 2 and 1 tenth (sets using base-ten blocks)
   c. 3 sets of 16—3 sets of 1 and 6 tenths (sets using base-ten blocks)
   d. 3 × 134—3 × 1.34 (sets using base-ten blocks)
   e. 3 × 7—3 tenths × 7 tenths (array)
   f. 4 times 23—4 tenths times 2 and 3 tenths (array)

8. Use the constant key on a calculator to activate repeated addition to:
   a. count 5 sets of 0.3.
   b. find the product of 6 and 0.2.

9. Sue did the problem below. Correct the problem. Without using a model or a rule, how can you help Sue notice that her answer is obviously wrong?

$$
\begin{array}{r}
2.4 \\
\times 3.1 \\
\hline
24 \\
72 \\
\hline
74.4
\end{array}
$$

10. Use the base-ten blocks. If a flat is equal to 1, what are the values of the following?
   a. 2 units
   b. 2 longs
   c. Place two longs next to the flat. What number does this represent?
   d. Place another flat and 2 longs below the blocks used in part (c) to form an array. What multiplication problem does this represent?
   e. Multiply 1.4 times 1.3 using the base-ten blocks. Draw a diagram.

11. Use the base-ten blocks to illustrate the problem 1.6 × 2.3. Draw a sketch of the results, carefully delineating the partial products. Complete the multiplication problem below by filling in the four partial products and the final answer. Label the parts of your array to correspond to the written problem.

$$
\begin{array}{r}
2.3 \\
\times\ 1.6 \\
\hline
\underline{}\ A \\
\underline{}\ B \\
\underline{}\ C \\
\underline{}\ D \\
\hline
\underline{}\ \text{Final Answer}
\end{array}
$$

12. a. Write the answers to the following problems. What pattern do you observe? How can this pattern be used to teach multiplication by multiples of ten?
   (1) 23 × 100
   (2) 23 × 10
   (3) 23 × 1
   (4) 23 × 0.1
   (5) 23 × 0.01
   (6) 23 × 0.001
   b. *For your resource file:* In "Let's Do It: With Powers of Ten", Leutzinger and Nelson describe activities for teaching multiplying and dividing by 10, 100, and 1000.

13. Estimate the whole number answer and then place the decimal point appropriately in the product.
   a. 4.3 × 6 = 258
   b. 4.3 × 0.6 = 258

   c. 38.7 × 7.2 = 27864
   d. 38.7 × 0.72 = 27864

14. a. Analyze the introductory unit to multiplication of common fractions in at least two different textbooks. What problems are used to motivate the topic? What models are used? How is the algorithm introduced? How is estimation incorporated?
   b. Analyze the introductory unit to multiplication of decimal fractions. What problems are used to motivate the topic? What models are used? How is the algorithm introduced? How is estimation incorporated?
   c. How are common fractions and decimal fractions related in these units? If needed, how would you supplement these units?

15. For an explanation of how to use Cuisenaire rods to represent multiplication of fractions, read "Understanding Multiplication of Fractions" by Sweetland. Work through the examples using a set of Cuisenaire rods. Evaluate the procedures.

16. In Chapter 3 a daily plan was given that involved practice in mental arithmetic for a few minutes at the start of each period.
   a. Design two opening exercises with problems similar to those in Figures 9-14 through 9-16. In one of the exercises, present the problems orally, giving students time to write the answers. In the second exercise, show the students one problem at a time and then have them write the answer.
   b. Try out these exercises with a group of junior high students or your classmates. Have the students discuss the different strategies that they used. Also, discuss the differences in thinking depending on whether the problems were presented in a written or an oral format.

17. a. List and briefly describe the estimation strategies for decimal fractions that were presented in this section. Reread and

rework the problems presented in Figures 9-25 to 9-27.

b. How are these strategies similar to the strategies for common fractions?

c. Are you comfortable with estimation strategies? What factors would make students comfortable with estimation? What factors would make students uncomfortable with estimation? How could those factors be overcome?

18. *For your resource file:* Read "Estimating Decimal Products: An Instructional Sequence" by Vance.

DIVISION OF COMMON FRACTIONS

As with the other operations, early work with division of fractions (common and decimal) should emphasize the concept of the operation. Situations should be used to motivate the topic and models should be used to solve the situations. Again, the numerical recordings of the procedures for solving problems should be delayed. Primary concern should be with development so that students will be able to recognize division situations and extend their concepts of division to fractional numbers. The goal is that after they have learned the algorithm, they will also know *when* to apply the operation.

COMMON FRACTIONS AS DIVISORS

Situations where common fractions are the divisors will be discussed first. These situations are introduced through measurement problems similar to those in which children were asked to determine how many twos in eight. Initially, to solve this problem children measured off or subtracted twos from eight until no more twos could be subtracted (Figure 9-28). Students need to know that such measurement situations are division problems (Figure 9-28a) *and* that division situations can be interpreted as measurement situations (Figure 9-28b).

Another prerequisite is knowledge of the number of parts in a whole. Students have learned that other names for one include numbers such as $\frac{5}{5}$, $\frac{4}{4}$, and $\frac{2}{2}$. Knowing that there are 2 halves in a whole is similar to "How many halves in a whole?" Questions such as "How many thirds are there in one? How many fourths? How many tenths?" should be informally solved using fraction bars, paper strips, or Cuisenaire rods (Figure 9-29). The question of how many 1 fourths are in 1 should be related to the division problem $1 \div \frac{1}{4}$, as we are dividing the strip into parts each one-fourth long.

These concepts can then be extended to other numbers and situations. For exam-

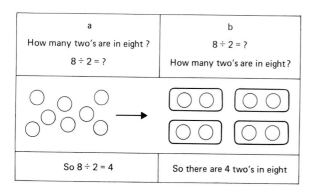

a	b
How many two's are in eight ?	$8 \div 2 = ?$
$8 \div 2 = ?$	How many two's are in eight?
So $8 \div 2 = 4$	So there are 4 two's in eight

FIGURE 9-28.
Measurement division.

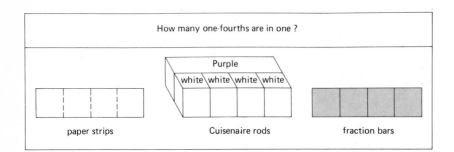

FIGURE 9-29.
Fourths in one.

ple, "Karon is making aprons for her friends for Christmas. If each apron requires $\frac{1}{2}$ meter of material, how many aprons can Karon make from the 2-meter remnant she bought yesterday?" Students can easily draw a diagram of this problem (Figure 9-30). By marking off the cloth in $\frac{1}{2}$-meter lengths and counting these, they will find that Karon can make four aprons from 2 meters of material. This problem could also have been solved using paper strips or Cuisenaire rods (Figure 9-31).

This thinking should be extended to problems in dividing a fraction by another fraction. For example, "Karon's twin sister Karol is making mittens for her friends for Christmas. If each pair of mittens uses $\frac{2}{5}$ of a 250-gram ball of yarn, how many pairs of mittens can she make from $\frac{4}{5}$ of a 250-gram

ball?" To solve this problem students could use a model such as paper strips to represent the yarn. Two strips that are the same length should both be folded into fifths. One is shaded to represent four fifths, the other to represent two fifths. The strip representing two fifths is then refolded so that only the shaded parts are shown. It is then used to determine how many two-fifths are in 4 fifths. By measuring off the four fifths in units of two fifths each, they could see that Karol can make two pairs of mittens (Figure 9-32).

The problem of how many two-fifths are in 4 fifths is relatively easy to picture and solve mentally. Problems such as $\frac{2}{3} \div \frac{1}{6}$ or

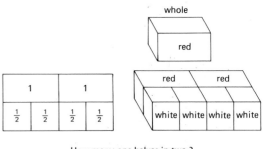

How many one-halves in two ?
$$2 \div \frac{1}{2} = ?$$
There are 4 halves in two.
so $2 \div \frac{1}{2} = 4$

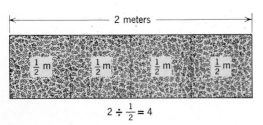

$$2 \div \frac{1}{2} = 4$$

FIGURE 9-30.
Division by a fraction.

FIGURE 9-31.
Halves in two.

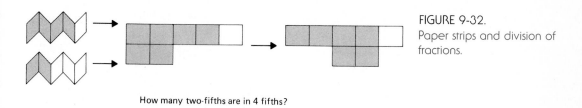

FIGURE 9-32.

Paper strips and division of fractions.

How many two-fifths are in 4 fifths?

$$\frac{4}{5} \div \frac{2}{5} = 2$$

$\frac{3}{5} \div \frac{2}{10}$ may not be as apparent, but they can be clearly shown with models (Figure 9-33). This situation should be discussed as how many one-sixths in 2 thirds and how many two-tenths in 3 fifths.

To introduce the algorithm for division, the teacher should have the class solve a number of problems using models. Their results should be recorded as shown in Figure 9-34a. The teacher should then write in the corresponding multiplication sentences for each problem (Figure 9-34b). After the students have solved the multiplication problems, they should compare the problems in the two columns. Through discussion they should conclude that the answers for each

pair are the same, the dividends are the same, the operations are the inverses of each other, and the divisors are multiplicative inverses. They should then conclude that any division problem can be solved by rewriting it as a multiplication problem.

Some students who have memorized rules for operations often have difficulty with division by decimal and common fractions. Their initial response is that answers should be smaller not larger when they divide. They need opportunities to explore situations where the divisors are less than one, equal to one, and greater than one. The types of experiences described above will help students develop division concepts. The problems above all had whole-number answers and were selected so that the manipulations

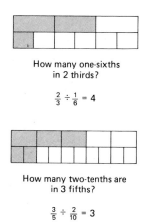

How many one-sixths
in 2 thirds?

$$\frac{2}{3} \div \frac{1}{6} = 4$$

How many two-tenths are
in 3 fifths?

$$\frac{3}{5} \div \frac{2}{10} = 3$$

FIGURE 9-33.

Dividing unlike fractions.

$2 \div \frac{1}{2} = 4$	$2 \times \frac{2}{1} = 4$
$\frac{4}{5} \div \frac{2}{5} = 2$	$\frac{4}{5} \times \frac{5}{2} = 2$
$\frac{2}{3} \div \frac{1}{6} = 4$	$\frac{2}{3} \times \frac{6}{1} = 4$
$\frac{3}{5} \div \frac{2}{10} = 3$	$\frac{3}{5} \times \frac{10}{2} = 3$
a	b

FIGURE 9-34.

Relating division to multiplication.

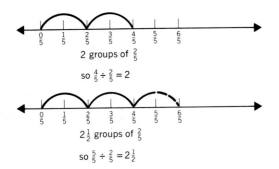

2 groups of $\frac{2}{5}$

so $\frac{4}{5} \div \frac{2}{5} = 2$

$2\frac{1}{2}$ groups of $\frac{2}{5}$

so $\frac{5}{5} \div \frac{2}{5} = 2\frac{1}{2}$

FIGURE 9-35.
Division of fractions using a number line.

with the models were relatively easy to work. Other problems should also be explored and their results discussed.

Remainders may present a special problem when students are dividing by a fraction using models. If, in one of the earlier examples, Karol had had a whole ball ($\frac{5}{5}$ of yarn, the division $\frac{5}{5} \div \frac{2}{5}$ could be shown on a number line. Both problems $\frac{4}{5} \div \frac{2}{5}$ and $\frac{5}{5} \div \frac{2}{5}$ are shown in Figure 9-35.

Some students, after doing this division with the model, will say the answer is $2\frac{1}{5}$. These students are forgetting the meaning of the original problem. The question asks, "How many groups of $\frac{2}{5}$ each are there in $\frac{5}{5}$?" With the number line, the student can see that there are two whole groups of $\frac{2}{5}$ each and one half of another group since $\frac{1}{5}$ is equal to $\frac{1}{2}$ of $\frac{2}{5}$. Karol could make $2\frac{1}{2}$ pairs of mittens from one ball of yarn.

Remainders should be considered relative to the situation. One-half pair of mittens would probably not be very useful. Instead, the extra $\frac{1}{5}$ ball of yarn would simply be left over as an undivided remainder.

The next example involves a mixed number divided by a fraction. One fifth-grade textbook uses circular regions to illustrate $\frac{5}{2} \div \frac{3}{4}$ (Figure 9-36). In order to measure

off three fourths, the halves are cut to show fourths. Then sets of 3 fourths are removed until all of the parts are used. There are 3 sets and one partial set. Since there is 1 out of the three parts needed for a set, there is one third of a set. So $\frac{5}{2} \div \frac{3}{4}$ is $3\frac{1}{3}$. The diagrams clearly show the process and the result. It is then noted that the same result can be found by multiplying by the reciprocal of the divisor.

As students work problems of this type, they will discover another algorithm for the division of fractions. The students could write the terms of the division problem so that they have a common denominator and then divide the numerator of the dividend by the numerator of the divisor (Figure 9-37a). This algorithm can be used to relate division of fractions to both division of whole numbers and multiplication of fractions. If the denominator is thought of as the *name* of the fraction pieces, dividing five fifths into groups of two fifths each is the same problem as dividing five units into groups of two units each. In either case the answer is $2\frac{1}{2}$ (Figure 9-37b).

Figure 9-38 shows a diagram of the solution to the problems $5 \div 2$ and $\frac{5}{5} \div \frac{2}{5}$. In the first number line the interval represents one whole; in the second number line the interval represents one fifth. Since the unit (denominators) are the same, they can be ignored, and the numerators can be considered.

Common denominators can be used to solve problems such as $\frac{3}{4} \div \frac{7}{8}$. Again, the students need to consider the question, how many 7-eighths are in 3 fourths? They should realize that since 7 eighths is larger than three fourths, they do not have enough for a whole group, so the answer will be less than one. This is similar to the reasoning for problems such as $32 \div 123$. Since 123 is larger

More about dividing by fractions

You can use pictures to divide a fraction by a fraction.

Draw $\frac{5}{2}$ circles:

Divide into $\frac{1}{4}$'s:

Separate into $\frac{3}{4}$'s:

Count groups
of $\frac{3}{4}$'s:

| 1 group of $\frac{3}{4}$ | 1 group of $\frac{3}{4}$ | 1 group of $\frac{3}{4}$ | $\frac{1}{3}$ of a group of $\frac{3}{4}$ |

$$\frac{5}{2} \div \frac{3}{4} = 3\frac{1}{3}$$

You would have gotten the same answer if you had multiplied $\frac{5}{2}$ by $\frac{4}{3}$.

Instead of drawing pictures to divide by a fraction, you can multiply by its reciprocal.

$$\frac{5}{2} \div \frac{3}{4} = \frac{5}{\cancel{2}_1} \times \frac{\cancel{4}^2}{3}$$

$$= \frac{10}{3}$$

$$= 3\frac{1}{3}$$

FIGURE 9-36.
Dividing mixed numbers using models. (From C.A. Dilley, D.W. Lowry, W.E. Rucker, **Heath Mathematics**, 1985, Grade 6, p. 174. Reprinted by permission of D.C. Heath & Company.)

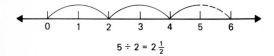

(a) $1 \div \frac{2}{5} \longrightarrow \frac{5}{5} \div \frac{2}{5} \longrightarrow 5 \div 2 \longrightarrow 2\frac{1}{2}$

(b) 5 fifths ÷ 2 fifths $\longrightarrow$ 5 ÷ 2 $\longrightarrow$ $2\frac{1}{2}$
5 units ÷ 2 units $\longrightarrow$ 5 ÷ 2 $\longrightarrow$ $2\frac{1}{2}$

(c) $\frac{5}{5} \div \frac{2}{5} \longrightarrow \frac{5 \div 2}{5 \div 5} \longrightarrow \frac{5 \div 2}{1} \longrightarrow 5 \div 2 \longrightarrow 2\frac{1}{2}$

FIGURE 9-37.
Dividing like fractions.

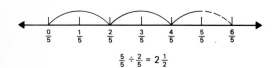

$5 \div 2 = 2\frac{1}{2}$

$\frac{5}{5} \div \frac{2}{5} = 2\frac{1}{2}$

FIGURE 9-38.
Number lines to show division.

than 32, the answer is less than one. The process of solving $\frac{3}{4} \div \frac{7}{8}$ with fraction bars is shown in Figure 9-39.

WHOLE NUMBERS AS DIVISORS

Just as their early experiences included problems such as how many thirds in one,

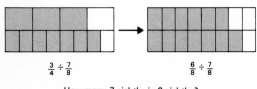

$\frac{3}{4} \div \frac{7}{8}$ $\frac{6}{8} \div \frac{7}{8}$

How many 7 eighths in 6 eighths?

$\frac{6}{8} \div \frac{7}{8} = \frac{6}{7}$

FIGURE 9-39.
Fraction bars showing quotients less than one.

students also encountered informal experiences dividing fractions by whole numbers. Two examples include "Jermone, Fred, and Elizabeth decided to share half of the pie. What part of the pie did they each eat?" and "Hal and Bill decided to split the $4\frac{4}{5}$ containers of food that were left." Both of these situations have been represented in Figure 9-40.

These problems and mixed numbers should also be related to the algorithm for dividing whole numbers. Division of mixed numbers should be taught right along with division of fractions since the process does not involve any new concepts. Students simply rename the mixed numbers as fractions and use the same algorithm they would use for any other division of fractions (Figure 9-41).

When a more formal explanation of division of fractions is presented to the students, it must be developed carefully. Four underlying concepts must be understood if this algorithm is to be taught meaningfully (Figure 9-42). Students must understand:

1. Multiplication of fractions.
2. Division by the identity, 1.
3. Reciprocals (multiplicative inverse).
4. Multiplication of the two terms of a division problem by a constant.

From discussing this example, students can see that this is the same algorithm that

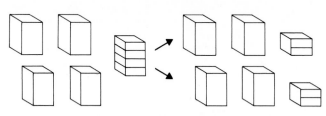

FIGURE 9-40.
Dividing fractions by whole numbers.

One half shared among 3

$\frac{1}{2} \div 3$

4 and 4 fifths shared between 2

$4\frac{4}{5} \div 2 = 2\frac{2}{5}$

they developed earlier with models. Thus, to divide fractions, they can simply multiply the dividend by the reciprocal of the divisor.

ESTIMATION FOR DIVISION OF COMMON FRACTIONS

By comparing the sizes of the divisor and the dividend, the students can estimate the size of the answer. Estimating the quotients for fractions can help students develop a better perspective of the concept of division of fractions. It can also help them determine the reasonableness of their results.

ROUNDING

The strategy of rounding is appropriate for mixed numbers. The numbers are simply rounded to the nearest whole number. This will give an estimate of an approximate answer or a check for the reasonableness of results. Examples with student thinking are given in Figure 9-43. The second and third

	original problem	$\frac{3}{4}$
$\frac{3}{4} \div \frac{2}{3}$		$\frac{2}{3}$
$\frac{3}{4} \times \frac{3}{2} \div \frac{2}{3} \times \frac{3}{2}$	concepts 3 and 4	$\dfrac{\frac{3}{4} \times \frac{3}{2}}{\frac{2}{3} \times \frac{3}{2}}$
$\frac{3}{4} \times \frac{3}{2} \div 1$	concepts 1 and 3	$\dfrac{\frac{3}{4} \times \frac{3}{2}}{1}$
$\frac{3}{4} \times \frac{3}{2}$	concept 2	$\frac{3}{4} \times \frac{3}{2}$
$\frac{9}{8}$	concept 1	$\frac{9}{8}$
(a)		(b)

FIGURE 9-42.
Division of fractions.

$2\frac{1}{3} \div 1\frac{1}{4}$ $2\frac{1}{3} \div 1\frac{1}{4}$

$\frac{7}{3} \div \frac{5}{4}$ $\frac{7}{3} \div \frac{5}{4}$

$\frac{28}{15} \div 1\frac{5}{4}$ $\frac{7}{3} \times \frac{4}{5}$

$28 \div 15$ $\frac{28}{15}$

$1\frac{13}{15}$ $1\frac{13}{15}$

FIGURE 9-41.
Division of mixed numbers.

Problems	Student Thinking
$5\frac{7}{8} \div 3\frac{1}{3}$	Round to $6 \div 3$ My estimate is around 2
$3\frac{1}{5} \div \frac{7}{9}$	$3 \div 1$ is 3 Estimate is 3
$13\frac{1}{4} \div 5\frac{3}{5}$	$13 \div 6$ $13 \div 6$ is $2\frac{1}{6}$

FIGURE 9-43.
Rounding for division of fractions.

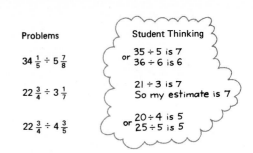

FIGURE 9-44.
Using compatible numbers for division of fractions.

students could improve their estimates by comparing the rounded numbers to the original problem. The second student should realize that since the divisor is less than one, the answer must be more than $3\frac{1}{5}$. In the third case the student could have thought, "Since I rounded the divisor up and I used a smaller dividend my estimate is too small."

COMPATIBLE NUMBERS

Due to the complexity of the operation and the percent of time we use division of fractions, it is sufficient simply to teach rounding as an appropriate strategy for division of fractions. Nevertheless, some students may devise more exact strategies or be ready for a further challenge. If the numbers are cumbersome to work with or a more exact estimate is desired, using compatible numbers is an appropriate strategy. Examples using this strategy are included in Figure 9-44.

COMPARING QUOTIENTS TO ONE

In the section "Division of Common Fractions," an example was discussed where the quotient was less than one. The students were to note that since the divisor was larger than the dividend the answer would be less than one. The concept can be extended as a strategy for estimating quotients. If the

numbers were the *same* value, the quotient would be one. When the numbers are similar in value, the quotient will be near one. Depending on whether the divisor is larger or smaller than the dividend, the estimate will be less than or greater than one (Figure 9-45). This strategy should also help students determine the reasonableness of their results.

DIVISION OF DECIMAL FRACTIONS

Students will encounter dividing money in their everyday life before encountering divi-

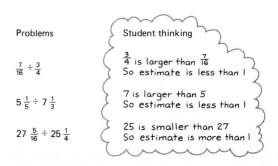

FIGURE 9-45.
Comparing quotients to 1.

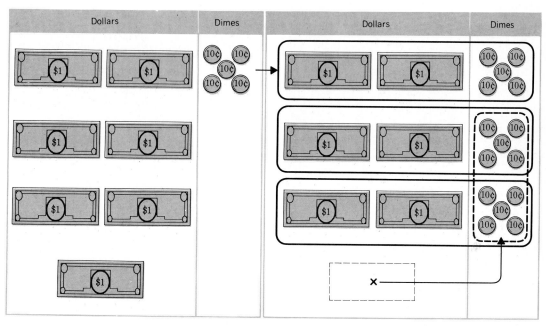

FIGURE 9-46.
Dividing money.

sion of decimals. For example, Patty, Ruth, and Kathy picked strawberries all day and earned $7.50. They divided the money equally as shown in Figure 9-46. Although students usually see this as division of dollars and cents, they can be guided to relate it to division of decimals. In addition to money, these are some of the other situations that we encounter that involve division of decimals.

> Evan was cutting up an 8.4-pound ham for the freezer. How much should he put in each package if he wanted to serve it four different times?

> It rained a total of 4.2 inches over a three-day period. What was the daily average?

> Mindy checked her pedometer. She had run 8.4 kilometers in the last 3 days. What was her average daily run?

> After driving 347 miles Carolyn put 10.4 gallons of gasoline in her new car. How many miles per gallon does the car get?

WHOLE NUMBERS AS DIVISORS

The first decimal fraction division introduced to students is dividing decimal fractions by whole numbers. The example of dividing the 8.4-pound ham by 4 could be represented by Cuisenaire rods (Figure 9-47a). In this case the orange or ten rod is defined as the unit of one. After representing 8 and 4 tenths, the ones are then shared among 4 sets. The tenths are then distributed among the sets. Since each set contains 2 orange rods and 1 white rod, the answer is 2 and 1 tenth. As with other operations, students should explore and solve problems before being introduced to the algorithmic form. When the al-

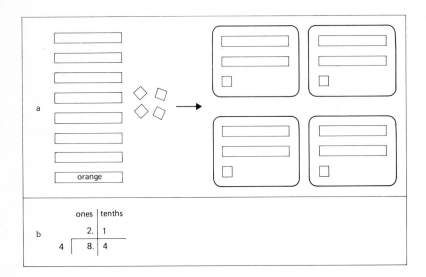

FIGURE 9-47.
Decimal division using
Cuisenaire rods.

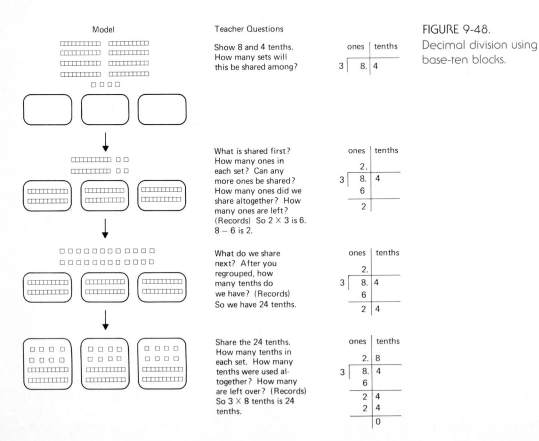

Model	Teacher Questions		
	Show 8 and 4 tenths. How many sets will this be shared among?		ones | tenths
			3 ⟌ 8. | 4
	What is shared first? How many ones in each set? Can any more ones be shared? How many ones did we share altogether? How many ones are left? (Records) So 2 × 3 is 6. 8 − 6 is 2.		ones | tenths
			2.
			3 ⟌ 8. | 4
			6
			2
	What do we share next? After you regrouped, how many tenths do we have? (Records) So we have 24 tenths.		ones | tenths
			2.
			3 ⟌ 8. | 4
			6
			2 | 4
	Share the 24 tenths. How many tenths in each set. How many tenths were used altogether? How many are left over? (Records) So 3 × 8 tenths is 24 tenths.		ones | tenths
			2. | 8
			3 ⟌ 8. | 4
			6
			2 | 4
			2 | 4
			0

FIGURE 9-48.
Decimal division using
base-ten blocks.

gorithmic form is introduced, the place-value form as shown should be used (Figure 9-47b).

To solve the example involving running 8.4 kilometers in 3 days, students would need to regroup. This problem is represented by base-ten blocks; in this situation the long was defined as one (Figure 9-48). Teacher questions and step-by-step recordings have been included for each step. This is the same sharing or distributive algorithm that was introduced in the section on division of whole numbers.

In some cases such as 0.12 ÷ 3, students may place the decimal point directly in front of the digit 4 in the quotient to obtain an answer of 0.4. When students are asked to illustrate the problem using base-ten blocks and are reminded that in this situation the flat is defined as one, they will see that their answer is 4 hundredths or 0.04 (Figure 9-49).

For additional assistance in the correct placement of the decimal point, students should be reminded to use their skills in estimation. Thus if they are dividing a number that is between 7 and 8 by three, for example 7.5 ÷ 3, the only reasonable answer would be close to two. If their computations yield an answer of 25 or of 0.25, they know immediately that this is not reasonable.

In the problems above, the quotients terminated after a certain number of places. In some division problems the students will encounter remainders. In some of these cases the students may decide to round their quotients; in other cases zeros may be annexed to continue the division (Figure 9-50a). In either case the students should be given explicit directions as to the number of decimal places needed or desired. Similar problems occur with the calculator. The calculator displays for these problems are shown in Figure 9-50b. When using calculators to solve division problems, students need instruction on how to interpret the results and how many place values are reasonable.

DECIMAL FRACTIONS AS DIVISORS

As problems become more complex, it is helpful to develop a *generalization* for the placement of the decimal point. To do this, students first recall that they know how to place the decimal point in the quotient when the divisor is a whole number. Obviously, if they could rewrite problems so that the divisor was always a whole number, this generalization would always work.

Patterns should be used to develop the rationale for decimal fraction divisors. In Figure 9-51, both the divisor and the dividend have been multiplied by the same factor. Often, students' first reaction is that the quotient will also be multiplied by the factor. On

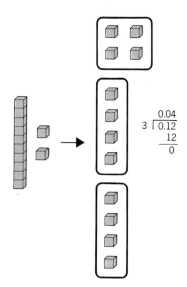

FIGURE 9-49.
Dividing decimals using base-ten blocks.

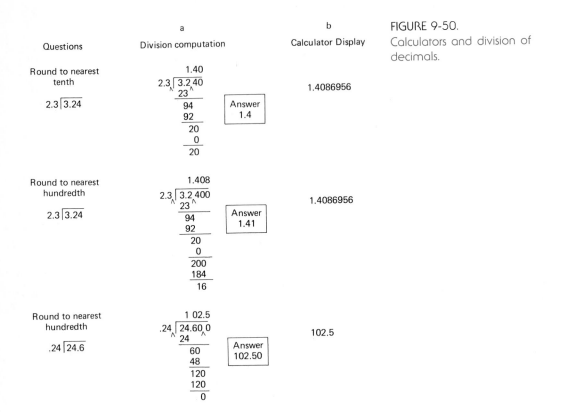

FIGURE 9-50.
Calculators and division of decimals.

examination of the problems, the students should realize that the division problems are equivalent.

The concept that both terms of a division problem can be multiplied by a constant without changing the answer is again useful. By choosing an appropriate power of 10 as the constant, students can always rewrite a problem so that the divisor is a whole num-

ber (Figure 9-52). For students who have difficulties with the concept of multiplying both terms of a division problem by a constant, a problem such as $0.2\overline{)3.46}$ can be related to common fractions (Figure 9-53). After students understand this concept, they may simply use a caret ($\wedge$) to indicate the new position of the decimal point in both the divisor and the dividend (Figure 9-54).

Estimation skills can also be used when the divisor is a decimal fraction instead of a whole number. To divide 3.46 by 0.2, Travis, a fifth grader, first used the standard division algorithm to find the sequence of digits (Figure 9-55). Then by estimation he placed the decimal point in the answer. In estimating, his sequence of thought was as follows. "I want to know how many groups of 2 tenths

$$3\overline{)15} \longrightarrow 6\overline{)30} \longrightarrow 18\overline{)90}$$

$$4\overline{)8} \longrightarrow 40\overline{)80} \longrightarrow 8\overline{)16}$$

FIGURE 9-51.
Patterns of division.

$0.2\overline{)3.46}$ $\longrightarrow$ 0.2 $\times$ $10\overline{)3.46 \times 10}$ $\longrightarrow$ $2\overline{)34.6}$

$1.76\overline{)892}$ $\longrightarrow$ 1.76 $\times$ $100\overline{)892 \times 100}$ $\longrightarrow$ $176\overline{)89200}$

FIGURE 9-52.
Placing the decimal point.

$0.2\overline{)3.46}$ $\longrightarrow$ $\dfrac{3.46}{0.2}$ $\longrightarrow$ $\dfrac{3.46}{0.2} \times \dfrac{10}{10}$ $\longrightarrow$ $\dfrac{34.6}{2}$ $\longrightarrow$ $2\overline{)34.6}$

FIGURE 9-53.
Rewriting decimal division.

$0.2_\wedge\overline{)3.46}$ $\qquad$ $1.76_\wedge\overline{)892.00_\wedge}$

FIGURE 9-54.
Caret to indicate decimal point.

each are contained in 3.46. There are 5 groups of 2 tenths each contained in one. In three, there would be three times as many groups or 15 groups. Since 3.46 is a little more than three, my answer should be a little more than 15. Therefore, the decimal point goes between the 7 and the 3 to give an answer of 17.3."

Dividing by 10s, 100s, and 1000s should also be explored. The patterns developed with whole numbers should be extended to decimal fractions by applying estimation strategies and using the calculator. The results of students' calculator work can be recorded as shown in Figure 9-56a. The students should analyze the pattern and discuss generalizations. The constant key on the calculator can be used to explore patterns using problems such as those shown

in Figure 9-56b. Students should observe that when a number is divided by tenths that it becomes 10 times larger. Again, students should form a generalization and extend it to dividing by hundredths, thousandths, and so on.

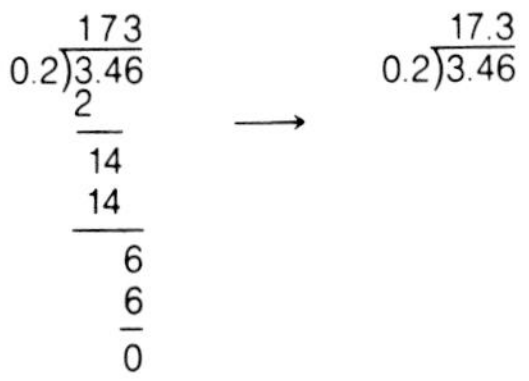

ESTIMATION FOR DIVISION OF DECIMAL FRACTIONS

As with the other operations for decimals, estimation is an important aspect for deciding the placement of the decimal point and for determining the reasonableness of results.

$$\begin{array}{r} 1\,7\,3 \\ 0.2_\wedge\overline{)3.46} \\ \underline{2} \\ 1\,4 \\ \underline{1\,4} \\ 6 \\ \underline{6} \\ 0 \end{array}$$ $\longrightarrow$ $$\begin{array}{r} 17.3 \\ 0.2\overline{)3.46} \end{array}$$

FIGURE 9-55.
Placing the decimal point by estimation.

a	b
	$3562 \div 0.1$
$3562 \div 100$	$356.2 \div 0.1$
$3562 \div 10$	$35.62 \div 0.1$
$3562 \div 1$	$3.562 \div 0.1$
$3562 \div 0.1$	
$3562 \div 0.01$	$482 \div 0.01$
$3562 \div 0.001$	$48.2 \div 0.01$
	$4.82 \div 0.01$
	$.482 \div 0.01$

FIGURE 9-56.
Division patterns.

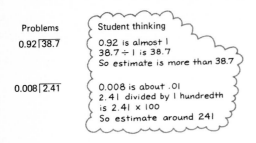

FIGURE 9-57.
Dividing by 1, 10, 100, or 1000.

DIVIDE BY 1, 10, 100, OR 1000

In the previous section, patterns of dividing by tenths, hundredths, and thousandths were discussed. In situations where the divisors are near 1, 0.1, 0.01, 0.001, this strategy can be applied. Examples of problems and student thinking have been included in Figure 9-57.

COMPATIBLE NUMBERS

As with the division of common fractions and whole numbers, the strategy of finding numbers that are easy to divide can be extended to decimal numbers. Examples of various problems and student thinking are shown in Figure 9-58. The last student may refine the estimate further by thinking, "Since there are

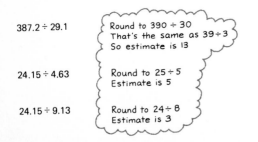

FIGURE 9-58.
Decimal division and compatible numbers.

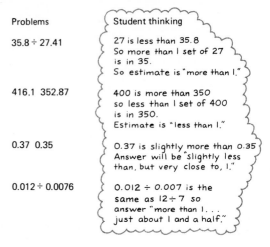

FIGURE 9-59.
Compare quotients to one for estimations.

more eights in 24 than 9s, my estimate should be less than 3."

COMPARE QUOTIENTS TO ONE

This strategy is the same as the one developed in "Estimation for Division of Common Fractions." If the dividend and divisor were the same, the quotient would be one. If the divisor is slightly smaller than the dividend, the answer will be greater than one. If the divisor is slightly larger than the dividend, the answer will be less than one. Examples of these problems and student thinking are shown in Figure 9-59.

QUESTIONS AND ACTIVITIES

1. Write a story problem for each of the following conditions. Include a variety of situations and questions.
   a. division of common fractions

b. whole number divided by a common fraction

c. common fraction divided by a whole number

d. division with mixed numbers

e. two-step with addition and division of fractions and mixed numbers

2. a. Reconsider Problem 1. Change the terms involving common fractions to decimal fractions. Rewrite the situations; include at least two situations that contain too little or too much information. Are partitive and measurement division situations included?

b. Compare your results to those that you wrote for common fractions and whole numbers. How are they alike? Different?

3. Use sets to illustrate each of the following.

a. How many thirds in a set of six?

b. How many 2 thirds in a set of six?

c. How many 3 fourths in a set of nine halves?

d. How many 3 fourths in a set of 2?

e. How many 2 fifths in a set of 7 tenths?

f. 3 fifths of a package of crackers were left. Jim shared it with his sister. How much did they each get?

4. Represent the following using paperfolding or region models.

a. 3 fifths of a carton of ice cream. Jim shared it with two of his friends. What part of the container was Jim's portion?

b. 2 thirds of a sandwich. Bill shared it with his sister. What part of a sandwich did they each eat?

c. Rebecca noted that it took 4 hours to rake the first 3 fifths of the yard. What part of the yard was done each hour? How many hours will it take to rake the remaining part of the yard?

d. How many 3 fifths in 4 fifths?

e. How many halves in 7 sixths?

f. $2\frac{3}{4} \div \frac{3}{4} = ?$

g. How many 5 sixths are contained in 2 sixths?

5. Compare $4 \div 3$ and 4 fifths $\div$ 3 fifths. How are the problems alike with relation to remainders?

6. Compare each pair of problems below. Write a number sentence for each.

a. 3 fifths of a carton of ice cream. Jim ate 1 third of it. What part of the container was Jim's portion?

a. 3 fifths of a carton of ice cream. Jim shared it with two of his friends. What part of the container was Jim's portion?

b. 2 thirds of a sandwich. Bill ate half of it. What part of the sandwich did Bill eat?

b'. 2 thirds of a sandwich. Bill shared it with his sister. What part of a sandwich did they each eat?

7. Evaluate the method of each of the following problems. If it is a correct procedure, do the sample problem using the same method.

a. $\frac{2}{3} \div \frac{2}{7} \rightarrow \frac{14}{21} \div \frac{6}{21} \rightarrow \frac{14}{6} \rightarrow 2\frac{1}{3}$

a'. $\frac{5}{6} \div \frac{4}{14}$

b. $\frac{5}{7} \div \frac{4}{9} \rightarrow \frac{\frac{5}{7}}{\frac{4}{9}} \rightarrow \frac{\frac{5}{7} \times \frac{9}{4}}{\frac{4}{9} \times \frac{9}{4}} \rightarrow \frac{\frac{45}{28}}{\frac{36}{36}} \rightarrow \frac{\frac{45}{28}}{1} \rightarrow 1\frac{17}{28}$

b'. $\frac{2}{3} \div \frac{5}{7}$

8. *Materials needed:* Fraction bars. Use fraction bars to solve the following. (*Hint:* Use the common denominator method and the measurement idea of division.)

a. $\frac{3}{4} \div \frac{1}{4}$

b. $\frac{2}{3} \div \frac{1}{4}$

c. $\frac{3}{4} \div \frac{1}{6}$

d. $\frac{5}{12} \div \frac{7}{12}$

9. Use the number line to solve the following problems. Write the appropriate number sentence.

a. How many 3 eighths in 6 eighths?

b. How many 3 eighths in 7 eighths?

c. $\frac{3}{5} \div \frac{1}{5}$

d. $3 \div \frac{1}{2}$

e. $1\frac{5}{6} \div \frac{2}{3}$

10. Solve the following using paperfolding. Write number sentences so that both common fractions and decimal fractions are considered.

a. How many 2 tenths in 4 tenths?
b. How many 2 tenths in 7 tenths?

11. Solve the following using a number line. Modify the number line so that both common fractions and decimal fractions are considered.
   a. How many 2 tenths in 4 tenths?
   b. How many 2 tenths in 7 tenths?
   c. How many 7 tenths in 2 tenths?

12. Solve the following using base-ten blocks. Write number sentences so that both common fractions and decimal fractions are considered.
   a. How many 3 tenths in 9 tenths?
   b. How many 4 tenths in 7 tenths?
   c. How many 7 tenths in 4 tenths?
   d. How many 7 hundredths in 21 hundredths?
   e. How many 7 hundredths in 2 tenths?

13. Use the constant key on a calculator to activate repeated subtraction to:
   a. determine the number of 0.2 in 4.
   b. determine the number of 0.5 in 3.5.
   c. find $6 \div 0.2$.
   d. find $0.3 \div 6$.

14. a. Redefine the base-ten blocks so the flat is one and then solve the following problems.
      (1) $3.2 \div 4$
      (2) $4.2 \div 3$
      (3) $7.36 \div 3$
      (4) $3.16 \div 3$
   b. Re-solve two of the problems in part (a) with another student. For each problem, one person should play the part of the student; the other the part of the teacher, recording the algorithm. Devise teacher questions to relate the procedures with the model to the recording of the algorithm.
   c. Compare your procedures with the model and the recording of the problems above with those below. How are they alike? Different?
      (1) $32 \div 4$
      (2) $42 \div 3$

(3) $736 \div 3$
(4) $316 \div 3$

15. A student has learned to solve $0.75 \div 0.5$. How would you use this fact to teach the concept of division of common fractions?

16. a. What patterns should students discover in working through the sequence of problems in Figure 9-56? How could a calculator be used in this activity?
   b. How could this activity be modified to focus on patterns of multiplication?
   c. Write up a sequence of problems involving multiplication patterns of decimal numbers that are parallel to those that you described in part (b).

17. Estimate the whole number answer and then place the decimal point in the appropriate position in the quotient.
   a. $74.16 \div 36 = 206$
   b. $74.16 \div 0.36 = 206$
   c. $74.16 \div 3.6 = 206$
   d. $741.6 \div 3.6 = 206$

18. How do problems such as those in Figure 9-59 show whether or not students understand division and decimal concepts?

19. *For your resource file:* Copy "Ideas" by Towsley. Read through the sections on estimating sums, differences, products, and quotients for fractions. Work through parts of each activity. What was your reaction to the problems?

20. The following advertisement was placed in shoppers sacks at the checkout counter. Identify the math error(s). If one of your students were consistently making this(these) error(s), how would you remediate?

21. a. Analyze the introduction to the division of common fractions in two different textbooks. Are story situations used to motivate the topic? What type of models are used—set or measurement? How and when are situations linked to the algorithm? Comment on the quantity and quality of story problems. Is partitive or measurement division used? Cite publisher, copyright date, and grade level.

  b. Analyze the introduction to the division of decimal fractions in two different textbooks. Are story situations used to motivate the topic? What type of models are used—set or measurement? How and when are situations linked to the algorithm? Comment on the quantity and quality of story problems. Is partitive or measurement division used? Cite publisher, copyright date, and grade level.

  c. Is the division of common fractions and decimal fractions related in the textbooks?

22. *For your resource file:* In "Teaching Division of Fractions with Understanding," Thompson describes readiness and developmental activities for common fractions using regions. Read this article and add the ideas to your resource file.

23. *For your resource file:* Trafton and Zawojewski discuss prerequisites and development for division of common and decimal fractions in "Teaching Rational Number Division: A Special Problem." Read this article and add the ideas to your resource file.

24. *For your resource file:* Read and copy one of the following articles. In "A Look at Division with Fractions," Silvia describes how to use regions and patterns to develop the concepts and procedures of division of common fractions. Feinberg, in "Is It Necessary to Invert?", uses the number line to develop division of common fractions.

25. *For your resource file:* A variety of topics are discussed in the articles by Thornton and Smart. In "The Why of Arithmetic," Smart discusses the *why* of such procedures as why you align decimal points in addition and not in multiplication or why you cannot divide by zero. These concise explanations to common questions from students should be helpful. In "A Glance at the Power of Patterns," Thornton presents patterns for developing multiplication of integers and common and decimal fractions, and division of fractions.

26. a. Read "Estimating with 'Nice' Numbers" by Reys, Reys, Trafton, and Zawojewski. Write a brief evaluation of the activities.

  b. Read "Developing Estimation Strategies" by Rubenstein. Use compatible numbers to estimate answers to the division problems and the fraction-times-whole-number problems. Add these and the other activities to your resource file.

TEACHER RESOURCES

Feinberg, Miriam M. "Is it Necessary to Invert?" *Arithmetic Teacher 27* (January 1980): 50–52.

Leutzinger, Larry P., and Glenn Nelson. "Let's Do It: With Powers of Ten." *Arithmetic Teacher 27* (February 1980): 8–12.

Lindquist, Mary Montgomery, Thomas P. Carpenter, Edward A. Silver, and Westina Matthews. "The Third National Assessment: Results and Implications for Elementary and Middle Schools." *Arithmetic Teacher 31* (December 1983): 14–19.

National Assessment of Educational Progress. *The Second Assessment of Mathematics, 1977-78: Released Exercise Set.* Denver, CO: Education Commission of the States, 1979.

Reys, Robert E., Barbara J. Reys, Paul R. Trafton, and Judy Zawojewski. "Estimating with 'Nice' Numbers." *Mathematics Teacher 78* (November 1985): 615–625.

Rubenstein, Rheta N. "Developing Estimation Strategies." *Mathematics Teacher 78* (February 1985): 112–118.

Silvia, Evelyn M. "A Look at Division with Fractions," *Arithmetic Teacher 30* (January 1983): 38–41.

Smart, James R. "The Why of Arithmetic." *Arithmetic Teacher 26* (January 1979): 21–23.

Swart, William L. "Fraction vs. Decimals—The Wrong Issue." *Arithmetic Teacher 29* (October 1981): 17–18.

Sweetland, Robert D. "Understanding Multiplication of Fractions." *Arithmetic Teacher 32* (September 1984): 48–52.

Thompson, Charles. "Teaching Division of Fractions with Understanding." *Arithmetic Teacher 27* (January 1979): 24–27.

Thornton, Carol A. "A Glance at the Power of Patterns." *Arithmetic Teacher 24* (February 1977): 154–157.

Towsley, Ann E. "Ideas." *Arithmetic Teacher 34* (October 1986): 26–32.

Trafton, Paul R., and Judith S. Zawojewski. "Teaching Rational Number Division: A Special Problem." *Arithmetic Teacher 31* (February 1984): 20–22.

Vance, James H. "Estimating Decimal Products: An Instructional Sequence." In *Estimation and Mental Computation,* 1986 Yearbook of the National Council of Teachers of Mathematics, pp. 127–134. Reston, VA: The Council, 1986.

10
TEACHING MEASUREMENT

"$4 \times 6 = 24$ and that needs to be added to the 15. Twenty-four plus 15 is 39. So 39 . . . cubic centimeters, centimeters, square centimeters? I never know what label to use."

Evaluate this student thinking. How would you respond to such a student?

Before entering school, children have had experiences with measures such as length, weight, time, and money. For example, when Susan, a 3-year old, is asked how old she is, she responds by holding up three fingers. She has learned an appropriate response, but she probably has no accurate time concept of a year. A similar response occurs when John states that he weighs 20 kilograms but has no concept of a kilogram.

The first part of this chapter is an overview of various aspects of measure that need to be considered as part of *all* measurement. These ideas are encountered in the study of any measures, such as weight, volume, time, or length. A number of these sections describe concepts that need to be introduced to children before they study a measurement system.

OVERVIEW OF MEASUREMENT

ATTRIBUTE BEING CONSIDERED

The first activities should focus on the attribute to be considered. If a box is presented to a group of children, some may focus on the design of the box: Is it an attractive color? An interesting design? If they didn't like the design, they may consider the attribute of surface area and consider how much paper is needed to recover the surfaces. Others may consider its origin or use: Where is the box from? What was it used for? What could it be used for? Some may consider the attribute of length: Is it long enough to hold my toy truck? A baseball bat? Is it too high to fit underneath the bed? Others may focus on volume and consider the types of or number of objects that it could hold. Others may focus on the material from which it was made: Is it flexible? Is it strong enough to hold two jars of apple cider? Would it float?

ORDERING

For teaching measurement to children, intuitive conceptual activities should precede actual measurement activities. When children cannot reach an object on a high shelf, they often seek a taller person to help them. They thus are showing an awareness of comparisons of different lengths. As the children's skills increase, lengths of more than two objects can be compared. Objects that have smaller differences in length and that have various other differences in size or shape should be included in ordering activities (Figure 10-1).

A similar activity involves mass and the use of a balance scale (Figure 10-2). Children can guess which of the two box-shaped masses is heavier and then place the masses on the two pans of the balance scale to check the estimation. Later experiments could involve ordering three or more masses.

To order the three masses shown in Figure 10-2, the children should pick up two masses, one in each hand. After estimating the relative weights, they should place the two masses in order noting the lighter and the heavier. To determine the placement of the third mass, they will have to decide if the third mass fits before the first mass, after the second mass, or in between the two masses. The balance scale should then be used to check the estimations.

BASIC UNIT OF MEASURE

After the children have had many experiences in ordering objects according to some measurable property, they are ready to begin doing some actual measurement. First

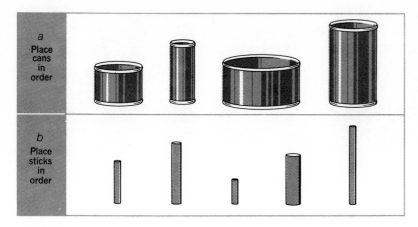

FIGURE 10-1.
Ordering cylinders from tallest to shortest.

experiences in measurement can be done with a problem-solving approach. For example, the teacher might say, "Today we are going to make a tin-can telephone. We will use a string long enough that someone in the front of the room can talk to someone in the back of the room. How can we decide how long a string we need to cut from this ball?" Students will probably suggest stretching the string from the front of the room to the back and then cutting it. This is a very direct method of measurement. If no other method is suggested, the teacher could vary the problem. "We have no string but must go to the store and buy some. How can we tell the storekeeper how much string we need?"

As they discuss various ways to solve these problems, children should begin to understand that measurement is a process of comparing an unknown quantity to a known one. Furthermore, they will see the need for a basic unit of measure to compare two quantities that cannot be placed together physically for comparison purposes. This need for a basic unit of measure can be developed through activities involving non-standard measurement.

NONSTANDARD/STANDARD MEASUREMENT

Nonstandard measurement activities in the classroom should be used to help children develop and extend the concept of measurement and develop the need for standard measures. Historically, the earliest units of measure used by people were based on parts of the body. Thus, units such as the cubit (Figure 10-3), the foot (the length of a person's foot), and the yard (the length

FIGURE 10-2.
Ordering masses.

FIGURE 10-3.
Cubit.

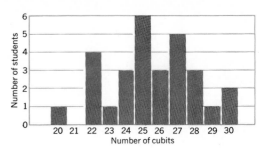

FIGURE 10-4.
Bar graph of cubits.

between the nose and the fingertips of a person's outstretched arm) were always readily available. The problem arose when two different people tried to measure the same quantity. Obviously an adult who measures 2 meters in height will have a larger cubit than a child who measures 1 meter. The basic unit of length, the cubit, is not the same length for each person; therefore, it is called a nonstandard unit of measurement. Other examples of nonstandard units of length would include feet, hand spans, pencils, or belts.

To aid their understanding of the importance of standard measurement, the children could measure the length of the classroom in cubits. If each student measured this length, the results would vary considerably as the students' cubits would not all be the same length. The results could be tallied and a bar graph could be formed (Figure 10-4). The class could discuss such questions as: Is it reasonable that the length of the room could vary between 20 and 30 cubits? Who has the longest cubit? The shortest? What is the most common length of the room in cubits? What should we do so that all of us obtain the same number of cubits for the length of the room? If we selected one of the cubits to be the class's official cubit, would

our communications about measurement be solved?

From these experiments and appropriate discussion, students should develop the idea that if measurements are to have any meaning, a standard unit of measure is necessary. In other words, each person making the measurement must use a basic unit of length that is the same length as the basic unit used by any other person.

Similar activities can be developed for area, volume, and mass. For example, as children find the areas of their desks by covering them with pieces of paper (Figure 10-5), they are developing the concept of area as covering a surface. By using various-sized sheets of paper such as file cards, envelopes, and notebook paper, the students will discover that the *number of sheets* needed to cover an area varies with the *size*

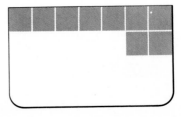

FIGURE 10-5.
Finding area of desk with paper.

of the sheet. In these activities children are also learning that for objects larger than the basic unit, they must repeat the basic unit over and over. To find the total length, area, volume, or mass, they simply count as they repeat the basic unit.

For volume experiments, students could use such nonstandard measuring units as paper cups or cottage-cheese cartons to measure the amount of water needed to fill a bucket. Children's experiences with volume and capacity should vary. In one activity they may fill a plastic container with layers of blocks and then count the number of blocks that the container held. In another they may fill the same container with water, measuring the amount of water the container will hold by counting the number of paper cupfuls that were poured into the container. In both of these cases they are considering how much a container will hold; in one case they count the number of cubes; in the other they count the number of repeated cupfuls.

Mass experiments can be done using a balance scale (Figure 10-6). Students can weigh items in terms of paper clips, nickels, pencils, or spoons. They can then compare the results.

Another concept involving nonstandard

1 inch	=	1 thumbs width
12 inches	=	1 foot
5 feet	=	1 pace
1000 paces	=	1 mile

FIGURE 10-7.
Roman system of measurement.

measure can be demonstrated by having students pace off the length of the room. They will find that they cannot always replicate their own results. Ancient systems of measurement, such as the Roman system (Figure 10-7), can be discussed with regard to this experiment. The students should note in the Roman system the familiar terms that are also in the customary system, formerly known as the English system, of measurement.

At this time the need for multiples and subdivisions of the basic unit should be developed. To develop the need for subdivisions of the basic unit, students could be asked to determine such measures as the length of someone's little finger, the thickness of a quarter, or the width of a mathematics textbook. In order to measure these objects, the students may need to subdivide their basic unit into smaller parts. Similar situations can be created to develop the need for subdivisions of their chosen basic units of other measures such as area, volume, mass, and angle.

To create the need for multiples of the basic unit, we will describe an example using volume. Perhaps the class was using a large cottage-cheese carton as the basic unit. The teacher could ask how they would measure the volume of a large wastepaper basket, a bathtub, or a swimming pool. The students may determine how many cartons are contained in a small pail (such as 15 cartons equals 1 pail) and use the pail as a larger unit of measure. The volume of the pail could then be used to determine the

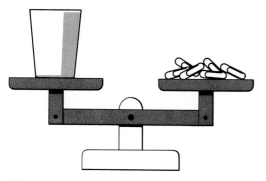

FIGURE 10-6.
Balance scale.

measure of the large wastepaper basket. After doing these volume experiments, the students may decide that they will need another method to determine the volume of the swimming pool. Again, similar activities could be used to develop the need for multiples of other basic units such as those for length, area, mass, and angle.

As students work with nonstandard units of measurement, they will soon see the need for standard units. For example, after the students measured the room with their cubits, they may have decided that one of their classmates' cubits should be chosen as the basic unit. The length of this particular student's cubit would become the official length, the standard unit. This length could be replicated on adding-machine tape so that each student would have a cubit the same length. But when the students want to communicate with others outside of their classroom, they will find that their system is not adequate. If the class ordered a sign with the dimensions of 2 cubits by 15 cubits, would they receive the size they wanted? For this reason a standard unit that is adopted by society is needed.

ARBITRARY SYSTEMS OF MEASUREMENT

After sufficient experimentation with nonstandard measurement, students will understand the need for a standard system. All systems of measurement are arbitrary. There is nothing inherent in a person's height that makes any one of the measures 6 feet 2 inches, 1.9 meters, or 37 googles any more or less valid than any other. As long as a basic unit has been defined and named and can be replicated, it is valid for use in measuring. No *one* system of measurement is "natural." Instead, all systems are imposed on nature by people. For this reason,

many different measurement systems have been developed. The problem occurs when measures from different systems are to be compared. For example, "If one man weighs 14 stone, another man weighs 90 kg, and a third man weighs 190 lb, which man weighs the most?" Although each of these is a valid measure, it is impossible to compare them unless one is familiar with all three systems. But the real confusion starts when countries with different systems start interacting with each other.

The standard system of measurement in common use in the United States is called the customary system. However, the metric system is the standard system for over 90% of the world's people. Even in the United States, the metric system is already employed to some extent. U.S. firms that trade with foreign countries usually produce products with metric specifications. Tools such as wrenches are commonly available in this country in both customary and metric sizes.

Many everyday items such as food products come in packages with customary-unit specifications, such as crackers in 2-pound boxes or milk in 1-quart bottles, but are labeled in both customary and metric units. A few products come in packages with metric-unit specifications, such as soda pop in 1-liter bottles or yarn in 100-gram balls.

The basic unit of length in the metric system is the meter. The meter was originally defined as one ten-millionth of an arc representing the distance between the North Pole and the Equator (Figure 10-8). In 1960 the meter was redefined as 1 650 766.73 wave lengths in vacuum of the orange-red line of the spectrum of krypton 86. This new definition has the advantages of being more precise and of allowing the meter to be exactly reproduced in any scientific laboratory in the world. The basic unit of volume, the liter, is defined as the quantity that a 10-deci-

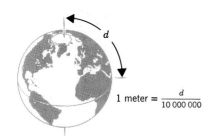

$$1 \text{ meter} = \frac{d}{10\ 000\ 000}$$

FIGURE 10-8.
Defining the meter.

meter cube will hold. A liter of water with no impurities at sea level is defined as having a mass of one kilogram.

After the basic units have been established, various multiples and subdivisions of these units are needed. One major advantage of the metric system is that it is based on the decimal system; that is, all multiples and subdivisions of the basic units are powers of ten. Various prefixes are used with the name of the basic unit to define the multiples and subdivisions as shown for length in Figure 10-9. Prefixes derived from Latin are used for subdivisions of the basic unit, and multiples of the basic unit are expressed with Greek-derivative prefixes. Since "centi" comes from the Latin for hundred, a centimeter is 0.01 of a meter, or there are 100 centimeters in every meter. A kilometer is 1000 meters since "kilo" is Greek for thou-

sand. In teaching the metric system, only the commonly used prefixes should be introduced to young children.

CONVERSIONS

Students should be given the opportunity to learn to think metric and to think in customary units. To accomplish this, the metric system and the customary system should be taught as separate or dual systems with emphasis placed on the metric system. When students are asked to make an estimation in kilograms, they should think in metric terms rather than estimate in pounds and then convert to kilograms. The students should use only metric units since this encourages thinking within the system. Obviously, when these estimations are checked, the measurements should be made in metric units. Similarly, when working in the customary system, students should estimate and measure completely in terms of these units.

Conversion from one unit to another within the metric system is a simple matter. It is only necessary to multiply or divide by the appropriate power of ten. Thus, 3 liters would be equal to 0.003 kiloliter or to 3000 milliliters. By contrast, in the customary system conversion from one unit to another involves multiplying or dividing by such numbers as 5280, 8, 12, 2000, 16, 16.5, and so on.

Conversions between the two systems should usually be avoided. Doing computation exercises to convert miles to kilometers offers no real understanding of the relationship between the two units. With the exception of scientific or technical work, if a conversion cannot be done mentally, it should not be done. The following is a list of approximate relationships that can be used for mental conversions.

Millimeter	0.001 of a meter
Centimeter	0.01 of a meter
Decimeter	0.1 of a meter

Meter is the basic unit for length

Dekameter is	times a meter
Hectometer is	times a meter
Kilometer is	times a meter

FIGURE 10-9.
Prefixes used with meter.

8 kilometers is approximately 5 miles.

A meter is a little longer than a yard.

5 centimeters is about 2 inches.

A liter is slightly more than a quart.

250 milliliters is about 1 cup.

A kilogram is a little more than 2 pounds.

For scientists and technicians, charts showing exact conversion factors or calculators that have conversion keys are readily available.

STRATEGIES FOR ESTIMATION

Part of learning measurement is estimating measures. When children are first learning about such measures as liters, pounds, inches, or meters they need to learn to conceptualize these units. They should be able to estimate which measures are about the same as, more than, or less than the size of the unit being considered. After they have conceptualized the size of a unit they are ready to begin learning estimating strategies.

Comparison

When students are deciding if an object is more than or about one liter, they are using comparison. This strategy is extended by making comparisons with other known quantities as well as with the basic unit. For example, in a lesson on measurement the third graders were asked to estimate the height of the teacher's file cabinet. Looking at the file cabinet, Sue reasoned, "The cabinet is taller than I am . . . How can I decide how much taller it is? . . . Oh, Stan is over by the cabinet. If I knew how tall Stan is, I could compare his height to the height of the cabinet. I am 126 centimeters tall . . . Stan is a little bit shorter, so he's about . . . 120 cen-

timeters tall. The cabinet is about . . . 25 centimeters taller than Stan, so . . . 120 plus 25 . . . the cabinet is about 145 centimeters tall."

Another student, Audrey, estimated area by reasoning, "I measured the den and it is 90 square feet. The kitchen looks 2 and a half times as large, so I'll estimate 180 plus 45 is . . . 200 plus 25 more or 225 square feet." After lifting her dog Fierce, Cecilia estimated that he weighed 20 pounds, as she knew that her cat Pony weighed 9 pounds.

In working with volume conversions Drake wrote that there were 6 cubic feet in 2 cubic yards. He reflected on his results, thinking of a cube one yard on an edge and a cube one foot on an edge. The comparison was not 1 to 3. He visualized how many cubic feet he could repeat along one of the bottom edges and then determined that there were 9 square feet in the bottom layer. Then he visualized how many layers high, to give him a measure of 27 cubic feet in one cubic yard.

Repeating a Unit

Another strategy is that of mentally repeating the unit. To estimate the length of the classroom, Stan first visualized a 1-meter distance and then mentally "repeated" the unit down the entire length of the classroom. In estimating this same distance, Lela visualized her height of about five feet and mentally repeated the five-foot length. She repeated the length 6 times, so her estimate was 6 times 5 feet or 30 feet.

Tom used this method for estimating the height of a building. Looking at the outside of the building, he estimated the height of one floor and then counted the number of floors by considering the rows of windows.

To estimate the area of a room, Glenna first estimated that the tabletop had an area of one and a half square meters. She counted as she mentally moved the table along one of the walls. She counted four tables along the wall. She then determined that the room would hold four rows of four tables. She then reasoned "16 times $1\frac{1}{2}$ square meters is 16 + 8 or 24 square meters."

Subdivisions

A third strategy, subdivisions, involves looking at small sections of the whole to be estimated, estimating each part and then using addition or multiplication to find the whole. For example, to estimate the length of a classroom wall that contains several equal-sized windows, the students can estimate the width of one window and multiply that estimation by the number of windows. Often, the windows do not extend the entire length of the wall. In this case the length of the remaining portions of the wall should be estimated and added to the previous estimation. This strategy can be used to estimate any length that is already divided into equal-sized subdivisions. The strategy is helpful because shorter distances are easier to estimate than longer ones.

Vonda used this strategy to estimate the amount of floor area in Wright Hall, a classroom building on campus. She counted the number of offices on the second floor and multiplied this number times her estimate of the average size of an office. She then classified the classrooms into three categories according to size; after estimating the size of each category, she multiplied and added accordingly. After determining the area of one floor, she multiplied by the number of floors in the building.

Deanne used this strategy to estimate the amount of money in her piggy bank. She subdivided the coins by their values and then estimated the number of pennies, nickels, dimes, and quarters. She then used her calculator for determining the total value.

Halving

In many cases the length to be estimated has no existing equal-sized subdivisions. A fourth strategy that could be useful in this situation is visually approximating half of the total length and estimating this distance. If this half is still too great a distance for easy estimation, the student could repeat the process by visually dividing again, estimating that distance, and multiplying by four. The process of dividing in half can be repeated several times until the portion being considered is small enough to be easily estimated. However, the students should be aware that each approximation of half introduces some error. Therefore, the larger the number of approximations used, the greater the total error.

This procedure could have been used to answer a problem discussed earlier, finding the area of Wright Hall. The students could have mentally divided the building's length and width in half and estimated these shorter lengths. After determining the area of one floor, they could multiply to find the area of the entire building.

In all measuring activities, students should experience measurements in different units by making estimations of length, area, volume, mass, and so on. Estimation should be based on selecting an appropriate unit and estimating the number of those units. After choosing an appropriate unit, students should give reasonable estimations. The estimations should be checked by measuring the objects. Estimation errors of more than 10 percent of the total measure mean that the students need additional practice in estimation to improve their skills. If estimation skills are omitted, students are only reading numbers from a measuring instrument. Estimations help them to develop an understanding of and a feeling for the various units of measure.

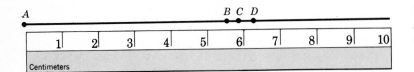

FIGURE 10-10.
Measuring objects to the nearest centimeter.

APPROXIMATIONS AND PRECISION

In working with measurements, children should begin with gross measurements and gradually be introduced to more precise measurements. For example, young children are not capable of reading millimeters when they begin doing measurement activities. The first rulers they use to measure objects will be marked only in centimeters. Thus each answer is read to the nearest centimeter.

No matter how precise the measuring instrument used, no measurements are exact. For example, in Figure 10-10, $\overline{AB}$ has a measure of 6 cm since it is closer to 6 than to 5, but $\overline{AC}$ and $\overline{AD}$ would also be called 6 cm long even though D, B, and C are at different distances from A. Each measurement was rounded off to the nearest centimeter. The ruler is said to have an error of one-half centimeter. Therefore the greatest possible error in measuring with this ruler is one-half of a centimeter. If the ruler were marked off in millimeters, the greatest possible error would be one-half of the smallest unit or one-half of a millimeter.

If an object is measured with a meter stick that is marked only in decimeters, the measurement will not be as precise as when we use a meter stick that is marked in centimeters. A meter stick marked in millimeters would be more precise than either of the previously mentioned meter sticks. But an instrument that is capable of measuring parts of a millimeter would be still more precise. Measurements are limited by the precision of the tools used. Thus, all measurements are approximate.

Since no measurement is exact, no measuring instrument can be exact. In a previous example, students chose a particular cubit as the standard and replicated that cubit for each class member. However, each time the standard cubit was replicated, some error occurred. Similarly in the real world, no matter what is used as the defined standard basic unit, it can never be replicated exactly. Thus, no measuring instrument is exact.

QUESTIONS AND ACTIVITIES

1. A set of objects can be ordered in different ways depending on which attributes are being considered.
   a. List the different attributes for which the cans in Figure 10-1 could be ordered.
   b. List at least ten different attributes that could be used to order the students in your class.
   c. Consider a grapefruit. What are some of the different attributes that could be considered in response to the question, "How much?"

2. List at least 20 different measuring instruments. Name the attribute being measured for each instrument.

3. In "Teaching Measurement to Elementary School Children," Inskeep lists 12 objectives of measurement. List the objectives. Read through the sections on

teaching these objectives for various types of measures.

4. a. Read the children's book *How Big Is a Foot?* by Myller for an example of a nonstandard unit of measure.

b. Develop a teaching lesson involving the hand span as a nonstandard measure. Describe the activities, charts for recording data, and questions that help children realize the need for standard measurement.

c. *For your resource file:* Excellent suggestions for teaching a lesson on nonstandard measure are contained in "Let's Do It: Developing the Concept of Linear Measurement" by Bruni and Silverman.

5. Given the basic unit shown below, George found the perimeters of both figures to be 10. Was he correct? If not, what was his mistake?

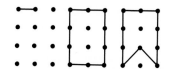

6. Read the children's book *Area* by Srivastava. What is the purpose of the activities on pages 8–9, 12–15, 21–24, and 26–28?

7. a. What nonstandard objects or units could be used to measure volumes of containers such as cereal boxes, margarine boxes, shoe boxes, or bread pans.

b. Name a nonstandard object or unit that could be used to measure the capacity of containers such as pop bottles, cottage-cheese containers, vases, and plastic milk bottles.

c. How are the foregoing situations alike? Different?

d. Eventually, we use linear measure to measure both volume and capacity. Briefly describe or show how you would

use the unit chosen in part (b) to calibrate the containers below to measure in your chosen nonstandard unit.

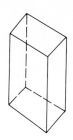

8. *For your resource file:* Read and copy "Let's Do It: Student-Made Measuring Tools." In the article Shaw describes activities that involve children in making their own measuring instruments for length, mass, and volume. How could you adapt these ideas for nonstandard measure or customary measures?

9. a. Choose a nonstandard basic unit of mass. How would you create the need for subdivisions? Need for multiples?

b. Choose a nonstandard basic unit of volume. How would you create the need for subdivisions? Need for multiples?

10. What is meant by the statement "All measurement systems are arbitrary"?

11. a. Why teach estimation? O'Daffer lists five reasons in "A Case and Techniques for Estimation: Estimation Experiences in Elementary School Mathematics— Essential, Not Extra!" What are the reasons?

b. *For your resource file:* In addition to the O'Daffer article, two other good resources would be "Estimation as Part of Learning to Measure" by Bright and "Estimation in Measurement" by Coburn and Shulte.

12. Read the children's book *Estimation* by Linn. Summarize some of the activities described in the book.

13. Read "The Use of Strategies in Estimating Measurements" by Hildreth for descriptions of appropriate and inappropriate strategies for estimating length and area. What inappropriate strategies had some fifth- and seventh-grade students developed? What recommendations did Hildreth make for teaching estimation?

14. Consider the strategies that were described for estimation. What strategy or strategies could you use to estimate the floor area of your dorm or home? Estimate the area and describe how you obtained this estimate.

15. a. Use the halving estimation technique to estimate the height of large trees.
   b. Use two different strategies to estimate the height of the tallest building on campus. What strategies did you use?
   c. To check your estimate, read "How High Is a Flagpole?" by Hunt to determine a way to measure the building and the tree.

16. Cecelia made the measurement shown below and wrote her answer as 5.25 units. Cite two errors in her thinking. What is an appropriate answer?

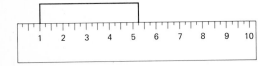

17. What is meant by the statement "All measurement of continuous quantities is approximate"?

18. Explain the difference between estimation and approximation. Read the article, "Estimation and Approximation—Not Synonyms" by Hall for clarification of the differences between the two concepts.

19. a. In "Sticks and Stones" Lappan and Winter discuss precision for linear and area measures. Read this article and then measure your desk using only a foot ruler. Remeasure with a ruler calibrated in inches. Then remeasure

with a ruler whose inches have been subdivided in eighths or sixteenths.
   b. Draw a circle with a four-inch radius on inch-square graph paper. Draw two more congruent circles on graph paper marked in half-inch and quarter-inch squares. Find the area of the circle by counting and estimating squares for each case. Compare your results.
   c. *For your resource file:* For more pre-formula activities on finding the area of a circle, read "Finding the Area of a Circle: Use a Cake Pan and Leave Out the Pi" by Szetala and Owens.

TEACHING MEASURES

Concepts of measurement are developed in this chapter by using the metric system rather than the customary system. An activities approach to teaching measurement is highly recommended since it is essential for student understanding of measurement concepts. Appropriate measuring activities are included in this chapter; others are included in the questions and activities section and in *The Elementary Math Teacher's Handbook.* A similar teaching approach for measurement should be used when the customary system is taught.

LENGTH

Beginning activities for developing the basic concepts of length have already been described in the overview. The basic unit of length is the meter. Other commonly used units are millimeter, centimeter, and kilometer. The first of these units that children usually encounter in school is the centimeter, which is introduced by means of a model (Figure 10-11). In order to internalize the concept of 1 centimeter, children must esti-

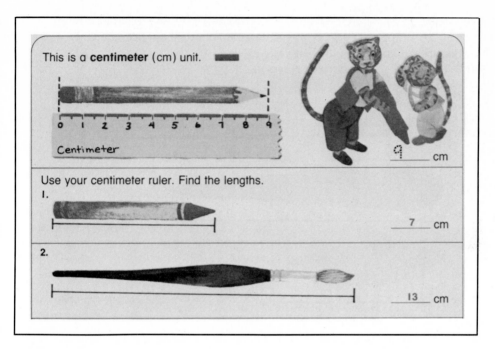

This is a **centimeter** (cm) unit. ▬

Centimeter

9 ___ cm

Use your centimeter ruler. Find the lengths.

1.

7 ___ cm

2.

13 ___ cm

FIGURE 10-11.
Measuring in centimeters. (From Robert Eicholz, Phares O'Daffer, Charles Fleenor, Randall Charles, Sharon Young, Carne Barnett, **Addison-Wesley Mathematics: Book 2,** 1985, p. 227. Copyright © 1985, Addison-Wesley Publishing Co. Inc.)

mate the dimensions of various small objects in centimeters and check their estimations by measuring.

A 1-centimeter ruler would obviously not be practical for actually measuring objects. On the other hand, the next larger common unit, the meter, is too long to be convenient for making measurements such as the length of a piece of chalk or the thickness of a book. Even for a measurement such as the width of the teacher's desk, a meter stick is awkward for young children to use. Instead, children could use interlocking centimeter cubes to build a 10-centimeter ruler (Figure 10-12). After estimating small lengths, the children should then use their 10-centimeter rulers to check the estimates. Ten-centimeter paper strips with dittoed centimeter mark-

ings could also be used for these measuring activities.

After children have done many activities estimating and measuring small lengths, they should begin to estimate longer lengths. For this, they should learn to visualize 10 centimeters as a whole unit (Figure 10-12). The orange Cuisenaire rod would make a convenient model since it is 10 centimeters

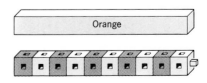

FIGURE 10-12.
10-centimeter ruler.

long but has no markings so children will see it as a whole unit. Children can practice estimating 10-centimeter units by separating a variety of objects by length and placing them into three sets. These sets would be those objects that are shorter than 10 centimeters, those that are longer than 10 centimeters, and those that are approximately equal to 10 centimeters. To check their estimates, the children should then measure the objects with the orange Cuisenaire rod or some other model of a 10-centimeter unit.

Next, instead of just classifying objects longer than 10 centimeters, children must measure these longer objects in 10-centimeter units. For this activity children should have a large supply of 10-centimeter paper strips or orange Cuisenaire rods. To measure a length such as the width of the teacher's desk, the children could place the 10-centimeter units end to end along the edge of the desk (Figure 10-13). To determine this length, the children can count the units as "ten, twenty, thirty . . . sixty centimeters." As children measure other longer objects, they will further internalize the concept of the 10-centimeter unit.

Children should also estimate to the nearest 10 centimeters the lengths of various objects that are shorter than a meter. They can then check their estimates by measuring with their 10-centimeter unit. As this skill is practiced and extended, children will gradually start estimating these longer lengths to the nearest centimeter. For example, in estimating the length of a book children would think, "10, 20 . . . no, 30 is too much . . . it's closer to 30 than to 20 . . . so 28 centimeters."

Thirty-centimeter rulers are commonly available commercially. These rulers are convenient for measuring many common objects such as books, pencils, and so on. However, they are not useful for extending measurement concepts to the next larger common unit, the meter. If children use 10-centimeter paper rulers, they can tape ten of these rulers together to form the next larger unit, the meter (Figure 10-14). If the 30-centimeter unit is repeated, the multiples are 30 cm, 60 cm, 90 cm, 120 cm, but not 100 cm or 1 meter. Another problem is that if children constantly use a 30-centimeter ruler, they will not conceptualize a 10-centimeter unit but rather a 30-centimeter unit.

As children are measuring small objects in centimeters, they will begin to see the need for larger units for measuring such things as the length of the classroom. When first introduced to the meter, children should practice estimating various lengths as longer than, shorter than, or approximately equal to 1 meter. This activity will help them to internalize the concept of this unit. For actually measuring longer lengths such as the length of the classroom, the children will need to learn to repeat the meter unit by laying off one meter, marking that, moving the meter stick to lay off another meter, and so on. Children should also learn to estimate longer lengths to the nearest meter.

After initial experiences in estimating the lengths of small objects to the nearest cen-

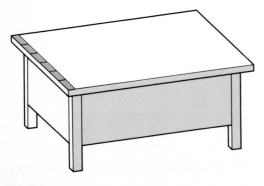

FIGURE 10-13.
Measuring desk with 10-centimeter units.

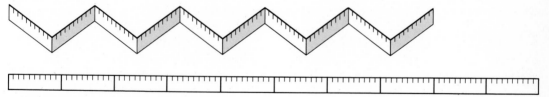

FIGURE 10-14.
Ten 10-centimeter rulers linked together.

timeter and the lengths of longer objects to the nearest meter, students should learn to distinguish when to use each unit. For example, if children are trying to estimate the length of a knife, the height of a door, or the length of a chalk tray, they must first decide on an appropriate unit. Once the unit has been chosen, they can use one or more of several estimation strategies discussed earlier.

Estimation skills can be extended to the multiples of a meter. These longer units of length can be measured in school hallways or on the playground. As a preparatory activity, students can practice adjusting their paces to a 1-meter length. For this activity, strips of masking tape can be placed one meter apart on the classroom floor. By maintaining an even stride, the students can use their 1-meter pace as a measuring tool to approximate such distances as home to school or classroom to lunchroom.

To develop a concept of a 10-meter length, students can pace off 10 meters. The accuracy of their strides can be checked by trundle wheels or 10-meter lengths of rope as shown in Figure 10-15. After measuring the 10-meter length, the students should study this distance and then estimate such distances as classroom lengths, tree heights, or gym lengths. After students have developed a concept of 10-meter lengths, this can be extended to 100-meter lengths by similar activities in estimation and actual

measurement. It would be helpful to find near the school a city block or some other referent model that measures approximately 100 meters. The 1000-meter unit, the kilometer, can be related to paper routes, long walks, jogging distances, or distances between towns.

As intermediate students are developing the concepts of units longer than a meter (multiples of a meter), they should also be introduced to units shorter than a centimeter (further subdivisions of a meter). The millimeter can be introduced as one tenth of a centimeter. One millimeter is about the measure of the thickness of a dime. Various objects should be estimated and measured using millimeters as the unit of measure.

AREA

To measure area, children must first develop the concept of the property to be measured. Activities were mentioned earlier where chil-

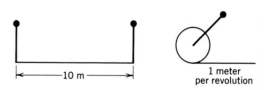

FIGURE 10-15.
Measuring tools for longer lengths.

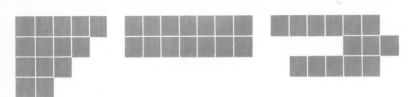

FIGURE 10-16.
Finding area by counting square units.

14 units   14 units   14 units

dren were introduced to area by covering surfaces with sheets of paper (Figure 10-5). Preliminary experiences with area should also involve ordering. For example, children should begin by ordering various-sized file cards by area. As children extend their concept of area from this and similar activities, they will recognize other surfaces such as classroom walls, desktops, floors, and so on. These surfaces can also be compared by size (area) without regard to other characteristics of the objects.

Young children often perceive that as the shape of a surface changes so does its size. The following is an appropriate activity to help children learn that size does not necessarily change just because shape does. Children can be given several equal-sized units and asked to place them together to form various areas. By counting the units, the children will find that all the areas are the

same size even though they are different shapes (Figure 10-16).

When a distance must be measured, an appropriate unit of *length* must be selected. When a surface needs to be measured, an appropriate unit of *area* needs to be selected. Children's preliminary experiences with area should be counting activities. For example, Mr. Schulz introduced simple area concepts to his class by asking the children to guess how many pieces of paper would be required to cover the surface of a student desk. To check their estimates, the children used papers to cover their desktops. Chuck covered his desk with sheets of notebook paper and reported to the class, "The area of my desk is four." Karen said, "But my desk is the same size as Chuck's. I covered my desk with file cards, counted them, and got an area of 24." Through guided discussion, Mr. Schulz helped the class to discover that

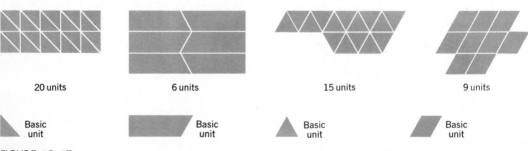

20 units   6 units   15 units   9 units

Basic unit   Basic unit   Basic unit   Basic unit

FIGURE 10-17.
Nonsquare basic units.

the reported measures were different because Karen and Chuck used two different nonstandard units of measure. The class also observed that the smaller the chosen unit of area, the more units were needed to cover the desk.

Children should participate in activities using other nonsquare basic units to measure area. Some examples are shown in Figure 10-17. The children should observe that these units cover the surface without overlapping or leaving gaps. Children should also attempt to cover surfaces with units such as circles, ellipses, pentagons, and so on that will not cover the surface exactly. From these experiences children will see that a unit for measuring area must cover the surface exactly.

At this stage it will probably appear to children that many different polygons would be appropriate as units of area measure. However, we must consider other factors. Usually fractional parts of the basic unit are needed to cover a surface completely. Through activities children can discover that it is easier to find fractional parts of a square than it is to find fractional parts of triangles, parallelograms, or other polygons. Also, when we find the areas of rectangular regions, we measure the base and the height in the *same* linear units. When these measures are multiplied to find area, the result is square units. Therefore, standard basic units of area are defined as squares.

The basic unit of area in the metric system is the square meter. Other units commonly used to measure area are square centimeters, ares, and hectares. The first of these units usually introduced to children is the square centimeter (Figure 10-18). As discussed in the section on length, children need activities in estimation and in counting square centimeters that will lead them to in-

Area

To find the **area** of the blue rectangle, we can count the **square centimeter** tiles that it takes to cover it.

square centimeter

1 cm
1 cm

The area is 15 square centimeters.

FIGURE 10-18.
Square centimeter model. (From C. A. Dilley, D. W. Lowry, W. E. Rucker, **Heath Mathematics,** D. C. Heath & Company, 1988, Grade 3, p. 248. Reprinted by permission of D. C. Heath & Company)

ternalize the concept of one square centimeter.

Students also need experiences estimating the areas of larger surfaces such as a tabletop. The square centimeter is too small to be practical for this type of estimation. Therefore, the students should be introduced to the square decimeter (10 centimeters by 10 centimeters) since it is more appropriate for such estimations. As students improve their concept of a square decimeter through activities in estimating and measuring, their estimation skills will improve. A large number of square decimeters should be available for students to use in checking their area estimates.

The relationship between square centimeters and square decimeters can be shown using centimeter graph paper. Students can cut a square decimeter from the graph paper and observe that there are 100 square centimeters in 1 square decimeter. Students are often surprised by this fact. Since they already know that there are 10 centimeters in 1 decimeter, they expect that there will be 10 square centimeters in 1 square decimeter. By studying their model of a square decimeter, the students can see their error and can conceptualize the correct relationship between linear and area measures.

To measure still larger areas such as the floor of the classroom a large unit—the square meter—is needed. To begin developing this concept, the students could use masking tape to outline a square meter on the classroom floor. The area of the classroom walls and of the floor can be estimated and discussed in terms of square meters. Students can discover the relationship between square meters and square decimeters by covering their model of the square meter with square decimeters.

To conceptualize larger units such as ares, the students can lay out a square 10 meters by 10 meters. They can then discuss this in relation to the size of the classroom floor, the entire school building, or the playground. If the students have found a square city block approximately 100 meters on a side, this would be a good model for 10,000 square meters or one hectare.

VOLUME/CAPACITY

Everything occupies or encloses space. The measure of this space is called volume. Volume concepts should be developed through activities in a manner similar to the development of area concepts. An appropriate activity for beginning to conceptualize volume is ordering various-sized boxes according to the space they occupy. Similarly, the cans shown in Figure 10-1a could be ordered by the space they enclose, that is, how much they contain or their capacity.

Children should also realize that various-shaped objects can occupy or contain the same amount of space. For example, given 12 blocks, children can build different-shaped rectangular solids (Figure 10-19). By counting the blocks they will observe that the

12 cubic units

12 cubic units

FIGURE 10-19.
Conservation of volume.

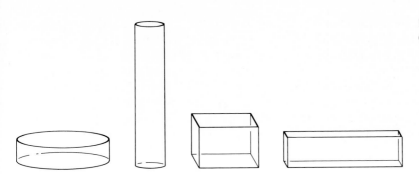

FIGURE 10-20.
One-liter containers.

two shapes have the same volume. Similarly, given the containers in Figure 10-20, by pouring water from one container to another the children can discover that all four containers have the same capacity.

Volume is usually introduced by filling boxes. To measure the volume of a shoe box, children could fill it with their toy blocks. The children would then count the blocks, their basic unit of measure, to determine the volume of the box. By filling the same box with smaller blocks, the children will realize that, as with length and area, the smaller the basic unit, the more times it must be repeated.

To measure the volume or capacity of a pail, children could fill it by pouring in paper cupfuls of water. The paper cup is thus the basic unit of measure. By counting each cupful as they pour it into the pail, the children can determine the volume of the pail. By using a cottage-cheese carton to fill the same pail, the children will again see that the larger the basic unit of measure, the fewer times it must be repeated.

If the children had filled the shoe box with Ping-Pong balls or soda cans, they would have observed that there were unfilled spaces. Spheres and cylinders are thus shown to be inappropriate units of volume. Just as a square was the most convenient basic unit of area, similarly a cube is the most convenient basic unit of volume.

When children filled the shoe box with toy blocks, they placed three rows of six blocks on the bottom of the box. It took a second layer of 18 blocks to fill the box so the box has a volume of 36 blocks as found by direct measurement (Figure 10-21). Since the basic unit of measure, the block or cube, has edges of 1 unit by 1 unit by 1 unit, the volume of this box could also be found indirectly by using the linear dimensions and an appropriate formula. Since $V = l \times w \times h$ and the box measures 6 units by 3 units by 2 units, the volume of the box is 6 units $\times$ 3 units $\times$ 2 units or 36 cubic units.

Direct measurement using cubes is not a convenient method for measuring the volume of most objects such as dining rooms,

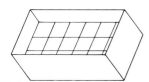

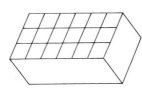

FIGURE 10-21.
Volume by direct measurement.

tin cans, water towers, or concrete blocks. However, cubic units are still appropriate units for calculating the volumes of such objects using formulas and appropriate linear dimensions. Unfortunately, to measure the volume of irregular-shaped objects—for example, a large pottery vase—formulas and linear measures are unlikely to be appropriate.

A more convenient method is to measure the capacity, how much the object will hold. When children measured the volume of the shoe box, they packed the blocks into it. Unfortunately, the blocks will not fit compactly into the pottery vase. After pouring as many blocks as possible into the vase, the children count the blocks to find a rough approximation of the capacity of the vase. If, instead of blocks, the children used marbles, popcorn, or sand as their basic unit, they would have obtained successively better approximations of the capacity of the vase.

However, as the basic unit becomes smaller and smaller, it becomes harder to count the individual units. Instead of counting grains of sand, the children need to compare the quantity of sand in the pottery vase to a known quantity. If they chose a paper cup as their basic unit, they could repeatedly fill the paper cup with the sand from the vase and count cupfuls to measure the capacity of the vase. Finally, since a liquid will fill the space completely, it will give the best approximation of the capacity of the vase.

Units of capacity are also needed to measure the volume of liquids since liquid has shape only in a container. When the capacity of a particular container is defined as the basic unit, the volume of an unknown quantity of liquid can be measured using this container.

The common metric units of volume that are convenient for estimation and measurement are cubic centimeters, cubic decimeters, and cubic meters. The cubic centimeter is usually introduced at about the fourth-grade level, and the larger units are introduced later. To help children conceptualize these metric units, models of cubic centimeters, cubic decimeters, and cubic meters should be available in the classroom. Children will become familiar with these units through activities in estimation and counting similar to those described for area. By observing the relative sizes of the models, the children should decide which units would be appropriate to measure different volumes such as desk drawers, shoe boxes, closets, swimming pools, or crayon boxes.

The relationship of the cubic centimeter to the cubic decimeter should be discovered by observing first how many cubic centimeters will form the bottom layer of a cubic decimeter and then how many layers would be required to complete it. A similar activity should be discussed for cubic decimeters and a cubic meter.

The basic unit of capacity in the metric system is the liter, which is introduced to children in the primary grades. When quantities smaller than the liter are to be measured, the children should be introduced to a common subdivision, the milliliter. Since the milliliter is an extremely small quantity, the children's first graduated measuring containers should be marked in multiples of 250 or 100 milliliters. As children mature, they will become capable of reading scales calibrated in smaller units such as 10-milliliter or 5-milliliter units.

A dissectible cubic decimeter that is commercially available can be used to show students the relationship between capacity and volume (Figure 10-22). The clear plastic box has inside dimensions of 10 cm by 10

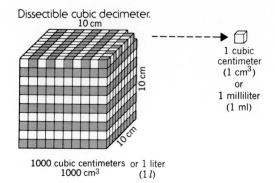

Dissectible cubic decimeter.

10 cm

10 cm

10 cm

1 cubic
centimeter
(1 cm^3)
or
1 milliliter
(1 ml)

1000 cubic centimeters or 1 liter
1000 cm³   (1 *l*)

FIGURE 10-22.
Dissectible cubic decimeter.

cm by 10 cm. It is filled with nine flats, nine longs, and ten units that are available in contrasting colors. By making comparisons, the children can discover that one long is equivalent to 10 units, one flat is equivalent to 100 units, and, therefore, the entire box holds 1000 units or 1000 cubic centimeters. The box will also hold 1 liter of water so 1 liter is equivalent to 1000 cubic centimeters. Since the small cube is one-thousandth of the large cube, the small cube is 1 cubic centimeter or 1 milliliter.

WEIGHT/MASS

In everyday use, weight and mass are considered equivalent measures. Technically, they are not the same. Weight is the force on an object due to the pull of gravity. An object will weigh less on the moon than on the earth because the moon's gravitational pull is less. Mass measures the actual quantity of matter, so the mass of an object is the same on the earth and on the moon. For example, on a balance scale, if a mass of 90 kilograms will balance a person on earth, that same mass will balance the person on the moon. How-

ever, using a spring scale the same person will weigh 90 kilograms on the earth but only 15 kilograms on the moon. Mass remains constant; weight changes according to gravity. Since these two quantities are considered the same in everyday use, the term "mass" and the technical difference between mass and weight are introduced to students only in the upper elementary grades.

Children's initial experiences with weight involve arranging objects of various sizes, shapes, and weights in order from lightest to heaviest or heaviest to lightest. In the first of these activities children should distinguish gross differences in weight between objects. As their estimation skills improve, these differences should become smaller and smaller. Children can order by weight one set of objects with similar attributes such as three books and another set of objects with widely varying attributes such as a coat, a pair of shoes, and a book. Even when the weight differences between the objects in the two sets are similar, the first set, similar-shaped objects, will be easier to order by weight than the second set, dissimilar objects. Even if the second set consisted of three coats, it would still be harder to order by weight than the first set since coats vary more in attributes other than weight than books do. A balance scale should be available for children to check their estimations.

Just as they did with other measures, children need experiences with nonstandard weight measures and with repeating the basic unit of measurement (Figure 10-6). Similarly, other activities should help children develop the concept that the weight of the basic unit will determine the number of basic units needed to balance a given object.

The basic unit of mass in the metric system is the gram. However, since this is a very small unit, children should first be introduced to the kilogram (1000 grams). By using a kilogram mass on a balance scale for comparison, children can find various objects whose mass is less than, more than, or approximately equal to one kilogram.

For older children when more accuracy is desired, masses of 500, 200, 50, 25, 10, 5, or 1 gram(s) can be used. For most activities in measuring weight, children should use a balance scale. After estimating the weight of an object such as a book, the student chooses the single mass closest to this estimate and places it on the opposite pan of the balance scale. By observing whether this mass is too large or too small, the student can make a closer estimate of the book's weight. The student can then add or subtract appropriate standard masses until the two sides balance. The unknown weight of the book can be found by adding the known standard masses.

As children work with the balance scale, they are also developing the concept of weight (mass). In contrast, when children weigh objects using other types of scales, they are just reading numbers from a dial. However, children should have some practice using these other scales so that they can learn to interpret the calibrations correctly.

Mass is also related to linear dimensions and volume (Figure 10-22). If the decimeter cube were filled with one liter of distilled water at 4° Celsius, the water would have a mass of 1 kilogram. Similarly, 1 cubic centimeter or 1 milliliter of water would have a mass of 1 gram. For measuring large quantities, 1 cubic meter or 1 kiloliter of water would have a mass of 1 metric ton (1000 kilograms). Thus the measures of length, volume, and mass are defined so that they are interrelated within the metric system.

QUESTIONS AND ACTIVITIES

1. How is the metric system related to the base-ten number system?

2. Order the following activities in an appropriate learning sequence.
   a. Line up paper clips to measure the length of an object.
   b. Choose your basic unit of length to be a paper clip.
   c. Measure objects longer than your measuring device.
   d. Link 5 paper clips together to form a ruler.
   e. Measure objects that are shorter than your measuring device.

3. *For your resource file:* Read "Learning About Rulers and Measuring" by Thompson and Van de Walle. The authors describe a number of activities involving comparing lengths, repeating units of length, constructing and using a ruler, and the transition to standard rulers.

4. Find objects that are the same length as a millimeter, centimeter, decimeter, and a meter. Try to use common objects that you carry with you or use dimensions of your body. What is the purpose of this activity?

5. a. Attach ten interlocking centimeter cubes together to form a ruler. Estimate various lengths that are less than 50 centimeters. Check your estimates with your ruler.
   b. *For your resource file:* A number of activities using the ten-centimeter length are contained in the article "Let's Do It: The Neglected Decimeter" by Lindquist and Dana.

6. a. Use the Cuisenaire ten-rod or another ten-centimeter length to mark off a meter length on a roll of paper tape. What is the purpose of having children make their own measuring instruments?

b. Estimate lengths that are about one meter. Check your estimates by using your meter tape.

c. Estimate lengths that are less than one meter. Estimate to the nearest decimeter (10 centimeters). Check your estimates by using your meter tape.

d. Estimate lengths that are between one and three meters. Estimate to the nearest decimeter (10 centimeters). Check your estimates by using your meter tape.

7. Is 5 centimeters less precise than, the same as, or more precise than 50 millimeters? Why? (*Hint:* Use greatest possible error in explaining your answer.)

8. a. Find the perimeters of the following polygons.

(1)

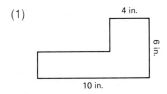

4 in.

6 in.

10 in.

(2)

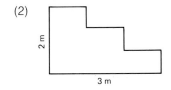

2 m

3 m

b. Cut a length of string that you would estimate as your waist measurement. Check your estimate. Was your estimate too large or too small? Repeat estimating the measure of your head, neck, or wrist.

9. The mathematics portion of the National Assessment of Educational Progress shows that children and adults do not understand the concepts of area. Given the polygon and two different basic units, describe activities that would help a child develop the concept of area.

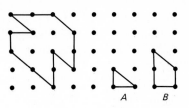

A   B

a. If A is the basic unit, what is the area of the polygon? _____

b. If B is the basic unit, what is the area of the polygon? _____

10. a. Could rectangles or circles be used as a unit of area? Why or why not?

b. Explicitly, why are square units used instead of rectangular units in standard area measurement?

11. John used a file card to measure the surface of his notebook, as shown. What is wrong with his thinking?

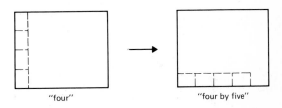

"four"   "four by five"

12. Use newspaper and tape to make a model of one square meter. Use this model to estimate such areas as floors in rooms and tabletops.

13. On centimeter graph paper draw various-shaped rectangles that each have an area of 24 square centimeters. That each have a perimeter of 24 centimeters.

14. Cut out a square that measures ten centimeters by ten centimeters. Estimate and then measure four surfaces using this unit.

15. On a recent quiz the following question was posed: "2 cm² = _____ mm². Draw a sketch to justify your answer." Below are three students' responses. Analyze their thinking in each case, decide whether or not each is correct, and, if incorrect, tell what the student's error in thinking was.

a. Jody's work

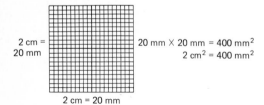

$20 \text{ mm} \times 20 \text{ mm} = 400 \text{ mm}^2$
$2 \text{ cm}^2 = 400 \text{ mm}^2$

b. Troy's work

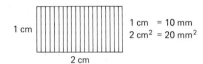

$1 \text{ cm} = 10 \text{ mm}$
$2 \text{ cm}^2 = 20 \text{ mm}^2$

c. Jeremy's work

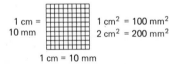

$1 \text{ cm}^2 = 100 \text{ mm}^2$
$2 \text{ cm}^2 = 200 \text{ mm}^2$

16. Ann comments that she doesn't know whether to label her answer as cm^2 or cm^3. What type of experiences were lacking or did she fail to understand in her conceptual development?

17. a. Lee read 2 cm^2 as "two centimeters squared." How should the phrase be read?
    b. Draw and label diagrams to show the difference between a two-centimeter cube and two cubic centimeters.

18. *For your resource file:* Students' conceptions of measurement are discussed in a number of excellent articles. Read one or more of the articles below to gain a perception of student thinking—correct and incorrect.
    a. One article by Hiebert is "Units of Measure: Results and Implications from National Assessment." Test results of 9- and 13-year-olds with regard to graphs, temperature, area, and volume are discussed. Recommendations for instruction are included.
    b. Hart discusses test results for 13- and 14-year-olds in the article "Which Comes First—Length, Area, or Volume?"
    c. Five different errors in thinking are discussed in "Student Misconceptions About Area Measure" by Hirstein, Lamb, and Osborne.
    d. First graders' thinking about length is discussed in "Why Do Some Children Have Trouble Learning Measurement Concepts?" by Hiebert.

19. Use centimeter cubes to build a shape that contains 5 cubes. How many different shapes can be made if the faces always match?

20. Explain why the thinking for solving either of the following problems is the same.
    a. How many cubic inches would fit in a cubic foot?
    b. How many cubic centimeters would fit in a cubic decimeter?

21. a. Use centimeter or inch graph paper and cut out several copies of each of the following rectangles: 5 by 5, 7 by 5, 5 by 4, 7 by 4, and 4 by 4. Use tape and build all possible combinations of boxes.
    b. How many unit cubes will each box hold?

22. Devise an activity to help students discover the relationship between the mass (grams) of a given amount of water and its volume (milliliters).

23. Measurement activities should be included throughout the year instead of in one separate unit. Read "Let's Do It: Organizing a Metric Center in Your Classroom" by Bruni and Silverman for suggestions on setting up learning centers. Briefly describe how you could use such a center to teach measurement throughout the year.

24. Which should be used first dial or balance scales? Conceptually, how do they differ?

25. a. How would you help children develop the concept of a liter?
  b. Estimate and then measure the volume of a number of objects in liters and milliliters.
  c. Examine the measuring instruments used to measure volume. How are they calibrated? How precise are the instruments?

26. How does Problem 25 differ when developing the concepts of a quart? A cup?

27. a. How would you help children develop the concept of a kilogram? A gram?
  b. Estimate and then measure the mass of a number of objects in kilograms and grams.
  c. Examine the scales used to measure mass. How are they calibrated? How precise are the instruments?

28. How does Problem 27 differ when developing the concepts of a pound? An ounce?

29. Which of the following statements are true for the mass of water at 4 degrees Celsius with no impurities and at sea level?
  a. A cubic centimeter of water measures 1 centiliter and weighs 1 gram.
  b. A cubic meter of water measures 1 kiloliter and weighs a metric ton.
  c. A cubic decimeter of water measures 1 liter and weighs 1000 grams.
  d. A cubic centimeter of water measures 1 milliliter and weighs 1 kilogram.

30. *For your resource file:* Some articles could include the following. The article "Let's Do It: Making Measurement Meaningful" by Horak and Horak contains a number of teaching ideas for length and area. "Brian's Question" by Goodman includes problem-solving situations involving weight and volume such as "Could a suitcase hold 30 000 twenty-dollar bills? Could you lift it?" Activities for weight and volume for grades 1 through 8 are presented in "Ideas" by Tabler and Jacobson. Introductory activities for weight are described in "Weighing Ideas" by Epstein and in "Let's Do It: An Introduction to Weight Measurement" by Bruni and Silverman.

TEMPERATURE

To determine how hot or cold something is, the temperature must be measured. Children's first experiences with temperature should involve comparison. For example, the differences among various containers of hot and cold water could be noted. By dipping their fingers into the water, the children can determine which container holds the hottest or coldest water and order the others accordingly.

A similar experiment could be used to introduce the thermometer as a measuring instrument. The children could place the thermometer in the various containers of water and observe the corresponding rise and fall of the fluid in the thermometer. Later the children can learn to read the number line marked along the thermometer. To practice this skill, they could take turns reading the outdoor thermometer and recording the daily temperature on a graph. By reading the line graph, they can discuss the coldest day or the warmest day of each week, month, or year. (*How Little and How Much: A Book About Scales* by Franklyn Branley gives an excellent development about scales in general and temperature scales in particular.)

The Celsius scale is used to measure temperature in the metric system. The temperature at which water freezes is defined as 0° Celsius (0°C); by definition, water boils at 100°C. Other common referents on this scale are 20°C for normal room temperature and 37°C for normal body temperature.

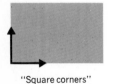
"Square corners"

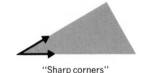
"Sharp corners"

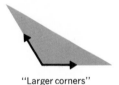
"Larger corners"

FIGURE 10-23.
Angles as corners.

ANGLE

One of children's first introductions to angles in the classroom is through their explorations of polygons. They note that some polygons have "square" corners, others "sharp" corners, and others "large" corners (Figure 10-23). As children become more mathematically mature, they can check to find out which polygons contain right angles (Figure 10-24). By using a file card, they can test which angles are right angles and which angles are more than or less than a right angle.

As children classify angles, they should be developing the concept of an angle. The "sides" (rays) that define the angle separate the plane into three regions. These regions are the points on the angle itself, the angle's interior and its exterior. It is the position of the two rays in relation to each other that students will learn to measure. They should observe that the size of an angle is not a function of the "length" of the rays that define that angle. Angles are also formed by the intersection of two planes. A common example is the corner of a room or the angle formed by two adjacent walls. (Angles formed by rays and planes are explored in Robert Froman's *Angles Are Easy as Pie,* an

excellent children's book on the concept of angles.)

At first, children compare the sizes of various angles to a right angle to determine the relative sizes of the angles. Next they are ready to begin measuring angles. From previous measuring activities they know that they need a basic unit of measure. The right angle they used to compare angles is obviously too large to be a convenient basic unit. For flexibility in measuring, the students will recognize that the unit angle should be fairly small. With this information, each student or group of students should draw and cut out their own nonstandard unit angle.

Now the students can measure any angle by comparing it to their unit angle. The students lay the unit angle inside and against one side of the angle to be measured (Figure 10-25). They mark off the first unit and then repeat the unit until the entire angle is measured. This activity further develops the concept of what property is to be measured. Since the students made several different nonstandard unit angles, they will obtain several different measures for a given unknown angle. This also shows the need for a standard unit of angle measure.

The standard unit of measure for angles

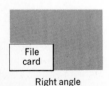
File card

Right angle

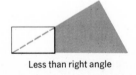
Less than right angle

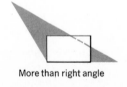
More than right angle

FIGURE 10-24.
Right angles.

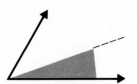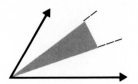

FIGURE 10-25.
Nonstandard measurement of angles.

is the degree. The entire region around a point (a circle) is defined as 360 degrees (360°). One degree is $\frac{1}{360}$ of the entire circle. To understand this definition, children should be able to "see the angles" in a circle. The degree as the standard unit of angle measure should be introduced through activities. For example, each child could cut out a circle and fold it into four equal-sized parts. The children should recognize that each of the four angles formed by the fold lines is a right angle. Since the circle is defined as 360°, each right angle is 90°. Each circle could be folded again to make eight smaller equal-sized parts. Each angle would then be 45°. Through class discussion, the children should observe that if they continued this activity, the circle would be divided into more and more equal-sized parts and each part would have a measure that be-

comes smaller and smaller. A measure of one degree will be very small.

After the students understand what property of an angle is to be measured and what the standard unit of angle measure is, they are ready to begin using a protractor, a standard tool for angle measurement. A protractor is merely a semicircle with degree measures marked on it. Since the entire circle measures 360°, the protractor has a scale that ranges from 0° to 180°. Because the degree is an extremely small unit, children's first experiences with a protractor should involve measuring angles to the nearest five or ten degrees (Figure 10-26). This is similar to the children's experiences in measuring length when they measured first to the nearest centimeter and later to the nearest millimeter, a more precise unit.

The first measuring activities in which

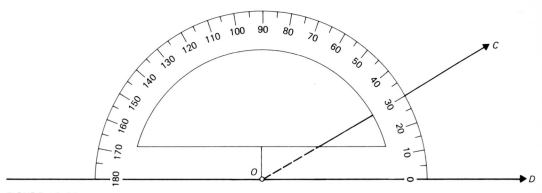

FIGURE 10-26.
Using a protractor.

students use a protractor should be carefully structured. To place the protractor correctly, the students should first observe that the vertex of the angle (the point where the two rays meet) relates to the center of the circle. This circle is indicated on the protractor by the symbol "O," which stands for "origin" (Figure 10-26). This point "O" on the protractor should be placed at the vertex of the angle to be measured.

Next, the students should notice that just as a ruler starts with zero, so the scale marked on the protractor starts with zero. To measure the length of a line segment, they first positioned the ruler so that the zero was at one end of the line segment. Similarly, to measure an angle the protractor must be placed so that, with the origin at the vertex of the angle, the zero (base line) is on one of the rays (the boundary or "end" of the angle region) as indicated in Figure 10-26. The measure of the angle can now be read by following the scale from zero degrees to the point at which the other ray crosses the protractor.

Later, students will be using protractors marked with a double scale (Figure 10-27).

They must choose the appropriate scale to read. Again, they should start reading the scale at zero degrees. In this case the bottom scale is read since it is numbered 0, 10, 20 . . . from the ray OD. Thus the measure of angles COD is seen to be 30°. Although the scale also shows 150°, the students should recognize that this is obviously not the measure for this angle. From previous experience in comparing various angles to a right angle, the students can easily see that the measure of angle COD must be less than 90°. By estimation, the student can see that angle COD is less than half of a right angle. Therefore, a measure of 30° is a reasonable answer since 30° is less than half of 90°. Some students may notice that it would also be possible to use the top scale by noting that the difference between 180° (the position of OD) and 150° (the position of OC) is 30°.

A transparent plastic protractor is useful for demonstrations. By placing the protractor on the overhead projector, a student can demonstrate correct angle measurement for the rest of the class. Another advantage of the transparent protractor is that it is easier

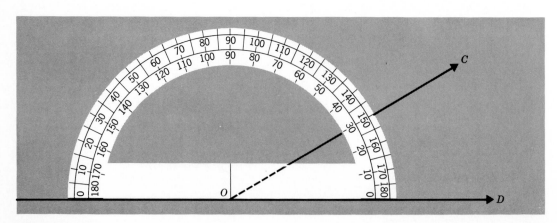

FIGURE 10-27.
Using a double-scale protractor.

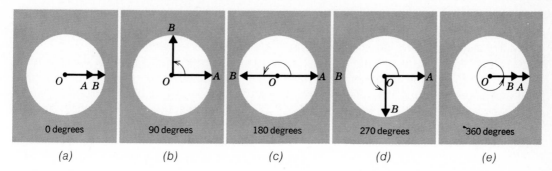

FIGURE 10-28.
Reference angle measures.

for the students to place it correctly on the angle.

Students should be encouraged to estimate the number of degrees in an angle before measuring the angle. They should be familiar with angle measures of 90°, 180°, and 270° (Figure 10-28). By recognizing that an angle to be measured lies between 90 and 180°, they can make an appropriate estimate. In addition to experiences estimating and measuring angles between 0 and 360° the students should draw angles of various given measures. Students must develop a thorough concept of angles in order to understand what is to be measured and what is the basic unit of measure. By doing so, common errors, such as misplacing the base line of the protractor of reading the wrong scale, can be avoided.

TIME

Children's first experiences in time should deal with ordering events according to when they occur. They should consider such concepts as before, now, and after. The class should note that *before* school in the morning they did such things as getting up, eating breakfast, and walking to school. *Now* they are studying mathematics. *After* lunch, they will study science and then go out for recess.

Besides discussing their activities, the children could draw sequential pictures of what they did during the course of the day. They could also order pictures depicting sequence such as pictures of a flower gradually unfolding or a meal being prepared. Some comic strips that are complete in four pictures could be cut apart and the children could be asked to put the pictures in the proper order.

After they have had experiences with sequence of events, children need to develop an understanding of and a feel for specific units of time. To help them develop this concept, the teacher should use various specifically timed activities. For a small group activity, the children can be instructed to shut their eyes and raise their hands when they think one minute has passed. The teacher can write down each child's name and the length of time that has passed when the child raises his or her hand. At the end of one minute the teacher can announce the time. Alternatively, if some children have not yet raised their hands at the end of one minute, the teacher may continue the activity until all hands are raised.

The class can then discuss their individual perceptions of 1 minute. The teacher should be exact in timing these activities as people often say "wait a minute" or "just a minute" and mean any time from one-half minute to one-half hour. Time intervals of 5, 10, 15, and 30 minutes can be introduced by planning activities that start and end in exactly 5, 10, 15, or 30 minutes.

Children can also estimate the time that it takes to complete a certain task. For example, they can predict how long it will take them to walk across the room and then have someone time their action. Similar discussions could be developed for the length of time needed for such activities as running across the playground, walking to the library, or running around the gym. The class could also compare the different lengths of time it takes various students to walk to school. They would need to consider the different rates at which people walk in order to decide which students lived the closest to or farthest from school.

Children's first experiences in reading the clock involve whole hours—two o'clock, five o'clock, and so on. They should understand that the long hand completes one cycle while the short hand moves from one numeral to the next consecutive numeral. This can be demonstrated by using a real clock. As the minute hand is moved, the children can observe the position of the hour hand before and after the minute hand has completed one cycle.

The order of and time for various activities can be written on the chalkboard, such as reading—eleven o'clock, lunch—twelve o'clock, mathematics—one o'clock, and recess—two o'clock. Appropriate drawings of clocks can be given with each time as shown in Figure 10-29. Even at this early stage, children should be learning to use the all-numeral notation (11:00) as well as the numeral-and-word notation (11 o'clock) for writing time. This will help prepare them for activities in telling time in more detail for which all-numeral notation is used almost exclusively.

After learning to tell time to the hour, children are usually introduced to telling time to the half and quarter hour. This can be confusing to children who have had previous experiences with money since a half hour is only 30 minutes while a half dollar is 50 cents. An alternate procedure is to teach telling time in five-minute intervals.

After the children have reviewed counting by fives, they can be introduced to a clock that has an outer ring showing the multiples of five (Figure 10-30). The outer ring of numbers is for the minute hand, while the inner ring is for the hour hand. The clock should be set to a certain hour, for example,

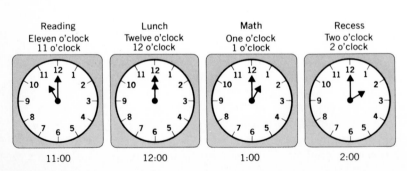

Reading Eleven o'clock 11 o'clock	Lunch Twelve o'clock 12 o'clock	Math One o'clock 1 o'clock	Recess Two o'clock 2 o'clock
11:00	12:00	1:00	2:00

FIGURE 10-29.
Reading clocks—hours.

FIGURE 10-30.
Telling time. (From C. A. Dilley, D. W. Lowry, W. E. Rucker, **Heath Mathematics**, D. C. Heath & Company, 1983, Grade 2, p. 121. Reprinted by permission of D. C. Heath & Company)

eight o'clock. The minute hand should be moved from eight o'clock to five minutes after eight. The minute hand has moved from eight o'clock to five minutes *after* eight, which is read as "five minutes after eight". The minute hand should then be moved five more minutes. The children should note that it is now ten minutes after eight.

This activity should be continued through a complete rotation with the children counting by fives—that is, five-minute intervals. Children will probably need guidance in the transition from 55 minutes after eight to nine o'clock. The children should also note that as the minute hand proceeds around the clock, the hour hand moves closer and closer to the next numeral. The activity should be repeated with other examples, and the outer ring should be gradually phased out.

To tell time to the nearest minute, children will need to observe that there are four marks delineating five spaces or minutes between each pair of numerals on the clock face. They can then count on the appropriate number of spaces toward the next mark. For example if the clock indicates 8:07, the children can observe that the minute hand has passed the numeral one indicating five minutes, and they can count on two more spaces (minutes) or 5 . . . 6, 7. For 9:14 the children would need to think of ten, then 10 . . . 11, 12, 13, 14, or they may count back one from 15.

To relate telling time to the written form and the digital clock, it can be explained that 20 minutes after eight is written as 8:20—the twenty is written *after* the eight. Adults commonly read this as "eight twenty." Similarly the numerals 6:04, 9:55, and 3:45 are read as six o'four," "nine fifty-five," and "three forty-five."

The 9:55 is also commonly expressed as "five minutes to ten." The time 3:45 can be similarly expressed as "fifteen to four." Another common way of expressing quarter hours such as 2:15, 2:30, and 2:45 is to say "quarter after two," "half past two," and "quarter to three." Children will gradually learn all these ways of expressing time.

Time concepts in relation to the calendar are introduced to children in the early primary grades. A calendar showing all 12 months at once is desirable to help children develop the concept of the year as a whole. As the year progresses, the children can see the repetition of the week in 7-day intervals and the year in 12-month intervals. Special holidays and class events can be marked on the calendar. The children can then refer to events as "three weeks ago" or "in one month."

The study of a calendar can incorporate counting activities. For example, even in kindergarten, children can be given a dittoed calendar for the particular month and asked to draw an appropriate picture depicting that month. These calendars can be taken home and as each day passes the children can mark off another numeral (day) on the calendar. From time to time as the days are marked off, the children may count how many more days to a certain holiday or to the end of the month. This activity can later be modified by giving the children a grid and asking them to write in the appropriate numerals to make a calendar.

Patterns on the calendar should be discussed such as if today is Monday, then 7, 14, 21, etc. days from now it will also be Monday. If today is Thursday the sixteenth, then last Thursday was the ninth and next Thursday will be the twenty-third.

MONEY

Although many preschool children can identify certain coins, they may not recognize all the denominations. In addition to the color and size of each coin, they must also recognize the designs on both sides of each coin. Real money or play money that looks just like real money should be used for the initial activities. If the play money is crudely designed, the children may have difficulty transferring these learned skills to real money. For worksheets, coin stamps are available depicting either side of the various coins.

The values of different coins are learned next. Young children often do not recognize that different coins have different values. Thus, they think that 3 nickels is more money than 2 dimes. They may be focusing on just the number of coins (3 is more than 2) or on just the physical size of the coins (nickels are bigger than dimes). Children need activities designed to help them focus on the different values of the various coins.

The basic unit of the U.S. monetary system is the dollar. The cent, commonly called a penny, is defined as one-hundredth of a dollar. Other coins are defined in terms of the cent. The nickel is introduced as five cents, the dime as ten cents, and so on. As the students become more familiar with the various coins, they will recognize that 10 cents is also the equivalent of 2 nickels and that, therefore, 2 nickels are equivalent to 1 dime. To reinforce this skill, trading games using coins can be played where children exchange two nickels for one dime or two dimes and a nickel for a quarter.

Activities using only pennies, dimes, and dollars will help to reinforce the concept of the decimal base of our monetary system. From these activities children will realize that

10 cents is equivalent to 1 dime and 10 dimes is equivalent to 1 dollar so 100 cents is also equivalent to 1 dollar. From emphasis on this relationship between dollars and cents, children will come to understand the different representations for dollars and cents since 56 cents can also be expressed as $0.56. Since children know that 1 dollar is equivalent to 100 cents, they can extend this knowledge to larger amounts; for example, $5.00 is 500 cents and $2.41 is 241 cents.

To determine the value of a given group of coins, children need various skills. They should recognize that it is easier to start counting with the largest-value coins. They will also need to be able to count by 1s, 5s, 10s, 25s, and 50s as shown in Figure 10-31. Children should experiment with the various ways they can express the same amount of money. Given a particular total, they should determine which combination requires the fewest coins.

Making change utilizes this skill since it is customary to give change in the smallest possible number of coins. For example, when the children are playing store, if the cash register shows that the "customer" is to receive 34 cents in change, the appropri-

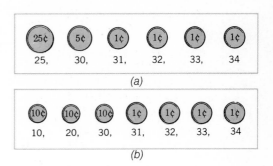

FIGURE 10-32.
Making change.

ate coins are shown in Figure 10-32a. However, if that exact set of coins is not available, the "clerk" should be able to use other coins having the same total value (Figure 10-32b).

Another skill for making change is required if the "clerk" counts on from the purchase. For example, if the "customer" gives one dollar for a 56 cents purchase, the "clerk" may count as shown in Figure 10-33. The "clerk" needs to know appropriate key numbers such as 75 rather than using all dimes after 60 cents and counting 60, 70, 80, 90, . . . 1 dollar.

Additional activities should include counting to totals greater than one dollar. For example, if the purchase total is $1.32 and the customer pays with a 5-dollar bill, the change would be correctly counted as shown in Figure 10-34. As the clerk counts $1.32, $1.33, $1.34, . . . $5.00, she or he should place the appropriate coins and bills in the customer's hand.

FIGURE 10-31.
Counting money.

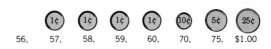

FIGURE 10-33.
Counting on change.

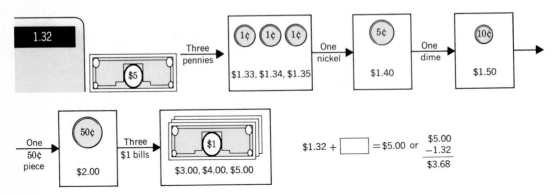

FIGURE 10-34.
Using money to make change

OPERATIONS WITH MEASURES

ADDING MEASURES

One of the advantages of using a measurement system based on ten, such as the metric system, is that adding measures in the system is no more complicated than adding whole numbers and decimals. Since everything is based on ten, it is a simple matter to rewrite all measures in terms of a single unit. For example, if 3 meters, 6 meters, and 58 centimeters are to be added, the addition could be done as shown in Figure 10-35.

However, students must learn to do operations in the customary system of measurement as well; this requires an understanding of regrouping with various values other than ten. For example, when adding measurements that contain yards, feet, and inches, students must regroup first by twelves and then by threes. A specially defined abacus is useful when the addition of these measurements is started (Figure 10-36). When 7 inches is added to 2 feet, 6 inches, 12 inches of the 13 inches are re-

grouped as 1 foot, and 3 feet are regrouped as 1 yard. In the metric system this inconsistency is not encountered since all regrouping is done by tens.

When adding measures that have variable place values, one approach is to add first within each column. Then, starting from the smallest unit of measure, students rename until the measurement is written in simplest form (Figure 10-37). In the example shown, the first step is to add the measures by columns, obtaining 12 yards 6 feet 27 inches. Next the 27 inches is rewritten as 2 feet 3 inches. The 8 feet (2 feet plus 6 feet) is then rewritten as 2 yards 2 feet. In the last step 2 yards is added to the 12 yards. Another form, equally good, is to add the first column on the right, simplify and rename, and then add the second column.

$$
\begin{array}{r}
3.00 \\
6.00 \\
\underline{0.58} \\
9.58 \text{ meters}
\end{array}
\qquad
\begin{array}{r}
300 \\
600 \\
\underline{58} \\
958 \text{ centimeters}
\end{array}
$$

FIGURE 10-35.
Adding metric measures.

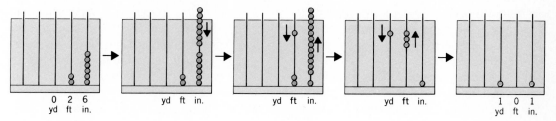

0	2	6
yd	ft	in.

yd	ft	in.

yd	ft	in.

yd	ft	in.

1	0	1
yd	ft	in.

FIGURE 10-36.
Abacus for adding linear measures in the customary system.

Still another form, similar to that used when adding metrics, is to rewrite the entire measure in terms of a single unit. Thus 2 feet 9 inches plus 1 foot 4 inches could be rewritten as 33 inches plus 16 inches or as $2\frac{3}{4}$ feet plus $1\frac{1}{3}$ feet. Then the measures are added just like any other numbers, and, if desired, the answer can be rewritten in other units.

Some measurements present special problems because they are cyclic in nature. Time and angle measurement are two examples of this concept. Questions such as "If it is 11:00 P.M. now, what time of day will it be 3 hours from now?" are special and should be discussed separately. While discussing these measurements, the underlying concept of rotation must be emphasized since it will be the basis for many future concepts.

100 cm	10.0 dm	1.00 m
− 53 cm	− 5.3 dm	− .53 m

FIGURE 10-38.
Subtraction problems using the meter stick and Cuisenaire rods.

SUBTRACTING MEASURES

Like addition, subtraction using the metric system of measurement is relatively simple. By using a meter stick and Cuisenaire rods, children can be involved with subtraction problems of differing complexity. For example, several different subtraction problems can be generated from the same set of measurements (Figure 10-38). Another example involves the liter container that was filled with 750 milliliters of water (Figure 10-39). How much more water must be added

5 yd	2 ft	9 in.
3 yd	2 ft	7 in.
4 yd	2 ft	11 in.

2 yd $\begin{cases} 2\,\text{ft} \\ 6\,\text{ft} \end{cases}$ 27 in.
12 yd
↓ ↓
14 yd 2 ft 3 in.

FIGURE 10-37.
Adding measures.

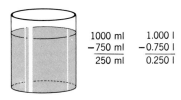

1000 ml	1.000 l
−750 ml	−0.750 l
250 ml	0.250 l

FIGURE 10-39.
Subtracting decimals using liter container.

to obtain a liter? In the metric system, the subtraction algorithm for decimals or whole numbers can be used to solve these problems. In the customary system, special problems arise because the student cannot rename by tens.

Subtraction of customary measurements involves the problem of working with variable place values. In working the problem shown in Figure 10-40, students must first rename 1 foot as 12 inches and later must rename 1 yard as 3 feet. Since this requires a thorough knowledge of equivalent measures and because the renaming is not all done by tens as in the decimal number system, students make many errors.

A common error is to rename by tens instead of twelves when working with feet and inches. If this error had occurred in the problem in Figure 10-40, the 7 inches would have become 17 inches instead of 19 inches. When these errors occur, the students should be given a yardstick that is clearly marked in feet and inches. Students can observe that since there are 12 inches in 1 foot, they should have renamed 1 foot as 12 inches. A similar situation, but requiring different renaming, exists in such problems as 5 gallons, 2 quarts, 2 cups minus 1 gallon, 3 quarts, 3 cups or 7 cubic yards minus 14 cubic feet.

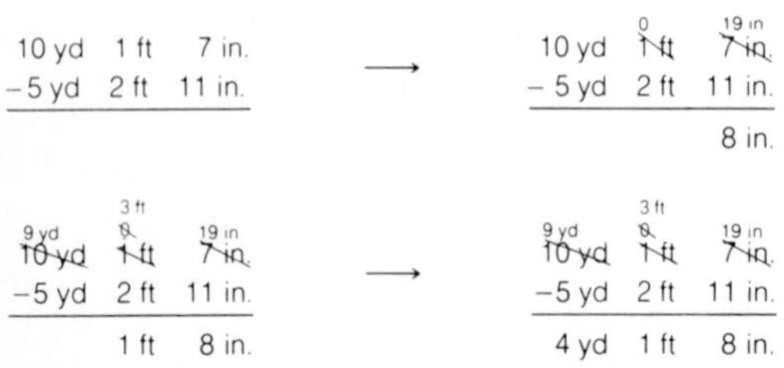

The measurement of temperature can be used to introduce subtraction of numbers. The thermometer is used as a vertical number line since the temperature goes up and down. Children can explore subtraction with temperature by testing what happens with a temperature drop of six degrees starting at various points on the thermometer. When the starting point is 4 degrees or 1 degree, measurement of temperature can also be used to introduce negative integers.

MULTIPLYING MEASURES

As with addition and subtraction, multiplication with metric measures is the same as multiplication with whole numbers and decimals. In fact, practical problems involving decimals often arise from measurement activities. For example, "If Jimmy is making bread and the recipe calls for 0.6 liter of water, how much water will he need for a recipe $2\frac{1}{2}$ times as large? If the same recipe calls for 15 milliliters of yeast, 2.3 kilograms of flour, 45 grams of dried milk, and 0.085 liter of honey, how much of each of these ingredients does he need?" To solve these problems, Jimmy needs no new skills. He only needs to multiply whole numbers and decimals.

One new concept that does occur in multiplying linear measures is multiplying the unit of measure by itself. For example, "Helen is planning to put new carpeting in her living room. She measures and finds that the room is 7.5 meters by 5.3 meters. How much carpeting does she need to buy?" Students must not only multiply the *numbers* in the problem but also the *units* of measure, thus changing linear measures to area measure (Figure 10-41).

An area diagram (array) of Helen's living room floor is also shown. To increase prob-

FIGURE 10-40.
Subtracting measures.

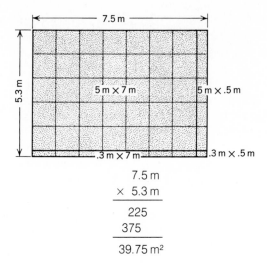

$$\begin{array}{r} 7.5\,\text{m} \\ \times\ 5.3\,\text{m} \\ \hline 225 \\ 375 \\ \hline 39.75\,\text{m}^2 \end{array}$$

FIGURE 10-41.
Multiplying metric measures.

lem-solving skills, this same problem could be made more complex. For example, "If carpet comes in 2-meter, 4-meter, 6-meter, 8-meter, and 10-meter widths, what is the smallest amount of carpet that Helen can buy to cover her floor? What width will it be? If this same carpet must all be laid going the

same direction, what is the smallest amount she can buy? What width will it be? How much leftover carpet will she have? What will be the shape of the remnant or remnants?" These additional questions each require many steps in the solution. The students must select the relevant information and use the appropriate operations on it.

Unfortunately, most carpet in this country is still sold by the square yard rather than by the square meter. For this reason students need some understanding of multiplication of measures in the customary system. "Since no one in Helen's city sells carpet by the square meter, she remeasures her living room and finds that it is 5 yards 2 feet by 8 yards 1 foot." Students could solve this problem using the customary system by changing 5 yards 2 feet to $5\frac{2}{3}$ yards and changing 8 yards 1 foot to $8\frac{1}{3}$ yards. The multiplication problem would then be $5\frac{2}{3}$ yards $\times$ $8\frac{1}{3}$ yards, a type they have solved before.

Alternatively, the students could have left the measures as originally given. Now students must multiply these measures as shown in the algorithm and the area diagram in Figure 10-42. Any renaming done with

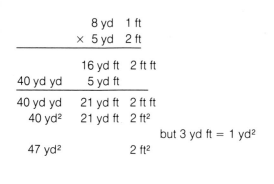

(a)

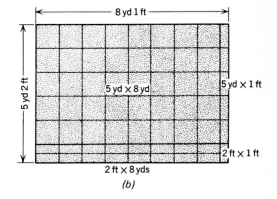

(b)

FIGURE 10-42.
Multiplying customary measures.

these measures must account for variable place value. In simplifying the final answer, 40 yd-yd and 2 ft-ft are rewritten as 40 yd^2 and 2 ft^2, respectively. The 21 yd-ft creates special problems since the units are not the same. A "yard-foot" is equivalent to a rectangle that is one yard by one foot. Since it takes three such rectangles to make one square yard, 21 yd-ft can be renamed as 7 yd^2. The array that was used is the same type that was used before with metric measures.

DIVIDING MEASURES

Most of the concepts needed for division of measures have already been developed. In fact, many examples of practical division problems have involved measures. Students should be aware that problems involving division of measures can be either measurement or partitive division situations. "Mr. Stokes is polishing the school hallway. In 10 minutes he can polish 8 meters down the length of the hall and across the entire width. If the hall is 3 meters wide and 60 meters long, how long will it take Mr. Stokes to polish the hall?" "The Plainfield community garden space is a rectangular field measuring 60 meters by 100 meters. If each individual plot contains 20 square meters, how many plots are there in the entire space?" Both of these are measurement division situations. In each case students know, or can easily find, the size of the total group or measure and the size of each smaller group or measure. They are asked to find the number of groups.

For partitive division students know the size of the total group and the number of groups it is to be divided into and they must find the size of each group. "Ms. Westermeier has a board that is 5 cm thick, 30 cm wide and 4 m long. She wants to cut it into two pieces of equal length to make walking boards for her Sunday School class. How long will each walking board be?" "Ms. Lehman's Girl Scout troop has made 20 kilograms of Christmas candy to pack in boxes

linear measure	×	linear measure	=	area measure
		m × m = m²		
		cm × cm = cm²		
		4m × 5m = 20m²		
area measure	÷	linear measure	=	linear measure
		m² ÷ m = m		
		cm² ÷ cm = cm		
		20m² ÷ 4m = 5m		
linear measure	×	area measure	=	volume measure
		m × m² = m³		
		cm × cm² = cm³		
		5cm × 100cm² = 500cm³		
volume measure	÷	area measure	=	linear measure
		m³ ÷ m² = m		
		cm³ ÷ cm² = cm		
		500cm³ ÷ 100cm² = 5cm		
volume measure	÷	linear measure	=	area measure
		m³ ÷ m = m²		
		cm³ ÷ cm = cm²		
		500cm³ ÷ 5cm = 100cm²		

FIGURE 10-43.
Multiplication and division of related measures.

$$6\tfrac{2}{3} \text{ yd} \div \tfrac{2}{3} \text{ yd} \rightarrow \tfrac{20}{3} \div \tfrac{2}{3} \rightarrow 10$$

$$6 \text{ yds } 2 \text{ ft} \div 2 \text{ ft}$$

$$(18 \text{ ft} + 2 \text{ ft}) \div 2 \text{ ft} \rightarrow 20 \div 2 \rightarrow 10$$

FIGURE 10-44.
Renaming for division of measures.

and sell. They plan to sell each box for $1.25. All their expenses in the project total $12.50. If they want to sell all the candy and make a profit of $50, how much candy should they pack in each box?"

In all these problems, the students do not need any new skills to do the required division. They simply need to apply what they already know about division of whole numbers, fractions, and decimals. Of course, since some problems are multistep and require other operations, they must use these skills as well.

One new concept that does occur in division of measures is the idea of dividing an area measure by a linear measure or dividing a volume measure by an area or a linear measure. For example, "The individual garden plots in Plainfield are rectangles that measure 20 m². If each plot is 4 m wide, how long is it?" To solve this problem students must divide not only the number 20 by the number 4, but also the area measure by the linear measure to yield another linear measure. Probably the easiest way to clarify this concept is to relate this type of division problem to its corresponding multiplication problem which students already understand. This relation is shown in Figure 10-43.

If division of measures using the customary system must be done, the process can be related to students' previous learning. The concept of dividing an area or volume measure by another measure in the customary system is the same as in the metric system. The difficulty in division of measures in the customary system arises from the variable place values. As with the other operations, often the best approach for overcoming this difficulty is to eliminate it by renaming the measures in terms of a single unit (Figure 10-44). As students do a few calculations in the customary system, they will soon see how much easier calculations are in the metric system.

SUMMARY

Although this chapter deals separately with many different measurement topics, these measurement concepts are interrelated. Obviously children must understand linear measurement and have a basic concept of area before they are ready to develop formulas for finding area. However, although concepts are sequenced within any one topic, the concepts among the various topics are not necessarily sequenced. For example, money, time, length, capacity, and area concepts are all introduced in the first grade. Furthermore, it is not important which topic is taught first.

Measurement is not uniquely situated in the elementary school curriculum. While measurement concepts are studied in mathematics, they are also studied in other subjects such as science, social studies, and art. The presentations of these concepts in the various subjects should be compared and coordinated for better instructional effectiveness. The presence of measurement throughout the elementary curriculum occurs because of the importance of measurement in everyday life. Although various applications of measurement were discussed in the text, this is only a small fraction of the applications of measurements that occur in the world around us.

QUESTIONS AND ACTIVITIES

1. a. Read the children's book *How Little and How Much: A Book About Scales* by Branley.
   b. How are scales used to introduce measuring instruments?

2. Is angle *B* larger than angle *A*? Explain your reasoning. Devise a method for teaching this concept.

3. Describe an activity using nonstandard measure of angles.

4. What is the role of estimation in angle measurement?

5. a. How would you explain the rationale for the correct placement of the protractor in measuring angles?
   b. How would you help a student who was having difficulty deciding which of the scales to read?

6. Consult two different elementary textbook series. When and how are each of the following ideas introduced?
   a. concept of angles
   b. right angles
   c. classifying angles
   d. estimating angle measure
   e. measuring angles with a single scale
   f. measuring angles with a double scale
   g. measuring angles to the nearest ten degrees
   h. measuring angles to the nearest degree

7. *For your resource file:* In "Introducing Angle Measure Through Estimation" Zweng describes a teaching sequence that proceeds from arc measure to angle measure. Copy and read the article. What are some of the unique aspects of this sequence that should help students develop a better understanding of angle measure?

8. *For your resource file:* Read one or more of the articles about time. Write up or copy some of the teaching ideas. Several factors to be considered in teaching time are discussed in "It's About Time" by Riley. Read the article noting the factors with which you are unfamiliar. "A Single-Handed Approach to Telling Time" by Thompson and Van de Walle discusses using just the hour hand to tell time. The minute hand and digital clocks are also introduced. A sequence of activities are given in "Teaching Time-Telling" by Nelson. "Teaching Time with Slit Clocks" by Horak and Horak includes concept-of-time activities as well as telling-time activities. "Let's Do It: Developing Intuitive Ideas About Time" by Bruni and Silverman also includes many activities on the concept of time.

9. "Ideas" by Tabler and Jacobson contains several activities involving estimation and reasonableness of results. The activities include estimating computational answers as well as estimating measures and gathering data. Work through one of the activities.

10. *For your resource file:* Play and evaluate at least two of the games included in the article "Primary Coin Card Activities" by Daane. Add these ideas to your resource file.

11. *For your resource file:* Read and evaluate the activity on how to teach the value of the different coins as described in the article "Making Sense Out of Dollars and Cents" by Bradford. Add these ideas to your resource file.

TEACHER RESOURCES

Bradford, John W. "Making Sense Out of Dollars and Cents." *Arithmetic Teacher* 27 (March 1980): 44–46.

Bright, George W. "Estimation as Part of Learning to Measure." In *Measurement in School Mathematics,* 1976 Yearbook of the National Council of Teachers of Mathematics, pp. 87–104. Reston, VA: The Council, 1976.

Bruni, James V. "Geometry for the Intermediate Grades." *Arithmetic Teacher 26* (February 1979): 17–19.

Bruni, James V., and Helene J. Silverman. "Let's Do It: An Introduction to Weight Measurement." *Arithmetic Teacher 23* (January 1976): 4–10.

———. "Let's Do It: Developing Intuitive Ideas About Time." *Arithmetic Teacher 23* (December 1976): 582–591.

———. "Let's Do It: Developing the Concept of Linear Measurement." *Arithmetic Teacher 21* (November 1974): 570–577.

———. "Let's Do It: Organizing a Metric Center in Your Classroom." *Arithmetic Teacher 21* (February 1976): 80–87.

Coburn, Terrence G., and Albert P. Shulte. "Estimation in Measurement." In *Estimation and Mental Computation,* 1986 Yearbook of the National Council of Teachers of Mathematics, pp. 195–203. Reston, VA: The Council, 1986.

Daane, C. J. "Primary Coin Card Activities." *Arithmetic Teacher 27* (February 1980): 34–36.

Epstein, Susan L. "Weighing Ideas." *Arithmetic Teacher 24* (April 1977): 293–297.

Goodman, Terry A. "Brian's Question." *Arithmetic Teacher 29* (March 1982): 14.

Hall, Lucien T. "Estimation and Approximation— Not Synonyms." *Mathematics Teacher 77* (October 1984): 516–517.

Hart, Kathleen. "Which Comes First—Length, Area, or Volume?" *Arithmetic Teacher 31* (May 1984): 16–18, 26–27.

Heise, Patricia, Christine Coughlin Smith, and Carol A. Thornton. "Basic Money Concepts and Skills in Meeting the Needs of Special Children." *Journal for Special Educators of the Mentally Retarded 12* (Spring 1975): 163–167, 186.

Hiebert, James. "Units of Measure: Results and Implications from National Assessment." *Arithmetic Teacher 28* (February 1981): 38–43.

———. "Why Do Some Children Have Trouble Learning Measurement Concepts?" *Arithmetic Teacher 31* (March 1984): 19–24.

Hildreth, David J. "The Use of Strategies in Estimating Measurements." *Arithmetic Teacher 30* (January 1983): 50–54.

Hirstein, James J., Charles E. Lamb, and Alan Osborne. "Student Misconceptions About Area Measure." *Arithmetic Teacher 25* (March 1978): 10–16.

Horak, Virginia M., and Willis J. Horak. "Let's Do It: Making Measurement Meaningful." *Arithmetic Teacher 30* (November 1982): 18–23.

———. "Teaching Time with Slit Clocks." *Arithmetic Teacher 30* (January 1983): 8–12.

Hunt, John D. "How High Is a Flagpole?" *Arithmetic Teacher 25* (February 1978): 42–43.

Innskeep, James E., Jr. "Teaching Measurement to Elementary School Children." In *Measurement in School Mathematics,* 1976 Yearbook of the National Council of Teachers of Mathematics, pp. 60–86. Reston, VA: The Council, 1976.

Jackson, Robert L., and Glenn R. Prigge. "Manipulative Devices with Associated Activities for Teaching Measurement to Elementary School Children." In *Measurement in School Mathematics,* 1976 Yearbook of the National Council of Teachers of Mathematics, pp. 187–209. Reston, VA: The Council, 1976.

Lappan, Glenda, and Mary Jean Winter. "Sticks and Stones." *Arithmetic Teacher 29* (March 1982): 38–41.

Lindquist, Mary Montgomery, and Marcia E. Dana. "Let's Do It: The Neglected Decimeter." *Arithmetic Teacher 25* (October 1977): 10–17.

Nelson, Glenn. "Teaching Time-Telling." *Arithmetic Teacher* 29 (May 1982): 31–34.

O'Daffer, Phares. "A Case and Techniques for Estimation: Estimation Experiences in Elementary School Mathematics—Essential, Not Extra!" *Arithmetic Teacher* 26 (February 1979): 46–51.

Riley, James E. "It's About Time." *Arithmetic Teacher* 28 (October 1980): 12–14.

Robinson, G. Edith, Michael L. Mahaffey, and L. Doyal Nelson. "Measurement." In *Mathematics Learning in Early Childhood.* Thirty-seventh Yearbook of the National Council of Teachers of Mathematics, pp. 227–250. Reston, VA: The Council, 1975.

Sengstock, Wayne L., and Kenneth E. Wyatt. "Meters, Liters, and Grams, The Metric System and Its Implications for Curriculum for Exceptional Children." *Teaching Exceptional Children* 8 (Winter 1976): 58–65.

Shaw, Jean M. "Let's Do It: Student-Made Measuring Tools." *Arithmetic Teacher* 31 (November 1983): 12–15.

Szetala, Walter, and Douglas T. Owens. "Finding the Area of a Circle: Use a Cake Pan and Leave Out the Pi." *Arithmetic Teacher* 33 (May 1986): 12–18.

Tabler, M. Bernadine, and Marilyn Hall Jacobson. "Ideas." *Arithmetic Teacher* 28 (September 1980): 27–32.

Thiessen, Diane, and Margaret Wild. *The Elementary Math Teacher's Handbook.* New York: Wiley, 1982.

Thompson, Charles S., and John Van de Walle. "Learning About Rulers and Measuring." *Arithmetic Teacher* 32 (April 1985): 8–12.

———. "A Single-Handed Approach to Telling Time." *Arithmetic Teacher* 28 (April 1981): 4–9.

Zweng, Marilyn J. "Introducing Angle Measure Through Estimation." In *Estimation and Mental Computation,* 1986 Yearbook of the National Council of Teachers of Mathematics, pp. 212–219. Reston, VA: The Council, 1986.

CHILDREN'S LITERATURE

Armstrong, Louise. *How to Turn Lemons into Money.* Illustrated by Bill Basso. New York: Harcourt Brace Jovanovich, 1976.

Behrens, June. *True Book of Metric Measurement.* Illustrated by Tom Dunnington. Chicago: Children's Press, 1975.

Bendick, Jeanne. *Measuring.* Illustrated by Jeanne Bendick, New York: Watts, 1971.

Branley, Franklyn M. *How Little and How Much: A Book About Scales.* Illustrated by Byron Barton. New York: Crowell, 1976.

———. *Measure with Metric.* Illustrated by Loretta Lustig. New York: Crowell, 1975.

Fey, James T. *Long, Short, High, Low, Thin, Wide.* Illustrated by Janie Russell. New York: Crowell, 1971.

Froman, Robert. *Angles Are Easy as Pie.* Illustrated by Byron Barton. New York: Crowell, 1976.

———. *Bigger and Smaller.* Illustrated by Gioia Fiammenghi. New York: Crowell, 1971.

Grender, Iris. *Measuring Things.* Illustrated by Geoffrey Butcher. New York: Pantheon Books, 1975.

Hoban, Tana. *Is It Larger? Is It Smaller?* New York: Greenwillow Books, 1985.

———. *Over, Under, and Through and Other Spatial Concepts.* New York: Macmillan, 1973.

———. *Push-Pull Empty-Full: A Book of Opposites.* Photographs by author. New York: Macmillan, 1972.

Linn, Charles F. *Estimation.* Illustrated by Don Madden. New York: Crowell, 1970.

Myller, Rolf. *How Big Is a Foot?* Bloomfield, CT: Atheneum, 1962.

Phillips, Jo. *Right Angles: Paper-Folding Geometry.* Illustrated by Giulio Maestro. New York: Crowell, 1972.

Piendowski, Jan. *Sizes.* Illustrated by the author. New York: Harvey, 1975.

Schlein, Miriam. *Heavy Is a Hippopotamus.* Illustrated by Leonard Kessler. Reading, MA: Addision-Wesley, 1954.

Shapp, Martha, and Charles Shapp. *Let's Find Out What's Big and What's Small.* Illustrated by Carol Nicklaus. New York: Watts, 1975.

Srivastava, Jane Jonas. *Area.* Illustrated by Shelley Freshman. New York: Crowell, 1974.

————. *Spaces, Shapes, and Sizes.* Illustrated by Loretta Lustig. New York: Crowell, 1980.

————. *Weighing and Balancing.* Illustrated by Aliki. New York: Crowell, 1970.

Thurber, James. *Many Moons.* Illustrated by Louis Slobodkin. New York: Harcourt Brace Jovanovich, 1971.

Trivett, Daphne, and John Trivett. *Time for Clocks.* Illustrated by Guilio Maestro. New York: Crowell, 1979.

Walter, Marion. *Make a Bigger Puddle, Make a Smaller Worm.* Illustrated by the author. New York: M. Evans and Company, 1971.

Youldon, Gillian. *Sizes.* New York: Watts, 1979.

11

TEACHING GEOMETRY

Ms. Duncan, a third-grade teacher, replied to the second-grade teacher, "Teach geometry? . . . I didn't have it in elementary school, so I skip the topic. Besides, the kids think it's boring just memorizing all those terms." Ms. Lott responded, "My kids like it—right now we are studying three-dimensional shapes using a set of wooden solids. Why don't you visit our class during your planning period tomorrow?"

Evaluate the philosophies of these teachers.

When most people hear the term "geometry," they think of the formal deductive course that has been traditionally taught in high school. Geometry in the elementary schools is completely different from this course. Before they begin school, children are already exploring their environment and becoming increasingly aware of the sizes and shapes of objects. Geometric shapes of various dimensions abound in the environment—both natural and human-made. Common objects such as seed pods, honeycombs, snowflakes, books, oatmeal boxes, windows, balls, dinner plates, and so on are some of the children's first geometric models. Additional geometric concepts should be built on these basic experiences. Geometry is not formally developed in the elementary school. Instead, it is developed by an intuitive approach in which children explore and experiment with materials to discover various geometric concepts.

Children live in a three-dimensional world. Therefore, their first geometric experiences should be with three-dimensional models. As children explore space figures, they also begin investigation of plane figures as they learn to consider just a surface of a space figure. All of this is done very informally. Then the children are ready to consider lines and points, the building blocks of geometry. Finally they return, on a more abstract level, for additional exploration into the properties of plane figures and space figures. This chapter is organized according to this sequence.

SPACE FIGURES (INTRODUCTION)

Children's first activities with space figures consist of play and classification. The activities described in this section involve analyzing the shapes of various solids. The space figures are discussed intuitively and informally: intuitively in that children are using objects to explore the concepts and informally in that the rigidity of definitions and formal language is not imposed on the discussion.

We will use such formal words as "parallel," "truncated," and "prism" in this text for clarity and brevity. However, in working with young children, the emphasis should be on their recognizing and understanding these concepts rather than on naming and defining them. This does not mean that the teacher should avoid using these words since some children will be ready to adopt formal vocabulary before others. Even the children who are not ready to use these words themselves can benefit from hearing others use them.

Everyday objects such as cereal boxes, soup cans, oranges, ice cream cones, wedges of cheese, and the like should be collected and classified according to similar characteristics (Figure 11-1). The children should tell how they have classified the set. In this case their rule of classification could have been all cans, all containers that hold water, or all cylinders. All these classifications are correct. In the first two the children have classified according to the type of container or its use. In the third case the children have classified according to a geometric concept—shape. The emphasis of this activity should be classifying objects of the same shape; it should not be simply a naming activity. However, the word "cylinder" can be used by the teacher.

As the children classify these everyday objects, they may observe that two of the cylinders seem to be the same size. By matching the ends and the heights of these two cylinders, the children can determine that the cylinders are the same size and shape (Figure 11-2). Objects that have the same size and shape are said to be con-

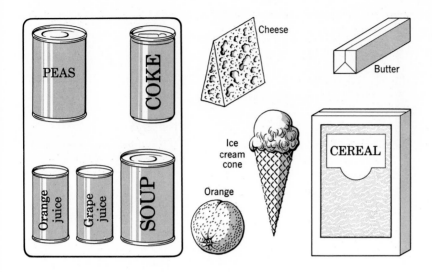

FIGURE 11-1.
Classification of three-dimensional objects.

gruent. The formal words may be introduced at the teacher's discretion. The "same size and shape" is appropriate vocabulary that describes this concept for young children.

After children have participated in many classification activities, they can study some of the properties of a particular group of space figures. For example, they might begin by looking at the properties of cylinders. For young children various-sized cylinders should be used so that the concept of cylinders is abstracted (Figure 11-3). The cylinders vary with respect to height or diameter or height and diameter. By variations such as these, the children will become more aware that the circular base and the height of the cylinder are distinct variables. Similar activities can be developed for cubes, spheres, and the like so that children conceptualize the properties that define these geometric shapes.

As the children participate in these activities, they should be informally acquiring concepts related to space figures. As an extension of the previous activities, children can classify a larger and more varied set of

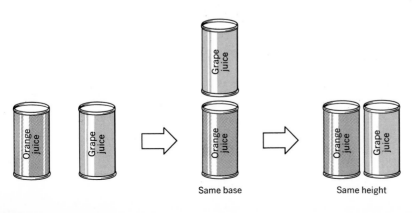

FIGURE 11-2.
Three-dimensional objects of the same shape and size.

Same base

Same height

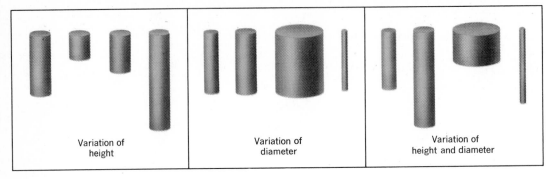

FIGURE 11-3.
Cylinder variation.

geometric solids (Figure 11-4). One set the children might choose is shown in Figure 11-5b. In this case, the children have noticed that these objects are all similar to cans or as one child said, "They are round but have flat ends." Through a discussion, the teacher led the class to discover the properties of cylinders; that is, each has circular, congruent, parallel bases and curved sides.

On another day the children selected a set of "blocks" (right rectangular prisms). In trying to define the properties of their set, one of the children said, "Every side has four square corners." Another child picked out the rest of the prisms as shown in Figure 11-5a and said, "These have some sides with four square corners too." Other observations were made by the class. "Three solids have two sides without square corners." "The two different sides are the same size and shape and are parallel." "One has only three rectangles and the other sides are triangles." Through class discussion, the children generalized that some solids have two faces that

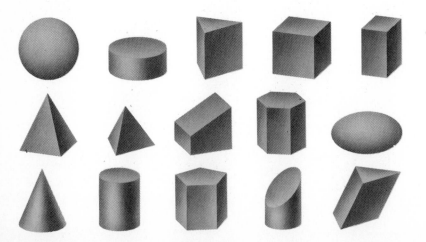

FIGURE 11-4.
Geometric solids.

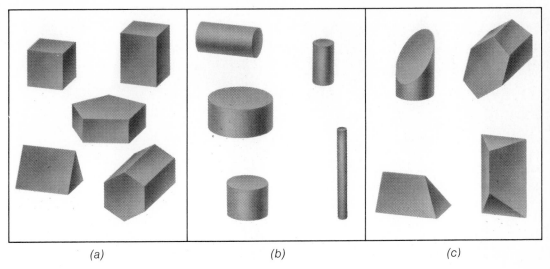

(a) (b) (c)

FIGURE 11-5.
Prisms and cylinders.

are congruent polygons and are parallel and their other faces are all rectangles. These solids are called right prisms.

Through other activities and discussions, children should extend their knowledge by comparing and contrasting solids to distinguish their properties. Some appropriate generalizations include the following. Prisms and cylinders both have congruent, parallel bases (Figure 11-5a and b). Some prisms and cylinders have lateral faces that are not perpendicular to their bases (Figure 11-6). Some solids have some of the same properties as prisms and cylinders but have bases that are not parallel or congruent (Figure 11-5c). The children should observe that other solids such as pyramids and cones have only one base and the faces meet at a point (Figure 11-7). Other solids such as spheres and ellipsoids are curved but they are different from both cylinders and cones.

Children can extend their concepts of

the properties of solids by trying to stack various combinations of these solids. They will find that some solids (right cylinders and prisms) are much easier to stack than others. They will also learn that the order in which solids are stacked makes a difference sometimes (pyramid and cone) but not other times (prism and cylinder). In stacking some solids, the position of the solid makes a difference. A prism will stack on top of a cylinder only when the cylinder is standing on one of its bases. As children move the solids into

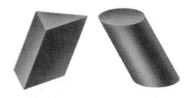

FIGURE 11-6.
Nonright prisms and cylinders.

FIGURE 11-7.
Pyramids and cones.

various positions in building stacks, they will learn to recognize each solid even when it is not standing on its "base." The shape of the solid is not dependent on its position in space.

Other properties of solids can be discovered by placing a solid in a box and moving the box so that the solid moves from side to side. In this activity the children cannot see the solid so they cannot use visual cues for identification. When given an unknown solid in a closed box, children can try to determine what is in the box by listening to the sounds as the object moves from side to side. Depending on their shapes, some solids roll, others slide, others slide and roll.

In another activity, the children can use the sense of touch instead of the sense of sight for shape identification. Several objects of various shapes are placed in a box. A cloth is draped over the open box so the contents of the box cannot be seen. The cloth should have two slits that are large enough for a child's hands. The children take turns putting their hands through the opening and picking up an object. After handling the object, the child can try to guess, based on touch, what shape the object is. To check

the guess, the child pulls the object out of the box and looks at it. Children must recognize various properties of a shape before they are able to identify that shape. For example, if an object has six rectangular faces, the child still has to determine that all the edges are the same length before accurately identifying a cube. A child may decide that an object is round, but roundness alone does not determine a sphere. The shapes to be placed in the box will depend on the concept to be abstracted.

A variation of this activity would be to place the shapes shown in Figure 11-8 in the box and ask the children to try to find the cylinder. As a child feels the objects, she or he should reject certain solids. For example, the cone is pointed so it is not a cylinder. As soon as the child determines that a certain solid is not a cylinder, it can be removed from the box to check the guess visually. This activity continues until the child correctly identifies the cylinder. This same activity can be done later using models of plane figures.

Solids can be related to flat shapes (plane figures) by using a sorting box (Figure 11-9). The top of this sorting box has inter-

FIGURE 11-8.
Identifying solids by touch.

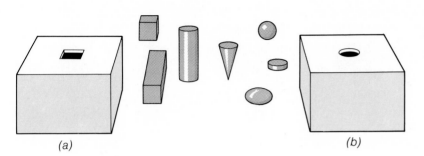

FIGURE 11-9.
Classification using a sorting box.

(a)   (b)

changeable inserts so that the cutout form can vary from activity to activity. Special attention should be given to the construction of the solids and the inserts. In early activities with sorting boxes, the inserts and solids should be chosen so that only one solid will go through the opening in a given insert. In later activities, it may be that more than one solid will go through the opening, but only one solid will fit the opening exactly. Still other inserts should be constructed so that more than one solid will exactly fit through the hole. For example, in Figure 11-9a both the cube and the rectangular prism will fit exactly through the opening. Some inserts may have more than one opening. For example, if the insert has both a rectangular and a circular opening, the children should find which one solid will fit exactly through both openings. As the children participate in these activities, they should notice that some solids such as the rectangular prism (not a cube) and the cylinder shown in Figure 11-9 will fit through the openings only two ways. In contrast, the cube can be inserted six different ways and the sphere in innumerable ways.

By further analyzing solids, children can begin studying the relationships between three-dimensional objects and their two-dimensional surfaces. For example, a set of solids and flat pieces can be used in a matching activity (Figure 11-10). By laying the square piece on one of the faces of the cube, the students find that the face has the same size and shape as the square piece.

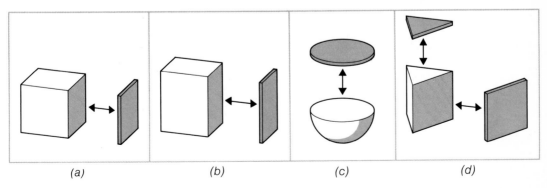

(a)   (b)   (c)   (d)

FIGURE 11-10.
Matching solids and flat pieces.

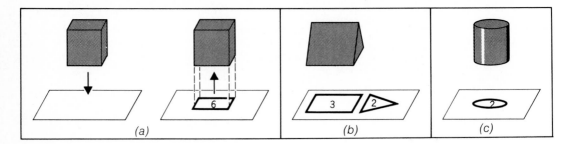

FIGURE 11-11.
Tracing faces of solids.

They can also show that all six faces are congruent by measuring each face with the square piece. As noted in Figure 11-10b through d, the students will need a variety of flat pieces. For the rectangular prism shown in Figure 11-10b, three different-sized rectangles will be needed. Through experimentation, the children will find that each rectangle matches two opposite faces. In Figure 11-10c the students can only match part of the hemisphere since only surfaces that are flat can be matched.

For an extension of this activity, the children can trace the faces of a solid on a sheet of paper (Figure 11-11). After tracing one face of a cube, the children turned the cube and found that another face also fit the tracing. They continued turning the cube until

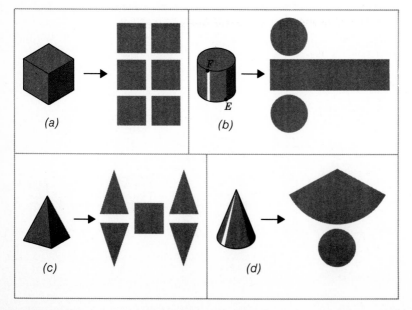

FIGURE 11-12.
Cutting apart solids.

they had checked all six faces. They then recorded the total number of faces inside the tracing. Figure 11-11b and c show the results obtained from tracing a triangular prism and a cylinder.

The relationships between the surfaces of a solid can be further explored by cutting apart solids made of paper (Figure 11-12). The children can again make comparisons among the various sides. They may be surprised when they discover that the curved surface of a cylinder becomes a rectangle (Figure 11-12b). A different result could have been obtained if they had cut from point E to point F on the curved surface. The children should make predictions about the number and shape of the sides of various solids. For example, they can discover how the base of a pyramid is related to the number of triangles in the pyramid if they are given time to explore pyramids with various-shaped bases. The more mature students can learn to make their own solids. At first they may need a pattern, but later they can learn to develop their own patterns.

In an earlier activity, when children observed the ellipsoid passing through the hole in the sorting box (Figure 11-9), they may have observed that the ellipsoid's thickness varies. This same shape can be made from clay so that children can cut the solid (Figure 11-13a). The slant of the cut should vary as well as where the cut is made. Before the cuts are made through the ellipsoid, the children should predict what shape the cut surface will be. In this case various-sized circles and ellipses will result. This predicting and cutting activity should be repeated using other solids.

A variation of this activity can be done with shadows. A solid is held between a light source and a screen. As the object is moved closer to the light, the children discover that the shadow becomes larger. As the object is turned, they will also see shadows of different shapes formed. (An excellent children's book on this subject is *Shadow Geometry* by Daphne Trivett.)

In studying the properties of solids, the children's perception of a shape usually includes the entire object. The use of wooden blocks as the only models of space figures only strengthens this erroneous concept. Other models such as empty shoe boxes, oatmeal boxes, or Ping-pong balls can be used to illustrate space figures. The shoe box would represent a right rectangular prism. The children can easily see that the closed box divides space into three regions (Figure 11-14). The three regions are inside

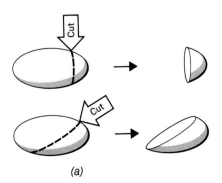

(a)

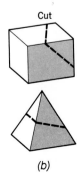

(b)

FIGURE 11-13.
Cutting solids.

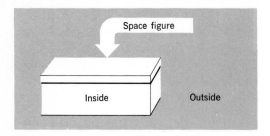

FIGURE 11-14.
Regions in space.

the box, the box itself, and outside the box. The box itself is the model of a right rectangular prism.

In more formal terms, the right rectangular prism divides space into three regions: the interior points, the points on the prism, and the exterior points. The interior of the region is discussed when students are considering volume measures. They will be asking themselves how many milliliters or cubic centimeters are needed to fill the region. The box itself is discussed when students are considering the surface of the box. They will need to know the area of the faces in order to cover the surface of the box.

QUESTIONS AND ACTIVITIES

Note: For the following problems a set of solids is needed. For some problems pictures of solids could be used, but it is preferable to use the actual solids.

1. Consider a sorting box (Figure 11-9) for which each solid will fit exactly.
   a. Which of the solids in Figure 11-4 would exactly fit through a square opening? A rectangular opening? A circular opening? A triangular opening?
   b. In a sorting box insert, a cylinder will fit through a rectangular opening and a circular opening. Draw sorting box

inserts that contain more than one opening for each of the following: rectangular prisms, triangular prisms, rectangular pyramids, triangular pyramids, hemispheres, cones, and square pyramids.

2. The following activities should be done with other students. Repeat these activities several times to explore different attributes. If possible, do these activities with a group of elementary school children.
   a. Place a solid in a box that is large enough for the solid to roll or slide in. Do not let the others see the solid. The other students should determine what is in the box without opening the box.
   b. Think of one of the solids. Have the others guess the solid by giving them one clue at a time about the attributes of the solid.
   c. Place a solid in a sack. Do not let the others see the solid. Have the other students determine what is in the sack by touching but not seeing the solid.
   d. Think of one of the solids. Describe this solid by its attributes so that the others would be able to draw a picture of it.
   e. Separate some of the solids into a subset by focusing on an attribute that they all have in common. Have the other students determine what attribute you used to separate the sets.

3. Predict the number of and shape of the faces of different solids. Trace the faces as shown in Figure 11-11 to check your predictions.

4. Draw two-dimensional patterns that could be used to construct three-dimensional shapes for each of the following: a rectangular prism, a triangular prism, a triangular pyramid, a cone, and a square pyramid.

5. Consider cross sections of different shapes, such as those represented by an orange, a tube of sausage, and a stick of margarine. If you are doing this activity with elementary children, check your predictions by cutting.

a. What different surfaces could be obtained when an orange is cut? Where would you cut to obtain the largest circle?

b. What different surfaces could be obtained when a sausage is cut? Why do we often cut sausages on a slant?

c. What different surfaces could be obtained when a rectangular prism is cut?

6. Describe how you would help children distinguish between the concepts of a cylinder and the interior of a cylinder. Between the concepts of a sphere and the interior of a sphere.

7. a. Obtain a set of Geoblocks from the *Elementary Science Study* and work through some of the activities using the blocks. As you work through these activities, discuss your thinking with other students. What is the purpose of the activities?

b. *For your resource file:* Other activities involving building with blocks are described by Carter in "Move Over, Frank Lloyd Wright!" Read this article and add it to your resource file.

8. a. Find a variety of solids such as those shown in Figure 11-4. Hold the solid between a light source (such as a flashlight) and a screen. Discover which solids make a triangular shadow; a rectangular shadow; a circular shadow.

b. Draw all of the different shapes of the shadows generated by a rectangular pyramid, a cone, and a cylinder.

c. *For your resource file:* Read "Projective Geometry in the Elementary School" by Mansfield. Seven lessons that involve children in exploring space through projective geometry are described.

9. In "Improving Spatial Abilities with Geometric Abilities," Young describes eighteen activities for improving spatial abilities for students in elementary school. Read the article. Since the activities are given in increasing order of difficulty,

choose and do three activities that you would find challenging.

10. In "Strategies for Teaching Elementary School Mathematics," Troutman describes geometric activities that reflect strategies for teaching mathematics. What strategies are discussed?

PLANE FIGURES (INTRODUCTION)

The space figures that have just been discussed are three-dimensional figures since they have length, width, and thickness. Plane figures have only two dimensions. They do not have thickness. Shadows and images on a movie screen are examples of two-dimensional objects. Since children need models, plane figures will be explored in this section by using three-dimensional objects. However, the thickness will be ignored and only two dimensions of the shape will be considered. Many of the activities that were discussed in the section on space figures can be adapted and used with plane figures. Most activities with plane figures can be introduced at the same time as activities with related space figures.

Many school children have already experienced figure perception activities with commercially available toys in their homes or in preschool. A readiness activity for those children who do not have sufficient experience is shown in Figure 11-15. In this activity the children place the correct shape into its matching form on the board. The shapes that are to be placed in the form board are three dimensional, not two dimensional. But each piece is the same thickness so that children will focus their attention on the base of the object. This activity is much simpler than the activities described with a form box for solids. In this board, there is only one correct

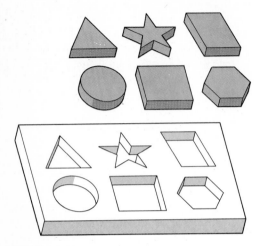

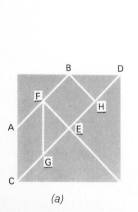

FIGURE 11-15.
Using a formboard.

place for a given shape and only one correct shape for a given place.

A more sophisticated activity can be developed using tangrams. A tangram puzzle is made up of seven pieces as shown in Figure 11-16a. Children can place the tangram pieces inside the outlines of various figures. As they attempt to duplicate various figures,

the children will need to focus attention on the properties of individual pieces and on the relationships among the pieces. The diagrams can become more complicated as children mature mathematically. Children can also be encouraged to create their own patterns.

Children's perception of shape can also be developed through attribute blocks. In the activity illustrated in Figure 11-17, the children discriminate according to shape by placing the squares in the square loop and the circles in the circle loop. Rule cards that indicate the classification can be inserted in the loops (Figure 11-18). The attribute pieces can also be placed in a box and children can try to guess which shape they are touching. A similar activity was described in detail in the section on space figures.

Shape recognition of flat surfaces was included in the section on space figures. As children matched flat surfaces to the faces of solids, sliced through solids, and cut solids apart, they were recognizing the plane surfaces of solids. By tracing around the various attribute pieces, the children will be ab-

FIGURE 11-16.
Shape exploration using tangrams.

(a)   (b)   (c)

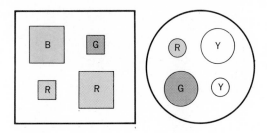

FIGURE 11-17.
Classifying circles and squares.

stracting the concept that the outline of the piece is the shape being considered, not the piece itself. This activity should precede the tracing of a solid figure that was described in the section on space figures. (There are several excellent children's books that explore simple concepts of shape. Some of these books are *Shapes, Shapes, Shapes* and *Circles, Triangles and Squares* by Tana Hoban, *Are You Square?* by Ethel Kessler, *Round Things Everywhere* by Seymore Reit, *My Very First Book of Shapes* by Eric Carle, *The Shape of Me and Other Stuff* by Dr. Seuss, and *Sesame Street Book of Shapes,* by the Children's Television Workshop.)

Most commercially available attribute blocks are limited in their variety of shapes. Dienes mathematical variability principle states that if a mathematical concept has several variables, all these variables must be exemplified. For example, when they read the word "triangle," many people think of an equilateral triangle. If this is their only concept of a triangle, their concept is incomplete because they have not accounted for all the variables. To develop an accurate concept of triangles, children should be given many examples (Figure 11-19). Since the important concept is "a simple closed figure with three sides," the size of the angles and the lengths of the sides of the triangles should vary. As they study these triangles, the children will find that they can separate the set of triangles into smaller subsets. For example, triangles *a, b, c, d, e, f,* and *k* have two sides the same length (isosceles triangles) (Figure 11-20). Furthermore, triangles *a, b,* and *c* have three sides the same length (equilateral triangles), which is a subset of the isosceles triangles. Triangles *g, h j, l,* and *m* have no sides equal (scalene). Children should be involved in classifying the triangles according to their differences and similarities, *not* in merely naming the triangles.

As the children made the classifications described above, they were classifying the triangles by taking each one and comparing the lengths of its sides. After they had finished this classifications activity, one of the

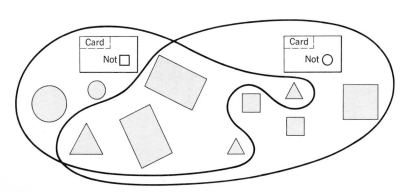

FIGURE 11-18.
Attribute blocks with rule cards.

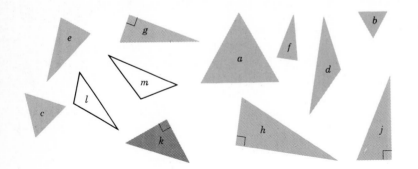

FIGURE 11-19.
Dienes mathematical
variability principle.

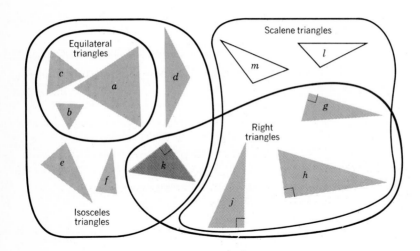

FIGURE 11-20.
Classifying triangles.

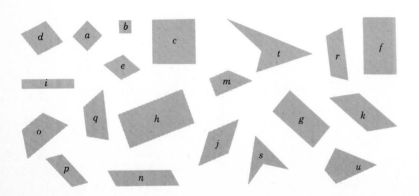

FIGURE 11-21.
Quadrilaterals.

children said, "Hey, some of these triangles have square corners." Other children joined the discussion. "Why can't we classify those triangles with square corners (right triangles) as a group?" "Look, there aren't any right triangles in the set of equilateral triangles." "Could we find other groups by looking at the angles?"

A similar activity can be developed using four-sided figures (quadrilaterals). Students should be given a variety of quadrilaterals to classify (Figure 11-21). As Ms. Newcomer's class studied the set, they first selected rectangles *i, f, g,* and *h* and placed them in a loop. Next, they selected the squares and placed them in another loop. The students selected squares and rectangles first since these were familiar shapes. To make further classification, they needed to study the attributes of the remaining pieces. As they did this, they realized that the squares had all the attributes of rectangles and, therefore, belonged inside the rectangle loop as well as in a loop of their own (Figure 11-22).

As the children studied the remaining figures, they noted that figures *d, e, j, k, p,* and *n* have two pairs of parallel sides (parallelograms). However, so do rectangles, so they formed a large loop around the first loops. As they examined figures *d* and *e* (rhombuses), they noted that both had four equal sides just as squares do. Consequently, they placed a fourth loop so that it contained the squares and rhombuses (Figure 11-23). This loop was placed in such a manner that the rhombuses remained inside the parallelogram loop and outside the rectangle loop. Finally, they separated the quadrilaterals that had exactly one pair of parallel sides (trapezoids). Thus they finished with a complete classification of quadrilaterals.

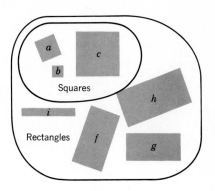

FIGURE 11-22.
Classification of rectangles.

One method of defining and naming shapes is the "this is—this is not" format. A rectangle is defined in Figure 11-24 using this format. The rectangles are in various positions: vertical, horizontal, and diagonal. This helps to ensure that the children will not associate shape with any one position but will be able to abstract just those properties necessary to define that particular shape. In all the "these are rectangles," parallel opposite sides joined at right angles are present. None of the figures in the "these are not rectangles" set contains *all* the properties of a rectangle. This same format can be used to define other shapes such as trapezoids, isosceles triangles, regular polygons, non-convex polygons, ellipses, and so on.

The geoboard can be used to investigate many concepts of plane geometry: line segments; open and closed figures, including polygons; properties of polygons; and so on. A geoboard has nails placed in a grid pattern or spaced equidistantly around a circle. By stretching rubber bands around the nails, children can form various polygons. In the previous activity the children were given specific quadrilaterals; in this activity they are asked to generate their own. The chil-

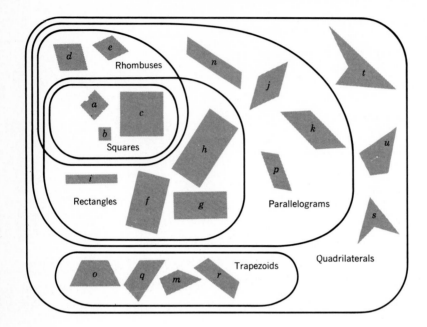

FIGURE 11-23.
Classification of quadrilaterals.

dren should be encouraged to form a large variety of quadrilaterals. These can be recorded on dotter paper, and the children can mark the rectangles (Figure 11-25). Observe that in this example none of the students formed rectangles with a diagonal orientation. They should be encouraged to find some of these rectangles.

Similarly, properties of triangles can be

explored on geoboards. As children form a large variety of triangles on the grid geoboard, they will discover that they are unable to form equilateral triangles (Figure 11-26). On the circular geoboards, children will find that they can form equilateral triangles as well as other isosceles triangles and scalene triangles (Figure 11-27).

Geoboard activities can be extended to

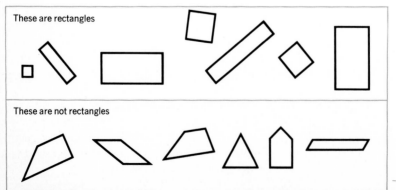

FIGURE 11-24.
Defining rectangles.

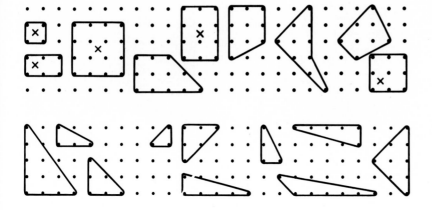

FIGURE 11-25.
Quadrilaterals on dotter paper.

FIGURE 11-26.
Triangles on dotter paper.

include many other polygons. In all these activities, students should compare and contrast the polygons in several different ways—lengths of sides, sizes of angles, and so on. Each new comparison that is introduced by a student should be discussed by the class.

The children have already been introduced to the concept of roundness in space figures. They also encounter it in plane figures such as circles and ellipses. If the children cut a sphere such as a grapefruit into various sections, they will obtain circles of various sizes. If they cut a cylinder, such as a sausage, they will obtain circles or ellipses depending on the slant of the cut.

To draw circles, the children can trace around circular pieces such as lids or cups. A large circle can be formed by two children

holding the two ends of a string. Keeping the string taut, one child walks around the other, while the second child pivots on a marked position. When the first child returns to the starting position, a circular path has been generated (Figure 11-28).

In the preceding activities, plane figures have been classified only by shape. We can also classify these figures according to both size and shape in order to explore congruency. Early activities in congruence include cutting out two identical shapes. One shape is then placed on top of the other to demonstrate that they are congruent.

When figures are placed in different positions, the children may have difficulty in recognizing congruent figures. For example, in Figure 11-29 all the triangles are con-

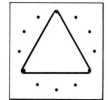 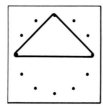 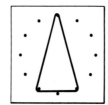 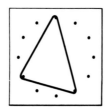 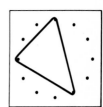

FIGURE 11-27.
Triangles on circular geoboard.

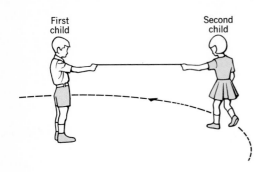

FIGURE 11-28.
Generating a circular path.

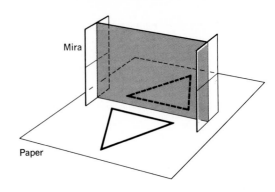

FIGURE 11-31.
Mira.

gruent to each other. To check whether the figures are congruent, the children decided to trace triangle 1 and try to match the tracing to the other triangles. To see if triangle 1 was congruent to triangle 3, they slid the tracing across the surface (Figure 11-30a). To check triangle 4, they flipped the tracing of triangle 1 over, which is similar to the movement involved in turning a page (Figure

11-30b). Finally, to check triangle 2, the tracing of triangle 1 was turned in a movement similar to the movement of the hands of a clock (Figure 11-30c).

A mira can also be used to study figures that have the same size and shape. The mira is a vertical piece of red plexiglass with a recessed edge. The recessed edge should always be placed on the bottom facing the child. When the mira is placed on a piece of paper beside a triangle, an image of the original triangle can be seen in the mira (Figure 11-31). With a pencil, the child can trace the image on the paper on the opposite side of the mira from the original triangle (Figure 11-32). After the child has drawn the reflection of the triangle, the result will be a diagram similar to the one shown in Figure 11-

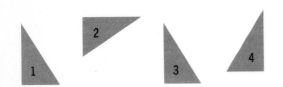

FIGURE 11-29.
Congruent figures.

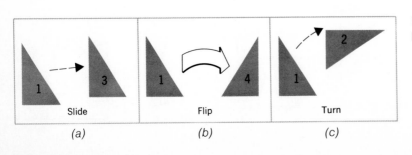

FIGURE 11-30.
Flips, slides, and turns.

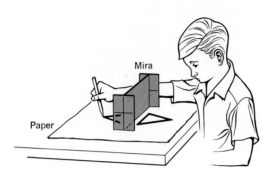

FIGURE 11-32.
Using the mira.

30b. Since the new triangle was drawn the same size and shape as the original triangle, the two triangles are congruent.

As with solid objects, the children's perception of a shape often includes the entire object instead of just the outline of the object. For this a picture frame could be used as a model of a plane figure. The frame (a rectangle) divides a plane into three regions (Figure 11-33). The three regions of the surface are inside the frame, the frame itself, and outside the frame. The frame itself is the rectangle.

In more formal terms, a rectangle divides a plane into three regions: the interior points, the points on the rectangle, and the exterior points. The interior of the region is discussed when students are considering

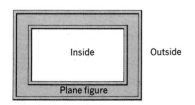

FIGURE 11-33.
Regions on a plane.

area measures. They will be asking how many square centimeters are needed to cover the surface. The rectangle itself is discussed when the students are trying to find the distance around the rectangle or the perimeter.

QUESTIONS AND ACTIVITIES

1. Dienes mathematical variability principle can be used to develop concepts in geometry. For example:
These are rectangles.

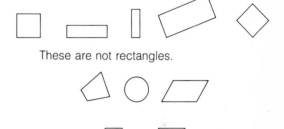

These are not rectangles.

Devise a "these are . . . these are not . . ." definition for parallelograms and one for trapezoids. Further explanation for using examples and nonexamples is contained in "Some Guidelines for Teaching Geometry Concepts" by Charles.

2. *For your resource file:* Relatively simple polygons such as triangles and quadrilaterals can be used to generate a number of activities. Read "Let's Do It: A Triangle Treasury" by Van de Walle and Thompson or "Geometry" by Burger. Add these activities to your file.

3. In Figure 11-20, triangles were first classified by the length of their sides. In addition to classifying by lengths of sides, children should also focus on angles. What categories would be formed if they

classified this same set by angle size? What special names would be given to each set?

4. You can readily make your own tangram puzzle. See Figure 11-16a. Use a lightweight cardboard such as a file folder. Draw a 10-centimeter square. Points *A* and *B* are midpoints of the sides. Points *F* and *E* are midpoints of line segments *AB* and *CD*, respectively. Points *G* and *H* are midpoints of line segments *CE* and *ED*, respectively. Connect appropriate points and cut pieces accordingly. Directions for forming a tangram through paperfolding are given in "Teaching Geometry with Tangrams" by Russell and Bologna; the pattern is also found in most elementary textbook series.

5. a. Use all of the tangram pieces to form the following figures.
   (1) a square
   (2) a nonrectangular parallelogram
   (3) a trapezoid
   (4) a nonsquare rectangle
   (5) a triangle
   b. Can you make a triangle with one of the pieces? Two pieces? Three pieces? . . . Seven pieces?

6. Miranda found four different-sized squares on her 5 × 5 geoboard. The squares she found had areas of 1, 4, 9, and 16 square units. Sam said that there were other squares, but Miranda was disbelieving. What hints or guiding questions can you give Miranda to help her find the other squares.

7. a. Windows and doors are usually rectangular. Why? Although garage doors, house doors, and doors to public buildings are all usually rectangular, their proportions are different. Why? Read "Let's Do It: Let's Take a Geometry Walk" by Nelson and Leutzinger. Plan a geometry walk on your campus; map out the route and state which places your class will visit, what geometric concepts will be related, and what the function of these concepts is.
   b. The children's books *Circles, Triangles and Squares* and *Shapes, Shapes, Shapes* by Hoban are helpful for increasing people's awareness of their environment. Read one of these books. How could you use and extend this book with children?

8. a. Read the children's book, *The Ellipse* by Charosh. Do the experiments described in the book. Write a brief paragraph summarizing the book and stating your opinion of it.
   b. Read five books from the list of Children's Literature at the end of this chapter. Devise a lesson based on one of these books.

9. Use a geoboard or dotter paper to determine which of the following can be formed on a geoboard. For each type form one example that has a side parallel to a side of the geoboard and a second example that is not parallel to any of the sides. For each case, form the general case; that is, the rhombus should be a nonsquare rhombus.

Quadrilateral	Square
Rhombus	Parallelogram
Rectangle	Kite
Isosceles trapezoid	Right triangle
Obtuse isosceles triangle	Acute triangle
Pentagon	Hexagon

10. Compare the various strategies below with regard to their use in deciding whether or not two figures are congruent. How do they differ perceptually? Which appears to be the easiest for children to explore first?
   a. Measure the sides and angles of two triangles to determine if they are the same size and shape.
   b. Trace around the plastic triangle and compare the tracing to the original figure.
   c. Draw a triangle and then use a mira to draw its image.

11. Describe how you would help children distinguish between the concepts of a quadrilateral, the interior of the quadrilateral, and the exterior of the quadrilateral.

12. Students can use problem-solving techniques to analyze properties of regions. For example, given the simple closed curve in the figure below and point *A* located in the same plane, the problem is to determine whether point *A* is in the interior or the exterior region. One solution technique is to draw point *B*, which is obviously in the exterior region, and then join *B* and *A* with a line segment or curve. As the students proceed from point *B* to point *A*, whenever the curve crosses the boundary of the figure it goes from one region to the other. Is point *A* inside or outside the curve? Can you form a generalization about the relationship between the number of boundaries crossed by the segment and whether the point in question is in the interior or the exterior of the figure?

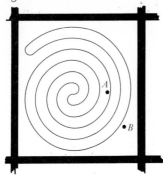

13. a. Two resources that introduce children to an intuitive definition of circles are the children's book *Circles* by Sitomer and Sitomer and the article "A 'Fair' Way to Discover Circles" by Cangelosi. Read one of these resources. How is the definition of a circle explored? Evaluate the other activities in the resource. Why could these be considered problem-solving activities?

  b. Read and explore some of the activities

in "Let's Do It: The Surprising Circle" by Dana and Lindquist.

14. a. Given the definition below, find all pentominoes. (There are 12.) These are pentominoes.

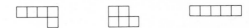

These are all the *same* pentomino.

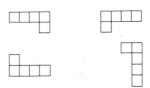

These are not pentominoes.

  b. Read "Pentominoes for Fun and Learning" by Cowan. Solve some of the problems posed in the article. What is the purpose of such activities?

15. *For your resource file:* Real-life situations and classroom activities involving slides, flips, and turns are explored in "Living in a World of Transformations" by Sanok. Read this article and add the ideas to your teaching file.

CURVES, LINES, AND POINTS (INTRODUCTION)

Flat pieces were used as models to represent plane figures. Since flat pieces have three dimensions—length, width, and thickness—they could not be formally used to define two-dimensional ideas. Just as flat pieces were used as models to represent two-dimensional objects, shoelaces could

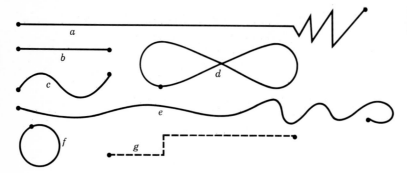

FIGURE 11-34.
Shapes of various paths.

be used as models to represent a one-dimensional concept—a curve. If the shoelace were pulled taut, this model would represent a line segment. The plastic ends of the shoelaces could be considered models of points.

Paths can be used to informally introduce curves, line segments, and points. A path can be described as long, short, crooked, curved, straight, continuous, broken, and so on (Figure 11-34). Points can be introduced similarly. Enlarged dots at the ends of the paths can represent endpoints.

If children start tracing the paths at one of the points, they will either come back to the starting point or they will arrive at a point on the opposite end of the path.

There is only one dimension being considered. Consequently, the only comparison of dimensions that can be made is with respect to length. The paths are either the same length or one is longer than the other. If the children want to compare the lengths of paths *a* and *d*, they would find it difficult to measure them in their present positions. It would be easier to compare the paths if

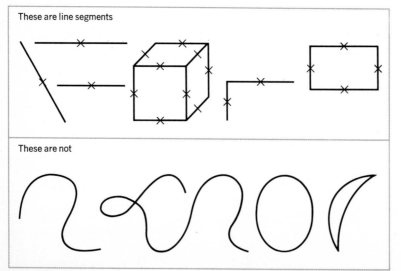

FIGURE 11-35.
Line segments.

These are line segments

These are not

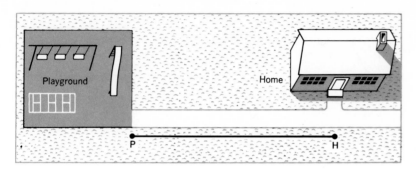

FIGURE 11-36.
Path representing line segment.

they were straight. This can be accomplished by using strings to represent the paths and then simply placing the strings side by side.

The children's first experiences with straight lines only include line segments. In Figure 11-35 the line segments are marked by X's. Since line segments have definite lengths, children can be involved in measuring these lengths as discussed in Chapter 10. The line segment could be represented by the straight path from the playground to home and this path could be labeled (Figure 11-36). The distance from the playground to home (PH) is the same as the distance from home to the playground (HP). Since only the direction is different, the children can measure the path from H to P or from P to H.

Letters were used to describe locations (points) at the ends of the paths (line segments) (Figure 11-36). Paths can also contain several locations (points) along their length (Figure 11-37). By moving from letter to letter, the children are learning that a point is a specific location. These activities should precede children's introduction to the number line. On the number line, as the children move from point to point, they are also adding and subtracting numbers (Figure 11-38).

In Figure 11-37 three points were located between the points representing the playground and home. This could be extended to introduce the "number" of points on a line segment. For example, the children could be asked to indicate two more points by drawing two more dots on line segment PH ($\overline{PH}$). They could be asked if they could place three more points, five more points, and so on. The children will soon recognize that a large number of points can be represented on the segment and still more could be shown. With guidance from the teacher, the children can conclude that there is a large number of points on the line segment. This type of activity can serve as an introduction to the concept of infinity.

Given a random set of points, like those

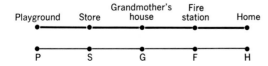

FIGURE 11-37.
Locations along a path.

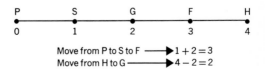

FIGURE 11-38.
Paths to represent number lines.

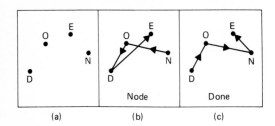

FIGURE 11-39.
Locations and order along paths.

Plotting locations.

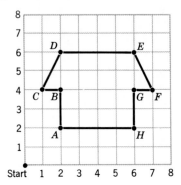

FIGURE 11-41.
Plotting locations.

in Figure 11-39a, the children can connect all four points with line segments. However, different children given this same task may get different results (Figure 11-39b and c). The order of the points determines the direction of movement. Locations of the points were the same, but the order in which the children connected them produced different results.

Another activity involving location of points can be used to introduce a grid (Figure 11-40). The children are instructed to move along the path horizontally ($\rightarrow$), then vertically ($\uparrow$), but not diagonally ($\nearrow$). Pictures can be drawn by plotting given points and connecting them in order as shown in Figure 11-41. Since most children find this kind of activity fun, it can be used for motivation as well as for learning. Besides plotting points to find someone else's picture,

children can invent their own pictures and make lists of the points necessary to make those pictures. Then they can exchange these lists and try to plot each others' pictures. Sometimes a list of points will have to go back to its designer for correction of errors. Working out their own designs and finding and correcting errors will do more to increase the children's understanding of a grid system than merely plotting lists of points given in a textbook will.

After studying line segments, the students can extend this concept to the concept of a ray. A line segment has two endpoints, but a ray has only one endpoint and extends infinitely into space in the other direction. Since no concrete model of a ray is

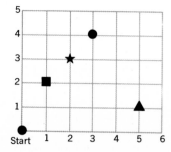

FIGURE 11-40.
Introductory graphing.

complete (all models are finite), the concept of a ray extending infinitely is difficult for children to understand.

Students are familiar with models of rays such as the beam of a flashlight. A flashlight beam originates from a point, the flashlight bulb, and extends indefinitely in one direction. The concept of rays can also be illustrated by one of the double lanes of an interstate highway. As the children stand on a bridge overlooking the road, they can observe that the road extends into the distance as far as they can see. If they moved to another bridge 20 kilometers away from the first one, they would be able to see beyond their first observation, but they still could not see the end of the road.

Rays in the classroom can be introduced on the geoboard. A line segment can be represented on a geoboard; a ray is simply an extension of this segment in one direction. The nails marked *A* and *B* represent the endpoints of the line segment. The students can take the rubber band at nail *B* and stretch it in the same direction away from point *A*. If the rubber band had unlimited elasticity, it could be stretched indefinitely. This represents ray *AB* ($\overrightarrow{AB}$) (Figure 11-42b). Figure 11-42c shows a diagram of $\overrightarrow{BA}$.

Similarly, the geoboard can be used to represent lines by stretching the rubber band representing $\overline{AB}$ in both directions (Figure 11-42d). If the rubber band had unlimited elasticity, it could stretch indefinitely. As the interstate highway model was used to represent the concept of a ray, it can also be used to represent the concept of a line. After the children have looked as far as they can see down the road in one direction, they can turn around and look down the road in the other direction. The road stretches as far as they can see in both directions.

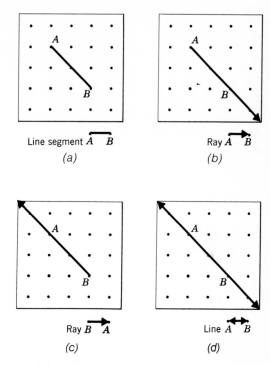

Line segment $\overline{A\ B}$
(a)

Ray $\overrightarrow{A\ B}$
(b)

Ray $\overrightarrow{B\ A}$
(c)

Line $\overleftrightarrow{A\ B}$
(d)

FIGURE 11-42.
Introduction to rays and lines.

More formally, a line has no endpoints but stretches infinitely in both directions. As shown in Figure 11-42, a line segment is a subset of a ray and a ray is a subset of a line. Thus, since there is an infinitely large number of points on a line segment, there is also an infinitely large number of points on a ray or on a line.

After they have grasped the concept of lines, children are ready to explore the relationship between two or more lines. The concepts of parallel, intersecting, and perpendicular lines should be developed through activities that build understanding of the concepts. Again, this study should not be turned into just a naming exercise.

Parallel lines could be introduced by again using the interstate highway as a

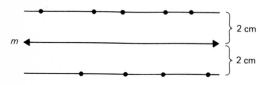

FIGURE 11-43.
Drawing parallel lines.

model. The two double lanes of the interstate represent a pair of parallel lines since in most locations the two lanes are an approximately equal distance apart. Similarly, other models of parallel lines that the children can readily identify include railroad tracks, city streets, lines on notebook paper, and the like. As the children look at railroad tracks, they can see that the tracks are the same distance apart although they appear to meet in the distance. If the children walk along the tracks, they can see that the rails continue to remain the same distance apart no matter how far they walk.

To introduce parallel lines in the classroom, students could be given a line m and asked to find a point that is 2 centimeters from the closest point on m (Figure 11-43). The students should repeat this process by finding more points that are 2 centimeters from the given line. They will soon realize that the points are forming two straight lines. The result is two new lines that are both parallel to line m.

In another activity, when the children folded a rectangular piece of paper into halves as shown in Figure 11-44, they noted that the line created by the fold is equidistant from (parallel to) both edges of the paper. The children then folded the paper again as shown in Figure 11-45. The two fold lines crossed or intersected each other. Most children are already familiar with the word intersection since two streets meet at an intersection (Figure 11-46). An intersection of two streets names a particular point just as two lines intersect at one point.

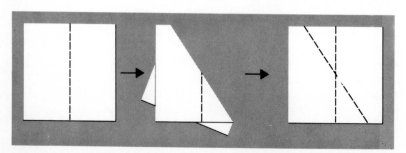

FIGURE 11-44.
Folding parallel lines.

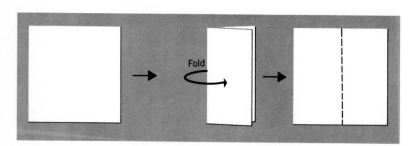

FIGURE 11-45.
Folding intersecting lines.

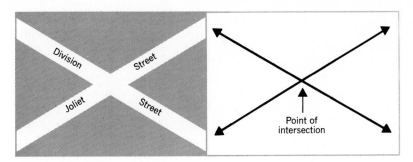

FIGURE 11-46.
Intersections.

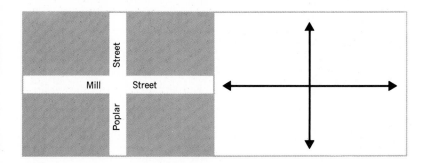

FIGURE 11-47.
Perpendicular lines.

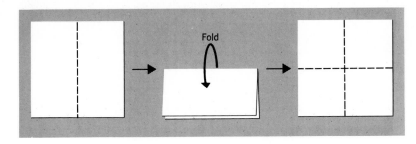

FIGURE 11-48.
Folding perpendicular lines.

Streets often intersect forming square corners (Figure 11-47). Square corners are called right angles and are formed by the intersection of perpendicular lines. Lines that intersect to form square corners can be illustrated by paperfolding (Figure 11-48). The rectangular sheet of paper was folded in half vertically and then horizontally. The two fold lines represent a special case of intersecting lines called perpendicular lines. (Children's books on these topics that are extremely well written are *Straight Lines, Parallel Lines, Perpendicular Lines* by Mannis Charosh; *Lines, Segments, Polygons* by Mindel and Harry Sitomer; and *Right Angles: Paper Folding Geometry* by Jo Phillips.)

A plane surface is related to linear concepts in various ways. Several examples of curves are shown in Figure 11-49a. Curves may or may not separate a plane into regions. A closed curve is a curve that returns to its starting point (Figure 11-49b). It sepa-

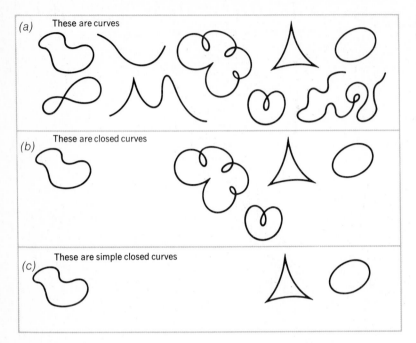

FIGURE 11-49.
Classification of curves.

rates the plane, but it may intersect its own boundary. A simple closed curve does not intersect its own boundary (Figure 11-49c).

A simple closed curve divides the plane into three regions: inside the curve, the curve itself, and outside the curve. Activities with regions should gradually develop from experiences with general regions to experiences with simple convex regions. Simple convex regions are those in which any two

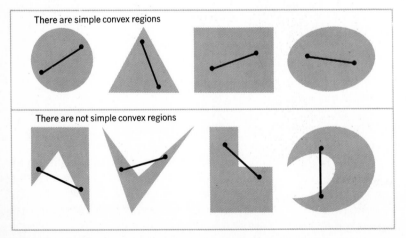

FIGURE 11-50.
Convex (and nonconvex) regions.

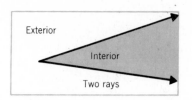

FIGURE 11-51.
Two rays forming an angle.

points in the interior region can be joined by a line segment that does not cross the curve forming the region (Figure 11-50). Simple convex regions such as circles, triangles, and parallelograms are the regions usually studied in the elementary classroom. The linear and area measures of these regions are usually found.

The relationship of a ray to the plane surface should also be studied. Two distinct rays that have a common endpoint divide a plane into three regions (Figure 11-51). The two rays form an angle. Just as two rays with a common endpoint separate a plane into three regions, one line also separates a plane into three regions (Figure 11-52a). The regions are the points on the line, the points on one side of the line, and the points on the other side of the line. Parallel lines and intersecting lines also separate a plane into regions (Figure 11-52b and c).

The separation of a plane by perpendic-ular lines is used in developing a coordinate system (Figure 11-53). The two lines divide the plane into four regions or quadrants. To locate points within the four quadrants, the lines can both be numbered. The horizontal line (x axis) follows the number line approach that is normally used. The vertical line (y axis) is simply a vertical number line. Every point on the plane can be named by an ordered pair that can be used as a system for locating positions on a plane. The point where the two lines intersect is called the origin: (0,0). All other locations are found from this reference point. This is an extension of the simple grid for plotting points that was described earlier. That grid was simply the upper, right-hand (first) quadrant of the coordinate system.

A game that involves plotting points-is four-in-a-row. Two teams of students or two players take turns giving ordered pairs that are then plotted by another member of the class. The first team to plot four consecutive points in a line wins the game. The students soon realize that not only do they need to plot four points in a row but they must also develop a strategy for blocking their opponents. Whichever student gives the winning point can become the plotter for the next game. The teacher may need to plot the first game. After the students have learned to play the game, they are able to follow the

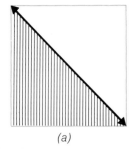

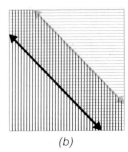

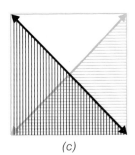

(a) (b) (c)

FIGURE 11-52.
Lines forming regions.

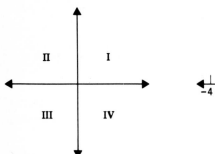

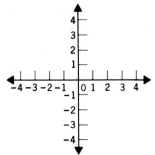

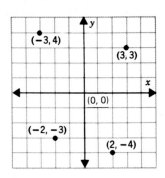

FIGURE 11-53.
Coordinate system.

teacher's example in organizing it. If the students are consistently using the first quadrant and need more practice in the other quadrants, the game can be restricted to certain regions.

CURVES, LINES, AND POINTS (EXTENSION ACTIVITIES)

The activities introduced in this section are other suggestions for topics and methods suitable for the elementary school student. We will mention several topics briefly since it is not possible to explain all the problem-solving activities developed for exploring geometry. Any one of these situations could be explored by students and, through their investigations, extended into related topics in geometry. Children's books and articles in the *Arithmetic Teacher* can provide a large number of interesting topics for the students as well as for the teacher.

Children can use paperfolding to investigate the angles formed by intersecting lines (vertical angles). First they would fold two lines that intersect on a sheet of paper (Figure 11-54). Students can compare angle AOC with angle DOB by folding the two angles on top of each other so that the rays match. The students will observe that the angles have the same measure. The activity can be repeated to compare angles AOD and COB. Students should note that the sum of angles AOD and DOB is 180 degrees. Some students may observe that the two fold lines used to compare the angles turned out to be perpendicular to each other. As an extension, students should be encouraged to discover whether this is always true and why.

Another pattern involving vertical angles can be studied when a pair of parallel lines (*m* and *n*) are intersected by line *l* forming eight angles (Figure 11-55). Ms. Lautenbach, Jim's teacher, told him that the measure of angle 1 was 130 degrees and asked him to find the measures of the other

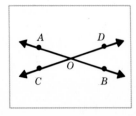

FIGURE 11-54.
Comparing vertical angles.

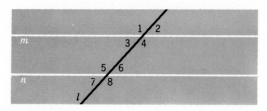

FIGURE 11-55.
Parallel lines cut by a transversal.

angles. By tracing angles 5, 6, 7, and 8 on another sheet of paper, Jim compared them to angles 1, 2, 3, and 4 by placing the tracing on top of the angles. He found that angles 1, 2, 3, and 4 were the same size as angles 5, 6, 7, and 8, respectively. From his previous experiences with vertical angles, he knew that angle 4 measures 130 degrees. Since $\angle 1$ and $\angle 2$ form a straight angle (180°), he concluded that $\angle 2$ measures 50 degrees. From this information he could readily find the measures of the other angles.

In Figure 11-30 the motions of flips,

slides, and turns were illustrated. The relationships among these motions and lines can be explored using the mira. Carmen placed a mira on line m and traced the image of trapezoid $ABCD$ to form trapezoid $A'B'C'D'$ (Figure 11-56). She then flipped trapezoid $A'B'C'D'$ over line n to form trapezoid $A''B''C''D''$. Carmen realized that the two movements of the trapezoid to its final position are equivalent to the one motion of sliding the trapezoid from its first position to its final position. The class had also been studying intersecting lines so Carmen decided to see what would happen if the trapezoid were flipped twice over intersecting lines (Figure 11-57). She found that the two movements of the trapezoid over intersecting lines were equivalent to the one motion of turning the trapezoid from its first position to its final position.

The branch of mathematics known as topology contains many interesting topics that students can pursue on their own. Some of these topics are networks, map coloring,

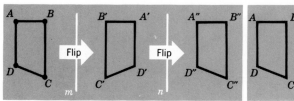
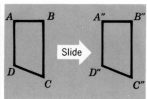

FIGURE 11-56.
Two flips over parallel lines.

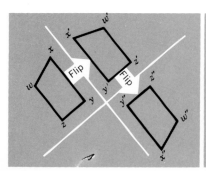
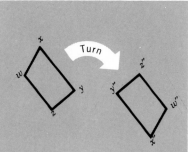

FIGURE 11-57.
Two flips over intersecting lines.

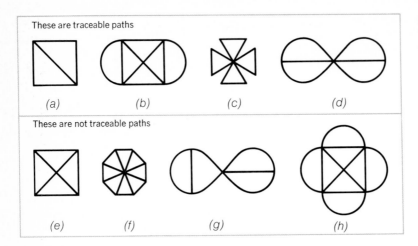

These are traceable paths

(a)   (b)   (c)   (d)

These are not traceable paths

(e)   (f)   (g)   (h)

FIGURE 11-58.
Traceable paths or networks.

and Möbius strips. A discovery lesson on networks can be designed by exploring traceable paths (Figure 11-58). A traceable path is a path that can be completely traced without retracing any section of the path or lifting the pencil off the paper once the path is started.

After the students have traced a few paths, they should be encouraged to find what properties a path must have to be traceable. As they analyze the paths, they will observe that the number of line segments that intersect at the vertices determines whether a path is traceable. The students will need to collect data that should be organized and studied in order to formulate a pattern. The sides of polygons or other plane figures and the edges of polyhedrons are simply networks. The same tracing activity can be used with solids.

Networks divide the plane into regions. A student can explore these regions through map coloring (Figure 11-59). The only rule in map coloring is that no region should share part of a border with a region of the same color. Regions of the same color are allowed to touch only at one point. The purpose is to find the smallest possible number of colors needed for the map.

Möbius strips can be fascinating for any age group. A Möbius strip is simply made by taking a narrow strip of paper, giving one

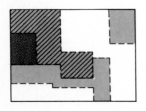
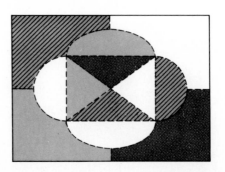

FIGURE 11-59.
Map coloring.

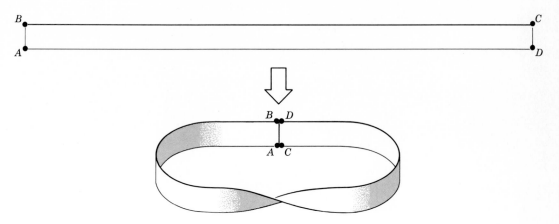

FIGURE 11-60.
Möbius strip.

end a half twist, and taping the ends to- gether (Figure 11-60). Students can then start drawing a line lengthwise on the strip. As they continue drawing, they will eventu- ally come back to the starting point. They will discover that although any short section of the strip has two sides, the entire strip has only one side. This can be seen because the single line that they have just drawn can now be found on "both sides" of the entire strip.

Students can continue exploring the Möbius strip by cutting down the center of the strip until they come back to the starting point. They should predict what type of fig- ure will result before cutting since they will probably be surprised at the results. (Other activities with networks, map coloring, and the Möbius strip are explored in detail in *Stretching a Point* by Mitch Struble.)

Many constructions traditionally re- served for the high school curriculum can be done in the elementary school if appropriate methods are used. Paperfolding and mira activities should precede construction activ- ities with straightedge and compass. Pa-

perfolding is a relatively simple procedure that can be handled by young children whereas the compass and straightedge re- quires greater motor coordination and math- ematical maturity. These three construction techniques can be applied to a variety of situations. As discussed below, all three ac- tivities result in the forming of perpendicular bisectors.

Students can divide a line segment in half (bisect it) by simply folding the segment on top of itself so that the endpoints match (Figure 11-61a). The fold line that bisects $\overline{AB}$ is called a line of symmetry because the fold line divides the line segment into two congruent parts that overlap exactly.

A mira is used in the same manner. The mira is slid over the line until the reflected image exactly matches the part of the seg- ment seen through the mira (Figure 11-61b). A line is drawn along the base of the mira. This line of reflection is also a line of sym- metry.

Another method for bisecting line seg- ments is through the use of a straightedge

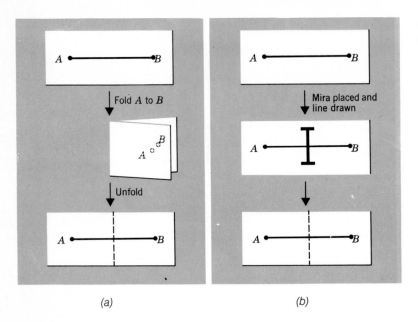

FIGURE 11-61.
Bisecting a line segment.

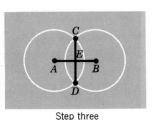

FIGURE 11-62.
Bisecting a line segment with straightedge and compass.

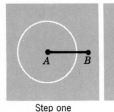

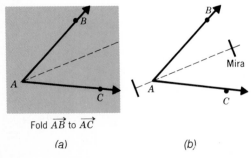

Fold $\overrightarrow{AB}$ to $\overrightarrow{AC}$

(a)   (b)

FIGURE 11-63.
Bisecting an angle.

and compass (Figure 11-62). The students could bisect $\overline{AB}$ using the following steps. (1) With point A as the center, construct a circle whose radius is more than one half the length of $\overline{AB}$. (2) With point B as the center, construct a circle with the same radius. (3) Label the points where the two circles intersect C and D. (4) Draw $\overline{CD}$. Point E, the point where $\overline{CD}$ intersects $\overline{AB}$, is the bisecting point of $\overline{AB}$. One explanation for this construction is based on the properties of a rhombus. The students should be encour-

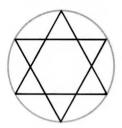  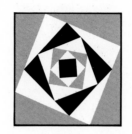

FIGURE 11-64.
Constructed designs.

aged to discover why the construction works. Figure 11-63 shows the result of using paperfolding and the mira to bisect an angle. The student can also construct the angle bisector using a straightedge and compass.

Students can use constructions to create patterns. Rulers, compasses, and protractors are used in forming various designs (Figure 11-64). Polygons and string designs can be constructed using colorful materials. As an art project, students can make such designs and decorate the classroom. (Good resource books for constructions and designs are *Fun with Lines and Curves* by Elsie Ellison, and *Line Designs* by Dale Seymour, Linda Silvey, and Joyce Snider.)

QUESTIONS AND ACTIVITIES

1. Broken lines, paths, and simple closed curves were some of the ideas discussed in this section. Consider the printed letters of the alphabet; which ones are closed paths?

2. Describe to other students a path that you made on a geoboard. By your clues they should be able to make the same path on their geoboards. Variations of this activity could include making polygons and other designs.

3. a. Draw a part of a line. Draw one point on the paper that is two centimeters from

the closest point on the line. Two more points. Five more points. Consider all points that meet this condition. What figure is being formed?

b. Repeat part (a), but consider all points in space. You may find it helpful to use a pencil to represent the line. What figure is being formed?

c. Draw a point. Draw one point on the plane that is five centimeters from the point. Two more points. Five more points. Consider all points that meet this condition. What figure is being formed?

d. Repeat part (c), but consider all points in space. Consider one point five centimeters from the point. Two more points. Five more points. Consider all points that meet this condition. What figure is being formed?

4. Figure 11-40 shows how a picture was formed by plotting coordinates. Form a design of your own and determine the appropriate coordinates. *For your resource file:* "Coordinate Geometry—Art and Mathematics" by Terc describes how one class extended this idea to paint murals for the school. "Distortions: An Activity for Practice and Exploration" by Battista introduces distortions by graphing on nonsquare graph paper.

5. With another student, play the coordinate game four-in-a-row. Is there a winning strategy?

6. Use paperfolding to determine how you could help students illustrate the following.

a. lines that would intersect in a point on the paper
b. lines that would intersect in a point off the paper
c. lines that do not intersect
d. perpendicular lines
e. the number of lines that pass through one point
f. the number of lines that pass through two points
g. whether three points are collinear (on the same line)

7. a. Using sheets of paper to represent planes and pencils to represent lines, find *all* possible relationships between planes and lines. For example, a line can be on the plane; therefore, the intersection of the line and the plane is a line.
   b. Find all possible intersections of two planes. Find all possible intersections of three planes.
   c. Find all possible intersections of two lines. (*Note:* Did you find lines that were nonparallel and nonintersecting? These are called skew lines.)

8. a. Our environment contains numerous examples of relationships between points, lines, and planes. Consider your environment and describe examples of rays, line segments, points, and planes. Discuss the functions of such designs; for example, a doorknob is a point on a plane or curtains (planes) hang from a rod (line) that is attached to a wall (plane) at a certain location (points). Consider road maps, furniture, kitchen utensils, and so on, with regard to their design and function.
   b. Most cities are designed with parallel and perpendicular streets. Consider cities that are not. What advantages or disadvantages are there in the designs? What happens if window or door frames are not parallel? When are houses not built perpendicular to the ground? Brainstorm with other students and

make a list of "what ifs" and their consequences.

9. Given two lines, their maximum number of points of intersection is one point. The maximum number of intersections for three lines is three points. What is the maximum number of intersections for four lines? Ten lines? What strategies could students use to find the solution?

10. a. Fold a paper into four parts using parallel folds; punch a hole in each of the four corners of the folded paper. Predict the design before unfolding.
    b. Fold a paper into four parts using perpendicular folds; punch a hole in each of the four corners of the folded paper. Predict the design before unfolding.
    c. Create some of your own designs by varying the number of folds, the type of folds, and the location of the cuts. More ideas are given in "Snapshots" by Ranucci.

11. Construct a convex polygon with six sides on a geoboard. What is the maximum number of sides of a convex polygon constructed on a 5-by-5-grid geoboard?

12. Angela shaded the interior of an angle as shown here. How would you help her extend her concept of angles?

13. Figure 11-55 shows parallel lines cut by a transversal. A tracing activity was described in the text with regard to corresponding angles. Students should also do this activity with nonparallel lines. What should they conclude?

14. a. How many triangles in the accompanying figure? How does perception enter into this activity?

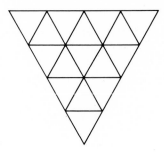

b. Did you make a simpler problem? Can you find a pattern? Can you extend it to a larger figure? How is this like the classic problem, how many squares on a checkerboard?

c. *For your resource file:* A number of activities complete with problem solving suggestions are included in "Using Tables to Solve Some Geometry Problems" by Bright.

15. Figure 11-32 illustrates how to use a mira to draw congruent figures. Use a mira to do the following constructions. Compare the final images with the original images. According to Figure 11-30, what one motion could have produced the same results? *Materials needed:* Mira. Use the mira to:

a. flip trapezoid *FRED* over line *w* and that image over line *j*.

b. flip parallelogram *TROY* over line *s* and that image over line *t*.

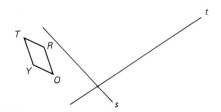

16. Figure 11-58 shows illustrations of traceable networks. Demonstrate that networks *a* to *d* are traceable. Construct some networks of your own; decide whether they are traceable or not. How does the number of even and odd vertices relate to whether or not the network is traceable?

17. Consider the map coloring shown in Figure 11-59. Draw some diagrams of your own. What is the minimum number of colors needed to cover the surface so that the same colors do not share a common border? What is the purpose of such an activity?

18. a. Make a Möbius strip as shown in Figure 11-60. Start on one side and draw a path. Did you come back to your starting point?

b. Predict your result and then cut down the center of the strip until you return to the starting point. What is the result? What would the result be with two half twists? Three half twists?

c. What would happen if you cut around the strip at a distance of one third of the distance from the edge. In each case guess and then check. Did you find a pattern?

d. What is the purpose of this activity?

19. Some geometic designs are shown in Figure 11-64. Use compass and straightedge to create two designs of your own.

20. Use paperfolding to determine how you could help students construct:

a. a perpendicular through a point on a line.

b. a perpendicular through a point not on the line.

c. bisection of a line segment.

d. bisection of an angle.

21. Redo the constructions listed in Problem 20 using a mira.

22. Construct a rhombus that measures ten centimeters on a side. Draw in the diagonals. Cut out the rhombus. How are

the opposite sides of the rhombus related? Consider the diagonals. What is their relationship to each other? Consider the lengths of the diagonals; are they equal? Consider the point of intersection of the diagonals. How does the point appear to divide each diagonal? Consider the vertex angles. How do the diagonals appear to divide them? Use paperfolding to check your conjectures.

23. Do the constructions listed in Problem 20 by using a compass and straightedge. Also construct parallel lines. Use your problem-solving skills and the properties of the rhombus that you found in Problem 22 to determine appropriate constructions.

24. a. Do the paperfolding activities described in the children's book *Exploring Triangles: Paper-Folding Geometry* by Phillips.

    b. Describe how you could use paperfolding to divide the following angle in fourths.

PLANE FIGURES (EXTENSION ACTIVITIES)

We discussed plane figures previously when we examined introductory activities for primary-grade children. This section discusses other activities that can be explored by more mathematically mature students. The extended study of shapes leads to more sophisticated methods of measurement, namely formulas. Through the analysis of various shapes, formulas for circumference

and for area formulas are developed in this section and in the question set.

One concept involving polygons is the idea of symmetry. A region is symmetric if one half of the region can be folded exactly over the other half (Figure 11-65). The fold lines are the lines of symmetry. By folding lines of symmetry, students will discover that the diagonals are lines of symmetry for the square but not for other rectangles. Some figures such as the scalene triangle have no lines of symmetry, but others such as the circle have an unlimited number of lines of symmetry.

Another concept of polygons that should be introduced is similarity. The concepts of similarity can be applied to various closed curves and polygons. Similar objects have the same shape but varying sizes. Some familiar examples of similarity are a photo and its enlargement, a slide and its image on a screen, and the state of Illinois and the state highway map. Similarity can be used to introduce ratios between the sides and the areas of two or more similar figures, which is discussed in Chapter 12.

Tangrams, which were illustrated in Figure 11-16a, can be used to explore congruence and similarity of triangles. For example, the two small triangles are congruent because they are the same size and shape. The small, medium-sized, and large triangles are all similar since they have the same angle measure and the lengths of their sides are proportional. To demonstrate this similarity, the students can simply match the angles of one triangle to the corresponding angles of another.

For triangles, matching angles is sufficient to demonstrate similarity. However, having like angles is a necessary but not a sufficient condition to show similarity for other polygons. The square and the rectan-

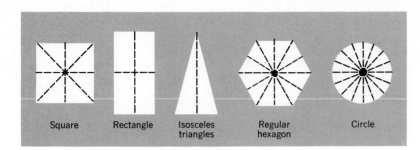

FIGURE 11-65.
Lines of symmetry.

gle shown in Figure 11-65 are not similar. Although their angles are equal, their sides are *not* proportional. The large rectangle would be similar to one of the small rectangles that is outlined by the dashed lines. Since each side of the small rectangle is one half of the corresponding side of the large rectangle and their angles are equal, the two rectangles are similar.

The student can extend this concept by studying regular and irregular polygons. A regular polygon is one whose sides are all the same length and whose angles all have the same measure. All other polygons are irregular (Figure 11-66). The students should look for a pattern to distinguish between regular and irregular polygons with regard to similarity.

Geostrips can be used to build various regular and irregular polygons. Geostrips are strips of plastic or cardboard of various lengths that can be fastened together (Fig-

ure 11-67a). In exploring various polygons with the geostrips, one student formed an equilateral triangle using three equal-length strips (Figure 11-67c). Another student found that there were certain combinations of strips that could not be used to form triangles (Figure 11-67d). After much experimentation, the students generalized, "If the combined length of two strips is shorter than the longest strip, a triangle cannot be formed."

Another student formed a four-sided regular polygon, a square. The square was then transformed into an irregular polygon, a rhombus, as the angles changed (Figure 11-67e). The students also noted that the area of the polygon changed as the shape changed even though the perimeter remained constant in all three transformations.

Just as various polygons can be constructed by using geostrips, students can also construct plane figures with a straight-

Regular polygons

FIGURE 11-66.
Regular and irregular polygons.

Irregular polygons

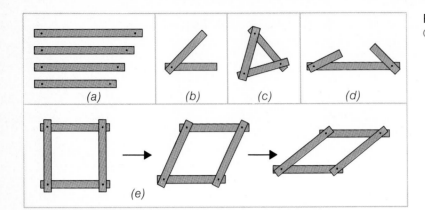

FIGURE 11-67.
Geostrips.

edge and a compass or with a mira. In any construction, the purpose of the activity is to develop a better understanding of the properties of plane figures, not merely to learn to do the construction. For example, Curt noted that, in order to decide whether two triangles were congruent, he did not need to check all three sides and all three angles. He decided to try to find the minimum amount of information needed to determine whether two triangles were congruent.

Curt drew triangle *ABC* (Figure 11-68a) and used a straightedge and a compass to construct a second triangle congruent to triangle *ABC*. After constructing $\overline{B'C'}$ congruent to $\overline{BC}$ and ∠*B'* congruent to ∠*B,* he obtained the result shown in Figure 11-68b. Next he measured $\overline{AC}$ and tried to locate *A'* by measuring that length from *C'.* He discovered that he could form two different triangles (Figure 11-68c). He constructed

$\overline{A'B'}$ congruent to $\overline{AB}$ and then erased the incorrect line segment he had drawn from *C'* (Figure 11-68d).

Curt discovered that two sides and an angle that are congruent constitute sufficient conditions to form congruent triangles provided that the two sides form the angle. This is just one set of conditions that will determine congruent triangles. Curt might have stopped here or, with some encouragement from the teacher, he might have continued exploring to find other sets of conditions that will determine triangle congruency.

The total number of degrees in a polygon determines the total number of sides. Given a specific number of sides, the polygon's shape is related to how the degrees are distributed among the angles. The number of degrees in a polygon can be determined in several ways. Measuring with a protractor is one procedure. However, due to

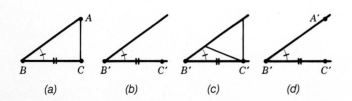

FIGURE 11-68.
Constructing a triangle.

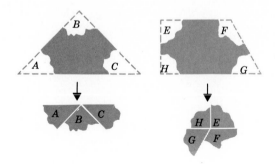

FIGURE 11-69.

Tearing corners to determine degrees in triangles and quadrilaterals.

the smallness of one degree, the inaccuracies of the measuring instrument, and the inaccuracies on the part of the person doing the measuring, an approximation of the sum of the angles rather than the exact sum will be obtained when a protractor is used.

An appropriate activity for determining the number of degrees in triangles and quadrilaterals is to tear off their corners and place them together to form a single angle (Figure 11-69). Since the three angles of a triangle form a straight angle, the students can deduce that the number of degrees in a triangle is 180. Using similar reasoning, they can conclude that a quadrilateral contains 360 degrees. If the triangles or quadrilaterals were regular polygons, the degrees would

be equally distributed among the angles; therefore, each angle in an equilateral triangle is 60 degrees, and each angle in a square is 90 degrees.

This method is not convenient for finding the total number of degrees in a polygon with more than four sides. However, students can readily discover the number of degrees in any polygon after they know that there are 180 degrees in a triangle. They simply divide the polygon into the smallest possible number of triangles (Figure 11-70). Since the students know that there are 180 degrees in one triangle, they simply multiply 180 degrees times the number of triangles that were formed. They can generalize this pattern to a formula by observing that the number of possible triangles is always two less than the number of sides (Figure 11-70).

The concepts of perimeter and area should be informally introduced as counting activities. To find the distance around a polygon (perimeter), the students simply add the measures of the various sides (Figure 11-71). In the special cases of finding perimeters of regular polygons, students may devise a shortcut by multiplying the length of any one side times the number of sides in the polygon. For example, the perimeter of the hexagon in Figure 11-71d is found by multiplying 6 × 3.

Finding area is related to covering the

5 sides
3 triangles

6 sides
4 triangles

N sides
$N-2$ triangles

Number of sides	3	4	5	6			N
Number of triangles	1	2	3	4			$N-2$
Degrees	180	360	540	720			$(N-2) \times (180°)$

FIGURE 11-70.

Degrees of polygons.

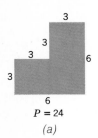 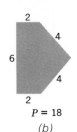 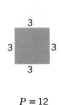 

$P = 24$
(a)

$P = 18$
(b)

$P = 12$
(c)

$P = 18$
(d)

FIGURE 11-71.
Finding perimeters of polygons.

surface of the plane. Several different polygons or combinations of polygons can be used to tile (completely cover) the plane. The polygons should be placed side by side so that they do not either overlap or leave gaps (Figure 11-72). These patterns are called tessellations.

Students can build patterns using only one shape, or they can combine two, three, or four shapes to build more sophisticated patterns. The patterns in Figure 11-72a and e could be described as having areas of "7 hexagons" and "9 squares, 4 octagons," respectively. In preliminary activities, the students place the polygons by deciding whether a shape with large or small angles is needed. Later, they can use their knowledge of the total number of degrees in a polygon to determine which polygons or

combinations of polygons will tessellate the plane. As discussed in Chapter 10, children's first activities in area should involve counting the total number of units that cover a region. In Figure 11-73c, the children count every two half-units as being one square unit. If the shape is irregular, the students will have to approximate the area (Figure 11-73d).

Geoboards, graph paper, and dotter paper can serve as square units and are useful in helping children develop the concept of area and discover formulas for finding the areas of various polygons. Since they have used rectangular arrays for solving multiplication problems, children can readily discover that the formula for the area of a rectangle is simply length times width (Figure 11-74).

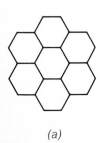   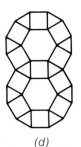 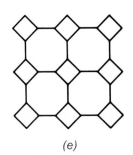

(a) (b) (c) (d) (e)

FIGURE 11-72.
Tessellation patterns.

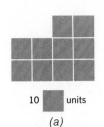 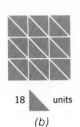 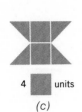 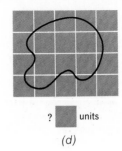

10 [] units   18 [] units   4 [] units   ? [] units

(a)   (b)   (c)   (d)

FIGURE 11-73.
Counting activities for
area.

To find the area of a triangle, students must know that the diagonal of a rectangle cuts the region into two congruent parts. In Figure 11-75a, the students simply divide the area of the rectangle (3 square units) in half to find the area of the triangle. In Figure 11-75b, they form rectangles *IJMN* and *JKLM*. They take half of each rectangle and add these parts to obtain the area of the whole triangle. To find the area of triangle *DFI* in

Figure 11-75c, the students may consider the rectangle *DEFG* and then subtract the areas of triangles *DEF* and *DGI*.

Children can discover the formula for the area of a triangle by forming a series of triangles as shown in Figure 11-76. Although the shapes of the triangles are different, the bases, heights, and areas of the triangles are the same. Consequently, the students can conclude that the area of a triangle

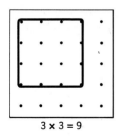 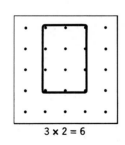 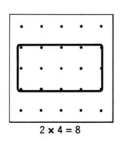

3 x 3 = 9   3 x 2 = 6   2 x 4 = 8

FIGURE 11-74.
Formula development
for area of a rectangle.

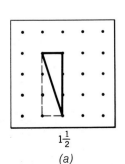 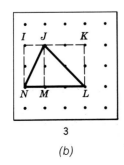 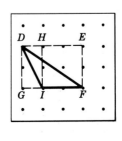

$1\frac{1}{2}$ 3

(a)   (b)   (c)

FIGURE 11-75.
Finding areas for
triangles.

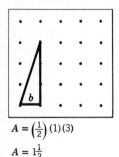

$A = \left(\frac{1}{2}\right)(1)(3)$

$A = 1\frac{1}{2}$

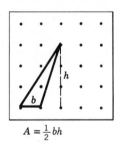

$A = \frac{1}{2}bh$

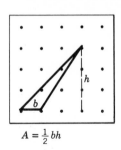

$A = \frac{1}{2}bh$

FIGURE 11-76.
Formula development for area of a triangle.

equals one half of the base times the height, $A = \frac{1}{2}bh$.

The formula for the area of a parallelogram can also be developed on the geoboard (Figure 11-77a). By using paper parallelograms, the students can cut and move triangle *ABE* to the position indicated by triangle *DCH* (Figure 11-77b). They have thus formed a rectangle so the area can be found by multiplying the base times the height. Additions or subtractions of rectangles and right triangles can also be used to find the areas of trapezoids on a geoboard as shown in Figure 11-78a.

The formula for the area of a triangle is useful for developing formulas for the areas of more complex figures. For example, the trapezoid in Figure 11-78b can be divided by line segment *WY* into two triangles. The students notice that the height *h* of both triangles is the same and that the base of triangle *WXY* is *b*, and the base of triangle *WYZ* is b_2. Since the area of trapezoid *WXYZ* is obviously the sum of the areas of triangles *WXY* and *WYZ*, the students reason that the formula for the area of a trapezoid is $A = \frac{1}{2}b_1h + \frac{1}{2}b_2h$. This can be further simplified as $A = \frac{1}{2}h(b_1 + b_2)$.

Formula development should be approached as a problem-solving activity. The most important concept for students to learn is how to divide regions into parts for which they can find the area. If students learn this concept, they have a method for finding areas of many figures. A memorized formula is a limited concept that a student can only apply to specific situations. Another ap-

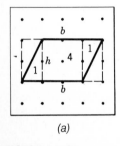

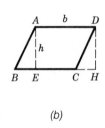

(a)   (b)

FIGURE 11-77.
Formula development for area of a parallelogram.

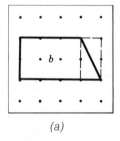

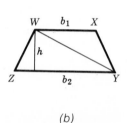

(a)   (b)

FIGURE 11-78.
Formula development for area of a trapezoid.

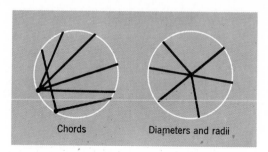

FIGURE 11-79.
Properties of a circle.

proach to formula development is through paper cutting. This approach is explored in the problem set and in *The Elementary Math Teacher's Handbook*.

Students must understand various properties of circles before developing formulas for the circumference and the area of a circle. By measuring the various line segments (chords) that have their endpoints on the circle, students will discover that the longest segment is the chord that passes through the center of the circle. By further exploration

they should observe that the distance from the center of the circle to the circle itself (the radius) is one-half of the diameter (Figure 11-79).

The formula for the distance around the circle can be developed through measurements. Students can measure the diameters, radii, and circumferences of circular objects such as food cans, bicycle tires, and wastepaper baskets. Some possible results are shown in Figure 11-80. The students will soon observe that the circumference is always a little more than three times the diameter. The ratio between the circumference and the diameter is called *pi*. Those students who measured in metric terms can use a calculator to find a better approximation of *pi*. Those students who used the customary measures will need to divide the circumference by the diameter, which will involve division of fractions in most cases. The students should then generalize that the circumference can be found by multiplying *pi* (π) times the diameter or $C = \pi d$.

To find the area of a circle, the students can subdivide and rearrange it (Figure 11-81). The rearranged circle approximates the shape of a parallelogram whose base is one-half of the circumference of the circle and whose height is the radius of the circle. By using several examples, the students can see that as the triangles into which the circle is divided become smaller, the rearranged pieces of the circle more nearly approximate a parallelogram. Since the formula for the area of a parallelogram is base times height,

Radius	Diameter	Circumference
3.1 cm	6.2 cm	19.5 cm
2¾ in	5½ in	17¼ in
13.8 cm	27.6 cm	86.7 cm
5⁹/₁₆ in	11⅛ in	35 in

FIGURE 11-80.
Relationship between circumference and diameter.

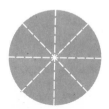 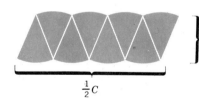

$$A = \tfrac{1}{2} C \cdot r$$
$$= \tfrac{1}{2} \pi d \cdot r$$
$$= \tfrac{1}{2} \pi 2r \cdot r$$
$$= \tfrac{1}{2} 2\pi \cdot r^2$$
$$= \pi r^2$$

FIGURE 11-81.
Formula development of area of circle.

the formula for the area of a circle is shown to be one-half of the circumference multiplied by the radius. This formula can be simplified to *pi* times radius times radius or $A = \pi r^2$ (Figure 11-81).

QUESTIONS AND ACTIVITIES

1. a. Devise an activity that will help young children differentiate between similarity and congruence of squares. Use appropriate vocabulary, such as "size and shape."

   b. Extend this lesson to rectangles or other quadrilaterals.

2. a. Stretch a rubber band parallel to a side and down the middle of a geoboard. Form a triangle on one side of the board. Form a second triangle on the other side of the geoboard so that the design is symmetrical. Repeat using a quadrilateral.

   b. Change the line of symmetry to one of the diagonals.

   c. Do one of the last two activities described in "Ideas" by Bazik and Tucker.

   d. *For your resource file:* Patterns, line symmetry, and rotational symmetry are explored in "Let's Do It: Cut and Paste for Geometric Thinking" by Van de Walle and Thompson.

3. A number of introductory and intermediate activities using geostrips are described in "Let's Do It: Strip Tease" by Lindquist and Dana. Use geostrips, straws, or strips of posterboard to construct the following polygons.

   a. A square; transform it to a rhombus.

   b. A rectangle; transform to parallelogram.

   c. A triangle; will any three strips work?

   d. A regular pentagon; transform it to an irregular pentagon.

   e. A regular pentagon; build another pentagon that is similar but not congruent to the first one.

4. a. Ms. Schoen assigned her class to draw triangle *ABC* with line segment *AB* measuring 5 centimeters, line segment *BC* measuring 8 centimeters, and angle *B* measuring 30 degrees. Will they construct congruent triangles?

   b. The class started to experiment to determine whether, if they started with any other three factors, such as all three sides or all three angles, they would have unique triangles. What are the various combinations they will need to try? Which ones will they discover will work?

5. Chuck was trying to count the diagonals in the following polygon, but he kept losing his count. He decided to look at a simpler polygon to see if he could find a pattern. He began making a chart as shown.

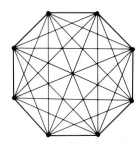

Polygon	Number of diagonals	Number of sides
Triangle	0	3
Quadrilateral	2	4
Pentagon		
Hexagon		
Heptagon		
Octagon		
Nonagon		
Decagon		

Fill in the chart and find the pattern. Write an equation expressing the relationship of the number of sides to the number of diagonals.

6. a. An experiment was described for determining the total number of degrees in triangles and quadrilaterals. Try this for a number of triangles and quadrilaterals. Does it always work? What about for nonconvex quadrilaterals? What results are obtained if this is extended to pentagons or hexagons?

b. Consult an elementary school textbook to determine how this topic is taught.

7. *For your resource file:* Programs to draw various shapes are contained in "The Turtle Deserves a Star" by Billstein and Lott and "Polygons, Stars, Circles, and Logo" by Craig.

a. Locate one of the articles and work through the Logo programs described.

b. Read the articles and add them to your resource file.

8. a. Use a template, a pattern, or a set of polygons to determine which polygons will tessellate if using the following combinations.
(1) equilateral triangles
(2) squares
(3) regular pentagons
(4) regular hexagons
(5) regular octagons
(6) any combination of two different shapes
(7) any combination of three or more different shapes

b. Consider any triangle or any quadrilateral. Will it tessellate the plane?

c. Other shapes and designs are included in "Let's Do It: Concepts, Art, and Fun from Simple Tiling Patterns" by Van de Walle and Thompson. What are the various reasons that are discussed for teaching tessellations?

9. In "Generating Patterns from Transformations" by Martin Johnson, transformations are combined with rectangular tessellations to create designs. Read this article. Design a new pattern card or one similar to those shown in Figure 9 of the article. Create three designs (one each) by reflection, reflection and rotation, and rotation.

10. a. Use graph paper to draw a rectangle with a perimeter of 14. What is the area? Is there more than one solution?

b. Consider a perimeter of 28. Which rectangle has the maximum area? Consider a perimeter of 20. Which rectangle has the maximum area? Do you see a pattern. Test your conjecture.

c. Consider rectangles with an area of 12. Are all their perimeters the same? Reconsider this question using areas of 7, 15, and 25. Which shapes have the smallest perimeters? The largest?

d. Reconsider the problems above if you were not limited to rectangles. Which shape would have the largest area given a specific distance around?

e. *For your resource file:* Activities that are similar to these and are appropriate for children in grades one through six are described by Shaw in "Let's Do It: Exploring Perimeter and Area Using Centimeter Squared Paper."

11. a. Draw the following figures: square, rectangle, parallelogram, rhombus, acute triangle, isosceles triangle, right triangle, trapezoid, and regular hexagon.

b. Determine the minimum number of measurements that would need to be taken for each polygon in order to find their perimeters. Indicate each measurement that would need to be made by labeling that part of the diagram with an X.

c. Determine the minimum number of measurements that would need to be taken for each polygon in order to find their areas. Indicate each measurement that would need to be made by labeling that part of the diagram with a Y.

12. a. Find the areas of the following polygons.

(1)

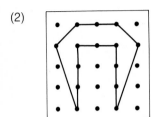

(2)

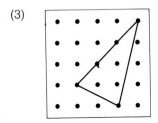

(3)

b. *For your resource file:* Numerous geometric concepts can be explored using geoboards with students from a variety of age groups. Read "Geoboard Geometry for Preschool Children" by Liedtke and Kieran or "Use of Geoboards to Teach Mathematics" by Walter. Write up those activities that you want to add to your resource file.

13. Read and summarize "Better Perception of Geometric Figures Through Folding and Cutting" by Ibe. Do activities A through D, including 7A through 7D. Indicate with dotted lines where the cut or fold lines should be marked.

14. An excellent method for developing formulas for area is through paper cutting. Work through the problems below with scissors, rectangular sheets of paper, and a ruler.

a. The area of a triangle can be developed from the area of a rectangle $A = bh$. Label (clockwise) the four corners of the paper *A*, *B*, *C*, and *D*. Pick any point along side *CD*, call it *E*. Draw triangle *ABE*. How does the area of triangle *ABE* compare to rectangle *ABCD*? Cut along *AE* and *EB*. Will the two smaller triangles cover triangle *ABE*? How does the area of the triangle compare to the rectangle? Compare the height and base of the rectangle to the height and base of the triangle. What is the formula for the area of the triangle? Note that this activity is appropriate if the altitude being considered is inside the triangle or is one of the sides.

b. The area of a parallelogram can also be developed from the area of a rectangle. Draw a parallelogram and cut it out. Label the four vertices of the parallelogram *A*, *B*, *C*, and *D*. Consider *AB* as the base and fold a line perpendicular to the base. Cut along this line. Rearrange the pieces to form a rectangle. How does the area of the parallelogram compare to the area of the rectangle? Compare the height and base of the rectangle to the height and base of the parallelogram. What is the formula for the area of the parallelogram?

c. The area of any triangle can also be developed from the area of a parallelogram. Draw any triangle (obtuse, right, or acute), and cut out this triangle and a copy of it. Rearrange the pieces to form a parallelogram. How does the area of the triangle compare to the area of the parallelogram? Compare the height and base of the triangle to the height and base of the parallelogram. What is the formula for the area of the triangle?

d. Draw a trapezoid. Label the trapezoid's bases and the altitude. How can the formula for the area of triangles be used to develop the formula for the area of a trapezoid?

15. *For your resource file:* Read "Geometry in the Middle School: Problem Solving with Trapezoids" by Thomas. Evaluate the six different methods that students devised for finding the area of a trapezoid.

16. a. *For your resource file:* Read "The Shear Joy of Area" by Spitler.

b. Use a geoboard to explore these procedures and those shown in Figures 11-74 through 11-78. Analyze the areas of triangles and parallelograms as the bases and the heights are held constant but the polygons are sheared.

17. Consult an elementary school textbook to determine how area formulas are developed.

18. a. To develop the relationship between the diameter and the circumference of circles, students need to measure several circular objects. Describe how you would help students discover this relationship. Then measure various circular objects to determine how close their results could be.

b. *For your resource file:* Ott, Sommers, and Creamer describe a problem-solving lesson involving ratios in "But Why Does $C = \pi d$?"

19. How would you develop the area of a circle through paper cutting? Work through this activity with another student, explaining how you would derive the formula from your results.

20. Pick's theorem deals with polygons on a geoboard and states a relationship between the number of boundary points (pegs touched by the rubber band forming the polygon), the number of interior points

(pegs inside the rubber band but not touched by it), and the area of the polygon. Use problem solving to discover this relationship. Two examples of polygons are shown below.

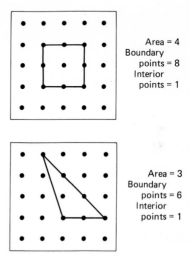

Area = 4
Boundary points = 8
Interior points = 1

Area = 3
Boundary points = 6
Interior points = 1

SPACE FIGURES (EXTENSION ACTIVITIES)

Various properties of space figures were discussed in the introductory activities for primary-grade children. By classifying solids into such sets as pyramids, prisms, cylinders, cones, and spheres, students are analyzing the various properties of space figures. As in the previous section, "Plane Figures (Extension Activities)," the further study of three-dimensional shapes leads to a more sophisticated method of measurement. Through the analysis of three-dimensional shapes, surface area and volume formulas are developed in this section and in the question set. In studying three-dimensional objects, students can gradually proceed to two-dimensional drawings of the objects. Many students have difficulties in correctly interpreting the drawings because they have had inadequate experience with the actual solids. A set of solids should always be available for student use as well as for class demonstrations and discussions.

Part of students' experiences with three-dimensional shapes can include learning to draw these shapes. For example, prisms and cylinders have parallel congruent bases which are the foundation for drawing these shapes (Figure 11-82a and b). In drawing bases, students should be aware of perception. The rectangular base in Figure 11-82a is drawn as a parallelogram. In the second step of each of these drawings, students should observe that the edges of the bases are parallel. In the third step the vertices are connected; it should be observed that these

edges are parallel to each other. Pyramids and cones are easier to draw, as they have only one base with one opposite vertex or apex (Figure 11-82c). As students gain expertise they can use dotted lines to indicate the hidden edges.

A relationship among the faces, vertices, and edges of polyhedrons was discovered by Euler, a Swiss mathematician in the eighteenth century. Students can find this relationship for themselves. They should choose a variety of polyhedrons to analyze and then record the numbers of faces, vertices, and edges for each polyhedron (Figure 11-83). Students should analyze several polyhedrons in order to collect enough examples to develop a pattern that can be expressed as a formula, Euler's formula.

The cutting apart of space figures was

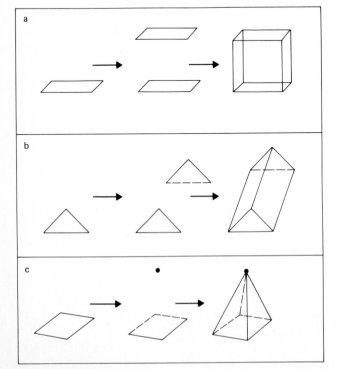

FIGURE 11-82.
Drawing three-dimensional shapes.

Polyhedron	Faces	Vertices	Edges
Triangular pyramid	4	4	6
Square pyramid	5	5	8
Cube	6	8	12
Pentagonal prism	7	10	15

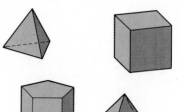

FIGURE 11-83.
Discovering Euler's formula.

discussed previously as one way of exploring their properties. After students have taken apart various solids, they can begin to construct solids. After constructing the cube and other rectangular prisms, they can construct more complex figures.

One special set of solids is called the platonic solids. A platonic solid must have faces that are all formed by one of the regular polygons, and it must have the same number of edges meeting at each vertex (Figure 11-84). By making various models, the students are not only exploring space but are also using measurement skills and developing problem-solving skills. (A good resource book on the construction of a variety of solids is *Polyhedron Models* by Magnus Wenninger.)

Finding the surface area of solids depends on the polygons and other closed curves that form the faces and curved surfaces of the solids. Students can find the surface area of a solid by adding the areas of the individual parts. Again, the students

should have the solid to observe or preferably to cut apart. In Figure 11-85a to find the surface area of a cylinder, the students observe that they need to find the area of two circles that are the same size and a rectangle. The rectangle has as its dimensions the height of the cylinder and the circumference of the circle. Thus students have several measurements to consider before starting computations. In Figure 11-85b they need to find the areas of three different pairs of rectangles. In Figure 11-85c they need to find the area of five faces, but four of them have the same area. In Figure 11-85d they are also finding the surface area of a pyramid, but they have four different areas to find. The cone in Figure 11-85e can be cut apart to show that it is composed of a circle and a fractional part of a circle. To find the area of the fractional part of the circle the student needs to measure the radius of the circle (the slant height of the cone) and the angle formed by the two radii. If the measure of the angle is 120 degrees, then the student has

FIGURE 11-84.
Platonic solids.

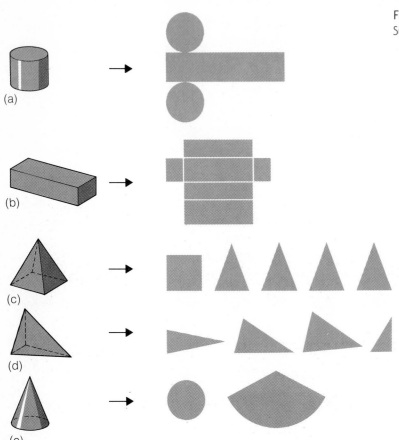

FIGURE 11-85.
Surface area of solids.

$\frac{120}{360}$ or $\frac{1}{3}$ of a circle. Students should develop their own procedures for solving these problems rather than being told by the teacher what specific steps to follow. By cutting the solids apart, they can find their own solutions based on information they have already learned in the study of plane figures.

Introductory activities in volume involve counting the number of cubes that form a solid (Figure 11-86). Building blocks or interlocking cubes can be used to build solids and to develop the idea of a basic cubic unit. These activities were described in Chapter 10. After various counting activities to find the volume of solids, the children can be guided to develop the formulas for the volume of cubes and rectangular prisms. In Figure 11-86b, the solid contains one layer of 20 cubes. The solid in Figure 11-86c is simply six layers of 20 cubes or 120 cubes. Since the students already know that the area of a rectangle can be found by multiplying the length times the width ($A = lw$), they can now conclude that the volume of a rectangular prism is found by multiplying the length times width of the base by the height of the prism; that is, $V = lwh$.

A more general volume formula can be

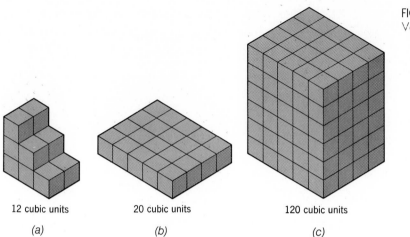

FIGURE 11-86.
Volume of solids.

12 cubic units   20 cubic units   120 cubic units

(a)   (b)   (c)

developed through the idea of a solid generated by moving a plane figure through space. Thus a rectangular prism is formed by moving a rectangle through space (Figure 11-87a). The volume generated is equal to the area of the rectangle times the perpendicular distance it moves through space.

Similarly, the cylinders in Figure 11-87b and c can be generated by moving a circle through space. In each case the volume of the cylinder can be found by multiplying the area of the circle by the perpendicular dis-

tance it moves through space. In all three cases, the volume of the solid generated can be found by multiplying the area of the base (B) by the height (h) or $V = Bh$. This idea is useful for finding the volumes of all types of prisms and cylinders.

Another method of finding the volume of solids is water displacement. From previous experience students know that when a rock is dropped into a container of water, the water level rises. By measuring the change in water level, they can find the volume of

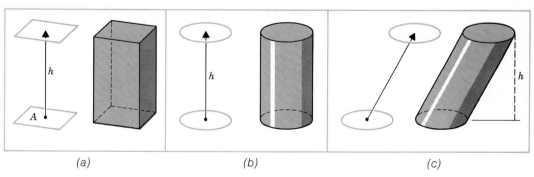

(a)   (b)   (c)

FIGURE 11-87.
Generating solids.

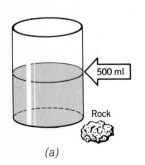

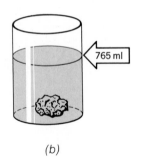

$$
\begin{array}{r}
765 \text{ ml} \\
-500 \text{ ml} \\
\hline
265 \text{ ml}
\end{array}
$$

FIGURE 11-88.
Finding volume by water displacement.

(a)   (b)

the rock (Figure 11-88). Since the water rose from 500 milliliters to 765 milliliters, the rock has displaced a volume of water equivalent to 265 milliliters. Since 1 milliliter is the equivalent of 1 cubic centimeter, the rock has a volume of 265 cubic centimeters. If the units used to measure the rectangular prism in Figure 11-86c were cubic centimeters, the prism would displace 120 milliliters or 120 cubic centimeters of water.

The volume of a pyramid can be found in the same way. To discover how the volume of a pyramid is related to the volume of a rectangular prism, students should select a pyramid and a prism that have the same base area (B) and height (h) (Figure 11-89). They will find that a rectangular pyramid with a base (B) of 5 centimeters by 4 centimeters or 20 square centimeters and a height (h) of 6 centimeters will displace 40 milliliters or 40

cubic centimeters of water. Using the formula already developed, the students find the volume of the prism to be 120 cubic centimeters. Therefore, the volume of the pyramid is one-third the volume of the prism that has the same dimensions or for the pyramid $V = \frac{1}{3}Bh$. Through further experiments, they will discover that this relationship is always true. They will also find that the volume of a cone is one-third of the volume of a cylinder with corresponding dimensions.

Volume formulas can be developed similarly using commercially available materials, a Sage kit. The kit includes plastic containers similar to the models shown in Figure 11-89. By filling one container with water and pouring the water into the related container, the students can find the relationship of the two volumes.

For example, the base of the square

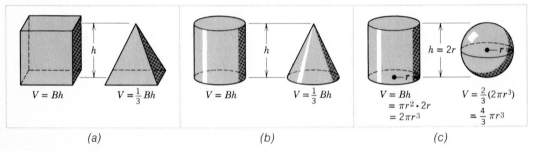

$V = Bh$ $V = \frac{1}{3}Bh$ $V = Bh$ $V = \frac{1}{3}Bh$ $V = Bh$ $V = \frac{2}{3}(2\pi r^3)$
                                                                                    $= \pi r^2 \cdot 2r$ $= \frac{4}{3}\pi r^3$
                                                                                    $= 2\pi r^3$

(a)   (b)   (c)

FIGURE 11-89.
Relationships between various solids.

pyramid is the same as one of the faces of the cube; the height of the pyramid is the same as the height of the cube (Figure 11-89a). The pyramid can be filled with water and its contents poured into the cube. Since it takes three pyramids to fill the cube, the volume of the pyramid is one third of the volume of the cube. Similarly the cone will need to be filled three times to fill the related cylinder (Figure 11-89b).

To find the relationship between the volumes of cylinders and spheres, the students must obtain a sphere that fits exactly inside a cylinder; that is, the radius of the cylinder must equal the radius of the sphere and the height of the cylinder must equal the diameter (twice the radius) of the sphere (Figure 11-89c). When the students measure the water displacement of the sphere, they find that it is two-thirds of the water displacement of the corresponding cylinder. The formula for the volume of a cylinder is the area of the base (πr^2) times the height (d or $2r$). By rearranging, $V = (\pi r^2)(2r)$ to $V = 2\pi r^3$, the students have the formula for the volume of this cylinder. The volume of the sphere is simply $\frac{2}{3}$ of that ($\frac{2}{3}$ of $2\pi r^3$) or $V = \frac{4}{3}\pi r^3$.

With the Sage kit the students will also use a cylinder and its related hemisphere. It takes three hemispheres to fill the cylinder. Since one hemisphere fills one third of the cylinder, one sphere would fill 2 thirds of the cylinder. So the reasoning shown above and in Figure 11-89 is thus demonstrated to be true.

Another approach to developing volume formulas is through the dissection of solids. To develop the formula for the volume of a pyramid from the formula for the volume of a cube, the students must envision how many congruent square pyramids can be formed from one cube. Since there are six faces to a cube, six pyramids can be formed. Each face of the cube becomes the

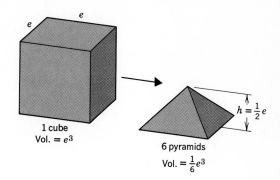

FIGURE 11-90.
Volume of a pyramid.

base of one pyramid (Figure 11-90). The volume of one of the pyramids is, therefore, one-sixth the volume of the cube. Examining the formula $V = \frac{1}{6}e^3$, the student sees that e^2 is the area of the base of the pyramid (B). The third edge (e) of the cube is twice the height ($2h$) of the pyramid. Thus $V = \frac{1}{6}e^3$ becomes $V = \frac{1}{3}Bh$, the traditional formula for the volume of a pyramid.

The formula for the volume of a cone can be developed formally from the formula for the volume of a pyramid. The formula for the area of a circle was developed by partitioning the circle into triangles. Similarly, the sphere can be partitioned into pyramids in a manner similar to the partitioning of the cube. From these pyramids the formula for the volume of the sphere can be developed mathematically.

SUMMARY

The topics that have been included in this chapter and throughout the text should be presented to students in a manner that has students involved in discussions and problem solving. In order to maximize student thinking and involvement, teachers need to learn to ask good questions and to plan for student participation. As we can see from this chapter, geometric activities are available in widely varying levels of difficulty. Some activities are appropriate for very young children; others are designed for more mathematically mature students. Geometry should be included throughout the elementary mathematics curriculum because it contains many excellent problem-solving situations that students will enjoy. Also, many of the geometric concepts discussed in this chapter are essential in developing measurement skills. As children explore various geometric concepts, they become more aware of and learn to better appreciate the geometric beauty of their environment.

QUESTIONS AND ACTIVITIES

1. a. Consider a cube made of 27 smaller unit cubes. Paint the surface. How many of the smaller cubes have six faces painted? Five faces? Four faces? Three faces? . . . Zero faces? Solve the problem and then reflect on your plan. Did you use a model? Draw a picture?
   b. Consider some extensions. How do the problem and the students' perceptions change if the number of cubes is 64? If all six corner cubes are removed before painting the surface? If only one pair of opposite sides are painted? If all sides except the bottom are painted?

2. a. Take a set of 16 cubes and arrange them to find all possible rectangular prisms. Which has the smallest surface area? The largest surface area?
   b. What shape would you predict would have the greatest surface area for 25 cubes? The smallest surface area?

3. a. Use a set of cubes to build cubes starting with a cube 1 by 1 by 1. What is the next largest cube? The next one? How many cubes are needed to build each one? What number pattern is being formed?
   b. Consider the surface area of the cubes. Can you find a pattern?

4. a. Find some models for cylinders and rectangular prisms such as oatmeal boxes, canisters, margarine boxes, or shoe boxes. What measurements would students need to take to find the volume of these objects? The surface area? Have the students take only the smallest possible number of measures. Is there more than one set of measures that could be taken?
   b. Consider truncated cones such as glasses and yogurt containers. How could students develop a volume formula for these shapes? What measures would they need to take?

5. a. Consider the pentominoes that you made in the preceding section. Which of these can be folded to form a cube with one missing face?
   b. Consider the following patterns. Predict how you could cut a cube to obtain these results? Check your guesses.

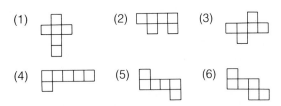

6. Problem solving as well as a number of other skills are involved in forming three-dimensional shapes.
   a. Construct patterns for each of the Platonic solids and then cut and fold them to form the model. Patterns for the solids and a lesson are described in the article "Build a City" by Reynolds.

b. Alternatively, choose and construct two of the patterns discussed in "Cardboard, Rubber Bands, and Polyhedron Models" by Campbell.

7. Tim and Sara were predicting what a cone would look like when it was cut apart. Their results are shown below. What are their errors? How would you help them with their perceptions?

8. Construct and cut out two congruent circles with a radius of four centimeters. Cut so that you have $\frac{1}{4}$, $\frac{1}{2}$, and $\frac{3}{4}$ of the circles remaining. If these sectors (parts of a circle) were each taped to form a cone, what would they look like? Predict the differences and then check your guesses.

9. Ms. Hansen assigned her class to make the shapes described below. What prerequisites are needed to complete these problems? How could you help students devise a plan for each situation?
a. a cylinder that had a volume of 63 π cubic centimeters
b. a cone that had a height of 8 centimeters and radius of 6 centimeters
c. a square pyramid that had a surface area of 96 square centimeters

10. What relationship exists among the faces, edges, and vertices of polyhedrons? Collect information and write the relationship as an equation.

11. a. How would you develop the volume formula for a rectangular prism? How would you extend this to prisms with other bases? How would you extend this to cylinders? How are the volumes of cylinders and prisms related?
b. Use the materials from a Sage kit or other related three-dimensional figures. Determine and explain how to develop the volume of a pyramid, a cone, and a

sphere. How are the volumes of cones and pyramids related?

12. In "Geometric Activities for Later Childhood Education," Henderson and Collier outline five types of problem-solving situations. For each type they describe representative activities. Read the directions for the student; select and solve one of these activities for each type of problem-solving situation. Do not read "information for the teacher" unless you need help in solving the problems.

13. *For your resource file:* One problem-solving strategy is to use tables for organizing information. Read "Using Tables to Solve Some Geometry Problems" by Bright. Work through at least two problems. Since the solutions are given in the article, cover them up while you read the original statement of the problem. If you need hints or want to check your solutions, uncover the appropriate sections. Add these ideas to your resource file.

14. How to draw some three-dimensional shapes was illustrated in Figure 11-82. Use a similar procedure to draw the following shapes.
a. a cube
b. a triangular prism sitting on one of its bases
c. a pentagonal prism sitting on one of its lateral faces
d. a cylinder sitting on one of its bases
e. a cylinder lying on its side
f. a triangular pyramid sitting on its base
g. a hexagonal pyramid sitting on one of its lateral faces

15. a. Solve the problem on perimeters posed by Maier and Nelson in "Problem Solving: Tips for Teachers." Read through the examples of student thinking reflecting on how you solved the problem compared to how others solved it.
b. Other problems in the same article involve visual perception. Solve one of the problems listed under "Try This."

16. Locate "Activities: Spatial Visualization" by Lappan, Phillips, and Winter. Select and solve any three problems from each sheet in this article on three-dimensional shapes.

17. In "Geometry Is More Than Proof," Hoffer describes the van Hiele levels of mental development in geometry. The five levels are recognition, analysis, ordering, deduction, and rigor. Activities relating to the lower levels need to be included in the elementary school curriculum.
    a. Read the article. Define each of the levels.
    b. Study the descriptions given in Table 1 for the first three levels and the sample activities described in Table 2.

TEACHER RESOURCES

Battista, Michael T. "Distortions: An Activity for Practice and Exploration." *Arithmetic Teacher* 29 (January 1982): 34–36.

Bazik, Edna F., and Benny F. Tucker. "Ideas." *Arithmetic Teacher* 30 (January 1983): 27–32.

Billstein, Rick, and Johnny W. Lott. "The Turtle Deserves a Star." *Arithmetic Teacher* 33 (March 1986): 14–16.

Bright, George W. "Using Tables to Solve Some Geometry Problems." *Arithmetic Teacher* 25 (May 1978): 39–43.

Bruni, James. *Experiencing Geometry*. Belmont, CA: Wadsworth, 1977.

Brydegaard, Marguerite, and James E. Inskeep (Eds.). *Readings in Geometry from the Arithmetic Teacher*. Reston, VA: National Council of Teachers of Mathematics, 1972.

Burger, William F. "Geometry." *Arithmetic Teacher* 32 (February 1985): 52–56.

Campbell, Patricia F. "Cardboard, Rubber Bands, and Polyhedron Models." *Arithmetic Teacher* 31 (October 1983): 48–52.

Cangelosi, James S. "A 'Fair' Way to Discover Circles." *Arithmetic Teacher* 33 (November 1985): 11–13.

Carter, Beth W. "Move Over, Frank Lloyd Wright." *Arithmetic Teacher* 33 (September 1985): 8–11.

Charles, Randall I. "Some Guidelines for Teaching Geometry Concepts." *Arithmetic Teacher* 27 (April 1980): 18–20.

Clements, Douglas C., and Michael Battista. "Geometry and Geometric Measurement." *Arithmetic Teacher* 33 (February 1986): 29–32.

Cowan, Richard A. "Pentominoes for Fun and Learning." *Arithmetic Teacher* 24 (March 1977): 188–190.

Craig, Bill. "Polygons, Stars, Circles, and Logo." *Arithmetic Teacher* 33 (May 1986): 6–11.

Dana, Marcia E., and Mary Montgomery Lindquist. "Let's Do It: The Surprising Circle." *Arithmetic Teacher* 25 (January 1978): 4–10.

Gibb, E. Glenadine, and Alberta M. Castaneda. "Experiences for Young Children." In *Mathematics Learning in Early Childhood,* Thirty-seventh Yearbook of the National Council of Teachers of Mathematics, pp. 95–124. Reston, VA: The Council, 1975.

Henderson, George L., and C. Patrick Collier. "Geometric Activities for Later Childhood Education." *Arithmetic Teacher* 20 (October 1973): 444–453.

Hoffer, Alan. "Geometry Is More Than Proof." *Mathematics Teacher* 74 (January 1981): 11–18.

Ibe, Milagros D. "Better Perception of Geometric Figures Through Folding and Cutting." *Arithmetic Teacher* 17 (November 1970): 583–586.

Immerzeel, George. "Geometric Activities for Early Childhood Education." *Arithmetic Teacher* 20 (October 1973): 438–443.

Johnson, Donovan A. *Paper Folding for the Mathematics Class*. Reston, VA: National Council of Teachers of Mathematics, 1957.

Johnson, Martin L. "Generating Patterns from Transformations." *Arithmetic Teacher* 24 (March 1977): 191–195.

Lappan, Glenda, Elizabeth A. Phillips, and Mary Jean Winter. "Activities: Spatial Visualization." *Mathematics Teacher 77* (November 1984): 34–36.

Liedtke, W., and T. E. Kieran. "Geoboard Geometry for Preschool Children." *Arithmetic Teacher 17* (February 1970): 123–126.

Lindquist, Mary Montgomery, and Marcia E. Dana. "Let's Do It: Strip Tease." *Arithmetic Teacher 25* (March 1978): 4–8.

Maier, Gene, and Ted Nelson. "Problem Solving: Tips for Teachers." *Arithmetic Teacher 34* (October 1986): 34–36.

Mansfield, Helen. "Projective Geometry in the Elementary School." *Arithmetic Teacher 32* (March 1985): 15–19.

Mira Math for Elementary School. Canada: Mira Math Co., 1973. Distributed by Creative Publications, Palo Alto, CA.

National Council of Teachers of Mathematics. *Experiences in Mathematical Discovery: Geometry.* Reston, VA: The Council, 1966.

Nelson, Glenn, and Larry P. Leutzinger. "Let's Do It: Let's Take a Geometry Walk." *Arithmetic Teacher 27* (November 1979): 2–4.

Nuffield Mathematics Project. *Shape and Size (3).* New York: Wiley, 1971.

Ott, Jack M., Dean D. Sommers, and Kay Creamer. "But Why Does $C = \pi d$?" *Arithmetic Teacher 31* (November 1983): 38–40.

Ranucci, Ernest R. "Snapshots." *Arithmetic Teacher 25* (February 1978): 40–41.

Read, Robert C. *Tangrams.* New York: Dover Publications, 1965.

Reynolds, Jean A. "Build a City." *Arithmetic Teacher 33* (September 1985): 12–15.

Roper, Susan. *Paper and Pencil Geometry.* Chicago: Franklin Publications, 1970.

Russell, Dorothy S., and Elaine M. Bologna. "Teaching Geometry with Tangrams." *Arithmetic Teacher 30* (October 1982): 34–38.

Sanok, Gloria. "Living in a World of Transformations." *Arithmetic Teacher 25* (April 1978): 36–40.

Shaw, Jean M. "Let's Do It: Exploring Perimeter and Area Using Centimeter Squared Paper." *Arithmetic Teacher 31* (December 1983): 4–11.

Spitler, Gail. "The Shear Joy of Area." *Arithmetic Teacher 29* (April 1982): 36–38.

Suydam, Marilyn N. "Forming Geometric Concepts." *Arithmetic Teacher 33* (October 1985): 26.

Terc, Michael. "Coordinate Geometry—Art and Mathematics." *Arithmetic Teacher 33* (October 1985): 22–24.

Thomas, Diane. "Geometry in the Middle School: Problem Solving with Trapezoids." *Arithmetic Teacher 26* (February 1979): 20–21.

Tinsley, Tuck, IV. "The Use of Origami in the Mathematics Education of Visually Impaired Students." *Education of the Visually Handicapped 4* (March 1972): 8–11.

Trafton, Paul R., and John F. LeBlanc. "Informal Geometry in Grades K-6." In *Geometry in the Mathematics Classroom,* Thirty-sixth Yearbook of the National Council of Teachers of Mathematics, pp. 11–15. Reston, VA: The Council, 1973.

Troutman, Andria Price. "Strategies for Teaching Elementary School Mathematics." *Arithmetic Teacher 20* (October 1973): 425–436.

Van de Walle, John, and Charles S. Thompson. "Let's Do It: A Triangle Treasury." *Arithmetic Teacher 28* (February 1981): 6–11.

———. "Let's Do It: Concepts, Art, and Fun from Simple Tiling Patterns." *Arithmetic Teacher 28* (November 1980): 4–8.

———. "Let's Do It: Cut and Paste for Geometric Thinking." *Arithmetic Teacher 32* (September 1984): 8–13.

———. "Let's Do It: Promoting Mathematical Thinking." *Arithmetic Teacher 32* (February 1985): 7–13.

Walter, Marion. "An Example of Informal Geometry: Mirror Cards." *Arithmetic Teacher* 13 (October 1966): 448–452.

———. "Frame Geometry: An Example in Posing and Solving Problems." *Arithmetic Teacher* 28 (October 1980): 16–18.

———. "Use of Geoboards to Teach Mathematics." *Education of the Visually Handicapped* 6 (May 1974): 59–62.

Wilmot, Barbara. "Creative Problem Solving and Red Yarn." *Arithmetic Teacher* 33 (December 1985): 3–5.

Young, Jerry L. "Improving Spatial Abilities with Geometric Abilities." *Arithmetic Teacher* 30 (September 1982): 38–43.

CHILDREN'S LITERATURE

Abbott, Edwin A. *Flatland*. New York: Dover, 1953.

Adler, David A. *3D, 2D, 1D*. Illustrated by Harvey Weiss. New York: Crowell, 1975.

Brown, Marcia. *Listen to a Shape*. New York: Franklin Watts, 1979.

Burns, Marilyn. *Math for Smarty Pants*. Illustrated by Martha Weston. Boston: Little, Brown, 1982.

Carle, Eric. *My Very First Book of Shapes*. Illustrated by the author. New York: Crowell, 1974.

Charosh, Mannis. *The Ellipse*. Illustrated by Leonard Kessler. New York: Crowell, 1971.

———. *Straight Lines, Parallel Lines, Perpendicular Lines*. Illustrated by Enrico Arno. New York: Crowell, 1970.

Children's Television Workshop. *The Sesame Street Book of Shapes*. New York: Signet Book, 1971.

Ellison, Elsie C. *Fun with Lines and Curves*. Illustrations adapted by Susan Stan. New York: Lothrop, 1972.

Emberley, Edward. *Ed Emberley's Big Green Drawing Book*. Illustrated by the author. Boston: Little, Brown, 1979.

———. *Ed Emberley's Big Orange Drawing Book*. Boston: Little, Brown, 1980.

Froman, Robert. *Rubber Bands, Baseballs and Doughnuts: A Book About Topology*. Illustrated by Harvey Weiss. New York: Crowell, 1972.

Grender, Iris. *Playing with Shapes and Sizes*. Designed by Geoffrey Butcher. Illustrated by Judy Jennings. New York: Knopf/Pantheon, 1975.

Hoban, Tana. *Circles, Triangles and Squares*. Illustrated by the author. New York: Macmillan, 1974.

———. *Round & Round & Round*. New York: Greenwillow Books, 1983.

———. *Shapes, Shapes, Shapes*. New York: Greenwillow Books, 1986.

Holt, Michael. *Maps, Tracks, and the Bridges of Königsberg: A Book About Networks*. Illustrated by Wendy Watson. New York: Crowell, 1975.

Juster, Norman. *The Dot and the Line*. New York: Random House, 1963.

Kessler, Ethel. *Are You Square?* Illustrated by Leonard Kessler. Garden City, NY: Doubleday, 1974.

Klugman, Hertha. *Can You Swallow a Squiggle?* Illustrated by Ann Wolf. New York: Wonder Books, 1971.

Lexau, Joan M. *Archimedes Takes a Bath*. Illustrated by Salvatore Murdocca. New York: Crowell, 1969.

MacAgy, Douglas, and Elizabeth MacAgy. *Going for a Walk with a Line: A Step into the World of Modern Art*. Garden City, NY: Doubleday, 1959.

Phillips, Jo. *Exploring Triangles: Paper-Folding Geometry*. Illustrated by James Rolling. New York: Crowell, 1975.

———. *Right Angles: Paper Folding Geometry*. Illustrated by Giulio Maestro. New York: Crowell, 1972.

Reit, Seymour. *Round Things Everywhere.* Illustrated by Carol Basen. New York: McGraw.

Seuss, Dr. *The Shape of Me and Other Stuff.* Illustrated by the author. New York: Random, 1973.

Seymour, Dale, Linda Silvey,and Joyce Snider. *Line Designs.* Palo Alto, CA: Creative Publications, 1974.

Sitomer, Mindel, and Harry Sitomer. *Circles.* Illustrated by George Giusti. New York: Crowell, 1971.

———. *Lines, Segments, Polygons.* Illustrated by Robert Quackenbush. New York: Crowell, 1972.

———. *Spirals.* Illustrated by Pam Makie. New York: Crowell, 1974.

———. *What Is Symmetry?* Illustrated by Ed Emberley. New York: Crowell, 1970.

Struble, Mitch. *Stretching a Point.* Philadelphia: Westminster Press, 1971.

Trivett, Daphne H. *Shadow Geometry.* Illustrated by Henry Roth. New York: Crowell, 1974.

Walter, Marion. *Look at Annette.* Illustrated by Navah Haber-Schaim. New York: Evans, 1972.

———. *Make a Bigger Puddle, Make a Smaller Worm.* Illustrated by the author. New York: Evans, 1972.

Wenninger, Magnus J. *Polyhedron Models.* London: Cambridge University Press, 1970.

Youldon, Gillian. *Shapes.* New York: Watts, 1979.

12

TEACHING RATES, RATIOS, PROPORTIONS, AND PERCENTS

"Let's leave a tip of 15%."
"There were three of us . . .
The bill is $14.63." "Your pizza
was $7.35, the sandwich was
$3.65 . . ." "Do we have
enough to cover the bill?"
"Okay the tip . . . let's see 15%
. . ." "Never mind, let's each
throw in a dollar."

$\frac{1}{2}$% of 60 is 30. Right?

Rates, ratios, proportions, and percents are special forms of comparisons used by people in everyday life. For the most part they differ only in that special names are given to them. A rate is the comparison of one measure to another, such as 80 kilometers per hour or 2 kilograms of peaches for one dollar. A ratio can also be considered as the comparison of one measure to another; if three out of five people have black hair, this can be expressed as the ratio 3 to 5, or the ratio between the values of a quarter and a dollar is 1 to 4. The ratios 3 to 5 and 1 to 4 can also be expressed respectively in the form $\frac{3}{5}$ and $\frac{1}{4}$. A proportion simply involves two equivalent ratios. It is a mathematical sentence that sets one ratio equal to another. For example, $\frac{1}{4} = \frac{25}{100}$ expresses equivalent ratios when comparing the values of quarters and dollars. Or 1:2 to 3:6 can represent the cost of three pencils if one pencil sells for two cents. Percent is regarded as the comparison of a part to the whole when the whole is one hundred. For example, four percent, 4%, could represent the amount of sales tax, 4 cents, that an individual pays for each dollar's worth of purchases.

It should be noted that in each case above, a comparison is being made. Only the form in which the comparison is being named differs. Throughout this chapter various situations will be used to explore different aspects of these topics. These applications and similar ones should be used to motivate and to introduce these concepts to your students.

RATIOS AND EQUIVALENT RATIOS

Some of a child's earliest experiences with comparisons involve rates and ratios. For example, if a child pays five cents for two pen-

FIGURE 12-1.
Comparisons of pencils and pennies.

cils, the rate is two pencils for five cents or the ratio of pencils to pennies is 2 to 5 as shown in Figure 12-1. The child could also compare the pennies to the pencils to obtain a ratio of 5 to 2. Another comparison can be made with regard to some of the students in the classroom. One group of students that often works together is made up of four boys and three girls as shown in Figure 12-2. The number of girls is $\frac{3}{4}$ the number of boys or the ratio of girls to boys is 3 to 4 or 3:4. By comparing the number of boys to the number of girls, students should find that the ratio is 4 to 3 or 4:3. These comparisons are between one *part* of a set and another *part*.

Comparisons can also be made between a *part* of something and the *whole* thing. Thus we can compare the girls (part) and the entire group of children (whole). In this case the students must compare the number of girls (3) to the number of boys and girls (7). Therefore, the ratio is 3 to 7 or 3:7. This last situation is similar to the concept of a fraction since a part of the set is being compared to the whole set.

Just as with number concepts, activities involving models, oral names, and number names are essential in introductory work (Figure 12-3). Students should be involved

FIGURE 12-2.
Ratios comparing girls and boys.

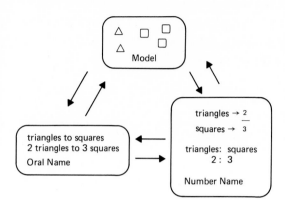

FIGURE 12-3.
Model—oral name—number name.

in experiences with models and oral language before these are linked to the written language. When results are recorded, it is important that the numbers being compared are labeled to indicate which comparisons are being made. The recording should be an extension of the oral language that the students are using to describe the situation.

To interpret ratios correctly, students must ask themselves what two quantities are being compared and what is the order of the comparison. Students—and adults—often make incorrect comparisons, as they are not interpreting the information correctly. For example, "In unpacking a carton of peaches Naomi observed that she unpacked one bruised peach for every three good peaches. If Naomi unpacked twelve peaches, how many were bruised?" An incorrect answer of 4 peaches is often made as an individual incorrectly interprets the ratio 1:3 as a comparison between bruised peaches and all of the peaches. The correct reasoning and solution is shown in Figure 12-4. The ratio 1:3 is correctly interpreted as a comparison between bruised peaches and good peaches. When a picture of the ratio of one bruised peach to three good peaches

is drawn, the students will observe that they are considering a set of four peaches. By drawing three such sets, 12 peaches, they observe that there would be 3 bruised peaches out of a total of 12 peaches.

Another common misinterpretation of ratios occurs when two ratios are combined to form a third ratio. Since ratios are often written in fraction form, students may try to add them in the same way they previously added fractions. However, since a ratio is not a number but a comparison it cannot be treated as a fraction. For example, "John won three out of five games on Tuesday and four out of seven games on Thursday. What is his record of wins?" Two completely different ratios were combined to form a new third ratio as shown in Figure 12-5. As was discussed earlier, students must decide what is being compared before setting up a ratio. In this case the total number of wins, 7, was being compared to the total number of games, 12.

Care must be taken that students do not confuse ratios with fractions in spite of some similarities between the two concepts. As discussed previously, a ratio can be expressed in fraction form. Thus, in Figure 12-

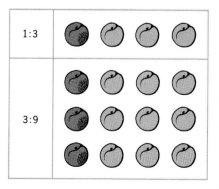

FIGURE 12-4.
Interpreting ratios.

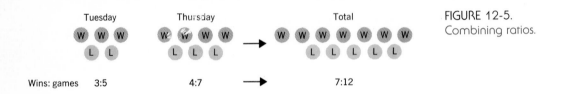

FIGURE 12-5.
Combining ratios.

2, the ratio of girls to the whole group is 3 to 7 or 3:7 or $\frac{3}{7}$. Also, as students learn to find equivalent ratios, they will soon discover that the processes involved are the same as those for finding equivalent fractions. However, whereas a fraction expresses a part of a whole, a ratio expresses a relationship between two quantities when one quantity may or may not be a part of the other. Confusion arises because there is some overlap in these meanings. In Figure 12-2 if the ratio of girls to the whole group is 3:7, it is also true that $\frac{3}{7}$ of the group is girls. Similarly, students find that $\frac{4}{7}$ of the group is boys and that these can be combined (added) to say that $\frac{7}{7}$ of the group is girls and boys. This looks just like the addition of fractions. What students must be aware of is just what the reference is. In this case they should see that first the number of girls, then the number of boys, and finally the number of boys and girls are all being compared to the same number, the number of the whole group.

Students should contrast this with the situation shown in Figure 12-5. In this case they should see that the number of wins Tuesday is being compared to the number of games played Tuesday for a ratio of 3:5. Similarly, the number of wins Thursday is being compared to the number of games played Thursday. To combine these ratios, the students must compare the total number of wins both days to the total number of games played both days for a completely new ratio of 7:12.

Another important procedure in working with rates and ratios is learning to find equivalent rates and ratios. In the example shown in Figure 12-4, Naomi found that a ratio of one peach to three peaches was equivalent to the ratio of three peaches to nine peaches. Children's initial experiences in finding equivalent ratios should involve models.

Given the following problem, "If 2 pencils cost 5 cents, how much would 4, 6, 8, or 10 pencils cost?" the students could begin with a direct approach using pencils and

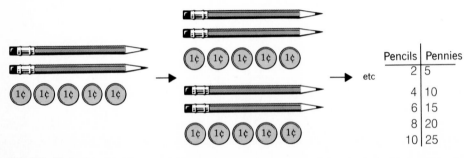

FIGURE 12-6.
Finding equivalent ratios with models.

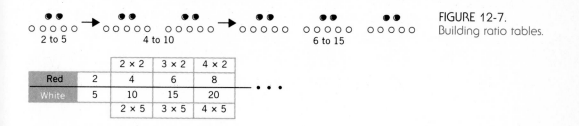

FIGURE 12-7.
Building ratio tables.

pennies as their models (Figure 12-6). Next, moving to a slightly more conceptually abstract model, the students could use red and white counters to represent the pencils and pennies. Thus, to show the ratio of 2 to 5, the students could set out 2 red and 5 white counters. Then the students should lay out 2 more red counters and 5 more white counters (Figure 12-7). They should note that for every 2 red counters there are 5 white counters or a total of 4 red and 10 white counters. The number of red counters and the number of white counters have both doubled. Students should repeat this procedure by laying out 2 more red counters and 5 more white counters. Again, they should note that there are 2 red counters for every 5 white counters. There are now 6 red counters and 15 white counters; the number of red counters and the number of white counters have both tripled. As the students gain confidence with the problems, they can record the corresponding information in a table, noting that the entries are 2, 3, 4, and so on times their first entry (Figure 12-7).

After working through various examples, the format can be changed by presenting problems with missing information. For example, "the ratio of 3 red counters to 4 white counters is to be maintained; if there are 12 white counters, how many red counters are needed?" Jessica solved this problem using counters (Figure 12-8). First, she set up the basic ratio of 3 to 4 and added enough white counters to make twelve whites (Figure 12-8a and b). Jessica thought, "But now I have a ratio of 3 to 12 . . . that's not right, but how do I know how many more red counters I need? . . . Let's see. . . . I need 3 red counters for every 4 white counters. Why don't I separate the white counters into groups of four (Figure 12-8c). . . . Oh—yes, . . . now I have two groups of white counters without any red counters. I need three red counters for each group so I need six more red counters. . . . That's it! The ratio of 3 to 4 is equivalent to the ratio of 9 to 12" (Figure 12-8d).

Cuisenaire rods could also be used to find equivalent ratios. The red rod that represents two is compared to the yellow rod, which represents five (Figure 12-9a). To find an equivalent ratio for 2 to 5 another combination of a red rod and a yellow rod are

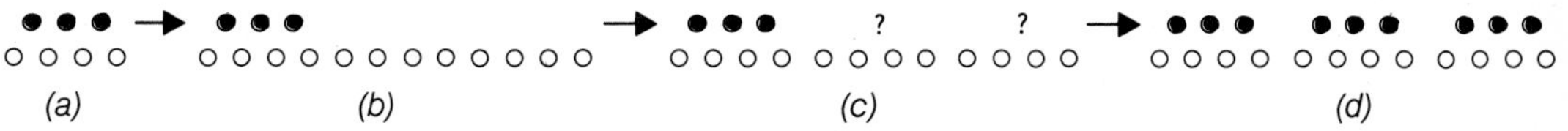

3 to 4 is equivalent to 9 to 12

FIGURE 12-8.
Finding the missing part.

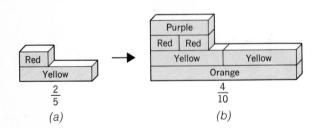

FIGURE 12-9.
Cuisenaire rods representing equivalent ratios.

formed (Figure 12-9b). The student can readily see that each pair is in a 2-to-5 ratio. The sections are then combined and traded for equivalent rods to show the ratio of 4 to 10. This same process can be used to find other equivalent ratios, which students can record in a chart as shown in Figure 12-6.

Equivalent measures can also be expressed as ratios. For example, to rename meters as centimeters, students can simply look at a meter stick marked in centimeters as shown in Figure 12-10. They observe that 1 meter is equivalent to 100 centimeters so that ratio is 1 to 100. Therefore, 2 meters is equivalent to 200 centimeters, 3 meters is equivalent to 300 centimeters, and so on. Some students may fill in this table by counting and recording 1, 2, 3, 4 . . . and then 100, 200, 300 . . . , rather than thinking 1, 100, 2, 200. . . . Although this type of table is appropriate for some introductory work, the students should also be working with tables where the entries are not consecutive and/ or regularly spaced (Figure 12-11). Also, the

teacher should ask questions to determine whether or not the students are focusing on the ratio.

Figure 12-12 shows two additional examples of comparing metric units by means of ratios. In the first example, water was measured to the nearest hundred milliliters. Therefore, the liter measures are accurate to the nearest tenth of a liter. Similarly, students should recognize that in the second table, since two measures are recorded as 395 and 425, they can assume that all the centimeter measures are accurate at least to the nearest 5 centimeters. Therefore, 380 centimeters was renamed as 3.80 meters instead of as 3.8 meters, and so on.

Equivalent ratios could also be used to solve rate problems. Jody was figuring out how far it is from Alvord, IA, her home, to Omaha. Her family was planning to leave for Omaha at 9 A.M. She heard her father mention that they would need to travel at a speed of 80 kilometers per hour in order to arrive by noon. To calculate the total distance she

1 meter = 100 centimeters

Meters	1	2	3	4	5	6
Centimeters	100	200	300	400	500	600

FIGURE 12-10.
Ratio of meters to centimeters.

cars	1	3		6	7	9		100
wheels	4	12	20	24			100	

shirts	8	16	40			56	48	
slacks	3	6		9	24			12

books	30	15	105			225	45	1500
shelves	2		7	4	25			

FIGURE 12-11.

Ratio tables with irregular intervals and/or random order.

Milliliters	1000	1500	2000	3000	3500
liters	1	1.5	2.0	3.0	3.5

Centimeters	380	395	420	425	450
Meters	3.80	3.95	4.20	4.25	4.50

FIGURE 12-12.

Metric system conversion.

drew an arrow representing the distance traveled in one hour and labeled that interval 80 kilometers (Figure 12-13). She then drew in two more arrows to represent the remaining distance to be traveled between 10 A.M. and 12 noon. Since each arrow represented a distance of 80 kilometers, Jody calculated that the total distance was 240 kilometers.

Graphing, as well as diagrams and tables, can be used to show the relationship between various ratios. For example, Ken noticed that his father often did not completely turn off the water faucet in the

kitchen. His father frequently complained about high utility bills. Ken thought that the dripping faucet could be contributing to the high bill, so he set out a measuring container to catch the dripping water. At 5-minute intervals, he recorded the amount of water collected. He plotted his results as shown in Figure 12-14. After Ken measured water for 15 minutes, he noted that, since the rate of dripping water was constant, he could simply connect the three points on this graph with a straight line. In discussing his graph with his father, Ken pointed out that a liter of water was wasted every 25 minutes and that 2.4 liters were wasted every hour. Consequently his father started being more careful in turning the water faucet off.

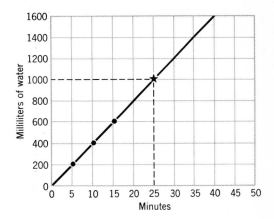

FIGURE 12-14.

Using graphs to show equal ratio.

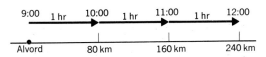

FIGURE 12-13.

Ratio of kilometers to time.

QUESTIONS AND ACTIVITIES

1. Lay out eight white chips and twelve white chips. Rearrange the chips so that you can find a ratio that is the same as 8 to 12.

2. Consider a set such as 3 pencils and 7 pens or 5 cats and 2 dogs.
   a. Write a ratio problem that involves a part/part comparison.
   b. Write a ratio problem that involves a part/whole comparison.
   c. Why is it important that comparisons be labeled?

3. Why is determining the number of your heartbeats for one week a ratio problem?

4. Solve the first table using two different methods. What type of thinking is needed in order to solve the second table?

Cars	3	9	6	12				21
Trucks	5	15	10		25	50	40	

Pencils	12	15	18		9		30	
Erasers	8	10	12	16		30		40

5. Use equivalent ratio tables to solve the following process problems. For approximately what grade level would these problems be appropriate?
   a. Jack and Carol have a total of 12 nickels, dimes, and quarters. If the sum is $1.45, how many of each coin do they have?

	Number of coins	Value of coins
Nickels		
Dimes		
Quarters		

   b. There were a total of 32 chickens and cows in the barnyard. Erica counted a total of 60 legs. How many chickens were in the barnyard?
   c. Measure the edges and diagonals of various-sized squares. Find the ratio of the length of the diagonal to length of the side. Is there a relationship?

6. Cut out a copy of a tangram puzzle. [See Problem 4 in "Plane Figures (Introduction)" in Chapter 11 for instructions on making the puzzle.] For parts (a) through (e), record your answers in a table. As you answer the questions, look for a pattern in your answers.
   a. Define the small square as your basic unit of area so the area of the square is one. What is the area of each of the other pieces?
   b. Redefine the small triangle as your basic unit of area. What is the area of each of the other pieces?
   c. Redefine the nonsquare parallelogram as your basic unit of one. What is the area of the other pieces?
   d. Redefine the medium triangle as your basic unit of one. What is the area of each of the other pieces?
   e. Redefine the large triangle as your basic unit of one. What is the area of each of the other pieces?
   f. Why is this considered an activity involving ratio?

7. In addition to using models to find equivalent ratios, students can draw a set of repeated diagrams. Show how students could draw a picture to solve the following problems.
   a. 2 cans for 50 cents; 6 cans for ? cents
   b. 1 dozen—12 items; 2 dozen—? items
   c. 2 tickets—$5; 8 tickets—$?
   d. 50 miles in 1 hour; ? miles in 5 hours

8. Ratio and proportion are usually considered upper elementary topics. Read "Let's Do It! From Blocks and Model Making to Ratio and Proportion" by Bruni and Silverman for intuitive ideas regarding ratio and proportion for children in lower elementary grades. Describe some of these activities.

PROPORTIONS

After forming charts of equivalent ratios, students are ready to begin using proportions. A proportion is simply an equation that expresses two ratios as being equivalent. For example, by use of the counters it was shown that $\frac{2}{5} = \frac{4}{10}$, $\frac{2}{5} = \frac{6}{15}$, and $\frac{4}{10} = \frac{6}{15}$. Although charts help a student in organizing information and in formulating a pattern, they are not practical in solving most proportion problems. For example, if Robyn's car averages 9 kilometers per liter, how many kilometers can Robyn travel with a full tank of gas if the gas tank has a capacity of 40 liters? In order to work the problem, Robyn started to make a table (Figure 12-15a). She soon realized that there would be 40 entries in her table. Robyn decided to double each entry (Figure 12-15b), but the ratio that she needed was between the ratios 288:32 and 576:64. Since all the ratios in the table were equivalent, she added 8 and 32 to obtain 40 liters and added 72 and 288 to obtain 360 kilometers. Therefore she knew her car would travel 360 kilometers on a full tank of gas. Although Robyn had obtained the answer, she was curious about whether there were other shortcuts. She then worked the problem as shown in Figure 12-15c. Robyn multiplied the first two pairs of entries by 2. She then multiplied each part of the ratio 36:4 by 10 to obtain 360:40. Reflecting on her work, Robyn recorded her step-by-step thinking (Figure 12-15d). Since she multiplied by $\frac{2}{2}$, $\frac{2}{2}$, and then $\frac{10}{10}$, this was equivalent to multiplying by $\frac{2}{2} \times \frac{2}{2} \times \frac{10}{10}$ or $\frac{40}{40}$ as shown in Figure 12-15e.

Bob, another student who had been watching Robyn work, pointed out to her that in her original problem the missing number was 360 so she could have set up the problem as shown in Figure 12-15f and solved it accordingly. Glancing back at her original

Kilometers	9	18	27		
Liters	1	2	3		40

(a)

Kilometers	9	18	36	72	144	288	576
Liters	1	2	4	8	16	32	64

$$\frac{288}{32} \quad \frac{72}{8} \longrightarrow \frac{360}{40} \quad \frac{\text{Kilometers}}{\text{Liters}}$$

(b)

Kilometers	9	18	36	360	
Liters	1	2	4	40	

(c)

$$\frac{9}{1} \times \frac{2}{2} = \frac{18}{2} \longrightarrow \frac{18}{2} \times \frac{2}{2} = \frac{36}{4} \longrightarrow$$

$$\frac{36}{4} \times \frac{10}{10} = \frac{360}{40}$$

(d)

$$\frac{9}{1} \times \frac{40}{40} = \frac{360}{40}$$

(e)

$$\begin{array}{c}\text{Kilometers} \rightarrow \\ \text{Liters} \rightarrow\end{array} \frac{9}{1} = \frac{N}{40} \longrightarrow \frac{9}{1} \times \frac{40}{40} = \frac{360}{40}$$

(f)

FIGURE 12-15.
Robyn's table and proportions.

table she exclaimed, "Of course, adding 40 nines is the same as forty times nine." Robyn now has developed an efficient procedure for solving proportion problems.

Many problem-solving situations use proportion in measurements. For example, Glenna, who was preparing for the RAGBRAI (Register's Annual Great Bicycle Ride Across Iowa), was installing an odometer on her bicycle. As she worked, she started thinking about odometers. She wanted to know how many times the wheel would revolve before 1 kilometer would register on the odometer. She knew that her bicycle's wheels had a diameter of 66 centimeters. In order to find one revolution, she had to know the circumference of the wheel. She was doing the calculations mentally and was only interested in an approximation, so instead of multiplying the diameter by *pi,* about 3.14, she simply multiplied 3 × 66 and rounded her answer up to 200 centimeters. The ratio of revolutions to centimeters was 1:200. Since 200 centimeters were equivalent to 2 meters she reasoned that the ratio of one revolution to meters was 1:2. Since there are 1000 meters in 1 kilometer, she reasoned that 1:2 was equivalent to *N*:1000 as shown in Figure 12-16. Since 1000 is 500 times larger than 2, she multiplied 1 times 500 to obtain 500 revolutions.

In the preceding example Glenna knew the rate per one unit. That made her calculations relatively easy. In some problems the rate per unit is not directly given. For example, "Ms. Grohe was planning on freezing 5 kilograms of peaches. Peaches were advertised at 3 kilograms for $2.85. How much will she have to pay?" One approach to this type of problem is to determine the cost per unit. Using this technique, Ms. Grohe would find how much 1 kilogram would cost and then multiply by the number of kilograms desired. Ms. Grohe reasoned, "3 kilograms for 3 dollars would be 1 dollar for each kilogram. Since the actual price of 3 kilograms is $2.85

Step 1
$$\frac{3 \text{ kg}}{\$2.85} = \frac{1 \text{ kg}}{X} \longleftarrow \text{weight} \atop \longleftarrow \text{cost}$$

$$\frac{3 \text{ kg}}{\$2.85} = \frac{1 \text{ kg}}{\$0.95}$$

Step 2
$$\frac{1 \text{ kg}}{\$0.95} = \frac{5 \text{ kg}}{X} \longrightarrow \frac{1 \text{ kg}}{\$0.95} \times \frac{5}{5} \longrightarrow \frac{5 \text{ kg}}{\$4.75}$$

FIGURE 12-17.
Using unit-rates to solve proportions.

or 15 cents less than 3 dollars, the price of each kilogram will be 1 dollar minus $\frac{1}{3}$ of 15 cents or 1 dollar minus 5 cents, which is 95 cents. For 5 kilograms I will pay 5 times as much as for one so 5 times 95 cents is . . . 5 times $1 minus 5 times 5 cents or $5 minus 25 cents or $4.75." The written procedure for unit cost approach is shown in Figure 12-17.

Finding a unit rate is not suitable for all proportion problems. For example, "If Janie bought three small cans of tomato juice for 49 cents, how much would a case, 24 cans, of tomato juice cost?" The unit price contains a fractional part of a cent. The problem can be solved by using the unit-rate approach, but this would involve multiplying 24 times $16\frac{1}{3}$. Instead, this problem could be solved mentally. Since there are 8 sets of three cans in 24, Janie will be paying 8 times the price of 49 cents. She then reasoned, "8 times 49 is . . . 8 times (50 − 1), so 8 × 50 minus 8 is 400 − 8 or 392."

The written approach for her thinking is shown in Figure 12-18. Since the rate was expressed as the number of cans per price, the desired number of cans, 24, is placed over the new price, the unknown or *x*. Because 3 × 8 is 24, the rate $\frac{3}{0.49}$ is multiplied by the identity $\frac{8}{8}$ to obtain $\frac{24}{3.92}$.

Some problems cannot be readily solved by this procedure either. For example, Kara's grandfather has promised her

$$\begin{array}{c} \text{revolutions} \longrightarrow \\ \text{meters} \longrightarrow \end{array} \quad \frac{1}{2} = \frac{N}{1000} \longrightarrow \frac{1}{2} \cdot \frac{500}{500} = \frac{N}{1000}$$

$$\frac{1}{2} = \frac{500}{1000}$$

FIGURE 12-16.
Glenna's proportion problem.

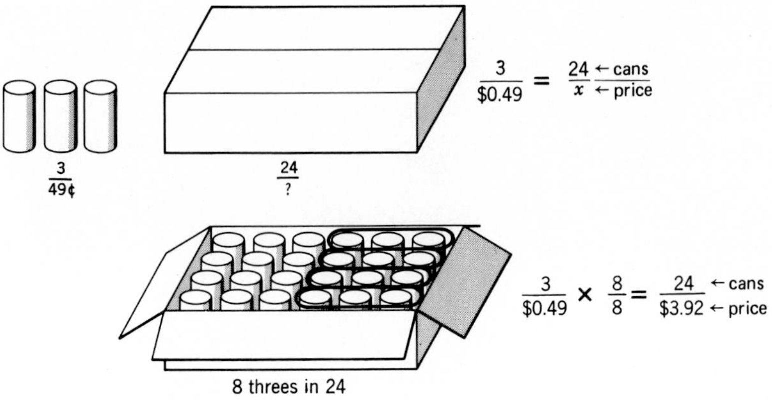

FIGURE 12-18.
Janie's proportion problem.

$$\frac{3}{\$0.49} = \frac{24}{x} \begin{array}{l}\leftarrow \text{cans} \\ \leftarrow \text{price}\end{array}$$

$$\frac{3}{\$0.49} \times \frac{8}{8} = \frac{24}{\$3.92} \begin{array}{l}\leftarrow \text{cans} \\ \leftarrow \text{price}\end{array}$$

that on her tenth birthday she would receive a meter's length of dimes that were laid side by side. About one month before her birthday Kara became extremely curious about how much money her grandfather had promised her. She placed a meter stick on the floor and started placing dimes next to it (Figure 12-19), but she ran out of dimes before she solved the problem.

She noticed that four dimes were the same length as 7 centimeters. Since she wanted information about 100 centimeters, she set up a proportion (Figure 12-20). Since 7 is not a factor of 100, Kara multiplied $\frac{4}{7}$ by the identity $\frac{100}{100}$ and $\frac{x}{100}$ by the identity $\frac{7}{7}$. Because the 400 and the 7x are now both being compared to 700, Kara asked herself what number times 7 is 400. She divided 400 by 7 to obtain an answer of $57\frac{1}{7}$. She decided that her birthday present would be 57 dimes or $5.70.

To check the reasonableness of her result, she observed, "4 dimes were 7 centi-

$$\frac{\text{Dimes}}{\text{Centimeters}} \qquad \frac{4}{7} = \frac{x}{100}$$

$$\frac{100}{100} \times \frac{4}{7} = \frac{x}{100} \times \frac{7}{7}$$
$$\frac{400}{700} = \frac{7x}{700}$$
$$400 = 7x$$
$$57\frac{1}{7} = x$$

FIGURE 12-20.
Kara's proportion problem.

meters, so. . . . If 4 dimes were 8 centimeters, 1 dime for every 2 centimeters. For one hundred centimeters . . . 1 to 2 is the same as 50 to 100. My estimate of 50 is too low, as 4 dimes were originally compared to 7, not 8 centimeters, so 57 is a reasonable answer."

Carolyn used this same procedure, proportions, in working with scale drawings. While making a dress for her niece Jody, she decided to appliqué a design as shown in Figure 12-21. The dimensions of the boat were given on a drawing Carolyn had selected. She wanted to increase the size of

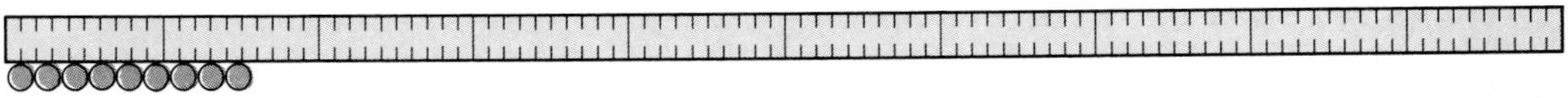

FIGURE 12-19.
Kara's measuring problem.

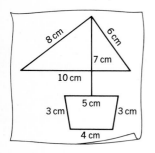

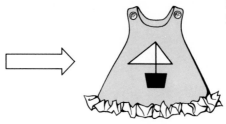

FIGURE 12-21.
Scale drawing of a sailboat.

the drawing so that the base of the appliquéd boat would be large enough for a pocket. Instead of a 4-centimeter length, she decided 10 centimeters would be more suitable. Since the appliqué was to be in the same proportion as the original drawing, she set up the proportions shown in Figure 12-22a.

In part (b), Carolyn multiplied twice by the identity in the forms of $\frac{x}{x}$ and $\frac{10}{10}$. Since both ratios have bases of $10x$, Carolyn asked herself what number times 4 equals 30. Her answer was $7\frac{1}{2}$ or 7.5 centimeters. Since there were five more problems left, she started to look for a shortcut. She noted that in Step 4 of her work in Figure 12-22b, the equation $4x = 30$ can be factored to $4(x) = 10(3)$. These factors are located diagonally across from each other in the original ratio as shown in Figure 12-22c. To check her work Carolyn substituted 7.5 in her original

proportion, $\frac{4}{10} = \frac{3}{7.5}$. When she used cross products, the equality became $4(7.5) = 10(3)$ or $30 = 30$. Since a proportion is made up of equivalent ratios, an equality must result.

If two unequivalent ratios such as $\frac{2}{3}$ and $\frac{1}{2}$ are set equal to each other ($\frac{2}{3} = \frac{1}{2}$), when cross products are applied, the result is $2(2) = 3(1)$ or $4 = 3$. Since the original statement was false, the last statement must be false. Thus, if cross products yield a false statement, students know that their original ratios are not equivalent.

The following week in Mr. Field's mathematics class, Carolyn was trying to find which rectangles shown in Figure 12-23

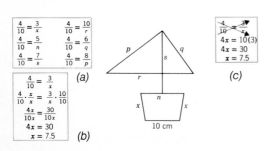

FIGURE 12-22.
Solving scale drawings by proportion.

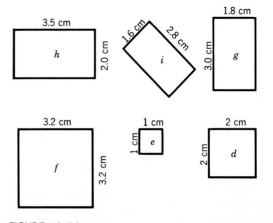

FIGURE 12-23.
Finding similar rectangles.

$$\frac{\text{width of } h}{\text{width of } i} = \frac{\text{length of } h}{\text{length of } i}$$

$$\frac{2.0 \text{ cm}}{1.6 \text{ cm}} = \frac{3.5 \text{ cm}}{2.8 \text{ cm}}$$

$$2.0 \times 2.8 = 1.6 \times 3.5$$

$$5.6 = 5.6$$

(a)

$$\frac{\text{width of } h}{\text{width of } g} = \frac{\text{length of } h}{\text{length of } g}$$

$$\frac{2.0 \text{ cm}}{1.8} \overset{?}{=} \frac{3.5 \text{ cm}}{3.0}$$

$$2.0 \times 3.0 \overset{?}{=} 1.8 \times 3.5$$

$$6.0 \neq 6.3$$

(b)

$$\frac{\text{width of } h}{\text{length of } h} = \frac{\text{width of } i}{\text{length of } i}$$

$$\frac{2.0}{3.5} = \frac{1.6}{2.8}$$

$$5.6 = 5.6$$

(c)

$$\frac{\text{width of } h}{\text{length of } h} = \frac{\text{width of } g}{\text{length of } g}$$

$$\frac{2.0}{3.5} \overset{?}{=} \frac{1.8}{3.0}$$

$$6.0 \neq 6.3$$

(d)

FIGURE 12-24.

Using proportions to solve for similar rectangles.

were similar to each other. Before, when she had compared similar shapes, one figure was always two or three times larger than the other figure. For example, if one triangle had sides of 2, 3, and 4 centimeters the other triangle would be formed by doubling each corresponding side to 4, 6, and 8 centimeters. Carolyn then remembered the scale drawing that she had done the previous week. The original sketch and the appliqué were similar figures. Therefore, to find out if two rectangles were similar, she realized she could set up a proportion comparing the two lengths and the two widths in the same order. To check the truth of the proportion, she used cross products (Figure 12-24a and b).

Carolyn found that rectangles h and i are similar because an equality results when cross products are applied. The "proportion" in Figure 12-24b does not result in an equality, so rectangle h is not similar to rectangle g. In Figure 12-24c and d Carolyn set up proportions stating that the width compared to the length of one rectangle is equivalent to the width compared to the length of another rectangle. This proportion should also result in a true statement if the rectangles are similar. This procedure gave her the

same result; that is, rectangles h and i are similar, and rectangles h and g are not.

Carolyn then started setting up the proportions for the squares (Figure 12-25). While setting up the proportion she realized that *all* squares have to be similar since she was writing the same ratio each time. The properties of polygons e and d in Figure 12-23 further intrigued her. She noted that the ratio of the sides was 1:2. The diagonals were also in a 1:2 ratio since square e had a diagonal of about 1.4 cm while square d had a diagonal of about 2.8 cm. However, the areas of the squares were not in a 1:2 ratio (Figure 12-26). Carolyn found that she could lay four squares the size of e on top of square d. Thus, she discovered that when the linear dimensions of the square doubled, the area quadrupled. Mr. Field encouraged

$$\frac{\text{side of } f}{\text{side of } e} = \frac{\text{side of } f}{\text{side of } e}$$

$$\frac{3.2}{1} = \frac{3.2}{1}$$

$$3.2 = 3.2$$

$$\frac{\text{side of } f}{\text{side of } f} = \frac{\text{side of } e}{\text{side of } e}$$

$$\frac{3.2}{3.2} = \frac{1}{1}$$

$$3.2 = 3.2$$

FIGURE 12-25.

Proportions for squares.

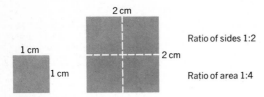

Figure 9-22.

FIGURE 12-26.
Ratio of areas of two squares.

Carolyn to continue exploring the areas of other similar polygons and the volumes of solids to see if this relationship could be extended.

QUESTIONS AND ACTIVITIES

1. a. Real-life situations and experiments should be used to generate proportion problems. Solve the following rate problem using a ratio table.

   Jo swims $\frac{3}{4}$ of a mile in a 40-minute exercise period at least 5 times a week. What is the minimum length she swims in a week? Maximum length in a week? Minimum time in a month?

   b. Re-solve the problem above by writing proportions.

   c. This situation could easily be rewritten involving your future students' activities. The activity could become running, walking, reading books, eating pizza, or mowing lawn. The time could become days, weeks, minutes, or years. A good teaching technique is to have students write their own problems. Write a similar problem that would be appropriate for middle school or junior high students.

2. Students should also collect their own data which can be used for proportion problems.

Choose one of the following situations and design a proportion problem where the students would collect data for a certain time period and then extend that to another time period.

   a. the amount of time doing homework as compared to watching television

   b. the number of times the school cafeteria serves Mexican food, pizza, or your favorite food

   c. the number of times your heart beats normally . . . after a minute of exercise

   d. the number of paper clips that you can link together to form a chain in a certain time period

   e. the number of times you can print your first name in a given time period

   f. the number of people who can stand in a square meter

3. Compare these two situations: (1) the amount of time it takes you to walk around a city block or down a long school hallway and (2) how far you can walk in 30 seconds. Design two similar proportion problems that include both ideas. What teacher questions could you ask to help students understand the comparisons? To help them decide what measures need to be taken and how they will collect the data?

4. Write two different proportions that students could use to solve each of the following questions: Kim had visions of winning a million dollars in the Iowa lottery. She wondered whether, if she were to receive all of the money at once in one-dollar bills, it would fit in a large suitcase? In her car trunk? Would she be able to carry it?

5. Conversion activities are closely related to rate and ratio problems. Intelligent shopping requires that the consumer is able to compare costs for various-sized products. For example, which is the better buy, 5 lb 4 oz of soap for $3.23 or 2 lb 12 oz for $1.95? Find at least three different ways students could solve this problem.

CONCEPTS OF PERCENT

Although comparisons and percents are commonly used applications, National Assessment results show that students have difficulties with percent concepts and their applications. About one third of the 13-year-olds and one half of the 17-year-olds responded correctly to questions about the basic concepts of percent. About one sixth of the 13-year-olds and one third of the 17-year-olds could solve problems that involved operations or applications of percent (Carpenter and others, 1981). To understand and apply percent concepts, students must have mastered the prerequisites of fractions and comparisons.

National Assessment results and research at the University of Michigan show that most students have a stronger concept of common fractions than of decimal fractions (Carpenter and others, 1981; Payne, 1984). In the development that follows, common fractions are used to explore initial percent concepts to build on the students' backgrounds. Common fractions are also emphasized because in real-life situations individuals are more likely to change a percent to an equivalent common fraction for estimations or mental computations. Decimal fractions should be linked to the percent concepts to extend students' concepts of decimals and percents. Also, if calculators without percent keys are used, percents can be rewritten as decimal fractions.

Percent is simply a comparison or ratio of part to whole where the whole is always 100. The part–whole language that was used with certain ratios (part-to-whole comparisons) and with fractions should be extended. Early emphasis should be on the word "percent" and its meaning. "Percent" comes from Latin words that mean "for each one hundred." The term should be linked to other words from the same root, such as "century" and "cents" (money). The term "percent" should also be linked to the symbol for percent, %. A ratio of 4 to 100 is equivalent to four percent, which is written symbolically as 4%. This is also the same as four hundredths or 0.04. Thus four *parts* per hundred (whole) can be written as $\frac{4}{100}$ or 0.04 or 4%.

To develop the percent concept, students should be involved in activities that link models to the oral and written names for percent (Figure 12-27). The first lessons should be limited to percents between and including 1 and 100 percent. The common fractions in these lessons should be limited to situations where the whole is 100.

In later lessons the relationship between other common fractions and percent should be explored. Since each dollar is made up of 100 cents, money can be used to show the relationship between fractions, decimals, and percents. For example, one-fourth of

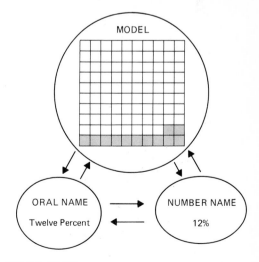

FIGURE 12-27.
Model—oral name—number name.

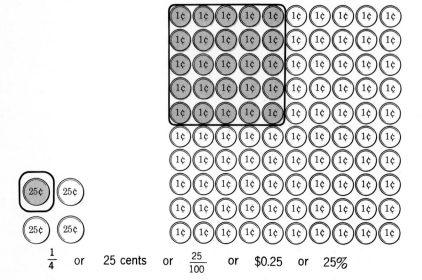

FIGURE 12-28.
Money representing fraction, decimal, and percent.

$\frac{1}{4}$ or 25 cents or $\frac{25}{100}$ or $0.25 or 25%

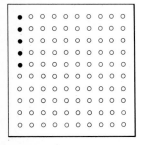

FIGURE 12-29.
One hundred peg board and graph paper.

$\frac{5}{100}$ or 0.05 or 5% or $\frac{1}{20}$

one dollar is 25 cents or $\frac{25}{100}$ or $0.25 or 25% of a dollar (Figure 12-28).

Students can use graph paper or a hundred-peg board to study these three relationships. Five percent is shown in Figure 12-29. One-tenth of the whole would be one row of the peg board or graph paper. Since there are ten parts in each row, $\frac{1}{10}$ would be $\frac{10}{100}$ or 10%.

Measures in the metric system can also be used to represent percents. If the meter stick is defined as one, 10 centimeters would be $\frac{1}{10}$. This could be renamed as 0.10 meter, which is 10% of a meter (Figure 12-30).

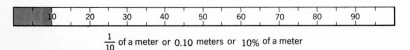

$\frac{1}{10}$ of a meter or 0.10 meters or 10% of a meter

FIGURE 12-30.
Meter stick representing fractions, decimals, and percents.

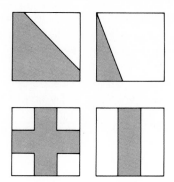

FIGURE 12-31.
Estimating percent—regions.

Twenty-three centimeters would be $\frac{23}{100}$ of the meter stick or 0.23 meter or 23% of the meter.

Estimation activities can be used to extend students' concepts of percents. Good estimation skills are also important for doing mental computations with percents and for being aware of reasonableness of results in percent computations. Grids with various shadings can be shown and the students can classify the examples as close to 0, 50, or 100 percent (Figure 12-31). These estimations can be refined by having the students decide whether the examples are a little more or less than 50% or about halfway between 0 and 50 percent. Number lines with region models and later number lines alone can also be used for estimation activities (Figure 12-32). Various examples could be shown on an overhead; the students could estimate these percents and also make up situations that involve these percents.

Percents greater than one hundred percent or less than one percent need to be developed carefully after students have mastered percent concepts between 1 and 100 percent. Results from the Second National Assessment show that a little more than $\frac{1}{4}$ of the 13-year-olds and less than one half of the 17-year-olds could change 125% to a decimal fraction. Percents greater than one hundred should be introduced through models and real life examples.

Percents larger than 100 can be introduced just as fractions larger than 1 were introduced. If one 10-centimeter square represents 100%, then two 10-centimeter squares represent 200%. Similarly, one and a half 10-centimeter squares would represent 150% (Figure 12-33).

Class discussion could include examples such as the following:

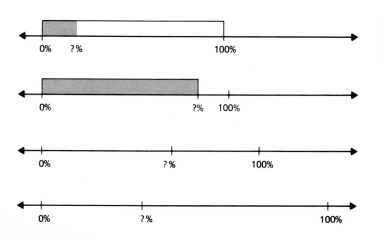

FIGURE 12-32.
Estimating percents—number lines.

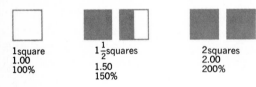

1 square	1½ squares	2 squares
1.00	1.50	2.00
100%	150%	200%

FIGURE 12-33.
Percents larger than 100%.

The seating capacity of a room is 100%. If all of the chairs are filled and some people are standing, the room is filled to more than 100 percent capacity.

If 100 percent is the wholesale or base price of the item, will the store be selling it at that price (100%) or at a greater price (more than 100%)?

The organization originally had 20 members (100%) now it has expanded to 35 members (175%).

Models should be used to represent these concepts.

In another example, Andy is comparing his height of 1 meter to that of his older brothers Matt and Mark, who are 1.5 meters and 2 meters tall respectively. When Andy compares his height to Mark's, he finds that he is half as tall as Mark or that their heights are in a ratio of 1 to 2. Since Andy is considering Mark's height as the whole, or 100%, Andy is 50% as tall as Mark (Figure 12-34a). Next, Andy compares his height to Matt's. Their heights are in a ratio of 1 to 1.5 or 2 halves to 3 halves or 2 to 3. Since the ratio of their heights is 2 to 3 and Matt's height is being considered the whole or 100%, Andy is $66\frac{2}{3}$% as tall as Matt (Figure 12-34b).

Later, Andy decided to set up the ratios in the opposite direction. This time Andy's height was considered as the whole or 100%. When Andy compared Mark's height to his, he found that Mark was twice as tall or Mark was 200% as tall as Andy (Figure

12-34c). When Andy compared Matt's height to his, he found that the ratio of their heights was 1.5 to 1 so Matt was 150% as tall as Andy (Figure 12-34d).

Percents less than one percent can be introduced using a grid. By shading in one half of a square on a ten-by-ten grid and comparing it to one square, the students should conclude that it is one half of one percent or ½% (Figure 12-35). Some students confuse ½% with 50% or ¾% with 75%. In order to prevent these misconceptions, examples like these should be modeled and discussed. Students should be able to explain that 50% is ½ of one hundred percent and ½% is ½ of one percent.

To relate percent concepts to decimal fractions, activities using ten-by-ten grids can be used. The whole or 1 is 100 percent. One tenth of the grid is one row or $\frac{1}{10}$, 0.1, or 10%. One tenth of a row or one square is one hundredth of the grid, namely $\frac{1}{100}$, 0.01, or 1%. The pattern of dividing by ten should be extended. The students should reason that when they shade in one tenth of a square that if all of the squares were divided into 10 parts that each part is one thou-

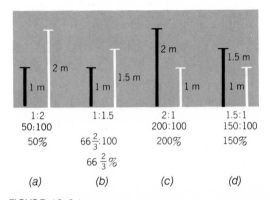

1:2	1:1.5	2:1	1.5:1
50:100	66⅔:100	200:100	150:100
50%	66⅔%	200%	150%
(a)	(b)	(c)	(d)

FIGURE 12-34.
Using percents to compare heights.

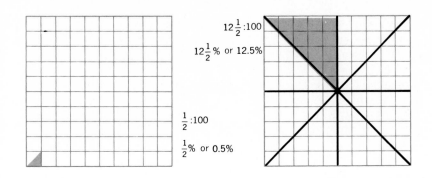

FIGURE 12-35.
Graph paper representing fractional percents.

$12\frac{1}{2}$:100

$12\frac{1}{2}$% or 12.5%

$\frac{1}{2}$:100

$\frac{1}{2}$% or 0.5%

sandth of the grid. One tenth of a square or one thousandth of the grid is $\frac{1}{1000}$, 0.001, or 0.1%.

Percents less than 1 percent can also be modeled by using a meter stick marked in millimeters. If one centimeter is being considered, it is one out of 100, or 1% of a meter is represented. Five millimeters or 0.5 centimeter or one half of a centimeter out of 100 centimeters would be 0.5% or $\frac{1}{2}$% of a meter.

In exploring percents, students will start to associate common fractions with their related percent. Some fractions such as $\frac{23}{100}$ or $\frac{3}{10}$ can be easily changed mentally to their percent equivalent. In addition to tenths and hundredths, other fractions such as halves, fourths, fifths, twentieths, twenty-fifths, and fiftieths are easy to change to percents as these denominators easily divide one

hundred. The study could start with the easy denominators for unit fractions and their related percents and then be extended to fractions with numerators other than one. Since halves, tenths, hundredths, fourths, and fifths are commonly used fractions, students should be able to quickly and accurately give the related percent.

Halves and fourths can be readily shown by folding ten-by-ten grids into two or four equal-sized pieces. The students can then shade the appropriate parts on the unlined side, using a magic marker or dark pen. When the grid is flipped to the lined side, the students can determine the equivalent percent by counting the number of shaded squares (Figure 12-36). After these initial activities, the students can think "fourths . . . $\frac{1}{4}$ of a hundred is 25, so 25 per-

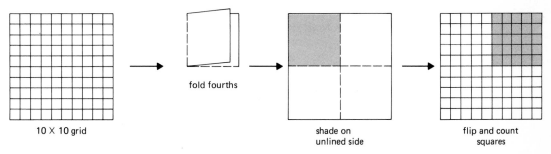

10 X 10 grid   fold fourths   shade on
                                            unlined side   flip and count
                                                                  squares

FIGURE 12-36.
Folding fourths to find percent.

cent." To extend this thinking to $\frac{3}{4}$ the student could reason, "$\frac{1}{4}$ was 25 hundredths so $\frac{3}{4}$ is 3 times 25 hundredths or 75 hundredths or 75 percent."

The students should observe that every two rows is a fifth, so each 20 squares is a fifth or 5 × 20 is 100. Some students may reason "$\frac{1}{5}$ is $\frac{2}{10}$, which is $\frac{20}{100}$ or 20 percent." Mental computation should be emphasized; for example, to change $\frac{2}{5}$ to a percent the students should reason: "Fifths . . . 5 divides 100 20 times. 2 times 20 is 40."

Fractions with such denominators as 25, 50, or 20 can also be readily computed mentally. For $\frac{3}{25}$ a student may reason "4 twenty-fives is 100 and 4 times 3 is 12 . . . so 12 hundredths or 12 percent." Another student may reason, "$\frac{3}{25}$ . . . $\frac{6}{50}$ . . . $\frac{12}{100}$, so 12 percent."

Other examples that the students should explore are the percent equivalents for common fractions such as $\frac{1}{8}$, $\frac{3}{8}$, and $\frac{1}{3}$. Eighths can readily be shown by folding a ten-by-ten grid into eight equal-sized parts. To represent $\frac{1}{8}$ one of the parts can be shaded using a magic marker on the unlined side of the grid. When they flip this square to the grid side, the students can determine that $\frac{1}{8}$ equals twelve and a half squares out of a hundred or $\frac{1}{8}$ equals $12\frac{1}{2}$% or 12.5% of the whole square (Figure 12-35b). In the first lessons these relationships should be explored with models. As they work with these models, the students should gradually memorize these percent equivalents of fractions that are common in our everyday experiences.

Students should also have experiences in changing percents to the simplest name for the common fractions. In order to help students develop competence in mental arithmetic, the teacher must include opportunities for them to practice changing per-

a	Part	3	6	18	
	Whole	5	10	30	100

b	Part		19		$\frac{19}{35} = \frac{X}{100}$
	Whole		35		35 X = 19 (100)
					X = 54.3

FIGURE 12-37.
Percents and ratio tables.

cents to fractions and fractions to percents. Examples of how to solve these problems mentally should be shared by the teacher and by the students.

In the previous examples, most of the fractions could be easily changed to parts per one hundred due to the nature of the numbers. For other numbers using proportions or a calculator is an appropriate method. Since percents are simply the special case in the ratio tables where the whole is one hundred, a proportion can readily be written. Figure 12-37a shows various names for $\frac{3}{5}$. Since $\frac{60}{100}$ is one of the names, $\frac{3}{5}$, $\frac{6}{10}$, and $\frac{18}{30}$ can all be written as 60%. To find the percent equivalent of $\frac{19}{35}$, a proportion was written (Figure 12-37b). The answer was rounded to the nearest tenth of a percent 54.3%. If a calculator with a percent key was used to find the percent for $\frac{19}{35}$, a display of 54.285714 may result. The student then needs to decide to what place value to round the number.

It was stated earlier in this chapter that students had great difficulty with thirds and eighths. For thirds the dilemma is the repeating decimal; for eighths it is the thousandths place. It was recommended that the directions should be explicit as to whether an exact or approximate answer is desired. The decimals could be rounded to the nearest hundredth for a whole-number percent. If a more exact number is needed, the desired accuracy must be stated.

1. Design an activity that involves all six translations: model ↔ oral name, model ↔ written name, written name ↔ oral name. Use 10-by-10 grid paper for your model.

2. Consider the numbers 1 through 100. Use patterns to determine the percent of numbers that belong to each of the following sets.
   a. odds
   b. numbers divisible by five
   c. numbers that contain the digit 9
   d. numbers that contain the digit 0
   e. numbers that have two digits that are the same

3. a. Use one hundred interlocking cubes or base-ten cubes to build a model that is 10 cubes by 10 cubes by 1 cube. If this solid were painted on all its faces, what percent of the individual cubes would have all faces painted? 5 faces? 4 faces? 3 faces? 2 faces? 1 face? 0 faces?
   b. Rearrange the cubes to form a solid that measures 4 by 5 by 5 or 2 by 5 by 10. Determine the percent of individual cubes that will have paint on 0, 1, 2, 3, 4, 5, and 6 faces if this new solid is painted on all its faces.

4. Materials needed: Several pieces of graph paper cut into 10 × 10 squares.
   a. Fold one 10 × 10 square into two equal-sized parts. Shade in one half on the back side of the graph paper; use a magic marker or black pen so that the shading clearly shows through on the

opposite side. Flip the sheet over. How many parts per hundred have been shaded in?
   $\frac{1}{2} = \frac{\square}{100} = $ _____%
   b. Repeat part (a) for $\frac{3}{4}$, $\frac{1}{8}$, and $\frac{3}{8}$
   $\frac{3}{4} = \frac{\square}{100}$ _____%
   $\frac{1}{8} = \frac{\square}{100}$ _____%
   $\frac{3}{8} = \frac{\square}{100}$ _____%
   c. Shade in one row of a 10 × 10 square.
   $\frac{1}{10} = \frac{\square}{100}$ _____%
   d. Use the 10 × 10 graph paper to represent $2\frac{3}{10}$.
   $2\frac{3}{10} = \frac{\square}{100}$ _____%
   e. Why is the unlined side shaded in parts a and b? Why not just shade in the grid side?

5. Maude reads 0.34 as "point thirty-four." Why is this oral language not appropriate for helping students change decimal fractions to percents?

6. Maude reads 0.34 as "point thirty-four." Why is this oral language not appropriate for helping students change decimal fractions to percents?

7. a. Claude wrote that 0.2 is equivalent to 2%. Devise an activity using grid paper to help him correct his thinking. Explicitly state what questions will be asked. What generalization should he form?
   b. What special problems can be anticipated for changing decimal fractions such as 0.234, 1.3245, or 0.3 to percent form? How would you help students understand and develop a procedure?
   c. Analyze a lesson on decimals and percents from an elementary school textbook. What suggestions do you have for improving this lesson?

8. a. A model made of two congruent paper circles can be used for estimating fractions. This model was adapted by John Van de Walle by marking one circle in 10 equal sections and then subdividing each section into ten parts. Make such a model that is at least divided into ten parts; see the following figure. Use the lined parts to represent 30%, 60%, and 90%.

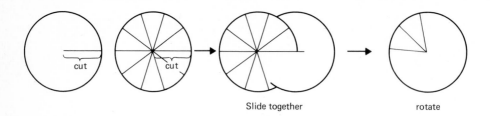

cut   cut

Slide together   rotate

b. Flip the model to the unlined part; estimate whether the amount shown is close to 0%, 50%, or 100%. Check your answer by flipping the model over.

c. Estimate or show such percents as 13%, 24%, 78%, 33%, or 7%.

9. Sam expressed the ratio of 3 to 5 by the following diagram.

So the ratio of 3 to 5 is 60%. George diagrammed the ratio of 5 to 3 as follows:

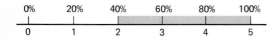

George said the ratio of 5 to 3 was 40%.
a. What is wrong with George's example?
b. What one question would help him *discover* his mistake?

10. Sarah had been taught the rule that to change decimals to percents you move the decimal point two places. Part of her assignment is shown below. Sarah had 75% of the problems correct, but how well does she understand the concept behind the rule she memorized? What questions could you ask Sarah to determine whether she understood the problems that she got correct? What could you do to help her understand this concept?

$0.3 = 30\%$
$0.45 = 45\%$
$3 = 3\%$
$7 = 7\%$
$2.35 = 235\%$
$0.23 = 23\%$
$12.3 = 1230\%$
$0.57 = 57\%$

11. a. Use a large ten-by-ten grid to develop the concept of percent less than 1%. Consider the grid as 100%. One row or one tenth is what percent? One tenth of a row or one square is what percent? One tenth of a square would be what percent? If each square were divided into 10 pieces, how many parts would be in the whole? What fraction of the whole grid is $\frac{1}{10}\%$ or 0.1%?

b. Shade in $\frac{1}{2}$ of one square. What would be the percent name for this number? Express this fraction of a percent as both a common fraction of 1% and a decimal fraction of 1%. What is the decimal fraction name (not percent) of this number?

c. Extend this thinking to $\frac{3}{4}\%$. Subdivide a small square into 10 parts. You could shade in $\frac{7}{10}$ but that would be too small and $\frac{8}{10}$ is too large. Since $\frac{3}{4}$ or $\frac{75}{100}$ lies between $\frac{7}{10}$ and $\frac{8}{10}$, divide the same square again to create a 10-by-10 grid. Each of these small squares is what fraction of one percent? Of the whole or the entire grid?

d. Reflect on your thinking in the activity above. How will this help students with their concept of percent? Their concept of decimals?

12. Jeremy had shaded in one eighth of a hundred grid. He counted $12\frac{1}{2}$ squares. He wrote $12\frac{1}{2}\%$ for his answer. How would you help extend his thinking so that he realizes that 12.5% is also an appropriate answer? Extend this idea to finding the percent equivalent for $\frac{1}{3}$.

13. When asked to shade in 0.5%, Joss shaded 50 out of a hundred squares. How could you help correct his thinking?

14. For the last several months, Sioux Falls shoppers have been paying a "temporary" 1% sales tax for street repairs. Recently, in discussing the current status of this tax, a reporter said, "Out of every dollar you spend in Sioux Falls, 1 cent goes for street repairs." What is wrong with this statement? How would you help a student who shared this misconception?

OPERATIONS WITH PERCENT

In the section "Ratios and Equivalent Ratios" examples were given to show that ratios can be added only if the comparisons are part to whole and the wholes are the same. Percents should be approached similarly. They can be added, but special precautions must be taken. For example, if 30% of the people in one city read newspaper A and 25% read newspaper B, it does not follow that 55% read A or B. It could be the case that 25% of the people read only newspaper A; 5% read both A and B; and 20% read only newspaper B. Given this information the student can then correctly state that 50% of the people read A or B (Figure 12-38). Since the parts to be added were not disjoint, some of the people would have been counted twice if 30% and 25% had been added directly.

25% A only
5% A and B
20% B only
50% A or B

FIGURE 12-38.
Combining percents.

If students know only that 15% of the people in city A read a certain newspaper and 25% of the people in city B read the same newspaper, they cannot say anything about what percent of the people from both cities read that paper. If the 15% represents 15 people out of 100 people and the 25% represents 50 people out of 200 people, the new ratio is 65 people out of 300 people. This percent is slightly more than 21%; it is not 40% (15% + 25%). Since the wholes were not the same, the percents or parts of the whole could not be added directly. This is similar to the problem regarding wins and games played shown in Figure 12-5.

Alternatively, the following example shows how the numbers of the percents can be simply added or subtracted to yield a correct new percent. "Marsha, a sixth-grader, spent 40% of her weekly allowance on Monday and 35% on Tuesday. What percent of her allowance did she have left for the rest of the week?" In solving this problem, the students added 40% and 35% to yield 75% and then subtracted that number from 100% to find that Marsha has only 25% of her allowance left. In this situation the whole was the same, and the percents to be added or subtracted were disjoint.

In the past, percent problems have been categorized into three different types.

Type 1: 35% of 20 is _____.

Problem situation:	Given that Sarah made 35% of her shots in a ball-game, how many shots did she make if she attempted a total of 20 shots?

Traditional procedure: $\begin{array}{r} 20 \\ \times\ .35 \end{array}$

Proportion procedure: $\frac{35}{100} = \frac{x}{20}$.

Type 2: _____% of 20 is 7.

Problem situation:	Given that Sarah made 7 out of 20 shots in a basket-ball game, what percent of her shots did she make?

Traditional procedure: $20\overline{)7.00}$

Proportion Procedure: $\frac{x}{100} = \frac{7}{20}$

Type 3: 35% of _____ is 7.

Problem situation:	Given that Sarah made 35% of her shots and alto-gether made 7 shots, how many shots did she attempt?

Traditional procedure: $.35\overline{)7.00}$

Proportion procedure: $\frac{35}{100} = \frac{7}{x}$

If the "three different types" are compared, the only difference is the unknown. The unknown in type 1 is the part; in type 2, the percent; and in type 3, the whole. Often these types were developed without meaning, and the students were simply expected to memorize rules about when and what to multiply or divide for any one type. When students encountered percents in problem sets or in real life, they did not know which rule to apply. The students were unable to decide what numbers were to be multiplied or divided.

However, these concepts can and should be developed meaningfully rather than rotely. Part–whole concepts can be extended to teach students how models and proportions, often combined with mental computations, can be applied to solve percent problems. For example, models can be used to build the concept that 50% of 38 can be mentally computed as $\frac{1}{2}$ of 38 or 38 ÷ 2. When proportions are used, the "procedure" is the same for all three types. The proportion is set up so that the part-to-whole ratio is equal to the percent-to-100 ratio. Then the student solves the proportion for whichever number (part, whole, or percent) is unknown. Using proportions to solve percent problems not only makes them easier to solve but also helps to reinforce the concept that a percent is simply a special form of a ratio.

In "Position Paper: Teaching and Learning Percent" by a committee, chaired by David Dye from the Minnesota Department of Education, the following position is stated with regard to percent.

Case III is hardly ever encountered in life situations and is most difficult for students to understand and use. Case I is most commonly used in everyday life and Case II is occasionally met. Teachers should not emphasize nor require the identification of problem situations by Case I, Case II, or Case III. . . . In using the proportion method of solution as advocated above for students in seventh grade, the three cases are all basically solved by the same method. So in drill and practice without problem situations, students should be introduced to all three cases. However, when applications and problem solving are to be worked on, Case I should receive the most attention, Case II a lesser amount and Case III should probably not be required of all students.

In light of this position paper and of the order in which percent is discussed in elementary textbook series, the situations for finding a percent of a number will be presented first in this text. Since most people use mental computations to solve percent problems in everyday life, mental computations as well as proportions will be explored. In the next sections, models will be used to develop *meaning for the relationships between percents and numbers*. The emphasis will be on part/whole. These sections will emphasize how to teach mental computation while developing these relationships. The same models and similar procedures and questions are appropriate for paper-and-pencil computation. At the end of this section these types will be extended and rediscussed with regard to story situations.

PERCENT OF A NUMBER

Mental computations are used by most adults to get an answer or an estimate in percent applications. A large number of the percents that are commonly used are percents such as 10%, 50%, 25%, and $33\frac{1}{3}$%, which are easy to compute mentally. Since students are also somewhat familiar with these common percents and their related fractions, these percents should be emphasized in introducing the concept of a percent of a number. By focusing on such percents, students can also learn to solve these problems using mental computations.

Just as children's first introduction to

one fourth was always with an object partitioned into exactly four sections, students' first introduction to percents should be with objects that are composed of exactly 100 parts. A ten-by-ten grid is a convenient model. If 54% or $\frac{54}{100}$ of the whole is shaded, 54 squares is the part being considered, or 54% of 100 squares is 54 squares. If 30% or $\frac{30}{100}$ of the whole is shaded, the part, 30% of 100 squares or 30 squares, is being considered. If 50% or $\frac{50}{100}$ or $\frac{1}{2}$ of the whole is shaded, the part, 50% of 100 ($\frac{1}{2}$ of 100) or 50, is being considered.

When this thinking is extended to wholes other than 100, the percents should be compatible with the wholes (for example, 10% of 50 rather than 10% of 55 or 25% of 40 rather than 25% of 67), so that the numbers are easy to compute. Class discussions using models should be used to introduce easy percents such as 100%, 10%, and 1% of a number. These first experiences are easy to compute mentally and form the basis for estimating and computing with other percents. The part/whole language should be used to explore these relationships. For the example in Figure 12-39a, if we want 100%, we want the whole thing, so 100% of 100 is 100, 100% of 40 is 40, and 100% of 4 is 4. For examples involving 10%, the students should reason, "If the whole is 100, then the part is 10% of 100 or $\frac{1}{10}$ of 100 or 10. If 30 is the whole, then the part is 10% of 30 or $\frac{1}{10}$ of 30, which is 3" (Figure 12-39b). Similarly, for 1% if the whole is 100, the part is 1% or $\frac{1}{100}$ of 100, which is 1. When the whole is 200, the part is 1% of 200 or $\frac{1}{100}$ of 200, which is 2 (Figure 12-39c).

Percents that are near 1%, 10%, or 100% can be rounded to obtain numbers that are easy to compute mentally. To solve 12.3% of $234.56, Sue decided an estimate of 10% of $235 or about $24 was sufficient for her purposes. After solving 96.7% of 345

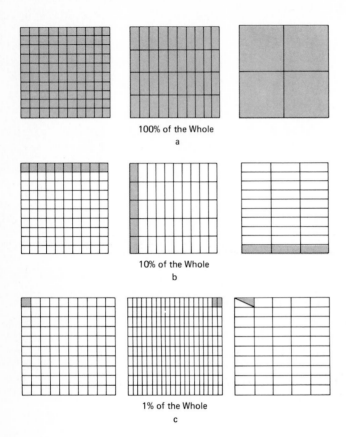

FIGURE 12-39.
100%, 10%, or 1% of the whole.

100% of the Whole
a

10% of the Whole
b

1% of the Whole
c

on her calculator, Ilka observed that her answer of 333.6 was reasonable as 100% of 345 is 345 and her answer should be a little less than 345.

Mental computations for 1%, 10%, and 100% are the basis for mentally calculating 2%, 20%, or 200%. In these situations the students need to be able to reason as follows, "20% of 320. . . . 10% or $\frac{1}{10}$ of 320 is 32, so 20% is twice as much or 64. 2% of 560. . . . 1% of 560 is 5.6, so 2% is twice as much or 11.2." In some cases the students should round the numbers to be able to do the calculations easily. For example, 20% of $4.68. . . . 10% or $\frac{1}{10}$ of $4.68 is about $0.47, so 20% is twice as much or 94 cents.

Through discussion, students can be taught to extend this thinking further to include percents such as 3%, 4%, 30%, 400%, 5%, or 15%. A number of individuals use this type of thinking for various applications. For example, to figure the sales tax at a 4% rate, Lou reasoned, "4% of $56.79. . . . 1% . . . $\frac{1}{100}$ of $56.79 is 57 cents, so 4% is 4 times that amount, so 57 . . . 114 . . . 228, $2.28." To figure a 5% sales tax, Kara thought, "5% of $4.85. . . . 10% of $4.85 is $0.49, so 5% is one half that amount. $\frac{1}{2}$ of 49. . . . $\frac{1}{2}$ of 50 is 25, so about 25 cents." Kevin used similar reasoning to figure a 15% tip. The bill was $12.35 so Kevin reasoned, "10% of $12.35 is $1.24, so 5% would be one half of $1.24 or $0.62. $1.24 + $0.62 is $1.86."

Other common percents such as 50%,

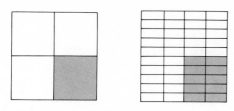

25% of the Whole

FIGURE 12-40.
25% of the whole.

25%, 20%, and $33\frac{1}{3}$% can also be easily calculated mentally for finding percents of numbers. As in the cases discussed above, the percents should be changed to the common fraction equivalent. The fractional part of the whole is then found by multiplying the fraction times the whole. To help students conceptualize this process, models such as those shown in Figure 12-40 can be used. Teacher questions should include, "What percent or fraction do we want? What is the whole? What is the part?" From these models the students can readily see that 25% of 4 or $\frac{1}{4}$ of 4 is 1 or that 25% of 20 or $\frac{1}{4}$ of 20 is 5. This can be extended to 75% of a number by considering $\frac{1}{4}$ of the whole and then three times that result.

For 20% of the whole, students can think of $\frac{1}{5}$ of the number or find 10% of a number and then double that result. For example, to mentally compute 20% of 36, the student could think "20%.... $\frac{1}{5}$ of 36 ... too hard, so $\frac{1}{5}$ of 35 would be 7. So 20% of 36 is a little more than 7." Alternatively, the student may think, "10% of 36 is 3.6, so 20% is twice as much or 7.2." This thinking could also be extended to percents such as 40% and 60% or $33\frac{1}{3}$% and $66\frac{2}{3}$%.

Set models should also be used to develop this thinking (Figure 12-41). To solve these problems students will need to determine the whole by counting. To find 50% of

the whole, they simply count the whole and take $\frac{1}{2}$ of that amount. For the model in Figure 12-41a the student would think "50% of the whole or $\frac{1}{2}$ of 8 is 4. 50% or $\frac{1}{2}$ of 7 ... $3\frac{1}{2}$ in each part." To find 25% of the whole, they will need to determine $\frac{1}{4}$ of the set. For the second example (Figure 12-41b), the thinking could be "25 percent of the whole ... $\frac{1}{4}$ of 6 is less than two.... $\frac{1}{2}$ of 6 is 3, so $\frac{1}{4}$ of 6 is $1\frac{1}{2}$." This thinking can be extended to similar problems. For example, for finding 75% of the whole of 12, the student will need

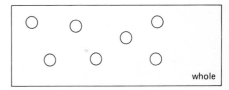

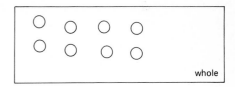

a   50% of the whole

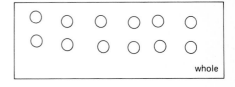

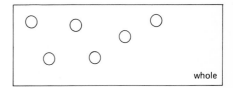

b   25% of the whole

FIGURE 12-41.
Percent of the whole set.

to think, "75% is $\frac{3}{4}$, $\frac{1}{4}$ of twelve would be three . . . so 3 fourths or 3 times 3 is 9."

After students have learned to find percents of numbers using common fractions, this skill can be extended to estimating other problems. In these cases students should estimate answers by *rounding* percents to common fractions. For the problem 35% of 75, 35% could be rounded to $\frac{1}{3}$, as 35% is near $33\frac{1}{3}$. One third of 75 is 25, so 35% of 75 is a little more than 25. In some cases students may also want to round the whole to a compatible number. For the problem 18% of 62, students could round 18% to 20% and then reason, "Twenty percent of 62 or $\frac{1}{5}$ of 62. . . . $\frac{1}{5}$ of 60 is 12.

Activities should also be included to help students develop the concept of the percent of a number when the percents are

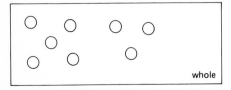

300% of the Whole

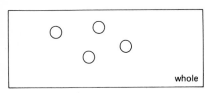

150% of the Whole

75% of the Whole

FIGURE 12-42.
Is the part greater than the whole?

more than 100%. Models should be used in discussions about whether the part will be smaller or larger than the whole (Figure 12-42). At first the students should simply identify the problems for which the part is greater than the whole. Next, they should estimate how large the part will be. In the first problem, the part is larger than the whole as 300% is 3 times as large as 100%. To solve the problem shown in Figure 12-42b, students could reason, "150% of 4 . . . answer will be more than 4 . . . $1\frac{1}{2}$ times as much. 100% is 4 . . . need 150%, so . . . 50% or $\frac{1}{2}$ more is 2 more, so . . . 4 plus 2 or 6." For part c they should recognize that the part will be less than eight, as 75% is less than 100%.

When applications are introduced, they should also be explored conceptually and related to students' earlier work. Models can be used to introduce and illustrate the amount of interest at a 10 percent rate. For example, "What is 10% of 10 dollars?" Since the students know that 10% means 10 parts per 100, they write $\frac{10}{100}$, but this is equivalent to the fraction $\frac{1}{10}$. One tenth of 10 dollars is simply one dollar (Figure 12-43a). Similar logic was used to determine 10% of 5 dollars. The students exchanged one 5-dollar bill for five 1-dollar bills. They then exchanged each dollar bill for two 50-cent pieces. They had changed the 5-dollar bill to the form of ten 50-cent pieces and could then easily see that one tenth or 10% of 5 dollars was 50 cents. The students are simply finding equivalent fractions or ratios.

In all of the mental computation problems discussed above, multiplication was used. These problems, such as 50% of 16, are multiplication problems ($\frac{1}{2} \times$ 16) just as 3 sets of 5 and $\frac{1}{4}$ of a set of 20 are multiplication problems. Proportion also needs to be considered to extend students' concepts of percents. As the students encounter other types of percent problems, they could use

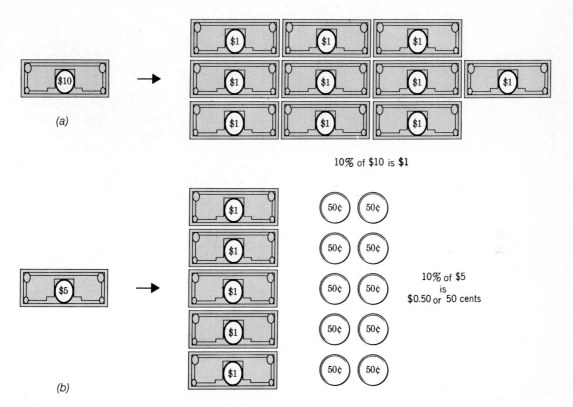

10% of $10 is $1

10% of $5
is
$0.50 or 50 cents

(a)

(b)

FIGURE 12-43.
Solving percent problems using money.

proportions to solve these problems. By continuing to build an understanding of the concepts and by analyzing the problems by part and whole, students will be able to select appropriate processes.

As discussed earlier, percents are simply special cases in ratio tables where the whole is one hundred (Figure 12-37). Consequently, the students could have set up the problem in Figure 12-43 as a proportion (Figure 12-44). In writing proportions to find the percent of a number, students should label the part and whole as they have done in the past. On the left-hand side of each proportion the students rewrote 10% as $\frac{10}{100}$. In the second part, they knew that the whole

was 5 dollars so they wrote 5 across from 100% or the whole. The unknown part of 5 dollars was written directly across from 10% or the part that was being considered.

$$\frac{\text{Part}}{\text{Whole}} = \frac{\text{Part}}{\text{Whole}}$$

$$\frac{10}{100} = \frac{x}{10}$$

$$100x = 10 \times 10$$
$$100x = 100$$
$$x = 1$$

(a)

$$\frac{\text{Part}}{\text{Whole}} = \frac{\text{Part}}{\text{Whole}}$$

$$\frac{10}{100} = \frac{x}{5}$$

$$100x = 10 \times 5$$
$$100x = 50$$
$$x = 0.50$$

(b)

FIGURE 12-44.
Using proportions in money problems.

$$\frac{\text{Part}}{\text{Whole}} = \frac{\text{Part}}{\text{Whole}}$$

$$\frac{x}{18} = \frac{25}{100}$$

$$100x = 18 \cdot 25$$

$$100x = 450$$

$$x = \$4.50$$

$$\$18.00 - \$4.50 = \$13.50$$

(a)

$$\frac{\text{Part}}{\text{Whole}} = \frac{\text{Part}}{\text{Whole}}$$

$$\frac{x}{18} = \frac{25}{100}$$

$$\frac{x}{18} = \frac{1}{4}$$

$$4x = 18$$

$$x = 4.50$$

$$\$18.00 - \$4.50 = \$13.50$$

(b)

FIGURE 12-45.
Using proportion to find sale price.

There are numerous examples of the use of percents in everyday life; a number of these are two-step story problems. One problem is "Jeanine went shopping for a new pair of slacks. She found a pair she liked that was marked $18.00. All slacks were on sale for 25% off. What price should Jeanine expect to pay?" Jeanine could have used the solution shown in Figure 12-45a. After she determined that her discount was $4.50, she subtracted $4.50 from $18.00 to determine the sale price. Since Jeanine did not have paper and pencil handy, she did the problem mentally, using a thought pattern similar to the proportion shown in Figure 12-45b. Since $\frac{1}{4}$ is equivalent to $\frac{25}{100}$, she divided 18 by 4 to obtain $4.50, and then she subtracted.

When proportions are used to find the percent of a number, students can use a calculator to find the cross products. When an equation or multiplication approach is used, students will probably change the percent (25% of 18) to its decimal equivalent (0.25 × 18). Percents can be computed directly on a number of calculators; for example, 25% of 18 becomes ⊡ ⊡ ⊠ ⊡ ⊡ ⊡ on some calculators. The advantage is that students can enter the percent directly rather than having to change it to a decimal fraction. Using the percent key on calculators is discussed in Appendix A.

FINDING WHAT PERCENT ONE NUMBER IS OF ANOTHER

In a previous section, ratios and fractions were represented as percents. In these cases a part-to-whole comparison was being made. The same comparison is being made to determine what percent one number is of another number. The decision that needs to be made is what is the part and what is the whole. Once the part and whole are determined, it is simply a matter of changing the ratio or fraction to a percent.

Grids, money, number lines, and regions are some of the models used in *Ratio, Proportion and Scaling* to introduce what percent one number is of another. Some similar activities are shown in Figure 12-46. The unknown or percent is the comparison between the part and whole. In each case the whole is defined. The students should use estimation to note which parts are greater than the whole, that is, which percents would be greater than one hundred percent. They should also estimate which parts would be about 50% or less than 10%.

In these introductory activities the whole is usually one hundred and the students are asked to compare the part and the whole. After students have explored this concept, their experiences should be extended to include applications and problems where the size of the whole varies. Some of the problems will involve familiar fractions for which the students know the equivalent percent. For example, what percent of the original seating capacity does a room have if 10 of the 25 chairs in the room have been removed? Fifteen, the part or the current number of chairs, is compared to 25, the whole or original number of chairs. Fifteen twenty-fifths is $\frac{60}{100}$ or 60%.

In other cases the students may find it easier to set up proportions or use a calcu-

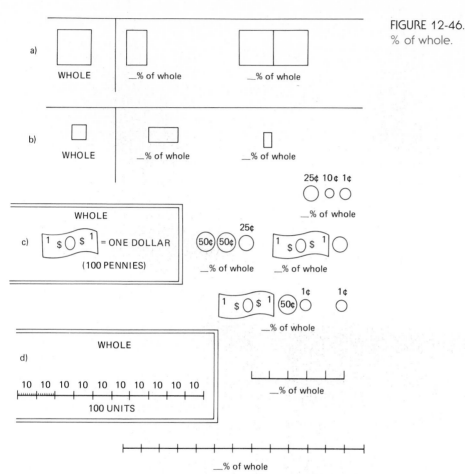

FIGURE 12-46.
% of whole.

lator to find the percent. One example came from an advertisement students found in a local newspaper. "A bicycle originally selling for $95 was on sale for $57. What was the discount rate?" Two different approaches the students used to solve this problem are shown in Figure 12-47. In the first example, the part or discount of $38 was compared to the whole or original price of $95. In the second case the sale price of $57 was considered the part. Since the sale price was 60% of the whole or original price, the discount is 100% − 60% or 40%.

As can be seen from the previous examples, there is more than one method to solve these problems. For each problem the students must carefully analyze the relationships between the numbers and not just assume that the smaller number is the part. In one situation Deanna wanted to compare her current running time of 55 minutes to her original time. When she first started, she ran 25 minutes. The whole is 25 minutes, her original time. The part is her new time of 55 minutes. Since the part is larger, the percent will be greater than one hundred.

```
 $ 95   original price
-$ 57   discount price
 $ 38   discount
```

$$\frac{Part}{Whole} = \frac{Part}{Whole} \qquad\qquad \frac{Part}{Whole} = \frac{Part}{Whole}$$

$$\frac{x}{100} = \frac{38}{95} \qquad\qquad\qquad \frac{x}{100} = \frac{57}{95}$$

$$95x = 38 \times 100 \qquad\qquad 95x = 57 \times 100$$

$$95x = 3800 \qquad\qquad\qquad 95x = 5700$$

$$x = 40 \qquad\qquad\qquad\qquad x = 60$$

40% discount   60% sale

FIGURE 12-47.
Using proportion to find discount rate.

As discussed earlier, students should not memorize three different categories of percent problems and how to solve them. They should be introduced to one type at a time with a large number of experiences with models and using part/whole language. After they have been introduced to both percent of a number and finding what percent one number is of another, they should be involved in activities where they analyze the situations. By determining whether the percent, part, or whole is given, they can then decide what relationships are known and how to solve the problems. Figure 12-48 shows a lesson designed to discriminate between the two different types. In the example, drawings for the knowns and the unknown are used to illustrate the problems. In the problems that follow the students are asked to decide what is to be found. This is followed by solving the problems and using mental arithmetic to check reasonableness of results.

FINDING A NUMBER WHEN A PERCENT OF IT IS KNOWN

The third percent case is finding a number when a percent of it is known. In this situation the percent and the part are known but not the whole. To help students develop this concept, activities with models and part/whole language are again needed. Figure 12-49 shows some examples that have been modified from *Ratio, Proportion and Scaling*. The teacher should use part/whole language to help the students conceptualize, estimate, and answer these problems. Questions should be conceptually oriented; for example, "Is this a part or a whole? Is the whole larger? About how large (or small)—a little or a lot larger (smaller)? What is the whole?"

To solve problem (b) of Figure 12-49, students would need to recognize that the class is the whole and the 4 students are the part. The four students comprise 20 percent or $\frac{1}{5}$ of the class. The whole class is 100% or 5 fifths so 5 times 1 fifth or 5×4 is 20 students. For problem (d) the students should estimate that since the part is 30% the whole would be a little more than 3 times larger. 3 times 6 is 18 or 90%, so the answer will be more than 18. For an exact answer, 6 is 30 percent, so 2 would be 10 percent. Since 10% is 2, 100% is 20. For problem (f), the part is 150%, so the whole of 100% is smaller. Since 150% is $1\frac{1}{2}$ or $\frac{3}{2}$, the part should be split into three parts to show 3 halves. Two of the parts should be shaded to show 1 whole or 100%.

An application of finding the whole is, "The 80 students in the fifth-grade class at Brush School represent 12.5% of the school's enrollment. What is the total enrollment?" The solution was found using proportions (Figure 12-50). In part (a) one student renamed $\frac{12.5}{100}$ to $\frac{125}{1000}$ to avoid decimals. In part (b) another student recognized that 12.5% or $\frac{12.5}{100}$ was equivalent to $\frac{1}{8}$, substituted $\frac{1}{8}$ in the problem, and solved accordingly.

When students are introduced to all "three cases" of percent problems, the main difficulty is being able to determine what procedure to use. Rather than memorizing pro-

STRATEGIES for PROBLEM SOLVING

9 PROBLEM SOLVING
Do You Find a Percent or Percent of a Number?

How do you determine what kind of percent problem you need to solve? Look at the information in the problem. Then use a diagram to help you.

Fairfax School has 800 students. 20% are seventh graders. How many students are seventh graders?

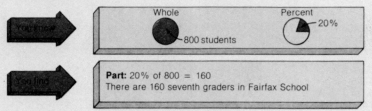

Part: 20% of 800 = 160
There are 160 seventh graders in Fairfax School

Of the 800 students in Fairfax School, 600 take music. What percent of the students take music?

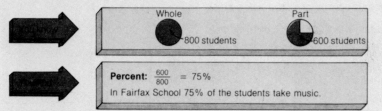

Percent: $\frac{600}{800}$ = 75%
In Fairfax School 75% of the students take music.

TRYOUT EXERCISES Write PART or PERCENT to show what must be found. Then solve. Check using 1%, 10%, or 50%.

1. If 15% of the 800 students are in the band, how many are in the band?
Part; 120 students

2. Of the 800 students, 400 are ninth graders. What percent are ninth graders?
Percent; 50%

3. A band uniform is priced at $89. The school gets a 20% discount. What is the amount of discount?
Part; $17.80

4. The list price for a glee club robe is $60. The discount to the school is $15. What is the percent of discount?
Percent; 25%

FIGURE 12-48.
Percent discrimination. (From Joseph Payne et al., **Harper & Row Mathematics**, Grade 7, p. 364. Copyright © 1985 Macmillan, Inc. Reprinted with permission of Scribner Educational Publishers, a division of Macmillan, Inc.)

a

This is 1% of the bikes.
How many bikes altogether?

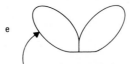

e

This is about 66% of the whole.
Draw 100% of the whole.

FIGURE 12-49.
The whole thing.

b

This is 20% of a class.
How many in the entire class?

f

This is 150% of the whole.
Shade the whole.

c

This is 75% of the cost.
Each one will be ___ % of the cost.
The total cost is $

d

This is 30% of the apples in a bag.
How many apples are in the bag?

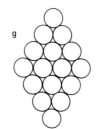

g

This is 160% of
the whole.
Shade 100% of the whole.

cedures, students should analyze the relationships among percents, parts, and wholes. In each of the "three cases," either the part, whole, or percent is missing, and the other two factors are known or can be derived. For students to solve percent problems successfully, they need to be able to classify the knowns and the unknown as being a part, a whole, or a percent. If students can successfully analyze or draw diagrams of the relationships, they can easily solve the problem.

Four approaches that use diagrams to analyze these relationships are shown in Figure 12-51. *Harper & Row Mathematics* uses circular diagrams to draw what is known and

what is unknown (Figure 12-51a). For each type of percent problem the knowns are diagrammed and the unknown is defined. The same story situations given in part (a) are used to illustrate the other diagrammatic ap-

$$\frac{\text{Part}}{\text{Whole}} = \frac{\text{Part}}{\text{Whole}}$$

$$\frac{12.5}{100} = \frac{80}{x}$$

$$\frac{125}{1000} = \frac{80}{x}$$

$$125x = 80,000$$

$$x = 640$$

(a)

$$\frac{\text{Part}}{\text{Whole}} = \frac{\text{Part}}{\text{Whole}}$$

$$\frac{12.5}{100} = \frac{80}{x}$$

$$\frac{1}{8} = \frac{80}{x}$$

$$x = 8 \cdot 80$$

$$x = 640$$

(b)

FIGURE 12-50.
Using proportion to find total enrollment.

proaches to percent problems. A second approach, Venn diagrams, is shown in part (b). One diagram is labeled percent and represents the percent being considered and 100 percent. The other diagram is quantity, the part and the whole. The proportions that can be written from these drawings are shown beside each diagram.

The last two methods shown in Figure 12-51c and d are similar as they are based on number lines. In part (d) the number line was modified to include a shaded area. In both of these approaches, the number line has two scales. The top scale involves percent, and the other scale involves quantity. Along the scale the quantities for 0, the part, and the whole are matched, respectively, with 0%, the percent, and 100%. The cor-

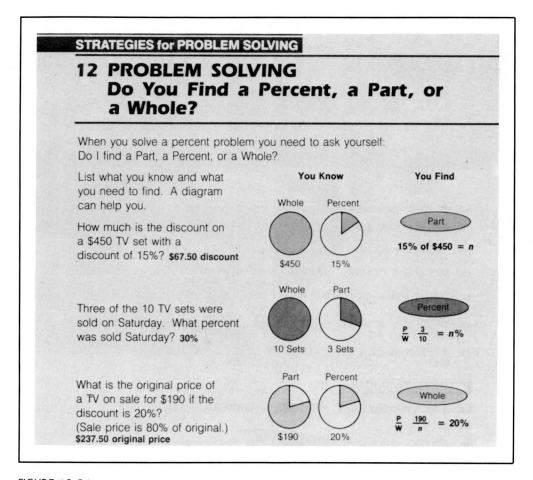

FIGURE 12-51a.

Diagramming percent relationships. (From Joseph Payne et al., **Harper & Row Mathematics**, Grade 8, p. 262. Copyright © 1985 Macmillan, Inc. Reprinted with permission of Scribner Educational Publishers, a division of Macmillan, Inc.)

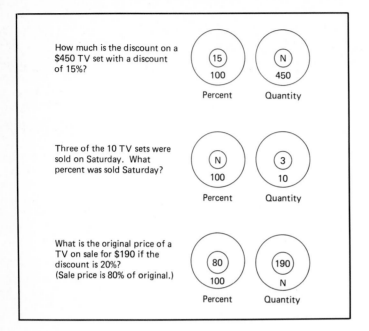

FIGURE 12-51b.

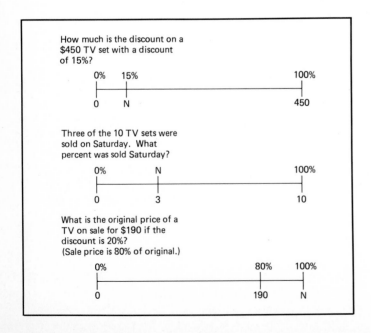

FIGURE 12-51c.

FIGURE 12-51d.

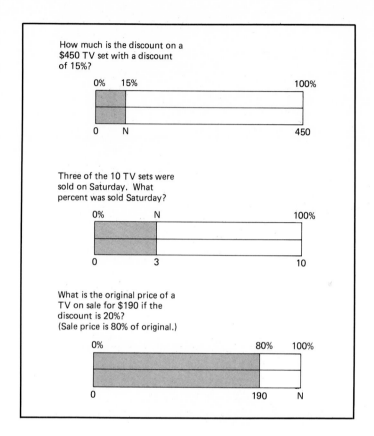

responding proportions are written beside each diagram.

Students should learn to use at least one of these diagrammatic procedures. If they are able to draw a picture of the situation, they should be able to solve the problem successfully. Once the problem is diagrammed, they can simply use proportions or the relationship that a percent times a whole is the part.

After students have been introduced to the three percent cases, they should be involved in discrimination tasks to determine what is given—part, whole, or percent. Later, students should analyze the same problems,

but this time they could also draw diagrams and/or estimate answers. They should also set up the proportion and/or equation. To emphasize the process and analysis, the students should have some lessons in which they do *not* solve the problems but simply analyze the situation and set up the process for solution.

The purpose of studying percent is to be able to apply it to situations in the real world. The applications and their specific vocabulary are reflected in the examples found in textbooks. In reviewing elementary textbook series on lessons and situations involving percent, a variety of situations and vocabulary were found. The majority of situ-

	PERCENT	PART	WHOLE
Sales Tax	tax rate	sales tax	amount of purchase
Income Tax	tax rate	income tax	taxable income
Discounts	discount rate	discount	original price regular price
		sale price = original − discount	
Markups	percent of markup	markup	purchase
		selling price = purchase price + markup	
Inflation	rate of inflation	inflation or price increase	original price
Percent of Increase and Decrease	percent of increase or decrease	increase or decrease	original
Simple interest	interest rate $i = p \cdot r \cdot t$	interest	principal
Compound interest	interest rate	interest	principal

FIGURE 12-52.
Terms found in percent problems.

ations involved finding the percent of the whole. There were relatively few examples of finding the whole.

The situations surveyed involved sales and income taxes, discounts, markups, simple interest, compound interest, inflation, and budgets (circle graphs). A number of these situations have their own special vocabulary which can prove confusing to adults as well as to middle school and junior high students. Throughout this chapter the vocabulary has focused on part, whole, and percent. New terms should be linked to these concepts. Figure 12-52 shows some of these terms classified as percent, part, or whole. Linking these terms to part, whole, and percent language will expedite student learning. Students need to become familiar with these terms and the relationships among them. (*Note:* The last two entries on simple and compound interest will also add a factor of time.)

QUESTIONS AND ACTIVITIES

1. a. Consider Figure 12-39a. How would you use these diagrams to help students generalize that 100% of *n* is *n*? How would you help students extend their thinking to 200% of *n*? 300% of *n*? Draw a diagram and write out appropriate student thinking for 300% of 4.

b. Consider Figure 12-39b. How would you use these diagrams to help students generalize that 10% of *n* is $\frac{1}{10}$ of *n*? How would you help students extend this thinking to 20% of *n*? 30% of *n*? Draw a diagram and write out appropriate student thinking for 30% of 40. Write out student thinking for 20% of 32.

c. Consider Figure 12-39c. How would you use these diagrams to help students generalize that 1% of *n* is $\frac{1}{100}$ of *n*? How would you help students extend this thinking to 2% of *n*? 3% of *n*? Draw a diagram and write out appropriate student thinking for 3% of 400. Write out student thinking for 2% of 32.

2. Consider Figure 12-40. Explain how to use the diagrams to help students find 25% of any number. How could you help students extend this to 75% of a number?

3. For each of the following problems, represent the set with the indicated number of counters. Find the part being considered by using the counters.

a. Whole is 10 counters; find 20% of the whole.
b. Whole is 5 counters; find 20% of the whole.
c. Whole is 15 counters; find 20% of the whole.
d. Whole is 12 counters; find 25% of the whole.
e. Whole is 12 counters; find 75% of the whole.
f. Whole is 10 counters; find 60% of the whole.

g. Whole is 15 counters; find 60% of the whole.
h. Whole is 6 counters; find 150% of the whole.
i. Whole is 8 counters; find 125% of the whole.

4. Find 35% of 568 by entering ⑤ ⑥ ⑧ ✕ ③ ⑤ ％ on your calculator. (Adjust your calculator code if necessary.) What happens if the 35% is entered before the 568? Do you get the same result?

5. Solve the following problems using the percent key on a calculator. What are your answers to the nearest whole percent? The nearest tenth of a percent?
a. 45% of $665
b. $12\frac{1}{2}$% of 345
c. $33\frac{1}{3}$% of 637
d. $87\frac{1}{2}$% of 74

6. Do this problem with another student. One person should do the problems below with a calculator and the other using mental computation. Which procedure is faster?
a. 25% of 600   b. $33\frac{1}{3}$% of 360
c. 50% of 436   d. 1% of 345
e. 10% of 23   f. 100% of 671
g. 20% of 60   h. 10% of 562

7. a. Analyze a unit on percent from an elementary textbook. How is the percent of a number introduced? Are models used? Is mental arithmetic incorporated? Is estimation used?

b. Design, copy, and find supplementary materials to use with these lessons. The activities outlined in "Estimation and Mental Arithmetic with Percent" by Allinger and Payne would be helpful in planning.

8. Consider Figure 12-46. Estimate or determine the percents for the given parts and wholes.

9. Use cubes to represent the following problems.
a. Represent set *X* using four cubes and set *Y* using one cube. If set *X* is the whole and set *Y* is the part, *Y* is what

part or percent of X? If set Y is the whole and set X is the part, X is what part or percent of Y?

b. The numbers in set X and set Y are redefined as shown below. For each case, represent the sets and then fill in the chart by determining "X is what part of Y?" and "Y is what part of X?"

X	Y	X is what percent of Y?	Y is what percent of X?
2	5		
3	4		
3	1		
5	4		
3	8		

c. Can you find a pattern? If set X is 25% of set Y, set Y is what percent of set X? What can be stated about the size of sets X and Y? If set X is 400% of set Y, set Y is what percent of set X?

10. Reflect on the statements "A is _____% of B" and "A is what part of B." Which is conceptually more concrete? Why is it important to include both statements in the development of percent concepts?

11. Work through each of the examples in Figure 12-49 reflecting on the student thinking needed to solve each problem.

12. a. Write a story problem for each of the following examples.
    (1) 25% of 40 = _____
    (2) 25% of _____ = 10
    (3) _____ % of 40 = 10
    b. How could a student use ratio and proportion to solve each of these problems?

13. a. Sue in Ms. Jewell's class made a score of 96 out of 150 on the math test. John in Mr. Gauett's class made 275 out of 465 on his math test. John said, "I made

a better score than you did, Sue." Is he correct? Explain.
    b. Which would you rather have, Sue's score, John's score, or a 48 out of 75 on this test? Why?

14. a. 5 is _____ % of 4.
    b. How would you introduce this concept?

15. In an elementary textbook, find a lesson that includes more than one type of percent applications. In Figure 12-51, diagrams were used to illustrate percent problems. Choose two of these methods and draw diagrams to analyze these problems. *For your resource file:* For further information about drawing diagrams to analyze percent problems, read "Another Look at the Teaching of Percent" by Dewar.

16. In an elementary mathematics textbook, find a lesson that involves all three types of percent problems. Analyze each problem and determine what is known (part, whole, or percent) and what is unknown.

17. In reviewing five elementary textbook series, both proportions and the equation method were found. Some textbooks used only the equation approach for all three cases. The lessons showed situations rewritten as $X = N\% \times W$, with two of the variables known. Percents with proportions were not found in two series. Another text used only proportions.
    a. What advantages and disadvantages are there to using one approach? Two approaches?
    b. Consult a textbook series. What approach(es) is(are) used? Are the situations related to diagrams?

18. Joe's father makes $12,000 a year. He receives a raise of 10%. Two months later his company is having financial difficulty. All salaries are reduced 10%. Joe says, "My father's raise didn't make any difference. He still makes $12,000 a year." Devise a lesson to help Joe correct his mistake.

19. Jim receives $.75 an hour for babysitting for a family with two little boys. One night their

cousin was visiting so he received $1.00 an hour. Jim said, "I received a 25% increase." Try to figure out how Jim reached this erroneous conclusion. Draw diagrams of parts and wholes that would help Jim find his error.

TEACHER RESOURCES

Allinger, Glenn D., and Joseph N. Payne. "Estimation and Mental Arithmetic with Percent." In *Estimating and Mental Computation,* 1986 Yearbook of the National Council of Teachers of Mathematics. Reston, VA: The Council, 1986.

Brown, Gerald W., and Lucien B. Kinney. "Let's Teach Them About Ratio." *Mathematics Teacher 66* (April 1973): 352–355.

Bruni, James V., and Helene J. Silverman. "Let's Do It! From Blocks and Model Making to Ratio and Proportion." *Arithmetic Teacher 24* (March 1977): 172–180.

Carpenter, Thomas P., Mary Kay Corbitt, Henry S. Kepner, Mary Montgomery Lindquist, and Robert E. Reys. *Results of the Second National Assessment of the National Assessment of Educational Progress*. Reston, VA: National Council of Teachers of Mathematics, 1981.

Coburn, Terrence G. "Using the Calculator to Teach Decimal and Percent Concepts, Skills, and Applications." Presentation at the National Council of Teachers of Mathematics Regional Meeting at Cedar Rapids, IA, February 1985.

Dewar, Jacqueline. "Another Look at the Teaching of Percent." *Arithmetic Teacher 31* (March 1984): 48–49.

Driscoll, Mark. "What Research Says." *Arithmetic Teacher 28* (February 1981): 34–35, 46.

Duea, Joan, George Immerzeel, Earl Ockenga, and John Tarr. *Problem Solving Using Special Computations*. Cedar Falls, IA: Price Laboratory School, University of Northern Iowa.

———. *Problem Solving Using Tables*. Project Impact. Cedar Falls, IA: Price Laboratory School, University of Northern Iowa.

Dye, David, Chair of Committee for Minnesota Department of Education. "Position Paper: Teaching and Learning Percent." St. Paul, MN: Department of Education, 1981.

Glatzer, David. "Teaching Percentage: Ideas and Suggestions." *Arithmetic Teacher 31* (February 1984): 24–26.

Mathematics Resource Project. *Ratio, Proportion and Scaling*. Palo Alto, CA: Creative Publications, 1977.

National Assessment of Educational Progress. *The Third National Mathematics Assessment: Results, Trends, and Issues*. Denver, CO: Education Commission of the States, April 1983.

Payne, Joseph N. "Curricular Issues: Teaching Rational Numbers." *Arithmetic Teacher 31* (February 1984): 14–17.

Skypeck, Dora Helen B. "Special Characteristics of Rational Numbers." *Arithmetic Teacher 31* (February 1984): 10–12.

Smart, James. "The Teaching of Percent Problems." *School Science and Mathematics 80* (March 1980): 187–192.

Van de Walle, John. "Fraction and Decimal Numeration Suggestions for Curriculum Revision." Presentation at Annual Meeting of National Council of Teachers of Mathematics, San Antonio, TX, April 1985.

Van Engen, Henry. "Rate Pairs, Fractions, and Rational Numbers." *Arithmetic Teacher 7* (December 1960): 389–399.

13
TEACHING STATISTICS AND PROBABILITY

"I don't see any reason to go to the inservice session on statistics and probability. After all, I'm a second-grade teacher."

How would you respond if this teacher were one of your colleagues?

Statistics and probability may seem to be rather advanced topics for the elementary mathematics classroom. In actual fact, however, children encounter these topics every day outside the classroom. If they also encounter these topics in the classroom, they will be better prepared to deal intelligently with their environment.

STATISTICS

Statistics is the study of the meaning and interrelationships of data. Even small children encounter statistics in daily living. When a father says to a child, "You have only been in bed on time two days this week," he is quoting a statistic. When a child says, "But, Mom, every girl on the block has a bicycle except me," she is quoting a statistic. In modern society practically everything is organized and analyzed numerically; this is statistics.

Many of the statistical concepts that we use daily are quite easy to understand. Children should be introduced to these concepts in the elementary school in order to develop an awareness of and a capacity to judge statistical information. Of course, the teacher must also understand these concepts to guide the student's development.

GRAPHING

One way of looking at data is through the use of graphs. Graphing is a part of statistics since graphs are one way of organizing and studying data. Reading, interpreting, and constructing tables, graphs, and charts is one of the ten basic skill areas recommended by the National Council of Supervisors of Mathematics. Students need to learn not only how to read, analyze, and make inferences from graphs and charts but also how to organize numerical information into graphs, charts, and tables.

Simple graphing of data can be introduced to very young children through activities. For example, the class might want to collect information about when students' birthdays occurs. They could do this simply by writing on the board each child's name and the month in which that child's birthday occurs (Figure 13-1). This would not be very useful for answering general questions about birthdays. The children would find that it is a long process to determine which month contains the most birthdays. Just answering the question, "Are there any months that have no birthdays and, if so, which ones?" would require checking each of the twelve months until either a birthday in that month was found or the entire list had been checked. From a few questions like these, even very young children can soon see the need to organize their information.

Probably the easiest way to organize this information would be in a simple pictograph in which each picture (symbol) in the graph represents one item. The children could write their names on paper birthday cakes to represent their birthdays. Then each one could place a cake beside the appropriate month (Figure 13-2). By simply looking at the graph and counting, children could now answer many questions about birthdays. "Which month has the most birthdays?" "Do any months have no birthdays?" "How many birthdays are there in June?" "How many months have exactly two birthdays?"

One problem that may arise in interpreting this graph is that a child may say that March contains more birthdays than June or August. Instead of counting the number of cakes in a row, this child is looking at how long a line the cakes make. This problem can be avoided by making sure that the sym-

FIGURE 13-1.
Unorganized list of birthdays.

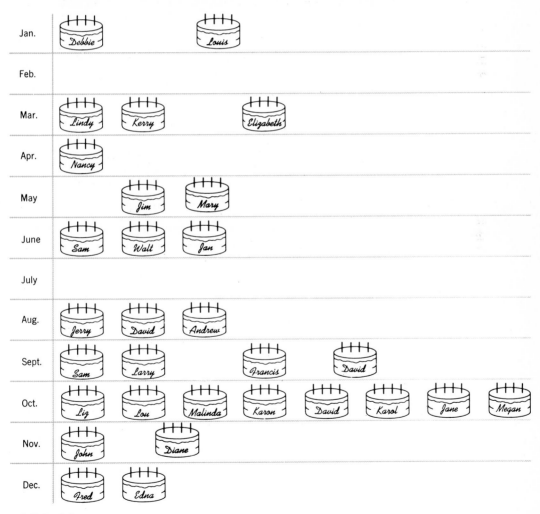

FIGURE 13-2.
Pictograph of birthdays.

Jan	Debbie	Louis								
Feb										
Mar	Lindy	Kerry	Elizabeth							
Apr	Nancy									
May	Mary	Jim								
Jun	Sam	Walt	Jan							
Jul										
Aug	Jerry	David	Andrew							
Sep	Sam	Larry	David	Francis						
Oct	Liz	Lou	Malinda	Karon	David	Karol	Jane	Megan		
Nov	John	Diane								
Dec	Fred	Edna								

FIGURE 13-3.
Bar graph of birthdays.

bols being used to make the graph are lined up exactly. This could be done, using the same graph shown in Figure 13-2, by marking each row into spaces and consecutively putting exactly one cake in each space starting beside the name of the month.

Alternatively, in the same type of chart children could simply write their names in the appropriate spaces (Figure 13-3). In this graph it is easy to see at a glance that the number of birthdays contained in March, June, and August is the same and the number in September is one more. This is a beginning form of a bar graph. Each space that contains a name could be colored in to make horizontal bars whose lengths would correspond to the number of birthdays represented.

8							
7	Evelyn						
6	Craig						
5	Carol			Debbie			
4	Terry		Robyn	Glenn			
3	Louie		Frances	Bob	Gussie	Beth	
2	Diane		Edna	Ann	Carolyn	Nerrida	Gary
1	Jane		Joe	John	Don	Kara	Kim
	Red	Orange	Yellow	Green	Blue	Purple	Black

FIGURE 13-4.
Bar graph of favorite colors.

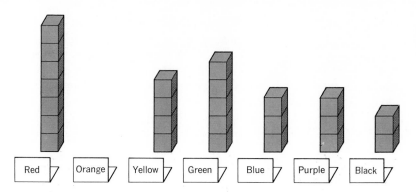

FIGURE 13-5.
Bar graph using blocks
(favorite colors).

A similar bar graph could be made using vertical bars. Figure 13-4 shows a vertical graph of favorite colors. The children write their names in the column above their favorite colors. Bars could be filled in using the appropriate color for each column.

As children's understanding of graphs matures, they will probably realize that in most cases it does not make any difference who has chosen red as a favorite color. The important information is how many people have chosen red as a favorite color. This idea could be developed by forming the same graph with a different procedure. Each child could pick out a wooden cube of the appropriate color. These cubes could then be stacked beside cards of the corresponding colors (Figure 13-5).

To help children progress from this form of a bar graph to a more abstract form, two-centimeter cubes or one-inch cubes and the corresponding graph paper could be used. First, the stacks of cubes could be lined up on the graph paper (Figure 13-6a). Later,

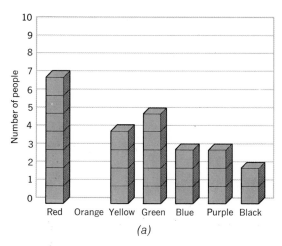

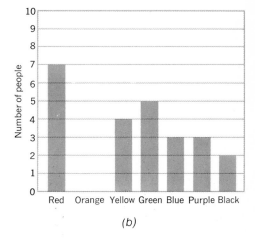

FIGURE 13-6.
Bar graphs of favorite colors.

graph paper alone could be used and bars of the appropriate height colored (Figure 13-6b).

These first graphs are very simple and go from concrete to pictorial representations. Before children are involved in drawing and labeling graphs such as in Figure 13-6b, they will be involved in reading and interpreting graphs. As part of interpreting graphs they will need to discuss what attributes are being measured and how the data are recorded. The importance of labeling graphs and knowing the source of the data should be discussed as the children interpret graphs. As they construct their own graphs, labels and sources should be part of the graphs.

As the children gain skill in reading, interpreting, and making bar graphs, they can use them to represent many kinds of information. The bar graphs shown in Figure 13-7 are more sophisticated. The graphs include axes marked in intervals other than by ones. Two of the scales do not start with zero. Students should be given opportunities to read such graphs before constructing them. They should discuss why such intervals were chosen. As they start to construct their own graphs, discussions about desirable scales should precede making their own graphs.

At the intermediate level after the student has used simple pictographs and bar graphs, a more sophisticated form of pictograph can be introduced. In this type of pictograph, each symbol used represents multiple units instead of only one unit. For example, Mr. Re's third-grade class wanted to make a pictograph of birthdays similar to the one shown earlier. However, they wanted to include all the students in the entire third grade instead of just those in their classroom. Since there were three third-grade classes with a total of 98 students, they didn't want to draw one cake for each student. They decided to have each cake represent four students, and they made the graph shown in Figure 13-8.

In constructing this graph, the students encountered some difficulties. With each cake representing four birthdays, it was easy to draw the symbols for months such as June with 12 birthdays or July with 4 birthdays. But since February contained only 2 birthdays, they had trouble. Don suggested that they could draw a small cake that was only half as big as the others. Becky thought it would be too hard to tell exactly what size "half-as-big" should be so she suggested drawing half a cake. Some of the students still thought it would be difficult to tell the difference between a half cake and a fourth of a

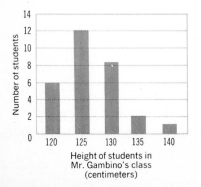

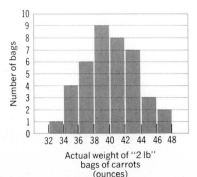

FIGURE 13-7.
Bar graphs.

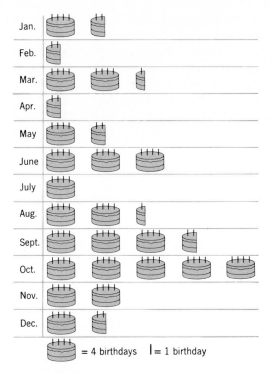

FIGURE 13-8.
Pictograph of birthdays.

candle on top of a cake or part of a cake represents one birthday.

In this case the students found a simple solution to the problem. However, since each symbol in a pictograph may represent several hundred, thousand, or million items, this type of solution is not usually possible. Figure 13-9 shows a pictograph of the ships of several countries. Each symbol represents 200 ships. In interpreting the partial ships the student must decide what aspect of the figure to consider. For example, are 100 ships represented by a figure half as long or one with half as much area?

Another type of graph introduced in the elementary school is the line graph. A line graph, sometimes called a frequency polygon, can be easily made from a bar graph like the one shown in Figure 13-7b. This is done by simply connecting the mid-points of the tops of the bars as shown in Figure 13-10.

Line graphs have the advantage of being able to show change over time. For example, the changing stock market prices are usually represented on a line graph. The line graph can easily be used to compare two sets of similar data on the same graph. Figure 13-11 shows a line graph that compares the data on how students in two different classes spent their time. The black line represents one class; the white line represents a different class.

cake. Then Gwendolyn suggested that they put four candles on each whole cake. In this way they could have two candles on a half cake and one candle on a fourth cake. They decided to use Gwendolyn's idea. Thus their graph has a dual key since one cake with its candles represents four birthdays but each

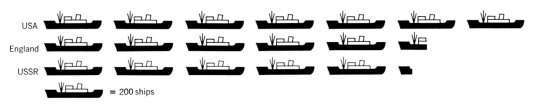

FIGURE 13-9.
Pictograph of trading ships.

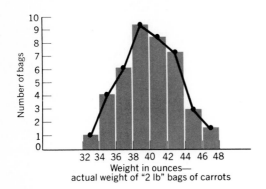

FIGURE 13-10.
Line graph of bar graph.

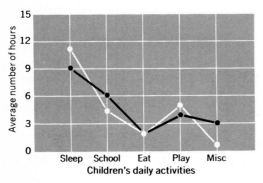

FIGURE 13-11.
Line graph of two sets of data.

As students work with different types of graphs, there are some concepts that must be developed. Through class discussion of a few examples like those shown in Figure 13-12, students can quickly see the necessity of complete labeling on all graphs. Without complete labels the graphs are difficult or impossible to interpret. Thus students realize that all graphs need to be titled and labeled appropriately. A legend explaining any symbols used should be included.

Another concept that needs some development is the idea of the scale for the graph. The scale should be uniform and appropriate for the desired value. Figure 13-13 shows several different graphs of the same data each using a different scale.

Students should notice that the three graphs give quite different pictures of the data. For instance, in Figure 13-13b it looks as if there were more than twice as many chocolate pies sold as there were lemon pies. Figure 13-13a shows only a few more chocolate pies than lemon pies. Figure 13-13c is much harder to read because the scale is so small. However, for some types of data, it is necessary to use multiple units because otherwise the graph would be too large. (*Statistics* by Jane Jonas Srivastava describes graphs and statistics and in-

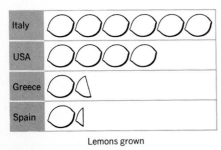

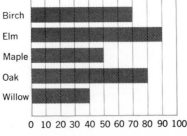

FIGURE 13-12.
Incomplete graphs.

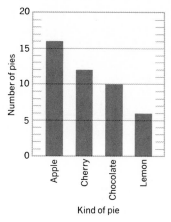

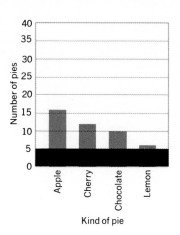

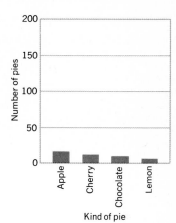

FIGURE 13-13.
Choosing an appropriate scale.

cludes activities for the elementary student. *Graphs* by Dyno Lowenstein contains a detailed development of graphs appropriate for the upper elementary student.)

One more type of graph used in the elementary school is the circle graph. The entire circle is considered the whole of some quantity such as weekly earnings. The whole is then broken down into appropriate parts indicating how it is used. For example, if half the circle is marked as "savings," students should interpret that half of that student's weekly earnings is put into savings. Figure 13-14 shows circle graphs indicating how two children spend their weekly earnings. To interpret a circle graph, students must consider what the whole is. Miriam and Jerry both spend the same amount of money ($0.50) for school supplies. However, this amount is one third of Jerry's weekly earnings but only one fourth of Miriam's weekly earnings.

When students first construct circle graphs, the circle is usually subdivided for them into parts such as 6, 8, 10, or 12. If

there were ten pieces of data such as 3 cats, 2 dogs, 4 hamsters, and 1 parrot, the circle would have been divided into ten parts. The students would then color the number of parts that correspond to each pet (Figure 13-15). Equivalent fractions are often encountered in interpreting or constructing circle graphs. If the whole circle represented 12 pieces of fruit and one fourth of it represented apples, there would be $\frac{1}{4}$ of 12 or 3 apples. Three of the 12 parts would be shaded.

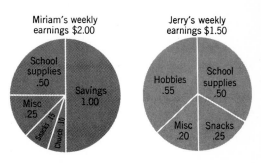

FIGURE 13-14.
Circle graphs.

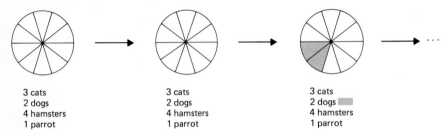

3 cats
2 dogs
4 hamsters
1 parrot

3 cats
2 dogs
4 hamsters
1 parrot

3 cats
2 dogs
4 hamsters
1 parrot

FIGURE 13-15.

Beginning construction of circle graph.

In a more sophisticated construction task, students must decide how to divide the circle. In constructing a circle graph, it is often helpful to set up a table first. This table should show each fractional part the circle is to be divided into, the number of degrees for each part, and perhaps the percent of the whole for each part. Figure 13-16 shows such a table and the corresponding circle graph. These are based on the information about time use by students in Mr. Gambino's class as shown in the line graph in Figure 13-11.

The hours the students spend in each of the activities were given in the graph. Since the students know there are 24 hours in a day, 100 percent in any whole, and 360 degrees in a circle, filling in the rest of the table is a simple matter of using proportions. For example, nine hours spent in sleep is equivalent to $\frac{9}{24}$ of the day. Therefore, $\frac{9}{24} =$

$\frac{x}{100}$ and $\frac{9}{24} = \frac{x}{360}$. Students do not need to find the percent to find the number of degrees needed. They could simply set up the proportion $\frac{9}{24} = \frac{x}{360}$. However, since circle graphs are difficult to interpret exactly from the drawing, usually data are included on the graph to define each section. Often these data are given as percents (Figure 13-16). One way students can check the figures in the table is to add each column to see if they get the correct total or whole.

QUESTIONS AND ACTIVITIES

1. *For your resource file:* A number of articles from the *Arithmetic Teacher* and the NCTM yearbook *Teaching Statistics and Probability* discuss the skills that primary children should acquire through graphing.

	Hours	Fraction of day	Percent of day	Degrees of circle
Sleep	9	$\frac{9}{24}$ or $\frac{3}{8}$	$37\frac{1}{2}$	135
School	6	$\frac{6}{24}$ or $\frac{1}{4}$	25	90
Eat	2	$\frac{2}{24}$ or $\frac{1}{12}$	$8\frac{1}{3}$	30
Play	4	$\frac{4}{24}$ or $\frac{1}{6}$	$16\frac{2}{3}$	60
Misc	3	$\frac{3}{24}$ or $\frac{1}{8}$	$12\frac{1}{2}$	45
Total	24	$\frac{24}{24}$	100%	360°

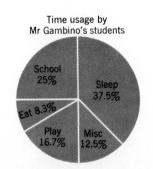

Time usage by Mr Gambino's students

School 25%
Sleep 37.5%
Eat 8.3%
Play 16.7%
Misc 12.5%

FIGURE 13-16.

Constructing a circle graph.

Additionally, "The Graph Examined" by Slaughter, "Bar Graphs for Five-Year-Olds" by Smith, "Bar Graphs for First Graders" by Johnson, "This Is Us! Great Graphs for Kids" by Sullivan and O'Neil, and "Graphically Speaking: Primary-Level Graphing Experiences" by Choate and Okey include activities to develop these concepts. Evaluate one of these articles. Read and copy for your resource file one or more of these articles.

2. In "Graphing for Any Grade," Nibbelink describes a procedure for plotting points for a line graph. Read the article and then use this technique to make a graph. Either collect your own data or use data from an elementary school textbook lesson on line graphs.

3. What are some topics that young children would be interested in and for which they could readily collect data for graphs? What topics would be appropriate and of interest to middle school children? Describe how you would help the class decide how to collect the data. *For your resource file:* "Stand Up and Be Counted" by Scalzitti, " 'Top Ten' Mathematics" by Siwakowsky, and "Stimulating Problem Solving and Classroom Settings" by Liedtke and Vance suggest topics and methods of helping students organize.

4. a. At what grade level is the topic of bar graphs introduced? Pictographs? Line graphs? Circle graphs?
   b. Analyze the first lessons for circle, pictorial, or line graphs from two different elementary textbooks. Evaluate the lessons with regard to strengths and weaknesses.

5. In the "Ideas" department of the *Arithmetic Teacher,* activity sheets for students at various grade levels and lesson plans for these sheets are given. Read "Ideas" by Shaw for activities on bar and circle graphs. Note that each lesson contains both interpreting graphs and constructing graphs. Evaluate the lesson on constructing circle

graphs. How was the activity structured so that this could be used as a beginning activity on circle graphs?

6. Ms. Schurrer assigned the following problem to her students. What prerequisite skills must the students have to solve the problem?

Copy and complete the following table and construct a circle graph based on this information.

	Amount
Food	$15
Clothing	$12
Entertainment	$ 6
Misc.	$ 3
Total	$36

Fraction	Percent	Degrees

7. *For your resource file:* Three teaching aids for pictorial, bar, and circle graphs are given in "Collecting and Displaying the Data Around Us" by Horak and Horak. Copy and add these ideas to your resource file.

8. Read "Making and Interpreting Graphs and Tables: Results and Implications from National Assessment" by Bestgen. What are common misconceptions and errors regarding graphing? What recommendations for the mathematics curriculum are given?

MEAN, MODE, MEDIAN, AND RANGE

Once data has been collected and organized, there are many ways to describe it numerically. One of the questions often asked is, "What is the average?" In other words, "What one number is typical of this whole group of numbers?"; "How much does the average bag of carrots weigh?"; "In what month is the average student's birthday?"; or "What was the average score on the quiz?"

Statisticians call these "averages," or our attempts to describe what is typical, the measures of central tendency. These measures include three different statistics: mean, median, and mode. The most commonly used is the mean, sometimes called the arithmetic average, or just the average. A person asked to find the average weight of several bags of carrots would probably compute the mean.

Students can develop an understanding of the mean through simple activities. Figure 13-17a shows the heights of three stacks of arithmetic books. An appropriate question might be, "if these stacks were all the same height, how many arithmetic books would there be in each one?" The students can take the books and physically move them until they have three stacks of equal height (Figure 13-17b). Thus they see that the "average" stack of books is six books high.

Similarly, students can find the average height of students in their class. In this case they cannot solve the problem physically by taking a few centimeters off a tall student and adding them to a short one. They can represent each student's height with some model. Since each student in Mr. Gambino's class is more than 1 meter tall, the students decided to represent only that part of their

heights that was over 1 meter. Using Cuisenaire rods for the representation, they could then manipulate the rods until they had formed trains of equal length (Figure 13-18). They added 1 meter to this result to obtain an average height of 132 centimeters. However, if the students wished to find the mean height for the entire class of 30 students, using Cuisenaire rods would be a lengthy procedure. At this stage the students need to examine what they have done with models in order to work out an algorithm that will give the same results.

In the example shown in Figure 13-17, the students might have solved the problem in one of two ways. They might have simply taken books off a tall stack and added them to a shorter one until they had three equal stacks. Figure 13-19a shows the books as they were originally stacked. The students take one book from the tallest stack and put it on the shortest stack (Figure 13-19b). Since the third stack is still short, they take another book from the second stack and put it on the third (Figure 13-19c). Now the first stack is tallest so they take a book from it and put it on the third stack (Figure 13-19d) so that all three stacks are equal. Someone might have noticed in the second step that the first and second stacks were equal. That person might have taken one book from each and put both on the third stack at the same time, thus going immediately to the last step.

Both these methods yield the correct answer, but they do not help students to develop an algorithm for solving more complex

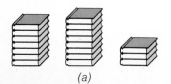

(a)

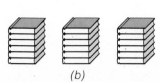

(b)

FIGURE 13-17.
Finding the mean.

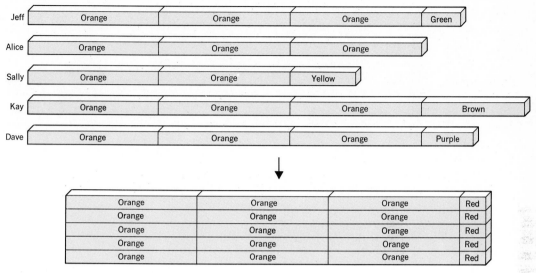

FIGURE 13-18.
Finding the mean with Cuisenaire rods.

problems. Another student, Mike, solved the same problem another way. He stacked all the books together (Figure 13-20). Then using partitive division, he separated them into three stacks of equal size. He obtained the same answer as the rest of the class.

Not only has Mike found the correct mean for this example, but also by examining his process he can discover an algorithm for finding any mean. First he added all the books together into one stack. Then he di-

vided them into the same number of stacks he started with, but he made them of equal size. Since addition and division are both processes he already knows, he can now find the average height of the students in his class without the help of a model. He can simply *add* all the heights and *divide* by the number of students.

Practical problems involving the mean can be found in all school subjects and in many other areas. A health class might want

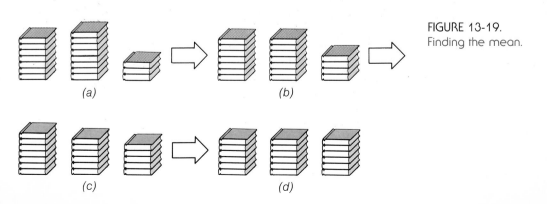

FIGURE 13-19.
Finding the mean.

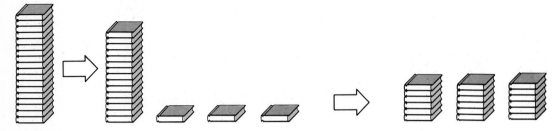

FIGURE 13-20.
Finding the mean.

to find the average height and weight of class members and compare this to the national averages. In physical education one student's average running speed can be compared to another's. In science and social studies, the mean as an average occurs frequently as in the average annual rainfall, the average age of employees of a certain business, the average life expectancy of a fruit fly, and so on. In fact, when people speak of the average, they usually are talking about the mean.

However, there are other kinds of averages. For example, if students used the bar graph in Figure 13-3 to show that the typical student would probably have a birthday in October, they are not using the mean as a

measure of what is typical or average. Instead they are using a statistic called the mode. The mode is simply the value that occurs most frequently.

Figure 13-21 shows the vehicles owned by each of several families in Wilmington. The mean number of vehicles owned by these families is $(2 + 2 + 2 + 2 + 7) \div 5$ or 3. However, students can see that it would be unreasonable to say that the typical family owns three vehicles. It would be logical to say that the typical family owns two vehicles since this is the situation that occurs most often in the given data.

Finding the mode is a simple matter of inspecting the organized data to see which value occurs most frequently. In Figure 13-7

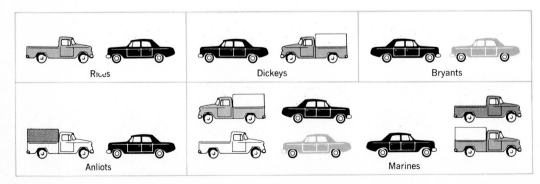

FIGURE 13-21.
Vehicles owned by five families.

David's	OOOOOOOOOO	10
Doug's	OOOO	8
Derek's	OO	4 ←—— Median
Chris's	OOOOOOO	3
Jeremy's	OOO	2

FIGURE 13-22.
Finding the median.

the mode for the heights of students in Mr. Gambino's class is 125 centimeters. The mode for the actual weight of a "two-pound" bag of carrots is from 38 ounces to 40 ounces.

The third measure of central tendency is the median. The median is the value in the middle such that exactly half the values fall below it and half above it when all the values are placed in order. Figure 13-22 shows how many marbles each of five boys has. If the numbers are put in order, the median is seen to be 4 since this is the number in the exact middle. (Jane Jonas Srivastava's *Averages* explores mean, median, and mode through excellent activities appropriate for the elementary school child.)

For the elementary student, this brief introduction to the idea of the median is probably sufficient. The teacher, however, should have a more sophisticated understanding of this topic. This is important so that teachers can structure student activities that are on an elementary level but are still mathematically correct.

To understand the median in more detail, we must first understand the nature of the data in question. Using the bar graph in Figure 13-3, October was selected as the mode because that is the month in which the most birthdays occur. However, with this same data, it would not make sense to talk about a certain month as being the mean or another month as being the median. This is true because this type of data is discrete data. This means that if the months were placed along a line, it would not be possible to say that it is the same distance along the line from April to May as it is from September to October.

On the other hand, the graph in Figure 13-7a shows continuous data. If the heights reported were placed on a line, it would be the same distance along the line from 120 centimeters to 125 centimeters as from 135 centimeters to 140 centimeters. With continuous data, it is reasonable to talk about mean and median. In the same way the number of marbles each boy has in Figure 13-22 can be viewed as continuous data because the difference between one marble and two marbles is exactly the same as the distance between six marbles and five marbles.

In Chapter 10 we discussed the idea of measurement as being continuous and subject to possible error. Thus any of the line segments shown in Figure 13-23 would have

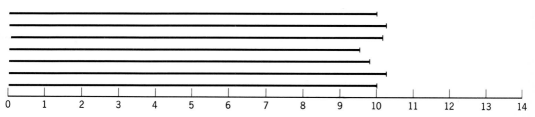

FIGURE 13-23.
Measurement—continuous and approximate.

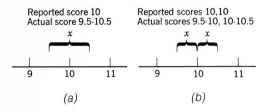

Reported score 10
Actual score 9.5-10.5

x

9   10   11

(a)

Reported scores 10,10
Actual scores 9.5-10, 10-10.5

x   *x*

9   10   11

(b)

FIGURE 13-24.
Statistical meaning of individual scores.

been reported as 10 centimeters to the nearest centimeter. Some of these line segments are obviously less than or more than 10 centimeters. However, none are less than 9.5 centimeters nor more than 10.5 centimeters so they all would be reported as 10 centimeters. Thus a reported measure of 10 centimeters is seen as representing the entire interval on the scale from 9.5 centimeters to 10.5 centimeters.

In a similar manner statisticians look at other types of data as continuous. To the statistician any value reported as 10 represents the interval from 9.5 to 10.5. Thus if Sally makes a score of 10 on a quiz, the statistician considers that her score covers the entire interval from 9.5 to 10.5 (Figure 13-24a).

If Virginia also makes a 10 on the quiz, the two scores are considered to cover the entire interval or one score covers 9.5 to 10 and the other score covers 10 to 10.5 (Figure 13-24b). If other students also had scores of 10, the interval would be divided accordingly.

This information can be used in finding

an exact median. Since the median is the exact point that has just half the scores below it and half above it, it can be found by graphing the scores on a number line. Such a graph for the boys' marbles in Figure 13-22 is shown in Figure 13-25. Since there are five scores and half of five is two and one half, the median is the point below which two and one half scores fall. As we see from the diagram, it is exactly 4. Obviously elementary students would not use a number line to solve a problem this simple. This example was chosen as a beginning illustration of the nature of continuous data and its use in finding the median.

However, if five marbles belonging to John are included in this data, the appropriate graph will look like Figure 13-26. Since there are now six scores, the median is the point below which three of these fall. But the diagram shows that there are only two and a half scores below 4. The exact point below which three scores fall is $4\frac{1}{2}$.

Two more examples for finding the exact median for a set of data are shown in Figure 13-27. In each set of data there are eight scores so the median is the exact point below which four scores fall. In Robyn's test scores the median comes between two scores both reported as 18. Since four scores are reported as 18, the interval from 17.5 to 18.5 is sectioned into four parts with each representing one score. Since the second of these eighteens is the fourth score of the set, the median falls at the point between

Derek's   Jeremy's   Doug's   Chris's   David's

0   1   2   3   4   5   6   7   8   9   10   11

Median = 4

FIGURE 13-25.
Finding the median.

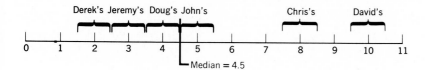

FIGURE 13-26.
Finding the median.

the second 18 and the third 18, namely at exactly 18. In Eva's scores there are also four scores reported as 18. But in Eva's scores the third 18 is the fourth score of the set. Therefore the median falls at the point between the third 18 and the fourth 18, namely at exactly 18.25.

This finding of the exact median would not be taught in the elementary school except possibly for enrichment. However, the teacher must be aware of the principles involved because elementary students can find medians for simple sets of data such as the number of the boys' marbles as shown in Figure 13-22. Median problems for elementary students should include only sets of data for which the exact median is a whole number. It would be appropriate for students to find the median for Robyn's spelling scores but not for Eva's since elementary

students would probably report Eva's median as 18, which is not exact. By leaving out problems in which the exact median is not a whole number, the teacher avoids building false concepts that must later be unlearned. At the same time the students are allowed to learn a basic concept of the median without being confused by more advanced concepts for which they are not yet ready.

As students learn about averages—mean, median, and mode—to represent what is typical, they should develop some understanding of when to use these various measures. As pointed out before, sometimes mean and median are simply not appropriate for the data being discussed. Other times, although all three measures could be used, one is more appropriate than another for describing what is typical for each. Figure

Robyn's spelling scores	Robyn's scores ordered
Test 1-20	20
2-18	19
3-18	18
4-15	18
5-16	18
6-18	18
7-18	16
8-19	15

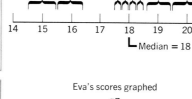

FIGURE 13-27.
Finding the exact median.

Eva's spelling scores	Eva's scores ordered
Test 1-19	20
2-18	19
3-20	19
4-19	18
5-18	18
6-16	18
7-18	18
8-18	16

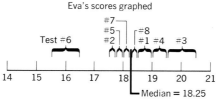

	Quiz #1	Quiz #2	Quiz #3
	20	19	20
	20	18	19
	20	17	19
	20	16	17
	20	14	14
	12	14	13
	11	12	12
	10	3	12
	9	3	11
	2	3	11
Mean	14.4	11.9	14.8
Median	12.5	14	13.5
Mode	20	3	11,12,19

FIGURE 13-28.
Selecting mean, median, or mode.

	Quiz #1	Quiz #2	Quiz #3
	20	15	10
	14	12	10
	10	10	10
	5	8	10
	1	5	10
Mean	10	10	10
Range	20	11	1

FIGURE 13-29.
Same mean, different ranges.

13-28 shows three sets of quiz scores for ten students and the mean, the median, and the mode for each set of scores. In each of these sets of scores, a different "average" is most representative of the typical score. Class discussion can bring out such concepts as, "One or two low scores has more effect on the mean than on the median." Of course, students should also realize that in many cases these three measures will have very similar values. For example, if they use the data for carrots presented in the graph in Figure 13-7. They will find the mean to be two pounds eight ounces, the mode two pounds seven ounces, and the median two pounds eight ounces.

One more statistical measure, which is very easy to compute and often used by the elementary student, is called the range. The range simply tells how spread out the scores are. It is the distance from the lowest score to the highest score including both endpoints. Figure 13-29 shows three sets of scores with the same mean, but very different ranges. From examples like these, students can easily see why it would often be

helpful to know the range as well as the mean. The range is also considered in determining how to number the axis for bar and line graphs.

QUESTIONS AND ACTIVITIES

1. a. The concepts of mean, median, and mode are presented via activities in the children's book *Averages* by Srivastava. How could you use these ideas to develop lessons for elementary children?

   b. How many children (yourself, brothers, and sisters) are there in your family? Collect and organize the data for the entire class. Find the average number of children per family. Mean, median, mode, and range are statistics terms previously discussed. How would you use each of these terms in interpreting this data?

2. *For your resource file:* The article "Let's Do It: Making Graphs" by Shaw contains a number of suggestions for helping young children collect and analyze data. A program for finding means with a computer is also included. Copy and add these ideas to your resource file.

3. Stack cubes or link interlocking cubes together in lengths of 3, 5, 8, 7, and 12

cubes. Describe how you would use these to find the mean for that set of numbers.

4. *For your resource file:* The article "Developing Some Statistical Concepts in the Elementary School" by Bohan and Moreland describes some activities to develop the concept of the mean, median, and mode. Read and copy these ideas.

5. a. At what grade levels are mean, median, and mode introduced?
   b. Read the introductory lesson for means in two different elementary school textbooks. Is a rule given or is the concept introduced meaningfully? Compare the introductory lessons and write a summary of how the concept is introduced. How could either of these lessons be supplemented to improve the lesson?

6. What would be a suitable height for a doorframe for your classroom if you allow a 15-centimeter clearance? Calculate the height by using the (a) mean, (b) median, and (c) mode for the class. If each student in the group walked through each doorframe, what would happen? Which of these statistics is appropriate as a standard for the doorframe? Would any other statistic be better than any of these? If yes, what statistic, and why?

7. Rob and Angela started working on the problem below. Rob said it could not be solved as the number of people wasn't given. Angela disagreed. She said that it didn't matter whether the graph was marked in units of 1, 2, 5, 10, 1000, or 1 000 000. Who was correct? Why? Given the table below, give the numerical value of the mean, median, and mode. Which of these measures, if any, describe the "typical" wage earner? Defend your answer.

Mean = _____
Mode = _____
Median = _____

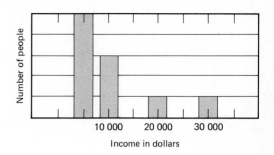

Income in dollars

8. To find the average of 50 and 100, consider the number midway between the two numbers . . . 75. For 90 and 96, consider . . . 93. In the article "Making Averaging Easier," Smith extends these ideas to numbers such as 46 and 68. By considering the place values separately, he describes methods to find the average of the two numbers mentally. Read this article and try this method for averaging 52 and 70, 23 and 67, 25 and 51, 342 and 582.

9. *For your resource file:* Read and add one of the following to your resource file: In "Developing Concepts in Probability and Statistics—And Much More," Bruni and Silverman describe activities for the primary grades. Dickinson describes how to use the computer for graphs in "Gather, Organize, Display: Mathematics for the Information Society"; programs are included.

PROBABILITY

Another statistical concept that elementary students can understand is the idea of sampling. When Mr. Gambino's students measured their heights and made a graph, Figure 13-7, they measured every student in the class. When they made their study of the actual weight of "two-pound" bags of carrots, they checked only 40 bags. There were many other bags of carrots in the store, and there were three other stores in town. Even so they can make predictions about all "two-pound" bags of carrots. Since they randomly chose a reasonable number of bags to check, their results are a good estimate of what is true of all bags of carrots. Since checking all the bags of carrots and doing the computations to find the mean, median, and mode would be very time consuming, they used just a sample to get a close estimate.

It is assumed in the case above that the sample from one store is representative of the other stores. In the case of the students' heights, the source needs to be considered in order to compare the sample to other populations. If this were a class of second graders, the results could be used to predict heights of other second graders. However, the sample might not be a good predictor of heights for *all* second graders as heights can vary among different nationalities and over large spans of time. Also, whether these data were collected at the beginning of the year, midterm, or end of the year would affect the predictions that could be made. To use this information for prediction, we would need to know more about the population sampled and when the sample was taken.

In order to justify using only a sample and then making predictions about an entire group, statisticians must rely on the concepts of probability. Probability deals with

making predictions about future events. "There is a 20% chance of rain tonight" and "Northern is a two-to-one favorite over State in Saturday's football game" are statements of probability. The validity of these predictions depends on the reliability of the data and the individual's ability to analyze the data. Through introductory activities, the elementary student can understand the concepts of simple probability.

In children's first activities they should simply list what *outcomes* are possible. For the spinners shown in Figure 13-30 the possible outcomes are red, white, and black. For the cards different attributes could be considered. If the attribute is number, the outcomes would be 7, 9, 3, 4, 6, and 5. If the attribute is color, the outcomes are black and red. In one third-grade textbook the children are asked to find all possible outcomes for tossing a dime, a nickel, and a penny (Figure 13-31). Students will need to use a problem-solving strategy such as "make an organized list" or "use a chart" to find all possible outcomes.

Another aspect that should be considered is "Are the outcomes equally likely?" For the first spinner in Figure 13-30, red, white, and black are *equally likely* outcomes. For the second spinner, black is a *more likely* outcome than either white or red. Selecting an even-numbered card is a *less likely* outcome than selecting an odd-numbered card

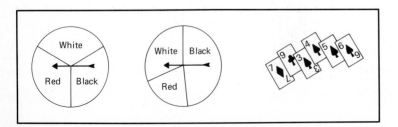

FIGURE 13-30.
Outcomes.

FIGURE 13-31.
Listing outcomes. (From Joseph Payne et al., **Harper & Row Mathematics,**
Grade 3, p. 231. Copyright © 1985 Macmillan, Inc. Reprinted with permission
of Scribner Educational Publishers, a division of Macmillan, Inc.)

(Figure 13-30).

These concepts are prerequisites to introducing probability more formally in the upper grades. Figure 13-32 shows how one fifth-grade textbook introduces probability. Note that fraction concepts are involved as the total number of possible outcomes must be equally likely. Probability is introduced as a ratio of the number of desired outcomes to the total number of possible outcomes.

In beginning activities in probability, students should first predict the results of an experiment. Then they should actually do the experiment and record the results. For example, students can predict how many times a coin will land heads if they toss it 20 times. Young children, who are being intuitively introduced to the concepts of probability, would simply predict 10 heads and 10 tails. As they experiment, the teacher should ask questions such as "We had 3 heads in a row. What do you think the next outcome will be?" At first children will predict that it is "time for a tail." Through experiences, they should ob-

serve that these outcomes are independent of each other.

Older children who are being introduced more formally to probability can write the probability as a ratio. After they have made the prediction, they can toss the coin and keep a tally of the results as shown in Figure 13-33. Then the total number of heads and the total number of tails can each be expressed as a fraction. In the example the fraction $\frac{9}{20}$ represents a ratio of the number of heads to the total number of tosses.

Most children can easily grasp intuitively that since there are only two ways a coin can land, heads or tails, it will probably land heads one-half of the time. In other words, in 10 tosses it is likely that heads will turn up five times. By actually doing the tossing and recording the results, they can see the difference between theoretical and experimental probability. By doing the experiment several times with different numbers of tosses, they will discover what happens to this relationship between experimental and

5 PROBABILITY

To start the game, a coin is tossed.
Team A chooses heads.
Team B chooses tails.
Is the probability better for
Team A or Team B to win the toss?

The coin has two sides, heads and tails.

In a toss, the *probability* for heads is

1 out of 2, or $\frac{1}{2}$.

The probability for tails is 1 out of 2, or $\frac{1}{2}$.

The *outcomes* are equally likely.

Each team has an equal probability
for winning the toss.

There are two possible outcomes for the spinner. It can
stop on blue or on red, but the outcomes are not equally
likely. Which outcome is less likely? Which outcome is
more likely?

- Blue is *less likely*. The probability

  for blue is 1 out of 4, or $\frac{1}{4}$.

- Red is *more likely*. The probability

  for red is 3 out of 4, or $\frac{3}{4}$.

> Here's how to find the probability that something will
> happen. Find the ratio of the number of ways it can
> happen to the total number of possible outcomes.

FIGURE 13-32.
Introducing probability. (From Joseph Payne et al., **Harper & Row Mathematics,**
Grade 5, p. 356. Copyright © 1985 Macmillan, Inc. Reprinted with permission
of Scribner Educational Publishers, a division of Macmillan, Inc.)

Heads	|||| ||||	$\frac{9}{20}$
Tails	|||| ||||		$\frac{11}{20}$

FIGURE 13-33.
Tossing a coin.

theoretical probability as the size of the sample changes. For ease in comparing experimental probability to theoretical probability, middle school students who understand the relationships between common and decimal fractions can use calculators. Even if they obtain experimental probabilities of $\frac{14}{39}$, $\frac{27}{62}$, or $\frac{68}{127}$, these cumbersome numbers can be readily changed to decimal fractions and compared to $\frac{1}{2}$.

Similar experiments should be done with materials such as spinners, dice, or colored chips drawn from a bag. Students will easily make predictions like those shown in Figure 13-34. These predictions can be checked by experimentation. Younger children should be asked such questions as "Which color is more likely?" and "Are the numbers on the cube equally likely?" Middle school students should be asked such questions as, "What is the probability that the spinner will point to red or green? To green, yellow, red, or blue? To black?" Students should observe that the probability of an outcome varies from zero to one. Again, middle school students can use a calculator to compare the experimental probability to the theoretical probability.

In another experiment students can be asked to predict what will happen if two pennies are tossed at the same time. Most students will predict three possible outcomes: two heads and no tails, one head and one tail, no heads and two tails. They will probably predict that each of these will occur about one-third of the time. When this prediction is checked by actually flipping two pennies, the students will soon discover that the outcomes are noticeably different from their predictions. They will find that the outcome of one head and one tail is occurring at approximately twice the rate of either of the other outcomes.

To discover why this is happening, students should consider a question similar to the one posed in Figure 13-31. The question can be reconsidered using two different coins such as a penny and a nickel. By making an organized list of the outcomes, students should note why the one-head–one-tail outcome occurs more often (Figure 13-35). Students should again be asked to predict what the outcomes will be before ac-

FIGURE 13-34.
Making predictions.

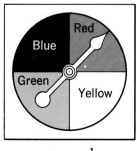

Red = $\frac{1}{4}$

Heads = $\frac{1}{2}$

Two = $\frac{1}{6}$

Event	Outcome Coin A	Outcome Coin B	Fractional Probability
1	H	H	$\frac{1}{4}$
2	H	T $\Big\}$ $\frac{2}{4}$	$\frac{1}{2}$
3	T	H	
4	T	T	$\frac{1}{4}$

FIGURE 13-35.
Expected events for two coins.

tually flipping the coins. As the students do the experiment, they should record exactly what happens with each toss (Figure 13-36).

The experiment will show that the outcome "one head and one tail" can occur either when the penny lands heads and the nickel lands tails or when the penny lands tails and the nickel lands heads. Thus students will see that there are four equally likely ways the coins can land and that two of these satisfy the requirement "one head and one tail."

Students should be able to extend and to analyze what will happen if they flip three coins. By thinking about three coins, a penny, a nickel, and a dime, students can set up a table similar to the one shown in Figure 13-37. From such a table they can see that there are eight equally likely events.

If one is only interested in the number of heads that occur, there are only four outcomes. These four outcomes are three heads, two heads, one head, and no heads. The four outcomes are not all equally likely (Figure 13-37). Again the students can actually flip the coins and compare the experimental outcomes to the predicted outcomes.

Students can also make predictions about other outcomes that are not equally likely. The spinner in Figure 13-38a is divided into eight equal-sized parts so each part is equally likely. Since two of the parts are blue, the probability of blue is $\frac{1}{8} + \frac{1}{8}$ or $\frac{2}{8}$. The probability of red is 4 one-eighths or $\frac{4}{8}$. Each of the 12 marbles in Figure 13-38b is equally likely to be drawn out so the probability of drawing a black marble is $\frac{5}{12}$. (*Probability* by Charles Linn contains an excellent collection of probability experiments for elementary children.)

In the preceding examples, students have been making predictions based on a known sample space and outcomes whose theoretical probability is known. After making these predictions (theoretical probability), they have done the experiments and recorded the results (experimental probability). After experiences of this type, they can participate in activities for trying to predict the theoretical probability based on the ex-

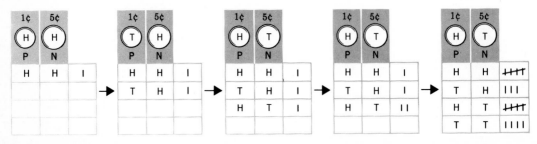

FIGURE 13-36.
Tossing two coins.

Event	Outcome				Fractional Probability
	Penny	Nickel	Dime		
1	H	H	H	3 Heads	$\frac{1}{8}$
2	H	H	T	} 2 Heads	$\frac{3}{8}$
3	H	T	H		
4	T	H	H		
5	H	T	T	} 1 Head	$\frac{3}{8}$
6	T	H	T		
7	T	T	H		
8	T	T	T	0 Head	$\frac{1}{8}$

FIGURE 13-37.
Theoretical probability for three coins.

perimental probability. To exemplify this concept they could consider the results of tossing a thumbtack or a paper cup. After listing the different outcomes that could occur from tossing the object, the students could discuss which outcomes are more likely. Although they can easily see that the outcomes are not equally likely, they have no theoretical way to determine what the appropriate probability of each outcome will be. By collecting data, they could arrive at an experimental probability.

Sometimes the sample space, as well as the probability, is unknown. To develop this concept, students could work alone, in pairs, or in small groups. Each group would be given a sack containing 12 color cubes. Without looking in the sack, students would

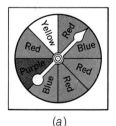 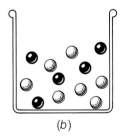

(a)   (b)

FIGURE 13-38.
Predicting unequal outcomes.

draw out a cube, record its color, and replace it in the sack. They would continue to do this until they had enough information to make predictions about what was in the sack.

An activity of this sort should start out at a simple level, perhaps with just two colors and an equal number of each. Gradually the difficulty could be increased by such variations as using three or four colors, including different numbers of each color, or increasing the total number of cubes in the sack.

This activity could also be used to develop some concepts of statistical sampling. For this activity the bag should contain at least three different colors of cubes. Students would be asked after only two draws to make predictions about what colors the cubes are and how many of each color are in the bag. Then they would make three more draws and make new predictions, if necessary, based on this sample of five draws. This type of experiment could be extended until they had a sample of 10 or 20 or even more draws on which to base their predictions. Then each group would check their bag to see how close their various predictions were to the actual number of cubes. By comparing results with other groups and through class discussion, they could develop the concept that the larger the sample size, the better the predictions that can be made from the sample.

They should also observe that although a larger sample may have given them better information it also took more time. They should extend this thinking to costs in industry, for example testing flash cubes or sampling truffles. Similarly, in taking polls, if the whole population were surveyed, it would be costly and time consuming.

Other concepts of probability can also be explored and developed informally. By structuring the examples and questions, teachers can lead their students to discover simple laws of probability. Four counters— two blue, one yellow, and one red—can be used to generate the concepts involving "*and*" and "*or*." First, the probability of drawing a red or yellow at random will be considered. The desirable outcome of red *or* yellow is more likely than simply red, so the probability will be greater than $\frac{1}{4}$. Since the probability of red is $\frac{1}{4}$ and the probability of yellow is $\frac{1}{4}$, the probability of red *or* yellow is $\frac{1}{4} + \frac{1}{4}$ or $\frac{1}{2}$. The probability of red *or* blue would be $\frac{1}{4} + \frac{2}{4}$ or $\frac{3}{4}$. From such examples students should generalize that "*or*" increases their options and the probabilities are added.

The class should then consider what happens if we consider two draws in a row, replacing the first draw before the second draw. What would be the probability of first drawing a red counter and then a yellow counter? To analyze this question a sample space should be generated (Figure 13-39a). To differentiate the two blue counters, subscripts were used. From the chart the class can determine that the probability of drawing a red counter and then a yellow counter is $\frac{1}{16}$, as only one outcome of the 16 is red and then yellow. The probability of a yellow and then a blue would be $\frac{2}{16}$. The probability of

First Draw	Second Draw
Red	Red
Red	Yellow
Red	Blue$_1$
Red	Blue$_2$
Yellow	Red
Yellow	Yellow
Yellow	Blue$_1$
Yellow	Blue$_2$
Blue$_1$	Red
Blue$_1$	Yellow
Blue$_1$	Blue$_1$
Blue$_1$	Blue$_2$
Blue$_2$	Red
Blue$_2$	Yellow
Blue$_2$	Blue$_1$
Blue$_2$	Blue$_2$

$P(R, Y) = P(\frac{1}{4}, \frac{1}{4}) = \frac{1}{16}$

$P(Y, B) = P(\frac{1}{4}, \frac{1}{2}) = \frac{2}{16}$ or $\frac{1}{8}$

$P(B, B) = P(\frac{1}{2}, \frac{1}{2}) = \frac{4}{16}$ or $\frac{1}{4}$

$P(R, R) = P(\frac{1}{4}, \frac{1}{4}) = \frac{1}{16}$

a   b

FIGURE 13-39.
Drawing counters.

two blues in a row would be $\frac{4}{16}$. As the students determine these probabilities, the individual probabilities and results should be recorded (Figure 13-39b). As the students analyze their results they should conclude that the individual probabilities of single outcomes should be multiplied to obtain the results of an "*and*" situation.

This situation can be readily extended to probabilities without replacement. If the same situation as shown in Figure 13-39a is considered, the only change would be to exclude the examples where the same counter was drawn in the first and second draws. By excluding outcomes such as red, red, the sample space is limited to 12. The probability of drawing a red and then a yellow would be $\frac{1}{12}$. After selecting a red (one out of four counters or $\frac{1}{4}$), three counters are left. Since one of the three is yellow, the probability of red *and* then yellow is $\frac{1}{4} \times \frac{1}{3}$ or $\frac{1}{12}$.

Tree diagrams are also an excellent way of using a diagram to explore probabilities with or without replacements. Each location where the branch divides indicates a choice.

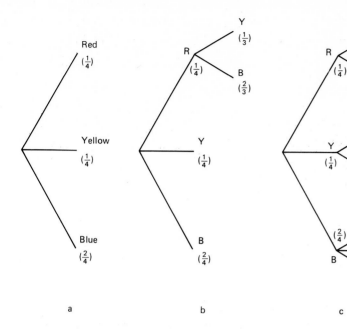

FIGURE 13-40.
Tree diagrams.

a

b

c

To represent the choices red, yellow, or blue, three branches are drawn and labeled with the corresponding probabilities (Figure 13-40a). Note that the probability of drawing a blue is twice as much as the probability of either a red or a yellow as there are two blues and only one each of red and yellow. After a red counter is selected for the first choice, there are two colors for a second choice, so two branches are drawn at the end of the red branch and labeled with the appropriate probabilities (Figure 13-40b). The other branches should be drawn and labeled similarly. There are a total of 12 outcomes only one of which represents red and then yellow. The probability of each selection can be written directly on the branches (Figure 13-40c). As the tree is traced to find the probability of drawing a yellow and then a blue, the thinking could be "yellow first so $\frac{1}{4}$ probability . . . then blue . . . blue is now 2 out of 3 so probability of blue on this draw is $\frac{2}{3}$, so prob-

ability of drawing yellow *and* then blue is $\frac{1}{4} \times \frac{2}{3}$ or $\frac{2}{12}$."

Another situation that could also be used to motivate these generalizations is tossing a coin and a number cube at the same time. The students could set up a table of possible outcomes (Figure 13-41a). Just by looking at the table, they can find the probability of any single event. For example, the probability of tossing a 6 is $\frac{2}{12}$, since there are 12 events and 2 of them include a 6 on the number cube. Similarly, the probability of tossing a tail is $\frac{6}{12}$, the probability of tossing a number greater than 4 is $\frac{4}{12}$, and so on.

To find the probability of two events happening at the same time, students could again examine the sample space. For example, if students wish to find the probability of getting a head and a 3 on a single toss, they would first need to find the probability of getting a head and the probability of getting a 3. As shown in Figure 13-41b, they

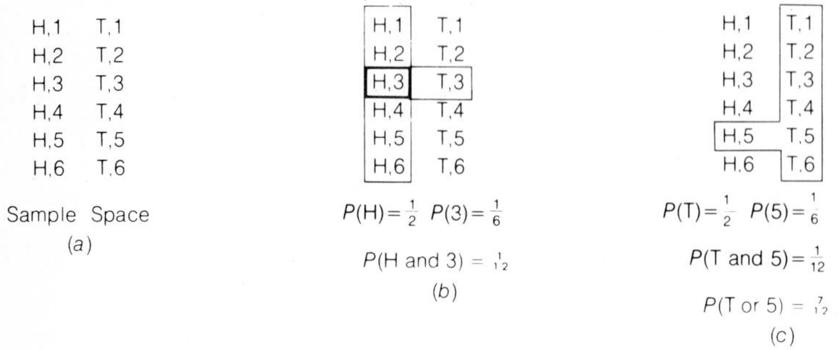

H,1	T,1		H,1	T,1		H,1	T,1	
H,2	T,2		H,2	T,2		H,2	T,2	
H,3	T,3		H,3	T,3		H,3	T,3	
H,4	T,4		H,4	T,4		H,4	T,4	
H,5	T,5		H,5	T,5		H,5	T,5	
H,6	T,6		H,6	T,6		H,6	T,6	

Sample Space

(a)

$P(H) = \frac{1}{2}$ $P(3) = \frac{1}{6}$

$P(H \text{ and } 3) = \frac{1}{12}$

(b)

$P(T) = \frac{1}{2}$ $P(5) = \frac{1}{6}$

$P(T \text{ and } 5) = \frac{1}{12}$

$P(T \text{ or } 5) = \frac{7}{12}$

(c)

FIGURE 13-41.
Finding probabilities.

could then find the place where these events overlap to determine the probability of a head and a 3 on the same toss. They may also recognize the probability of a head and a 3 as the intersection of the set of the probability of a head and the set of the probability of a 3, so $\frac{1}{2} \times \frac{1}{6} = \frac{1}{12}$.

To find the probability that at least one or the other of two events will occur, they could proceed similarly. Figure 13-41c shows the probability that at least one of the events a tail or a 5 will occur. Again students will find the probability of each event separately. Then the probability of at least one of the two events occurring can be seen to be the union of the sets of the probability of either one alone, so $\frac{1}{2} + \frac{1}{6} - \frac{1}{12} = \frac{7}{12}$. Although *or* indicates addition, $\frac{1}{12}$ had to be subtracted from $\frac{1}{2} + \frac{1}{6}$ so that the outcome T,5 which is included in the set of tails *and* in the set of fives would not be counted twice.

Most students find simple statistics and probability to be enjoyable activities. Experiences at the elementary level should be kept simple, but the examples used should always be mathematically correct. There are a number of excellent games and activities that can involve students in the lower as well as the upper grade levels in exploring and applying the concepts of probability and statistics.

QUESTIONS AND ACTIVITIES

1. What topics in probability are taught in elementary school? Consult the scope-and-sequence chart of an elementary textbook to determine the topics and the grade levels.

2. How would a chart help students answer the following problem?

   A local ice cream store offers the following ice cream choices: (1) chocolate, (2) coconut, (3) almond fudge, (4) raspberry ice, and (5) chocolate chip. This ice cream can be topped with whipped cream, nuts, both, or neither. Assuming equally likely outcomes, what is the probability that the next customer will pick chocolate chip with nuts given all the possibilities?

3. a. Read the children's book *Probability* by Linn. Do one of the activities described in the book.
   b. Describe how you could use this book with a class to introduce the concept of probability. To provide activities in probability.

4. a. Toss two coins 20 times and record the outcomes in a table. Calculate the experimental probabilities. How close were your results to the theoretical probabilities?

b. Compare your results with other students' results. Compile these results and calculate new experimental probabilities. Were your group results closer to the theoretical probability?

5. Develop a laboratory activity for a class experiment in probability that involves tossing thumbtacks.

6. a. *For your resource file:* In the article "Let's Do It: Take a Chance," Horak and Horak describe a number of excellent probability activities for children in the lower elementary grades. Some of the concepts explored are impossible events and certain events, sampling, collecting data, and simple probabilities. Experiments include work with counters, cards, dice, three-dimensional shapes, spinners, coins, and bottle caps. Read the article and write your reaction to the article. Add this article to your resource file.

   b. *Additional options for your resource file:* Other articles that involve probability and graphing for young children are "A Second-Grade Probability and Graphing Lesson" by Woodward and "Let's Do It: Looking at Facts" by O'Neil and Jensen.

7. *For your resource file:* For other probability lessons, consider the following articles. "Ideas" by Jacobson and Tabler includes activity sheets appropriate for grades 1 through 8. The articles "Activities in Applying Probability Ideas" by Choate, "Ya Gotta Play to Win: A Probability and Statistics Unit for the Middle Grades" by Fennell, and "Probability in the Intermediate Grades" by Enman describe a series of lessons for students in the intermediate grades.

8. Suppose that you as a teacher were setting up a class probability experiment with red and green disks using at least 30 disks. How many red disks and how many green disks would you need so that the probability of drawing a green disk is $\frac{2}{5}$? How many of each would you need to make

the probability of drawing a green disk equal to $\frac{2}{7}$?

9. Devise a lesson to show why the probability values derived from an experiment may differ from the expected theoretical values.

10. Ms. Lee had her students find the probability of obtaining 2 heads when tossing three coins and the probabilities for the ways a paper cup lands when tossed into the air. Both problems involve probability. How do the two experiments differ with respect to probability concepts?

11. *For your resource file:* Need more information on why or how to teach probability? Read "A Case for Probability" by Jones to explore why the topic is essential. For a description of a class dialogue about probability, read "Put Some Probability in Your Classroom" by Burns.

12. *For your resource file:* "Statistical Sampling and Popsicle Sticks" by Shryock includes a description of a lesson on sampling that was used with fourth-grade students.

13. *For your resource file:* Some intriguing and fun games are described in "Fair Games, Unfair Games" by Bright, Harvey, and Wheeler. Play two or three of these games with another student. Add these activities to your resource file.

14. *For your resource file:* Two resources for probability and statistics are the February 1979 issue of the *Arithmetic Teacher* and the 1981 Yearbook of the NCTM, *Teaching Statistics and Probability*. They both have a number of excellent articles on activities for elementary students. Consult the tables of contents for articles that are relevant to you. Read any two of these articles and add them to your resource file.

15. Read a section on probability or statistics from *The Good Time Math Event Book* or *The I Hate Mathematics Book* by Burns. The book you chose would appeal to what age levels? Write your reaction to and evaluation of the section that you read.

TEACHER RESOURCES

Bestgen, Barbara J. "Making and Interpreting Graphs and Tables: Results and Implications from National Assessment." *Arithmetic Teacher* 28 (December 1980): 26–29.

Bohan, Harry, and Edith J. Moreland. "Developing Some Statistical Concepts in the Elementary School." In *Teaching Statistics and Probability,* 1981 Yearbook of the National Council of Teachers of Mathematics, pp. 60–63. Reston, VA: The Council, 1981.

Bright, George W., John G. Harvey, and Margariete Montague Wheeler. "Fair Games, Unfair Games." In *Teaching Statistics and Probability,* 1981 Yearbook of the National Council of Teachers of Mathematics, pp. 49–59. Reston, VA: The Council, 1981.

Bruni, James V., and Helene J. Silverman. "Developing Concepts in Probability and Statistics—And Much More." *Arithmetic Teacher* 33 (February 1986): 34–37.

Burns, Marilyn. *The Good Time Math Event Book.* Illustrated by Richard Wilson. Palo Alto, CA: Creative Publications, 1977.

———. "Put Some Probability in Your Classroom." *Arithmetic Teacher* 30 (March 1983): 21–22.

Choate, Laura Duncan, and JoAnn King Okey. "Graphically Speaking: Primary-Level Graphing Experiences." In *Teaching Statistics and Probability,* 1981 Yearbook of the National Council of Teachers of Mathematics, pp. 33–41. Reston, VA: The Council, 1981.

Choate, Stuart A. "Activities in Applying Probability Ideas." *Arithmetic Teacher* 26 (February 1979): 40–42.

Dickinson, J. Craig. "Gather, Organize, Display: Mathematics for the Information Society." *Arithmetic Teacher* 34 (December 1986): 12–15.

Enman, Virginia. "Probability in the Intermediate Grades." *Arithmetic Teacher* 26 (February 1979): 38–39.

Fennell, Francis (Skip). "Ya Gotta Play to Win: A Probability and Statistics Unit for the Middle Grades." *Arithmetic Teacher* 31 (March 1984): 26–30.

Horak, Virginia M., and Willis J. Horak. "Collecting and Displaying the Data Around Us." *Arithmetic Teacher* 30 (September 1982): 16–20.

———. "Let's Do It: Take a Chance." *Arithmetic Teacher* 30 (May 1983): 8–15.

Jacobson, Marilyn Hall, and M. Bernadine Tabler. "Ideas." *Arithmetic Teacher* 28 (February 1981): 31–36.

Johnson, Elizabeth M. "Bar Graphs for First Graders." *Arithmetic Teacher* 29 (December 1981): 30–31.

Jones, Graham. "A Case for Probability." *Arithmetic Teacher* 26 (February 1979): 37, 57.

Knowler, Kathleen A., and Lloyd A. Knowler. "Using Teaching Devices for Statistics and Probability with Primary Children." In *Teaching Statistics and Probability,* 1981 Yearbook of the National Council of Teachers of Mathematics, pp. 41–44. Reston, VA: The Council, 1981.

Liedtke, Werner, and James Vance. "Stimulating Problem Solving and Classroom Settings." *Arithmetic Teacher* 26 (May 1978): 35–38.

Nibbelink, William. "Graphing for Any Grade." *Arithmetic Teacher* 30 (November 1982): 28–31.

Nuffield Mathematics Project. *Pictorial Representation.* New York: Wiley, 1972.

O'Neil, David R., and Rosalie Jensen. "Let's Do It: Looking at Facts." *Arithmetic Teacher* 29 (April 1982): 12–15.

Scalzitti, Joyce. "Stand Up and Be Counted." *Arithmetic Teacher* 27 (May 1980): 12–13.

Shaw, Jean M. "Ideas." *Arithmetic Teacher* 32 (January 1985): 27–32.

———. "Let's Do It: Dealing with Data." *Arithmetic Teacher* 31 (May 1984): 9–15.

———. "Let's Do It: Making Graphs." *Arithmetic Teacher* 31 (January 1984): 7–11.

Shryock, Jerry. "Statistical Sampling and Popsicle Sticks." In *Teaching Statistics and Probability,* 1981 Yearbook of the National Council of Teachers of Mathematics, pp. 45–49. Reston, VA: The Council, 1981.

Shulte, Albert P. "Learning Probability Concepts in Elementary School Mathematics." *Arithmetic Teacher* 34 (December 1986): 32–33.

Siwakowsky, Evelyn. " 'Top Ten' Mathematics." *Arithmetic Teacher* 28 (March 1981): 25.

Slaughter, Judith Pollard. "The Graph Examined." *Arithmetic Teacher* 30 (March 1983): 41–45.

Smith, Michael S. "Making Averaging Easier." *Arithmetic Teacher* 29 (December 1981): 40–41.

Smith, Robert F. "Bar Graphs for Five-Year-Olds." *Arithmetic Teacher* 27 (October 1979): 38–41.

Sullivan, Delia, and Mary Ann O'Neil. "This Is Us! Great Graphs for Kids." *Arithmetic Teacher* 28 (September 1980): 14–18.

Van Engen, Henry, and Douglas Grouws. "Relations, Number Sentences, and Other Topics." In *Mathematics Learning in Early Childhood,* Thirty-seventh Yearbook of the National Council of Teachers of Mathematics, pp. 251–271. Reston, VA: The Council, 1975.

Woodward, Ernest. "A Second-Grade Probability and Graphing Lesson." *Arithmetic Teacher* 30 (March 1983): 23–24.

CHILDREN'S LITERATURE

Burns, Marilyn. *The I Hate Mathematics Book.* Illustrated by Martha Hairston. Boston: Little, Brown, 1975.

James, Elizabeth, and Carol Barkin. *What Do You Mean by "Average"? Means, Medians, and Modes.* Illustrated by Joel Schick. New York: Lothrop, Lee and Shephard, 1978.

Linn, Charles. *Probability.* Illustrated by Wendy Watson. New York: Crowell, 1972.

Lowenstein, Dyno. *Graphs.* Illustrated by the author. New York: Watts, 1976.

Pallas, Norvin. *Calculator Puzzles, Tricks, and Games.* Illustrated by Joyce Behr. New York: Sterling Publishing, 1976.

Srivastava, Jane Jonas. *Averages.* Illustrated by Aliki Brandenburg. New York: Crowell, 1975.

———. *Statistics.* Illustrated by John Reiss. New York: Crowell, 1973.

Willerding, Margaret F. *Probability: The Science of Chance.* Chicago: Franklin Publications, 1970.

14

TEACHING INTEGERS AND THEIR OPERATIONS

Mr. Scott to colleague, "I don't see why it's important that I should say negative two and positive six instead of minus two and plus six. I've always done it this way . . . The kids know what I mean."

How would you respond if this teacher were one of your colleagues?

CONCEPT OF INTEGERS

Another set of numbers studied in the elementary school is the set of integers. Students may have encountered negative integers earlier when experimenting with a calculator and trying such problems as 3 − 5 or 25 − 100. There are also practical examples of negative integers that they should already have encountered. Probably the most common example is temperatures below zero. Other examples include money owed to someone, an overdrawn bank account, location below sea level, and football yardage penalties.

The concept of integers is a topic in which students can discover patterns. A student already familiar with positive integers can develop the idea of negative integers by an extension of the number line in the opposite direction. If positive integers are thought of as position indicators along a line, negative integers can be introduced as position indicators in the opposite direction. If a positive one is thought of as the location of one unit to the right of zero, then it is logical to think of the location of one unit to the left of zero as a negative one (Figure 14-1).

Using the ground floor of a building as the reference point (corresponding to zero

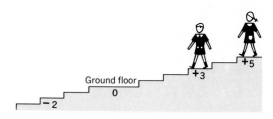

FIGURE 14-2.
Examples of negative integers.

on the number line), students could be asked to go up or down a certain number of steps and then describe their positions numerically. If the school building has no steps, this activity could be done on a floor number line (Figure 14-2). Through this kind of activity, students can learn that a negative one and a positive one cancel each other or make zero. If Jared starts at zero and moves one space right ($^+1$) and one space left ($^-1$), his final location will be the same place that he started, zero.

Counters can also be used to represent integers. Each counter represents a positive one or a negative one (Figure 14-3). If both positive and negative counters appear in the same set, they can be paired. Each pair represents zero, since a negative one and a positive one together make zero. This is similar to the situation where a positive one

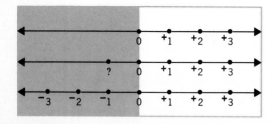

FIGURE 14-1.
Number lines.

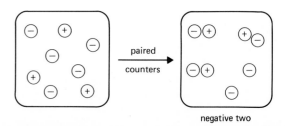

FIGURE 14-3.
Negative and positive counters.

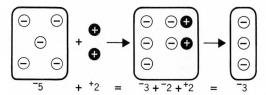

FIGURE 14-4.
Adding integers using counters.

means you have one dollar and a negative one means you owe one dollar. When the debt of one dollar ($^-1$) is paid with a dollar ($^+1$), the result is having zero dollars. Students should be given many examples of determining the value of different sets before being introduced to addition with integers.

The sign of the integer indicates the direction of the number. The numeral of the integer indicates the magnitude or length of the number vector. In some situations the direction of the number is not important; only the magnitude is important. For example, if Tim decided to jog seven miles a day it would not matter in what direction he jogged. When the direction of the number is ignored and only the magnitude is considered, this is the absolute value; that is, the absolute value of a positive seven or a negative seven

is seven. The symbol representation of this concept is $|^-7| = 7$ and $|^+7| = 7$.

ADDING INTEGERS

Counters can be used to explore and develop addition of integers. A situation such as the following can be represented with counters. "Jo wanted to buy an item that cost $5. Since she had $2, how much money would she still owe?" (Figure 14-4) By pairing the counters, the students can readily see the answer is $^-$$3. This is similar to the problems encountered in Figure 14-3.

Addition of integers can also be introduced on the number line. Students can think of a positive integer as indicating a move to the right and a negative integer as indicating a move to the left. They can then easily work addition-of-integer problems (Figure 14-5).

By working many examples both with counters and on a number line, students can soon formulate simple rules for adding integers.

1. If the numbers are positive, add the absolute values, and the result is positive.

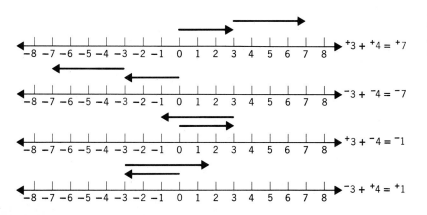

FIGURE 14-5.
Adding integers on the number line.

2. If the numbers are negative, add the absolute values, and the result is negative.

3. If the signs are opposite, find the difference between the two absolute values, and the result takes on the sign of the number that has the larger absolute value.

Students should become well acquainted with the addition process for integers before encountering subtraction problems.

In order to solve some of these problems, students were using the concept of the additive identity. For the problem $^-5 + {}^+2$, two positive counters were paired with two negative counters (Figure 14-4). To solve $^-5 + 2$ on a number line a move of 2 intervals to the left is canceled by a move 2 intervals to the right. Positive two is the additive inverse of negative two, as their sum is zero, the additive identity. Students should generalize that the sum of any number and its additive inverse or negative is zero, or $x + {}^-x = 0$.

For more emphasis on the additive inverse and the identity, the teacher can demonstrate and discuss addition problems using the properties of addition instead of the informal rules developed earlier. In the example shown in Figure 14-6, $^-8$ is rewritten as $^-3 + {}^-5$ because $^-5$ is the additive inverse of $^+5$. This explanation for the addition of two integers is a good introduction for formal proofs which students will encounter in later study of mathematics.

SUBTRACTING INTEGERS

The number line can be used to help students discover the concepts involved in the subtraction of integers. In Figure 14-7a, students are introduced to a problem that they already know, $^+5 - {}^+3$ or $5 - 3$. They ask themselves how far $^+5$ is from $^+3$. Students start drawing their vector from 3 and continue to 5. Since the vector is two units long and it is in the positive direction, the answer is $^+2$. In Figure 14-7b, $^-5 - {}^+3$, the answer is $^-8$ as the vector was drawn 8 units in the negative direction. As students study these

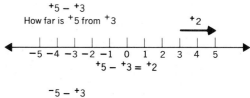

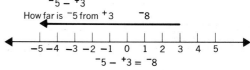

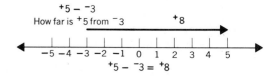

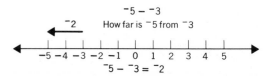

$^-8 + 5 =$	$(^-3 + {}^-5) + 5$	Rewinding $^-8$
	$^-3 + (^-5 + 5)$	Regrouping
		Adding inverses
	$^-3 + 0$	Adding identity
	$^-3$	

FIGURE 14-6.
Explaining addition of integers.

FIGURE 14-7.
Subtraction of integers using vectors.

examples and similar ones, they may observe a pattern. Since students already understand addition of integers, they should be guided to discover the relationship that exists between addition and subtraction of integers. Each of the subtraction problems was considered as a missing-addend problem. The example $^-5 - {}^+3$ was solved by considering $^+3 + \square = {}^-5$. In this case, $^+3 + {}^-8 = {}^-5$.

The subtraction of integers can be solved on the number line by relating it to addition. For example, when students solve the problem $^-5 + {}^+3$ they graph $^-5$ and then add $^+3$ to obtain $^-2$ (Figure 14-8a). Since subtraction is the inverse of addition, they should move the vector in the opposite direction for the problem $^-5 - {}^+3$ (Figure 14-8b).

In studying these examples, it can be seen that some problems have the same solutions. For example, the subtraction problem in Figure 14-8c has the same answer as the addition problem in Figure 14-8b. In fact, every subtraction problem in Figure 14-8 has a corresponding addition problem. Therefore, every subtraction problem can be rewritten as an addition problem. Instead of subtracting a number, the opposite (additive inverse) of the number can be added. For example, $^-5 - {}^+3$ can be written as $^-5 + {}^-3$. By rewriting these subtraction problems as equivalent addition ones, students are simplifying the situation. Then they can use previously learned techniques for the addition of integers.

Counters should also be used to help students develop an understanding of subtraction of integers. For this model, the first number (subtrahend) is represented with the appropriate positive or negative counters, and the take-away approach for subtraction is used. Again, to subtract a positive integer

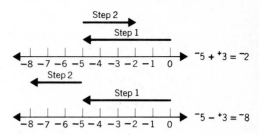

FIGURE 14-8a.
Addition and subtraction of negative and positive integers.

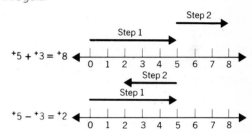

FIGURE 14-8b.
Addition and subtraction of two positive integers.

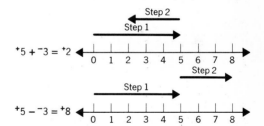

FIGURE 14-8c.
Addition and subtraction of positive and negative integers.

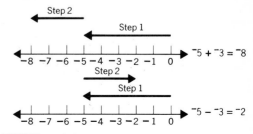

FIGURE 14-8d.
Addition and subtraction of two negative integers.

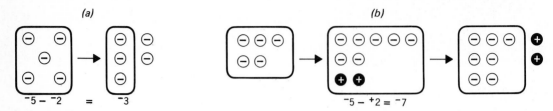

FIGURE 14-9.
Taking away counters when subtracting integers.

from a positive integer, students simply use subtraction of whole numbers. To solve the problem $^-5 - {^-2}$, students would first represent $^-5$ with counters. After taking away two negative counters (subtracting $^-2$), they can see that they have $^-3$ left (Figure 14-9a).

In solving $^-5 - {^+2}$, the students find that after they have represented $^-5$, there are no positive counters to be taken away. Since a negative counter and a positive counter add to zero, pairs of positive and negative counters can be added to the set without changing its value. Therefore, these pairs are added until it is possible to take away the appropriate amount. In this example two pairs of positive and negative counters are added to the original set so that two positive counters can be taken away (Figure 14-9b). The case of a positive integer minus a negative integer can be developed in the same way.

The foregoing process is similar to the equal-additions algorithm for subtraction (Figure 6-59). In this algorithm, instead of regrouping to solve $64 - 38$, students added

10 ones to 64 and 1 ten to 38, thus forming an equivalent, easier-to-solve problem. For integers the numerical process is shown in Figure 14-10. In part (a), positive two was added to both numbers. Consequently, the number to be subtracted is zero—an easy number to subtract. The subtraction computation was simplified by adding the inverse of the number to be subtracted to both numbers.

Some special attention should be given to the cases where the integers to be subtracted both have the same sign, but the one with the *larger* absolute value is being subtracted from the other. Models should also be used to develop this type of problem. To solve $^+4 - {^+7}$, students would first represent $^+4$ with counters. When they begin subtracting, they find that they can not take away 7 positive counters. The additive identity in the form of three pairs of positive and negative integers must be added to the original set so the subtraction can be completed. Now the students can see that $^+4 - {^+7} = {^-3}$ (Figure 14-11).

This type of situation for negative inte-

$$
\begin{array}{r}
^-5 \\
- \ ^-2 \\
\hline
\end{array}
\xrightarrow[\text{add } ^+2]{\text{add } ^+2}
\begin{array}{r}
^-3 \\
- \ 0 \\
\hline
^-3
\end{array}
$$

$$\therefore {^-5} - {^-2} = {^-3}$$

(a)

$$
\begin{array}{r}
^-5 \\
- \ ^+2 \\
\hline
\end{array}
\xrightarrow[\text{add } ^-2]{\text{add } ^-2}
\begin{array}{r}
^-7 \\
- \ 0 \\
\hline
^-7
\end{array}
$$

$$\therefore {^-5} - {^+2} = {^-7}$$

(b)

FIGURE 14-10.
Adding the inverse in subtracting integers.

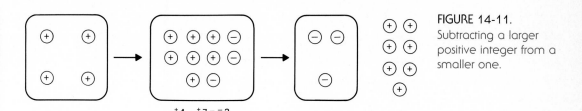

FIGURE 14-11.
Subtracting a larger positive integer from a smaller one.

$^+4 - ^+7 = ^-3$

gers should be developed in a similar way with counters or on a number line. To solve $^-3 - ^-8$ on the number line, Warren thought, "I need to know how far $^-8$ is from $^-3$. To get from $^-8$ to $^-3$, I need to move 5 spaces to the right . . . that's $^+5$ so $^-3 - ^-8 = ^+5$" (Figure 14-12a). Ivy, in solving this same problem on the number line, related it to addition. She thought, "To solve $^-3 + ^-8$, I start at zero, move 3 spaces left, and then move 8 more spaces left. To solve $^-3 - ^-8$, I need to start at zero, move 3 spaces left, and then move 8 spaces right (the inverse). So my answer is $^+5$" (Figure 14-12b).

After students have solved a number of subtraction problems with models, the teacher should write the corresponding addition problem with each subtraction problem. The students should generalize that adding the inverse results in the same solution as subtracting an integer.

MULTIPLYING INTEGERS

Students should have a good understanding of the models and the patterns of addition and subtraction of integers before studying multiplication of integers. Patterns, models, and properties can be used to develop the multiplication generalizations. The first type of integer multiplication encountered is the

a

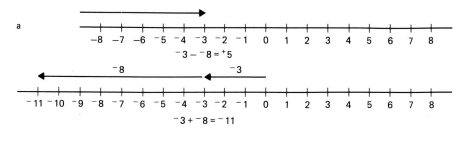

$^-3 - ^-8 = ^+5$

$^-3 + ^-8 = ^-11$

Subtract ion inverse of additon

b

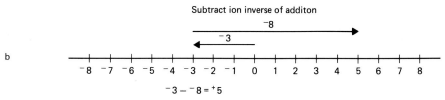

$^-3 - ^-8 = ^+5$

FIGURE 14-12.
Subtracting a smaller negative integer from a larger one.

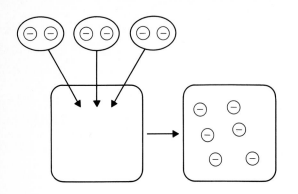

3 sets of negative two is negative six.

$$3(^-2) = ^-6$$

FIGURE 14-13.
Multiplying a positive times a negative—counters.

$$\begin{array}{r} -2 \\ -2 \\ -2 \\ \hline -6 \end{array}$$

case of multiplying a positive integer times another positive integer, which is no different from multiplying whole numbers. Students can easily see that when multiplying two positive integers, the product is also positive.

The second type of problem, that of multiplying a positive times a negative, can be explained by repeated addition. Counters can be used to illustrate and solve the problem (Figure 14-13). Another effective model, a number line, is shown in Figure 14-14 illustrating the problem 5 ($^-4$).

The third type of problem involves multiplying a negative times a positive. Since they have already developed a pattern for multiplying a positive times a negative, students should be able to apply the commutative law of multiplication to show that since 5 ($^-4$) = $^-20$ and 5 ($^-4$) = $^-4$ (5), therefore $^-4$ (5) = $^-20$. Battista, in "A Complete Model for Operations on Integers," extends

the models of counters to include multiplying by negative numbers. To show ($^-4$) 2, he reasons that 4 × 2 and 4 × $^-2$ would mean *adding* 4 sets of 2 or $^-2$ so $^-4$ × 2 means *subtracting* 4 groups of 2. In order to subtract from the set, pairs of positive and negative counters are originally placed in the set so that 4 sets of two can be taken away (Figure 14-15). After subtracting 4 sets of positive two, the students should observe that eight negative counters remain, so $^-4$ × 2 is $^-8$. From experience in solving many problems of this type using both models and the commutative law, students can form the generalization that when multiplying two integers, if the signs are different, the product is negative.

The fourth type of problem, that of multiplying a negative times a negative, can be developed similarly to the example discussed above. To illustrate $^-3$ × $^-2$, the students would again consider a set containing pairs of negative and positive counters (Figure 14-16). In this case 3 sets of $^-2$ would be taken from the set. Six positive counters remain, so $^-3$ × $^-2$ is $^+6$.

A mathematical explanation for why a negative times a negative equals a positive begins with writing an equation showing that

$$5 \times (^-4) = (^-4) + (^-4) + (^-4) + (^-4) + (^-4) = {}^-20$$

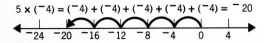

FIGURE 14-14.
Multiplying a positive times a negative—number line.

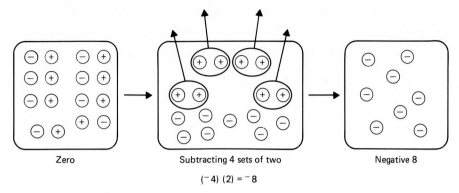

FIGURE 14-15.
Multiplying a negative times a positive.

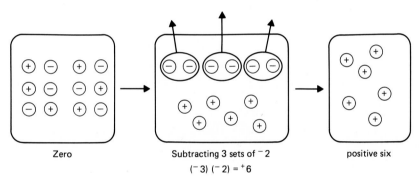

FIGURE 14-16.
Multiplying a negative times a negative.

⁻5 × 0 = 0 as any number times zero is zero (Figure 14-17, Step 1). Since students know that a number added to its additive inverse is zero, they can substitute "⁺4 + ⁻4" for "0" as shown in Step 2. The distributive law can then be applied to obtain the equation in Step 3. Since students know that a negative times a positive is a negative, they know that ⁻5 × ⁺4 is ⁻20. In Step 4, they observe that ⁻20 plus some number (⁻5 × ⁻4) is zero. Since the missing number must be the additive inverse of ⁻20, the missing number is ⁺20. Thus, (⁻5)(⁻4) is

⁺20 (Step 6), or a negative times a negative yields a positive product. Although this is a specific example, the general case can be

Step 1	−5 × 0 = 0
Step 2	(⁻5) × [⁺4 + (⁻4)] = 0
Step 3	(⁻5) × (⁺4) + (⁻5) × (⁻4) = 0
Step 4	⁻20 + (⁻5) × (⁻4) = 0
Step 5	⁺20 = ⁺20
Step 6	(⁻5) × (⁻4) = ⁺20

FIGURE 14-17.
Developing negative times negative.

(a) $30 \div {}^-5 = \square \longrightarrow {}^-5 \times \square = 30 \longrightarrow {}^-5 \cdot {}^-6 = 30 \longrightarrow 30 \div {}^-5 = {}^-6$

(b) ${}^-30 \div 5 = \square \longrightarrow 5 \times \square = {}^-30 \longrightarrow 5 \cdot {}^-6 = {}^-30 \longrightarrow {}^-30 \div 5 = {}^-6$

(c) ${}^-30 \div {}^-5\square \longrightarrow {}^-5 \times \square = {}^-30 \longrightarrow {}^-5 \cdot {}^+6 = {}^-30 \longrightarrow {}^-30 \div {}^-5 = {}^+6$

FIGURE 14-18.
Dividing integers.

proven by replacing the numbers with variables to represent any integers.

The last concept to be developed is that of multiplying more than two integers, for example, $({}^-3)({}^-2)({}^-2)({}^-4)({}^-5)$. In this case, the sign rule for the multiplication of two integers is being extended to a general rule for multiplying any number of integers. Students should be able to discover a generalization for this multiplication related to whether the problem contains an even or an odd number of negative integers. They can readily discover this pattern on a calculator by multiplying a negative integer times a negative integer, that product times another negative integer, and so on.

DIVIDING INTEGERS

The division of integers does not involve a new procedure. It is simply related to division of whole numbers and multiplication of integers. Thus when 30 is to be divided by ${}^-5$, students can rewrite the problem as a missing factor problem (Figure 14-18). From their understanding of the multiplication of integers, they know that ${}^-5 ({}^-6) = {}^+30$. Therefore, $30 \div {}^-5 = {}^-6$. Students can generalize that a positive integer divided by a negative integer yields a negative integer.

In this same manner all the generalizations for the division of integers can be re-

lated to multiplication. The teacher must realize that this is a concept and not a separate algorithm that needs extra computational work. Too often in arithmetic, practice with algorithms has been emphasized when what is to be learned is really a concept that must be developed for understanding.

QUESTIONS AND ACTIVITIES

1. a. Read Froman's *Less Than Nothing Is Really Something,* a children's book about integers.
   b. Play the game P.A.M. with a friend.
   c. Use the activities described in this book to teach a group of children.

2. Mark said that ${}^-8$ is greater than ${}^-7$ as 8 is larger than 7. Ted said that ${}^-7$ is greater than ${}^-8$. Who is correct? How would you help the other student see his mistake and understand the concept?

3. a. Some situations involving integers are given below. Write a number sentence for each.
   (1) Chad already had a debt of 5 dollars. From what he has he must pay a bill of 3 dollars. How much does he owe?
   (2) The temperature was ${}^-6$ degrees; then it dropped 5 degrees. What is the new temperature?

(3) The temperature was ⁻3 on Monday, 5 on Tuesday, 2 on Wednesday, ⁻5 on Thursday, and ⁻8 on Friday. How many degrees did the temperature drop by the end of the week?

(4) The stock lost 3 points every day for 4 days. How many points did it lose during this interval?

b. Write other situations involving comparing integers and the four operations.

c. Consult a textbook series on story problems involving integers. Describe the situations given to motivate the topic.

4. Solve the following problems using positive and negative counters.
   a. $3 + {}^-3$
   b. ${}^-5 + {}^-2$
   c. ${}^-3 + 7$
   d. ${}^-6 + {}^-2$
   e. $4 + {}^-3$

5. Show how a student could use the number line to solve the following problems.
   a. $15 + {}^-7$
   b. $15 + {}^-15$
   c. $15 + {}^-17$
   d. ${}^-8 + {}^-6$
   e. ${}^-8 + 13$

6. Describe how you would use a model to solve addition of integer problems and how you would extend this to help your students arrive at a generalization for addition of integers. Include appropriate examples so that all cases are represented.

7. Use positive and negative counters to solve the following problems.
   a. ${}^+6 - {}^+3$
   b. ${}^-5 - {}^-2$
   c. ${}^-3 - {}^-7$
   d. ${}^-2 - {}^-5$
   e. ${}^+4 - {}^+5$
   f. ${}^-6 - {}^+2$
   g. ${}^+5 - {}^-4$

8. Use a number line or counters to solve the following problems.

   a. $4 + {}^-3$
   b. $4 - {}^-3$
   c. ${}^-4 + {}^-3$
   d. ${}^-4 - {}^-3$

9. Use the number line and the missing addend approach to solve the following problems.
   a. ${}^-5 - 2$
   b. ${}^-3 - {}^-5$
   c. $4 - {}^-2$

10. Describe how you would use a model to solve subtraction of integer problems and how you would extend this to help your students arrive at a generalization for subtraction of integers. Include appropriate examples so that all cases are represented.

11. *For your resource file:* Read one of the articles from the Teacher Resources. "The Integer Abacus" by Dirks describes how to use a special abacus to show addition and multiplication as well as subtraction by adding the opposite. In "A Complete Model for Operations on Integers," Battista uses charged particles (signed counters) to develop the concept of integers and to show all four operations.

12. Use positive and negative counters to solve the following problems.
   a. $5 \times {}^-2$
   b. ${}^-4 \times 3$
   c. ${}^-3 \times {}^-2$
   d. ${}^-2 \times {}^-5$

13. Solve the following problems using the number line.
   a. $2 \times {}^-4$
   b. ${}^-8 \div 2$
   c. ${}^-9 \div 2$

14. Describe how you would use a model to solve multiplication of integer problems and how you would extend this to help your students arrive at a generalization for multiplication of integers. Include appropriate examples so that all cases are represented.

15. Patterns can be used to generate answers for problems involving integers. Solve the first four problems in each part below by using addition of whole numbers. Solve the next three by continuing the pattern of the answers.

a. 5 + 3   b. 4 + 6
   5 + 2   4 + 4
   5 + 1   4 + 2
   5 + 0   4 + 0
   5 + ⁻1   4 + ⁻2
   5 + ⁻2   4 + ⁻4
   5 + ⁻3   4 + ⁻6

16. Revise Problem 15 so that a sequence of number is used to explore subtraction of integers.

17. Revise Problem 15 so that a sequence of number is used to explore multiplication of integers.

18. Use the constant function on your calculator to multiply negative one times itself. Push the $\boxed{=}$ key again, what is your result? Continue depressing the equals key; what patterns do you note? Predict the answers to the problems below and then check using your calculator.

a. (⁻1) 9th
b. (⁻1) 12th
c. (⁻2) 3rd
d. (⁻2) 6th

TEACHER RESOURCES

Battista, Michael T. "A Complete Model for Operations on Integers." *Arithmetic Teacher 30* (May 1983): 26–31.

Dirks, Michael K. "The Integer Abacus." *Arithmetic Teacher 31* (March 1984): 50–54.

Grady, M. B. Tim. "A Manipulative Aid for Adding and Subtracting Integers." *Arithmetic Teacher 26* (November 1978): 40.

Peterson, John C. "Fourteen Different Ways for Multiplication of Integers or Why (⁻1)(⁻1) = ⁺1." *Arithmetic Teacher 19* (May 1972): 396–403.

CHILDREN'S LITERATURE

Froman, Robert. *Less Than Nothing Is Really Something.* Illustrated by Don Madden. New York: Crowell, 1973.

15

TEACHING NUMBER PATTERNS AND THEORY

"Zero? . . . Odd or Even? I don't think it's either."

Evaluate this student thinking. How would you respond?

Ms. Manning commented to her colleague, "My students always get greatest common factor and least common multiple confused." Mr. Payne replied, "I usually just introduce them to factors and multiples and than we look at common factors and common multiples." "Well . . . even if that does work with your students, both LCM and GCF are in our textbook, so I feel I should teach it that way."
Evaluate this thinking.

EVENS AND ODDS

One of the first number patterns children encounter is counting by twos. As discussed in the numeration section on counting, children should explore both the evens and odds by counting by twos. Counting is an introductory activity to evens and odds, but it is not an appropriate strategy for determining whether or not an individual number such as 47 or 82 is even or odd. To determine whether a whole number is even or odd, children can use counters. If all of the counters in the set can be paired, the number is even (Figure 15-1a). If there is an extra counter that cannot be paired, the number is not even; it is odd (Figure 15-1b).

Through such explorations the children are learning various number concepts. They are representing numbers with counters. They are pairing counters, which involves one-to-one correspondence. If one more counter is added to an even number of counters, the new one is unpaired, so the number is odd. Figure 15-1 shows the representations of eight (even) and one more than eight (odd). Through further exploration of adding one more counter, the children should see that the even–odd sequence is an alternating one. These ideas can be extended in later grades with questions such as "Which kind of number will the answer be when you add an even number plus an even number? An even plus an odd? When you multiply an even times an odd? An odd times an odd?" Children may initially use guess and check by trying sample numbers. They should be asked to verify these results by showing their results using counters and explaining why the generalizations will be true. (Two children's books that explore evens and odds are *Odds and Evens* by O'Brien

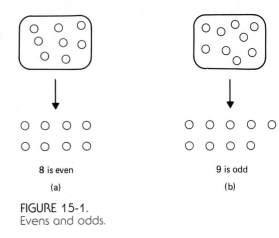

8 is even

(a)

9 is odd

(b)

FIGURE 15-1.
Evens and odds.

and *Number Ideas Through Pictures* by Charosh.)

FACTORS: PRIMES AND COMPOSITES

As students learn multiplication, they are learning that every counting number has factors. Factors are numbers that can be multiplied to yield a given number as a product. For example, $4 \times 3 = 12$ so 4 and 3 are factors of 12, $3 \times 3 = 9$ so 3 is a factor of 9, and $1 \times 5 = 5$ so 1 and 5 are factors of five. The students will soon learn that some numbers have several whole-number factors. For example, 12 has factors of 1, 2, 3, 4, 6, and 12. Other numbers have only two whole-number factors. For example, 1 and 5 are the only two whole numbers that can be multiplied to yield 5 as a product. Any counting number (except 1) that has only two whole-number factors (1 and itself) is called a prime. Those counting numbers that have more than two whole-number factors are called composites.

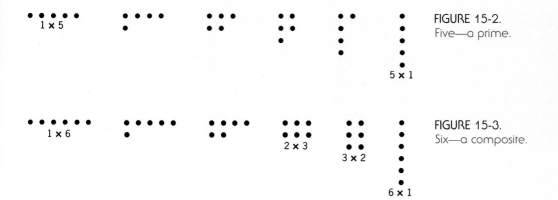

FIGURE 15-2.
Five—a prime.

FIGURE 15-3.
Six—a composite.

The students can easily distinguish between primes and composites using counters, the hundred pegboard, or graph paper. Since primes have only two whole-number factors, there is only one way that the objects representing a prime can be arranged in a rectangular array. Since multiplication is commutative, a 5 × 1 array is equivalent to a 1 × 5 array. Figure 15-2 shows Rachel's steps as she tries to arrange five pegs in a rectangular array. Since she has only found one distinct, rectangular arrangement, she can conclude that 5 is a prime. Figure 15-3 shows possible arrangements of six pegs. Since the pegs can be arranged in two distinct arrays, this shows that 6 has more than two factors and is a composite.

Another model that Rachel could have used to find whether a given number is prime or composite is counting rods such as Cuisenaire rods. First she would select a rod to represent the number she wished to test. Then she would line up smaller rods along this rod to see what its factors are (Figure 15-4). Rachel will find that the only rods she can line up exactly with the black rod are the white rods; therefore, 7 is a prime. Since white and green will both line up exactly with

the blue, she can see that 9 is composite. By counting the rods, she can discover that 1 × 9 or 9 × 1 = 9 and 3 × 3 = 9.

A simple device that students can use for finding primes is called the sieve of Eratosthenes. Students begin by writing the counting numbers in order as far as they wish to go. They omit 1 because it is considered neither prime nor composite. They skip 2, the first prime, and beginning with 4, cross out all the rest of the multiples of 2. then they

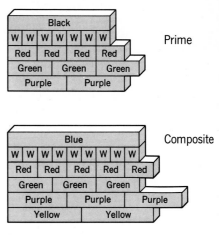

FIGURE 15-4.
Finding factors with Cuisenaire rods.

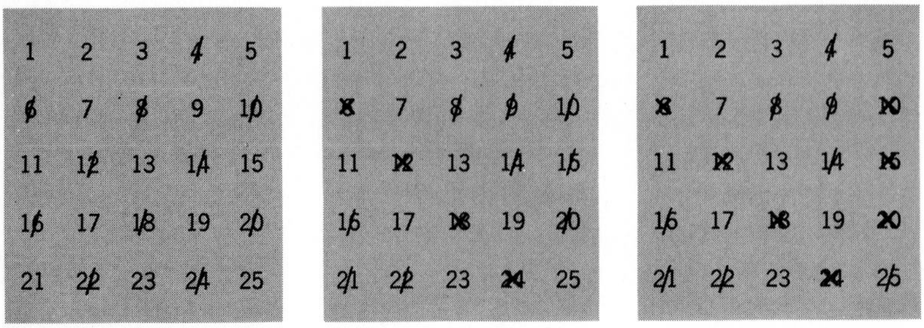

FIGURE 15-5.
Sieve of Eratosthenes.

move to the next number, which is not crossed out. It is a prime so they skip it and then cross out all the larger multiples of it. They continue in this manner until all the composites are crossed. Several steps of this process are shown in Figure 15-5.

At a more abstract level after students have learned to recognize primes and composites, they will notice that some composites have composite factors. For example, two factors of 12 are 3 and 4. Although 3 is a prime, 4 is not. However, 4 has factors of 2 and 2. By substitution, students know that $12 = 3 \times 2 \times 2$, and all these factors are prime. If they started with a different set of factors for 12, 2 and 6, they would see that 2 is prime but 6 is composite. But 6 has factors of 3 and 2, so $12 = 2 \times 3 \times 2$. Finding prime factors in this way will lead the students to the discovery of the fundamental theorem of arithmetic. This states that every composite number has a unique set of prime factors.

This set of prime factors can be found in several ways. One easy method is the factor tree (Figure 15-6). The students write the number and any pair of factors of it. If either of these factors is composite, they write any pair of factors of that factor. They continue this until all the numbers on the ends of the branches are primes. These primes are the unique set of prime factors of the original number.

To find the prime factorization of a number, some students use their number sense. For the examples shown, some students would immediately "see" 36 as being 4×9 (Figure 15-6a) or 6×6 (Figure 15-6b) and start their factor trees with these numbers. They would then write the factors of 4, 9, and 6 accordingly.

Other students may use their knowledge of primes and the problem-solving strategy "guess and check." They may have thought "The smallest prime is 2. Since 2 divides 36, the factors are 2×18 (Figure 15-6d). Two also divides 18. . . ." For a number such as 102 they may think "2 divides 102, so . . . 2×51. 2 doesn't divide 51. . . . 3 divides 51 . . . 17 times. 17 is prime, so 102 is $2 \times 3 \times 17$." They are simply checking the primes in order; this list is the same set of numbers that they found in the Sieve of Eratosthenes.

$36 = 2 \times 2 \times 3 \times 3$

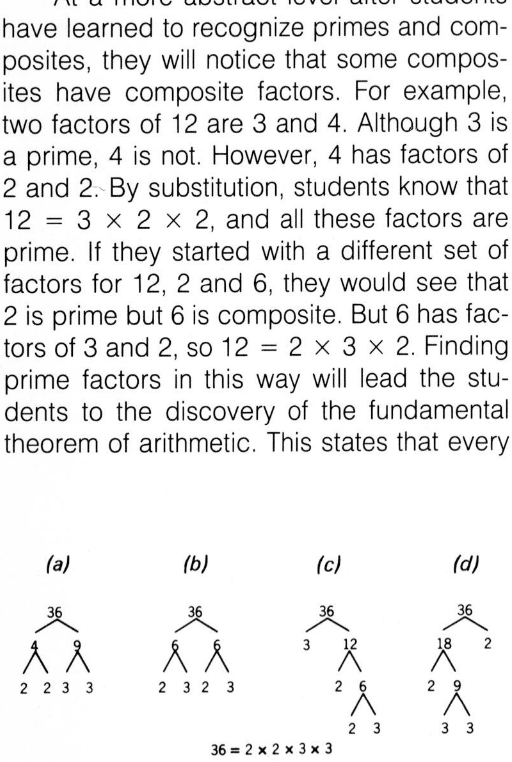

FIGURE 15-6.
Factor trees.

COMMON FACTORS AND COMMON MULTIPLES

Cuisenaire or other counting rods can be used by students to find two special numbers: greatest common factor and least common multiple. Students often confuse these two terms. They perceive *greatest* common factor as a large number, so they think of large numbers or multiples. Similarly, some think of *least* common multiple as being a small number. To counter this confusion, emphasis should be on common *factors* and common *multiples*.

COMMON FACTORS

As students experiment with finding factors of composite numbers, they will probably notice that some numbers have some of the same *factors*. For example, since 3 is a factor of both 12 and 18, it is called a *common factor* (Figure 15-7). Other common factors of 12 and 18 are 1, 2, and 6. In addition to finding the common factors using Cuisenaire rods, students can look at the rods representing these common factors and immedi-

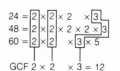

FIGURE 15-8.
Greatest common factor.

ately see that 6 is the largest, so it is the greatest common factor.

The greatest common factor is the largest whole number that will exactly divide two or more given numbers. For example, the greatest common factor of 12 and 8 is 4; the greatest common factor of 5 and 4 is 1; the greatest common factor of 6 and 18 is 6. For these relatively small numbers, it is easy to find the greatest common factor by inspection or by using models. For larger numbers, using models becomes cumbersome and time consuming.

Prime factorization can be used to find the greatest common factor at an abstract level (Figure 15-8). Given the numbers 24, 48, and 60, Dean first wrote the prime factors of each. Then he selected the set of prime factors that is a subset of each of these sets. These factors were multiplied to give the greatest common factor.

This concept is useful when students

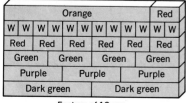

Factors of 12 are
1,2,3,4,6,12

Factors of 18 are
1,2,3,6,9,18

Common factors of
12 and 18 are 1,2,3,6

FIGURE 15-7.
Common factors.

are renaming fractions in simplest form. They can simply find the greatest common factor of the numerator and denominator and divide both by that greatest common factor (GCF) to give an equivalent fraction in simplest form. For a fraction such as $\frac{18}{24}$, some students will immediately see that 6 is the greatest common factor, so $(3 \times 6)/(4 \times 6)$ is $\frac{3}{4}$. Others will note that both 18 and 24 have a factor of 2 and will rename the fraction $\frac{9}{12}$. Since 9 and 12 both have a common factor of 3, the fraction can be renamed to $\frac{3}{4}$. In the second situation the student took two steps using, one at a time, the prime factors (2 and 3) of the greatest common factor (6) to achieve the same result.

COMMON MULTIPLES

In children's early experiences with counting, they learn to count by multiples such as 10, 20, 30, and so on. They can use Cuisenaire rods to count by multiples by making a rod train using a single color. For example, as they place red rods end to end they may count 2, 4, 6, and so forth. They can also use rod trains to find common multiples of two or more numbers. Figure 15-9 shows how children can find several common multiples of 2 and 3. Each time the length of the 2 train and the length of the 3 train match, the students have found another common multiple. The *common multiples* shown are 6, 12, 18, and 24. The first and smallest of these common multiples is the least common multiple. The least common multiple (LCM) is the

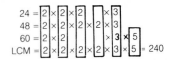

FIGURE 15-10.
Least common multiple (denominator).

smallest number such that the given numbers are all factors of it. For example, the least common multiple of 12 and 8 is 24; the least common multiple of 5 and 3 is 15; the least common multiple of 6 and 18 is 18. As with the greatest common factor, the least common multiple can be found using prime factors. Again, the student would write the prime factors of each given number. The prime factors of the least common multiple are found by selecting all factors that occur in any one of the numbers and using each the largest number of times it occurs in any one number (Figure 15-10). In the example, to be a multiple of 24 the least common multiple must contain factors of 2, 2, 2, and 3. The other numbers (48 and 60) are accounted for similarly.

This concept is also useful for renaming fractions since the least common denominator is simply the least common multiple of two or more denominators. Applying this same procedure to addition of unlike fractions, Bob found the prime factors of the given denominators (Figure 15-11). From the 12 he selected the prime factors 2, 2, and 3 so that his new denominator would be divisible by 12. From the 15 he selected the

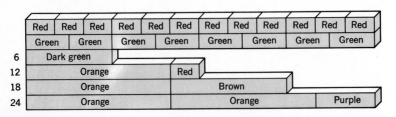

FIGURE 15-9.
Common multiples.

$$\frac{1}{12} + \frac{4}{15} + \frac{7}{10} = \frac{5}{60} + \frac{16}{60} + \frac{42}{60} = \frac{63}{60}$$

$12 = 2 \times 2 \times 3$
$15 = 3 \times 5$ LCM or LCD $= 2 \times 2 \times 3 \times 5 = 60$
$10 = 2 \times 5$

FIGURE 15-11.
Finding common denominator with primes.

prime factor 5, and since he had already selected a factor of 3, his new denominator will be divisible by 15. From the 10 he selected no prime factors because he had already selected factors of 2 and 5 so his denominator will be divisible by 10. He multiplied the selected factors to obtain a lowest common denominator for twelfths, fifteenths, and tenths. He renamed his fractions with a denominator of 60 and added.

LeAnn used *multiples and factors* to find the lowest common denominator for these same fractions. She recognized that the common multiple of 10 and 15 is 30. She then considered 30 and 12. Since 12 does not divide 30, she considered their factors, "12 is 3 × 4. 3 divides 30 but 4 doesn't. 30 . . . 3 × 10 . . . has one 2 as a factor . . . . In order to be divisible by 4 it needs another 2. So 30 × 2 is 60."

For fractions such as $\frac{3}{10}$ and $\frac{7}{15}$ or $\frac{5}{6}$ and $\frac{7}{8}$, the lowest common denominators or least common multiples are 30 and 24, respectively. Some students may use 48 as the common denominator when adding $\frac{5}{6}$ and $\frac{7}{8}$. They have chosen *a* common denominator

but not the *least* common denominator. Their procedures are not incorrect, but they may be more likely to make errors due to the larger numbers involved or they may not rename to the simplest form for their answer. The simpler form is desirable, as it is usually easier to comprehend.

SQUARE AND TRIANGULAR NUMBERS

In previous sections primes and composites were linked to arrays or rectangular models. Children encounter square numbers when they are introduced to the array of a number times itself and to areas of squares. Square numbers are informally defined in Figure 15-12. From such examples students should be able to determine that square numbers are those which can be arranged in an array with the same number of counters in each row and column. Children can use counters, drawings, or graph paper to explore such questions as "What is the next largest square after 25? What is the smallest square number? Is 18 a square number? What are the lengths of the sides of the square number 64?"

These ideas can be extended into problem-solving activities at various grade levels. If the students are looking at the sequence of square numbers, they should be able to write the square number if they know which term it is in the sequence (Figure 15-13). Stu-

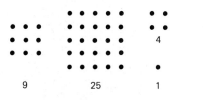

9   25   1

These are square numbers

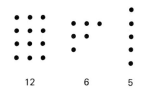

12   6   5

These are not.

FIGURE 15-12.
Square numbers.

Model	•	∴	••• ••• •••	•••• •••• •••• ••••	
Term	1	2	3	4	
Value	1	4	9	16	

FIGURE 15-13.
Square number sequence.

FIGURE 15-14.
Triangular numbers.

dents in upper grades should write this relationship in general terms.

Like square numbers, triangular numbers derive their names from their geometric representations. Counters or diagrams can be used to introduce triangular numbers. The first three triangular numbers are shown in Figure 15-14. The children should discuss how these were formed. They should then find the next triangular numbers in the sequence by drawing their pictures and determining their values. Students should be encouraged to find a general pattern for generating the next triangular number. This activity can be extended to determine the triangular number by knowing what number it is in the sequence. Students in upper grades should be encouraged to generalize this in terms of an unknown.

QUESTIONS AND ACTIVITIES

1. *For your resource file:* Two children's books that introduce evens and odds are *Odds and Evens* by O'Brien and *Number Ideas Through Pictures* by Charosh. The article "My Favorite Lesson: Odds and Evens" by Huff also deals with this topic. Read and evaluate one of these resources. Add the ideas to your resource file.

2. a. What problem-solving strategies could children use to answer "What is an even plus an even? An odd plus an odd? An even plus an odd? An even times an even? An even times an odd? An odd times an odd?"
   b. What generalizations should they make?
   c. How would you help children form a generalization for an even times an odd?

3. *For your resource file:* An activity extending the Sieve of Eratosthenes is described in "Patterns in Multiples" by Robold. Read and work through the article. A 10 by 10 array of the numbers 1 through 100 is needed for the activity. Copy the article or some of the ideas for your resource file.

4. Use counters, a pegboard, or graph paper to show that 7 is a prime number and 12 is a composite number.

5. "My Favorite Lesson: Odds and Evens" by Huff gives ideas on appropriate models and activities for introducing odd and even numbers. Devise a lesson plan for introducing this concept.

6. *For your resource file:* Read and copy one of the following articles: "An Inductive Approach to Prime Factors" by Hohlfeld, "Definitions for Prime Numbers" by Burton

and Knifong, and "Prime Factorization" by Lappan and Winter.

7. Play the following game with another student. First, list the numbers 1 through 31. One person selects a number and crosses out that number and all of its factors. The first person takes as a score the number itself, and the other person's score is the sum of all the factors that were crossed out. Play continues to the second person; only the unmarked numbers are considered. The second person selects a number, adds that number to his/her score, and crosses out that number and all of its factors. The other player adds all of these factors to his or her score. Play continues until all the numbers are crossed out. The player with the greatest score wins. (*Note:* To introduce the game to a class, the teacher can play against the class. After they understand the game, students can play in pairs. After players determine winning strategies, the list of numbers can be changed.)

8. Reys et al. included a number of activities involving factors, primes and composites, prime factorization, and divisibility tests in *Keystrokes: Calculator Activities for Young Students—Multiplication and Division.* Use your calculator to work through some of the activities. Add some of these ideas to your resource file.

9. *Materials needed:* Cuisenaire rods. Solve each problem using the indicated model. Diagram your process and solution.
   a. Use Cuisenaire rods to find the first 3 common multiples of 3 and 2.
   b. Use Cuisenaire rods to find the least common multiple of 4, 5, and 8.
   c. Use a number line to find the least common multiple of 2, 5, and 3.
   d. Use Cuisenaire rods to find the common factors of 6 and 24.
   e. What is the greatest common factor of 6 and 24?

10. *For your resource file:* Read and copy "Star Patterns" by Bennett. In this article least common multiples and greatest common factors are linked to geometric shapes.

11. Analyze each of the following multiplication examples. Do the sample problem using the same method.

a.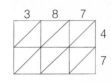

b.
$$\begin{array}{r} 36 \\ \times 12 \end{array} \rightarrow \begin{array}{r} 72 \\ \times\ 6 \\ \hline 432 \end{array} \qquad \begin{array}{r} 42 \\ \times 18 \end{array}$$

c.
$$\begin{array}{r} \cancel{45 \times 22} \\ 90 \times 11 \\ 180 \times\ 5 \\ \cancel{360 \times\ 2} \\ 720 \times\ 1 \\ \hline 990 \end{array} \qquad 52 \times 38$$

12. *For your resource file:* Various articles from the *Arithmetic Teacher* contain ideas for problem-solving lessons on number patterns. Read, copy, and evaluate one of the following articles for your resource file. In "Painless Drilling—Not Your Dentist, but the History of Mathematics" by Krulik the history of such topics as magic squares and hexagons, Egyptian multiplication, lattice multiplication, perfect numbers, and amicable numbers are described and explained. Bernard describes several games in "Constructing Magic Square Number Games." Whitin describes more patterns in "More Magic with Palindromes."

13. a. Draw a picture of the first five triangular numbers. The first five square numbers.
   b. An extension involving number patterns is to find the relationship between triangular and square numbers. In *Number Ideas Through Pictures,* Charosh shows combining pairs of

consecutive triangular numbers to represent square numbers. What is the relationship between square and triangular numbers?

c. As a further extension determine the sum of the sequence of square numbers or triangular numbers. In the problem-solving chapter, Elizabeth found the sum of the first 12 counting numbers and then the sum of the first 100 numbers. Finding the sum of the sequence of the squares is a similar problem for students who are more mathematically mature.

14. *For your resource file:* Triangular numbers are related to another number pattern, Pascal's triangle. Read about this pattern and its relationship to other topics in "Thank You, Mr. Pascal" by Jordan. Add these ideas to your resource file.

NUMBER PATTERNS AND FUNCTIONS

As children explore number concepts and operations, they will encounter various patterns. Similarly as they explore number patterns, they will learn more about number. Some of these relationships can be written as numerical expressions or sentences. As students mature mathematically, they will learn to write these relationships in more general or more abstract terms. Writing equations is an important problem-solving strategy as number sentences can help children express the relationships that they find in verbal problems. A special type of number sentence is called a function.

Functions can be informally introduced in the elementary school with practical situations. In one second-grade textbook, the problem-solving strategy "make a table" is used to solve a problem involving functions (Figure 15-15). The children know that 1 pencil costs 2 cents; they are to determine the cost of 4 pencils. The relationship between pencils and cents is called a function because the cost depends on (is a function of) the number of pencils. As the number of pencils increases or decreases, the number of cents changes accordingly. Note that this is a ratio-and-proportion problem that was solved by repeated units.

Many other practical examples of functions can be found. The number of student desks needed in the classroom is a function of the number of students in the class; the cost of a tank of gasoline is a function of the number of gallons the tank holds; the number of kilometers traveled on a given bicycle is a function of the number of revolutions of the wheels.

Functions can be explored informally through the use of pattern or function "machines." The function "machine" follows a specified rule to perform certain tasks on any number fed into it. For example, Figure 15-16a shows a function "machine" whose rule is "add 2." No matter what number is fed into it, the "machine" always adds 2 and gives a corresponding output.

Function "machines" are simply a format to introduce a particular pattern to the students. The format could be a written or oral whole-class activity. If the function is "multiply by three," the teacher can say or write various numbers one at a time. The children are to write the result after they multiply the number by three. The function machine could be a calculator. If "subtract four" is the constant function programmed into the calculator, students can enter any number, guess the answer, and then depress the equal key to check their answer. All of these formats are excellent ways of including mental arithmetic in the classroom.

Figure 15-16b shows the function writ-

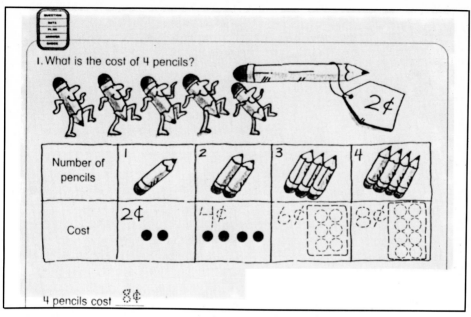

FIGURE 15-15.
Building a table. (From Robert Eicholz, Phares O'Daffer, Charles Fleenor, Randall Charles, Sharon Young, Carne Barnett, **Addison-Wesley Mathematics: Book 2,** p. 220 Copyright © 1985, Addison-Wesley Publishing Co. Inc.

ten as an equation in which placeholders are used to represent the input and output numbers. After selecting various values for the square placeholder, the students can find the corresponding values for the triangular placeholder. Notice that for any particular value selected for the input there is one and only one output.

One of the early number patterns that young children explore is finding the various partitions of a number. For the number six, they arrange and rearrange the counters forming different combinations that all add to six. They will note that as one addend is relatively small the other is relatively large. At first they may record their results as an organized list (Figure 15-17a). Later they will

write number sentences that express their results. This relationship could be written as the function $\square + \triangle = 6$.

If students had first been given the function $\square + \triangle = 6$, they could have substituted

RULE   ADD 2

Input   Output
$2 \longrightarrow \boxed{+2} \longrightarrow 4$

$3 \longrightarrow \boxed{+2} \longrightarrow 5$

$4 \longrightarrow \boxed{+2} \longrightarrow 6$

(a)

$\square + 2 = \triangle$

$\square$	$\triangle$
2	4
3	5
4	6

(b)

FIGURE 15-16.
Function "machine" and table.

$\Box + \triangle = 6$

□	△
0	6
1	5
2	4
3	3
4	2
5	1
6	0

(a)

$\Box + \triangle = 5$

□	△
0	5
1	4
2	3
3	2
4	1
5	0

(b)

FIGURE 15-17.
Functions using placeholders.

Replacement Set

Positive Rationals		Integers		All Rationals	
□	△	□	△	□	△
1	4	1	4	1	4
$2\frac{1}{2}$	$2\frac{1}{2}$	-3	8	$2\frac{1}{2}$	$2\frac{1}{2}$
$3\frac{3}{4}$	$1\frac{1}{4}$	14	-9	-3	8
$2\frac{46}{793}$	$2\frac{747}{793}$	-342	347	$2\frac{46}{793}$	$2\frac{747}{793}$
				-342	347

$\Box + \triangle = 5$

FIGURE 15-18.
Various replacement sets.

various values for the square placeholder to find the value of the triangular placeholder. Their results would be the same as those above (Figure 15-17a). Students can easily see that this function has several solutions. In looking at the same table, they can see that $\Box + \Box = 6$, where the square placeholder represents the same number each time it is used, has only one solution. By making a similar table for $\Box + \triangle = 5$ (Figure 15-17b), they can see that $\Box + \Box = 5$ has no whole-number solution.

The set of numbers from which the values for the placeholders are chosen is called the replacement set as the numbers "replace" the placeholders or unknowns. If the set of rational numbers were chosen as the replacement set in the preceding example, then $\Box + \Box = 5$ would have one solution, $2\frac{1}{2}$. The replacement set used for any given function will depend on the mathematical maturity of the students. In the examples $\Box + \triangle = 6$ and $\Box + \triangle = 5$, the replacement set, whole numbers, yielded a finite number of solutions. For more mathematically mature students, the set of positive rationals, the set of integers, or the set of all rationals might have been chosen as a replacement set. In these cases the set of possible solutions becomes infinitely large. Some examples of so-

lutions for $\Box + \triangle = 5$ using each of these replacement sets are shown in Figure 15-18.

We can also use the concept of inverse operations to solve functions. Because students know that addition and subtraction are inverses and multiplication and division are inverses, they can easily complete the tables shown in Figure 15-19. Through class discussion students can discover that the first table can be filled in by adding 5 to the value of the square placeholder *or* by subtracting 5 from the value of the triangular placeholder. The second table can be filled in similarly by multiplying the value of the square placeholder by 2 *or* by dividing the value of the triangular placeholder by 2.

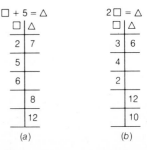

$\Box + 5 = \triangle$

□	△
2	7
5	
6	
	8
	12

(a)

$2\Box = \triangle$

□	△
3	6
4	
2	
	12
	10

(b)

FIGURE 15-19.
Completing function tables.

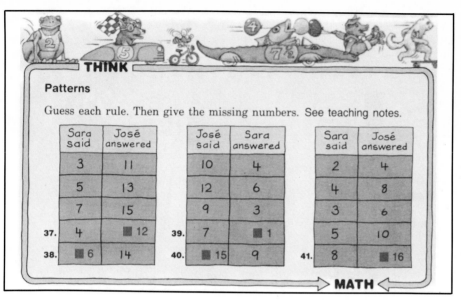

FIGURE 15-20.

Guess each rule. (From Robert Eicholz, Phares O'Daffer, Charles Fleenor, Randall Charles, Sharon Young, Carne Barnett, **Addison-Wesley Mathematics: Book 4,** p. 11. Copyright © 1985, Addison-Wesley Publishing Co. Inc.)

More sophisticated patterns or functions can be introduced by using various other patterns. The rule might be to multiply a number by itself, or it might be to multiply by one number and then subtract some other number. These activities can be extended to include numbers other than whole numbers such as rationals or integers. Students might be given the output and the rule and asked to find the input.

Functions can be used for problem solving as well as for practice in arithmetic operations. After students understand this format, they can begin playing the "what's-my-rule" game. In this game the students are given several corresponding input and output numbers and asked to find the pattern or function.

Figure 15-20 shows an example from one fourth-grade textbook. The students are given the input or original number and the corresponding answer or output. In the first situation the students should observe that the outputs are increasing. Since their replacement set is the set of whole numbers, they would be thinking that the operation must be addition or multiplication. By noting how the numbers are increasing they should decide that addition (in this particular example adding eight) is the missing pattern.

Students may observe that there is a difference of 1 between the first two inputs and outputs in the example taken from a sixth-grade textbook (Figure 15-21). But the difference is in a different order. Also, the next entries should indicate that the pattern was

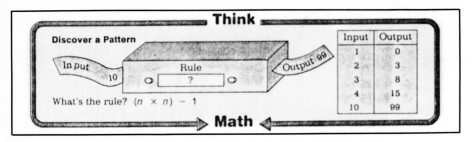

FIGURE 15-21.
What's the rule? (From Robert Eicholez, Phares O'Daffer, Charles Fleenor, Randall Charles, Sharon Young, Carne Barnett, **Addison-Wesley Mathematics: Book 6,** p. 5. Copyright © 1985, Addison-Wesley Publishing Co. Inc.)

formed by more than one operation and multiplication is one of the operations. As students analyze these types of patterns, they will learn more about number and its operations and also develop problem-solving and mental arithmetic skills.

In upper grades these number patterns will be extended as students graph the results. Graphing activities in the coordinate system can also be used in the study of patterns and functions. Figure 15-22 shows the graph of the function $\square + 2 = \triangle$. Notice in the figure that x has been substituted for the square placeholder and y has been substituted for the triangular placeholder. Students

are usually surprised that their results lie in a straight line. They should be encouraged to check the points that lie between the plotted points. The student will find that coordinates such as $(2\frac{1}{2}, \frac{1}{2})$ and $(4\frac{2}{3}, 2\frac{2}{3})$ are also correct solutions. Through further exploration, they can conclude that the points can be connected to form a straight line. After hypothesizing that all points on the line are correct, the students should check points not on the line. They should conclude that the solution set for $x + 2 = y$ lies only on the line that they have drawn. This number sentence can be called a linear equation with two unknowns since the graph of its solution is a straight line.

In the elementary school generally only linear equations are studied to any extent. However, for enrichment, simple nonlinear equations might also be introduced. These include nonlinear functions such as $x^2 = y$ and $xy = 12$ and also sentences such as $x^2 + y^2 = 25$ and $6x^2 + 9y^2 = 36$, which are not functions. The students will enjoy predicting what the graphs of these equations will look like and then actually graphing the equations to check their predictions.

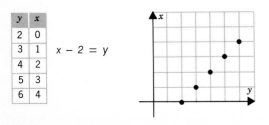

FIGURE 15-22.
Graph of the linear equation $x + 2 = y$.

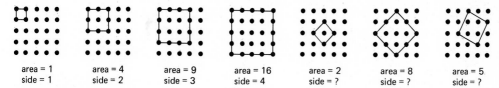

| area = 1 | area = 4 | area = 9 | area = 16 | area = 2 | area = 8 | area = 5 |
| side = 1 | side = 2 | side = 3 | side = 4 | side = ? | side = ? | side = ? |

FIGURE 15-23.
Squares on a geoboard.

A SPECIAL FUNCTION— SQUARE ROOTS

A special function encountered in middle school is square roots. In earlier grades students explore numbers and their squares. Later, they encounter numbers and their square roots. This topic is often student-generated. Students may observe that 11 times itself is 121 and then wonder what number times itself is 120. Or when finding all possible squares on a geoboard they may observe that the squares with areas of 1, 4, 9, and 16 have sides of 1, 2, 3, and 4, respectively, so what are the lengths of the sides of the squares with areas of 5, 8, or 2? (Figure 15-23) Since the square roots of these numbers are not whole numbers, they are more difficult to find.

Approximations can be found of the square roots of these numbers. To find the square root of 8, students might use one of several approaches. They could use a calculator with a square root key or look up the square root of 8 in a table. If they did not have these options available, they should use their calculators and estimation skills.

Figure 15-24 shows how students used the problem-solving strategies, "guess and check" and "make an organized list," to find an approximation for the square root of 8. Since they knew that $2^2 = 4$ and $3^2 = 9$,

they reasoned that the square root of 8 must be between 2 and 3. First they guessed 2.5, multiplied that times itself on their calculators, and recorded their results (Figure 15-24a). Since $2.5^2 < 8$, they could see that they needed to try a larger number. Their next guess was 2.7; but 2.7 squared is 7.29, which is still too small. They continued with the other steps shown and, from the last two steps, concluded that for two decimal places 2.83 is the closest approximation of the square root of 8. Other students solving this same problem might use more or fewer steps, depending on how many decimal places they wanted in their answer. Also, in the beginning some students might have reasoned that since 8 is closer to 9 than to 4, the square root of 8 will be closer to 3 than to 2. This could eliminate the first one or two steps.

An algorithm for finding square roots

a	$2.5 \times 2.5 = 6.25$	too small
b	$2.7 \times 2.7 = 7.29$	too small
c	$2.9 \times 2.9 = 8.41$	too large
d	$2.8 \times 2.8 = 7.84$	too small
e	$2.85 \times 2.85 = 8.1225$	too large
f	$2.83 \times 2.83 = 8.0089$	too large
g	$2.82 \times 2.82 = 7.9524$	too small

FIGURE 15-24.
Finding square root with a calculator.

used to be taught but has now become virtually obsolete. This algorithm was so complicated that it was difficult to learn, use, or remember. Now it has been replaced with new technology, the calculator. Not only is finding square roots with a calculator easier than using the algorithm, but the method can be generalized to cube roots.

In elementary school, squares and square roots are also explored in the Pythagorean theorem. In working with right triangles the students can be introduced to Pythagoras' theorem. Pythagoras, who was a Greek mathematician, lived about 540 B.C. He observed that the sum of the squares of the two sides of a right triangle is equal to the square of the hypotenuse (Figure 15-25). This relationship holds true for all right triangles. The ancient Egyptians used this relationship in their construction of pyramids. They used a rope with knots at intervals of 3, 4, and 5 units to make sure that the corners of the bases of the pyramids were square. The Egyptians knew from experience that the relationship was true for this particular triangle (3, 4, 5), but it was Pythagoras who first proved that it was true for all right triangles. To informally prove this relationship a student can construct squares on

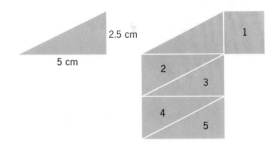

FIGURE 15-26.
One dissection showing Pythagorean theorem.

the three sides and rearrange the smaller squares so that they fit into the larger square as shown in Figure 15-25.

Another solution for some right triangles is shown in Figure 15-26. This solution is only appropriate for right triangles whose legs are in a ratio of two to one. The students constructed squares on both legs and then cut the larger square into four pieces. They rearranged the five pieces so that they formed a square on the third side of the triangle.

A more sophisticated dissection is shown in Figure 15-27. This construction will work for any right triangle. After constructing squares on each of the legs, the students locate point D in the large square. Point D is

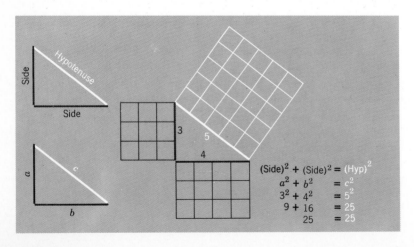

FIGURE 15-25.
Pythagorean theorem.

$$(Side)^2 + (Side)^2 = (Hyp)^2$$
$$a^2 + b^2 = c^2$$
$$3^2 + 4^2 = 5^2$$
$$9 + 16 = 25$$
$$25 = 25$$

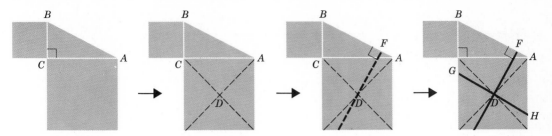

FIGURE 15-27.
General dissection showing Pythagorean theorem.

the intersection of the diagonals of the large square. Line segment EF is constructed so that it is perpendicular to $\overline{AB}$ and passes through point D. Line segment GH is constructed so that it is perpendicular to $\overline{EF}$ and passes through point D. The students can then cut out and rearrange these four pieces and the small square so that they form a larger square on $\overline{AB}$. These dissections can be done informally with students as problem-solving activities before formal study of the Pythagorean relationship.

Once students understand this relationship they can use it to find the length of one side of a right triangle when they know the lengths of the other two sides. In order to find the missing length, students must find the square root of a number. In the first example, the two given sides are 3 and 4. Since $3^2 + 4^2 = c^2$, $9 + 16 = c^2$ or $25 = c^2$. Therefore, the length of c was 5, the square root of 25. In the second example, $2.5^2 + 5^2 = c^2$ or $6.25 + 25 = c^2$. To find the length of c, the student must solve $c^2 = 31.25$.

PATTERNS IN FINITE SYSTEMS

It looks strange to write "4 + 7 = 4" or "2 + 13 = 1." However, this is the type of thinking we use when considering, "Wednesday, 7 days from now is Wednesday. Monday, 13 days or 2 weeks minus 1 day is Sunday." The days in the week and the days in a month are two examples that we encounter that involve finite systems.

A finite system is a number system that contains a limited number of elements. All operations within the system use only these limited elements. One of the simplest and most familiar finite systems is the ordinary clock which is part of every child's daily life. This system contains just twelve elements, namely the numbers 1 through 12. Addition in this finite system can easily be introduced by using questions such as, "It is now four o'clock. What time will it be nine hours from now?" It cannot be thirteen o'clock because thirteen is not an element of this system. Since it will be twelve o'clock in eight hours, in nine hours it will be one o'clock. So 4 + 9 = 1 in a finite system based on twelve.

This type of thinking can be explored as an enrichment activity on finite systems. After solving similar problems, the students can develop an addition table for a clock twelve system (Figure 15-28). As the students enter results in the table, they should become aware of certain patterns and make predictions about answers. More complex questions such as "It is now eight o'clock;

+	1	2	3	4	5	6	7	8	9	10	11	12
1	2	3	4	5	6	7	8	9	10	11	12	1
2	3	4	5	6	7	8	9	10	11	12	1	2
3	4	5	6	7	8	9	10	11	12	1	2	3
4	5	6	7	8	9	10	11	12	1	2	3	4
5	6	7	8	9	10	11	12	1	2	3	4	5
6	7	8	9	10	11	12	1	2	3	4	5	6
7	8	9	10	11	12	1	2	3	4	5	6	7
8	9	10	11	12	1	2	3	4	5	6	7	8
9	10	11	12	1	2	3	4	5	6	7	8	9
10	11	12	1	2	3	4	5	6	7	8	9	10
11	12	1	2	3	4	5	6	7	8	9	10	11
12	1	2	3	4	5	6	7	8	9	10	11	12

FIGURE 15-28.
Addition table clock twelve.

what time will it be 39 hours from now?" can then be introduced.

As the students determine answers or as they examine the clock arithmetic table, they should discover the identity element and the additive inverse for each number. To discover the identity element of addition, students must ask, "What number can be added to any other number and yield a result of that same number?"

By studying the table, students should soon realize that when "12" is added to any number, the result is that same number. To find the additive inverse the student must ask what number must be added to a number to obtain the additive identity "12." Therefore, the additive inverse of 7 is 5 since 7 + 5 = 12.

The students should check to see if the commutative and associative principles hold for clock arithmetic (Figure 15-29). Some simple examples or an analysis of the addi-

tion table will demonstrate that 0 and 12 are the same number in a modular twelve system. Therefore, the addition table for clock arithmetic in Figure 15-28 can be changed to the modular twelve system by substituting 0 for the numeral 12. Experiences in a finite system other than twelve should also be included. For example, modular three will include just the number 0, 1, and 2. (An excellent children's book that explores finite systems is *Solomon Grundy Born on Oneday: A Finite Arithmetic Puzzle* by Weiss.)

Multiplication in modular systems can

$$\overset{?}{5 + 8 = 8 + 5}$$
$$1 = 1$$

Commutative

$$\overset{?}{(5 + 8) + 7 = 5 + (8 + 7)}$$
$$1 + 7 = 5 + 3$$
$$8 = 8$$

Associative

FIGURE 15-29.
Examples of the commutative and associative principles for clock arithmetic.

$$7 \times 8 = 56$$
$$= 48 + 8$$
$$= (4 \times 12) + 8$$
$$= (4 \times 0) + 8$$
$$= 0 + 8$$
$$= 8$$

FIGURE 15-30.
Multiplication—mod twelve.

(a) $6 \times 0 = 0$
(b) $6 \times 2 = 12$ but $12 = 0$
      $= 0$
(c) $6 \times 4 = 24$
           2×12 factors of 24
           2×0 $12 = 0$
           0
(d) $6 \times 6 = 36$
           3×12 factors of 36
           3×0 $12 = 0$
           0

FIGURE 15-32.
Multiplication by sixes, modular system twelve.

be introduced along with the other operations. To multiply 7×8 in the modular twelve system, the student simply multiplies as usual but then changes the answer to its modular twelve equivalent (Figure 15-30). The students should note that some numbers in modular twelve do not have unique factors. For example, six can be written as $6 \times 1, 6 \times 3, 6 \times 5, 6 \times 7, 9 \times 2, 9 \times 6$, and so on (Figure 15-31). The explanation is shown in Figure 15-32.

The commutative and associative properties of multiplication can be verified by the students. The identity element of multiplication is 1, since 1 times any element is that element. But some numbers do not have multiplicative inverses. For example, $2 \times \square = 1$ cannot be solved. Therefore, "2" does not have a multiplicative inverse. This system also has zero divisors. Whenever a

×	0	1	2	3	4	5	6	7	8	9	10	11
0	0	0	0	0	0	0	0	0	0	0	0	0
1	0	1	2	3	4	5	6	7	8	9	10	11
2	0	2	4	6	8	10	0	2	4	6	8	10
3	0	3	6	9	0	3	6	9	0	3	6	9
4	0	4	8	0	4	8	0	4	8	0	4	8
5	0	5	10	3	8	1	6	11	4	9	2	7
6	0	6	0	6	0	6	0	6	0	6	0	6
7	0	7	2	9	4	11	6	1	8	3	10	5
8	0	8	4	0	8	4	0	8	4	0	8	4
9	0	9	6	3	0	9	6	3	0	9	6	3
10	0	10	8	6	4	2	0	10	8	6	4	2
11	0	11	10	9	8	7	6	5	4	3	2	1

FIGURE 15-31.
Multiplication table modular twelve.

×	0	1	2	3	4	5	6
0	0	0	0	0	0	0	0
1	0	1	2	3	4	5	6
2	0	2	4	6	1	3	5
3	0	3	6	2	5	1	4
4	0	4	1	5	2	6	3
5	0	5	3	1	6	4	2
6	0	6	5	4	3	2	1

FIGURE 15-33.
Multiplication table modular seven.

product is equal to zero and neither of the factors is zero, then the factors are called zero divisors. For example, $6 \times 2 = 0$; therefore $0 \div 2 = 6$ and $0 \div 6 = 2$; therefore, 6 and 2 are zero divisors. Some experimentation by the students should allow them to discover that these special situations occur whenever the modular number is divisible by other numbers. Thus if a prime number is chosen as the modular number the products will yield unique answers. Figure 15-33 shows a modular seven multiplication table. There are no duplicate answers on any one row or column of the products.

Another example of a finite system is the

measurement of angles (Figure 15-34). As the second ray moves counterclockwise, the measure of the angle becomes larger and larger. The angles in Figure 15-34a and g are the same angle. The angle measuring 360 degrees is the same as the angle measuring 0 degrees. This is an example of a modular 360 system.

A mathematical system can also be generated by using the rigid motions of transformational geometry. The geometric shape chosen will determine the number of elements in the system. After a geometric shape is chosen, all possible positions of the shape are analyzed. For example, if an equilateral triangle is cut from a sheet of paper (Figure 15-35), the students should consider all possible positions for returning it to the cut out space. The students can place the triangle in its first position (Figure 15-36a). They can rotate the triangle 120 degrees or 240 degrees clockwise around its point of symmetry (Figure 15-36b and c). The other positions are obtained by flipping the triangle around its various axes of symmetry (Figure 15-36d, e, and f).

After the six positions have been obtained, students can start experimenting with various combinations of movements. For example, if the triangle is in the rotated 120-degree ($\frac{1}{3}$ T) position and then it is flipped

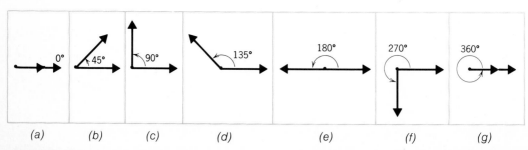

(a)   (b)   (c)   (d)   (e)   (f)   (g)

FIGURE 15-34.
Angle measure.

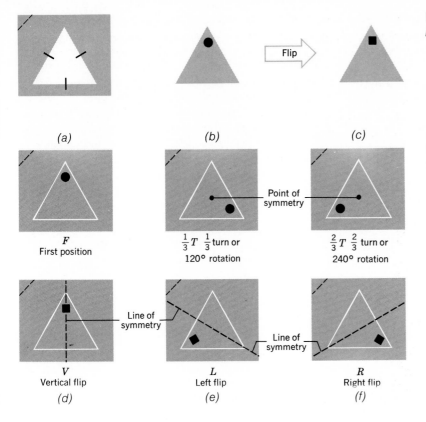

FIGURE 15-35.
Model for rigid motions.

FIGURE 15-36.
Rigid motions for trans-
formational geometry.

vertically (*V*), the result will be position *L*. To test if this movement is commutative the students could start with position *V* and then rotate the triangle 120 degrees ($\frac{1}{3}$ *T*). The result is position *R*, not *L*. Therefore the movements are not commutative.

The students can check for associativity in a like manner. A chart can be made in which students can record all combinations of two motions (Figure 15-37). By studying the table, they should note that the identity element for this operation is *F*, the first position. They also should deduce that $\frac{1}{3}$ *T* is the inverse of $\frac{2}{3}$ *T* but *V, F, L,* and *R* are their own inverses. Other finite systems can be developed by using squares, isosceles triangles, pentagons, rectangles, and the like.

	F	$\frac{1}{3}T$	$\frac{2}{3}T$	*V*	*L*	*R*
F	*F*	$\frac{1}{3}T$	$\frac{2}{3}T$	*V*	*L*	*R*
$\frac{1}{3}T$	$\frac{1}{3}T$	$\frac{2}{3}T$	*F*	*L*	*R*	*V*
$\frac{2}{3}T$	$\frac{2}{3}T$	*F*	$\frac{1}{3}T$	*R*	*V*	*L*
V	*V*	*R*	*L*	*F*	$\frac{2}{3}T$	$\frac{1}{3}T$
L	*L*	*V*	*R*	$\frac{1}{3}T$	*F*	$\frac{2}{3}T$
R	*R*	*L*	*V*	$\frac{2}{3}T$	$\frac{1}{3}T$	*F*

FIGURE 15-37.
Operation table—rigid motions.

The shape of the figure will determine the number of possible movements or elements in the finite system. (An excellent description of lessons on generating finite systems through geometric figures may be found in Walter's *Boxes, Squares and Other Things*.)

QUESTIONS AND ACTIVITIES

1. a. Use the Pythagorean theorem to find the missing side of the right triangle drawn below.

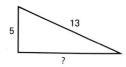

   b. Show why your answer is correct by using graph paper or one of the dissection methods discussed previously.

2. a. Complete tables for each of the following equations.

$$3\,\square + \triangle = 17 \qquad 4\,\square - 2 = \triangle$$

□	△
1	
3	
⁻4	
5	

□	△
2	
3	
8	
⁻1	

   b. Find the rule for each of the following tables.

□	△
3	9
0	3
1	5
5	13

□	△
5	5
4	6
2	8
7	3

   c. Play "what's my rule" with two or more other students.

d. What is the purpose of these activities?

   e. *For your resource file:* Read and copy "Functioning with a Sticky Model" by Reys.

3. Functions are informally defined and introduced in the children's book *A Game of Functions* by Froman. Read the book and then graph the results of two of the functions in parts (a) and (b) of Problem 2.

4. The coordinate system may be introduced by arrows indicating over and up. Plot the given coordinates on graph paper.

→	↑
1	1
4	2
13	5
10	4

   What rule was used to generate the graph? Also find the value for

→	↑
70	

5. "Computer Corner: Graphing" by Shumway describes how to introduce students to graphing using the computer. Program commands which can be modified are included. Read this article and then do at least activities 1 through 5, which will involve you in drawing diagonals with a computer.

6. a. *For your resource file:* In *The Good Time Math Event Book*, Burns lists numerous "events" for numbers, operations on numbers, measurement, geometry, statistics, probability, functions, and graphs. Select three "events" under "Functions and Graphs" and add them to your resource file.

   b. *For your resource file:* Read and copy "Ideas" by Burns. This article includes activity sheets for problem-solving lessons on patterns and graphs for students in grades 1 through 8.

7. a. *For your resource file:* In "Back to Basics the Magical Way" Flexer describes various number puzzles and tricks that are problem-solving activities that children find highly motivating and entertaining. Work through at least two of these tricks. Copy these ideas for your resource file.

b. Describe how you could use the children's book *666 Jellybeans! All That? An Introduction to Algebra* by Weiss to make up your own number puzzles or write and solve equations.

8. *For your resource file:* Two excellent resources for exploring number patterns with a calculator are *How to Develop Problem Solving Using a Calculator* by Morris and "Powers and Patterns: Problem Solving with Calculators" by Lappan, Phillips, and Winter. Refer to one of these resources and add at least four new activities to your resource file.

9. a. Find the square root of 456 by two different methods: repeated estimations on the calculator and either the square root key on a calculator or a square root table.

b. Which method reinforces the concept of square root?

c. What are the advantages and disadvantages of each method?

10. Finite arithmetic is presented very simply in the children's book, *Solomon Grundy, Born on Oneday: A Finite Arithmetic Puzzle* by Weiss. Read the book and write an evaluation of it.

11. *For your resource file:* Read and copy "Ideas" by Jacobson and Tabler for problem solving activities involving the calendar. The article includes activity sheets appropriate for students in grades 1 through 8.

12. What are the various topics presented in *Boxes, Squares, and Other Things* by Walter? Work through the lessons on base three or five as outlined in the book.

TEACHER RESOURCES

Beattie, Ian D. "Building with Blocks." *Arithmetic Teacher 34* (October 1986): 5–11.

Bennett, Albert B., Jr. "Star Patterns." *Arithmetic Teacher 25* (January 1978): 12–14.

Bernard, John E. "Constructing Magic Square Number Games." *Arithmetic Teacher 26* (October 1978): 36–38.

Burns, Marilyn. *The Good Time Math Event Book.* Illustrated by Richard Wilson. Palo Alto, CA: Creative Publications, 1977.

———. "Ideas." *Arithmetic Teacher 22* (April 1975): 296–304.

Burton, Grace M., and J. Dan Knifong. "Definitions for Prime Numbers." *Arithmetic Teacher 27* (February 1980): 44–47.

Chow, Paul C., and Tung-Po Lin. "Extracting Square Root Made Easy." *Arithmetic Teacher 29* (November 1981): 48–50.

Flexer, Roberta J. "Back to Basics the Magical Way." *Arithmetic Teacher 27* (September 1979): 22–26.

Hohlfeld, Joe. "An Inductive Approach to Prime Factors." *Arithmetic Teacher 29* (December 1981): 28–29.

Huff, Sara C. "My Favorite Lesson: Odds and Evens." *Arithmetic Teacher 27* (January 1979): 48–52.

Jacobson, Marilyn Hall, and M. Bernadine Tabler. "Ideas." *Arithmetic Teacher 28* (November 1980): 27–32.

Jordan, Arthur E. "Thank You, Mr. Pascal." *Arithmetic Teacher 27* (December 1979): 32–34.

Krulik, Stephen. "Painless Drilling—Not Your Dentist, but the History of Mathematics." *Arithmetic Teacher 27* (April 1980): 40–42.

Laing, Robert A. "Preparing for Pythagoras." In "Activities," edited by Evan M. Maletsky, Christian Hirsch, and Daniel Yates. *Mathematics Teacher 72* (November 1979): 599–602.

Lappan, Glenda, Elizabeth Phillips, and M. J. Winter. "Powers and Patterns: Problem Solving with Calculators." *Arithmetic Teacher 30* (October 1982): 42–44.

Lappan, Glenda, and Mary Jean Winter. "Prime Factorization." *Arithmetic Teacher 27* (March 1980): 24–27.

Morris, Janet. *How to Develop Problem Solving Using a Calculator.* Reston, VA: National Council of Teachers of Mathematics, 1981.

Nuffield Mathematics Project. *Computation and Structure 4.* New York: Wiley, 1972.

———. *Graphs Leading to Algebra.* New York: Wiley, 1972.

Papy, Frédérique. "Nebuchadnezzar, Seller of Newspapers: An Introduction to Some Applied Mathematics." *Arithmetic Teacher 21* (April 1974): 278–285.

Reys, Robert E. "Functioning with a Sticky Model." *Arithmetic Teacher 29* (September 1981): 18–23.

Reys, Robert E., Barbara J. Bestgen, Terrence G. Coburn, Harold L. Schoen, Richard J. Shumway, Charlotte L. Wheatley, Grayson H. Wheatley, and Arthur L. White. *Keystrokes: Calculator Activities for Young Students: Multiplication and Division.* Palo Alto, CA: Creative Publications, 1979.

Richbart, Lynn A. "Fun and Arithmetic Practice with Days and Dates." *Arithmetic Teacher 32* (January 1985): 48–50.

Risoen, John W., and Jane G. Stenzel. "A Truck Driver Looks at Square Roots." *Arithmetic Teacher 26* (November 1978): 44.

Robold, Alice I. "Patterns in Multiples." *Arithmetic Teacher 29* (April 1982): 21–23.

Shumway, Richard J. "Computer Corner: Graphing." *Arithmetic Teacher 31* (January 1984): 56.

Thiagarajan, Sivasailam, and Harold D. Stolovitch. *Games with the Pocket Calculator.* Menlo Park, CA: Dymax, 1976.

Van de Walle, John, and Charles S. Thompson. "Let's Do It: A Poster Board Balance Helps Write Equations." *Arithmetic Teacher 28* (May 1981): 4–8.

Walter, Marion I. *Boxes, Squares, and Other Things.* Reston, VA: National Council of Teachers of Mathematics, 1970.

Whitin, David J. "More Magic with Palindromes." *Arithmetic Teacher 33* (November 1985): 25–26.

———. "Patterns with Square Numbers." *Arithmetic Teacher 27* (December 1979): 38–39.

CHILDREN'S LITERATURE

Adler, David. *Calculator Fun.* Illustrated by Arline and Marvin Oberman. New York: Franklin Watts, 1981.

Brooks, Daniel Fitzgerald. *Numerology.* Illustrated by Terry Fehr. New York: Watts, 1978.

Burns, Marilyn. *The Book of Think (Or How to Solve a Problem Twice Your Size).* Illustrated by Martha Weston. Boston: Little, Brown, 1976.

———. *The I Hate Mathematics Book.* Illustrated by Martha Hairston. Boston: Little, Brown, 1975.

Charosh, Mannis. *Mathematical Games for One or Two.* Illustrated by Lois Ehlert. New York: Crowell, 1972.

———. *Number Ideas Through Pictures.* Illustrated by Giulio Maestro. New York: Crowell, 1974.

Frédérique and Papy. *Graph Games.* Illustrated by Susan Holding. New York: Crowell, 1971.

Froman, Robert. *A Game of Functions.* Illustrated by Enrico Arno. New York: Crowell, 1974.

Horne, Sylvia. *Patterns and Puzzles in Mathematics*. Chicago: Franklin Publications, 1970.

Lewin, Betsy. *Cat Count*. New York: Dodd, Mead, 1981.

O'Brien, Thomas C. *Odds and Evens*. Illustrated by Allan Eitzen. New York: Crowell, 1971.

Srivastava, Jane Jonas. *Number Families*. Illustrated by Giulio Maestro. New York: Crowell, 1979.

Trivett, John V. *Building Tables on Tables: A Book About Multiplication*. Illustrated by Giulio Maestro. New York: Crowell, 1975.

Weiss, Malcolm E. *666 Jellybeans! All That? An Introduction to Algebra*. Illustrated by Judith H. Corwin. New York: Crowell, 1976.

———. *Solomon Grundy, Born on Oneday: A Finite Arithmetic Puzzle*. Illustrated by Tomie de Paola. New York: Crowell, 1977.

Willderding, Margaret F. *Mathematics Around the Clock*. Chicago: Franklin Publications, 1970.

TO THE STUDENT: AS YOU FINISH THIS COURSE AND BEGIN TEACHING

We hope your semester went well. The semester probably raised a number of new questions as well as answering others. You have been introduced to some of the newest and proven methods of teaching mathematics. It may not have looked at all like your experiences as an elementary student or some of the classrooms that you observed. Here are some other final thoughts that we would like to share with you.

Consider a teaching situation where no models are available and you perceive the rest of the staff teaching rotely. As a beginning teacher that could be overwhelming. Consider one thing at a time. If you need base-ten blocks for introducing decimals, how could you make some? Some of your resources explained how to make your own manipulatives. At first you may only have a demonstration set. For fractions you may choose to use paperfolding rather than fraction bars. Or your students could be involved in making the fraction bars. Don't try to do everything the first year. Adapt and gradually implement small attainable goals each month. Don't try to do everything the first year but each year grow and change a little.

You won't learn to use models in your classroom without giving it a try. The first time we used models with a class we were scared! What if it doesn't work. What if the kids get out of control. Carefully think through your plan. Afterward reflect on what needs to be modified to improve your plan. Write down these suggestions in your resource file and your teacher's edition.

Teaching with manipulatives has been found to be effective. We've found that when it didn't work for us it was something about how we used and presented them. We also noted that we needed to work on our teacher questions. Some suggestions for teacher questions are found in this text, in the suggested readings, and in your teacher's edition of your textbook. Use them; adapt them to your personality and your students; and develop your own teaching style. Listen to the kids; you will know when your questions are good or when they need to be restated.

Use this text as a resource to help you teach particular topics. Continue to review some of the listed resources and add these to your resource file. Also read the current journals to keep yourself informed of new ideas. If your school doesn't subscribe to the *Arithmetic Teacher,* ask them to do so, and then circulate it among the faculty. Or get together with some other teachers and each individual could join a professional organization, such as those for reading, science, mathematics, or social studies. Often, elementary teachers feel overwhelmed at the number of organizations they think they should join and consequently don't join any of them. Join one and share with others.

You should be aware that we also realize it is much easier to teach rotely than by the methods described in this text. But have we taught if the students simply memorize procedures? You will find the reward is hearing the students say "I got it!" or "Oh that's what that means!" and watching their faces as they reflect their understandings and confidence. Also, consider what type of skills do individuals need for the twenty-first century? Do we need robots who can spout back information or procedures, or do we need reasoning, flexible thinkers who can not only work on solving new problems, but also pose new questions?

Best wishes to you (and your students) in your teaching (and learning) career.

CALCULATORS
AND COMPUTERS

CALCULATORS

Work through this section with a calculator. Analyze each code. You should be able to explain what is happening for each set of keystrokes. Parts of this appendix were adapted from a handout by Ed Rathmell. The questions referred to are those at the beginning of the section "Special Keys" in Chapter 2.

CLEAR AND CLEAR ENTRY KEYS

Two of the questions dealt with clear and clear entry keys. These keys are used when you change your mind or make a mistake in the middle of a calculation. In order to clear the display *and* any previous numbers or operations entered, but not the memory, the clear key is used. This key is usually indicated by $\boxed{C}$. Another clear key, the clear entry key, is used to clear only the last number that has been entered. The clear entry key is usually indicated by $\boxed{CE}$. On some calculators the clear entry key is marked by $\boxed{C}$ and the clear key marked by $\boxed{AC}$ to indicate "all clear." However, it is important to know your own calculator because on some calculators the $\boxed{AC}$ key also clears the memory. Some calculators have just one clear key. If the key is depressed once, it acts as a clear entry key; if it is depressed twice, it acts as a clear key. To change the operation entered, simply depress the desired operation key. This operation will replace the operation previously entered provided that the second number in the operation has not been entered. Analyze each of the following codes, and predict the results.

a. $\boxed{3}\,\boxed{4}\,\boxed{\times}\,\boxed{5}\,\boxed{C}\,\boxed{2}\,\boxed{=}$
b. $\boxed{3}\,\boxed{4}\,\boxed{\times}\,\boxed{5}\,\boxed{CE}\,\boxed{2}\,\boxed{=}$
c. $\boxed{3}\,\boxed{0}\,\boxed{\times}\,\boxed{+}\,\boxed{1}\,\boxed{4}\,\boxed{=}$
d. $\boxed{3}\,\boxed{0}\,\boxed{+}\,\boxed{\times}\,\boxed{1}\,\boxed{4}\,\boxed{=}$
e. $\boxed{4}\,\boxed{5}\,\boxed{\times}\,\boxed{-}\,\boxed{+}\,\boxed{2}\,\boxed{CE}\,\boxed{5}\,\boxed{=}$

OPERATIONS AND EQUAL KEYS

The purpose of the first two questions, $\boxed{5}\,\boxed{6}\,\boxed{\div}\,\boxed{7}\,\boxed{=}$ and $\boxed{5}\,\boxed{6}\,\boxed{\div}\,\boxed{7}$, was to emphasize the fact that the operation of division is not carried out until the equal key is depressed. In the second case the display simply showed the last number that was entered. It should be observed that the second number in the expression is the divisor, just as we normally write $56 \div 7$. The next set of problems involves operations and the error message. For each of the following problems predict the result and then check it on your calculator.

a. $\boxed{2}\,\boxed{3}\,\boxed{+}\,\boxed{5}\,\boxed{=}$
b. $\boxed{3}\,\boxed{4}\,\boxed{-}\,\boxed{1}\,\boxed{6}$
c. $\boxed{3}\,\boxed{\div}\,\boxed{0}\,\boxed{=}$
d. $\boxed{1}\,\boxed{7}\,\boxed{-}\,\boxed{2}\,\boxed{0}\,\boxed{=}$
e. $\boxed{3}\,\boxed{\times}\,\boxed{5}\,\boxed{+}\,\boxed{2}\,\boxed{=}$
f. $\boxed{3}\,\boxed{+}\,\boxed{5}\,\boxed{\times}\,\boxed{2}\,\boxed{=}$
g. $\boxed{1}\,\boxed{8}\,\boxed{\div}\,\boxed{3}\,\boxed{\div}\,\boxed{2}\,\boxed{=}$
h. $\boxed{1}\,\boxed{2}\,\boxed{-}\,\boxed{3}\,\boxed{+}\,\boxed{4}\,\boxed{=}$

An error message should have been obtained for problem (c), as division by zero is undefined. Since it is possible to subtract a larger number from a smaller number when the set of negative numbers is considered, for problem (d) the display will read -3 or $3-$ to indicate a negative three. If your calculator has a $\boxed{+/-}$ key, negative numbers can be shown by entering the number and then depressing the $\boxed{+/-}$ key to obtain the appropriate sign.

The purpose of problems (e) and (f) is to help you determine whether or not your calculator considers order of operations. Order of operations is a hierarchy that states that all operations involving parentheses, brackets, or exponents are completed first. All multiplications and divisions are done next. After multiplications and divisions are completed, then all additions and subtractions are completed. If all the operations in a statement are the same level in this hierarchy (for example, all additions and subtractions), then they should be completed in order from left to right. All calculators should give the correct answer of 17 for the expression 3 × 5 + 2 as first the multiplication should be performed (3 × 5 = 15), then the addition (15 + 2 = 17).

In the problem 3 + 5 × 2, the correct answer is 13 as order of operations indicates that multiplication is done before addition, so 5 × 2 = 10 and 10 + 3 = 13. Some calculators have order of operations built in so that if you simply do the keystrokes in the order indicated (③ ⊞ ⑤ ⊠ ② ⊟), the display will show 13 as the answer. Calculators that do not have order of operations will perform the operations in the order entered. For the code above, the calculator will first add 3 and 5 to obtain 8 and then multiply that result by 2 to obtain an incorrect answer of 16. If your calculator does not have order of operations, you will need to adjust the order in which the numbers and operations are entered.

If your calculator has order of operations, you should obtain answers of 2, 2, 81, and 22 for the codes below. If it does not have order of operations, write codes that will give you the correct answers for each statement on your calculator.

a. ① ② ⊟ ② ⊠ ⑤ ⊟
b. ③ ⓪ ⊡ ⑥ ⊟ ② ④ ⊡ ⑧ ⊟
c. ② ⊠ ③ ⑥ ⊞ ① ⑧ ⊡ ② ⊟
d. ① ② ⊞ ① ⑥ ⊟ ② ⊠ ③ ⊟

In addition to knowing whether your calculator has order of operations, you should also know whether or not it has scientific notation. Some of the following calculator codes will result in a display of numbers written in scientific notation or a display of another aspect of error messages. Predict the answers and then check your predictions with your calculator.

a. ③ ⓪ ⓪ ⓪ ⊠ ④ ⓪ ⓪ ⊟
b. ② ⓪ ⓪ ⓪ ⊠ ⑧ ⓪ ⓪ ⓪ ⓪ ⊟
c. ④ ⓪ ⓪ ⓪ ⓪ ⊠ ⑦ ⓪ ⓪ ⓪ ⓪ ⓪ ⊟
d. ④ ⑤ ⊡ ② ⊟
e. ⑤ ⓪ ⊡ ② ⊟
f. ④ ⊡ ⑤ ⊟
g. ① ⊡ ⑧ ⊟
h. ② ⊡ ③ ⊟

For some calculators error messages may also have occurred for problems (b) and (c). This error message does not mean the problem is undefined, as with division by zero, but that the calculator did not have sufficient display to show the answer. If your calculator has a ten-digit display rather than an eight-digit display, the answer 180 000 000 will be shown. Some calculators switch to scientific notation when the capacity of their display is exceeded. For problem (c) the answer 28 000 000 000 or 2.8×10^{10} would be displayed as $2.8 \times 10\,(10)$ or 2.8   (10) or 2.8   10.

Since the answers for problems (f) and (g) are decimal fractions that terminate in less than eight or ten place values, they can be readily shown on the display. The decimal fraction obtained for 2 divided by 3 is a repeating decimal. The display would be 0.6666666 or 6.6666666 × 10 (−1), depending on the calculator.

MEMORY

The memory of a calculator can be used to store a number for later use while the individual is using the calculator to solve other problems. In order to store or add numbers to the memory the ⎡M+⎤ key is used. When a number is stored in the memory, the letter M appears on the display. To determine what is currently stored in the memory, the memory recall key is used. This key is usually indicated by [RM] (Recall Memory), [MR] (Memory Recall), [RC] (Recall), or [MRC] (Memory Recall).

On some calculators store ([STO]) and sum ([SUM]) keys are used instead of an [M+] key. If your calculator has a [STO] key, this can be used to store numbers in the memory. If a number is in the memory and you press another number and [STO], it will replace the number in the memory with the new number. If you want to add a second number to the number in the memory, enter the second number and then press [SUM].

To explore these functions, turn your calculator off, then back on, and follow the directions below. Adjust the directions if your calculator has [STO] and [SUM] keys.

a. [MR]
What number is shown on the display? What number is currently stored in the memory?

b. [6] [M+] [9]
What number is shown on the display? What number should be stored in the memory? How can you check your guess? Check your guess.

In order to clear the memory, the clear memory key ([CM] or [MC]) is used. If your calculator does not have a clear memory key and has a [+/-] key, this can be used to add in the negative of the number being stored. For example, if 6 is currently being stored in the memory, enter [6] [+/-] to show −6 on the display, then use [M+] to add −6 to the 6 in the memory. If your calculator has a [STO] key, use the code [0] [STO]. As noted earlier, for some calculators the [AC] key will clear the memory as well as the display. An-

other alternative is to turn the calculator off and then back on.

c. [MC] [6] [M+] [9] [M+]
What number is shown on the display? What number should be stored in the memory? Check your guess.

d. [MC] [3] [M+] [7] [M+] [8] [M+] [4] [M+] [9]
What number is shown on the display? What number should be stored in the memory? Check your guess.

e. [MC] [5] [M+] [3] [×] [7] [=] [M+]
What number is shown on the display? What number should be stored in the memory? Check your guess.

Some calculators have [M−] keys. These are similar to [M+] keys except they subtract numbers from the memory rather than adding them. If your calculator does not have a [M−] key, you can use the [+/-] key to change the number to its negative and then use the [M+] key.

f. [MC] [6] [×] [3] [=] [M+] [3] [0] [−] [5] [=] [M−]
What number is shown on the display? What number should be stored in the memory? Check your guess.

CONSTANT OPERATIONS

Another feature of most calculators is constant operations. Explore this feature by working through the following code.

[2] [+] [=] [=] [=] [=] · · ·

[Some calculators need to have the operation sign pushed twice ([2] [+] [+] [=] [=] · · ·) or the constant key must be used ([2] [+] [K] [=] [=] · · ·).]

What was on the display before you depressed the equal sign? What was on the display after you pushed the equal key for the first time? The second time? The third time? The fourth time? What would be the result if you pushed the equal key 20 times?

What would happen with each of the codes below? What will be on the display before you depress the equal sign? What will be on the display after your push the equal key for the first time? The second time? The third time? The fourth time? Check your predictions with your calculator.

2 − = = = = =
2 × = = = = =
2 ÷ = = = = =

What would happen if the 2s in the calculator codes were changed to 5s? To 1s? To 10s? To 0s?

As can be seen from the activities above, counting forward or backward or multiplying or dividing by a constant can be explored on a calculator. The calculator can also be used to count on or back from various numbers, such as counting on by 2s from 25 or counting back by 5s from 45. Multiplication and division can also be adapted. To help you understand how your calculator operates on these functions, check to see what happens when a second number is inserted in the constant function.

2 + 2 = = = = ···

[Some calculators need to have the operation sign pushed twice (2 + + 2 = ···) or the constant key must be used (2 + K 2 = ···).]

What was on the display before you depressed the equal sign? What was on the display after you pushed the equal key for the first time? The second time? The third time? The fourth time? What would be the result if you pushed the equal key 20 times?

What would happen with each of the codes below? What will be on the display before you depress the equal sign? What will be on the display after you push the equal key for the first time? The second time? The third time? The fourth time? Check your predictions with your calculator.

2 − 2 = = = = =
2 × 2 = = = = =
2 ÷ 2 = = = = =

What would happen if the 2s in the calculator codes were changed to 5s? To 1s? To 10s? To 0s?

Were your results from the first two activities similar? In this next activity the only change in the code is that the first number was replaced by a 4. Try the following addition code on your calculator. On some calculators the 2 is the constant that is added; on others it is the four. Determine whether the first or second number is being held constant on your calculator for the following codes.

4 + 2 = = = = =
4 − 2 = = = = =
4 × 2 = = = = =
4 ÷ 2 = = = = =

On some calculators the second number is constantly added or subtracted, or it is the constant divisor. In these cases the code is similar to our oral language, as two is being repeatedly added, two is being repeatedly subtracted, or the number is constantly being divided by two. In this case the last code above will produce answers of 2, 1, 0.5, 0.25. . . . as four and then each successive answer is being divided by two.

However, in multiplication a constant two is the opposite of our oral language as we read "four times two." For multiplication, the calculator code and the oral language match when the first number (in this case the four) is the one that remains constant. On some calculators it is always the first number that is the constant. For these calculators and the codes above, four would be continually added, subtracted, used as a factor, or used as a divisor. In these cases the code $\boxed{4}$ $\boxed{\div}$ $\boxed{2}$ $\boxed{=}$ $\boxed{=}$ $\cdots$ will use four as the constant divisor. On these calculators this code will produce answers of 0.5, 0.125, 0.03125. . . . as two and then each successive answer is divided by four.

Consider your calculator for the following codes; predict the series of answers and then check your predictions.

Write appropriate codes for your calculator to perform the following constant calculations.

1. Add six to a series of numbers starting with 4.
2. Divide by 10 starting with a dividend of 250.
3. Multiply by 10 starting with 4.
4. Subtract 5s starting with 95.

Another variation of using the constant also needs to be explored. Try the following code on your calculator.

What was on the display after you pushed the equal key for the first time? The second time? The third time? The fourth time? What would be the result if you entered $\boxed{2}$ $\boxed{3}$ $\boxed{=}$?

How would you adapt this to add 15 to a series of numbers? What would be the results if the addition were changed to subtraction? Guess and then check. Adapt the code to subtract 15 from a series of numbers.

For the code below predict the result before pushing the equal key each time.

What would be the result if you entered $\boxed{1}$ $\boxed{5}$ $\boxed{=}$? How would you adapt this to multiply 15 times a series of numbers? What would be the results if the multiplication were changed to division? Guess and then check. Is the dividend or the divisor held constant? Write your own code to use constant division with a series of numbers.

PERCENT KEY

Many inexpensive calculators have a percent key. However, there are variations in the way this key works. For some calculators the code $\boxed{4}$ $\boxed{\%}$ will give a result of 0.04. The percent is changed to its decimal equivalent. To solve problems such as 10% of 18, the code would be $\boxed{1}$ $\boxed{8}$ $\boxed{\times}$ $\boxed{1}$ $\boxed{0}$ $\boxed{\%}$ $\boxed{=}$ or $\boxed{1}$ $\boxed{0}$ $\boxed{\%}$ $\boxed{\times}$ $\boxed{1}$ $\boxed{8}$ $\boxed{=}$.

(*Note:* The examples in this section are purposely selected so that the calculations can easily be done mentally. Since you can easily determine what the calculator results should be, you will be able to explore what calculator code is necessary to obtain these results with your own calculator.)

On some calculators the percent key acts as a function key. The procedure for finding the percent of a number is based on the equation or multiplication approach. The advantage is that you can enter the percent directly rather than changing it to a decimal fraction first. For example, to find 10% of 45, enter ④ ⑤ ✕ ① ⓪ %. Remember that when you multiplied 45 × 10 on the calculator you needed to push the equals key to obtain the answer. To find the percent of a number requires the same process except that you push the percent key rather than the equals key. This procedure changes 45 × 10 to 45 × 10%. What happens if you enter ① ⓪ % ✕ ④ ⑤?

Write a calculator code to do the following problems on your calculator.

1. Find 25% of 18.
2. By how much is an article reduced if it is marked 30% off and the original price is $49.50?
3. The company charged 15% interest on the charge of $75.86. What was the interest charge?

The new value of something after a particular percent of increase or decrease can also be readily found using the percent key on some calculators. One method is simply to find the percent of the number and add that amount to the original number or whole to find the new amount. For example, find the new price if the original price of $80 has been raised by 25%. To solve this in two steps, twenty-five percent of 80 dollars would need to be found and that result added to 80. The calculator code would be ⑧ ⓪ ✕ ② ⑤ % ➕ ⑧ ⓪. The same result can be obtained on some calculators by the code ⑧ ⓪ ✕ ② ⑤ % ➕. On other calculators this result can be obtained with the code ⑧ ⓪ ➕ ② ⑤ %. This code does *not* add 80 and 25%. It finds 25% of 80 and adds that result to 80. Try this code on your calculator. If your result is 100, your calculator

has this function. Percents of decrease can be found by changing the addition sign to a subtraction sign. To find 80 minus 25% of 80 the code would be ⑧ ⓪ ➖ ② ⑤ %.

The percent key on some calculators can be used to change a common fraction to a percent. To change $\frac{4}{5}$ to a percent, the calculator code is ④ ÷ ⑤ %, and a result of 80 is obtained. If the percent key on your calculator doesn't operate that way, it is just as convenient to use the calculator to find the decimal equivalent and then change the decimal to a percent. For example, the calculator code to change $\frac{4}{5}$ to a decimal fraction is ④ ÷ ⑤ =; the result is 0.8. Eight tenths is 80%. Use an appropriate method to change the fractions below to percents on your calculator. When appropriate, round to the nearest tenth of a percent.

$$\frac{3}{5} \qquad \frac{7}{20} \qquad \frac{2}{3} \qquad \frac{8}{5} \qquad \frac{23}{45} \qquad \frac{22}{65}$$

More information on percent of numbers is included in Chapter 12.

SQUARE ROOT KEY

Many inexpensive calculators have a square root key usually indicated by √. The calculator code for finding the square root of 25 is ② ⑤ √. The square root of 25 is 5 as 5 × 5 = 25. Use the square root key to find the square root of each of the following numbers. Round answers to the nearest tenth.

36	289	258	569	1356
23.4	8.1	6250	625	6.25
62.5	34.567	0.645		

For a discussion of finding square root on a calculator without using a square root key, see Chapter 15.

COMPUTERS

An advantage of writing a program is that it helps develop confidence or self-esteem. When students run their own programs, they have the feeling of satisfaction that they have been able to give directions that can be followed. Since programs are rarely correct the first time for anyone, the students learn they can make mistakes, but that the errors can be corrected and then the program will run. This helps develop a healthy attitude about making mistakes; that is, you try not to make them, but if you do, it's no major problem—it's part of learning.

Since writing a program helps you think about a problem, let's try writing a program for practicing basic addition facts. This section is not intended to teach you how to write programs. It is designed to show you how to think about what is to be done and how to tell the machine to do it.

What do we want done?

1. We want the computer to give the student a basic-fact problem.
2. We want the student to respond.
3. We want the computer to respond to the student's answer.

Now, let's look at how this might be written in BASIC language for the computer.

```
10    PRINT "3+5="
20    INPUT R
30    IF R = 8 GO TO 60
40    PRINT "NO, THAT IS NOT
      CORRECT"
50    GO TO 70
60    PRINT "GOOD, THAT IS THE
      RIGHT ANSWER."
70    END
```

Line 10 tells the computer to write on the screen $3+5=$. Line 20 tells the computer it will receive a response and to call it R. Line 30 tells the computer to compare the response with 8 and, if it is 8, to go to line 60 and print that message. If the response was not 8, the program just moves on to the next statement (line 40), which tells the machine to print the message that the answer was not correct. The computer executes the statements in the order they are numbered unless it is told to do otherwise. This is why line 50 says GO TO 70. If we have printed the message that the answer is incorrect, we don't also want the message that it is correct. GO TO 70 tells the computer to skip line 60.

The limitation of this program is that it only has one basic fact for the student to respond to and every time the program is run it is the same basic fact. What we really wanted the program to do included a fourth step.

What do we want done?

1. We want the computer to give the student a basic-fact problem.
2. We want the student to respond.
3. We want the computer to respond to the student's answer.
4. Since we want the student to do more than one problem, we do steps 1, 2, and 3 for as many problems as we think is appropriate.

Since we don't want the same problem every time, we need a command to tell the computer to randomly select a number 0-9 for each addend. Let A be the first addend. Then we write the statement A = RND(9). Different computers do this somewhat differently, but the general idea is the same—a number 0-9 is randomly selected by the machine and assigned the name A. If we decide the program should have 10 basic-fact problems, we use two statements: FOR K = 1 TO 10 and NEXT K.

Now our program would look like this.

```
10    FOR K = 1 TO 10.
20    A = RND(9)
30    B = RND(9)
40    PRINT A "+" B "="
50    INPUT R
60    IF R = A+B GO TO 90
70    PRINT "NO, THAT IS NOT
      CORRECT"
80    GO TO 100
90    PRINT "GOOD, THAT IS THE
      RIGHT ANSWER"
100   NEXT K
110   END
```

Line 40 will print the numbers that were picked for A and B. Lines 40-90 are like the first program, but we have added 20 and 30, which randomly pick the numbers that are used. Steps 10 and 100 are used to make the program do steps 20 through 90 ten times. Line 100 makes K one larger and tells the machine to go back to line 10. When the value of K is 11, the program ends since line 10 says "FOR K = 1 TO 10."

There are several other features we might want to put in this program. For instance, as was stated before, it is good for students to have a record of their number of correct answers. To do this we need to set up a counter that will start at 0 and count the correct responses. So, we will put in a first step that tells the computer the counter is started at 0, and then we will need an instruction that tells the computer to increase the count by 1 when a correct response is made. Notice that if an incorrect response is made, the program does lines 70, 80, and then goes to 100, skipping any lines between 80 and 100 so we can put our statement to increase the counter between 90 and 100. One of the reasons for numbering the lines by multiples of 10 originally was so that if you want to add statements, there are places for them. So, let's add two lines to our program.

```
5    C = 0
95   C = C + 1
```

Line 95 says that whatever value C was, now it should be one more. If the student answered the first problem correctly, the C would equal 0 + 1 or 1 in the computer's memory. If the student got the second one correct also, then C would be 1 + 1 or 2. The computer now has a record of how many correct answers there were, but we have not provided it with directions to print out the results. Since we really don't want the results until the student has done all 10 problems, we will put this in after line 100 and before the end.

```
105   PRINT "YOU GOT" C "OF THE
      10 PROBLEMS CORRECT."
```

After the student has answered ten problems, the computer will show the value of C. The screen would look like this—"YOU GOT 8 OF THE 10 PROBLEMS CORRECT."

In another variation, we may want the students to decide how many problems to do. For this, we would have to ask them the number of desired problems. The computer would have to receive this information and remember it. We would add statements 6 and 7 to the program.

```
6   PRINT "HOW MANY PROBLEMS
    WOULD YOU LIKE TO DO?"
7   INPUT N
```

Line 7 tells the computer to store the answer and give it the name N. We now need to change the parts of our program that were set up for 10 problems so that it can do N problems. The program would then look like this.

```
5    C = 0
6    PRINT "HOW MANY PROBLEMS
     WOULD YOU LIKE TO DO?"
7    INPUT N
10   FOR K = 1 TO N
20   A = RND(9)
30   B = RND(9)
40   PRINT A "+" B "="
50   INPUT R
60   IF R = A + B GO TO 90
70   PRINT "NO, THAT IS NOT
     CORRECT"
80   GO TO 100
90   PRINT "GOOD, THAT IS THE
     RIGHT ANSWER."
95   C = C + 1
100  NEXT K
105  PRINT "YOU GOT" C "OF THE"
     N "PROBLEMS CORRECT"
110  END
```

There are other things we might want to add to this program. For instance, instead of printing GOOD, THAT IS THE RIGHT ANSWER, we might want to have a picture of a smiling face and the word RIGHT. We also might want the program to have a title such as BASIC ADDITION FACTS so the students will know what kind of problems they will be doing before answering the question, "HOW MANY PROBLEMS DO YOU WANT TO DO?" This program doesn't provide the students with a second chance to respond if the first answer is incorrect. Since it is a program to practice basic facts, the chance for a second response was deliberately omitted to prevent wild guessing. However, in a program for practicing two-digit addition, you may want your students to be given a second chance to answer the problem. As you can see, there are many possible variations in computer programs for the classroom. However, this brief sample is enough to show you how to think about what you want done and how to tell the computer to do it.

The language of Logo is also frequently used in the elementary school. While BASIC often comes built into the machine, Logo must be loaded into the computer from a disk. The most common use of Logo is the turtle graphics part. Logo is, however, a complete language in which you can do the same things that you can do in BASIC. It does the same arithmetic operations and has the random number generating function as well as many other functions.

In this section we will explore some of what can be done with the turtle graphics. When we start the Logo, the turtle starts at the center of the screen pointing toward the top. Now we must give the turtle commands to make it draw what we want. CS means to clear the screen and is used at the beginning of a set of directions. RT 30 means to turn the direction the turtle is pointing 30 degrees to the right. To turn the turtle farther a larger number would be used, indicating that it should turn more degrees. A square corner to the right would be made by RT 90. LT followed by a number would turn the turtle left that number of degrees. FD means move forward in the direction the turtle is pointed. BK means move directly backward. A number following either of these commands tells the turtle how many spaces forward or back-

ward to move. Thus FD 50 means move forward 50 spaces. Now we are ready to give
the turtle commands that will make it draw
a triangle.

```
CS
RT 30
FD 50
RT 120
FD 50
RT 120
FD 50
RT 120
```

This last command isn't necessary, but
when it is included you can observe that the
sequence "FD 50 RT 120" is repeated 3
times. This allows us to use a new command,
"REPEAT," and our instructions could look
like this.

```
CS
REPEAT 3[FD 50 RT 120]
```

If we wish to make 3 more triangles of
the same size next to this one, we will have
to move the turtle from where the first triangle
ends to where we want the next one to start.
The PU (pen up) command allows us to
move the turtle without leaving a trail. PD
(pen down) is the command we use when
we wish to have the trail show again. Now to
make 4 identical triangles in a row, we could
use the following commands.

```
CS
RT 30
REPEAT 3[FD 50 RT 120]
PU
RT 60
FD 50
LT 60
PD
```

```
REPEAT 3[FD 50 RT 120]
PU
RT 60
FD 50
LT 60
PD
REPEAT 3[FD 50 RT 120]
PU
RT 60
FD 50
LT 60
PD
REPEAT 3[FD 50 RT 120]
```

This seems like a large number of commands to make four identical triangles. We
can shorten these instructions if we can find
another repeating pattern. The first triangle
is made with two commands—RT 30 and
REPEAT 3[FD 50 RT 120], but the other three
seem to use only one of these commands.
However, since the turtle does not leave any
trail while executing a turn, it makes no difference whether the pen is up or down.
Therefore, we can write the command PD
before the command LT 60. Also, a 60-
degree turn to the left can be accomplished
by turning 90 degrees left and then 30 degrees right. Now the command LT 60 can be
rewritten as the two commands LT 90 and
RT 30. A middle segment of our program to
draw four triangles can now be written as
follows.

```
PU
RT 60
FD 50
PD
LT 90
RT 30
REPEAT 3[FD 50 RT 120]
```

By substituting this set of commands

throughout the program, we can now see the two commands RT 30 and REPEAT 3[FD 50 RT 120] occurring four times.

In Logo we can write little programs called procedures. These procedures can be used to simplify the writing of longer programs. Procedures must follow certain rules. The first line of the procedure must consist of TO followed by the name of the procedure. The last line must be END. In between we write the directions for something such as drawing our triangle. When we put all this information together, our procedure called TRIANGLE looks like this.

```
TO TRIANGLE
RT 30
REPEAT 3[FD 50 RT 120]
END
```

Now we can make the turtle draw a triangle just by typing in the name (TRIANGLE) of this procedure. This procedure can also be used by name in a longer program. Going back to our original long program for drawing four triangles in a row, we see that the set of commands PU, RT 60, FD 50, PD, LT 90 simply moves the turtle into position for the next triangle. Thus we could have written these commands again at the end of our long program without changing what is drawn by the turtle. Now this set of commands is also repeated four times.

Now that our long program consists of four repetitions of a set of commands, we can use the REPEAT command to write a new short procedure. This new procedure must have a different name from the one we used before. Since it draws four triangles in-stead of one, we will call it TRIANGLES. Our new procedure looks like this.

```
TO TRIANGLES
CS
REPEAT 4[TRIANGLE PU RT 60 FD 50
PD LT 90]
END
```

The word TRIANGLE in the REPEAT line of this procedure tells the computer to run the procedure called TRIANGLE. REPEAT 4 causes the turtle to do everything in the brackets (draw a triangle and move into position for the next one) four times. With these two procedures (TRIANGLE and TRIANGLES) in the computer, we can now enter just the word TRIANGLES, and the turtle will draw all four triangles in a row.

If you have access to a computer that has a Logo disk, use it to try these programs and procedures. Probably the only way you'll believe that these two procedures will take the place of all those program lines is to try it. If you also have available a teaching book on turtle graphics you may want to try some other programs or procedures. Or you might want to try some variations in this given program. For example, what would happen if in the TRIANGLE procedure REPEAT line you made the turtle turn left 120 degrees instead of right? Or suppose you run the TRIANGLE procedure several times in a row without inserting the commands from TRIANGLES which bring the turtle into the next starting position. This is just a sample of what you can do with Logo. If you like it, you can probably get more instruction from another course.

B

MAINSTREAMING— CAN INDIVIDUAL NEEDS BE MET?

All classrooms contain a variety of individuals who differ in many respects such as nationality, size, background, interests, motivation, and abilities. As students progress through school, many of these differences increase. For example, some children will be intrinsically motivated as they enjoy the subject or take pride in doing good work. Others will need extra encouragement because of their lack of interest in the subject or their lack of motivation resulting from previous failures. The more years students are in school, the greater these differences in motivation are likely to become.

Similarly, as a group of students progresses from kindergarten to junior high and beyond, the *difference* between the knowledge of the best students and that of the poorest students will increase. A convenient rule of thumb suggests that in grade one, children differ by one year in knowledge or achievement; in grade two the range is two years; in grade three, three years, and so on (Figure AB-1). If the teacher directs all lessons and assignments to the "average" of the class, the brighter students will seldom be challenged and may become bored and the less able students will often be confused and may become totally lost.

In addition to the variance in abilities, interests, and motivation, other attributes must be considered. Some children may have specific handicaps that make learning more difficult. Consequently, even though a certain film is excellent, it may not benefit the hearing-impaired child if the background music is competing with the narrator's voice. A child whose attention span is short may stop listening after the first minute even though the teacher is presenting an excellent lesson. Teachers must organize the learning environment to accommodate all children, including exceptional children.

It is not within the scope of this textbook or of a mathematics methods course to describe specific programs for teaching mathematics to exceptional children. Nor is there "a way" to handle all the variables involved. Instead, what will be presented is a brief description of some of the literature available on students with special needs—namely, physically handicapped, learning disabled, slow learning and retarded, and gifted students. Lists of resources have been included that relate specifically to each of these groups and the learning of mathematics. These partial lists of available resources are intended to be a guide for teachers as they encounter special students in their classrooms. One resource, *The Mathematical Education of Exceptional Children and Youth,* is highly recommended for teachers who work with exceptional children. This book, written by mathematics educators and special educators, describes the characteristics and needs of different types of exceptional children and discusses appropriate strategies for teaching mathematics to each group.

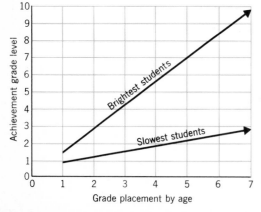

FIGURE AB-1.
Increasing achievement differences.

PHYSICALLY HANDICAPPED— MOTOR, VISUAL, HEARING

In 1975 Congress passed Public Law 94-142 that legislated educational assistance to all students with special educational needs. Two groups of exceptional children included under this law are the physically handicapped and the learning disabled. It was found that of the more than 8 million physically handicapped children in the United States over one-half did not receive appropriate educational opportunities. Public Law 94-142 states that specifically designed education is to be provided to meet the unique needs of these children. Rather than have schools give separate education for these individuals, they are to be mainstreamed into regular classrooms when feasible.

Also in 1975, the Council for Exceptional Children published a list of ideas inherent in the term "mainstreaming." According to the Council, mainstreaming is:

1. Giving each child the most appropriate education in the least restrictive setting.
2. Basing programs on the educational needs of the child, not on his or her clinical or diagnostic label.
3. Searching out and creating alternatives to aid general educators in serving exceptional children in the regular classroom.
4. Combining the expertise of general educators and special educators to give equal educational opportunity to all children.

On the other hand, mainstreaming is not:

1. Placement of all exceptional children in regular classes.
2. Placing exceptional children in regular classes without the necessary support services.
3. Ignoring children's needs that cannot be met in a regular classroom.
4. Any less expensive than self-contained special classrooms for exceptional children.

In order to mainstream special children, adaptations to the classroom must often be made. In some cases this will involve the physical structure of the building. For example, during the last few years, elevators and ramps have been added to many school buildings to accommodate students confined to wheelchairs. In the classroom, the regular desk may be replaced by a table.

Obviously, no major changes in the mathematics curriculum are needed for students whose handicap is physical. However, in some cases the students' mathematical background may be affected by the handicap. If students are absent from school periodically because of therapy or hospitalization, they will miss sections of the course of study. Although the teacher may help students catch up when they return, these students must study new, current material at the same time. In some cases the missed material is never fully assimilated. For example, fractions were introduced to Kathy's classmates while she was hospitalized for polio. Although she "studied" fractions in later grades and memorized the rules, she never really understood fractions. She still has this gap in her knowledge even though she has successfully completed college. Another important variable to consider is attitudes toward both self and others and also the attitudes of others toward the handicapped individual. These and other variables are discussed in "Teaching Mathematics to Children and Youth with Physical and Health Impairments" by Willoughby and Siller.

For students who are visually impaired, the written materials that they use must be adapted. Options include a reader, a braille writer, a typewriter, an Optacon, and a tape recorder. Teaching mathematics through actions on manipulative materials with appropriate language should be emphasized. Interaction with models is extremely important for the students to internalize concepts. For example, to represent the combination 3 × 5 to a visually impaired student, 3 rows of 5 pegs could be arranged on a pegboard or 3 rows of 5 cubes could be used. By feeling the model, the student can develop the concept of what 3 times 5 means. By adding more rows of five, this activity can be extended to the other multiples of five. The concepts the students are learning by working with the models are reinforced and extended by discussions and written work. Since the visually impaired student will have limited learning (if any) from written statements on the chalkboard, the teacher should take care to speak slowly and distinctly when relating the models to the written form. In "Teaching Mathematics to the Visually Impaired," Payne and Scholl give specific suggestions on how to teach various mathematics topics. The basic activities are similar to those suggested throughout this textbook. However, when it is appropriate, the activity is adapted to fit the needs of the handicapped individual. Payne and Scholl also describe various visual handicaps and discuss general considerations that are appropriate both inside and outside the mathematics classroom.

For hearing-impaired children the emphasis should be on models and written work. Learning experiences involving real-life situations and models have been found to be successful for hearing impaired children. The students are more likely to retain a new concept if the learning experiences are meaningful and are linked to appropriate written language than if repetitive drill is used exclusively. In "Teaching Mathematics to the Deaf and Hard of Hearing," Dietz and Williams relate the study and learning of mathematics to the characteristics of hearing-impaired students, discuss problems that may be encountered in the classroom, and describe principles for teaching mathematics.

For individuals working with students having motor, visual, or hearing handicaps, three chapters from *The Mathematical Education of Exceptional Children and Youth* published by the National Council of Teachers of Mathematics in 1981 were cited above. These chapters are:

Dietz, Charles H., and Clarence M. Williams. "Teaching Mathematics to the Deaf and Hard of Hearing."

Payne, Joseph N., and Geraldine T. Scholl. "Teaching Mathematics to the Visually Impaired."

Willoughby, Stephen S., and Jerome Siller. "Teaching Mathematics to Children and Youth with Physical and Health Impairments."

Additional articles that would be helpful include the following:

Awad, Michael M., and Joe L. Wise. "Mainstreaming Visually Handicapped Students in Mathematics Classes." *Mathematics Teacher* 77 (September 1984): 438–441.

Caster, Jerry. "Share our Specialty: What is 'Mainstreaming'?" *Exceptional Children* 42 (November 1975): 174.

Dodd, Carol Ann. "Multiply Success When Introducing Basic Multiplication Ideas to Visually Handicapped Children." *Education of the Visually Handicapped* 7 (May 1975): 53–56.

Dry, Edward. "Spanning the Math-Language Bridge in the Early Grades." *The Volta Review 80* (December 1978): 478–481.

Dugdale, Sharon, and Patty Vogel. "Computer-Based Instruction for Hearing-Impaired Children in the Classroom." *American Annals of the Deaf 123* (October 1978): 730–743.

Ling, Agnes H. "Basic Number and Mathematics Concepts for Young Hearing-Impaired Children." *The Volta Review 80* (January 1978): 46–50.

Moore, Mary. "Development of Number Concept in Blind Children." *Education of the Visually Handicapped 5* (October 1973): 65–71.

Post, Thomas R., Alan H. Humphreys, and Mickey Pearson. "Laboratory-Based Mathematics and Science for the Handicapped Child." *Science and School 13* (March 1976): 41–43.

Sheridan, Genevieve Canepa. "Number Recognition and Sequencing Through Games." *Teaching Exceptional Children 5* (Winter 1973): 90–92.

Tinsley, Tuck, III. "The Use of Origami in the Mathematics Education of Visually Impaired Students." *Education of the Visually Handicapped 4* (March 1972): 8–11.

Utz, W. R. "The Blind Student in the Mathematics Classroom." *American Mathematical Monthly 86* (June–July 1979): 491–494.

Walter, Marion. "Use of Geoboards to Teach Mathematics." *Education of the Visually Handicapped 6* (May 1974): 59–62.

LEARNING DISABLED

Another group of individuals with special educational needs are those who have learning disabilities. Public Law 94-142, which encompasses children with learning disabilities, defines this group as follows:

(A) The term "children with specific learning disabilities" means those children who have a disorder in one or more of the basic psychological processes involved in understanding or in using language, spoken or written, which disorder may manifest itself in imperfect ability to listen, think, speak, read, write, spell, or do mathematical calculations. Such disorders include such conditions as perceptual handicaps, brain injury, minimal brain dysfunction, dyslexia, and developmental aphasia. Such term does not include children who have learning problems which are primarily the result of visual, hearing, or motor handicaps, of mental retardation, of emotional disturbance, or environmental, cultural, or economic disadvantage.

Individuals with learning disabilities have specific problems that reflect a disorder in their thinking processes. As with physically handicapped individuals, children with learning disabilities range from low to high in intelligence and achievement. Similarly, instruction for students with learning disabilities must be adapted to compensate for each one's particular disability. For example, some students may have visual difficulties that cause reversals such as not being able to discriminate between 3 and E or between 6 and 9. Others may have difficulty with computational problems because they have poor motor skills or lack spatial abilities. These students, when adding or subtracting numbers, may be unable to line up the place values. Lined paper or color codes could be used to help them structure their written work (Figure AB-2).

"Teaching Mathematics to Children and Youth with Percpetual and Cognitive Processing Deficits" by Glennon and Cruikshank and "Computation: Implications for Learning Disabled Children" by Moyer and Moyer are good resources for describing

FIGURE AB-2.
Compensating for a learning disability.

some of the characteristics of learning disabled students and giving suggestions for teaching mathematics to them. Articles that describe activities in mathematics for learning disabled students include the following:

Aiello, Barbara. "The Tool Chest: Demystifying the Metric System for Exceptional Children." *Teaching Exceptional Children 8* (Winter 1976): 72–75.

Brown, Virginia. "Programs, Materials, and Techniques: Learning About Mathematics Instruction." *Journal of Learning Disabilities 8* (October 1975): 476–485.

Cawley, John F., Anne M. Fitzmaurice, Robert A. Shaw, Harris Kahn, and Herman Bates III. "Mathematics and Learning Disabled Youth: The Upper Grade Levels." *Learning Disability Quarterly 1* (Fall 1978): 37–52.

Dunlap, William, and Alison D. House. "Why Can't Johnny Compute?" *Journal of Learning Disabilities 9* (April 1976): 16–20.

Flinter, Paul F. "Educational Implications of Dyscalculia." *Arithmetic Teacher 26* (March 1979): 42–46.

Friedlandland, Seymour J., and Samuel J. Meisels. "An Application of the Piagetian Model to Perceptual Handicaps." *Journal of Learning Disabilities 8* (January 1975): 27–31.

Glennon, Vincent J., and William M. Cruikshank. "Teaching Mathematics to Children and Youth with Perceptual and Cognitive Processing Deficits." *The Mathematical Education of Exceptional Children and Youth*. Reston, VA: National Council of Teachers of Mathematics, 1981.

Jacobson, Ruth S. "Fun with Fractions for Special Education." *Arithmetic Teacher 18* (October 1971): 417–419.

Meyers, Ann C., and Carol A. Thornton. "The Learning Disabled Child—Learning the Basic Facts." *Arithmetic Teacher 25* (December 1977): 46–50.

Moyer, John C., and Margaret Bannochie Moyer. "Computation: Implications for Learning Disabled Children." *Developing Computational Skills,* 1978 Yearbook of the National Council of Teachers of Mathematics, pp. 78–95. Reston, VA: The Council, 1978.

Reilly, Vera. "Reversals in Writing: Some Suggestions for Teachers." *Teaching Exceptional Children 4* (Spring 1972): 145–147.

Sears, Carol J. "Mathematics for the Learning Disabled Child in the Regular Classroom." *Arithmetic Teacher 33* (January 1986): 5–11.

Smith, Marsha C. "Reversing Reversals." *Education and Training of the Mentally Retarded 7* (April 1972): 91–93.

Thornton, Carol A. "R$_x$ = Geometry: Perceptual-Motor Help for Many Handicapped Learners." *Arithmetic Teacher 27* (October 1979): 24–26.

GIFTED AND TALENTED

In the previous two sections students with the special needs of being physically handicapped or learning disabled were considered. Their academic abilities and achievement vary; they can be average, slow, or honor students. In the next two sections two other groups of students with special needs will be considered. These groups consist of the students at the upper and lower ends of academic ability. Guidelines for the instruction of physically handicapped and learning disabled students were legislated by Public Law 94-142. Legislation for gifted and talented students occurred with the passage of the Gifted and Talented Children's Education Act of 1978. This act provided for financial assistance to design, implement, and improve programs for the gifted. As with physically handicapped and learning disabled students, special considerations are needed for mathematically able students. Unlike many other types of exceptional children, the gifted have always been "mainstreamed" in the public schools. However, these students need programs that are designed specifically for them if they are to reach their fullest potential. Since these students comprehend concepts at a faster rate and need less practice than average students, they will be unchallenged and may become bored if given the same assignments as their classmates.

Two factors must be considered in planning instruction: acceleration and enrichment. The students should be allowed to work at a faster pace and to study more advanced topics as a particular unit is studied. They can also pursue enrichment topics either from chapters in the basic textbook that may not be covered by the rest of the class or from other resources. A combination of enrichment and acceleration is appropriate for these students. How gifted the student is should determine the balance between enrichment and acceleration. Extremely gifted students may be working three or four grade levels beyond their peers as well as doing enrichment work. Of course, when students are accelerated across grade levels, commitment and cooperation throughout the school district are needed. For example, if John has been accelerated in elementary school, he will probably be ready to enter an algebra class, not a normal seventh-grade mathematics class. For other students, broadening their background through enrichment with lesser modification to the basic assignments may be more appropriate.

The February 1981 *Arithmetic Teacher* was a special theme issue on mathematically able students. Several of these articles are cited below. Other articles in this issue include recommendations on curriculum and suggestions for activities for grades kindergarten through second, third and fourth, fifth and sixth, and seventh and eighth. Other resources given below also list characteristics of gifted students and discuss program considerations and materials. Many resource materials appropriate for gifted students are also listed in other chapters.

Bartkovich, Kevin, and William George. *Teaching the Gifted and Talented in the Mathematics Classroom.* Washington D.C.: National Education Association, 1980.

Fox, Lynn. "Mathematically Able Girls: A Special Challenge." *Arithmetic Teacher 28* (February 1981): 22–23.

Greenes, Carole. "Identifying the Gifted Student in Mathematics." *Arithmetic Teacher 28* (February 1981): 14–17.

Hlavaty, Julius (Ed.). *Enrichment Mathematics for the Grades,* Twenty-seventh Yearbook of the National Council of Teachers of Mathematics. Reston, VA: The Council, 1963.

House, Peggy. "Programs for Able Students: District or Regional Alternatives." *Arithmetic Teacher 28* (February 1981): 26–29.

Ridge, H. Laurence, and Joseph S. Renzulli. "Teaching Mathematics to the Talented and Gifted." *The Mathematical Education of Exceptional Children and Youth.* Reston, VA: National Council of Teachers of Mathematics, 1981.

Shufelt, Gwen. "Providing for Able Students at the Local School Level." *Arithmetic Teacher 28* (February 1981): 44–46.

Trafton, Paul. "Overview: Providing for Mathematically Able Students." *Arithmetic Teacher 28* (February 1981): 12–13.

Vance, James H. "The Mathematically Talented Student Revisited." *Arithmetic Teacher 31* (September 1983): 22–25.

SLOW LEARNING AND MENTALLY RETARDED

A fourth group with special needs are slow learners and mentally retarded children. As stated earlier in this chapter, the range in abilities and achievement varies in any classroom, and the range of achievement increases as the group of students progresses through school. In classroom achievement, slow-learning and mentally retarded students progress at a rate 50 to 80 percent of the average student's rate of growth (Kirk, 1972). Connally (1973) notes that mentally retarded students grow academically at a rate of half a grade level per year. These students are capable of learning, but they learn at a slower rate. New concepts must be broken down into very small steps, and these students will need more time than the average learner to develop the concepts and to obtain mastery. Also, they will need extra reinforcement to retain their learning.

To facilitate optimum learning, slow and retarded students should study a few topics in depth. Although not as many topics will be covered, it is more important to learn a few things well than to have vague concepts about a large number of topics. If these students are given the same assignments at the same pace as other students, the concepts that they cover will be only partially learned and soon forgotten. Also, by the following year, they may need to start learning completely over on some of the same topics.

The type of instruction most suitable for slow learners is basically no different from that discussed throughout this textbook; only the emphasis and the rate differ. These students need extra interaction with models to build concepts and to develop reasoning since they are more likely to think concretely than abstractly. If the rate of presenting new topics is adjusted to the rate at which the students learn, they will achieve greater success and learn more in their total school experience.

Basic resources to consider are "Teaching Mathematics to Slow-Learning and Mentally Retarded Children" by Callahan and MacMillan in *The Mathematical Education of Exceptional Children and Youth* and the 35th yearbook of the National Council of Teachers of Mathematics, *The Slow Learner in Mathematics*. These and other resources are given in the following list.

Aiello, Barbara. "The Tool Chest: Demystifying the Metric System for Exceptional Children." *Teaching Exceptional Children 8* (Winter 1976): 72–75.

Armstrong, Jenny R., and Harold Schmidt. "Simple Materials for Teaching Early Number

Concepts to Trainable-Level Mentally Retarded Pupils." *Arithmetic Teacher 19* (February 1972): 149–153.

Berkman, Gloria. "Teenagers Are Making It Work: An Activity Center in a Special School." *Teaching Exceptional Children 6* (Spring 1974): 126–133.

Callahan, John J., and Ruth S. Jacobson. "An Experiment with Retarded Children and Cuisenaire Rods." *Arithmetic Teacher 14* (January 1967): 10–13.

Callahan, Leroy G., and Donald L. MacMillan. "Teaching Mathematics to Slow-Learning and Mentally Retarded Children." In *The Mathematical Education of Exceptional Children and Youth,* pp. 146–190. Reston, VA: National Council of Teachers of Mathematics, 1981.

Coburn, Terrence G., and Albert P. Shulte. "Estimation in Measurement." In *Estimation and Mental Computation,* 1986 Yearbook of the National Council of Teachers of Mathematics, pp. 195–203. Reston, VA: The Council, 1986.

Connolly, Austin J. "Research in Mathematics Education and the Mentally Retarded." *Arithmetic Teacher 20* (October 1973): 491–497.

Finkel, William, and Karen Zimmerman. "Teaching Special Children to Tell Time." *Journal for Special Educators of the Mentally Retarded 12* (Spring 1976): 181–186.

Goodstein, Henry A. "Solving the Verbal Mathematics Problem: Visual Aids + Teacher Planning = The Answer." *Teaching Exceptional Children 6* (Summer 1974): 178–182.

Heise, Patricia, Christine Coughlin Smith, and Carol A. Thornton. "Basic Money Concepts and Skills in Meeting the Needs of Special Children." *Journal for Special Educators of the Mentally Retarded 12* (Spring 1975): 163–167, 186.

Kiraly, John, Jr., and Akira Morishima. "Developing Mathematical Skills by Applying Piaget's Theory." *Education and Training of the Mentally Retarded 9* (April 1974): 62–65.

Kirk, S. A. *Educating Exceptional Children.* Boston: Houghton Mifflin, 1972.

Kokaska, Sharen Metz. "A Notation System in Arithmetic Skills." *Education and Training of the Mentally Retarded 10* (April 1975): 96–101.

Kurtz, Ray, and Joan Spiker. "Slow or Learning Disabled—Is There a Difference?" *Arithmetic Teacher 23* (December 1976): 617–622.

Lowry, William C., Ed. *The Slow Learner in Mathematics,* 1972 Yearbook of the National Council of Teachers of Mathematics. Reston, VA: The Council, 1972.

Richbart, Lynn A. "Remedial Mathematics Program Considerations." *Arithmetic Teacher 28* (November 1980): 22–23.

Sengstock, Wayne L., and Kenneth E. Wyatt. "The Metric System and Its Implications for Curriculum for Exceptional Children." *Teaching Exceptional Children 8* (Winter 1976): 58–65.

Spicker, Howard H. "Selected Factors Influencing Learning and Retention Abilities of the Mentally Retarded." *Education and Training of the Mentally Retarded 1* (April 1966): 92–94.

Taylor, George R. "Active Games: An Approach for Teaching Mathematical Skills to the EMR." *Journal for Special Educators of the Mentally Retarded 10* (Spring 1974): 193–196, 207.

Thibodeau, Gerard P. "Manipulation of Numerical Presentation in Verbal Problems and Its Effect on Verbal Problem Solving Among EMH Children." *Education and Training of the Mentally Retarded 9* (February 1974): 9–14.

Thornton, Carol A., and Barbara Wilmot. "Special Learners." *Arithmetic Teacher 33* (February 1986): 38–41.

Vitello, Stanley J. "Quantitative Abilities of Mentally Retarded Children." *Education and Training of the Mentally Retarded 11* (April 1976): 125–129.

INSTRUCTIONAL PHILOSOPHY

The concepts and philosophy of teaching exceptional children are no different from those for teaching "average" children. The materials and lessons that have been found successful with special children are no different from the teaching activities described throughout this book. Many of the articles cited in this chapter give suggestions that are appropriate for any group of children, not just for exceptional children. Meaningful, developmental teaching is equally important for children who have special learning problems and for "average" children. For children with visual, hearing, or motor handicaps some modifications are needed to accommodate these handicaps. Similarly, for children who have specific learning disabilities, modifications on certain lessons are needed. For mentally handicapped and mathematically able children, the same teaching methods are also appropriate, but the rate of presentation of topics must be adjusted to fit the individual's rate of learning.

Accommodating exceptional children in the regular classroom is no small task. In addition to the wide range of student differences, various philosophies in designing an organizational plan for the classroom must be considered. As with most things in life, no one philosophy or organization pattern is the answer to everyone's problem. Often each idea can contribute to part of the whole.

Some theorists advocate individualized rather than whole class instruction. An advantage of individualized instruction is that students can work at their own rate and on appropriate content for them. Also students learn to organize their work and to work independently. A disadvantage is that teachers may become so busy with testing, planning, and organizing that little time is left for

instruction. Also, children have limited time to discuss their learning with each other and thus have limited interaction to develop communication skills.

On the other hand, whole class instruction does allow discussion and other interaction among students. In addition to developing communication skills, children can learn a great deal of mathematics from each other. Planning seems much simpler since there will be just one plan and one assignment for the entire class. However, too often whole class instruction offers neither sufficient challenge to gifted students nor adequate help to those students who do not have the prerequisite skills to understand a particular lesson.

A combination of different organizational patterns will probably do the best job of providing for all students. On some topics, such as developing the concepts of volume measurement, the whole class could be involved as the students estimate volumes and count cubes. Some individuals may need extra help but this could be readily accomplished within the whole class setting.

On the other topics, such as subtraction with regrouping, some children may need additional review or conceptual work on the prerequisite skills such as subtraction facts or subtraction algorithm with no regrouping. In this case the assignments should be varied to fit student needs. Some textbooks contain pretests to help organize student work for each unit. For example, on any given topic the students' assignments may vary as shown in Figure 3-8b. A pretest on the topic will indicate which skills students have mastered. The gifted students may do more challenging problems; the slower students should have assignments that are appropriate for their level. The appropriate grouping of students who are slow, average, or gifted will probably vary some from unit to unit. In addition to the suggestions in elementary textbooks for organizing instruction, an excellent resource is the 1977 yearbook *Organizing for Mathematics Instruction* published by the National Council of Teachers of Mathematics.

Additional resources include the articles below. Vance describes three categories and lists bibliographies for each: learners with special needs, diagnosis and remediation, and planning and organization.

Gilfoil, Anne. "How a Resource Teacher Can Use the *Arithmetic Teacher*." *Arithmetic Teacher* 29 (March 1982): 7.

Suydam, Marilyn N. "Research Report: Compensatory Education." *Arithmetic Teacher* 31 (April 1984): 44.

Vance, James H. "The Low Achiever in Mathematics: Readings from the *Arithmetic Teacher*." *Arithmetic Teacher* 33 (January 1986): 20–23.

INDEX